DEPENDENT INDEPENDENCE

C.O. MAKAME

CHEGUE PUBLISHING, NEW YORK

This seminal multi-disciplinary work is recommended for reflective minds. Rich in facts, lucid in flow, forceful in presentation, with no recognition for man-made barriers.

This is a most significant and unique contribution to our continuing discourse on the purpose and performance of Sovereign States, and, indeed, of all human societies. Relying on a solid academic and professional background in Philosophy, the Social Sciences, and Public Policy, the author exceedingly succeeds in weaving multi-disciplinary strands of knowledge and original insights as he traces and analyzes the various factors that impact nations in an increasingly-linked world. The book raises some germane questions and issues that should be of deep concern to all seekers of the Truth, Decency, Transparency, Accountable Governance, and the Dignity of all humans.

PRAISE FOR DEPENDENT INDEPENDENCE

"Well-researched, powerfully-delivered, provocative and stirring, deliberately devoid of subterfuge, doublespeak, and nuances. The author's voice and moral compass are evident literally on every page. This is an encyclopedic tome of intellectual rigor, curiosity, mental independence, and recurring query about the bipolar capacity of the animal called man. An irreverent, insightful, informative, and conscience-stirring accounting of the checkered journey of the human race, going back to billions of years through to the present; a very ambitious scope brilliantly and convincingly presented."

Juan Miguel Valle
Philosopher, Jurist

"This is brilliant intellectual alchemy at work. Definitely one of those few books you read and re-read over time, for reference purposes, for correlation with historical dynamics, for illumination into otherwise inaccessible areas of knowledge, and for sober reflection on the infinite range of capabilities exercisable and rationalized by our genus, the homo sapiens. A truly remarkable achievement in range, elocution, moral consistency, and clarity. Probing, incisive, analytical, elevated yet accessible, rich in scope and language, and eminently helpful. An unforgettable experience !!!"

R.J. Srinathan
Professor and Poet Laureate

"Part History, part Philosophy, part Political Science, part Economics, part Development Studies, part Sociology, part Psychology, part Archaeology, and effortlessly fused together in an excellent and forceful language. Wit, Satire, Polemics, Depth, Conscience, Moral Courage--all on display. Illuminating and powerful. Dr. Makame has done us all a great service by writing this very brilliant permanent companion for all those interested in a balanced narrative of History as well as the edification of decency and service to the common good. The stridency of focus on thematic subjects and the vibrant language only help to amplify the message."

Craig Fulton
Retired Diplomat and Ambassador

PRAISE FOR DEPENDENT INDEPENDENCE

"In Chinua Achebe's Opus, 'Things Fall Apart', which has sold over 10 million copies and has been translated into over fifty languages, Eneke the bird said: "since men have learnt to shoot without missing', it had learnt to fly without perching." When individuals and groups choose to engage in evil, the objective analyst has the right to use whatever language he or she chooses to expose and condemn such heinous transgressions against humanity. Dr. Makame has done just that in this very significant book. His vigorous and consistent position against racism, religious hypocrisy, anti-women practices, impunity, corruption, systemic cruelty, and all other forms of oppression, qualifies him as the human version of Eneke the bird."

Abdoulaye Sidibe
International Public Servant

"This book is written in a style that is very unique and refreshing for several reasons. Gone are the shackles and restraints of orthodoxy, without debasing the essence and quality of the core theme. We look forward to the sequel… this is a running abattoir of many societal and political sacred cows. A total liquidation of hypocrisy, mendacity, greed, covetousness, misogyny, and a life lacking in deep reflection. The author's humanity runs through every page.
A Monumental Feat..."

Efua N. Adjei
Nephrologist, Professor of Medicine, and Spiritualist

"I like a lot of things about this book: the scope, logical flow, extensive research, eclectic subjects covered with dexterity and illuminating insights, as well as the stridency of the advocacy, for that is what every commentary on the human condition is ultimately. I especially treasure the way the author has painstakingly related Philosophy to socio-politico-economic and historical systems, thus validating the position that Philosophy has tangible and real consequences for humanity. Very impressive!!!"

Hans Schopf
Historian

PRAISE FOR DEPENDENT INDEPENDENCE

"Just by following the substance, and not the propaganda, the author provides irrefutable commonality in principle and methodology among the white supremacists of America and Europe; the Islamic terrorists like Al Qaeda, ISIS, Boko Haram, and Fulani Jihadists of West Africa; as well as other hate groups driven by ideology, covetousness, and deep-seated sense of entitlement. Quite revealing. So, who judges who? I bear personal testimony to the sustained and systemic murderous carnage by Fulanis against my people in Plateau State, and indeed across the Christian Middle Belt of Nigeria, an onslaught ignored or enabled by the Fulani Muslim leadership of Nigeria--an ethnic group not indigenous to Nigeria and which never coexists peacefully with others."

Mordecai Yohanna Gantop
Lawyer and Priest

About the Author

C.O. Makame is a philosopher, Policy Consultant, and International Businessman. He was born of African parents, and attended top universities in Africa, Europe, and the United States, where he obtained undergraduate and advanced degrees in the Social Sciences, Classical Studies, Business Administration, and Government. The extensively-traveled Humanist lives in Washington, D.C. and California with his two Great Danes, and is an avid photographer, an audiophile, a classically-trained violinist, an average carpenter and furniture-maker, as well as a keen people-and-bird watcher.

First published in the United States in 2020 by Chegue Publishers, New York

Printed in the United States of America

Makame, C. O.
Dependent Independence: an analysis of the origins and performance of Sovereign States; History – Moral and Political Philosophy – Systemic Racism – Social Psychology - Impact of Philosophy on Social, Political, and Economic Systems – Performance of African States and the prognosis for the Continent.
j. ccx. Ph. 3 BNV

Includes Content, Images, References, and Citations
Hard Cover: 978-1-7352225-0-9
Paperback: 978-1-7352225-1-6
eBook: 978-1-7352225-4-7

Book Cover designed by Nadia Namko

Chegue Publishers, New York

If we are not ashamed to think it, we should not be ashamed to say it

--Marcus Tullius Cicero (106 B.C.-43 B.C.)

Prejudice is an emotional commitment to ignorance

--Nathan Rutstein (1931-2006)

If an offense comes out of the truth, better is it that the offense come than that the truth be concealed

--Thomas Hardy, Tess of the D'Urbevilles (1840-1928)

Care about people's approval, and you will always be their prisoner

--Lao Tzu (6th century-4th century, A.D.)

Don't let the noise of others' opinions drown out your own inner voice

--Steve Jobs (1955-2011)

This book is dedicated to

Dr. Nisha Apano,

Et fovebat me utcunque sublimis, et quaerere semper manere fueris curiosus.
Gratias tibi valde;

Gen. A. J. Danoff (rtd.)
Mentor, Brother, and Friend;

And to all oppressed people everywhere.

Preface

The impetus for this book came from a few unrelated but poignant developments that occurred with some rapidity over a two-week period in March, 2020. The world was coming to terms with the imminence or prevalence of a serious public health challenge; nations were competing among themselves on who would be the first to shut all air, land, and sea borders with other countries -- almost along the pattern that accompanies glaucoma-related blindness -- slowly but surely dimming one's vision; panic was palpable but our individual and aggregate exposure levels could still not be fully dimensioned; Public Health and Administration Officials in different countries were rapidly mobilizing for what promised to be a great challenge for the entire world; anxiety was evident among workers and business people, especially given the indeterminate scope and time-frame to plan with and for. Momentous and uncertain times were indeed unraveling right before us.

About this time, I was approached by a significant professional journal, to write an article assessing the level of preparedness of countries in Africa, the Middle East, Latin America, and the Indian subcontinent, for the emerging challenge. From my research for the article, it became glaring that several, or most, of the countries I had just written on had very weak public health systems and were simply ill-prepared for the enormity of the calamity that was about to befall them. Upon reflection, it was also evident that the same countries were performing rather poorly across virtually all known parameters of governance, and were failing substantially in the delivery of public goods to their citizens, as well as common duties to the human race. The question that followed was: what have these countries done with their sovereignty and political independence? What are the factors that inhibit development in these countries and Regions? Can they really continue to blame their past, including colonialism, sixty to seventy years after attaining political independence? Is there a political system that guarantees development? Are there outliers, and what have those countries done differently?

An older friend and mentor of mine, an eminent and distinguished Statesman in the US, developed a health challenge, thereby bringing to one's immediate consciousness the frailty of the human body and the need to literally say all that one wants to say while one still can. A close friend became one of the first victims of the Covid-19 pandemic in France, underscoring our guaranteed collective mortality. With these, and with the lockdown that suddenly made our days longer, one embarked on this effort.

The scope of this project is admittedly expansive, but it does serve a particular purpose. It is observed that a lot of political operatives and leaders, together with their citizens or victims, do not really understand the long trajectory, and the enormous sacrifices, that led to the current social and political norms like Democracy, Social Equality, Universal Suffrage, Fundamental Human Rights, Protection of Minorities, etc., etc.. It, therefore, became necessary, in my view, to start from the very beginning of human societal formation, and literally walk to the present, tracing, identifying, and analyzing the significant ideas and epochs in the process, before a valid and complete evaluation of modern States could be effectively done. Hopefully also, the long-suffering citizens of under-performing countries can effectively demand performance and accountability of their leaders. For objective minds in Europe, America, and around the world, an opportunity is presented in the following pages to give you a balanced narrative about History, as well as the critical drivers that underpin the suspicion towards the West. This is the kernel of the book, and, of course, extensive reliance has been made on existing writings on the various elements of the work. In essence, using Philosophy and multidisciplinary studies to attempt an analysis of State failure, or better still, to highlight the yawning gap between the purpose of governments and the reality in the under-developed countries, together with the serious implications of this state of affairs for the rest of the world.

Perhaps, this bears repeating in another phraseology. Essentially, I want to interrogate the concepts of political independence and sovereignty, focusing on the correlation with the provision, or non-provision, of public goods, as objectively defined. I will trace the earliest forms of political societies, through the centuries of Empire, the Berlin Conference of 1884-85, which essentially triggered off the era of colonialism, the circumstances and operative environment which made possible the whirlwind of the independence movement in the middle of the last century, access the performance of the "independent" States against objective parameters, identify and discuss the evolving nature of the public goods citizens expect from their political leaders, situate the rapid developments in ICT, Transportation, and Media platforms, as well as how these have contributed significantly to the shrinking of the world as we knew it. I will also argue that, given the interconnectedness of the world, the continuing sub-par performance of certain States eventuates in a significant threat to the rest of the world. We need to find a solution to this cascading profile of State Failure, in our collective interest, even in our enlightened interest. Sovereignty must connote responsibility, and not just perks for the leaders and their cronies.

Since most of the countries that have performed poorly will be found in Africa, Latin America, Central Asia, and South-East Asia, some mischievous, bigoted, and ignorant people may want to hijack the central thesis of the book, in advancing their invalid cause and theory. I will address this upfront, and use objective facts to highlight the pathologies in the "developed" countries, as well as the contributory impact of certain post-colonial Institutions and arrangements, on the profile of the world as we have it. In any case, many of these same countries in the Northern Hemisphere receive and bank the considerable amounts stolen by the leaders of failed States. Corruption is not a Swahili or Zulu word. The secrecy of the Banking protocols, as well as the corrupt obfuscation of beneficial asset/account ownership in Switzerland, Panama, Guernsey, Lichtenstein, China, and other Money Laundering destinations, have contributed maximally to the underdevelopment of those countries, while benefiting the destinations of these illicit funds. Foreign companies in the extractive industries have also significantly damaged the environment in the under-developed countries, while hobnobbing with connected local bullies and corrupt leaders. Hopefully, this will cure some of the arrogance.

The language employed in condemning some atrocities, past and present, is deliberately and unapologetically strong, irreverent, direct, and unambiguous. From this prism, this book may not be for all; if you seek a tepid, safe, and inoffensive narration of truly horrible FACTS, this author will not be your favorite writer. Having written Dissertations for advanced academic degrees in respectable Institutions in Africa, Europe, and the United States, the author is perfectly capable of the tone and style of academic writings: safe, middle-of-the road, "courteous", "professional", and generally bland in character. None of this temperance is needed when writing on genocide, slavery, colonialism, and their continuing glorification and value-less objectification up to this moment. The need for vigorous language is especially urgent and apropos because we see, in our midst, the reverential nostalgia for evil, edification of and non-apology for some of the past atrocities, the negation of historical facts, the chest-thumping, the lack of assignment of responsibility for these heinous crimes against humanity and Sins against God, as well as the conveniently-sanitized reference to History without acknowledging the old and enduring pain caused significant sections of humanity in the process. This is not a Doctoral Dissertation, mercifully, so we will write as we deem fit. No gagging or censorship has been entertained in this work; the fidelity is to the truth only.

Furthermore, no two artists, writers, or composers have exactly the same artistic or creative style, and it is rude to attempt molding others in one's image. It is trite to mention that creativity is a personal thing. Yes, a work such as this, while discussing objective facts, necessarily relies on the interpretation and subjective views of the analyst, as it should be actually , and the responsibility for the interpretation and conclusions remains that of the author. Hopefully, despite the stridency, the attempt at humor, where appropriate, comes through just as that, however acidic it may be.

Rigorous efforts have been made to ensure the correctness of the details herein, as well as the applicable attributions and chronology, where necessary. If and where there are slippages, they only confirm one's fallibility, and not any malicious intent or predilection for inexactitude. All borrowed ideas and words have been employed towards making the central argument, and nothing more or less. In addition, scrupulous attention has been paid to the necessary citations to ensure the necessary acknowledgment of intellectual property rights.

For the reader who is offended that I refer to King Leopold of Belgium (of Germanic ancestry) as a thug and a brute, keep your moralizing and censorship to yourself. Better still, exhume this long-dead animal and blame him for butchering over fifteen million (yes, 15 million) Congolese people as he stole their natural resources; if you do not have strong condemnatory words for the Transatlantic slave trade and the subsequent oppressive laws and policies in the US, but you have issues with the language we have employed to condemn this man-made evil, you are simply being duplicitous and cruel and, frankly, do not qualify to judge us. When, in 2019, the New York Times (NYT) launched the 1619 Project to re-examine the impact of slavery, both NYT and the lead writer of the project, Nikole Hannah-Jones, came under severe attack, with some people having the effrontery, habitual bad manners, and insensitivity to regard the work as a piece of propaganda, without having any condemnation for the evil practice of slavery itself as well as its continuing impact on millions of humans in America. If you regard the genocide and gross dispossession of Native Indians in America as just another chapter in History, your opinion on our chosen language is of no consequence to us. If your conscience is not seared by the rapacious, covetous, and arrogant era of Colonialism, plus its continuing negative consequences, we recommend that you gain first-hand experience before you can qualify to comment on our language. If the Opium Wars waged against China by Britain do not worry you, they worry us, and indeed instruct a better understanding of the Strategic Posture and Suspicion which a strong China demonstrates in its current engagements with the West.

Race Supremacists in America and around the world know neither History nor Genetics, and should read this book with some humility, openness, and understanding. It is offensive for the beneficiaries of the Berlin Conference (the so-called Scramble and Partition of Africa) to impose limits and guidelines on how this condescending, consequential, and violent disruption of Africa, should be narrated, to avoid offending them. Their feelings do not matter at all to us. Everything written about Religion in this book is supported by hard evidence; people need to know the destructive impact of Christianity and Islam in Africa and in most developing countries, before they can sermonize to us on the narrative and enlightenment provided in this work. Indeed, if people truly practised their own Religion and believed in a shared humanity, would the cited atrocities above have been done by them?

Is it false, for example, that the Jesuit Order of the Catholic Church trafficked and sold human beings as slaves when they newly started Georgetown University along the Potomac River in Washington, D.C, a travesty for which they have since apologized after exposure? Is it not true that, before the French Revolution, the same Catholic Church owned over 20% of all the land in France, through various contrivances? Is it not true that successive Popes fought vigorously against human beings being accorded individual rights and respect, choosing instead to align with oppressive Monarchs in Europe?

Is it not true that Muslims and Orthodox Jews treat women as an inferior gender, for whom they must make all vital decisions? For both, men do not even worship side-by-side with their women, and only choose to engage intimately with them in what the President of a major African country called "ze oza room" (the other room). Why can't these treasured mothers, wives, sisters, and daughters of ours be priests in Islam, in full affirmation of their potentials, freedom, options, and "Allah's Plan for all mankind"? Why do some men, especially "religious" men, derive joy and feel powerful from the emasculation of women? That cannot be God's Plan. Is it also not true that, while you have thousands of mosques across the Western world, there is no single church or synagogue in Saudi Arabia, for example? Wherein lies the principle of reciprocity? Why can't decent, assimilated, and accommodated Muslims in the West canvass for, and own, the push for this reciprocity in the Middle East, and, indeed, for the same freedoms they enjoy in the West? On the average, they accuse the West of not yielding more ground to them, when practitioners of other Faiths have no ground at all in most of the Middle East, and even Muslims themselves have circumscribed liberties, especially the women.

Why should the West be required or expected to remain liberal while basic freedoms are not accorded their own citizens in vast sections of the Middle East?

I secure my zone, and contest yours, it seems… (exactly the stratagem employed by Communists). Why should it be the duty of Western countries to accommodate displaced Yemenis, Syrians, and other Muslims from the Middle East, while rich countries in the mother-Region build mosques for them in rural Germany, Denmark, Sweden, and elsewhere in Europe? Why can't the oil-rich Middle Eastern countries either directly absorb their kith and kin or build massive Rehabilitation Centers or new cities for them across the deserts of the Region, thereby allowing these victims of wars and violence to remain in their own Region, praying as they please, practising their culture, eating their own food, and avoiding the pushback that we are beginning to witness in Europe? Part of the rekindling of toxic nationalism in Germany and Central Europe has been attributed to this deluge of refugees. History instructs us that this heartland of Europe has never handled diversity very well; the consequences have always been dire.

As at the time of writing these notes, Germany has opened some of its churches to Muslims -- mostly with ancestry in the Middle East and Turkey, for Eid-el-Fitri (end of Ramadan fasting period) services. This is because, due to physical distancing regulations (permitting a maximum of fifty worshippers inside a church or mosque), mosques filled out quickly. The question should be: can the same consideration or reciprocity be accorded Christians and Jews in core Muslim countries? Indeed, why is it difficult for these other Faiths to have the freedom of worship in Muslim countries or predominantly-Muslim parts of religiously-plural countries? Muslims should contribute to the global pool of freedom and rationality, from which they tap abundantly. This is the duty of all moderate Muslims, who are assumed to be in the majority in the Umra.

While still dealing with Stylistics and pungency of presentation, no words can be harsh enough for the so-called leaders (past and present) in most of Africa and in under-developed countries of the world, who have failed abysmally on the provision of basic services to their citizens several decades after their Independence. Blaming the past, and permanently attributing State failure to Conspiracy Theories will not hold any longer, as they have the willpower to pursue only positive policies for their people if they so choose, rather than serving only themselves and their favorites. Using the word "shameless" does not even begin to equate with the harm that these individuals have done to their countries, Region, future generations, and the world, by their criminal looting and glaring incompetence. In any case, they cannot keep blaming colonialism for their woes, when they enthusiastically and corruptly embrace more ruthless, brazen, and low-grade Chinese "colonialism" in the current era.

Yes, to the extent that one has used choice words, none of which is vulgar or outlawed in the objective sense, to render one's account of History, this is definitely not a usual book. It does not describe elevated low-lives and knaves with bloodied hands in flowery language. For this approach, the style of the ancient Philosophers, the writer sees and offers no apology. One more point, though. The reader will find several instances in the book where evil is roundly condemned, rather than just once, as some may prefer. In one's view, evil can never be condemned enough, especially when some people take pride in past evil and while new worrisome portents emerge. All decent people everywhere have a duty to vigorously and consistently condemn evil, in my view.

Allen Wood, while rendering the brilliant translation of Hegel's "Elements of the Philosophy of Right", from the original German to English, wrote that .." the author will regard any criticism expressed in a form other than that of scientific discussion of the matter itself merely as a subjective postscript and random assertion, and will treat it with indifference."

It was Socrates who said that "the only true wisdom is knowing you know nothing." For him, an assumption of a *tabula rasa* baseline is usually the best when seeking or pursuing knowledge. The Socratic Meno's paradox involves the following: "either you know what you are looking for, or you don't know what you are looking for." Students who have failed Open Textbook examinations because they had not opened those texts previously, can relate to this wisdom. McNeil instructs us that "facts do not speak for themselves, nor do they arrange themselves intelligibly." This is the job of humans, of analysts. Stephen Richards wrote that "there is no new knowledge; it already exists in the universe." I will beg to differ slightly; the definition of Epistemology, as the branch of Philosophy dedicated to identifying what we know, and how we know it, is fraught with controversies for multiple reasons, including Richards' position. If archaeologists discover something new about an ancient society in 2020, is that discovery the beginning of the knowledge, or is the knowledge of the ancient people -- who lived through the experience contemporaneously -- the true origin of that knowledge?

The Native Indian people lived in the Americas for centuries before Christopher Columbus emerged on the Continent; is it really correct to say that he discovered America? Discovered it for whom? For the people living there, or for his own kind, who embarked on a genocidal project and a grand program of displacement and covetous usurpation? In the same vein, it is quite rude and wrong to say that Mungo Park discovered the great River Niger, which cuts across West African countries. On the Nigerian side, the Ogbaru, Onitsha, Asaba, and Lokoja people lived on the coast of this River, and fished on its waters for hundreds of years before the British colonists claimed to have discovered it, and subsequently named it after that atrocious vehicle of oppression and exploitation, the Royal Niger Company. The Scottish Missionary and Intelligence Officer, David Livingstone, was the first European to get to the largest Water Falls in the world located in Zambia, East Africa in 1855. The Falls had existed for millions of years before then, and the locals had been visiting it for several centuries, yet this new visitor ignored the local name for the Falls and named it after the then Queen of the United Kingdom, Victoria, a name that has stuck. Renaming a geographical and physical reality, to suit one's preferences, language, dialect, and exploitative agenda, does not nullify the original existence of that river or mountain or town, or its original name, if only the people, the owners will have the confidence to keep calling it by its original name, and not succumb to the induced inferiority complex preference of the outside invader. Africa, for example, had very sophisticated civilizations before Europeans came calling; some of these were: Hausas, Igbos, Yorubas, Mali Empire, Songhai Empire, Fulas, Kingdom of Kush, Kingdom of Aksum, Ashanti Empire, Carthage, Benin Empire, Kingdom of Mutapa, Nok culture, Land of Punt, Kingdom of Zimbabwe, the Zulus, the Xhosas, etc, etc. People had great lives in THEIR places before their contact with Europeans, which, for most people, yielded very bad outcomes.

There is new knowledge, however. Any solution for the Coronavirus pandemic will be a new development, but it will build on the cumulative knowledge, the existing systems and protocols, as well as the institutional wisdom and memory of the Scientific community. Nobody with *tabula rasa* knowledge of Basic Science, Immunology, Biochemistry, Pharmacology, Pathology, and Medicine, can be of much help at these critical times. Synthesis, as in this case, becomes a realistic strategy.

When you set out to write about the earliest formations of the human society, to determine or track the factors and circumstances that led to our current fundamental social and political arrangements, it is best to assume absolute ignorance and rely on the informed, enlightened, and insightful wisdom of professionals and diligent academics who have made it their life's work to painstakingly piece together the coherent elements which give us a peek into those distant times, as well as the progressive journey to our present times. Without these very patient and detailed experts, how do you begin to know where to dig up, how to dig, what to dig out, how to analyze it, or how to place the significance of the archaeological finding, or socio-politico-philosophical idea, and their chronology, for example? And, yet, we must go all the way back in time because, as Aristotle instructs us, "we shall not obtain the best insight into things until we actually see things growing from the very beginning."

This narrative is not an expert commentary steeped in PalaeoAnthropology, Anthropology, Cultural Ecology, Archaeology, Cultural Ethnology, Paleontology, Ethnology, Ethnography, or related fields. It is also not an expert thesis on Political Science, Philosophy, History, Economics, Ethics, Development Studies, Health Policy, Public Policy, or Sociology. Indeed, the author makes no claim towards any form of expertise in this work. The object of the rendition is to lean on solid branches and trunks, to make a particular argument. An upfront admission is made regarding one's complete non-qualification for a thesis in these difficult and complex areas. One is, but, only relying on the writings, findings, and conclusions of deserving experts to proceed on a progressive journey towards the central thesis of this effort, namely, the assessment and interrogation of the concepts of political independence and sovereignty, especially how countries in the Southern Hemisphere have performed on the delivery of public goods for their citizens, even as they are sovereign and politically independent. While a distant historical perspective will aid in this enterprise, the ultimate focus will be on the contemporary performance and dynamics of sovereignty in the 21st century.

The accomplished French pianist, Richard Clayderman (born Phillippe Pages), has been pivotal in creating new music genres: New Age Classical and Easy Listening, by relying on existing classical and popular music to achieve melodic excellence across a broad range. The Dutch conductor and composer, Andre Rieu, is in the same category, the latter being the favorite of luxury cruise liners. Great and timeless pieces like "I did it my way", "When I fall in love", "New York", "In a Sentimental Mood", Franz Schubert's "Ave Maria", and Puccini's "Nessun Dorma", for example, have been replicated by many talented musicians, sometimes, with some flourish, all in an eternal tribute to the sheer brilliance and mastery of the original performance; here, imitation is the best form of flattery.

According to J. Salwyn, Shotwell Schapiro, and James T, "the heroic theory of invention - that a new idea springs fully developed from the brain of a " wizard " - is, like other heroic theories, a myth. An inventor is always one who has perfected a process, which others, as well as himself, have been experimenting with, studying, and investigating." In writing about our earliest progenitors and the philosophical ideas that informed our current social, political and economic systems, therefore, and without any competence or expertise in the underlying arcane subjects, I elect to follow in these eminent footsteps by relying, in many cases literally, on the established experts. While paraphrasing their thoughts and writings will be done where possible, in several cases, the message is best captured as originally formulated and in the words of these great academics. Hopefully, they will understand and pardon where specific i's are not dotted and t's crossed, as their products are rendered in the spirit of the Clayderman construct. The profundity, incisiveness, and eloquence of these great researchers, analysts, and writers make it difficult to limit oneself to mere interpretation, in several respects. Respect, gratitude, awe, and inspiration.

Every meal has a time frame to nourish and/ or poison the body, before the end-product is discharged within twenty-four hours. If this process is not completed within that time frame, highly-trained pharmaceutical and medical plumbers are typically consulted for either sludge-dissolving chemicals (laxatives) or to query the gastroenterological system. At the beginning, however, a great meal is a pleasurable experience, leaving in its wake rich memories and a longing for a repeat performance. The chef or cook, whatever the classification, is essentially an alchemist; knowing what ingredients - herbs, spices, fish, meat, all edibles, to mix, in what quantity and when, to achieve this great impact on the palate, and, hopefully, increasing patronage by satisfied customers. The chef is adept at picking what s/he regards as the best meat, shrimps, vegetables, herbs, etc., but does not necessarily have to become a shrimp farmer, or breed her own cows, produce her own cheese, or be an expert in the Soil Sciences. The same goes for the sommelier, who, while understanding the differences among wines, the climatic impact on varying grape types, as well as the brand offerings by different wineries, does not necessarily have to grow the grapes by herself. Hopefully, this detour elaborates the writing strategy, and mollifies any possible angst or perturbation by deserving experts over particularities or the inability of this chef to properly identify the specific chromosomal provenance of the Wagyu steak on her menu.

Since the Coronavirus Pandemic provides a good template for assessing the performance of States, and also eloquently demonstrates the integrated nature of the global system, it is only proper that we start the book with a chapter dedicated to this severe public health challenge. Thereafter, we shall resume the tracing of the formation and purpose of social and political systems from the times of antiquity to the present era, then make normative judgments and prescriptions as we round up.

Welcome.

Contents

DEPENDENT
INDEPENDENCE

I

An Integrated World; the Case of the Coronavirus Pandemic

It is 5.10 p.m. on Thursday, April 9, 2020. A very windy day in the mid-Atlantic Region of the United States. Earlier in the day, I had taken a long walk along the interminable C & O trail that abuts the tributary of the Potomac River in Bethesda, Maryland. The serenity, assurance, stability, quiet strength, constancy, and organic beauty of the environment belied the unusual times that we, as humans, currently live in. The synchronized balance and biodiversity of the ecosystem were in full display; sea turtles nestled on fallen trunks as they enjoyed the sun; talkative birds chirped away with joy, in the confidence that their water supply source was abundant and free of man-injected toxicities; the sedimentary rock formation and rich loamy soil bore eloquent testimony to the verified archaeological truth that this earth has been about 4.5 billion years in slow and steady formation; Nature remained particularly nonchalant over our anxiety, ambition, ephemerality, and the mostly artificial wreckage that we call development and beauty. The purity and simplicity of nature, but, mostly, its quiet confidence of permanence, eloquently conveyed the message that humans will come and go, but that Mother Nature, the bowel of the earth, will surely remain. In the overall scheme of things, we are nothing. Native Indians trod the same grounds thousands of years ago, displaced, dispossessed, and destroyed by their fellow humans, but the same grounds remain in service, mostly to the Cosmos, but, for a temporary time, the hikers, joggers, and other human guests; the nearby Tobytown remains a testament to man's arrogance, wickedness, and rationalization of convenient morality and objective evil.

You see, the world is currently facing a truly-unprecedented human tragedy on a global scale such as we have never experienced in history, which is still unraveling; the fluidity of the moment is such that, in the past few hours alone, but definitely today, the number of people who tested positive to the Coronavirus pandemic globally has grown by over 18,000; in the same time-frame, sadly, the global death toll has increased by almost 1,000. As at this moment, 1,582,904 persons have been diagnosed with this dangerous virus, while 94,806 have died. In the United States, 462,582 have tested positive, while 16,444 have died, with New York being the (current) epicenter; these figures remain in a state of flux as Global Institutions, Regional Bodies, National Governments, and sundry experts work assiduously to stem the direct human losses to this invisible but hugely-potent enemy, as well as to recover as much as possible the "normal" life we all had as at the distant period of four weeks ago!!!

This is not the first time we have had epidemics or pandemics in the world, but none has been as pervasive and impactful as what we are currently facing. Human beings have, over the centuries, been faced with very serious public health crises that culminated in the loss of tens of millions of lives, as well as a fundamental dislocation of life as it was known during each epoch. None of those, however, had as much impact on as many people and on as many facets of our modern lives, as the Coronavirus pandemic we are currently grappling with. Perhaps, a glossary of the past epidemics and pandemics will be useful at this point, before returning to the grave matter under review. We shall exclusively and most gratefully rely on Owen Jarus of LiveScience.com in this regard.

1. About 5,000 years ago (circa 3,000 B.C.), an epidemic wiped out an entire prehistoric village in the current northeastern part of China. The archaeological site is called "Hamin Mangha." The bodies of the dead were stacked inside a building and burnt together; given the contemporary mass burial sites in Miaozigou in the same Region, per definitive archaeological findings, it is safe to assume that this epidemic ravaged the entire Region.
2. Plague of Athens: 430 B.C. This killed an estimated 100,000 people at a time of relatively low population figures. The Greek historian Thucydides (460-400 B.C.) wrote that "people in good health were all of a sudden attacked by violent heats in the head, and redness and inflammation in the eyes, the inward parts, such as the throat or tongue, becoming bloody and emitting an unnatural and fetid breath" (translation by Richard Crawley from the book "The History of the Peloponnesian War," London Dent, 1914).
3. Antonine Plague: 165 -180 A.D. This was most likely smallpox, and was brought back by Roman soldiers from their various wars, especially in Mesopotamia, Asia Minor, Greece, Egypt, and modern Italy; this epidemic substantially decimated the all-powerful Roman Army, and killed an additional 5 million people in the Roman Empire. It contributed significantly to the end of the *Pax Romana* (the Roman Peace), and the eventual loss of empire. It is significant also that Christianity was introduced

during this ebb in the power of the erstwhile Imperial Rome, a collateral consequence of the plague.

4. Plague of Cyprian: 250-271 A.D. Named after Cyprian, the Bishop of Carthage (in modern Tunisia), this plague killed an average of 5,000 per day in Rome alone, and led Cyprian to conclude that "the end of the world" had come. "The bowels, relaxed into a constant flux, discharge the bodily strength [and] a fire originated in the marrow ferments into wounds of the fauces (an area of the mouth)," Cyprian wrote in Latin in a work called "*De mortalitate*" (translation by Philip Schaff from the book "Fathers of the Third Century: Hippolytus, Cyprian, Caius, Novatian, Appendix," Christian Classics Ethereal Library, 1885).
5. Plague of Justinian: 541 - 542 A.D. Named after the great Byzantine Emperor, Justinian, this bubonic plague was assessed to have killed 10% of the world population at the time, about 25 million people, and triggered the decline of the Byzantine Empire.
6. The so-called Black Death: 1346 - 1353. This epidemic, which wiped out half of Europe's population (about 85 million people), emanated from Asia, and was caused by the bacterium *Yersinia pestis* derived from infected rodents. The major impacts of this epidemic included the decimation of cheap labor, the end of European serfdom, and the acceleration of the introduction of technology in production.
7. The Cocoliztli epidemic: (1545 - 1548). This epidemic, which presented as hemorrhagic fever, gastroenterological problems, typhoid, and dehydration, killed roughly 15 million people in Mexico and Central America.
8. The American Plagues of the 16th century, brought to the New Continent by European settlers in the form of smallpox, killed about 90% of the indigenous peoples of the Western Hemisphere, and largely led to the end of the great Aztec and Inca civilizations.
9. Great Plague of London: 1665 - 1666. While it is difficult to fathom why this nomenclature of greatness was ascribed to a plague, King Charles II was among those who fled London at the peak of the epidemic. 100,000 people were killed (up to 15% of the population of the City), and the problems were compounded when yet another great, the Fire of London, engulfed the City on September 2, 1666, burning non-stop for four days.
10. Plague of Marseilles: 1720 - 1723. Yet another great, as christened !!! This was introduced by infested rodents on ships from the eastern Mediterranean, and killed about 100,000, which was about 30% of the then population of the Marseilles area.
11. Russian Plague: 1770 - 1772. This killed over 100,000 people, and severely tested Empress Catherine The Great's ability to restore order even afterwards.
12. Philadelphia Yellow Fever Epidemic : 1793. This mosquito-borne epidemic ravaged the then capital of the United States during the hot and humid

summer months of 1793, ending only when the temperature dropped during the Fall and Winter months, and the mosquitoes died off; this infestation signposted some of the ignorant race-based assumptions that some people would make 230 years later during the Coronavirus Pandemic.

13. Flu Pandemic: 1889 - 1890. With the improved transportation links and means afforded by the new industrial age, this influenza pandemic, which started in Russia, quickly spread to Europe and other connected parts of the world, and killed over a million people within five weeks. It must be emphasized that air transportation had not been discovered then.
14. American polio epidemic: 1916. This affected mostly children, and killed tens of thousands until the discovery of the Salk vaccine in 1954. A future US President, Franklin D. Roosevelt, was struck by polio in 1921. The polio epidemic has been substantially reversed in the world, thanks to advances in, and scope of, vaccination, but traces remain as at the time of writing.
15. Spanish Flu: 1918 - 1920. About 500 million were sick with this flu, while about 100 million died from it. The spread was worsened by the squalid conditions of the soldiers during WW1 (1914-1918), as well as the severe nutritional deficiencies that attended that war. There is no proof that the Flu started in Spain, but the name has stuck.
16. Asian Flu: 1957-1958. This blend of avian flu viruses started in China, and killed 1.1 million people around the world, with about 116,000 of those being in the United States. This pandemic spread very fast before it was contained.
17. AIDS Pandemic: 1981 - date. This end-stage of the Human Immunodeficiency Virus (HIV), has killed about 36 million globally. About 45 million still carry the virus around the world, but advances in therapeutic care make it possible for them to lead normal lives while on permanent medication. The quickest means of spreading the virus are homosexual activity, heterosexual relationships with infected persons, and through the careless infusion of contaminated blood.
18. H1N1 Swine Flu: 2009 - 2010. This new strain of the H1N1 flu, which started from Mexico, affected 1.4 billion world-wide, and killed between 160,000 and 580,000 out of that number, according to the US Centers for Disease Control (CDC).
19. The Ebola Epidemic: 2014 - 2016. This epidemic was mostly limited to some countries in West Africa, and affected roughly 29,000, while 12,500 died from it. The number of cases outside of that region was not significant enough to warrant a suggestion of dispersal.
20. The Zika Virus: 2016 to date: Mostly transmitted through mosquito bites and sexual activity, this virus is most active in the tropics. The impact assessment is still being undertaken.

After this comprehensive accounting of the major epidemics and pandemics that humans have experienced in the past five millennia, a few lessons can be gleaned therefrom as follows: public health hazards have debilitating effects on both population sizes and the political-economic dynamics of the impacted publics; they are very disruptive; they typically reinforce the religious fervor in those who are thus inclined; they generate considerable anxiety and uncertainty; for a brief moment, at least, survivors engage in epistemological probes about the meaning of life, but this inquiry fizzles away once normalcy is restored and people get back to their mechanistic existence; at least, until the next epidemic !!! One may also ask: given that previous epidemics and pandemics were named after the places, countries, and regions where they started from, why is there such reluctance and anxiety about calling this immanent pandemic either the Chinese pandemic or the Wuhan Pandemic? The first case was a 55-year old from Hubei province, China, on Nov. 17, 2019 (Wuhan is in Hubei Province) *Source: livescience.* 1 to 5 cases were reported daily by Dec. 15 (total infections = 27); there were 60 cases by Dec. 20. On Dec. 27, Dr. Zhang Jixian, Head of the Respiratory Department at Hubei Provincial Hospital reported 180 cases to Chinese Health Officials. It is useful to reflect that the Ebola Virus was named after Ebola, a river in the Democratic Republic of Congo (DRC), while the Lassa Fever was named after Lassa town in Borno State of Nigeria, the two places where these public health challenges were first identified. While the locational source of the coronavirus has been identified as Wuhan in China, its scientific provenance remains unclear; it was originally believed to have originated in a bat that possibly transferred it to the pangolin, then to humans; it is now spreading among people without any animal intermediary role.

Another lesson to draw is that, contrary to the eschatological declamation of religious leaders-- a group thoroughly ill-prepared to add any value in the face of serious challenges such as this - but who position to take full credit for scientific breakthroughs, as the self-proclaimed agents of a Deity that allowed the pandemic in the first place and still could not save her/his/its worshippers, the world does not end with any pandemic.

While humans are given to hyperbole in describing unusual situations of consequence, no exaggeration will be sufficient to underscore the uniqueness, novelty, and impact of the Coronavirus Pandemic that has paralyzed the world for the past four weeks, led to the quarantine of over 5 billion people around the world (out of the total population of 7 billion); eroded both domestic and international travel by over 90%; led to the closure of virtually all the schools and universities in the entire world; paralyzed commerce around the world; affected both rich and poor, powerful and weak; stretched the resilience and capacity of great nations and struggling ones; for the first time ever in human history, led to most of the world hunkering down at home, with no certainty on when this would end; unprecedented economic and financial ruin on individual, national, and global levels; indeterminate closure of Stock Exchanges; exposed the consequential vulnerabilities of the present structure of the Global Supply Chain wherein China manufactures for the entire world; introduced portents for a redefinition of the Global Order as well as the accepted norms of the workplace; threatened the essence of our sociability as humans; cancellation of pre-scheduled weddings, funerals, graduation ceremonies, investitures, etc., etc. across the world; the sudden end to the season for all Sports Leagues around the world; the cancelation of the 2020 Japan Olympics and reschedule to 2021; the cancelation of the various iconic and cultural events like the Wimbledon, French Open, US Golf Masters' Tournament, etc., etc.

The difficulty with writing at this time is that it is impossible to scope or dimension the full impact of the pandemic, because it is still in progress; it is also impossible to determine when it will end, as different parts of the world have varying capacities for containment, different countries and regions commenced the bold and difficult redemptive steps at different times, the world's integratedness has never been as strong as it is, and the development of a vaccine will take a few months at best. Up until now, the interconnectedness of the peoples and nations of the world had never been this strong ever. With this comes the risk of accelerated introduction of this dangerous virus, hence the quick decision by all the countries of the world to immediately shut their borders, and stop human traffic by air, sea, or land into their territories. In some cases, states within the same sovereign space have closed their boundaries with neighboring states, in the hope that the plateauing of the curve would occur before more deaths are recorded. It is also hoped that herd immunity would be achieved in no time, even as Scientists and Researchers intensify their efforts towards finding a permanent solution, to the benefit of all mankind. The globalization of the world was not supposed to be a harbinger of death, but here we are.

In the past few decades, and, especially in the past twenty years, the phenomenal advances in Information and Communications Technology (ICT) have truly shrunk the world beyond what could be contemplated by the greatest visionaries just forty years ago. These astounding leaps have revolutionized travel, commerce, banking, personal communications, office management, inventory management, logistics, medicine, supply chain, lifestyle, culture export, physical security, defense systems, education, telephony, the instancy of information, as well as the overall knowledge base of the human race. Silos of information have been emptied, and barriers to the mining and exchange of information substantially removed. These have come at a cost; governments have had to ramp up capacity and regulatory competence to be able to cope with the redefined landscape; reputation can be made and destroyed in an instant; the talented but criminally-minded also exploit the spectrum of possibilities that ICT offers, to cheat and defame others. With the cross-national impact of the Information Superhighway, governance has also been substantially redefined. For the first time in human history, we also have millions of people studying in distant lands, or, otherwise, living and working in places and countries different in character and temperature from their natural beginnings. Identity dynamics have been significantly affected by our new norms, even as the pull of the hearth remains strong for most.

In this new knowledge economy that emphasizes efficiency and innovation, relevant skill sets for success have been altered significantly, with the result that huge income disparities and economic dislocations have become rampant, with their consequences for peace, order, and domestic tranquility. The easy transfer of skills across borders has disadvantaged domestic workers who have remained stagnant in the face of the growing international competition for skills and resources. This finds occasional expression in the growing spate of nativitist inclinations, and the enduring hatred for "the other." Ultra-nationalism, as history instructs, is partly a sincere desire to preserve one's culture and heritage, but mostly an evocation of deep-seated inferiorities and singular incompetence in the face of competition; the recourse to group aggregation, anger, and violence, feels very empowering in an increasingly worthless and mediocre life.

Globalization has brought with it, considerable benefits for mankind, and significant trepidation for the unprepared. Would a debilitating pandemic, such as this is, reverse the trend towards global unity, or would it summon our individual and collective strengths towards solving what is truly a global threat, made even more potent by globalization? Insularity or making your country great again will not protect you from an enemy that is trans-national and invisible. This enemy carries no passport and does not submit itself at the Immigration Desk on arrival. Is it possible to reverse the gains of the past few years, then re-enact old and archaic protocols just to secure our borders, or should we embrace the challenge of this moment and provide requisite global leadership, seeing that mankind is on an irreversible movement towards functional solidarity across technological, educational, scientific, touristic, financial, commercial, and related lines?

The International Committee on Taxonomy of Viruses, on February 11, 2020, officially named the current pandemic SARS-COV-2, since it is essentially a more deadly strain of the Severe Acute Respiratory Syndrome (SARS), which had previously been mapped. The World Health Organization (WHO) promptly named it a global health emergency on March 11 2020, and gave it the Organization's highest risk classification. This is the first pandemic known to be caused by a new coronavirus; previous pandemics were caused by new influenza viruses, according to an assessment undertaken by RAND Corporation. The result is that most of the institutional knowledge, research, and guidance have focused mostly on influenza-based pandemics, hence the realistic medium-term horizon for the development of sustainable solutions like vaccines; palliatives like convalescent plasma introduction and non-pharmaceutical interventions would work, but cannot have the scope of application that would guarantee the non-resurgence of this deadly enemy. Like all pandemics, the Chinese virus has the following phases: investigation, recognition, initiation, and acceleration. To beat it finally, the virus has to be grown in cell culture, for further scientific investigation, including complementary genetic mapping. Separately, a serology test must also be undertaken; all of this will take some time, even with the abundance of talent and resources.

To date, over 175 countries have been impacted by this virus on all the Continents, the widest spread ever for any public health crisis. The coronavirus is infinitely more infectious than the influenza. McKinsey identifies some of the outcome-differentiators to be: scale-testing, sophisticated real-time surveillance, disciplined and rigorous contact-tracing, as well as focused quarantine. With over two-thirds of the world population currently on lock-down of one form or another, the multi-linear impact and geographical spread of this pandemic assume a hitherto unimaginable profile, with dire consequences for the world, as we knew it just a few weeks ago. It is difficult to over-emphasize our collective vulnerability to this pandemic. It has afflicted and killed across all demographics and will continue to do so until it is contained. It attacks the bigoted, hateful, entitled, and ignorant fellow who worships those totems of deep hatred, the Confederate and Nazi Flags, as much as it kills their victims; the significant segment of the human race called white people (though no one is really white in color,) as well as those that are pejoratively regarded as the "people of color", as if white, if accepted, is not a color !!!

The same kind of linguistic and sociological arrogance that seeks to make the descendants of European settlers in America, the default reference point in determining the American identity; every other American is given a hyphenated identity for this reason, so we have African-Americans, Asian-Americans, Indian-Americans, but not German-Americans, British-Americans, etc. The Irish, who were systematically discriminated against until JFK became president, have gradually morphed out of hyphenation, while the Levantine, Middle Eastern people, the illustrious Jews, assiduously seek their full assimilation and regard as a European people, no longer of Mediterranean ancestry, hence you hear the persistent reminder of the Judeo-Christian foundations of these united states, the inherent dislocations and inconsistencies notwithstanding. Never mind that an enthusiastic pursuit of belonging and acceptance (even in the face of history) has the logical corollary effect of the nullification of the parallel yearning for separateness. The sublimation of one's identity has consequences. But then, what is identity? Pray, if Jews have become Europeans, why are their half-brothers and cousins, the Palestinians, not Europeans as well? Extensive diaspora psychology and experience surely have serious implications… I digress...

The Covid-19 (baptismal name for the Chinese pandemic or Coronavirus or Wuhan virus) has struck and immobilized monarchs and plebeians; Prime Ministers and their cleaners; global cultural icons and their devotees; Bank CEOs and their lift operators; managers of the soul business and their manipulated tithers and *mugus*, etc. All need oxygen, to live. An acute respiratory problem, just like Mother Nature, is no respecter of status, bank balance, your placement or position along the spectrum of melanin density, height, weight, and all the ephemeral markers of differentiation. For, especially, those knaves, those rapscallions who pretend to be the leaders of perennially-undeveloped countries, this pandemic has been doubly troubling. Having privatized their countries' resources, and exported same to foreign banks and real estate; having refused to provide the very basics in healthcare infrastructure in their own countries, since they could previously seek medical attention in foreign countries for themselves, families, and co-looters, the speed with which countries around the world closed their airspaces and shut their borders, must have been deeply disturbing. Even if they could transport themselves to their usual foreign hospitals and clinics, those facilities are now grossly overwhelmed and, understandably, prioritizing their own citizens.

These unconscionable potentates, these insubstantial and tottering pretenders are finally forced to face the same possible health outcome as their citizens, their assumed employers. Some of these brassy and unchaste merchants have shamelessly resorted to begging foreign businessmen and AID Groups for ventilators, masks, gloves, and ICU beds which they could not provide even in the dedicated Clinics they built for themselves within the "foreign" zones they call their Presidential Palaces.

The billions of dollars voted for medical supplies and equipment are routinely diverted, due to the assumption of easy access to foreign hospitals. It worked, until now. Perhaps, they could explore seeking treatment in North Korea if struck with Coronavirus. If they cannot take care of themselves, who else can they take care of? This is the malady, the fate, of most of the world, as we shall explore further in due course.

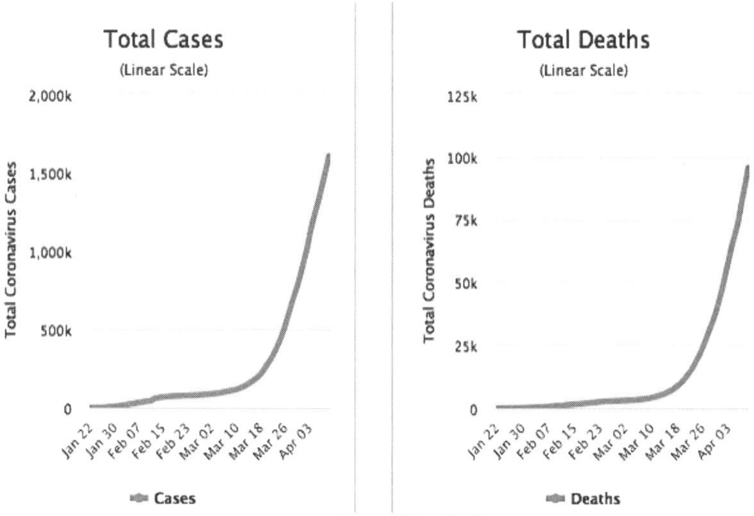

Source: Johns Hopkins

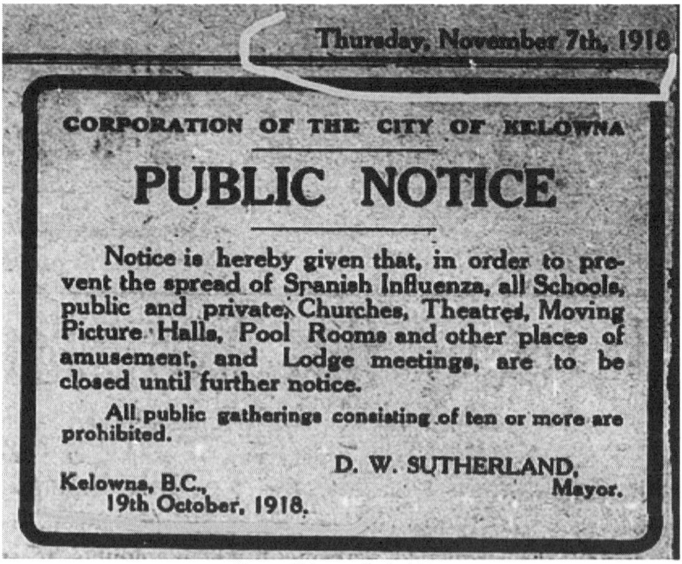

Thursday, November 7th, 1918

CORPORATION OF THE CITY OF KELOWNA

PUBLIC NOTICE

Notice is hereby given that, in order to prevent the spread of Spanish Influenza, all Schools, public and private, Churches, Theatres, Moving Picture Halls, Pool Rooms and other places of amusement, and Lodge meetings, are to be closed until further notice.

All public gatherings consisting of ten or more are prohibited.

D. W. SUTHERLAND,
Mayor.

Kelowna, B.C.,
19th October, 1918.

Source: Kelowna Capital News

Policemen stand in a street in Seattle, Washington, wearing protective masks made by the Seattle Chapter of the Red Cross, during the influenza epidemic in 1918. *Source: National Archives at College Park Maryland*

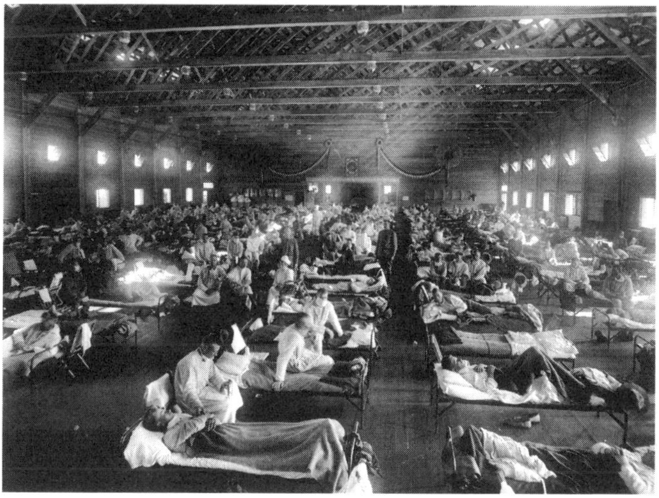

Emergency hospital during influenza epidemic, Camp Funston, Kansas, circa 1918. *Source: National Museum of Health and Medicine*

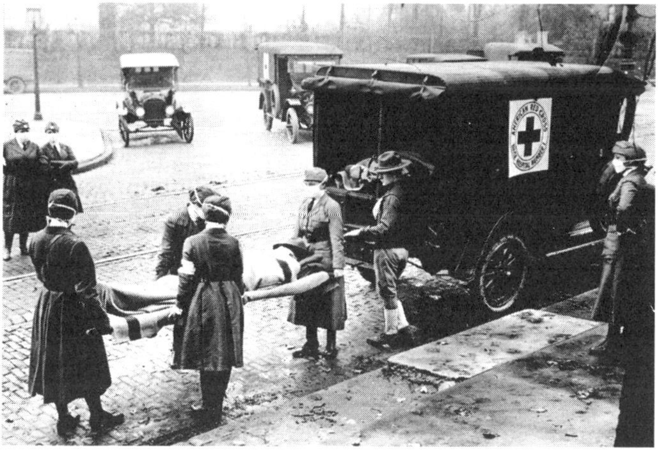

Members of the American Red Cross carrying a body during the 1918-20 "Spanish flu" pandemic which resulted in dramatic mortality rates worldwide. *Source: https://en.wikipedia.org/wiki/Pandemic*

Nurses leaving Blackfriars Depot, Chippendale NSW, Australia, during the flu epidemic, in April of 1919.
Source: New South Wales State Archives

OA telephone operator with protective gauze in 1918
Source: Bettmann Archive / Getty

Typist wearing mask, New York City, October 16, 1918.
Source: National Archives at College Park Maryland

And people stayed at home
And read books
And listened
And they rested
And did exercises
And made art and played
And learned new ways of being
And stopped and listened
More deeply
Someone meditated, someone prayed
Someone met their shadow
And people began to think differently
And people healed
And in the absence of people who
Lived in ignorant ways
Dangerous, meaningless and heartless.
The earth also began to heal
And when the danger ended and
People found themselves
They grieved for the dead
And made new choices
And dreamed of new visions
And created new ways of living
And completely healed the earth
Just as they were healed.

This poem, written by Kitty O'Meara in the midst of the COVID 19 pandemic, applies both retroactively to the pandemic of 1918 and to our current public health crisis.

These amplifiers are rendered here (along with **Figures 1,2, and 3*), to underscore the fact this is not the first time that humans have faced serious public health challenges. It needs to be repeated, though, that the world of 1918 was totally differently from the world we have in 2020. Our inter-relatedness could be assumed as the norm, but it was not always this way. For one thing, in 1918, global trade and travel were, at best, at less than 2% of the current levels. For context, the 19th Amendment of the US Constitution, which granted white women the right to vote, was passed by the Congress in June 1919, and ratified in August 1920, after decades of struggle and advocacy. The effective rights of the descendants of the black founding members of the Republic (male and female) to vote would not be guaranteed until the Voting Rights Act of 1965, despite the pro forma legislation to that effect almost a century earlier. It was not until the late 1950s that commercial air travel began in earnest, accelerating geometrically only in the last three decades.

The global realities in the first two decades of the 21st century have, therefore, considerably worsened the disruption, losses, and geographical spread caused by this pandemic. While the number of the dead from this pandemic is very unlikely to match levels that the world has seen in ages past, it is the totality of its disruptive impact, uncertainty quotient, and fatality rates, which stand this tragedy out as particularly unprecedented and dangerous. In a Brookings

Institution Report written by Katharina Fenz and Homi Kharas, titled "A Mortality Perspective on COVID:19: Time, Location, and Age", it is estimated that 18 million will die globally from heart diseases in 2020; 10 million from cancer; 6.5 million from respiratory diseases; 1.6 million from diarrhea; 1.5 million in road accidents; 1 million from HIV/AIDS; and 800,000 from suicides. In cold terms focusing strictly on death figures, the COVID-19 is really not the worst that can happen, but the story is far more complex than counting the number of dead bodies from the pandemic.

In the United States alone, for example, over 17 million discrete and individual applications have been filed in just three weeks for unemployment benefits; in the first week (just two weeks ago, 3.2 million applications were received). Analysts concur that a massive recession, if not a global depression, will ensue by later this year. GDP estimates for the first quarter of the year, and for the year in general, are expected to crash by upwards of 25% and 10% respectively. In a $21.4 trillion economy, such as the US is, this is a considerable erosion, which will have a long-term effect on employment levels, recovery, public expenditure, global strategic expenditure required of a Super Power, a major power seriously threatened by an invisible enemy, without a single bullet shot.

It will be unrealistic to be bullish in our aggregate demand estimates, going forward. The resiliency of a major country like the US cannot be assumed or replicated in most other countries, with the possible exception of China. Trade, global supply chains, tourism, transportation, manufacturing, construction, hospitality, food, services, animal husbandry, packaging, sports, culture, and, indeed, every sector has been negatively impacted both domestically and internationally.

The funeral homes in the cities with the concentrated fatality numbers are witnessing increased patronage levels. This spike in volume will taper off once the pandemic is over. Given the mandated physical distancing, as well as the closure of businesses, online retailers and aggregators like Amazon are the only reliable means of conducting our purchases, thus placing Amazon in the unique position to add 100,000 temporary workers to its workforce.

With factories completely shut down, offices, shops, and malls closed, and the vast majority of the human race forced to remain at home for weeks and months, most of them without any savings, salary or income from their businesses, demand has slumped across the board. It is reasonable to expect that there will be serial default on car notes, rents, insurance premiums, loans, mortgages, trade credits, etc. The credit system that functions on the basis of certainty and predictability has been upended completely. This is a season of furloughs, layoffs, and considerable social and economic dislocations. Access to new credit will be much tighter even after the pandemic. The capacity of governments to provide safety nets for the most vulnerable over the medium to long-term will be sorely tested, with the result that the poverty rate and security profile of most countries will deteriorate further, especially the most fragile States already grappling with the provision of basic public goods to their citizens before this pandemic.

The International Air Transportation Association (IATA) projects that the major airlines will lose over $110 billion in revenues if the pandemic is not contained within a quarter; the figures for regional and local airlines are not reflected here. The global demand for crude oil, for example, has crashed completely, since factories are all shut down around the world. The Brent grade is hovering at below $30 per barrel, a sharp drop of over 20%, the lowest since 1991. OPEC members have just agreed to reduce production by 9.7 million barrels per day, to create an artificial scarcity and then, hopefully, avoid a further slide in prices. The problem is that some member-nations will, as always, try to sabotage this cartel arrangement, but the High Seas are full of oil-laden ships, no factories are open around the world, the planes are on the tarmac, and all the cars are in garages. The continuing pressure on both supply and price from threats like shale and environmentally-friendly renewable energy, complicates the matter even further. In countries like Nigeria, Libya, Iran, Venezuela, Angola, and Indonesia, for example, where crude oil sales account for the bulk of their public revenue and foreign exchange, the outlook is very grim indeed. These same countries already had considerable (self-imposed) challenges with leadership, corruption, unsustainable debt over-hang, internal security failures and terrorism, population explosion, and extreme income polarities. The auguries for these countries are deeply worrisome, with near-term potentials for intensified tension, terrorism, revolution, outflow of refugees into their Regions, and complete breakdown of law and order. A state of anomie calleth….

Domestic and international financial flows will be imperiled into the foreseeable future, as individuals, companies, countries, and the world at large, re-strategize for survival and success in the new normal of the post-Coronavirus era, a major epoch that is unraveling before our eyes. We await the outcome of the World Bank's admonition that "governments should avoid protectionist policies, which would exacerbate the disruptions to global value chains, and amplify already elevated levels of uncertainty." The World Bank has announced an initial stimulus package of $160 billion over 15 months, with $14 billion immediately available. The bureaucratic maze for accessing these funds needs to be considered. While this is, ordinarily, a significant amount, it is a tiny drop in the ocean of what is required to maintain the global economic levels as at just a month ago, before this cataclysmic implosion. It is also far less, for example, than the half a trillion dollars ($500 billion) that the EU is planning to spend, to stimulate economic activities and support the displaced and poorest citizens in their Union.

In a Time magazine article, Ian Brenner correctly acknowledged that the evolving dynamics represent a significant blow to globalization, as we know it. It will be a stretch, in the mold of "The End of History" (apologies, Dr. Francis Fukuyama), to conclude from this premise and acknowledge that this is the end of globalization. What is clear is that being optimistic about accelerated demand recovery will be dangerous, foolhardy, and unrealistic. The US, with its National Debt profile at 100% of the GDP level, will be stretched even further by the expenditure of $2.2 trillion on a stimulus package, but concerted efforts, prudent fiscal management, and a systematic reversal of the dependence on China, a strategic competitor, for essential products (including ventilators, hospital beds, masks, and gloves!), should release the abundant creativity and entrepreneurship of the American people, thereby shrinking the recovery horizon and boosting both domestic employment and the GDP.

To get all of this done, however, we need to avoid what Thomas Pynchon characterized, in his "Gravity's Rainbow", as "a chaos of peeves, whims, hallucinations, and all-round assholery." MAGA adherents and Eminences have to decide whether or not a respectful and honest strategic engagement with America's allies is not better than the transactional heaves and humps that emanate from the temple of power. In an enduring partnership, such as will be needed in the post-Coronavirus era, the Truth can only be enabled and sustained by the truth. Kurt M. Campbell and Rush Doshi wrote in Foreign Affairs (The Coronavirus Could Reshape the Global Order), that America must take particular care to avoid this being her "Suez moment', the beginning of its decline as a major Power. They wrote that "the status of the U.S. as a global leader over the past seven decades has been built, not just on wealth and power, but also on the legitimacy that flows from the United States' domestic governance, provision of global public goods, and ability and willingness to muster and coordinate a global response to crises."

Enough said; assholery, buffoonery, endemic narcissism, vacuous ubiquity, transactionalism, tantrumism, immediatism, personal insecuritism, pettiness, borderline (or absolute) criminality, charlatanism, disdain for excellence and expertise, self-deceit disguised as alternative facts, attack on Institutions, personal lucre and survival at all costs, duplicity, demagoguery, chronic pettiness, absolutism, wannabe bullyism, and irredeemable nepotism, cannot be the ingredients of Statecraft required in the new challenging times such as we have.

As at the time of this accounting, over $7 trillion has been earmarked by countries and institutions around the globe, as intervention funds, to avoid the possible slip into a catastrophic depression on account of this pandemic; before this time, a lot of those countries were struggling economically. This aggregate amount is likely to increase as the full scope of the potential damage, and the quantum of requirements, are dimensioned over the medium-term. These funds will be channeled towards unemployment benefits, government expenditure, social security, loan guarantees, tax breaks, direct payments to citizens, new loans, new money by the Central Banks, and ancillary applications.

The US Stimulus Package approved by the Congress in March, 2020 was for $2.2 trillion; this totally dwarfed the 2008 expenditure to restart the US economy after that year's recession. The last time the global economy was depressed during peacetime was in 1938. In a CNN Business article by Julia Horowitz, Laura He, et al. on March 23, 2020, the other interventions were captured as follows: $112 billion approved by Congress towards vaccine research; the Federal Reserve Bank (the Fed) is committing $700 billion towards buying US Treasuries and Mortgage-backed Securities; an additional sum of $300 billion is further being committed by the Fed in additional financing to keep credit flowing to consumers and businesses.

The United Kingdom (UK) has announced an initial Stabilization Package of 330 Billion pounds ($397 billion), to be spent on loan guarantees, suspension of local business taxes for the retail, leisure, and hospitality sectors for 12 months, cover 80% of workers' salaries for at least three months at up to 2,900 pounds per person per month. For the self-employed in the UK, they will receive a cash grant of 80% of their average monthly profit up to 2,500 British pounds ($3,000) a month, over the first quarter since the pandemic. In addition, the Bank of England, the British Central Bank, will increase its stock of UK Government and Corporate Bonds by 200 billion pounds ($242 billion). Germany's immediate response, to protect its economy and its citizens from the impact of the Coronavirus pandemic involved a Rescue Package of 750 billion Euros ($ 825 billion) in lending and direct investments. For France, 45 billion Euros ($50 billion) was announced as immediate relief for small businesses and unemployed workers, as well as 300 billion Euros ($330 billion) guarantees in corporate borrowing. In Italy, which has been the European country hit the most by the pandemic, 25 billion Euros ($27.5 billion) was immediately committed towards helping workers and the over-stretched health system.

A direct intervention to mitigate the economic shocks will follow at a later date. Spain, another country with high infection and fatality rates, announced an immediate commitment of 200 billion Euros ($220 billion), to avoid the collapse of their economy. The umbrella European Central Bank would spend 750 billion Euros ($824 billion), buying government debts and private securities up until late-2020, apart from the 120 billion Euros ($133 billion) it had previously committed towards the same objectives. China, with 17% of the world's GDP, and the origin of the pandemic, announced the yuan equivalent of $1.64 trillion in financial relief and stimulus spending; another $1.62 trillion buffer for companies affected directly by the Covid-19 virus; as well as 800 billion yuan ($112.5 billion) in tax and fee reductions and other relief measures. It also declared its readiness to spend a lot more if necessary. Japan is finalizing its package, which is expected to exceed $270 billion in diversified interventions. India will start with $22.6 billion to be deployed towards food assistance subsidies and workers' benefits.

A vital question is: why did Italy become the epicenter of the Wuhan Virus in Europe? Tracy Beanz, the Founder and Editor-in-Chief of UncoverDC, wrote a well-researched and illuminating article on March 20, 2020, wherein she traced the dynamics that made this virus spike possible in Italy. Chinese nationals started settling in the Tuscany area of Italy, precisely Prato, in large numbers, in the 1980s; before long, this number grew significantly, with 300,000 Chinese nationals living officially in the Region, and many more living there illegally (some estimates have the number of illegals at close to 1 million people). The community operates with studied insularity, and has, over time, displaced local artisans with a lineage of centuries of proud craftsmanship behind them; this has generated considerable resentment in the community. Furthermore, to circumvent the psychological association of most mass-products made in China with inferior quality, these Chinese settlers in Italy now export the same goods around the world but under the label "Made in Italy", thereby taking advantage of Italy's earned reputation for quality and style. All of this, even as the local Italians do not benefit...and the perception of declining quality of Italian-made goods hurts the authentic Italian craftsmen and women.

Over the past few years, the Chinese Government has successfully co-opted some Italian politicians into their so-called One Belt One Road Project (a modern-day re-enactment of their Silk Road); China has, to date, spent over a trillion US dollars on this in various countries, and is still spending, according to the Council of Foreign Relations. China revitalized some northern Italian ports, mostly to serve Chinese commercial goals and objectives; a new logistics and export hub for exporting Chinese goods from the heart of Europe. Italy was also the first country in the G-7 Group of powerful nations to enlist in this Chinese Program. An Italian Court ordered the Bank of China operating in Italy, to pay a fine totaling 980,000 Euros, for illegally transferring roughly 4.5 billion Euros from Italy to China between 2006 and 2010, mostly in the form of "counterfeiting, embezzlement, exploitation of illegal labor, and tax evasion." In 2017, another fine of 600,000 Euros was levied on the same Bank of China (Milan Branch) for similar breaches.

All of these factors have inspired significant pushback by some politicians and locals; a prominent local politician, Giovanni Donzelli, was reported as saying that "The Chinese have their own restaurants and their own banks -- even their own police force. You damage the economy twice. Once, because you compete unfairly with the other businesses in the area; second, the money does not go back into the Tuscan economic fabric." It was against this backdrop that tens of thousands of Chinese traveled back home to China in November, 2019, for their New Year (of the Rat), feasted sumptuously on cherished local delicacies, contracted the Coronavirus, and came back to Italy with several cases of the virus, which became manifest and uncontrollable from February and March, 2020. Trade, Immigration, Politics, Economics, Tourism, etc., all clearly have serious implications for public health, as well as law and order, in the modern world. How does Italy begin to solve this problem?

It is quite clear that these significant amounts of money earmarked to stimulate the global economy could have been spent on infrastructure, education, healthcare systems, Science, or, simply saved by these countries. The size of the interventions is a further testimony to the magnitude of the problem; there is no doubt that, over the next few months and years, much more will be spent than is presently allocated. The world is truly in a crisis of monumental proportions. Given the inter-related nature of the global system, what happens in poorer countries, their capacity to tackle the pandemic, and their ability to recover economically, will have direct consequences for the rest of the world. If, due to several factors, for example, the spike in COVID-19 cases across Africa, Latin America, the failed States in the Middle East, and the Indian subcontinent happens when the richer countries have experienced plateauing, drastic reductions, and herd immunity, it is very likely that there will be a second, or even a third, wave of the virus across the world. This is a common problem for the whole world.

Various Intelligence Agencies, as well as consequential Think Tanks and Institutions like the Council on Foreign Relations, Brookings Institution, Jane's, Stratfor, Center for Strategic and International Studies, the World Health Organization (WHO), Johns Hopkins University, McKinsey, etc., are unified in their assessment that particular attention must be paid to how poorer countries handle the pandemic, as the entire world will be exposed to further vulnerabilities should they be allowed to fail in this regard. Africa has the highest contiguous concentration of failed or failing States in the world. Even before the pandemic, most of the 54 countries on the Continent were struggling, for several reasons, to provide acceptable levels of public goods for their citizens. The health care delivery system on the Continent is largely absent, the population explosion is at a negative variance with both opportunities and government support, access to basic services like potable water is abysmal, high public debts grossly depress the capacity to invest in developmental areas. Most of these debts are mis-directed, wasted, or stolen outright by government officials, public servants and their cronies.

As at February, 2020, African countries were owing China a cumulative amount of $145 billion, with an interest overhang of $8 billion annually. This profile is apart from other exposures to multilateral institutions like the World Bank and the IMF, as well as considerable and mounting local contractor obligations and domestic debts. There is very little to show for all these amounts. Public Revenues from natural resources, taxes, and other fiscal sources, are mostly diverted to personal accounts, with the result that the Continent suffers from the widest income disparity profiles in the world. You are either very rich or chronically poor.

With the mono-product economies that litter the Continent, the very consequential and drastic demand plunge for their natural products, with the attendant crash in prices on the international market, have worsened their economic outlook. Even at the best of times before now, most African countries (except, possibly, South Africa) did not invest in modern healthcare delivery systems; their leaders routinely traveled to the West, India, Singapore, China, and Dubai for their personal medical needs, or to die. Despite the typical African leadership norm of having dedicated clinics for their presidents (inside the massive and opulent presidential complexes inaccessible to the public), these clinics were still not properly equipped, staffed, or prepared for any health requirement beyond suturing primary wounds or dispensing pain killers. Hundreds of millions and billions of dollars voted for such clinics were and are still routinely diverted, even as the State ends up picking up the bills of these delinquent presidents and their families, supported by a coterie of staff and sycophants, as they embark on their extended medical tourism trips overseas. South Sudan, for example, has more Vice-Presidents than ventilators. The Nigerian President, Muhammed Buhari, for example, has spent up to 18 months out of the five years he has been in power, seeking medical attention and treatment in London, even as his country's medical system remains grossly sub-optimal.

A former president of the same country, Umaru Yar'adua, died in a Saudi hospital, after years of lies regarding his health and rule by proxy (by his lieutenants). Robert Mugabe, the freedom fighter turned tyrant in Zimbabwe, was a frequent visitor to Singaporean hospitals, where he finally died two years ago. As at February, 2020, only two laboratories could effectively confirm Coronavirus cases in the whole of Africa, according to the WHO. Since the global attention was called to this scourge, we now have only eight eligible laboratories on the Continent, with three in Nigeria, while a few more are being built. This is a Continent of 1.3 billion people, and growing, due mostly to the fatalistic and libidinal interpretation of the Koran among most of the Muslims on the Continent, with zero emphasis on responsibility, proper parenting, quality of life, and outcomes !!! The Economist magazine of March 26, 2020 correctly concluded that "Africa is woefully equipped to cope with COVID-19." It further wrote that "when life is a struggle, it is hard to worry about a threat you don't see…." The challenge of daily living is daunting enough. The Science magazine sees the risk posed by this virus to Africa as a "ticking time-bomb."

Many of the countries are grappling with very weak health systems, economic challenges, chronic political issues, serious security issues, as well as growing social dislocations. With the adverse sanitation issues, culture of physical contacts, population density in many of the cities and towns, living in denial which is buoyed by the preachings of manipulative pastors and Imams who engage in what Dr. Chidi Amuta calls " the organized crime of evangelical extortion" ("God Forbid", "It is not my portion", "Insha Allah", "No weapon fashioned against me shall prosper", etc., etc.), chronic poverty of the majority which entails struggling for daily income, the congestion on the minibuses that are commonly in use for public transportation, etc., etc., it becomes quite evident that some, if not all, of the containment measures made popular by the White House and the relatable Governor of New York, Andrew Cuomo, will not work in Africa, India, Bangladesh, Peru, El Salvador, or Ecuador, for example. You need to have pipe borne water and internal plumbing, to be able to wash your hands every twenty minutes, for example. There is no single city on the entire Continent of Africa that can boast of full provision of potable water supply from one end to the other. The rich typically recourse to providing their own water infrastructure, as they do with electricity, security, etc.

Physical distancing is an abstract, impractical, and unattainable theoretical concept for a poor family of six (or eight or ten) that is crammed into one tiny bedroom and living room, while they share bathroom, toilet, and kitchen facilities with other poor families, or embrace nature at will, in manifest expression of their ultimate freedom! These family members typically leave their ramshackle abode about 4 a.m., to pursue varying menial undertakings, and get home about 10 p.m. after their daily ritual of drudgery, and being sandwiched in overcrowded buses in endless traffic, all in very high temperature and deafening environmental noise. Now, they are forced to be at home all at one. Without deep broadband penetration, with epileptic power supply, with the very high temperatures brought on by climate change, the incentive to remain indoors and maintain physical distancing (which the world wrongly calls Social Distancing!!!), remains very remote. These factors also make it impossible for the school children, on an extended Coronavirus vacation, to take online classes, like their classmates in Western Europe or the US. Make no mistake, it is not everybody in Africa who faces these realities; after all, you have the fat cows in government, the genuinely-rich, corporate executives, successful business people with no ties to the governments, professionals, bankers, owners of all those private jets, parents of the millions of kids in schools all over the world because their very parents have directly or indirectly destroyed educational standards in their countries, etc., etc. The very rich and upper middle-class families live in outlandish splendor that only very few people outside the Continent can ever experience or relate to. The problem is that these families are relatively few in number, based on statistics.

According to Science magazine, Africa has the lowest average age in the world, with the median at below 20 years old and only 3% above 65 years old (compared with China that has achieved 12% in this segment in the past fifteen years due to their new wealth, better medicine, and improved quality of life). This healthy demographic split in Africa cannot be presently optimized to the Continent's benefit due to the corrosive public policies that have eroded potentials and opportunities across the board. Kenya, with 51 million people, has only 130 intensive care unit beds, according to the Science magazine, and 200 specialized ICU nurses. The profile is representative across the Continent, except, again, for South Africa (which is declining at a fast rate, one may add). The Academy of Sciences of the Republic of South Africa reports that people living with HIV are 8 times more likely to be hospitalized for pneumonia caused by the influenza virus than the general public, and also 3 times more likely to die from it.

Writing in the "Project Syndicate", Kevin Watkins (Africa's Race Against COVID:19) assessed that the Continent has a deficit of 3 million health care workers; the irony is that diaspora members from countries like Nigeria and Ghana contribute positively and significantly to the Healthcare Systems in Europe and the Americas (notably the UK and the US). There are, at least, 10,700 highly qualified Nigerian-born medical doctors working and living in the US alone, apart from a higher number of nurses and other healthcare professionals. A central thesis of this work is a philosophical investigation into what yields this outcome, and why more and more professionals, who should work towards improving Africa, are eager to flee as well. The average public health spend in Africa is $16 per person when a minimum of $86 is needed for an acceptable standard in countries within their indicative category.

With 7 hospital beds and one doctor for an average of 10,000 persons (it varies from country to country, but we are dealing with gross Continental averages here), and a massive under-investment profile, it is no wonder that the life expectancy rates are among the lowest in the world. By contrast, Italy, with over 34 beds and 40 doctors for 10,000 people, is massively overwhelmed by the Coronavirus attack, especially in the Lombardy Region. The United States, with even much better ratios, is struggling in places like New York, Detroit, Chicago, and New Orleans. Mr. Watkins writes that about 400,000 African children die each year from pneumonia, a condition that is largely manageable with antibiotics and medical-grade oxygen. The truth is that most of the available antibiotics are fake products imported from India, Indonesia, and China, while medical oxygen is very scarce. With the poverty spiral, zero safety nets, legacy economic challenges, burgeoning population numbers, public education standards on the decline, and the embarrassing state of the public health delivery system, there is a legitimate basis to remain concerned about what the industrial outbreak of this virus will mean for Africa, and, indeed, the world, given the interwoven links connecting us all.

Most countries in Africa (as, indeed, even the United States) did not take the threat posed by this virus seriously at the earliest stages. Governments wished it away, or assumed it was strictly China's problem, then it became Italy's problem, Spain's problem, and everybody's problem literally overnight !!! The decades of lack of preparation became glaring in their apoplectic and reactive responses. Without having much thought for their local dynamics, wherein the majority of their citizens depend on daily wages for survival, water does not run in majority of the homes, there is no electricity to power fans and air conditioners in crowded homes or to preserve perishables, there is no space at home for most people to maintain the physical distancing considered appropriate in Europe and US, etc., etc., poorer societies simply shut down their countries, deploying the Military and Police to enforce their diktat with ferocity. These brutes have since killed a few innocents who stepped out to fetch water, buy food, or take their pregnant wives to the hospital.

Despite shutting down countries and states for weeks -- to minimize human contacts and the spread of the virus, they took permission from the Spirit of Coronavirus and announced that Muslim Jumat services would hold on Fridays, while some states announced that Easter church services would hold. You see, the pandemic will pause once they are praying, and only pounce when they leave the mosques and churches. This reification of issues, this unthinking abdication of personal responsibility, this surrender to largely fantabulous myths, accounts for the malady that has befallen these countries. Some countries also announced that the crowded markets would open for four hours daily, to enable people buy foodstuff. During those hours, coronavirus will go on a short break. Well, poverty and frustration have mixed, and there are serious retail security problems across cities in Africa and India over the lockdown without provisions. Shops and homes are being invaded by both hungry people and professional criminals.

Initially, too, as the virus ravaged China and Europe, the street in Africa concluded that black people were immune from the virus. Some people propagated the unproven story that the high temperatures would not allow the virus to fester or attack people in Africa.

A lot of people actually believed this nonsense, and went about their business, incubating and spreading the virus on a progressive basis, albeit asymptomatically. With African-Americans representing the disproportionate percentage of victims of the pandemic in the US, these pseudo-virologists will soon propagate another theory. The abysmal ratio of testing in Africa is responsible for the low numbers of the patients and dead that we are seeing presently. The stigma factor attached to it is also a potent consideration. Perhaps, a major spike will call attention to the widespread prevalence of the virus on the Continent; this will mean a second or third wave for the rest of the world, as business people, international students, and tourists will commence their travels while being asymptomatic.

Religion has also played a negative role in the way people in the poorer countries have responded to this global threat; as it happens, the poorer societies have the highest concentration of religious people. Perhaps, it makes sense really. Islam and Christianity (its several variants) are dominant in Africa, with the common theme of accepting every situation as either God's Will (Insha Allah), or a test of faith. Personal responsibility recedes to the background; even as the Muslim Allah is assumed to be all-powerful, she/it/he still needs a few misguided adherents to help by perpetrating terroristic acts with the products of Science (bombs and weapons, not the Koran), on behalf of this seemingly-omnipotent Deity. Incongruous and nonsensical !!! Again, despite the great promise of heaven in both Christianity and Islam, for example, (everlasting peace and rejoicing for Christians; virginal allocations for Muslims), the reluctance to die seems illogical and un-religious. They need to die to get to heaven or Al-Janat Firdausi, yet they don't want to die !!! Why are these believers afraid of Coronavirus, which should accelerate the journey to perpetual enjoyment in heaven???

When believers eventually accepted the fact of the threat posed by the pandemic, some theorized and broadcast that it was from the devil. Some so-called religious leaders declared, without any foundation or qualification, that these were end-times. If true, you would expect their believers to be saved. Why is no one exempt? Why are the religious themselves in hiding? Some of them focused more on the remote and digital tithing by their gullible members during this period of quarantine, reminding them that paying their tithes (to him or her/ God !!!) was not negotiable or conditional, and that they should find electronic ways to remit their funds to the churches, to avoid incurring the wrath of God (namely, themselves)!!!. These Sole Proprietorships, these merchants of lies, these exploiters of human anxiety and frustration, these private jet and Rolls Royce-loving charlatans, these unworthy individuals, these impostors, these fellows who exploit the human fear of death (which must come to all living things!) these nihilists, these people who claim to raise the dead and restore sight to the blind, are all hiding in their homes, begrudging this virus for altering their financial projections for the year. When they finally manage to crawl out of bed, they shamelessly make foolish statements, to remain relevant by infamy.

The leader of one of the largest Pentecostal groups in Nigeria and Africa, Pastor Enoch Adeboye (private jet, Rolls Royce, etc.), with several millions of tithe-paying members/ victims "revealed" in March, two weeks into the arrival of the first Coronavirus case in Nigeria, that God told him (it had to be him) in January, 2020 that the whole world would be forced to go on vacation, but that he did not want to alarm the world. Subsequently, he said absolutely nothing when he declared that the same God had told him, yet again, that those who are killed by coronavirus are "those whose time to die has come." When he still needed to be heard, he declared magisterially that Coronavirus shall end someday. Of course, when Scientists and Researchers have done all the work !!! By that time, these hucksters, these snake oil peddlers, these godless creatures, will shamelessly turn around and weave a story for their gullible audience and victims, that their prayers and intercessions have finally saved the world.

Another successful manipulator, Pastor Oyedepo (private jets, etc.), with millions of followers/ victims could not take the chance of expecting his victims to pay their tithe electronically, so he summoned them to a church service in Lagos, Nigeria (and around all their branches) on the first Sunday after the lock down, in defiance of Government directives, ostensibly to grant them immunity from the coronavirus pandemic. Fools attended, and the result of their mutual infestation shall become clear in due course. Yet another character declared that he had covered Nigerians and Africans with "corrosive anointing", a play of words from Coronavirus. A dandy pastor, Chris Oyakhilome (private jet, etc.), with millions of gullible devotees/ victims, chose another path: after declaring Coronavirus to be the attack of the devil (who seems to have grossly overpowered the omnipotent God!), he went further by declaring, in a most illiterate and unintelligent manner, that the introduction of 5G technology was behind the lockdowns around the world, in order to enthrone the Rule of the Anti-Christ !!!

Oh, that great and unequalled humanist and philanthropist, Bill Gates, is the Arch-Devil, the current Anti-Christ. His predecessors included Napoleon Bonaparte, Il Duce Benito Mussolini, Saddam Hussein, and Barack Obama, while some of the earlier diabolical plots of this all-powerful Anti-Christ have included: the credit card, commercial aviation which shrank travel times significantly, street lights in London in 1830 which defied God's plan for day and night to be permanently separated, etc. So, the US shut down its entire system and the largest economy in the world to inaugurate a new leader of the world? Europe has been shut down and businesses closed for the same purpose? Mr. Oyakhilome said that the installation of 5G antennae and fiber optic cables was the reason that African Governments had shut down their countries, in obedience to foreign masters. Such imbecilic nonsense !!! But then, these tormented, narcissistic, and fraudulent people are richly rewarded by the society, all in the name of religion. They pay no price for their deceit. The same God revealed one thing to Adeboye, and the 5G nonsense to Oyakhilome. Interesting!!! Conceited Hustlers!!! This flashy man with no visible means of livelihood other than fleecing people in the name of God, actually flies a private jet, while Jesus rode on donkey backs.

Mr. Oyakhilome's competitor, with considerable following as well, and who ascribes all sorts of powers to himself, T.B. Joshua, was more definite than the rest; His own God told him that there would be a heavy rainfall on March 27, 2020, which would wash away every trace of Coronavirus in the world. Well, no rain fell on that day; we are in April, and the ravaging impact of the pandemic has only intensified. The pretender will soon hear God's reason for this disappointing outcome soon; perhaps, humans are still committing sin and have not learnt enough lessons yet. All of this, to buy time for Scientists and Researchers to save mankind from this viral onslaught!

It is instructive that Saudi Arabia, the global headquarters of Sunni Islam, as well as Iran, the competing headquarters of the Shiite Islamic strain, have shut down all their mosques, and canceled this year's Lesser Hajj (in Saudi Arabia), out of respect for Coronavirus, while Africans insist on opening their own mosques. It is, perhaps, lost on some people that millions of faithful Muslims who make the financial sacrifice (mostly Africans, again) to embark on this religious tourism to Mecca and Medina, simply to throw stones at the devil and to walk around an oversized concrete black box, could not even be saved by Allah and Muhammed from the virus which should kill only non-adherents of their faith.

In any case, why travel all the way to Saudi Arabia to identify and throw stones at the devil when they are surrounded by devils back in their own countries, with zero leadership, filth, poverty, and wholesale corruption? In fact, when some of them are devils themselves!!! The Vatican respected itself by just declaring that the world was going through deep trials in the form of the Coronavirus, and then promptly shut down all their thousands of branches/ churches worldwide. They declared ahead of time (7 weeks ahead of time), during the holiest period of Christendom when the Christian/ Catholic faithful were observing their mandatory 40-day fasting period (an ulceratic penance for Jesus' last 40 days on earth), a time one would expect an abundance of spiritual power and grace, that the Easter Mass and celebrations would not hold this year. Sikh temples around the world have been closed, to avoid worshippers getting sick.

The inference is that the Catholic prayers and incantations in the lost language of Latin, would not withstand the non-discriminatory ferocity of the coronavirus. The Pope had managed to issue a very rare and special (we were told) *Urbi et Orbi* message and blessing to the world in March, 2020, at the peak of the viral attack killing thousands of people next door in parts of Italy. It was quite a sight to behold the Pope holding an Easter Mass in a completely empty St. Peter's Basilica (beamed around the world by Science and Technology); therein, he made the very profound statement that the future of the European Union depended on how they tackled the coronavirus pandemic. Indeed!!! The Head of the Anglican Church is in London, issuing bland statements as well.

The remaining branch of the Abrahamic Religions, Judaism, has also not made any single positive contribution to the search for a solution to this catastrophe that has afflicted mankind. Their most sacred shrine, The Wailing Wall--usually protected by heavily-armed Security Forces, since the Force within the Wall cannot protect this most "sacred" of places--has been closed completely.

Even as these three religions have their grand rituals and festivals about the same time, during the era of Coronavirus, Christians were unable to attend Easter services worldwide; Muslims could not have their Tarawih prayers; and Jews were not saved during their Passover, and no seders were held by them. An eloquent and definitive statement for religion would have been made if the adherents of just one of these faiths were particularly protected from the virus. The same for races, gender, and other convenient differentiators. Yet, we are all in it together. Hmmmmmmm. It is proper to leave out the other faiths, like Buddhism, Hinduism, Shintoism, and the several forms of ancestral worship around the world, since none of those has the expansionist agenda, messianic arrogance, willful conceit, will to violence, ingrained condescension, and conversion orientation of some or all of these three; the three religions responsible for most of the problems in the world, due, at the end of the day, to the stubborn refusal to reach a justiciable agreement over a tiny parcel of dry land, the much too promised land (apologies to Aaron David Miller).

None of these, or other religions, has a solution to the virus attacking and killing mankind presently. None !!! In the twisted logic that underpins their essence, they feel entitled to approbate and reprobate, claim and disclaim, at their convenience. The pandemic is God's way of punishing the world, and God will stop it at her/his/ its own time (read, when Science has stopped it). We await as they all scramble to take credit once reason, expertise, rationality, inquiry, research, diligence, rigor, and tenacity, considerable financial resources, combine to find an effective and sustainable solution to the pandemic. Their prayers and interventions would have worked by then.... Amen, somebody!!!! Halleluyah!!! Insha Allah!!! Shalom!!!

We are told in a Decree of the Council of the Vatican that: " There never can be any real discrepancy between faith and reason since the same God who reveals mysteries and infuses faith has bestowed the light of reason on the human mind; and God cannot deny Himself, nor can truth ever contradict truth. The false appearance of such a contradiction is mainly due, either to the dogmas of faith not having been clearly understood and expounded according to the mind of the Church, or to the inventions of opinion having been taken for the verdicts of reason." Indeed, the Mother Church, "the Bride of Christ and Mother of His Elect", the Catholic Church contends that "as reason is inferior to, and must be enlightened by revelation, so philosophy is dependent on theology, and, if the need arises, must correct its conclusions by the higher and more certain truths of faith." "Philosophy," for them, "is the handmaid of Theology"--*Philosophia Theologice ancilla.* In the Encyclical " *A'terni Patris*, Pope Leo XIII approves and urges the teaching of the philosophy of St. Thomas for this reason.

This reminds one of the arbitrary declaration by Pope Pius IX on December 8, 1854 that Mary, mother of Christ, was also born of virginal birth. Invoking the doctrine of Papal Infallibility, and without much rigorous investigation or the convening of a General Council, he declared this personal position as a Church Dogma solely on the basis of his authority. While he did not affirm before his audience that any knowledge of this generational mythology existed before his declaration, he nevertheless decreed that they would become the dogma of the Church, going forward.

He then warned that "If any should dare to think otherwise in their heart than as we have determined, they shall learn and know that they are condemned by their own judgment, that they have made a shipwreck of the faith, and are separated from the unity of the Church." Since then, some faithfuls have been seeing apparitions of a woman in white, for example, in the Lourdes caves in France (1858); Fatima, near Lisbon, Portugal, 1917), generating a stream of devoted pilgrims until the present era. The fundamental issue with this circuitous declaration is that, if valid, the Ecclesiastical Community can always take credit for any and every positive outcome, without being subjected to the exacting standards and rigorous objectivity of the scientific method. In addition, any convincing facts regarding Evolution will nullify the central premise of the formulation in an irreversible and irrecoverable way. With this, there is no point proceeding to the objective determination of who receives these "divine" messages, and by what means they are transmitted. It is also impossible to know when God speaks and when it is humans, like ourselves, speaking, as in the case of the arbitrary imposition of the Mary Dogma by Pope Piux IX. For the mom and pop shops masquerading as Pentecostal Churches, the range of creativity and arbitrariness becomes infinite. There is nothing in the profound writings of eminent Church writers like Tillemont, Mabillon, Fleury, Natalis Alexander, Montfaucon, Bossuet, Muratori, Orsi, Cardinals Mai and Pitra, as well as Palma, Rohrbacher, Darras, Mohler, Alzog, Dollinger, Bishop Hefele, Cardinal Hergenrather, Jungmann, Briick, Kraus, and others, to sway one's conclusion otherwise.

There has also been a lot of prose, poetry, false statements, and misattributions recycled, all thanks to Social Media. The "all-knowing" Nostradamus has words fed into his mouth at will, depending on the circumstance; folks who failed O'Level Physics deign to comment on Ph.D.-level Physics (5G), alarmist declarations are forwarded and re-forwarded, thereby gaining in currency especially among the unthinking *hoi polloi*, and, frankly, even among the so-called educated -- with a unifier in a submission to religious manipulation

When asked her view on getting Coronavirus under control, Nancy Pelosi, the Speaker of the U.S House of Representatives commented thus "It won't happen unless we respect Science, Science, Science. And for those who say we choose prayer over Science, I say Science is an answer to our prayers". At least, Speaker Pelosi understands the real source of our survival from this tragedy, as she uses circumlocution to still attribute the eventual scientific breakthrough to her prayers. No mention of the rigorous scientific methodology, proof, inquiry, validation and testing, as well as peer review and repeatability which define Science, under the malleable refuge of religiosity. I understand she is an ardent Catholic.

Source: Cartoon Church, Illustrated by Dave Walker

Samples of Prose being peddled as a defense against Coronavirus:

"Jesus went on a Self-isolation in the grave for our sins. He was unduly quarantined even though He tested negative to sin. His Resurrection from His Isolation Centre after three days formed the foundation for our release from the lock down by sin. Anyone who has been infected by the virus of sin can be sanitized and recovered through the vaccine of the Blood of Jesus. He will subsequently live a Victorious Life through the Ventilator of the Holy Spirit."

"Surely, he has borne our infirmities and carried our diseases; yet we accounted him stricken, struck down by God, and afflicted. But he was wounded for our transgressions, crushed for our iniquities; upon him was the chastisement that made us whole, and, by his bruises, we are healed. Let us have faith in him and be healed by his stripes. No Coronavirus will come our way."

"10 Reasons why Corona cannot affect you:

1. *You are a spirit (Ps. 82: 6); Corona does not attack the Spirits;* 2. *You are a fire (Matt. 3:11); Corona does not resist fire;* 3. *You are a wind (John 3: 8); Corona does not attack the wind;* 4. *You are not earthly, but heavenly (Eph. 2: 6); Corona is on earth;* 5. *Your life is hidden in God (Col. 3: 3); Corona does not touch God;* 6. *You are a stone (1 Pt. 2: 4 - 5); Corona has no effect on stone;* 7. *You are the apple of His eye (Zach. 2: 8); Corona cannot enter God's eye;* 8. *You were bought at a great price (1 Cor. 6:20); Corona can't tear anything out of Jesus' hands;* 9. *You bear the marks of Christ (Gal. 6:17); Corona can't hurt Christ;* 10. *You live by His Blood (Rev. 12:11); Corona cannot overturn victory achieved over 2,000 years ago. Only reassure yourself that Jesus is your Lord and your Savior. Build your faith on His Word daily, and nothing evil shall come your way, including Coronavirus."*

We have also heard that the churches must be kept open and allowed to run their normal services (of selling hope, collecting money on God's behalf, mystifying normal and random developments, cursing one's endless enemies, and postponing the redemption of earlier prophecies and promises, in an enterprise that has become all about benefits), because "churches are not places of infection, but places of blessings." Ok, Pastor, go and kiss someone with a confirmed case of COVID-19, and seek no medical help. Several developing countries, having failed their citizens on the provision of basic health services, declared National Prayer Days, as their most vigorous response to a merciless pandemic. We are told that the faith-exploiter at the White House also saw this ruse as a way to consolidate his so-called evangelical base.

Others claimed that the virus would attack only those privileged people in the developing countries who could travel overseas; when this was debunked, the local populations earnestly prayed that their political leaders should become the victims of the pandemic. Well, wishes have no force, and only reflect desired outcomes, which usually do not happen. Oh, the coronavirus is also God's punishment for the numerous sins of the world. Purveyors of this nonsense do not recognize how much they de-market God and the entire business built around her/ him/ it. How can both God and the devil, the anti-

Christ, collaborate as equal partners, to wreak havoc in the world? What kind of God will destroy the world, just to prove a point? If they shift blame from God, how can an omnipotent, omnipresent, and omniscient God not stop the evil intentions and machinations of the Devil?

Their next response: Oh, s/he/it allows the Devil to wield some power. Indeed. What, precisely, are those sins? How compatible are these new sins with the sins by humans in the pre-Noah era? Why does the threshold keep shifting? Answering these germane questions cannot be as easy as using incompatible positions and just about any development to validate a convenient, compliant, pre-set position, however the imponderability and ridiculousness of the Construct. A definite position will help, with some accountability. There are multiple fallacies here: *Petitio Principii* (Circular Reasoning), *Ignorantio Elenchi* (Irrelevant Conclusion), *Reductio ad Absurdum* (Contradictory Premises and Reduction to Absurdity), *Patrocinia* (Special Pleading), as well as *Argumentum Ad Speculum* (Contrary to fact/ Changing the Meaning). God Save the King; God Save the Queen; God is involved in both ......

When all the distractions failed, Coronavirus cases started springing up across Africa, and governments imposed complete lockdowns (without much thought for the economic structure of their countries and the potentials of hunger killing more people than the COVID-19 attack), some situational historians and poets changed their tone, and cited the respected Queen of England to encourage people to stay at home. They wrote as follows:

'Queen Elizabeth II has survived:

The plague, Smallpox, Malaria, Nazi rule in Germany, WWII, Destruction of Berlin, Partition of Berlin, Creation of Israel, Partition of India , Korean War, Vietnam war, Unification of Berlin, Strife in Palestine, Invasion of Egypt, Arab- Israeli War, Cold War, Iran-Iraq War, First Gulf War, Disintegration of Soviet Union , Britain joining the EU, 9/11, Second Gulf War, Britain leaving the EU, Apollo 1-17, Revolutions in Africa, 14 British Prime Ministers, Charles and Diana, Charles and Camilla, Andrew and Fergie, Harry and Megan, 14 American Presidents, 7 Saudi Kings, 48 Italian Prime Ministers, 9 UN Secretary-Generals, 3rd, 4th, and 5th French Republics, Mad Cow Disease, Brexit; Meghxit, The Internet , Apple TV, Netflix ... and Covid-19'

Only because she rarely leaves her palace. Hahahahahahahahahaha!

Keep Safe. Stay at Home!!! False Hope to unthinking people.

A certain Pastor Daniel Obinim from Ghana also concocted some very powerful "Coronavirus Anointing Oil" which sold for $37 per bottle and which was "approved by the heavenly Department of the FDA." Indeed !!! A Kenyan pastoral charlatan based in the UK, whose preferred name actually exceeds his abundant idiocy -- can you believe that? – "Mr. Climate Irungu Wisemen", also issued the "Plagues Divine Protection Oil" in response to COVID-19; to get the guaranteed protection, though, you needed to pay him 91 British pounds for each bottle, with the encouragement to buy for all your relatives and loved ones. A few thousands of bottles were sold before the authorities clamped down on this fraudster.

Another Pentecostal church, with branches across Africa, asked the members to buy "Corona" Oil, and chant the following names or appellations twice daily in the same sequence after rubbing the oil all over their bodies, and the virus will avoid them completely. The oil sold out in hours, but most must be presently infected and active carriers!!! These cranky fellows have a deep fascination with oil…

Wonderful; Counsellor; Prince of Peace; Eternal Rock of Ages; King of Glory; Mighty God; King of kings; Lord of lords; Lord of hosts; Lily of the valley; Healer; Deliverer; Provider; Creator; Potter; Day Star; Cornerstone; Prophet of prophet; Saviour; I AM THAT I AM; Wisdom of God; Head of the church; Governor; Righteous Judge; Protector; Rock of offence; Shield; Merciful God; Gracious God; Faithful God; Giver; Victorious in Holiness; Consuming Fire; El Elyon; Jehovah Raphael; Jehovah Rohi; Jehovah Jireh; Jehovah Elgibor; Jehovah Shamah; Jehovah Shalom; El Olam; Defender; Redeemer; Comforter; Trinity in Council; Instructor; Teacher; Inspirer; Reminder; Invisible God; Hope of Glory; Lion of Judah; Root of Jesse; Man of war; Lamb of God; Sustainer; Convincer; Light of the world; Restorer; Silencer Stiller of storms; Proclaimer; Father of the fatherless; Husband of the widow; Smith of heaven;

The Way; The Truth; The Life; Bread of life; BreadWinner; Champion of champions; Winner of winners; Composer; Author; Finisher; Glorious in Holiness; Fearful in praises; Sleepless God; Ancient of days; Ageless God; Eternal God; Excellent God; Powerful God; Leader of leaders; Chief Inventor; Convener; Compassionate God; Commander-in-Chief of heavenly host; Worthy King; Overseer; Moulder; Shaper; Breaker; Praiseworthy God; Helper; Richer than the richest; Older than the oldest; Trustworthy God; Arranger; Master Builder; Master Planner; Master Minder; Arrester; Relentless God; Voice of hope; Beautiful God; Alpha and Omega; Game Changer; Our Refuge; Our fortress; Our Buckler; Our Banner; Strong Tower;

Unchanging changer; Rose of Sharon; All in All; Pillar of our lives; The First Born; Lamb that was slain; The Glory & lifter of our heads; The word of God; Our Advocate; Our High Priest; Bishop of our souls; High and Lofty one; Almighty; Our Best Friend; On time God; Lion of Judah; Omnipotent; Omnipresent; Omniscient; Consuming fire Adonai; The beginning & the end; Living water; Unquenchable fire; Awesome God; I salute your excellency Papa; Battle stopper; Unquestionable God; Jehovah shikenu; Mighty one in battle; Glorious in Holiness; Fearful in praises; Mighty man of valor; Miracle worker; Rock of ages; Merciful God; Advocate; Always doing wonders; Amen and Hallelujah; Answer to prayers; Intercessor; Interceptor; Balm of Gilead

Phew!!!!! As any moderately intelligent person knows, this eloquent manifestation of verbal diarrhea is just that, an uncontrollable profusion of effluent, with zero correlation with either palliatives or the cure. None of those words, or any combination thereof, is a convalescent plasma or a Salk vaccine. They do not even rise to the level of non-pharmaceutical interventions; just a foolish cacophony of gibberish, an outpouring of overwhelming stupidity, an impotent rendition of jarring and incompatible words, some wrongly pronounced in their original Aramaic or Hebrew. There was a reason the great philosopher accepted in the early 19th century that religion served a crucial purpose, that of decongesting the clinics of the psychiatrists and psychologists. Marx built on this by calling it the opium of the people.

This madness is not limited to Africa or the undeveloped parts of the world, though. In the United States, Televangelist Jim Bakker peddled what he called a "Silver Solution" that would protect his followers from the Coronavirus; well, the State of Missouri has sued him for that. Another huckster-pastor, Landon Spradlin, initially denied the existence of the virus; when he finally conceded that it was real, he blamed the Media for creating all the "panic" to hurt President Trump. Well, coronavirus killed the man in March, a few weeks ago.

Africa, Latin America, and the Indian subcontinent must test, test, and test NOW !!! The world must demand this. As the world continues to deal with this multifaceted and fluid disaster, a lot of strategic issues will need the attention of serious global leaders and thinkers. The virtual dependence on China for essentials must be reconsidered and broken, given the illiberalism in their political and economic space. The Government determines everything, and they are not shy about wielding their power in ways that some may consider whimsical and counter-productive to stability and predictability in the Global Order.

It has become evident that the assumption that interdependence and involvement of China in the coordinating Institutions of Global Peace, Trade, and Security, would elicit responsible behavior on their part, was naive in the first place. China is not likely to become a member or leader of the International Community on terms that promote decent engagement, respect for human rights and dignity, as well as balanced gain for all.

Foreign Affairs Magazine posed the question whether or not globalization, as we knew it, had been destroyed by Coronavirus. The interconnectedness of the world is now irreversible; new adjustments and protocols will need to be made and enacted to suit the new normal. No one country can afford absolute insularity, but nations have to rank their priorities, articulate their Comparative Advantages, and make strategic decisions on what they must produce locally and what they could keep importing. It has been hugely embarrassing to see major countries like the United States, the United Kingdom, Germany, France, and Italy (all nuclear powers) scramble desperately to buy ventilators, hospital beds, and personal protective equipment (elegant language for masks, gloves, and disposable gowns) from the same suppliers in China, where the pandemic started in the first place, for their hospitals and medical staff. This competition for limited supply made them all vulnerable to price gouging and even the virtual hijack of fully paid-for items.

President Trump of the United States had proudly announced late in 2019 that the US had spent over $2 trillion modernizing its military arsenal during his Administration. That is a whole lot of money, but the invisible COVID-19 virus has paralyzed the US and the world without shooting a single bullet, while the scarcity of gloves and face masks is threatening to expose the underbelly of an otherwise great power. A highly-leveraged US has committed over $2.2 trillion (more than all that weapons modernization figure) to stimulate its economy, while the world is estimated to have lost over $7 trillion already, and the problem has not been solved --- all without a single shot (pun intended).

It needs to be mentioned that Wuhan, where this pandemic started, in the Hubei Province of China, is the largest producer of optical cable and fiber in the world, controlling 25% of the global supply market; this holds serious implications for possible disruptions in this critical sector down the line.

For those who routinely castigate Governments, this moment shows the value of an efficient government, indeed of professionalism and expertise. How else would we have responded to this crisis in an ethical manner? Leave it to big business to handle, and they sell the vaccine to only the richest among us, while the rest of mankind dies? How about the trillions of dollars being spent to support displaced workers and struggling businesses around the world? Left to their devices, airlines and cruise ships would have continued with their operations in the midst of the pandemic thereby effectively moving infected people around the world, for speedy distribution of the virus. Good Governments intervened to provide the overarching protection and guidance needed critically during these perilous times.

Urgent and critical attention must also be paid to the utter incapacity of several countries to deal with even basic public health issues and related developmental imperatives, how much more a tragedy of such epic proportions as the Coronavirus pandemic. If we allow them to perpetuate their excuses and State failure, we shall remain imperiled as connected members of the human race. Sovereignty and Political Independence must mean something, must mean visible and measurable performance, and not just the leaders voting at the UN (where they parrot the illusions of notional parity and equality among nations, while they remain abject at the provision of very basic public goods), junketing all over the world at the expense of their poorly-served countries, flying the flags of their delinquent States, blaring siren on their streets in interminable convoys, and using government-paid Security Forces to drive their citizen-victims off the road, often in a very dangerous manner. The Post-coronavirus Era (P.C.E.), must lead to a fundamental revision or outright revocation of the relevant provisions of the Geneva Convention, which enable and sustain this assumption and illusion of hard territoriality and sovereignty of incompetence and failure once committed within a definite geographical space. This inviolability clause has been rendered redundant by the emerging and continuing challenges facing the entire world. **Independence** must not continue to **depend** on foreign resources, aid, and support.

Absurdities and Hilarities

In the face of this enormous tragedy that is still unraveling presently, one has observed quite a few absurd and hilarious developments.

We are now all “thugs." People use that word derisively to describe mostly young black men wearing hooded sweatshirts during winter. This characterization prepares the sociological conditioning for their casual killing by paid officers of the State in the US, without consequences, even as we condemn and jail people who arrange cock and dog fights. We spend billions of dollars pampering dogs and cats, and generally advocating for the “rights” of these animals, while the same people hardly flinch when an innocent life is taken willfully by agents of the State, for selling loose cigarettes, for “looking threatening”, even as they are completely innocent. Make no mistake, violent criminals should be dealt with as such, especially when the lives of our Police Officers are verifiably threatened, otherwise, the same justice and treatment should be accorded to all. What is a masked face but a hooded face, thugs? Whereas it would have been impossible to enter a bank with a face mask two months ago, you could be arrested for not wearing one now, you thug.

A prominent Monk of the Russian Orthodox Church, who is close to the political leadership there (that means one person: the puny, punting, putative, perennial, and recurring Czar), was hoisted on a private jet (picture that; a monk on a private jet!), and he flew over Moscow and St. Petersburg, blessing both cities and shielding them from the Coronavirus pandemic. Well, the reported cases in both cities have been on an increase…

The majority Hindu and Buddhist population in India has been attacking the minority Muslims, accusing them of being responsible for the coronavirus. Hatred of the "other" projected as religion...

A lot has changed in America in less than a month. When you walk or run on the sidewalks of suburbia America, hooded and masked people approaching from the opposite direction literally crawl into the drainage system or jump into the grass median, just to avoid you, the harbinger of death. The hilarious part is that some of these people never returned your polite greetings or wave of the hand just a month ago; now, they vacate the entire sidewalk for you, out of respect and fear for coronavirus. Many of these people are walking pharmacies, yet they assume you are the vector of pestilence. When those whose possible ancestral and social links with the implicated wet market also avoid you, the spectacle of hilarity is completed.

We have all been warned *ad nauseum* to maintain social distancing, in order to stem the spread of the virus. Well, humans, as social beings, cannot be distanced from one another. What we meant to say was Physical Distancing. Our socialness or sociability is not only expressed through handshakes and hugs; we remain social animals when we cook for our families, attend to the very sick at the hospitals, watch movies as families, speak with family, colleagues, and friends on phone. John O'Donohue wrote that: "to be human is to belong … belonging is the heart and warmth of intimacy." Obviously, we can be social or intimate in the pure sense without all the hugging and embrace. As mentioned earlier, there are lots of people who cannot afford the physical distancing prescription, but they remain social animals or humans nevertheless, and cannot be socially distant from other humans.

A vigorous contact tracing program is best achieved when you have details of everyone living within a country or region. In most under-developed countries, this is simply not the case. Some politicians deliberately retain the fluid citizenship data, to enable them rig elections or channel disproportionate government resources to their ethnic groups or Region on the basis of contrived and fraudulent numbers. In most of these countries also, the informal social structures and the reliance on congested buses as primary means of commute by the majority, make contact tracing even more difficult. It is very easy for a single carrier to make contact with a hundred different people daily, and then spread the virus in equal measure.

Many marriages and relationships are undergoing their first true test; divorce lawyers will be quite busy in the period immediately after our collective enforced quarantine. Some of the uber-rich but absent parents are also forced to spend time with their indulgent offspring, who are usually banished to very expensive private boarding schools, or are mothered by the governess on the few occasions they visit home, while the parents are busy closing deals, traveling, and attending Gala Nights --- none of which can now hold. It must be quite a spectacle to finally be introduced to your seventeen-year-old for the first time in ten years.

GenerationCorona kids are being sired across the globe without much thought or planning, especially in those parts where the contribution of the majority seems to be the endless production of children whose future remains bleak. In those same slums, parental responsibility is abdicated to some mythical provision for these almajiri horde; a pathetic social infestation or what Chidi Amuta calls the undifferentiated mass of impoverished humanity. It was Malthus who wrote that "it is the constant tendency in all animated life to increase beyond the nourishment prepared for it." These unthinking producers of abandoned children that litter the streets of the mostly-Muslim Northern Nigeria in their millions may not be aware that Malthus also wrote, as captured by Salwyn, Schapiro, and James T, that "as population grows there is not sufficient food for all; hence, poverty is unavoidable; the poor are the cause of their own poverty. War, disease, and famine are, therefore, natural, even beneficial, as they act as checks upon a too great increase of population." Talking about kids, some names have been devised by some societies around the Coronavirus, in a permanent tribute to this equalizer and trigger of a new epoch in human history.

It is telling that those wimpish pretenders, those animals, those tortured creatures who wreak mass violence in the name of religion (Islam in our modern times), have gone into their caves in the face of the Coronavirus pandemic.

Distressed individuals, sad malcontents like Duerte in The Philippines, and his duplicates around the world, see the pandemic as yet another opportunity to practise their sadistic lust for human blood, all in an effort to confirm their authoritarian hold on their hapless citizens.

Some countries like Panama have gone to the ridiculous level of separating their citizens by binary gender (good thing is that they still have natural, sensible, and known genders!), regarding who can come out on which day. What happens to emergencies? Hilarious.

When that phenom and eccentric, Michael Jackson, routinely wore masks and gloves, we assumed the masks only were meant to hide the considerable transfiguration of his nose from Michael's to Mickey's. When our Indian brethren practised Namaste, we thought it was a yoga move for spinal integrity. Now, we know….

Quite a few people have assumed that the collective problem facing mankind will force us to introspect, appreciate our common humanity, and, in the post-coronavirus era, racism, hatred, terrorism, greed, human trafficking, etc., will suddenly disappear. The so-called Grand Wizard or Imperial Wizard of the KKK will adopt babies from Tanzania and Bangladesh, and love will blossom in eternity. Immediately after the pandemic, the Israeli-Palestinian conflict will be resolved to the satisfaction of both parties; Saudi Arabia (including Mecca and Medina), as well as other absolute Islamic countries will have thousands of churches and synagogues, exactly the same way there are thousands of mosques all over Europe and the United States (anything to the contrary will evidence continuing foolishness on the part of the West and reward for these theocracies for their arrogance and anachronistic turf-protection at home while DEMANDING accommodation in the West);

Iran and the US will reset their bilateral relations on the basis of trust, respect, and cessation of direct and proxy hostilities; terrorists will stop being "hoodwinked with carnal desires" -- paradise *ex congruo*; China will start practising Jeffersonian Democracy; the pudgy little boy in North Korea will surrender all their nukes and ballistic weapons to the IAEA and conduct a free and fair presidential election monitored by Western parties; etc., etc. Not quite; humans have undergone several traumatic periods in history, and nothing changed. Irrational hatred is etched on some people's DNA, it and will not suddenly disappear because of a virus. This time will not be different.

Kumbaya chorus songs will only disadvantage the naive. Human nature will remain fundamentally wicked and predatory.

If anyone is in doubt, they only need to be aware that, even as the global human community is confronting this common invisible enemy, and recommendations are being formulated for an internationally-coordinated response, two French medical doctors, one heading an intensive care unit at a major French hospital -- Jean-Paul Mira and Camille Locht, suggested on public television that the Coronavirus vaccine should be tested on Africans whenever it is developed. The context of their suggestion is immaterial, as it evinces a very deep philosophical position on their part. As it is, France has far more cases of the virus than the entire Continent of Africa at this time, yet, the testing should be done on Africans!!! The fate of any black person who is rushed into the ICU under the care of these Mengele-wannabes is best imagined. As Musa Okwonga wrote in QZ.com, this actually follows "a long tradition of French experimentation upon Africans. To take just one example, between 1921 and 1956, millions of citizens were forced by French colonial governments "to receive injections of medications with dubious efficacy and with serious side effects, including blindness, gangrene, and death." Please see *https://scholar.harvard.edu/files/emontero/files/lowes_montero_colonialmedicine.pdf*, for an illuminating Report titled The Legacy of Colonial Medicine by Sara Lowes of Bocconi University and Eduardo Montero of Harvard University.

As Mr. Okwonga further reminds us, J. Marion Sims, the 19th-century American medical doctor who is generally celebrated as having pioneered Gynecology as a specialized field of study, practised his experiments and "theories" exclusively on enslaved African women (in America), with zero anesthetics. Notably, he abused and tortured a particular black woman, Anarcha, over thirty (30) times with these evil experiments. Less than a century later, several African-American men, who were promised free healthcare, were deliberately infected with syphilis, at a time there was no cure for it, and without their knowledge or consent. The purpose had to do with testing, yet again. When the cure for syphilis was finally discovered, it was not extended to these human guinea-pigs! No price was paid by the perpetrators; they probably won awards, like Dr. Sims, for their medical "breakthroughs", without any mention of the human casualtics. This may explain some of the suspicion a cross-section of Africans has towards vaccines and Western medical aid in general; a situation that is being exploited by the powerful and dubious anti-vaccine movement.

That horde of empty vessels who feed off inanities, and who have an insatiable need for recognition and sucking up all our air need to be accounted for as well, otherwise we would be remiss in our narrative; they call themselves celebrities. Is this a new profession? The slobby predators remain on the prowl targeting innocent young women until they are outed while the women feast on "fame." What, exactly, do some of these people do, other than struggling very hard (for the women) to convince us that they are, indeed, women? We must be regaled with their "famous curves", "stunning figures", "baby bumps", "peachy posterior/ derriere", "fabulous bodies", "flat tummies", "age-defying skin and body", "ample cleavages", they must "set pulses racing" when they step out; we need to know that they have "incredible figures" and "very ample assets", or when they "put their wonderful bodies on display." If that fails, then we will be regaled with their bikini pictures to cheer us, their followers, up in these traumatic times, or even make the earth-shaking revelation that they find weddings boring, or that they decided to freeze their eggs. Indeed !!!!! Thank you very much for all that you do for mankind.

When we finally determine that, indeed, they are women *sans* Caitlyn – even that one has an "ample cleavage" too !!!, these fellows will move to the next level and tell us how Weinstein invited them to his hotel room in Nice or Cannes in 2001, exactly 19 years ago. Ok, this Weinstein has fallen, and the PR benefits of the association must be squeezed even if it is deleterious. Shame means nothing, nor does it matter, in reality, that this same latter-day complainant seeking all the attention and pity for a nice Nice "dinner" actually cavorted with this and other Weinsteins, on the journey towards roles and "celebrity" status, indeed, even in maintaining their assumed perch on the ladder of vanity. If we still don't pay attention, then we must know when they make "coffee runs" in Malibu, or 5th Avenue, or West Village (of course, it has to be there, and we must be told who lives in the neighborhood, so that we know that the dullest kid in our High School has made it. Yeeeeeaaaaaah!!!), or when their LV-clad Pomeraranian (a pooch, no doubt!) has lost a tooth, or when they are "single" for the umpteenth time this year, and it is just April !!! We also need to know that they are quarantining well with their partners; who cares really? Part of the global information that will give us a vaccine for coronavirus is the knowledge that this hewer of rock-turned-"big" boy/girl spent last week in St. Tropez. If they deign to donate $5,000 to a soup kitchen, or build a playpen for their own children, they feel entitled to squeeze out an outlandish PR mileage from that token donation or choke us with the normalcy of providing for their own kids --- which we all do. Mtchhheeeeewwwww !!!!!

The appropriation of words like "single", "marriage", "his/her/their/they, etc., on a persistent assault on decency and culture, goes without any sustained refutation because the only acceptable voice is linear and subversive. Antonio

Gramsci, where are you? You succeeded after all; our society is weak and rewards ephemerality. Everything is relative…nothing is definite or defined; twisted psychology equates with personal freedom, which must trump the strategic health and quality of a civilization and a people.

When it is not about the plastic surgery-sustained body, we boast about "twenty billboards in the city …who the fXXX IS you? Self-made .... You are just affiliated"; "Ace of Spades, worth half a b; sold drugs and got away scot free." When rotating between freedom and the lam for gun offenses, we could even boast about having an "Audemars on my wrist", or repeat "I woke up in a new Bugatti" 25 times against the monotony of an auto-generated beat, all in the name of art.

The society needs all its strength, including its cultural strength, to excel in the Post-corona Era. As it is, the normal has become abnormal and the abnormal has become normal. The total human experience can now be categorized into four epochs: prehistoric, B.C., A.D. (which ended in 2020), and PCE (Post-coronavirus era). The character and challenges of this new era in history will be totally different from what we have ever seen before.

Having paid due homage to this great and invisible disrupter, it is important to pose a few questions: what will be the character of the new world order in the post-coronavirus era? Who will survive and who will lose out? What will be the role of nation-states and international organizations, going forward? Would there be a greater appreciation for professionalism and expertise? Would this pandemic cause some States to pursue protectionist policies? Would Regionalism help? Can the US continue to go it alone? If a pandemic can be this impactful, what will happen when a catastrophic climate-related challenge emerges? What are the new roles of sovereign States? How many are prepared for these roles? What should the rest of the world do, given that State failure in one defined space affects the rest of the world? -- pandemics, terrorism, refugee crisis, etc.

Before we attempt an interrogation and possible resolution of some of these thorny issues, let us go back, way, way back, in time, to when homo sapiens started forming social and political societies, and then start coming forward, to understand the purpose of all human societies in its unvarnished and simplest form.

II

The Earliest Times

It will be best to start with established facts and truths. Established by Science (carbon-dating), and validated by qualified experts, we know the following to be FACTS and the TRUTH:

The earth, the mother of us all, is at least 4.54 billion years old. As Bela H. Banathy writes, quoting Gould, life in its most rudimentary form started on earth 3.5 billion years ago in the form of prokaryotes which are loosely associated with bacteria. As Maryanski and Turner rendered based on scientific evidence, humans, in their current form, had their first distinct ancestor in the Homo genus, which first appeared in the world about two million years ago as Homo Habilis, then evolved into Homo Erectus about 1.6 million years ago, before mutating into our current form, the Homo Sapiens, about 300,000 years ago. Archaeological findings, mostly analyzed fossils in Ethiopia, confirmed that Homo Sapiens from the Middle Paleothilic era lived about 200,000 years ago; some members of this species, which replaced Neanderthals and Homo Erectus, left Africa about 90,000 years ago, starting the consequential dispersal into the rest of the world as we know it today. Anatomically, modern humans emerged about 50,000 to 14,000 years ago in Africa. Fukuyama traces the Homo Erectus in China to some 800,000 years ago, with our direct ancestors, Homo Sapiens, appearing there a few years after leaving Africa. Only recently, in May 2020, Australian Archeologists discovered the two million-year-old fossils of Hominin Australopithecus Sediba, which used its hands both to climb trees and to grasp objects.

China had human settlements and sophisticated metallurgy 5,000 to 3,000 years ago, building on the primary skills learnt in Africa. Substance over Form, humans are animals; large-brained hominids, no doubt, but still animals, with our closest relatives being the great apes, especially chimpanzees. As Science has proven, in the latter part of our evolution, which spanned over fifty-eight million years, we evolved from primates to anthropoid, then to hominoid, and finally to hominid.

Again, contrary to the pervasive tale, the religious hypothesis, or what Dr. Douglas Anele calls "the pious fictions of religious superstition", the TRUTH is that everything on earth evolved; nothing was created by some Deity residing somewhere. In the days of ignorance and little or no Scientific discovery, this belief in creation made sense; since the "mysterious" questions have been largely addressed by Science, a continued belief (for that is what it is) in creation derives from the overwhelming propaganda that has been woven around this false myth, as well as the massive emotional, psychological, political, and financial implications of thinking or admitting otherwise, even when the FACT of evolution has been proven. Adopting the circular argument that makes engaging with them really tiresome, these investors in a false narrative commit two more fallacies in making their "case" about a creator; *Post hoc ergo propter hoc* / the Fallacy of First Cause (after this, therefore, because of this!), and *Argumentum ad verecundiam* / the Fallacy of Appeal to Authority. It seems far much easier to hold on to both false premises and an invalid conclusion, since considering or accepting otherwise will be rather too weighty.

The human journey has been a long time in unraveling, contrary to the convenient but false orthodoxy. Definitely, the fairly-recent creation story in the Bible, which is 6,000 years old, is simply unable to explain a proven history of billions of years. As Banathy informed us in her "Guided Evolution of Society: A Systems View", a critical stage in our evolution was attained when homo sapiens started asking themselves questions like Who am I? Where am I? Who are you? Why are we here? This was a fundamental departure from their erstwhile "oneness with nature" and "oneness with wholeness", a stage that lasted for six million years. From the moment of consciousness and self-reflection regarding the "I and Thou", "We and Others", and "We and Nature", the seeds of rationality and overall awareness were sown. This marked the progression of homo sapiens from "biological evolution" to "cultural evolution." This social consciousness led to social cooperation and the developments that have followed ever since, citing Elgin's work on the subject. This evolution has taken social, cultural, technological, and political forms, and is presently unraveling, the limits of human creativity and rationality, as well as the laws of nature, being the only possible constraints.

The typical Eurocentric narrative is that the political arrangements in human societies evolve in a linear and "progressive" way from band through tribe through chiefdom and, then, the State. The Spencerian model queries and rejects this evolutionary accounting, which is mostly Darwinian in character and form. The Darwinian precept attributes differences in "cultural attainment" to biological differences between societies, thereby providing a theoretical justification for subsequent dominant and exploitative developments like colonialism, slavery, and some race-based genocidal atrocities. When it is presented that the progression is from "savagery" to "barbarism", and then to the end-stage of "civilization", the problem is that, from their prism, only European societies or societies vanquished and displaced by Europeans, and European mores imposed therein, are capable of attaining "civilization." This condescending and ignorant proposition has, very sadly, led to mass killings and considerable dislocations around the world, as we shall explore later on. As our modern history makes clear, cultural diversity enriches the human experience, and different cultures have their inherent systems and standards for evaluating "civilization" and cultural refinement. Adam Smith's "sequential linear model of development" was clearly wrong.

Serge Svizzero and Clement A. Tisdell provide further illumination and will guide us presently. They aver that hunter-gatherer societies were mostly at the mercy of nature; it coheres with reason that "ecological conditions and available natural resources influenced economic and social development" at the hunter-gatherer stage; this also impacted the economic wellbeing of the members of those primary societies. The impact and relevance of nature in determining outcomes might have receded in the modern era, but were dominant at the earliest stages of our social foundations; at that distant time, "the available tools, extent of geographical mobility, and the nature of property rights" played vital roles in the social structure that developed in each location.

According to Renfrew (2007), in West Asia, Egypt, and Africa, for example, the domestication of livestock species (sheep and cattle) preceded the cultivation of crops. Brewer (2008) thinks they happened simultaneously. The Phoenicians developed a relatively sophisticated style of long-distance trade very early (Markoe, 2005). Easterly and Levine criticize the eco-geographic theories of economic development (such as Smith's), so you see the diversity of opinion. Paraphrasing Zvelebil and Pluciennik, these eminent scholars instruct us that the hunter-gathering lifestyle was still practised in one-third of the globe in 1500 A.D. by about 1% of the then global population. By 2000, this dying lifestyle applied to only about 0.0017% of the human race. In the prehistoric era, however, that was the only option until the Neolithic period, when agriculture and pastoralism began to develop. The process of domestication of crops and animal husbandry took hundreds to thousands of years to develop fully, thereby providing the incubus of non-kin-based economies in the society; the earliest impulses of indigeneity and private enterprise!

While Marxists posit that social traditions are defined by the nature of the economy, Zvelebil and Pluciennik affirm that, at every stage of the human society, three activities have remained critical: how to get food resources; how to transform and preserve some of these food resources; and how to produce non-food resources (the economy); for them, therefore, it is very limiting to focus exclusively on the mode of subsistence. Shifting somewhat from the mainstream Eurocentric and linear tracing of social and political societies, the Boasian emphasis is on cultural differences, and not a linear social evolutionary model for all societies, terminating with the European ideal. This approach describes societies and does not haughtily explain why they are where they are on the journey towards conforming to the European template.

Several theories have been propounded on this process, for example, by Price, Drucker, Brown, Sahlins, Kelly, Kroeber, Flannery, Lee & De Vore, Powell, Morgan, Spencer, Darwin, Tylor, Martin Johnson, Krech, Wheat, Raven, Binford, Bettinger, Ames, Richerson, and Baumhoff; for our purpose, which does not entail a rigorous analysis or assessment of the respective viewpoints, a project for which we are poorly equipped, it should suffice to retain the salience of the predominant positions, and proceed along our journey.

In simple hunter-gatherer societies, there was no strict division of labor, and common property was the rule (Morgan, 1877; Lee and De Vore, 1968) -- "primitive communism." Woodburn (1980, 1982) associates egalitarianism with immediate return. Surplus food production and seasonality led to the need for storage, thereby gradually leading to exclusive (as opposed to communal) property rights, together with the correlating economic and social changes. When trade was introduced, common property resources reduced further as "this does not encourage the extension of markets." For North and Thomas (1977, p. 230), " the development of exclusive property rights over the resource base provided a change in incentives sufficient to encourage the development of cultivation and domestication...," the precursor of wealth accumulation and deferred gain.

The Structure of our Ancestral Society

Dimension	Description
Law:	
Legal codes	Undifferentiated from kinship norms and general cultural traditions
Enforcement	No coercive capacity
Courts	None; occasional "council of elders"
Legislative bodies	None
Education	Informal socialization and learning through observation and individual tutelage and practice
Medicine	No specialists, though shaman may use rituals to deal with ill health; most medicine practical and known by all members of band
Science	None beyond development of practical economic technologies, and here rate of innovation is very slow
4. STRATIFYING	
Resource distribution:	
Material	No inequality
Prestige	Some inequality
Power	None exists and, hence, no inequality
Class formation	None
Mobility	None, since there are no classes
5. CATEGORIC	Young and very old; male and female distinguished
6. CORPORATE	
Spatial units	The band, which at times decides when and where to locate or organizes a party for a gathering/hunting foray
Institutional units	Most activity organized in nuclear or household family units

Source: Human Nature and Evolution of Society, by Alexandria Maryanski and Jonathan H. Turner, Stanford University Press

It is, therefore, clear that societies form their structures by building on prior platforms while responding to both opportunities and threats in their environment; no new stage starts on a *tabula rasa* note, in a vacuum and out of void. Meek, Raphael, and Stein (1978), as well as Turgot (1750) described the economic development of human societies as comprising these four sequential stages: the age of hunting and gathering; pastoralism; agriculture; and commerce (including foreign trade, "foreign", in this context, meaning different things to different peoples in each epoch), as well as manufacturing. The various theories are not necessarily in contention but could be interpreted as legitimate differences in interpreting available patterns and data. An inherent defect of the supposition that there is a final stage of the evolution of human societies is that it begs the question: is this the end of history? Unlikely.

Thomas Hobbes suggested that humans lived like animals, with no culture. He said that humans, at the earliest stages, simply preoccupied themselves with reflexive biological endeavors like eating and procreating. Morgan (1877); Steward (1955); Tylor (1881), and White (1959) supported this position, which, in my view, was convincingly debunked by other researchers (notably Lee and Devore, 1968). What is clear is that, with private ownership of resources, new forms of differentiation on the basis of wealth, status, and hierarchy were introduced. This is without prejudice to whether we are analyzing the biological or economic theories of the evolution of hunter-gatherer societies.

Machiavelli (1519); Montesquieu ((1748); Turgot (1750); Smith (1776); Meek et al (1978), are in concurrence that local ecological and environmental factors strongly influenced the nature and prospects of prehistoric societies; a position that varies diametrically with the submission by Easterly and Levine (2003).

In tracing the origins of the concept of public goods as the fundamental driver of political, economic, and social arrangements, we need to consider the Concept of UltraSociality, where the structure of the social system, which is itself mostly the aggregation of the values and behaviors of the members, gets out of their control. The members now become "socially embedded", and Division of Labor, information-sharing, and sacrifice towards collective defense and common goals become the norm. From this, we begin to see population growth and consolidation within geographical units, information management, economic specialization, transportation, warfare, long-distance trade, the introduction of the market system, etc. With time, the size of the society grows, and, over millennia -- with improvements across board, the world is shrunk as we have it presently. It is this cumulative development that breaks the silos in the world, and also makes the entire world vulnerable to a major pandemic like the COVID-19.

A very quick scan of man's history, and reconciliation with modern realities, provide a convincing proof that the Western-type market systems have become dominant globally, changing the character of societies (including, or especially, in places like China and Russia, even as their Leadership still struggle with nostalgic political impulses!). UltraSociality has really come to stay, with individuals having less and less control and power in the system. Different societies around the world practise this system in one form or another. It is for this reason that we will, in due course, conduct an in-depth philosophical excursion into the history and dynamics that led to this ascendancy and global adoption. Economics and Politics, at the end of the day, reflect the dominant philosophical thoughts and preferences in a given environment. The market-driven European Thought has clearly been successfully transplanted in more parts of the world than any other. Jedediah Brillon-Purdy of the Columbia Law School writes that "the lower status of savagery," that is, when hunter-gatherers first mastered fire; when they learnt to domesticate animals and became herders, the so-called "middle status of barbarism"; and the invention of writing, when humanity "graduated out of barbarism" and entered history, capture the major epochs on man's journey towards "civilization."

At this point, they learnt how to cultivate grains, especially wheat and rice, and also began to appreciate the value of a fixed abode. With settling down and the emerging disputes, came the need for political systems, property ownership protocols, and a sense of identity. A sustained improvement on these elements led to the Industrial Revolution and Free Trade. Things became standardized and ordered with time, because "what you cannot measure and monitor, you cannot rule." The contrarian thinker, James C. Scott, insists that the highlighted developments did not work out for everyone, as the hard-working early peasant-serfs were exploited by the "leisured ruling class", thus providing an early template for subsequent oppressive and inhumane practices like slavery. For Scott, "civilization" is an exploitation machine, which is self-perpetuating, and which the benefiting oppressor very easily justifies and imposes wherever he may, until there is a consistent and powerful countervailing resistance.

Yuval Noah Hariri, in "The Sapiens", suggests that settled agriculture is "history's biggest fraud", because, unlike the common narrative, the quality of life actually dropped when agriculture replaced hunting and gathering for our earliest ancestors. Well, some others may have ideas of fraud-types that have had more impact on human history than agriculture. Chris Morgan, Raven Garvey, et al, write that "the hunter-gatherer's economic mode of production revolved around wild resources. Their behavior covered: mobility to sedentary; generalized equipment to specialized tools; egalitarian sharing economies to privatized competition; nuclear family/ band-level decision-making to centralized, hierarchical decision-making." We see clearly from this that the move towards specialization and private ownership of resources is integral to human nature, even when skewed attempts at institutionalizing communalism by force failed several millennia later. It might need to be pointed out that the hunter-gatherers preceded our species, the homo sapiens. Given the state of technology in the 21st century, it is remarkable that there was a time when burden baskets, manos and metates, baskets, seed-beaters, and winnowing trays, etc., comprised the AI, IOT, nanotechnology and quantum computing of mankind.

It is ironic that, in most of the theorizing about man's origins, apart from a casual or reluctant acknowledgment of Africa as the origin of ALL human beings, most of the commentaries are entirely Eurocentric; indeed, even the robust civilizations of Asia, Latin America, and the Levant are mostly ignored, the latter only reckoned with because of their seed contribution to Christianity, which predominates in the West. Most times when Africa is mentioned in commentary, it is with derision and condescension, rather than respect for the ancestor of us all. With this backdrop, it is gratifying that Philip Osafo-Kwaako and James A. Robinson of Harvard University dedicated their seminal research to tracing the track of the formation of most African societies. For them, the African experience deviates from the assumptions of the Eurasian template for State formation and centralization, whereby high population density, inter-state warfare, and trade are emphasized. Rather, where there was any semblance of centralization in Africa, this owed to "better public goods and development outcomes."

In their paper, titled: " Political Centralization in pre-colonial Africa", they cited Hopkins (1973), Thornton (1992), Jerome (2010), who suggest few historical differences and institutional dynamics between Africa and the rest of the world as of 1750 A.D. Inikori (2012) even posits that Africa was ahead of the Americas even if it was behind Eurasia. Technologically, Africa was behind the rest of the world, even the Americas (Good, 1971). Acemoglu and Robinson submit that Africa was backward in many areas of the modern period and lacked the political and economic institutions required for modern economic growth. The question should be: so, what happened? Easterly and Levine (1997) state that the ethnic fragmentation of Africa accounts for its relative poverty. Sachs and Warner (1997) attribute Africa's general condition to its "adverse" geography. Inikori (1992) and Nunn (2008) blame the slave trade instead, while Englebert (2000) finds culpability in the arbitrary delineation of post-colonial national boundaries by distant and rapacious European colonists.

While some or all of these factors might be valid, there is simply no excuse for African countries to continue blaming others and the distant past for their mostly sub-par performance across board. Most African countries attained political independence in the 1950s and 1960s, about 60 years ago. A serious, focused, and development-oriented leadership would have started yielding positive outcomes 60 years later, but a litany of woes is the lot of a majority of their citizens, income disparity is a very wide chasm, and delivery on primary public goods has been mostly absent. People cannot blame their past, or others, in perpetuity. Jews have been killed, dehumanized, and alienated through history. What has been their response? Acquire more education than their oppressors, hone artistic and business skills beyond levels that are attainable by their enemies, found and strengthen the Jewish homeland, their spiritual origins. They did not surrender and default to generating endless excuses. The best response to one's adversaries is superlative performance.

Even with their absolute interpretation of sovereignty, Francophone countries in Africa (the group of countries colonized by France) still, in 2020, comply with grossly-extortionate, insulting, and lopsided economic, monetary, and fiscal conditions dictated by France. Where is their independence? Why can't they say no? Why can't they expose France? A fraudulent contract is no contract. *Fraudem non esse contractum* !!! By the way, the same applies to the so-called British Commonwealth (where only the resources of the erstwhile colonies of Britain are "common" to all, meaning, available to Britain, while British resources are for Britain only). Why would people choose this level of self-flagellation??? For, who, in his or her full senses, accepts, complies with, and sustains the oppressive, inequitable, baseless, arrogant, exploitative, cruel, and condescending set of conditions which France imposed on the so-called Francophone countries (15 of them), as they got their political independence roughly sixty years ago; an independence which they always had before France invaded their territories, stole their resources, and, ultimately, "granted them independence" on usurious terms, which these so-called independent States have continued to respect and honor?

You are thanking and paying France for violating your dignity through colonialism, and for literally raping your countries for several decades!!! These countries deposit 85% of their foreign reserves with the French Central Bank in Paris, which invests this money for the sole benefit of the French Treasury!; if these same sustainers of the French economy need fiscal support to provide services for their own citizens, they must borrow their own money from France on commercial terms; French companies must be given priority in the exploitation of resources belonging to these African countries in a structure that is totally lacking in transparency; only French language must be spoken or taught in their schools; the French Military must have Bases in the countries, as a check on them; all military procurements must be from France; their collective currency, the CFA, is tied to the French Francs, and they are not allowed to have individual (national) currencies. Why wait to be "allowed?"

Who did this to Africans? How can a people be so thoroughly lacking in self-respect to accept this nonsense from France or any other country for that matter? Leaders like Presidents Sylvanus Olympio of Togo and Modibbo Keita of Mali, who resisted these impositions, were either marginalized or assassinated in bloody *coups d'etat* sponsored and supervised by France. How dare France continue to describe these countries as poor when it steals and retains all their wealth? It is estimated that a minimum of $500 billion is stolen by France from these countries on an annual basis. Who do you blame? I blame the so-called African leaders who allow this. A big shame on the leaders, political parties, pressure groups, and citizens of the following countries who allow this to continue, instead of stopping the corrosive practice immediately, closing all the French Military Bases in their countries, severing diplomatic relations with France, dare France to do their worst, and indeed drag France before the relevant International Bodies and Courts to demand a full accounting and return of all their money and resources stolen over the past few decades: Benin, Burkina Faso, Guinea-Bissau, Ivory Coast or Cote d'Ivoire,

Mali, Niger, Senegal, Togo, Cameroon, Guinea,, Central African Republic, Chad, Congo-Brazzaville, Equatorial Guinea and Gabon.

It is significant that other African countries colonized and cheated by France (but located in the northern part of the Continent), namely Tunisia, Morocco, and Algeria, are excluded from this disgraceful arrangement; is France afraid of the resistance of the street in those predominantly-Muslim countries? Is an incendiary temperament an insulation from perennial colonial exploitation? France had killed millions of Algerians during the Algerian War of Independence but dares not impose the afore-listed terms on independent Algeria. But, Mali, Chad, Niger, Guinea, etc., are also mostly-Muslim countries, so what is the difference? Why the cavalier expectation that the sub-Saharan countries will not resist? Indeed, are they not justified in their expectation, given the sheepish compliance by those so-called independent countries? Shame!!!

Indeed, this reminds one of the decision by the Zambian Government to allow Chinese nationals into their Police Force, wearing the uniform of the National Police, be outside of their disciplinary orbit, and ostensibly there to look after Chinese interests. Or the shameless, undignified, and odious acceptance of the Presidents of the fifty-four African countries for China to build, furnish, and equip the new Secretariat of their umbrella body, the African Union, in Addis Ababa, Ethiopia, as “a handshake of friendship." Indeed. Any wonder, then, that the Chinese Government bugged the columns, beams, and computers at this monument to indignity, thereby feasting on sensitive data and deliberations by the AU Leadership and Presidents. This expected breach of Information Security lasted for a minimum of five years before it was detected. Has it been completely eliminated? Which country on the Continent has the indigenous technical capacity and competence to provide this assurance? Is it conceivable that the European Union Secretariat in Brussels would be donated, built, furnished, and equipped by a non-EU nation? Never !!! When people willingly surrender or negotiate away their dignity, they should not complain when others disrespect them.

Several Presidential Complexes in many African countries are also maintained by foreign contractors, notably Europeans, who, definitely, use technical means to obtain sensitive information from the highest levels of government in those countries. For more on Chinese spying on sensitive African Buildings, The Heritage Foundation has an excellent article by J.Meservey, which can be accessed here: *https://www.heritage.org/asia/report/government-buildings-africa-are-likely-vector-chinese-spying*

The result of the acceptance of all these negatively-arrayed and exploitative practices is the preponderance of dysfunctional States with severely-degraded post-independence performance levels on public goods (Callaghy, 1984; Turner and Young, 1985). If we go by the Weberian doctrine that effective States determine State performance, then, most States in Africa are simply ineffective. Apart from the external factors, most African countries have consistently produced incompetent and corrupt leaders, whose predatory behavior compounds the dire fate of the Continent. The nepotism, prebendalism, cronyism, sense of entitlement, recourse to dominant sub-national identities like ethnicity and religion, bloated bureaucracies, tolerance for low standards, suppression of human and media rights, totalitarian tendencies, negative influence of imported religions: Islam and Christianity, as well as the replication of incompetence across board, are significant contributors to the depressing outcomes out of the Continent. In analyzing complex and culturally-diverse societies like Africa, the Middle East, Latin America, and the Indian subcontinent, it is unhelpful to employ the Eurocentric analytical framework. The pervasive environment on the Continent makes it extremely difficult to attain what Noam Chomsky and John Tomasi characterize as the five norms of market democracy: a participatory ideal of inclusion; democratic governance; market economics; the rule of law; and freedom of expression.

It is worth interrogating why some of these societies suffer from the debilitating affliction of corrosive, uber-corrupt, and inept leadership. Is it a function of the recruitment process that throws them up, their individual gross incapacities and defective personalities, lack of vision, inferiority complex, an extension of unresolved structural problems in their countries, or a combination thereof? The President of Nigeria, former military dictator, Muhammadu Buhari, in contrast to the ascetic and self-effacing persona he sold to the country before his election in 2015, enjoys the colonial pageantry of a full troupe of Scottish bagpipe-playing men clad in red costume, ushering him into functions, or conducting airport protocols for him on his numerous overseas trips (**Figure 6)*.

Harry Elmer Barnes, in writing about the Hebrew view of the natural State, states that it draws substantially from the Babylonians (who enslaved Jews), as well as the then prevailing thoughts in the Western Asiatic Orient. The Hebrew creation tale, as captured in the Book of Genesis (in the Bible), has continued to have particular significance in Western Thought, since it was subsumed into Christianity and Catholic Cosmogony. The same applies to Ethics, Theology, and Western European Social Sciences. According to this narrative, the Jewish man (who seemed to represent all living men in the world, even as we now have incontrovertible evidence that humans inhabited the earth for centuries before then), was created by a divine act wrought by a Deity roughly 6,000 years ago. This same Deity subsequently destroyed the world (known to them) because his creation and assumed father of all mankind, Adam, disobeyed some dietary preferences imposed by the Deity, by succumbing to the lure of his female companion and the devil. This led to the fall of the human race, as they knew it. The only survivors, Noah and his family, populated the world anew. There is a lot that can be validly challenged here, but that is not our focus presently.

For example, adopting the relatively-low standards we should reserve for human beings, and not for our Supreme Being, if the world was destroyed because Adam "ate the fruits of a forbidden tree", why has the same God, who is omnipotent, omnipresent, and omniscient, not destroyed the world several times afterwards as His/Her/Its creatures, human beings, were enslaved by others; the Bolsheviks killed millions of people to impose an utopian communist totalitarianism; over six million Jews and millions of other ethnic minorities were butchered by German Nazis and their collaborators in Czech Republic, Poland, Austria, Hungary, Belarus, Ukraine, Latvia, Russia, and the entire Region; an entire section of the United States fought a war over their "right" to enslave others; Mao and his entourage killed over forty million Chinese people to consolidate power; Pol Pot and his thuggish Khmer Rouge killed millions of their own people; Igbo people of Nigeria were killed in their millions by other Nigerians and completely dispossessed in a totally-unnecessary and unjust war; Hutus killed over a million Tutsis in Rwanda in less than a hundred days while the world watched; the British massacred Kikuyus (Kenyans) in 1963 during the so-called Mau Uprising in Kenya; the various terrorist activities; systemic exploitation and impoverishment of African and Latin American countries by European, American, and Chinese governments and their companies?

This alleged transgression or disobedience by Adam has, since then, been deemed so grave and applicable to all of mankind (Hebrew and Gentile alike; believer and unbeliever alike), that we cannot extricate ourselves from the "original sin" unless and until we comply with yet another strand of the rolling narrative. The sin of having a personal dietary choice!!! This supposed grave sin was committed thousands of years ago!!! Now, arrogantly propagated as being binding on all mankind in perpetuity. Indeed!!! This narrative actually says a lot about action and punishment; temperament; forgiveness; and other imperfections that should never be associated with an omniscient, omnipotent, and benevolent Father and Divine Creator. There is the genuine problem that much graver crimes and "sins" in my milieu have not formed a basis for my people to find the entire world guilty and, in particular, not for trivia, and in perpetuity!!! It is ironic that the great Jewish philosopher, Moses Maimonides, wrote that: "evils that beset this life flow from men's purposes, desires, opinions, and beliefs, and all of these derive from arrogance."

Five centuries ago, John Milton (1608 - 74), writing in the "Tenure of Kings and Magistrates", stated that men (and women, of course) were born free, equal, and in a state of primitivity, only brought down by Adam's "transgressions"; the same "sin" of disobedience, no doubt. In that same century, Baruch Spinoza, Enlightenment philosopher, Rationalist, Sephardic Jew, and Cartesian, wrote in *Tractatus Theologico Politicus* - published in 1670 - that Natural Right was identical with power, and that "might makes right." We can distill further from these writings that, for Spinoza, desire is as legitimate a guide as reason in the state of nature. Whatever a man desires in a state of nature, he has a right to obtain, and to use any means whatsoever to secure the object of his desire. All the same, it is still better to live by reason than by desire, for, only through the guidance of reason is a social life, with all its benefits, possible, and man who lives in an isolated state and guided by mere instinct, must have a most miserable existence. This allusion to the primitive felicity, the natural sociability of mankind, also highlights the benefits, purpose, and expectations of a social cum political structure. Spinoza continues by saying that men found it very necessary to join together in a civil society, to secure the advantages of a well-ordered society life. The natural right of the individual man is thus determined, not by sound reason, but by desire and power. This natural man may regard, as an enemy, anyone who hinders the accomplishment of his purpose. "There is no one who is not ill at ease in the midst of enmity, hatred, anger, and deceit, and who does not seek to avoid them as much as he can." The problem with this position includes the challenge of reconciling and resolving competing desires; this dialectic approximates the Hobbesian state of nature.

While a more expansive discussion of Western Political and Moral Thought, which underpins the Political and Economic systems, will be undertaken in subsequent sections, perhaps, a few more indicative evaluations should be done presently, especially focusing on their formulations regarding the early society. Samuel Pufendorf (1632 - 94) has two theories of the state of nature. The historical model considers patriarchy as the template, while the philosophical theory considers the condition in which "we may conceive man to be placed, by his bare nativity, abstracting from him, all the rules and institutions, whether of human invention, or of the suggestion and revelation of Heaven." The only problem is that this latter view is at variance with historical realities.

John Locke (1632 - 1704) has a position close to Pufendorf's formulation, but goes further: the state of nature, for him, was historic; not a state of war, but of peace. Men have always organized in political units (families and small social groups). The state of nature was one of equality and liberty, NOT "license." This narrative is the polar opposite of the Hobbesian position. For Locke, also, in the state of nature, man is without a political superior. The state of war is one where a man uses force against his neighbor without cause or right, and this can happen both in a state of nature and in civil society.

Cicero instructs us that the law is not a product of will but is given by nature; *Natura juris ab hominis repetenda est natura.* Writing further, he says that an immutable law exists; *jus naturale est quod semper bonum et aegum est.*, which is above all human laws. Apart from natural laws, there is *Jus gentium*, respected by all - which binds them - because it is predicated on their common needs, with contextual adjustments as necessary. This *Jus Gentium* is characterized by him as Universal Reason, a close equivalent to what we generally regard as our enlightened self-interest. There is also a *jus civile*, which is the law that applies to each nation. Cicero emphasizes that virtue is a critical quality that leaders must have, and, that, no political society or State can last if the leaders do not consider the common good. He places the political society at the core of justice, which he calls "Social Ethics", derived from the sociality of mankind, which considers the sphere beyond the individual; a clear love for others, more than one's love for oneself. This is the only way to achieve social cohesion. Accordingly, the law, which is based on justice, is a social necessity. *Res Publica* or public work, is the work of the people, but "the people are not any group of people gathered at random, but a union united in a legal system founded by a common accord for utility." He also wrote that peace was the basis for the society, but we need to know who defines "peace."

This social union is not only due to their natural proclivity towards unity and mutual benefits, but also a shared understanding of the equal application of the law. Christianity codified this precept as "love thy neighbor as thyself." In this society, true freedom cannot be destroyed by any pressure; this is the freedom that comes from "the overcoming of passions, involving living according to nature…." While Montesquieu (1694 - 1778) departed from the dystopian conception of humanity, as popularized by Thomas Hobbes, his philosophy emphasized the inalienability of man's rights, as well as man's inherent and enduring quest for freedom. He said that the state of war is a consequence of civil society, not of nature. Montesquieu's thoughts and writings substantially influenced the French Revolution, which had great significance for political development and the social arrangements in Western Europe, the Americas, and around the world since the 18th century. He was also among the first set of European philosophers to know about the rest of the world, and he was, perhaps because of this, an internationalist in his thoughts.

For Hobbes, man was not exactly warlike, or a fierce being, but was rather a timid creature frightened by the rude aspects of nature, and who focused only on the basic instincts of self-preservation and reproduction, as a result. The common response to the mutual fear of the manifestations of natural phenomena, conduces all men to social life which, with time, replaces instincts as the bonding factor in a society, with identified advantages for all. Once social life is entrenched, he says, men lose their feeling of weakness which attracts them to society; with their new "strength", they start originating a state of war.

David Hume (1711 - 1776), the Scottish Enlightenment philosopher, economist, empiricist, historian, and skeptic, had zero tolerance for the idea of a state of war before the society was formed. For him, this state of war was not a historical fact, but purely a conceptual and non-physical construct by philosophers, for analytical purposes only. Men's nature and needs impel a social arrangement from the beginning. While his thoughts were logical and consistent, Rousseau's had a lot of inconsistent views, as we shall be discussing in due course.

Thomas Paine (1737-1809), in his widely influential pamphlet, "Common Sense", wrote that man was originally sociable due to the benefits of mutual aid, but without political control. This yields, in his view, anarchy requiring a government for the restoration of order. In the prehistoric times, the form of this "government" clearly matched the fundamentals and realities of the extant period.

Immanuel Kant (1724 - 1804) copied Hobbes in his negative conception of humans. He wrote that, in an unregulated state of nature, men are in a state of violence and misery due to the anti-social and egoistic impulses of human nature. The only available form of escape is the establishment of the civil society through a contract, which would be inviolable once agreed to. He viewed this as a philosophical hypothesis, unlike Hobbes who saw it as a historical reality. This is their fundamental divergence. Bentham, on the other hand, said that humans had an ingrained habit of obeying superior authority in a political society, and that there was no such dynamic in a natural state.

The evaluation of Western Thought does not imply that other parts of the world lacked deep thinkers. We are merely following the evolution of the thoughts and mental processes which led to the Western political and economic systems, which have had the widest application and adoption in the world. Some early Chinese philosophers like Confucius, Sun Tzu, Mozi, Mencius, etc., were as rigorous, deep, and original as the European philosophers. Ancient Arabic Thinkers like Khaldun, al-Kindi, and ibn Sina

(Avicenna), ably combined Aristotelianism and neoPlatonism with Islamic Beliefs.

While we shall be consulting these eminent thinkers in subsequent chapters, the point being made is that, from the earliest times, man has always been drawn to the society both due to his nature, and the need to derive certain public goods therefrom. Aristotle had written that "to live alone, one must be a beast or a god", and that men were definitely not gods. As Inge Kaul put it, the whole purpose of government is determining "how best to enhance national well-being with limited resources."

Having made this point, we should proceed on our theoretical excursion by evaluating some of the dominant thoughts and philosophical traditions that led to the development, entrenchment, and refinement of the political, economic, and social systems, which have been successfully exported around the world. Thought influences policy choices and outcomes. The European model underwent considerable changes in the past millennia, owing to the prevailing tendency at each time. Studying Western Thought confirms the complexity and diversity of human temperaments, preferences, moral fiber, and capacity to moralize and rationalize their chosen path. While it is impossible to prescribe a specific philosophical orientation for all mankind, it is instructive that most humans are incapable of rising above their selfish impulses; the rationalization of their position needs to be evaluated against what is objectively true, just, fair, and sustainable.

Our philosophical discourse in the indicated regard shall not follow any strict chronology.

III

Political and Moral Philosophy

It will be helpful to start with the irrefutable fact that the history, politics, economic structure, and surviving moral foundation of Europe will be incomplete without the evolving and pivotal impact of Christianity, especially the Catholic Church. Accordingly, it will be useful to briefly narrate the dynamics that eventuated in this historical reality.

When the Western Roman Empire fell in 476 A.D., Christianity was a relatively minor (and almost subversive) movement. Believers and their few converts had faced persistent persecution from the religion of the Empire, Paganism. Whereas Emperor Constantine 1 had, by 313 A.D, legalized Christianity upon his own conversion the year prior, the resistance towards this fringe movement did not abate, and, indeed, heightened upon the death of the Emperor. Constantine 1 had decreed that laws which protected the official religion (paganism), should be applied towards protecting the property of Christian churches, as well as those of privileged Christian priests, but this had not fully taken effect before his death. Pagan practices were gradually becoming heretical and illegal. From this point onwards, Bishops assumed responsibility for the "souls" of their congregation; a status without provable responsibility but nonetheless extremely powerful. The next major thrust came in 380 A.D when Emperor Theodosius 1 made Christianity the State Religion of the Empire by decree, a charge that was executed with sustained violence, propaganda, and more decrees. Pagan shrines were converted into churches as a consequence of the Imperial Decree. This lasted until the fall of the Western Empire in 476, and, later on, the Eastern Roman Empire as well, through the Fall of Constantinople.

The significant thing to note is that, with Imperial protection, Christians had embarked on a massive proselytization program across Europe. Their monasteries progressively became centers for the preservation of classical culture, as well as the hallmarks of learning and expertise in spirituality, economy, agriculture, production, research, and overall guidance of the society. The Catholic Church also became involved in political and spiritual matters as intercessors, advocates, advisors, teachers, preachers, and leaders. The conversion of Clovis 1, the pagan King of the Franks, in 496 A.D., accelerated the spread of Catholicism in the West. When Visigoths and Lombards moved away from Arianism towards Catholicism, the capture of the West was complete, while the movement proceeded towards the Germanic and Slavic peoples. The Synod of Whitby of 664 reintegrated the Celtic Church of the British Isles into the Roman Orbit.

In the mid-8th century, due mostly to Byzantine dissidence and radicalism, there was a major division in the Church, which coincided with the massive attack launched against Christianity by Muslims. This schism divided the Church into the Eastern and Western Conferences. The East forbade the worship of religious images including pictorial images of the family of Christ, Saints, and biblical scenes. These were regarded by them as breaches of the Ten Commandments (specifically, Thou shall not make unto thee any graven images), and accorded with the teachings of the other Eastern Religions, namely, Judaism and Islam.

In fact, the Byzantine Emperor Leo III, removed the prominent image of Jesus at the Chalke Gate, which was the central entrance into the Great Palace of Constantinople, and replaced it with a cross. Pope Gregory III bitterly opposed this position before his death; his successor, Pope Hadrian 1 persuaded the Empress Irene (though a Byzantine), to summon an Ecumenical Council for the resolution of the divergent positions that threatened the unity of the Church. At the 2nd Council of Nicaea in 787, three hundred bishops adopted the Pope's position and retained the icons, a practice that persists to this day. Missionary activities and subsequent Colonialism spread Christianity beyond the Roman sphere. With slavery still very common in Ireland at the time, Irish missionaries like St. Columba and Columbanus still managed to introduce Catholicism into Scotland and the entire Europe, replacing the public rite of penance with private penance. The Germanic Anglo-Saxons, the predecessors of the English, who immigrated to the Island between 450 and 1066, ushered in a period of culture and scholarship, which the Church greatly benefited from.

With the Bishop of Rome as the Head of the Catholic Church (the Pope, successor to Peter the Fisherman), Rome became the center of the Church, except for the period when the Seat of the Church was relocated to Avignon in France between 1309 and 1377. With Catholicism as the official religion of the Empire starting from 380, the Pope's powers grew, even though, at that time, he was still notionally below the Emperor in status. With the fall of the Western Roman Empire, the powers of the Papacy grew even further. The ultimate push was when Pope Leo III crowned Charlemagne as the Imperator Romanorum; the Emperor of the Roman Empire in 800 A.D. With this Papal imprimatur, the Empire was re-christened the Holy Roman Empire; the Catholic Church had moved full circle from being a persecuted movement to sharing power with the Emperor, indeed, even conferring legitimacy on the Emperor. This practice, which has persisted in one form or another to this day, especially in the West and their former colonies (for example, swearing Oaths of Office by swearing on the Bible and/ or Koran, derived from this critical move), significantly elevated the status of the Pope vis a vis secular leaders. Charlemagne waged a thirty-year war of expansion of the Holy Roman Empire, attributing all successes to the blessings of the Pope. The competition for power between monarchs and the Pope was being resolved in favor of the latter, by default, until subsequent successful challenges which would split the Church into two; the origins of Protestantism...

Indeed, in a further push to concentrate both spiritual and temporal powers in the Successor to Peter, Pope Boniface VIII (1294-1303) issued *Unum Sanctam* in 1302 wherein he declared: "both swords . . . the spiritual and the temporal, are in the power of the Church. The former is to be used by the Church, the latter for the Church; the one by the hand of the priest, the other by the hand of kings and knights, but at the command and permission of the priest. Moreover, it is necessary for one sword to be under the other, and the temporal authority to be subjected to the spiritual . . .We therefore declare, say, and affirm that submission on the part of every man to the bishop of Rome is altogether necessary for his salvation." As reflected in Viorst (1965), "the Conciliar Movement, led by William of Ockham (1285-1347) and Marsilius of Padua (1280-1343), produced a reaction from the Avignon popes who emphatically asserted that popes were second only to God in authority and on par with the Virgin and the Saints in reverence due. The Papal Schism of the late fourteenth century so weakened the position of the Papacy that the College of Cardinals called a General Council to settle the dispute. The Council of Pisa (1409) failed to end the schism, but it succeeded in changing—at least for a time—the Constitution of the Church by empowering the College of Cardinals with the right to call a Council." This Movement, The Council of Trent (1545-1563) ended the threat of conciliarism when it granted the Pope the sole authority to call Councils and confirm their conclusions.

In the Middle Ages, the Catholic Church did not relent from waging wars and crusades, to entrench its doctrine, to forcefully convert new believers, and, especially, to capture or re-capture Jerusalem and the "Holy Land." Several Crusades were waged, starting from 1090 to 1300, mostly against Muslims who ruled Jerusalem for a long time. The first Crusade was in response to a call from the Eastern Orthodox Byzantine Empire for assistance in repelling the expansion of the Muslim Seljuk Turks into Anatolia. This expanded into attacks against pagan Slavs, Russian and Greek Orthodox Christians, Mongols, Cathers, Hussites, and political enemies of the Popes. These crusades, which were waged with extreme violence, have had significant political, economic, historical, and social effects over the centuries. Indeed, some modern-day Muslim clerics and their sympathizers rationalize the modern scourge of Islamic Terrorism by referring to these distant instances of Christian/ Catholic violence against heretics and unbelievers, especially Muslims. The swords that form a part of the regalia of Papal Knights of the various Orders also emanated from a time when they were used in actuality to "defend the Church", and not just as symbols.

With the return of the seat of the Catholic Church from Avignon to Rome by Pope Gregory XI in 1377, Romans insisted that all the popes must be produced from within their ranks. The first Roman Pope so elected (in 1378), Urban VI (born Bartolomeo Prignano, Bishop of Bari), turned out to be a poor and regrettable choice, according to the Electors, who cited his suspicious behavior, short temper, and his reform agenda. As a consequence, they elected a rival Pope, Robert of Geneva, tearing the Church and Europe apart. The ensuing crisis was finally resolved during the Council of 1414 called by Pope John XXIII.

This synopsis has been undertaken to underscore some elementals: history has consequences; power dynamics are never permanent, but remain in a state of fluidity; there is no vacuum in life, and the weak person of today will seize any available opportunity to enhance his or her strength; strife and violence have been fundamental and permanent features in the evolution of our political, social, and economic systems; there are enough blames to go round; the Church did not rely on Divine and pacifist means to grow and expand; human nature remains what it has always been through history, regardless of secular or ecclesiastical orientation; power intoxicates deeply, and its wielders will do anything, including shed blood (if allowed, or if they can get away with it), to retain and perpetuate their primacy.

Perhaps, drawing from the nature of man, especially the disposition towards mass violence or wars, the two greatest Catholic Fathers, theologians and philosophers, St. Augustine, the Bishop of Hippo (in modern Tunisia) - 354 A.D. to 430 A.D., and St. Thomas Aquinas (1225 - 1274), wrote extensively on human passions, as well as on Wars, perhaps to provide a theoretical justification and rationalization for the violence that enabled the expansion of the Church in its earliest days and years. In his very significant, comprehensive, and classic opus, "The City of God", written in 426 A.D., St. Augustine wrote that maintaining peace in the face of a grave wrong that could only be stopped by violence would be a sin. Defense of one's self or others could be a necessity, especially when authorized by a legitimate authority (meaning the Catholic Church or their endorsed secular rulers). He wrote that: "They who have waged war in obedience to the divine command, or in conformity with His laws, have represented in their persons the public justice or the wisdom of government, and in this capacity have put to death wicked men; such persons have by no means violated the commandment, "Thou shalt not kill."

He was also the first writer to use the term "Just Wars", though he did not dwell extensively on its components and criteria, a job that was eloquently done about a century later by Thomas Aquinas. St. Augustine wrote that "But, say they, the wise man will wage Just Wars. As if he would not all the rather lament the necessity of just wars, if he remembers that he is a man; for if they were not just he would not wage them, and would therefore be delivered from all wars." Thomas Aquinas, in his timeless *Summa Theologiae*, codified the Just War Theory, and provided the conditions under which wars could be just (all, from the prism of Catholic Orthodoxy):

- First, just war must be waged by a properly instituted authority such as the State. (Proper Authority is first: represents the common good: which is peace for the sake of man's true end—God.)
- Second, war must occur for a good and just purpose rather than for self-gain (for example, "in the nation's interest" is not just) or as an exercise of power (just cause: for the sake of restoring some good that has been denied. i.e. lost territory, lost goods, punishment for an evil perpetrated by a government, army, or even the civilian populace).
- Third, peace must be a central motive even in the midst of violence (right intention: an authority must fight for the just reasons it has expressly claimed for declaring war in the first place. Soldiers must also fight for this intention).

Man is an imperfect Being. This imperfection is manifest in personal conduct, excesses, thoughts, and in all other forms of intemperance. The relationships among humans are, therefore, occasionally characterized by envy, greed, domination, and other indications of selfishness and inconsideration. The translation of this framework to the macro level explains the strife, wars, suspicion, and overall disorder, which define inter-state relations. Classical and contemporary writers have theorized extensively on War and its many variants.

The consensus is that there are strict conditions that could accommodate and explain wars under the Classical Western Tradition. Again, human nature ensures the non-observance of this strict Code, leading to the proliferation of wars in History and in contemporary times. In many ways, war is the highest manifestation of sovereign power. The introduction of Ethics in Military Affairs is reflective of the Natural Law, and our connection thereto. Every State defends their war as just and blames the other State but, in reality, the same war cannot be just on two opposite sides. As Wyndam Lewis put it, "but what war that was ever fought, was a just war, except of course that waged by the enemy." Humanity has a shared dignity emanating from the spark of the Transcendental which is immanent in us all, not permitting of despoliation, abuse, or extinguishment. This is common and exclusive to humanity, regardless of their physical, intellectual, or moral qualities, social status, race, and other regular differentiators. Ultimately, each person is responsible for his/her actions, regardless of the instructions he/ she received from "superior" Officers. Ethics reinforces the nexus between moral justification for an action and its execution.

St. Augustine writes further that, while war is evil and an enabler of conflict, the imperfection of man ensures the inevitability of wars even as man strives towards the attainment of Peace. For him, all men innately strive for Peace, which is the "purpose of waging war…." He further asserts that the possibility of civic peace or *Tranquillitas Ordinas* can only be provided by God. God has, however, allowed Man to maintain this civic peace, expecting Man to know what is right and what is wrong. The Prince or Political Leader is God's representative on earth, according to St. Augustine. Disruptions to this Order could be redressed by wars. Clausewitz theorizes that war is an extension of politics and is motivated more by the ends than the means of war. In this regard, he sees no means as being too reprehensible or severe towards achieving victory in wars. Force can be used to any extent to achieve the objective of defeating the enemy. He regards the introduction of moral precepts into war considerations as an absurdity.

The eminent Dutch Jurist of the 16th century, Hugo Grotius, founded his Just War theories on the Natural Law, and avers that, as abominable as wars may be, they underscore man's departure from the Natural Law and that we should be realistic enough to recognize them. He advanced this position in his great work, *De Jure Belli ac Pacis*. For him, therefore, normative considerations regarding wars are unnecessary; rather, we should define the conditions for a just war.

He says that: "where the power of law ceases, there war begins." His early thoughts substantially guided *Jus in Bello* thinking. *While Jus ad bellum* is meant to guide those with power to make war declarations, *Jus in bello* is meant to guide Officers and soldiers on the battlefield. This idea of moderating human carnage as a philosophical (not necessarily practical) exercise has undergone some changes over the centuries, with criteria like cause for war (*casus belli*) and proportionality of war measures (*jus ad bellum*), particularly undergoing several iterations and generating considerable debate as the nature of conflict, state of Science, etc., become more complex and destructive.

Alberico Gentili (1552 - 1608) and Hugo Grotius (1583 - 1645) mainstreamed these concepts into International Law. With the current state of Intelligence Collection especially by very advanced technical means, where competent and capable Services can proactively and correctly determine the malevolent intentions of sundry State and non-State enemies, should they wait until they are struck before responding, or is proactive attack on that basis justified? Is pre-meditation necessarily a bad thing in the circumstance? With the irregular but potent threat posed to States by sundry non-State actors, e.g. terrorists, criminal hackers, and drug cartels, must the consideration and protection accorded State actors under the original Just War formulation be extended to these dangerous and amorphous enemies? I do not think so. For those interested in exploring these issues further (*Jus in Bello, Jus post bellum,*) etc., etc., a modern thinker and writer in this evolving field, Emeritus Professor Michael Walzer of Princeton University, is a very competent and helpful guide.

Perhaps, we should consult St. Augustine and St. Aquinas a bit more, given their critical roles in providing the foundational basis for Catholic Doctrinal Orthodoxy -- that was so very critical to Western political, economic, and social systems that dominate in the world presently. We must bear in mind that these were men of their times, and, regardless of their asceticism and clerical calling, were still human, with views, passions, and prejudices.

St. Augustine, Bishop of Hippo

His "*Tranquillitas Ordinis*" (Tranquility of Order) is one of the four ways of obtaining peace in the world, which he calls "the peace of all things." This is the classical western idea of peace. Peace is found in the tranquility of Order and the acceptance of the Order. Peace does not necessitate or imply perfect justice, for the polity is not capable of such justice. However, peace is achieved and maintained accordingly. This relies on harmony with the natural order of things; accepting order through hierarchy is key to peace; peace is not everyone being equal. We should want to ask this eminent man if, by peace, order, and hierarchy, he means the peace of the graveyard wherein some oppressors and exploiters hold their fellow humans down, subject them to varying levels of indignity and violence, and ask them to accept their lot in order to maintain order (pun is deliberate). Already, you can see here the seeds of the horrendous discriminatory practices in subsequent centuries. Convenient, situational, and Manichean writers like Nietzsche and Machiavelli borrowed extensively from these ideas, even as some truly horrible ideologies have sprung up from St. Augustine's ideas as well, or, to be charitable, interpretations of his views. It is easy to see how an entitled individual would buy and sell his fellow human being, or how a murderous tyrant would interpret his extermination of healthy opposition on the basis of this idea of Order at all cost. As a matter of fact, St. Augustine did not emphatically condemn slavery (which was pervasive in North Africa and the Levant during his time) as being intrinsically evil on its own. As a matter of fact, and perhaps inspired by the writings and prescriptions of this significant Catholic philosopher, the Catholic Church actually owned human beings as slaves many centuries later.

The Jesuit Order of the Catholic Church, which founded that otherwise excellent center of academics, Georgetown University, Washington, D.C. in January, 1789, sold 272 human beings (men, women, and children) from their "stock of slaves" in Maryland, to Henry Johnson (from Louisiana) in 1838, to settle some debts which threatened the survival of the then Georgetown College, on terms including the separation of family members who were thus sold. This was exposed only less than ten years ago by Investigative Reporters, whereupon, as a first measure, the highly-regarded University changed the names of the Halls honoring the Jesuit priests who were directly implicated in the slave sales transaction. (Rev. Father Thomas Mulledy Hall was changed to Freedom Hall in 2015, before the Board of Regents voted to name it permanently after Isaac (Hawkins), the first black man whose name appeared on the transaction document). (Rev. Father William) McSherry Hall was renamed Remembrance Hall in 2017, before its new permanent name, Becraft Hall, in a tribute to the black woman, Anne Marie Becraft, who opened the first school for black girls in Georgetown. The descendants of those sold individuals, the so-called GU(for Georgetown University) 272, mostly live in Maringouin, Louisiana, presently, and have been offered some apologies and restitution by the Jesuits for their acknowledged sin, a sin that was only exposed almost two hundred years later by external parties.

St. Augustine's philosophical doctrine that there is a certain Order in nature that provides norms for human conduct, needs further investigation and rebuttal, and should never be taken for granted. This doctrine received its most renowned form in St. Thomas Aquinas's "Treatise on Law," a part of his *Summa Theologiae*. For Aquinas, natural law was humanity's "participation" in the comprehensive eternal law. People could grasp certain self-evident principles of practical reason, which corresponded to the various goods toward which human nature inclined. Natural law was a standard for human laws: unjust laws, in principle, will not automatically command obedience, except by coercion. The problems here include the arrogance of finality, the acceptance of unjust and cruel man-made hierarchies, as well as the value-less insistence on 'Order', perhaps, maintained through violence? Human beings should have a divine duty to resist and challenge injustice and any degradation of their being and essence by any other human being. Shackling and exhorting the victim to be of good behavior and conform, seems to be out of touch with what an eminent religious priest should be prescribing or endorsing.

Canonized by Pope John XXII in 1323, Thomas Aquinas was heavily influenced by Aristotle. He disagreed fundamentally with Plato and St. Augustine on the architecture of the human society. While St. Augustine, for example, focused on the world to come -- the Christian El Dorado -- in which you either choose the world or heaven, Aquinas, the Angelic Doctor, did not share St. Augustine's fanaticism and absolutism (who wrote, for example, that we have no right to resist the existing order or laws), but believed that humans could have a rational, humane, and ordered world. His commitment to human dignity was also reflected in his writings. For him, you can do well both here on earth and in heaven, once your earthly activities are geared towards heavenly obligations and requirements. Our experience would confirm that St. Thomas Aquinas' template has prevailed.

He also aligns with Aristotle by acknowledging that man is a political animal. Achieving our earthly well-being requires a government, which entails our collective cooperation because we are social animals. He writes that: "the purpose of a secular government is not suppression and punishment, but the achievement of earthly well-being." It is safe to call this the provision of public goods. Virtue enhances the community. People get together to live according to virtue, and to live well in a way that would be impossible if they lived singly. The good life is a life of virtue. The end/ purpose of human association is a virtuous life. When St. Augustine writes that sin has tempered the human connection with Natural Law, so we need human laws to repress our negative inclinations by fear and force, Aquinas counters that the Natural Law is too general, so we need specific laws to guide our retail or individual conduct. For him, human laws are specific inferences made by practical reasoning from the Natural Law. Laws not derived from Natural Law are oppressive laws or those that fail to secure the public good; these are not laws at all and should not be obeyed, according to him. Their character is more of violence than of law. He further states that laws without justice have no claim to our allegiance and obedience.

Indeed, St. Thomas Aquinas, perhaps unwittingly, provided the theoretical basis for the subsequent unraveling of the Church-State Nexus, and the empowerment of the human person. He did this by raising the question of faith and reason against the backdrop of the injection of Aristotelian thoughts into Western Culture, and invariably questioning the accepted doctrine that had persisted for centuries without any effective challenge. In embracing the methodologies of the ancient Greek Philosophers to introduce some rationality in the processing of convenient and untested Orthodoxy, Thomas Aquinas demonstrated uncommon boldness and courage for his time. He was not an apostate, no doubt, but just placed some premium on human rationality; he was after all, one of the earliest Catholic priests to weave the concept of the soul. For him, however, God's existence needs no proof, and humans are incapable of knowing the essence of a god; the essence of a god is existence, he says, and humans only know material things. Following Aristotle, he writes that: "virtues are developed habits of powers disposing agents to good actions." that is, a balance between excess and defect in the exercise of power.

Nietzsche will seem to be following St. Augustine on the glorification of "strength", obedience by the weak, etc., as the natural order of things. He supports Monarchy (what he calls the Kingship of One) because it replicates God's government of the universe. Aquinas also writes that tyranny betrays the purpose of God's appointment of a political leader. He supports private property and sees Law as "a rule and measure" of reason. We are creatures who are naturally able to tell right from wrong. St. Augustine was emphatic on his doctrine that the Church and State must be the same, with the Church princes, priests, preferably, having the ultimate powers because their mandate came from heaven. He combated paganism and heresy, etc., especially Donatism, which was prevalent in his native North Africa, and pushed for the harmony of the physical, communal, moral, spiritual, and developmental dimensions of life -- all under the Catholic priests -- these being the responsibilities of leadership that, for him, only priests should discharge.

These priests must, however, inculcate the habits of self-examination, humility, surrender, and mercy; the earliest impulses of turning the other cheek when attacked or offended. For St. Augustine, politics was the art of the possible, made only possible because of an abiding faith in God. He believed in the transformative effect of Christianity but was realistic enough to admit that humans were particularly imperfect beings. Quite a paradox, but acceptable when you are speaking on God's behalf. He was heavily influenced by Cicero who wrote "*Res Publica*" (Public Thing), which actually meant "a thing of; something belonging to the people." Plato had also written in his "The Republic" that "a good man's service to his homeland has no limit or terminus." For St. Augustine, this homeland was one of faith controlled by Catholic priests, and not one by birth, heritage, habit, and physicality. Priests must administer the "*temporalis*"/ temporary sphere, to ensure the admittance of cleared souls into heaven. He also declared that "security lies in the happy condition of living rightly, rather than in being safe to act wrongly", and that "only the converted and reformed can have mercy." The earliest formulation of using intimidation, guilt, and the scare tactic of the horrible portents of hell to convert and retain adherents to the new Faith, had started... so, whereas, Epicureans saw death as the end of all evils, since the soul, in their conception, was mortal, St. Augustine and the early Catholic philosophers created a new narrative which involved the indestructibility of this same soul, and that only by accepting and practising the commands of the emerging Catholic Faith would people be saved from the damnation of hell fire, a prospect that cannot be, and has never been, proven, but which elicits the conditioned behavior of believers while they still have consciousness, the only period of consequence.

It is significant that St. Augustine distinguished between major and minor transgressions, only to be determined by Catholic priests, writing that: "if they are both equal because they are both misdeeds, then mice and elephants are equal because they are both animals, and flies and eagles, because they both fly." The Commonwealth, for him, is the property of the people;" a City is a group of men united by a specific bond of peace." There is no authority except from God, and only priests can interpret God's Intent; anybody who resists authority resists what God has established, and, by so doing, brings punishment unto himself (Romans 13: 1-8), with the declared assurance of some irredeemable and severe Divine Judgment, a punishment seemingly reserved for victims, and not perpetrators. This Augustinian position has been hijacked by sundry totalitarians over the centuries as a justification for their cruelty against people with dissenting views within the polity. The term "treason" has been serially debased and exploited by potentates with totalitarian inclinations. In some ways, St. Augustine could be regarded as having provided some of the earliest philosophical and theological validity for totalitarianism and political absolutism, all in his bid to negate and discourage any questions regarding his promotion of Catholic Orthodoxy.

There was rampant slavery by Arabs during his time, which he never categorically criticized, so it will be interesting to know if that was also part of God's intent, especially given the omnipotent attribute of the Divine Being. St. Augustine's emphasis on Order at all costs would appear to also require from the enslaved people, full compliance so that Order would be maintained. Indeed!!! Shouldn't Order be predicated on the unconditional protection of the dignity of the human person, equality, fair treatment, and objective justice? Some of these earliest promoters of the Faith did not seem much bothered by these imperatives, which they treated as distractions and, indeed, anomalous and *ultra vires* to the absolute and unconditional requirement of Order by all means.

He wrote that "I am human, and I consider nothing human alien to me", then added that a human being should love God, himself, and his neighbor, with the love commanded by Divine Law." As earlier mentioned, the problem with this charge is the duplicitous and incompatible comfort with slavery, as, indeed, with all forms of discrimination and injustice, once Order was maintained. When he writes that "whoever loves injustice, hates his own soul", the inconsistency becomes even more palpable and truly disappointing. The assumed soul should be a repository of all that is pure; yet St. Augustine has no harsh words for perpetrators of actual injustice and wickedness in the society beyond the sanitized and septic high-minded declaration with no anchor in reality. We should take his further declarations like "it is impossible to love oneself without loving God" in the same vein, for those who maintained his absolute and unconditional "Order" also loved themselves, actually loved themselves a whole lot, even as they committed several acts of wickedness against other humans, a practice that should ordinarily be regarded as being incompatible with the purity, essence, and quality of Divinity.

We are permanently warned to beware of God's Anger, both in life and after death, as this Divine Judgment is regarded as particularly harsh, and, one may add, disproportionate to the offence. St. Augustine was one of the earliest theoreticians who formulated this scare tactic to convert pagans, hold them in check, and control them throughout their lives, with the accredited representatives of God on earth, the men of the cloth, always men, the priests, insulated from the same standards of conduct while retaining the absolute monopoly on the interpretation of God's Will. How about the Chinese, Indians, Arabs, Aztecs, and Africans, who were leading their lives contemporaneously and who, mystified by their environment, also had their own Metaphysics and Cosmology, their own fear of death, of their environment, and of darkness in ways and forms not known to Christians, St. Augustine, and their cohorts? Were these people not also created by the same God? Are there different Gods for different societies? If so, how does this reconcile with the absolute attributes of Divinity, as well as the assumed indivisibility of God's Essence? Why did they not have the unmistakable choice to become Christians and Catholics wherever they might be?

Admitting discretion and choice in this instance detracts from God's omnipotence, and, possibly, his/her/its omniscience about their existence and spiritual practices which differed completely from Catholicism and Christianity. Indeed, why did it take Constantine and the other Emperors, plus Crusades and wars, to introduce and amplify Christianity? Why did humans, wherever they were born, not inevitably and automatically become Christians and Catholics, if that was the ineluctable will and wish of an omnipotent and omniscient Father? Why the need for the leprous and "invisible," actually, visible, hand of humanity to assist our Divine Being?

Perhaps, St. Augustine reveals his real intentions and tactics when he writes that: "rulers do not inspire fear in those who do good works, but in those who do evil; if you do evil, you should fear God." The intentions, anger, and punishment of God, are as interpreted and conveyed by the indoctrinated, invested, and empowered priests; when and how do we objectively achieve a determination of God's true intentions and the intentions of man projected to the pedestal of divinity? This question remains unanswered to this day. Raising a query falls within the specter of heresy. Why is this field the only one insulated from objective inquiry, even as it is our fellow fallible humans who make the declamation on behalf of Divinity? They, who remain the beneficiaries of the lack of inquiry and investigation; has any human problem ever been solved by this kind of imposed censorship? No…

The fear mongering continues when St. Augustine reminds us that: "everyone who puts his hope in a human being is cursed" (Jeremiah 17:5); the only problem with this is that he and his clerical colleagues interchange their divine and human cloaks with rapidity and convenience. So, when we hear that "all the kings of the earth will adore him; all nations will serve him" (Psalm 72: 11), we hear a mission statement to further their personal and institutional control over the thoughts and actions of ever-expanding vistas of humanity. The truth, however, is that, despite these magisterial declarations, the majority of the world population has not submitted to Yishu's suzerainty - despite the aggressive propagation methods, including colonialism, and the world continues to exist. When he tells us that "no one is just through his own justice", meaning that you must submit to Catholic or Christian control or justice, we assume he is just writing good poetry and nothing more. The same consideration we attach to his admonition not to love the world or the things in it, but to seek eternal salvation. But they want to control humans in this world…and beyond...but starting from this world, most importantly!!! There was a reason why De La Rochefoucauld (1615 - 1680) wrote that: "hypocrisy is the homage paid by vice to virtue."

Actually, as we proceed on this journey, it might be useful to consider some of the philosophical thoughts and ideas that preceded St. Augustine. In this regard, the last of the eminent Greek troika will suffice, having distilled and refined the thoughts of his predecessors and instructors, Socrates and Plato. It is by now obvious that we are referring to Aristotle. He wrote that every city is some sort of partnership, and every partnership is constituted for the sake of some good ("for everyone does everything for the sake of what is held to be good").

Aristotle saw the city as a political partnership, with the need for specializations. It is particularly offensive thousands of years later to read that "it is fit for Greeks to rule Barbarians", just as he proceeded to justify slavery. Quoting Charondas, he adopted the position that the members of the household are "peers of the mess" or "peers of the manger", as Epimenides of Crete called it. Just like Homer, Aristotle was very patriarchal. For Aristotle, the city has full self-sufficiency and exists by nature; the self-sufficiency is the purpose of the city! Man is a political animal and it is only humans who have the prerogative of "good and bad", "just and unjust." The city precedes the individuals, who are born to join; we cannot function without it. "Everything is defined by the city's task and its power." When the individual is separated from the city, s/he is no longer self-sufficient, but must become a beast or a god, with the latter status being unattainable. Accordingly, to avoid becoming a beast, man must be a part of the society/ city.

He writes that, without virtue, man is extremely unholy and savage (the most savage of all the animals). "The virtue of justice is a thing belonging to the City; for adjudication is an arrangement of the political partnership; this adjudication is judgment of what is just." He had no difficulty in categorizing a complete household as comprising free persons and slaves. He wrote that "for one who does not belong to himself by nature, but is another's, though a human being, is, by nature, a slave; a human being is another's who, though a human being, is a possession and a possession is an instrument of action and separable from it (its owner"). The circumlocution, the discursiveness, the prolixity, the gassiness, the wordiness, the pleonasm, the tautology, the verbiage, the diffuseness, and utter hollowness of the presentation of this overrated and ignorant little fellow, provide proof of the difficulty, of the impossibility, of reconciling this convenient and warped position with objective decency, morality, and eternal justice. Utter Rubbish. Some of these antediluvian gangsters have been honored more than their merit.

Aristotle was extremely chauvinistic, even for his time; the early European (and American) political structure, as well as the persisting structural discrimination against women in the Islamic world, owed their inspiration to Aristotle's views on the assumed lower status of women. He used analogies depicting assumed strength (must be only physical, which only a little fellow like Aristotle could understand), to configure his ideal society. This assumed philosopher and deep thinker perceives reason but is incapable of attaining it. He celebrated the rule of the so-called powerful (only, perhaps, physically powerful in the referential average dynamics between men and women). He needs to be instructed that brawn and brain are on different frequencies. A pity really that this nonsense persisted beyond his age, or continues to this date across the Middle East, where women are supposed to be grateful if they can drive in the year 2020, or if they can shake hands with men (still a rarity in those parts), even as more intimate forms of gender interaction, including sanctioned pedophilia, take place in private quarters, hence the explosion in population numbers and embarrassing levels of obstetric fistula.

Insecure men can really get creative and "philosophical" when it comes to repressing and controlling women, many of whom are, in reality, more resourceful, brilliant, productive, and creative than these entitled phallic wastrels. Aristotle also celebrated expertise in war, even as he was a wimp. He said that the good hunter should hunt down both beasts and other humans; when some humans, "naturally suited to be ruled, but unwilling to be ruled", they must be hunted down like wild animals, this war being "just." This improves the acquisitive expertise of the hunter, thereby enabling order and balance in the society; an early justification for slavery and the evil treatment of other humans. People pick examples that suit their agenda. Some of these progenitors of the Western Thought process were actually very interesting people, to be very polite.

Friedrich Nietzsche (1844-1900)

It is only logical that we proceed to discuss yet another demonic, depressed, and overrated character, Friedrich Nietzsche.

Since our objective remains tracing the evolution of Western Thought, limiting ourselves to Nietzsche's "Genealogy of Morality", written in 1887, should be a sufficient guidc as wc asscss his political and moral views. This German writer was unabashed in his promotion of the German machismo, as well as his deep-seated distrust of, if not hatred for, Jews. In many respects, he is centrally regarded as the philosopher who provided the theoretical justification for some of the aggressive political and military actions that Germany took in the 20th century, which had significant adverse consequences for global peace and ethnic minorities in particular. He inspired subsequent generations of

Germans, (especially the Nazi leadership, members, and collaborators) with an unapologetic mindset, which led to the cruelty towards Jews.

He used the term "democrat" as an abusive word and kept referring to what he regarded as "man's monstrous moral past." He sought a new humanity upon the "death of God" and Christian morality which, for him, tended to impose assumptions of equality among all races and mankind. He regarded some races as "special", "higher", and admonished them not to soften their feelings by respecting or considering the feelings, rights, needs, and well-being of other people regarded (by him) as being "inferior" to them. In his "*ridendo dicere severum*"/ "saying what is somber through jest" formulation, he attacks accepted norms of mutual respect and amity, while perpetuating his distortion of Darwinian principles. He insists that he who can do much good can also do much harm, and that we should consider the totality of a man's character, not just the assumed negatives. The problem with this is that he emphasizes and glorifies the "negative" side of man; we cannot just take his situational declarations; Socrates instructed us that an unexamined life is not worth living.

Nietzsche needs to be heard clearly and extensively in his own words, " I used the word "State" -- it is self-evident who is meant by that term -- some pack of blond predatory animals, a race of conquerors and masters, which, organized for war, and with the power to organize, without thinking about it, sets its terrifying paws on a subordinate population which may perhaps be vast in numbers but is still without any shape, is still wandering about. That's surely the way the "State" begins on earth. I believe that the fancy has been done away with which sees the beginning of the State in some "contract." The man who can command, who is naturally a "master", who comes forward with violence in his actions and gestures -- what has a man like that got to do with making contracts! We cannot negotiate with such beings. They come like fate, without cause, reason, consideration, or pretext. They are present as lightning is present, too fearsome, too sudden, too convincing, too "different" even to be hated. Their work is the instinctive creation of forms, the imposition of forms..."

There is hardly any need to add to this, or to highlight how this position correlates directly with some of the truly horrible things done by Nazi Germany during the 20th century, particularly their systematic killing of 6 million Jews, grand dislocation and larceny, as well as providing inspiration for very weak characters in Europe and America who only find their strength in demonizing and killing "others."

Nietzsche writes that human beings "arrogantly" assume to be superior to animals and proceed from that premise to ascribe unattainable moral ideals to themselves. He says that the concepts of morality, good, and bad, derive from these unrealistic expectations, and permanently blames Jews and Christians for what he regards as a distortion of the human essence in its raw form. For him, humans should think beyond "good" and "evil", as morality assumes knowledge of things they do not have. Morality, for this distorted and sad man, is a crippling and dangerous "thing" which shackles the present at the expense of the future. He writes that man is a "beast" who should not be "tamed" or "civilized" as a "house pet." He proceeds to attack modern culture and communal compassion, while seeking to produce what he calls "the Sovereign Individual", who shall not be constrained by morality, which is an "idiosyncrasy of degenerates which has caused immeasurable harm." Morality is a symptom of deeper issues beyond "good and evil", and the craving for a strong faith is meaningless, according to him.

He further writes that "herd animal morality" or a general moral code is unrealistic and impractical; this moral code, in his view, is the strategic and subtle weapon of the weak in the society, who cite divine authority to impose their own preferences on the strong. This is exactly why he has problems with organized religion, which he sees as the "clever" response by Jews to constrain Germans and all other "stronger" races. This was in 1887; 27 years before WW1, and 52 years before WW2 started.

Let's continue with Nietzsche: people over-value pity; he blamed people for lacking the courage to criticize the "popular superstition" of Christian Europe which instructed that selflessness and compassion defined morality, a condition he attributed to a fundamental naiveté about the real intentions of the weak people who started the religion. What is interesting is how some of these prominent individuals consistently used convenient positions, however contradictory, to project their real purpose. Referencing John Locke's Empiricism, Nietzsche writes that: "it is not true that the purpose of a thing -- its utility, form, and shape -- is the reason for its existence, since a Superior Force can repurpose this." From this windy presentation, he lands at his central position about the Will to Power; "the primordial fact of history." He instructs his devotees that exercising their Will towards any national or racial goals should not be constrained by any considerations whatsoever, the assumption being that his beloved Germans would always be stronger than others. He criticizes the drive towards a "rational, well-ordered egalitarianism"; instead, he celebrates autocracy and privilege.

He writes further that democracy has the "defect of morality" and furthers his manichean view of the world by stating that "active emotions" guide human actions. Examples of his *realissimum* or "most real being" will be God, Napoleon, or, as the world would see some decades later, Hitler. He doubts a common genealogy for all humans -- evidencing his limited knowledge even as he pretended otherwise -- and insists that history needs to constantly have major disruptions and changes. Morality represents the "*ressentiment*" of the weak against their oppressors, since they cannot fight back otherwise. "Slaves" condemn the lifestyle and prerogatives of their "Master" as "evil", which they then seek to overthrow or reverse. By employing guilt (*Schuld*), they seek to weaken the strong, and impose a "morality of custom" (*Sittlichkeitdersitte*) and, therefore, turn man into something "regular, reliable, and uniform, with a sense of responsibility -- as defined by the weak, who suddenly become strong, as a result (*Verantwortlichkeit*)." The strong must understand this and reject this effort to dilute his power or weaken him. Quite an argument indeed.... he sees no basis to situate ethical conduct within any code of intrinsic and objective parameters. For him, it is perpetually "us" vs "them", and nothing more.

Nietzsche further suggests that every human progress involves struggle, as well as both spiritual and physical torment, and that the strong should have no pity on those who suffer on the march towards "history", especially if these "losers' are not of their race!!! Blood and horror underlie all "good things", and all religions, for him, are substantially systems of cruelty, with the cruelty targeted at people and groups who were previously powerful and strong. The true intent is unraveling.... No wonder that, to this moment, Nietzsche remains the darling and inspiration of neo-Nazi members and their mendacious horde of ignoramuses and losers that dot the landscapes of the United States and Europe, a fraternity of intemperate, profoundly ignorant, and malevolent creatures who bastardize the concept of nationalism. While the National Socialist Party (Nazi) in Germany and Austria did not directly trace their grudges and politics of resentment to Nietzsche, his influence is very clear to the discerning.

His "Sovereign Individual" must also be supra-ethical (*ubersittlich*), not recognizing or embracing any ethical code "imposed from without"; having a bad conscience is an illness imposed by pressure, and is a repression of the Will to Power or the freedom to embrace the natural tendency towards animosity, cruelty, destruction, etc.; this profoundly morose, morbid, lugubrious, bitter, pessimistic, gloomy, and mournful creature preaches. He encourages his followers to express their worst instincts in "unapproved ways", since religion, for him, is substantively built around debt and guilt which is "man's sickness of itself."

In his ideal world, there is a Master-caste, "the highest exemplars of the species", which must not succumb to a guilty conscience deriving from any action they take against other races who are their "slaves" and who must suffer because they are inherently "weak." "... with sin, we have the most dangerous and disastrous trick of religious interpretation...", he writes. This very weak and tortured man states that when religion emphasizes "self-discipline, self-surveillance, and self-overcoming", and "purports to give morality as a target for humanity", the real target is the "stronger" race which must self-police and self-constrain its natural instincts and Will to Power. Religion becomes, in this context, the elevation of guilt to the metaphysical level, to weaken the strong and impose an artificial order of equality, which, as men discover themselves, must be disrupted through considerable violence and dislocation, in order to achieve or restore the "normal" order of things. God, in his view, is that "which is last, thinnest, and emptiest which is made the Cause or the *ens realissimum*." Such circumlocutous nonsense !!!

This very limited and sad man then rounds up by saying that politics should be geared towards the production of "great human beings", and an aristocratic culture, with economic servitude by the majority being essential. "The cry of compassion must not tear down the walls of culture", culture as defined by him. The Nietzschean narrative of the Creditor-Debtor dynamic needs some illumination here, because it was built on the Hegelian Construct. This is essentially his (Nietzsche's) position: from the tribal stages and continuing, people venerate their dead ones (ancestors), thanking them for their individual and collective progress; for this, sacrifices are made to the ancestors, places of worship designated and held sacred, plus the idea of indebtedness to them is ingrained in all, without ever holding these same ancestors accountable when an individual or the society at large suffers adversities. Reversals are attributed to human failings and transgressions of ancestral instructions and expectations, and, yet, more obedience and sacrifices.

The living are conditioned by society to remain grateful to their ancestors for sundry things; they are indebted to these mythically all-powerful ancestors, who are the creditors; much as one tries, this debt is never entirely repaid; the concept of punishment and eternal damnation (hell fire) gets introduced to ensure compliance; with time, the concept is hijacked and reified to the *causa firma* (first cause), as humans must now be grateful to the assumed First Cause for creating the world and giving them life; no amount of sacrifice, repayment, guilt-expiation, or atonement ever suffices; this debt simply can never be repaid, until, "out of love", the creditor repays himself on our behalf by giving us His own son, who is killed on behalf of the sinful world -- even binding those not yet born and those who do not believe in the narrative; the debt gets reinforced and permanent as a result.

Nietzsche calls this "the stroke of genius of religion", because religion is woven against this concept, with humanity required to be eternally grateful to the Deity for everything really; for him, the Jewish origin of Christianity was also worrisome, as he suggested that they had succeeded in placing their own ancestor(s) over and above all other peoples' ancestors, while the Roman Empire helped them spread the kernel of their religion around Europe; his German target audience must reject this imposition and be free according to their Will, and not be checked and constrained by religion or conscience. No debt should be assumed as being owed to any ancestor, especially the ancestors of people "weaker than them."

One may just add that it is actually interesting that people who were particularly weak while alive, are suddenly lionized and feared once they die in virtually every culture due to man's fear of death, exactly when they should be even weaker since death is the end of life and consciousness. In some form of reverse logic, they become very strong and indomitable in death, even as no one has convincingly established any nexus between life and death, or proven that there is a continuum or evidence of consciousness that survives physical death, and which remains active even after burial or cremation, remembering all of one's experiences while alive and apportioning blessings and punishment to the living on the basis of their veneration, or lack thereof. It is arguable that these philosophers may be onto something here, but their negative obsession with Jews, which found wholesale adoption and holocaustal expression in Germany and Central Europe after their time, should give one cause for sobriety and reflection.

Thoughts and ideas, however demented or unorthodox, surely have their followers and consequences, as the turbulence of the 20th century instructs. The import of these cursory scans of Western Thought is to bring to the fore the spectrum of ideas that defined what became manifest as political, economic, and social systems on the Continent and beyond. The similarities and sharp differences are reflective of the differences in outlook, training, temperament, context, historical circumstances, desires, influences, and psychological composition among the various writers and theorists. Ultimately, people chose, and will choose, what accords with their preferences and desired outcomes in life. When you convince yourself, for example, that other human beings are intrinsically inferior to you, you can dehumanize, buy, sell, and also systematically and legally exclude and maltreat them. You may even regard them as three-fifths of an individual and sleep easy.

But, they were born complete and equal, princes and princesses in their milieu, before the forced and shackled emigration, as well as the commencement of centuries of man-made deprivations, violence, legal disenfranchisement, negation of their humanity, forced name changes and obliteration of ancestral links; facts and realities that proceeded apace as the preachment of a Universal God of love, mercy, and common humanity reigned without irony. Indeed, these worshipful ones were so steeped in wickedness and entitled exploitation of the "other" that they would rather fight a war than respect the dignity of man. When they lost the Civil War in the United States, over 20,000 of these despicable characters emigrated to Brazil, which still practised slavery at the time, settling mostly in Sao Paolo. Their descendants are called *Confederados* (Portuguese pronunciation: *kõfede'radus*), and they continue to spread their ignorance and racial hatred to this day by worshipping their Confederate Flags.

It is conceivable that some of these losers have since found their way back to the US, reconnecting with their confederates in stoking race-based violence. Those who stayed back, and who have assumed fake Brazilian identities, remain condemned by ancestral infamy and depraved social conditioning.

Back to devout slave-owning Christians, how can the same God they worshipped and still worship in 2020 be for all mankind? For the Confederate Flag hearkens to "fond memories of a glorious past; our heritage." A heritage of infamy; a history of shameless exploitation and destruction of a part of the human essence. Maybe Nietzsche's; maybe Hegel's, but definitely not a God for all humans.

Hegel (1770 -1831)

It should be in order to review the other profoundly sad German philosopher, yet another Friedrich, Georg Wilhem Hegel (1770 - 1831). While he made pretensions of profundity by writing about the dialectics of thesis and antithesis leading to synthesis, his philosophy revolved around racial purity and subjugation of non-Germanic peoples. He thoroughly influenced Nietzsche.This conservative sycophant and apologist; this royal ass-licker (to Friedrich Wilhelm IV); this moronic character; this Hitlerian cosmic ancestor; this entitled and bigoted animal; this specimen of depravity; this reflection and manifestation of evil; this uncultured beast of no nation; this little fellow with a contrived and unmerited Messiah Complex; this companion of mendacity; this inspiration for bloodhounds and low lives; this low-class thug; this wretched creature; this concentration of bile; this reject; this profound idiot.......

In understanding the enormous scale of this man's low spirits, his ennui, his desperation, his wistfulness, his despair, and his dejection, we will look at the trashy work he called "The Elements of the Philosophy of Right." He promoted Statism, Absolutism, and Prussian *Machstaat toto coelo* - (by all the heavens, meaning absolute). He provided a theoretical justification, as if it was needed, for Totalitarianism, German Imperialism, their *Lebensraum*, as well as the demented Nazi Screed, which they impetuously called an Ideology. In his "Philosophy of the Right", his interpretation of freedom is totally different from the normal understanding of this loaded word. Freedom, for him, is a kind of action; one in which "I am determined through myself, and not at all through anything external"; not the general Construct, which situates freedom within the possibilities and choices of action. Remember Nietzsche's "Sovereign Individual"? What these individuals never quite addressed was how to reconcile competing, contentious, and contradictory tendencies among these assumed individual sovereigns.

He embarks on that tautologous and nonsensical formulation meaning nothing which is typical of these tormented individuals, when he writes that "we are free only when we overcome particularity", and act "universally", or "objectively", according to the "concept of the Will." Whatever!!! He queries the general assumption that God works *sub ration bon* (with good reason), and arrogantly postulates that Man (must be the German man only), being sovereign, is the only one qualified to determine what is right for him. While Immanuel Kant separates duty from inclination in his Categorical Imperative, Hegel insists that duty fulfills individuality, not suppress it, in a rational society. He proceeds to spew his prejudices about Hun superiority as a theory of Racial Purity; sadly, this found resonance and application in Europe and the United States, with severe consequences for lives, freedom, and public order. Truly, if some of these "great" German philosophers were formulating theories for a purely German society, and other Germans accepted their views, their conscious insularity might be respected; what were they doing in Cameroon, Ghana, East Africa, and South-West Africa? Or, just maybe, it was this kind of thinking that inspired those distant forays in pursuit of the resources belonging to those indigenous peoples; indeed, it was this mindset that motivated colonialism in its naked and raw form.

J. S. Mill and Hegel agreed that the ability to do as we choose is not intrinsically good but only because it is required for the achievement of other vital human goods. *Morsus conscientiae* (the bite of conscience) guides us towards what is right for us as individuals or a homogenous group in a racially-pure and segregated society. It would have been nice for these Knights of Evil and False Biology to live in the modern era, as their simplistic and devious proclamations have been largely debunked by Science, even as some distorted individuals hold dearly to craven concepts of an intrinsic group superior-inferior matrix in the human experience. H.B. Nisbet's translation of Hegel's work is as original as it can get, so we will rely extensively on it. He portrays the Hegelian supposition that human beings regarding themselves as persons and subjects is a product of European culture, and is a relatively-recent development influenced by Greek ethical life and Christian teachings. If this is so, how do they account for serfdom, feudalism, slavery, and the ecclesiastical control of the polity? One would think that the greatest triggers for the emphasis on the human person, the individual and her rights as a person, were the Lutheran reformation and the French Revolution.

The distinguishing feature of the modern state is Hegel's "Civil Society", which he defines totally differently from the earlier interpretation of civil societies (*burgerliche Gesellschaft*); he drops the correlation with the State and replaces this with the public community based directly on reason, and formed for collective or universal ends, and not necessarily by kinship or blood. The problem is that he still excludes non-relatives on racial grounds, thus nullifying his entire construct. In his civil society, people exist as persons and subjects who own private property; perhaps, some codification of the market economy, as opposed to the state-run economy. His civil society is a "universal family, which makes collective demands on its members and has collective responsibilities towards them"; the only thing to note here is that his universalism is blonde only.

This "universally blonde" family or society guarantees a secure, respected, and self-fulfilling way of life"; collectively, the constituents are responsible for preventing the members from falling into poverty - for whatever reason. The poor in this exclusive society are victims, not of some natural misfortune, but of a social wrong. It is remarkable how these men could project all these lofty ideals for their own people, even as they, concurrently, rationalized the exploitation, mass killing, and denigration of others. Germans and Belgians, as well as the other Western European Powers gleefully attended the Berlin Conference of 1884 -1885, where they arrogantly and remotely carved up distant African territories for rape, genocide, and plunder. Or, just maybe because, as he wrote, the State is the "march of God through the world." It may need to be said here that no other race or group has done to Europe or Europeans (and their descendants wherever they may be) what they have done to the rest of the world (in China, across Africa, in India, in South East Asia, Central Asia, in the Middle East, in Australia, in the Americas, etc.).

Whoever attacked Europe from outside Europe and laid claim to its resources, and killed its people? As recently as 1982, Britain even waged a naval war against Argentina over the distant Falklands (so-called by the Brits), the Spanish name for the war is *Guerra de las Malvina*. It will be interesting to know what the actual owners of the place call it, as the English and Spanish names cannot be original. As it is, this parcel of the South Atlantic Ocean belongs to Argentina, all the way at the southernmost part of the American Continent, yet Britain, in Europe which is atop America, waged a war on this archipelago ostensibly to protect some Dependencies aptly baptized South Georgia and South Sandwich. Indeed!!! The same Britain had waged Opium wars against China, and seized Hong Kong until 1997 when a newly-powerful China could demand their exit per contract. The British, Dutch, and Germans invaded South Africa and imposed their atrocious apartheid regime against the owners of the land, until the formal end of official racial segregation in 1994. For enlightenment on how Britain's hardest criminals, prisoners, and their descendants killed, dehumanized, and dispossessed Tasmanians and other Aborigines all the way in what they called Australia, please read: *https://www.vanguardngr.com/2020/07/a-fate-worse-than-slavery/*

Do we begin to talk about the United States and both its genocidal decimation of Native Indians and the enslavement of black people who had absolute freedom in Africa, only to very kindly "emancipate" them later, upon a bloody civil war? Why should the mostly English settlers in America be buying Louisiana from France or Florida from Spain, when there were original owners of the land? Just a little while prior, these settlers were still the subjects of King George III of England and other potentates in the Netherlands, France, Sweden, etc. Indeed, France has had centuries-old disputes with Germany over Alsace-Lorraine but would see no irony in laying claims over another person's land 8,000 kilometers (5,000 miles) away, to the extent of being the party to sell it. Shameless hypocrisy and usurpation!!! Has there been any atonement for America's original sin, just as there has been a token expression of guilt by Germany over its Nazi atrocities? The Catholic Church has apologized for its role during the Nazi Rule in Germany, and for engaging in slavery in the United States (the Jesuits/ Georgetown University case that has been unearthed).

Operation Ratline remains largely unmentioned, though; this was the program that the Catholic Church and some other conservative elements designed and executed, to enable hundreds of thousands, if not millions, of Nazi killers, their families, and sympathizers from Germany and across Central Europe, to escape to South America after World War II (notably Argentina under Juan Peron), Uruguay, Paraguay, Brazil, and other neighboring countries which were then ruled by Fascist Military Officers who were Catholic. This was all in a bid to shield them from due prosecution for War Crimes, Genocide, and Crimes Against Humanity at Nuremberg. This explains the significant

German populations you have presently in those very distant countries, though some have adjusted or changed their names, to obfuscate their origins (even as Nazi paraphernalia are privately treasured at home).

Those with interest in exploring this subject further and in understanding the roles played by two influential American brothers, Allen and Foster Dulles – wartime CIA Director and Secretary of State respectively (IAD, Dulles Airport, Washington, D.C.) should read the excellent book by Peter Levenda titled 'Ratline: Soviet Spies, Nazi Priests, and the Disappearance of Adolf Hitler.' This also explains why Dr. Adolf Eichman, the Nazi butcher, was kidnapped in Argentina, sedated, and ferried to Israel by Israel's respectable Intelligence Service, the Ha Mossad *leModi'in ule Tafkidim Meyuhadim*, known simply as the Mossad, in 1960, where he was duly tried and executed. If History is any guide, we shall soon be assailed with the Portuguese and Spanish equivalents of "Blood and Soil", "You shall not replace us" in Brazil, Argentina, and across that Region… the owners of the land should beware.

No responsibility has been assigned or accepted for America's very horrible foundational history, hence the glorification of an odious past, a despicable pedigree built on blood and injustice, celebrated even at the highest pedestals of governance presently. A shameless edification of evil!!! Why should we have European footprints in the Caribbean or Australia, lands that belonged to others? Has there been any accounting for the murderous activities of the genocidaire, Leopold of Belgium (actually a German, as are the royal family in England, who are ancestrally from the same Saxe-Coburg and Gotha in Germany)? Leopold's Gotha must be from Golgotha. This sad Germanic Belgian brute killed, murdered, and cannibalized a minimum of fifteen million Congolese people while criminally harvesting and removing the abundant natural resources of this very richly-endowed country. Why should Britain, France, Portugal, and Belgium be granting independence to African States and peoples who were always free and independent before the European invasion and disruption of their lives???

As the inimitable, legendary, prolific Nigerian philosopher, Afrobeat maestro, and crusader, who was also a tormentor and victim of Nigerian military brutes, Fela Anikulapo-Kuti, would have put it, "*Who are you ree*?" "*Wetin dey do you sef*?" The only problem is that this was not "*shakara, shakara oloje*," but the persistent wickedness of the "*animal in human skin*."

It bears emphasizing that people in the Hunza valley of Pakistan, the Nupe of Nigeria, the Ga of Ghana, the Aztecs of Mexico and Central America, etc., had their full lives before the Europeans invaded them, on the hubristic and self-serving mission of "civilizing" the owners of the land, who had lived for millennia on those lands, and had their metaphysics, social systems, concept of religion, architecture, art, jurisprudence, and other elements of a social life. The Chinese had musical instruments like the Sheng, Suona, and Guzheng; the Yoruba had their talking drums and Dundun; the Igbos had their ichaka, udu, oja, ogene, and ubo; the Cherokees and Sioux had their own flutes; Indians had their Ektara, Sitar, and Veenas; etc. All these instruments preceded the introduction of European pianos, violins, and drums to those societies. These facts are rendered, not to suggest that the intercourse between Europe and other societies was not beneficial in some respects; not at all; the objective is to render a balanced account and respond to the pervasive suggestion that other societies should remain eternally grateful to Europe for whatever they have "achieved."

When the term, Caucasian, is derived from Caucasus (literally, a hill, but meaning a place of large prospects), it is clear that this place of large prospects was not meant to be Europe. The story is far more nuanced and balanced than this convenient linearity. When beneficiaries of systemic injustice and cruelty casually tell the cumulative victims of these acts of injustice to "get over it; let's move on", without an acknowledgment of what has been done to be wrong; or, in cases, where these same people cling to the odious past "as value-less history", then some reminders become acutely necessary. Instead of an acceptance of guilt, we have people celebrating these atrocious practices in Charlottesville, in Savannah, in Mississippi, and across the United States and Europe in the second decade of the 21st century -- because no shaming or accounting has been applied to date. Indeed, it will be useful to know what the Apache, Navajo, Cheyenne, and Patawmak (re-named Potomac) actually called those lands, their lands, that have been re-christened and claimed by invaders.

Is Charlottesville (so-called) now a town in Germany, Wales, Scotland, or Italy, that German, Welsh, Scottish, and Italian descendants would chant "Blood and Soil", "You will not replace us", in these lands procured through the shedding of non-European blood on an industrial scale? In the midst of the Covid-19 pandemic in April, 2020, a slob who happens to be an elected Michigan State Senator --- instructively, not even in the South with its "heritage", one Dale Zorn, proudly wore the Confederate Flag as a face mask to the Chambers of the State Assembly in Detroit, before he was shamed into removing it, even as he clung to "history" as a defense for his offensive sartorial choice. In early May 2020, a middle-aged man proudly wore a Ku Klux Klan (KKK) hood to a grocery store as his choice of a face mask in Santee (nicknamed Klantee), California, in compliance with the State requirement to wear face masks while outside during this pandemic. It is significant that the town is nicknamed after the KKK in celebration of its racist past, in a mostly-liberal state such as California. What a despicable pedigree.... Don't tread on me, my state is for lovers ... Indeed !!!

A week later, yet another man in the same town, Dustin Hart, wore a swastika facial mask to another grocery store; when accosted by Law Enforcement, he claimed that he was exercising his First Amendment Rights. All of this was happening in America while the German President, Frank-Walter Steinmeier, was vigorously urging his compatriots to liberate themselves from the Nazi legacy and urging the Western world to reject the "return of evil in a new guise." If this could happen in California, it is anyone's guess what prevails in states like Mississippi, Arkansas, Alabama, Tennessee, Texas, and, actually, across quite a number of these "united" states. There will probably be an armed resistance to any attempt to rename the town, as people will defend "their heritage and history" -- unless a determined government imposes its Will. Some heritage and history indeed!!! No price has been paid for infamy, so, to that extent, the victims and objective commentators should retain their voices as well in rendering a full accounting of the dynamics. While, of course, it is not everyone in Klantee or Alabama who engages in these despicable acts, or condones them, the truth is that the voice of those who reject what is done in their name is not loud enough. The good should drown out the evil in our midst.

In an act of remarkable irony and profound arrogance, the European settlers in the current United States, pursued their Revolutionary War against England, to attain political independence for themselves, even as they felt entitled to enslaving their fellow human beings, people who foolishly actually joined these seekers of independence in fighting the war even as this independence and freedom did not apply to them. The protests that led to the Revolutionary War arose from the Tea Tax in Boston, opposition to the tax levy from England for the assistance rendered to the Colony during the French and Indian wars, as well as inspiration from the Enlightenment Movement which emphasized the freedom of speech, equality, and freedom of the Press. All this freedom was impetus for war even as they shackled other people, erased their sense of history, hanged them with glee, and utilized their forced labor free of charge!!! Indeed, they fought yet another war, the civil war, "to defend our way of life", which meant enslaving others, even as the churches were always full, notably in the southern states.

Indeed, all the states, cities, and small towns in the United States that end with "vania", "burg", and "ville", or that start with "New" this and that, were not always called those names by the natural and original owners of the land. What were they called? Where are those owners? Is it not a veneration of mendacity, grave evil, genocidal conduct, covetousness, and mass cruelty, to hug those lands, chant "blood and soil", and proceed as if history started with the annihilation of a race and rechristening of pre-existing places? When some of these places combine "lynch" and "burg" in their names even in 2020, it becomes clear what this much-cherished "heritage" means. Has there been any accounting? Any acknowledgment and apology? If there had been, all the violent and triumphant rhetoric *sans* values, would be tempered. While we explore the modern names of these ancient lands, the biggest mall in the United States (by rentable space), is located in a Pennsylvania town named, wait for it, King of Prussia. While this confluence town was rechristened a long while ago, should it not be a reasonable question to ask about the states, cities, and towns named after the original Native Indian owners of the land or the black Founding Fathers of these United States of America, for, indeed, they were there and played vital roles during the creation of the new country?

How about the early Chinese settlers and Mexican ancestors of this great country? While the violent displacement of a people and the renaming of their ancestral lands must remain condemnable, this moral position does not change nor is it mitigated when done by members of the same race against their race. What is wrong is objectively wrong, for situational morality is not morality. The 1994 Hutu genocide against Tutsis in Rwanda (in which over 1 million innocent people were butchered within three months) is a recent reminder of human bestiality and must remain condemned. As at 2020, this year of writing, the mostly nomadic Fulani ethnic group of West Africa (originally from Futa Jalon in Guinea), has persisted in its violent usurpation of other people's lands across the Region.

The focused violent attention of the Fulanis is on the arable Middle Belt and southern parts of Nigeria, areas settled by indigenous ethnic groups for several centuries. While people of Central African Republic and Ghana, for example, have been very firm in pushing back against these extremely violent and entitled Fulani terrorists masquerading as cattle herders (and their city sponsors/ protectors), they have been richly rewarded in Nigeria, an accommodation that has now morphed into extreme arrogance on their part. The Fulanis, though an ethnic minority in Nigeria, waged a very bloody war against the much more populous and trusting Hausas in the northern part of Nigeria in 1884, a crusade that was led by Uthman Danfodio. In Mincheva's apt characterization of the regional pattern of the risk involved, the militant arms of the Fulanis and others like them constitute 'the political organization of regionally concentrated groups [who] wish to demonstrate cultural cohesiveness and political solidarity by contesting the ethnic legitimacy of existing state boundaries"; one may add, with no consideration whatsoever for the effects of their violence and greed on local populations.

This minority Muslim group imposed Emirs on the far more populous peoples of the north; over time, three Fulanis have been presidents of Nigeria, namely, Shehu Shagari, Umaru Yar'adua, and the incumbent, Muhammadu Buhari (who was a Military Head of State from 1983 to 1985). Buhari has been in office as an "elected" president since 2015; he is in the second year of his second four-year term which started after a most corrupt and massively-rigged election in 2019. Since 2015, Mr. Buhari has presided over the most incompetent, opaque, and nepotistic government in that very-challenged country.

In a country with notoriously-unreliable citizenship records, a newly-appointed Fulani Minister of Humanitarian Affairs (her office is called) who took over a four-year Agency at the Buhari Presidency with extremely poor oversight, together with her predecessor, Maryam Uwais (another Fulani woman, but with no Cabinet rank), announced, at the peak of the Covid-19 pandemic, that their Office had distributed a cumulative amount of Naira 1.6 trillion ($4.5 billion) in CASH to the poorest people in the country (over the course of four years) as sustenance allowances and palliatives. The criteria and modalities for this "humanitarian aid" have never been disclosed, and the majority of the beneficiaries of N20,000 ($55) per head are Muslim northerners in a country where 100% of the vital crude oil revenue and 95% of tax revenue are generated in the Christian South. The thing is that, while a few people were shown on public television receiving some cash under the scheme, all efforts by the Civil Society for transparency and accountability have met with absolute stonewalling, because the same Minister claims that giving the details of the very poor beneficiaries would assault their "dignity." $4.5 billion...

While all the schools in the world were shut down since the pandemic started fully in March, this same woman, Ms. Sadiya Umar Farouq – with an inconsequential prior professional, financial, personal, and reputational pedigree -- claimed that her ministry, which seems to only distribute cash, has disbursed over $1 billion feeding school children in the past four years, including during this pandemic when schools are closed. All of this, with zero oversight, an absent database, and a non-existent accounting system. During her parliamentary appearance, she confirmed the authority of some of these suspicious allocations to be "Covid:19 Cash Transfer – President's Directive; the disbursement of funds to an additional 1 million households (cash transfer) in the sum of 30 billion Naira, data collection and validation, data cleaning and analysis, monitoring and evaluation, design and development of Covid:19 response register of beneficiaries, design of Covid:19 Cash Transfer, durable solutions and care maintenance for persons of concern, national durable solutions framework for persons of concern in the six geopolitical zones." The country's House of Representatives claims to be investigating half a trillion Naira (over 1.3 billion dollars) out of these spurious disbursements.

Most of Buhari's appointees have remained Fulanis and Northern Muslims; the Security Services are controlled by them as well, thereby threatening the careful and fragile balancing arrangement that has held that country together since political independence in 1960. The so-called cattle herders have also gained new confidence under Buhari, due to the rhetoric, funding programs, and obvious protection of the Buhari Government. They now openly carry submachine guns in a country where it is a crime to have the most basic weapons as a private citizen; they raid farmlands belonging to other ethnic groups and kill whoever protests the grazing of their cattle on people's farms; they attack communities, kill several people, burn down homes and churches, rape women and girls, then brazenly rename such communities; no single perpetrator has been arrested or prosecuted by the Government, thus validating the suggestions of official protection. The Buhari Government, which has several contending challenges, earmarked hundreds of millions of dollars of money generated in the predominantly-Christian South for a so-called RUGA project, aimed at building modern settlements for Fulani people across the entire country; on lands belonging traditionally to other peoples, which the native owners of the land find extremely offensive. Some senior government officials have also impudently advised survivors of these incessant attacks, to be their "brothers' keepers" by allowing Fulanis to act with impunity in their communities and on their farms.

The government also waived visa requirements for West Africans, in a program aimed at resettling all the willing Fulanis across West Africa in Nigeria. With their notoriously-porous land borders, as well as the issuance of nationality documents to these resettled people, the demographics of the country would be permanently altered, with grave implications for the census, allocation of federal resources, and electoral outcomes. The recourse to self-help by the consistent and unprotected victims, the indigenous peoples of Nigeria, will threaten the stability of that combustible and mostly-failed State. The world needs to pay close attention to this dynamic given the population of Nigeria, the lack of a reliable citizen database, the fragility of State systems and capabilities, the endemic corruption that has permeated the DNA of State Institutions, the implications for the entire Region if Nigeria collapses completely, as well as the possibility of the core Muslim North being an incubatory ground for Islamic Terrorism. The country has proven incapable of defeating Boko Haram terrorists after fifteen years and billions of dollars ostensibly spent on materiel, even as entire counties remain in the firm control of these rag-tag opportunistic terrorists. The Islamic State also has a foothold in the mostly ungoverned parts of the North, towards the borders with Niger Republic and Chad.

With these aforementioned examples, it becomes clear that wickedness has no unique racial character. Indeed, the "animal called man" (apologies to Olusegun Obasanjo) can be found everywhere. This easy recourse to bestiality goes beyond race, but the lack of accountability enhances the Cruelty Index in societies. It is the duty of all well-meaning people to condemn these evil practices, speak out, and demand accountability at all times.

After World War II, in which the US and Allied Forces (including hundreds of thousands of African and Indian soldiers under European colonization) engaged in a shooting war against Germany, Italy, and Japan, for six years, the United States established the Marshall Plan, funded it to the tune of $15 billion in 1948, for the purpose of rebuilding Europe, including Germany. The German Marshall Fund was established in 1972, to foster understanding between the United States and North Atlantic countries of Europe. Africa, India, China, the Caribbean countries, Native Indians, and native peoples in the current Latin American countries, never fought against Europe or America. How have they been treated? Have there been the equivalents of the Marshall Plan, to compensate in a token form for the grave injustice done against them for several centuries? No! Rather, the exploitation and gloating continue as "we will not be replaced" on another's land.

To quote the great Fela Kuti yet again, "*Teacher, don't teach me nonsense.*"

One may add, if the God of justice, mercy, and equity, if the God who made all in His or Her Image, sees nothing wrong with all this wickedness, systemic cruelty, disempowerment, and dispossession, is that God really for all, or "others" should worship their own Gods, Gods that may just favor them more and insist on mutual respect, universal justice, love, and amity? For, how can you seek your spiritual redemption and perpetual reward in the mythology of your oppressors? In the very Construct of your personal injury and depersonalization… It is difficult to reconcile some of the barbaric practices of the European proselytizers with the cardinal principles of their Faith. Let's even limit ourselves to: Thou Shall not kill; Thou Shall not steal; Thou Shall not covet thy neighbor's goods. Did the Opium War in faraway China; Transatlantic Slavery and resistance to its abrogation hundreds of years later; Colonialism in distant lands and the consequential takeover of other people's resources; displacement of indigenous populations in America and South

Africa, with genocide and apartheid to boot; etc., demonstrate compliance with these solemn Divine Mandates? If they did not, and still do not, practise the true essence of their Religion, why should the victims of their exploitation and dispossession then be obsessed with the discarded religion?

Muslims are even more honest when they declare their ambition to either convert all to Islam or kill unbelievers, on their journey towards establishing a "Haven of Peace", Dar es Salaam. Any Muslim who renounces Islam must be hunted down and killed, because population numbers matter to them and dictatorship must be preserved. The implication is that, since we have roughly 1.5 billion nominal Muslims around the world, and a global population of 7.6 billion people, about 6 billion people are yet to be converted or killed to achieve a "Haven of Peace." As at this time of writing, and for several years now, the violent attacks on, and displacement of, Christians in their ancestral lands across the Middle Belt and Southern parts of Nigeria, are proceeding apace, as the Central Government headed by a Fulani Muslim, Muhammadu Buhari, either feigns ignorance or recycles the boring condolences after the regular attacks in Kaduna, Adamawa, Taraba, Benue, Borno, and Plateau States (in particular) -- all targeted at either forceful conversion of survivors or the total annihilation of resistance and takeover of their land. Senior Administration Officials have openly canvassed for Muslim Fulas from across West Africa to proceed to Nigeria, to take over new lands and join the "uncompleted Dan Fodio Jihad." It is estimated that over seventy thousand people have been massacred by this horde of killers in the past few years alone. Heavenly peace indeed!!!

In what is regarded as apostasy in the Koran (5:10; 9:28), death is clearly prescribed, with a further charge to "fight and slay the pagans, seize them, beleaguer them, and lie in wait for them in every stratagem." In chapter 5, verse 51 of the Koran, faithful Muslims are specifically forbidden (for that is the tone and language of Islam) from having any relationship or friendship with Jews and Christians, with chapter 92:91 imploring them to "kill disbelievers wherever you find them", while 9:123 urges Muslims to "murder them and treat them harshly", the "they" here being non-Muslims. This same charge is also captured as follows: "O you who believe! Fight those of the disbelievers who are close to you, and let them find harshness in you, and know that Allah is with those who are the *Al-Muttaqun* (the pious)." Is it conceivable that a Muslim will plead that her/his compliance with these precepts is based on *Bila Kayf* (Arabic for 'believe without asking how')? Unconvincing and irrational…

These things are out there and need to be talked about. People should not be intimidated from acknowledging what is written in a public document. If the Muslim brethren disagree with these vile and violent charges (as I am sure most of them are), they should demand a fundamental reform of their Religion, especially as they interact more with non-Muslims, and live in non-Muslim societies, enjoying the benefits of Rationality and Reformed Christianity. Judaism also has a Reformed branch or denomination; why can't Islam reform even in 2020? The Koran, like the Bible, Torah, and Talmud, was written by human beings, fallible human beings with determinate ambition, limited worldview, exclusionary superstitions, and ancestral investment -- a combination that does not connote inexorability, infallibility, universal and timeless validity, as well as eternal application, despite pretensions to the contrary. A test case will be China, with no ecclesiastical religion, but which has moved from the Third World to the First in under forty years by adopting the proven successful methodologies of Science, Private Enterprise, and Capitalism.

As Anthony H. Cordesman wrote in the Journal of the Center for Strategic and International Studies (CSIS), "the patterns of extremist violence are dominated by violence in largely Muslim States and by extremist movements that claim to represent Islamic values. It shows that the START database counts a total of 70,767 terrorist incidents between 2011 and the end of 2016. A total of 60,320 of these incidents—85% of the global total—occurred in largely Islamic States. A total of 51,321 of these incidents—73% of the global total—occurred in the Islamic States in the Middle East and North Africa or MENA (Middle East and North Africa) Region." One may add that some of the identified countries may not be entirely Muslim States, for example, Nigeria has at least a 55% Christian population, but has been mired in terrorist attacks by Islamists.

Taking Nigeria as a Case Study, the following articulation of Muslim attacks on non-Muslims (especially Christians) since 1980 is emblematic of the norm in other places. Since Henry Omoregie compiled this long list of barbarity, the attacks have since intensified in both frequency and scale, while the Nigerian Government headed by Muhammadu Buhari, a Fulani Muslim, seems complicit, incompetent, and/or nonchalant in adopting vigorous means to stamp out this menace. It must be noted that the attacks started many years before Mr. Buhari became the civilian president in 2015 (he was a military dictator between 1983 and 1985), but the Fulanis have become more emboldened (like the white supremacists under Trump) since Buhari became president in 2015 -- openly displaying AK-47s, attacking farms, churches, and communities, killing at will, and also occupying and renaming people's hometowns especially in the Middle-Belt State of Plateau. He is in the second year of a second and final term, and objective observers seriously wonder if Nigeria will remain intact after his tenure in 2023, owing not just to this but also the gross ineptitude, nepotism, corruption, injustice, mounting public debts, and hypocrisy on evident display. All of this, while Boko Haram and ISIS in West Africa also attack both Muslims and non-Muslims alike in the northeastern states with impunity.

1. *December 18th-20th 1980*: Kano, Kano State_ Islamic Revivalists (Maitatsine group) attacked Christians and burnt churches; over 4,000 Christians were killed and their properties worth millions of naira (the national currency) lost.
2. *October 25th-30th 1982*: Kaduna, Kaduna State: another Maitatsine riot; over 50 Christians estimated dead.
3. *October 30th 1982*: Kano, Kano State (Sabon Gari Municipality): 2 Churches burnt to ashes, 6 more destroyed.
4. *December 26th-29th 1982*: Maiduguri, Borno State: Maitatsine riot: over 100 Christians lost their lives and properties destroyed.
5. *February 15th - 2nd March 1984*: The Gongola State (Jimeta-Yola): The Maitatsine group attacked Christians; over 500 Christians were killed.
6. *April 23rd-28th 1985*: Then Bauchi State (Gombe) - Maitatsine uprising: more than 100 Christians lost their lives.
7. *March 6th-12th 1987*: Kaduna State (Kafanchan, Kaduna, Zaria) & Katsina in Katsina State - Muslim students attacked Christian students at College of Education in Kafanchan and Christians fought back. The fight later spread to other places as indicated here under location. More than 150 churches were burnt and over 25 Christians killed.
8. *March 1988*: Kaduna Polytechnic, Kaduna: The Kaduna State Government destroyed a Christian Chapel under construction. This led to religious uprising.
9. *1988*: Kaduna State (ABU University Zaria): Benson Omenka, a final year student, was killed by Muslim students during Students Union elections. Christian students were also stoned, maimed and raped.
10. *1988*: Bauchi State, Gombe: Muslim students attacked Christian teachers and students in GSS Gombe, GTC Gombe and GSS Bauchi and other Secondary Schools in Bauchi State. Some of the Christian students were badly wounded.
11. *April 20th-23rd 1991*: Bauchi State, Bauchi: Fighting between Muslims and Christians; more than 200 people lost their lives and 700 churches and mosques were burnt.
12. *October 14th-16th 1991*: Kano State, Kano: The Reinhard Bonnke Crusade riots fighting between Muslims and Christians as Muslim activists rampaged and protested against a planned revival meeting during which a German Evangelist, Reinhard Bonnke, was expected to be the guest preacher. Over 700 Christians lost their lives.

13. *October 1991*: Plateau State: A young Igbo man was beaten to death by Muslims on a field opposite University of Jos during election primaries of the defunct Social Democratic Party (SDP).

14. *February 1992*: Kano State: Many Christians were massacred and churches destroyed.

15. *February 1992*: Plateau State, Jos: A young Christian, married with one child, was beaten to death by Muslims as he was going home from an evening church meeting, at Yan Taya junction, Jos.

16. *April 15th-16th 1992*: Kaduna state, Zangon Kataf local Government Area: What was supposed to be a communal riot between Christians and Muslims spread throughout Kaduna State. Hundreds of people lost their lives and buildings were burnt.

17. *May 18th 1992:* Kaduna, Zaria_Rev. Tacio Duniya of E.C.W.A, Rev. Musa Bakut and a host of others were murdered by Muslim fanatics.

18. *April 12th 1994*: Plateau State, Jos: Fighting between Muslims and Christians over the appointment of one Aminu Mato as Chairman of the Caretaker Committee for Jos Local Government Area. 16 lives were lost and properties were destroyed.

19. *1999*: Borno State: Religious riots as Borno State government mooted the idea of not allowing the teaching of Christian Religious Knowledge in Schools.

20. *February 4th -22nd 2000*: Kaduna State: Riots began after a Christian march opposing the implementation of Sharia law. Travellers were killed as they tried to escape from their vehicles. More than 1,000 people died in various clashes.

21. *Between February and May 2000*: Kaduna State, Kaduna: Christians in Kaduna were attacked on two different occasions as Muslim fanatics protested against the delay in the introduction of sharia in the state.

22. *May 16th 2000*: Kaduna: Muslim youths destroyed the ECWA church in Kaduna only hours after peacekeeping troops left the area.

23. *May 22nd 2000*: Kaduna State: Muslim youths torched the First Baptist Church and Christian homes, leading to retaliation by Christian youths. At least 11 people died and many others were injured in the incident.

24. *May 25th 2000*: Kaduna State: Several days of violence over the introduction of Sharia led to the death of at least 150 people. Homes, shops and churches were also destroyed.

25. *September 7th-9th, 2000*: Gombe State: In Bambam, 25 people died as a result of clashes between Muslims and Christians due to the possible

implementation of Sharia, which Christians resisted. Property destroyed was estimated in tens of millions of Naira.

26. *November 2000*: Kebbi State: Christians showing the Jesus film were warned not to continue showing the film, and were subsequently attacked and many killed.

27. *June 2001*: Jigawa State: 15 churches and 14 Pastors' residences were burned down in Gawaram. A similar attack on 11 churches occurred earlier in that year in Hadejia.

28. *August 5th 2001*: Bauchi State: According to the Church of Christ in Nigeria (COCIN), Muslim mercenaries had been attacking Christians in the Tafawa Balewa and Bogoro areas on two occasions. The attacks left more than 100 dead and 3,000 refugees.

29. *September 7th-12th 2001*: Plateau State, Jos: Muslims attacked Christians. Properties were destroyed and people lost their lives.

30. *September 7th-17th 2001*: Kano State: Seven churches were demolished; six other churches were set ablaze by a Muslim mob. Fifty-four churches were given demolition notices and seventeen of them were demolished by the Kano State Government. The Governor stated that all churches in Shagari quarters of Kano city were "illegal structures", probably due to the religious conflict in Jos.

31. *October 7th 2001*: Kaduna State: Muslim youths attacked three churches and 10 Christian-owned shops with gas bombs, setting fire to the buildings.

32. *October 14th-18th 2001*: Kano State: As a result of Anti-American protests (after America bombed Iraq due to 9-11), 600 Christians were missing and another 350 were killed; at least five churches were burned during the resulting riots.

33. *December 24th-25th 2001*: Gombe State: A visit to Gombe State by the Israeli Ambassador sparked a riot, at least 4 people were killed, 50 injured, and two churches damaged.

34. *2nd May 2002*: Plateau State, Jos: Muslims attacked Christians. Properties were destroyed and people lost their lives.

35. *May 2002*: Zamfara State: The whereabouts of two Christians charged with apostasy, converting from Islam to Christianity, were unknown. Lawali Yakubu and Ali jafaru disappeared after a judge refused to sentence them to death. To this day, no one has seen them.

36. *May-June 2002*: Niger State: At least 75 Christians were arrested for opposing the State's Sharia Law.

37. *June 6th 2002*: Katsina State: A Christian Police Officer in Katsina was clubbed to death by a mob of Muslims after being accused of trampling on a copy of the Koran. The Police Officer had warned a Muslim preacher to

stop inciting violence against Christians. Afraid of being arrested, the preacher fabricated the Koran story to provoke the crowd.

38. *September 2002*: Kaduna State, Federal Government College Zaria: Muslim students fought against Christian students when they realized that a Christian was likely to win the position of Students Union President during a student election. Many were killed and several female students raped.

39. *October 13th 2002*: Kaduna, Zaria: A clash over a student election at the Federal College of Education in Zaria ended in the murder of 20 Christian students.

40. *November 20th-21st 2002*: Kaduna State, Kadoka and Kano: Muslim mobs ransacked Thisday Newspaper's Office and then began to attack Christian targets in the town, damaging up to 20 churches. Over 200 people were killed and 1,200 injured in the attacks.

41. *December 26th 2002*: Bauchi State: An armed Muslim mob attacked Christians concluding Christmas celebration. The Celestial Church of Christ and many Christian homes were burnt.

42. *April 22nd 2003*: Kano State: A pastor and 6 of his church members were killed in a house fire which was believed to have been set by Muslim militants, who had previously warned them to close shop.

43. *December 2003*: Plateau State, Rim: Christians killed, houses and churches destroyed, individuals injured and many other damages.

44. *February 2004*: Plateau State, Yelwa Shendam: 47 Christians burnt in church with a lot of houses and properties destroyed.

45. *April 2004*: Kano State: Reprisal over the Jos crisis: many Christians killed, houses and properties lost.

46. *February 18th 2006*: Maiduguri: 56 churches burnt and 63 Christians killed in an orchestrated attack.

47. *September 2006:* Jigawa State: 26 churches burnt.

48. *September 28th 2007*: Kano State, Tudun Wada: 3 killed, 72 injured, 8 churches burnt.

49. *December 2007*: Bauchi, Yelwa: Ten Christians killed and 47 injured.

50. *May 13th 2008*: Bauchi State, Ningi, Tafawa Balewa: Six churches looted and burnt down.

51. *November 28th 2008*: Plateau State: Over 100 Christians killed, 71 churches burnt, 1,647 families lost their homes, 535 businesses burnt.

52. *December 2008*: Sokoto: CCF (NYSC) bus burnt.

53. *February 21st 2009*: Bauchi: 19 people dead, 12 churches burnt, 50 Christian homes destroyed.

54. *29th July 2009*: Borno, Bauchi and Adamawa States: A new Muslim terrorist group (at the time) called Boko Haram killed Christians who refused to accept Islam, burnt their churches and attacked Security Operatives.
55. *27th December 2009*: Plateau State: Muslims burnt Baptist Church at Yelwa and stabbed some Christians on the streets of Jos.
56. *29th December 2009*: Bauchi: A Muslim group called Kalikato attacked people, mostly Christians, in Bauchi, leaving 39 people dead and houses burnt.
57. *17th - 21 January 2010*: Plateau State: Muslims unleashed destruction over 24 communities in Jos North, Jos South, Barkin Ladi, Mangu, Pankshin and Dangi, claiming numerous lives and burning Christian homes and Churches including Bukuru Market.
58. *20th January 2010:* Sokoto state: A Christian man was killed in retaliation over an unrelated incident in Jos.
59. *22nd January 2010*: Kaduna State: Muslims attacked Christians at Mararraban Rido (close to NNPC depot).
60. *January 28th – February 1st 2010:* Gombe State: Muslims burnt ECWA primary and secondary schools at Bolori, burnt houses belonging to Igbos at Duku, burnt Yoruba Hall at Jekadafari and also burnt two churches with one vandalized.

These are just samples, and do not capture the deaths, arson, and looting by Muslims against non-Muslims in recent years. Senior Administration Officials in Nigeria (who are Muslims) have, since Buhari became the president in 2015, asked all Fulanis from across West Africa to proceed to Nigeria in droves without documents, with a promise to use public funds (generated in the predominantly Christian South) to resettle them. The federal government has considered using crude oil proceeds (from the South) to empower these non-Nigerians and to issue civic papers to them as new Nigerians. These fellows claim that Allah promised them Nigeria as their inheritance -- a repeat of how God promised Europeans that the Americas were theirs and that Africans and their resources were for European benefit. They act with the expected impunity, kill locals, rape women and girls, and not one has been arrested or prosecuted, thus generating serious resistance by the original Nigerians. The implosion of the country is not a theoretical assumption, but an expected outcome.

It needs to be stressed that the invidious activities, expansionist agenda, subversive activities, and Jihadist attitude of the Nigerian Muslim leadership started right from the inception of the country after Independence in 1960. As the well-respected Nigerian Nobel Laureate in Literature, Professor Wole Soyinka, was quoted as saying:

"There are people in power in certain parts of the country, leaders, who quite genuinely and authoritatively hate and cannot tolerate any religion outside their own. When you combine that with the ambitions of a number of people who believe they are divinely endowed to rule the country and who... believe that their religion is above whatever else binds the entire nation together, and somehow the power appears to slip from their hands, then they resort to the most extreme measures. Youths who have been indoctrinated right from infancy can be used, and have been used, again and again to create mayhem in the country. Those who have created this faceless army have lost control."

Fulani Muslims attacked a Christian community in Plateau State one night in March, 2010, and massacred over 500 men, women, and children (the Dogo na Hauwa massacre), who were sleeping in their own town. Fearing that the survivors would launch a reprisal attack after the mass burial, the then Jonathan federal government deployed soldiers to restore order. Afraid that the culprits would be identified and held accountable, a prominent Fulani man, who is presently the governor of Kaduna State, Nasir Ahmad El Rufai -- with suspected presidential ambitions, said that "Anyone, soldier or not, that kills the Fulani takes a loan repayable one day no matter how long it takes." Since he became the governor of the predominantly-Christian Kaduna State in 2015, Mr. El Rufai's tenure has been characterized by unceasing violence against Christians, with no one ever arrested or held culpable. The obvious and declared agenda is to murder or push out all Christians from the State, so that Fulanis from across West Africa can have an all-Muslim State there; the same diabolical agenda driving the push across the entire Middle Belt and the South.

To be fully honest, no one expects Mr. El Rufai to physically attack anyone, for this man is but only 5 ft, 2 inches tall, and weighs just over 100 pounds even with the bales and yards of heavy fabric and canopy, which cover his tiny frame. He is only relying on the outsized control of his minority ethnic group in Nigeria's political, administrative, and Security circles, as well as their ready army of uncultured, uneducated, and unthinking foot-soldiers ever ready to attack and kill innocents. Some Fulani Herdsmen -- minorities in Nigeria (all Muslims, an Arab and not an African faith) have likened Christians to dogs (who/ which) have no place in Nigeria due to their treachery of adopting the religion of the whites. Therefore, the herder-terrorists have taken on the mission of purging the country of the alleged treacherous beings. In a recent article published by Wall Street Journal, Bernard Henri-Lévy concluded that there is a brewing war targeted against Nigerian Christians by Fulani herdsmen after he spoke to the herders in different parts of the country. According to Levy, the high influx of herdsmen into Lagos, the commercial capital of Nigeria is not unrelated to the mission of the herdsmen to take over the city.

Levy in his article titled "The New War Against Africa's Christians, said "A slow-motion war is under way in Africa's most populous country. It's a massacre of Christians, massive in scale and horrific in brutality. And the world has hardly noticed."

That is the country called Nigeria, and that is the religion of peace !!! Their impunity, like that of their cohorts in America, must not be questioned. At some point soon, things will definitely get to a head, as injustice and impudence cannot last forever. The perpetrator never expects the long-suffering victim to react; if at all he must react, the aggressor always arrogantly assumes a symmetric response, not recognizing that the freedom of action and natural law reside with the victim.

Some newspaper articles were also provided by Omoregie to highlight these attacks:

1. 33 feared dead as herdsmen, farmers clash in Benue (a non-Muslim State) *http://www.vanguardngr.com/2013/09/33-feared-dead-herdsmen-farmers-clash-benue/Date Published September 30th, 2013*
2. Fulani herdsmen ravage Imo communities (far away in the South East, where the population is 100% Christian) *http://www.vanguardngr.com/2013/08/fulani-herdsmen-ravage-imo-communities/ Date Published August 15th, 2013*
3. Over 40 Killed in Renewed Nasarawa Attack, Articles | THISDAY LIVE *http://www.thisdaylive.com/articles/over-40-killed-in-renewed-nasarawa-attack/149651/#.UbHHTFEivlE.facebook / Date Published June 7th, 2013.* This state is not in the core Muslim North but is systematically being acquired by Muslims through violence.
4. Villagers flee as Fulani herdsmen invade Plateau (same as above) community *http://www.punchng.com/news/villagers-flee-as-fulani-herdsmen-invade-plateau-community/ Date Published June 3rd, 2013*
5. Herdsmen massacre 17, several hundred flee homes in Benue (same as above) *http://www.vanguardngr.com/2013/06/herdsmen-massacre-17-several-hundreds-flee-homes-in-benue/ Date Published June 1st. 2013*
6. Fulani/farmers clashes claim 300 lives in 5 months (these are not clashes, but Fulanis invading people's farms and homes) *http://www.sundaytrust.com.ng/index.php/news/13160-fulani-farmers-clashes-claim-300-lives-in-5-months/ Date Published May 26th, 2013*
7. Fulani herdsmen strike again, kill two, kidnap others in Benue *http://dailypost.com.ng/2013/05/25/fulani-herdsmen-strike-again-kill-two-kidnap-others-in-benue/ Date Published May 25th, 2013*

8. Gov. Gabriel Suswam of Benue (100% Christian state in the Middle Belt) on Wednesday alleged that some Fulani herdsmen attacked Agatu Local Government Area of the state, leaving "high casualties including women and children". *http://www.vanguardngr.com/2013/05/many-killed-in-benue-herdsmen-attack-20-policemen-killed-in-nasarawa/ Date Published May 8th, 2013* (Middle Belt)

9. Over 100 women, children and farmers killed in renewed Tiv/Fulani (in the Christian Middle Belt) bloodbath *http://www.vanguardngr.com/2013/05/over-100-women-children-and-farmers-killed in -renewed-tiv fulani-bloodbath/*

10. Fulani herdsmen sack Imo community (in the 100% Christian South East) *http://sunnewsonline.com/new/national/fulani-herdsmen-sack-imo-community/ Date Published April 23rd, 2013*

11. 10 killed in Delta as villagers, herdsmen clash (100% Christian State) http://www.vanguardngr.com/2013/04/10-killed-in-delta-as-villagers-herdsmen-clash/ *Date Published April 15th, 2013*

12. Horror: Fulani herdsmen murder, rape and destroy Ohaji/Egbema community *http://www.hoohaaonline.co/horror-fulani-herdsmen-murder-rape-and-destroy-ohajiegbema-community/ Date Published April 15th, 2013* (in the 100% Christian South East)

13. Three killed, houses burnt as Fulani herdsmen attack Tiv farmers (100% Christian State in the Middle Belt) *http://www.vanguardngr.com/2013/04/three-killed-houses-burnt-as-fulani-herdsmen-attack-tiv-farmers/ Date Published April 9th, 2013*

14. 5 killed in renewed Tiv/Fulani crisis (still seeking to sack indigenes from their ancestral lands in the 100% Christian State) *http://www.sundaytrust.com.ng/index.php/news/12447-5-killed-in-renewed-tiv-fulani-crisis/ Date Published March 24th, 2013*

15. 35 reported dead as Herdsmen Clash in Plateau State (target is to take over this Middle Belt State for Fulanis) *http://www.punchng.com/news/35-villagers-killed-in-fresh-plateau-communal-clash/ Date Published March 21st, 2013*

16. Over 100 Beroms Killed By Fulani Militias (in the Christian Middle Belt) – Lg Boss | 247 Nigeria *http://247nigerianewsupdate.com/over-100-beroms-killed-by-fulani-militias-lg-boss/ Date Published March 21st, 2013*

17. Hundreds Flee As Clash Between Herdsmen And Community Kills 2 In Delta *http://www.channelstv.com/home/2013/02/20/hundreds-flee-as-clash-between-herdsmen-and-community-kills-2-in-delta/ Date Published 21 Feb, 2013* (a 100 % Christian State in the oil-producing Niger Delta)

18. 30 killed, scores injured in Fulani herdsmen, Eggon farmers clash (against Christians) *http://www.vanguardngr.com/2013/02/30-killed-scores-injured-in-fulani-herdsmen-eggon-farmers-clash/ Date Published 08 Feb, 2013*
19. Two die, thousands displaced as Fulani, Gwari clash in Abuja *http://www.punchng.com/business/two-die-thousands-displaced-as-fulani-gwari-clash-in-abuja/ Date Published 30 Dec, 2012*
20. Save us from Fulani herdsmen, farmers plead *http://t.co/B04L1pyI/ Date Published 02 Dec, 2012*
21. Plateau: Gunmen shoot 12 Fulani herdsmen, kill 12 cows *http://tribune.com.ng/index.php/news/51231-plateau-gunmen-shoot-12-fulani-herdsmen-kill-12-cows/ Date Published 21 Nov, 2012*
22. Fulani Herdsmen Rape Newlywed In Ogun *http://www.informationnigeria.org/?p=36835/ Date Published 21 Nov, 2012*
23. Flash: 3 Dead As Fulani Herdsmen, Farmers Clash In Nasarawa *http://t.co/PiAv6PZj/ Date Published 19 Oct, 2012*
24. 30 feared dead in renewed Fulani/Tiv attack (in the Christian Benue State) *http://nigeriaindepth.com/30-feared-dead-in-renewed-fulanitiv-attack/ Date Published 17 Oct, 2012*
25. How I was almost killed by Fulani herdsmen – Motorcyclist *http://t.co/Nsah6Duf/ Date Published 16 Oct, 2012*
26. 2 killed in reprisal attack by Fulani in Plateau *http://tribune.com.ng/index.php/front-page-news/46483-2-killed-in-reprisal-attack-by-fulani-in-plateau/ Date Published 24 Aug, 2012*
27. Fear grips Enugu community as Fulani herdsmen kill 2 teenagers *http://dlvr.it/21P2yQ/ Date Published 18 Aug, 2012 (100% Christian Southeastern State)*
28. Police arrests herdsmen with sub-machine guns (nothing happened) *http://www.businessdayonline.com/NG/index.php/news/284-breaking-news/42272-police-arrests-herdsmen-with-sub-machine-guns/ Date Published: 03/08/2012*
29. Suspected Fulani herdsmen kill serving senator, state legislator in Plateau *http://www.punchng.com/news/suspected-fulani-herdsmen-kill-serving-senator-state-legislator-in-plateau/ Date Published 08 July, 2012*
30. Fulani herdsmen attack 9 villages in Plateau state *http://www.channelstv.com/home/2012/07/07/fulani-herdsmen-attack-9-villages-in-plateau-state/ Date Published 07 July, 2012*

31. Oyo to prevent recurrence of Fulani herdsmen, farmers' clash (in the Southwest) *http://nationalmirroronline.net/news/43744.html/ Date Published: 29 June, 2012*

32. Taraba: 13 fulani herdsmen killed in fresh tribal attacks (in the mostly Christian State) *http://www.ipaidabribenaija.com/index.php/latest-news/item/4551-taraba-13-fulani-herdsmen-killed-in-fresh-tribal-attacks/ Date Published 12 June, 2012*

33. 'Fulani herdsmen kill 75 Tiv farmers' (in the Christian Benue State) *http://www.thenationonlineng.net/2011/index.php/news/47428-'fulani-herdsmen-kill-75-tiv-farmers'.html/ Date Published: 22 May, 2012*

34. THE MENACE OF FULANI HERDSMEN *http://www.tribune.com.ng/index.php/editorial/40782-the-menace-of-fulani-herdsmen/ Date Published 14 May, 2012*

35. Potiskum attack: Fulani herdsmen give Jonathan ultimatum. They gave the serving President of the country an ultimatum to do what they wanted !!! *http://www.thenationonlineng.net/2011/index.php/news/45702-potisku-attack-fulani-herdsmen-give-jonathan-ultimatum.html/ Date Published 07 May, 2012*

36. Thousands of Fulani herdsmen flee Benue for C'river *http://www.channelstv.com/home/2012/03/28/thousands-of-fulani-herdsmen-flee-benue-for-criver/ Date Published 28 May, 2012*

37. Influx of Fulani herdsmen worries C' River (far away in the 100% Christian South South Region) *http://www.punchng.com/news/influx-of-fulani-herdsmen-worries-c-river/ Date Published 28 May, 2012*

38. C'River to 'repatriate' Fulani herdsmen *http://www.punchng.com/news/criver-to-repatriate-fulani-herdsmen/ Date Published 29 May, 2012*

39. Plateau State: Herdsmen slaughter family of 7 *http://pmnewsnigeria.com/2012/05/11/plateau-state-herdsmen-slaughter-family-of-7/ Date Published 11 May, 2012*

40. Fulani Herdsmen Kill 13, Destroy 30 Houses In Plateau *http://naijagists.com/fulani-herdsmen-kill-13-destroy-30-houses-in-plateau/ Date Published 03 May, 2012*

41. Fulani Herdsmen block Abuja-Jos road, waylay passengers *http://www.punchng.com/news/herdsmen-block-abuja-jos-road-waylay-passengers/ Date Published 07 May, 2012*

42. One Killed, Several Injured in Fulani-Hausa Clash In Sokoto *http://saharareporters.com/news-page/one-killed-several-injured-fulani-hausa-clash-sokoto/ Date Published 04 April, 2012*

43. Ogun pledges grazing routes, patrols to curb herdsmen's atrocities (in the Southwest) *http://www.vanguardngr.com/2012/03/ogun-pledges-grazing-routes-patrols-to-curb-herdsmens-atrocities/ Date Published 26 March, 2012*

44. Suspected Fulani herdsmen kill two policemen in Plateau state *http://www.channelstv.com/home/2012/03/21/suspected-fulani-herdsmen-kill-two-policemen-in-plateau-state/ Date Published 21 March, 2012*

45. Delta villagers protest attacks by Fulani herdsmen (in the 100% Christian Niger Delta State) *http://www.punchng.com/news/delta-villagers-protest-attacks-by-fulani-herdsmen/ Date Published 07 March, 2012*

46. M-A-S-S-A-C-R-E-! Fulani herdsmen, Boko Haram kill 39 •13 villages sacked in Benue (100% Christian State) *http://www.tribune.com.ng/index.php/front-page-news/37087-m-a-s-s-a-c-r-e—fulani-herdsmen-boko-haram-kill-39-13-villages-sacked-in-benue-20-feared-dead-on-akure-ilesa-expressway/ Date Published 06 March, 2012*

47. Fulani Herdsmen Vs Ogun State Villagers At War (in the Southwest) *http://www.nairaland.com/882080/fulani-herdsmen-vs-ogun-state/1 Date Published 29 February, 2012*

48. 5000 Flee As Fulani Herdsmen Attack Benue And Nassarawa *http://www.nairaland.com/815595/5000-flee-fulani-herdsmen-attack/ Date Published 01 December, 2011*

49. Herdsmen Kill 2, Molest Women In Imo (in the Christian Southeast) *http://www.nairaland.com/711381/herdsmen-kill-2-molestation-women/6 / Date Published 12 July, 2011*

50. Family of 8 killed in Jos midnight attack *http://www.momentng.com/en/news/3762/family-of-8-killed-in-jos-midnight-attack.html/ Date Published 05 September, 2011*

51. Fulani Herdsmen And Hausa Traders Clash At Golbin Boka *http://www.nairaland.com/764634/fulani-herdsmen-hausa-traders-clash/ Date Published 21 September, 2011*

52. Birom People's Reprisal Attacks *http://newsrescue.com/2011/09/birom-christians-eat-roasted-flesh-of-muslims-they-killed-in-jos-nigeria/#axzz203LOiZDE / Date Published 29 September, 2011*

53. Fulani Herdsmen kill 6 people in Plateau State *http://www.elombah.com/index.php/templates/system/css/media/system/js/news/node/index.php?option=com_content&view=article&id=4321%3Afulani-herdsmen-kill-6-people-in-plateau-state&catid=3%3Anewsflash/ Date Published 27 October, 2010*

54. Herdsmen strike in Ekiti, kill police corporal, two villagers wounded (in the Southwest)

http://www.nigeriavillagesquare.com/forum/archive/index.php/t-49367.html/ Date Published 21 March, 2010

55. How Stray Cows Caused Air Mishap In Port- Harcourt (in the 100% Christian oil-rich Niger Delta Region) *http://www.iasa.com.au/folders/Safety_Issues/RiskManagement/cowcrazy.html / Date Published 10 July, 2005*

56. How Buhari Confronted Lam Adesina Over Death of Fulani *http://www.naijapundit.com/news/how-buhari-confronted-lam-adesina-over-death-of-fulani*

Under the guise of being cattle herdsmen, these sponsored murderers unleash their cattle to graze on people's subsistence farms in the Middle Belt and all the southern parts of the country and dare the locals to challenge them. Buoyed by the lack of restraint despite several thousands of people killed by them, the umbrella body of these herder-terrorists publicly acknowledges their responsibility with impudence and renewed threats. They claim the whole of Nigeria as their inheritance, and have proceeded to sack, resettle, and rename towns in the Middle Belt. The expected and overdue organized pushback will have serious repercussions for this fragile country as well as the entire Region.

As far back as the 1960s, the foremost Northern (Fulani Muslim leader) had said as follows:

"The mistake of 1914 (the forced amalgamation of the Northern and Southern parts of the country by British colonialists) has come to light, and I should like it to go no further!"
– Sir Ahmadu Bello, addressing the Congress in Lagos, March 1953 (Quoted by Frederick Forsythe in his book, Biafra)

'Having abused us in the South, these very Southerners have decided to come over to the North to abuse us… We have therefore organized about a thousand men ready in the city to meet force with force…'
– Mallam Inua Wada, Kano Branch Secretary of the Northern People's Congress, addressing a meeting of section heads of the Native Administration during the imminent visit of a delegation of the Action Group to Kano, May 1953.

As the British writer, Frederick Forsythe, wrote in his book, 'Biafra':

"Since 1914, the British Government has been trying to make Nigeria into one country, but the Nigerian people themselves are historically different in their backgrounds, in their religious beliefs and customs and do not show themselves any signs of willingness to unite … Nigerian unity is only a British invention"

The first Prime Minister of the country, a Northern Muslim, Alhaji Sir Abubakar Tafawa Balewa, was reported by the TIME MAGAZINE of October 10, 1960 to have said there was no basis for Nigerian unity and it was only a wish of the British. Ahmadu Bello added that: "The new nation called Nigeria should be an estate of our great grandfather, Uthman Dan Fodio. We must ruthlessly prevent a change of power. We use the minorities (Christians) in the North as willing tools and the South as a conquered territory and never allow them to rule over us and never allow them to have control over their future" -- Parrot Newspaper, Oct 12, 1960

"I'm set and fully armed to conquer the Action Group, AG (the dominant political power in the enlightened and cosmopolitan Southwest), in the same ruthless manner as my grandfather conquered Alkalawa, a town in Sokoto province, during the last century"
– Sir Ahmadu Bello, in an interview to the DAILY TIMES of May 3, 1961

"We do not want, Sir, our Southern neighbors to interfere in our development… I should like to make it clear to you that if the British quit Nigeria now at this stage, the Northern people would continue their interrupted conquest to the sea"
– Alhaji Abubakar Tafawa Balewa, 1947, during the Inauguration of the Richard's Constitution. (Quoted by Frederick Forsythe in his book, 'Biafra')

Below is an extract from the proceedings of the Northern Regional House of Assembly between February and March 1964, less than four years after Nigeria's independence from the British.

Mallam Muhammadu Mustapha Mande Gyan:
On the allocation of plots to Igbos (of the Southeast, all Christians) or allocation of stalls, I would like to advise the Minister that these people know how to make money, and we do not know the way and manner of getting about this business. We do not want Igbos to be allocated with plots. I do not want them to be given plots…

Mallam Bashari Umaru:
I would like (you), as a Minister of Land and Survey, to revoke forthwith all Certificates of Occupancy from the hands of the Igbos resident in the Region… (Applause)

A. A. Agogede:
I'm very glad that we are in a Moslem country, and the government of Northern Nigeria allowed some few Christians in the region to enjoy themselves according to the belief of their religion, but building of hotels should be taken away from the Igbos, and even if we find some Muslims who are interested in building hotels and do not have money to do so, the government should aid them, instead of allowing Igbos to continue with their hotels.

Dr. Iya Abubakar (Special Member, Lecturer, Ahmadu Bello University, Zaria):
I am one of the strong believers in Nigerian unity, and I have hoped for our having a united Nigeria, but certainly if the present state of affairs continues, I hope the government will investigate first the desirability and secondly the possibility of extending the northernization policy to the petty traders (all Christians from other parts of the same country). (Applause)

Mallam Mukhtar Bello:
I would like to say something very important, that the Minister should take my appeal to the Federal Government about the Igbos in the Post Office. I wish the numbers of these Igbos be reduced.... There are too many of them in the North. They are like sardines and I think they are just too dangerous to the Region.

Mallam Ibrahim Musa:
Mr. Chairman, Sir. Well first and foremost, what I have to say before this Honorable House is that we should send a delegation to meet our Honorable Premier to move a motion in this very Budget Session that all the Igbos working in the Civil Service of Northern Nigeria, including the native authorities, whether they are contractors or not, should be repatriated at once...

Mallam Bashari Umaru:
There should be no contracts either from the government, native authorities, or private enterprises given to Igbo contractors (Government Bench: Good talk and shouts of "Fire the Southerners"). Again, Mr. Chairman, the foreign firms too should be given a time limit to replace all Igbos in their firms by some other people.

The Premier (Alhaji the Hon. Sir Ahmadu Bello, K.B.E., Sardauna of Sokoto):
It is my most earnest desire that every post in the region, however small it is, be filled by a Northerner (Muslim) (Applause)

Alhaji Usman Liman:
What brought the Igbos into this Region? They have been here since the colonial days. Had it not been for colonial rule, there would hardly have been any Igbo in this region. Now that there is no colonial rule, the Igbos should go back to their Region. There should be no hesitation about the matter. Mr. Chairman, North is for Northerners, East for Easterners, West for Westerners, and the Federation is for us all. (Applause)

The Minister of Land and Survey (Alhaji the Hon. Ibrahim Musa Cashash, O.B.E.):
Mr. Chairman. Sir, I do not like to take up much of the time of this House in making explanations, but I would like to assure members that having heard their demands about Igbos holding land in Northern Nigeria, my ministry will do all it can to see that the demands of members are met. How to do this, when to do it, all these should not be disclosed. In due course, you will all see what will happen. (Applause)

Well, just two years later, these same people contrived convenient excuses to kill over three million innocent Igbo Christians and wage a war against them in their homeland, aided, armed, and supported by Britain, the Soviet Union (as it then was), Egypt, and a host of other countries, while America saw no evil and spoke no evil, except for a 20 year-old Columbia University student, Bruce Mayrock, who set himself on fire in front of the UN Headquarters in New York in protest over the world silence at the genocide against Igbos in Nigeria. Bruce died a day later. *Requiescet in pace*, Bruce.

While we will revisit discussions about Nigeria and Africa in subsequent sections, we need to proceed along our journey. Accordingly, one more example of the state of affairs in Nigeria should suffice. Earlier this year, in 2020, some Muslims invaded a Catholic Seminary and abducted four young seminarians, whom they held in the forest together with a Christian housewife and mother who was also kidnapped with her two young children. While in the custody of these depraved animals, the woman was eventually killed. They also killed one of the seminarians. The Catholic Archbishop of his Province, a respected Nigerian man of conscience and integrity, Dr. Matthew H. Kukah, rendered the following eulogy, which captures the state of that country and the fragility of their Social Contract:

"The news of the capture of the kidnappers of the four Seminarians has been received with ecstasy and a sense of divine vindication both within and beyond the Catholic and Christian circles here in Nigeria. On the 25th April, I received a telephone call from Fr. Francis Agba, one of the Formators in the Good Shepherd Major Seminary, Kaduna, to say that a detachment of a Special team of the Nigerian Police Force from the Police Headquarters in Abuja had just arrived there to announce the capture of the criminals. I held my breath in shock and delayed excitement as Fr. Francis spoke. He had to ask whether I heard him well. I said yes, I did.

The Police, he said, had come with one of the kidnappers, Mustapha Mohammed, a 26 year old man and a member of the 45-man gang of kidnappers and bandits that has recklessly robbed, kidnapped, tortured and killed many people along the 180-kilometer stretch of road between Kaduna and Abuja, Nigeria's capital city, for the last four or so years. The Police said they brought him into the Seminary so he could explain how they got into the Seminary that night in January 2020.

According to Muhammad, they had killed Michael because he kept asking them to repent and turn their lives around from their evil ways. He said that what most annoyed them was that although Michael knew that they were Muslims, he continued to insist that they repent and abandon their way of life. Young Michael's courage represents a page out of the book of the martyrs of old. Also murdered with Michael by the same criminals was Mrs. Bolanle Ataga who had been kidnapped along with her two daughters. According to Muhammad, Bolanle was killed by the leader of their gang because she refused to be raped by him.

The story of Michael and Bolanle is a metaphor for understanding the deep scars that have been left behind by British colonialism, scars that have disfigured the face of Religion in Nigeria and continue to exacerbate tensions between Christians and Muslims. British colonialism was established after the British had conquered the extant one-hundred-year-old Caliphate established by Usman dan Fodio (1804-1903). Although northern Muslim historiography would continue to project Lugard as a Christian missionary of sorts and hold his colonial project responsible for the institutionalization of Christianity in the region, the colonial project, led by Lord Lugard at the beginning of the 20th century, saw Christian missionaries as obstacles to their adventure. What an irony! The truth is that missionaries preceded the colonial state in Nigeria by many years. Their mission of education and the conversion of local people to Christianity very often set them against the colonial state, and particularly so in Northern Nigeria, so much so that they were not permitted by the British to enter there until the 1930s. Thus, Christians in northern Nigeria have been left with a legacy by which they have suffered a double jeopardy.

Firstly, missionary work in Northern Nigeria was seen by the colonialists as an intrusion into the sacred space of Islam while the educated Christians were seen as irritants, challenging the racism and injustice embedded in colonialism, and slowing down their exploitation and trade. In Southern Nigeria, educated Christians were seen as more serious troublemakers because they constituted the trigger for the independence struggle. The weak muscles of northern hegemony were strengthened when the British introduced Indirect rule and imposed feudal Muslim leadership that oversaw taxation of the non-Muslim populations across the Middle Belt.

Secondly, in post-colonial Nigeria, the northern Muslim elite, using religion as a basis for social integration and power sharing, have continued to see Christians as outsiders. Today, it is popular myth in Northern Nigeria that whereas Muslims continue to marry young Christian girls and accept them and their cousins as converts to Islam, Muslim girls are warned that marrying a Christian or any Muslim converting to Christianity amounts to embracing a death sentence. Other forms of discrimination include the denial of places of worship for the building of Churches in most parts of northern Nigeria, the constant harassment and targeting of Christian places of worship for destruction by mobs of Muslim youth or by overzealous public servants of the state, the exclusion of Christians from public employment in the state civil service and limited opportunities for cultural self-expression. Christians remain outside the loop of power in most States despite their high levels of educational qualifications.

I have provided this backdrop to place the martyrdom of Michael and Bolanle in proper context, to appreciate the Sisyphean struggle that Christians are daily up against.

Against this backdrop, let me now return to the metaphor of the barking dog and why it is significant for our analysis. A barking dog announces a possible disturbance of the environment by a new arrival. It could be a friend or a foe, depending on the reaction of the intruder. In response to the barking dog, it is better to walk towards it, facing it as a sign of possible friendship or willingness to dialogue on your side. If you turn your back or attempt to run, the dog will consider your strategy as a declaration of war and it will hurt you. Walking towards the dog with confidence strengthens your chance to negotiate even before the master steps out. The British left a legacy of a feudal architecture of power that has been exploited by Nigeria's corrupt and incompetent ruling elite across the country. In the north, the Muslim elite has continued to exploit the deep religiosity of its members by presenting themselves as defenders of the faith, a strategy that has been exploited for political mobilization. In ignorance, their people have continued to see education as a western ploy to corrode their religion and culture.

This culture has bred ignorance, destitution, poverty, leading to a generation today across the northern states of over 13 million young people who have no meaningful survival skills. It is from this cesspool that Muhammad and his colleagues have emerged and are taking their revenge on a state that has failed them. To be sure, there are kidnappers roaming across Nigeria, but none have been as brutal, murderous, cold blooded, monstrous and brutish as those in the northern pool. They have slaughtered their fathers and mothers, irrespective of religion, status or gender. The challenging question before us in the north is, from where did they drink this poison?

Years of negative stereotypes against Christianity and its adherents have fed the anger of people like Muhammad who have come to believe that to be asked to repent is a call to war. True, by calling themselves Muslims while still carrying out acts of theft, banditry, rape and murder, these barking human dogs had lost the right to be called Muslims. However, there is no doubt that Muslim leaders and teachers in northern Nigeria must address the historical distortions and interpretations of the faith that have brought us to this cul de sac.

Else, why did Michael's appeal for a change of heart become a death sentence? It was borne out of the belief that Michael did not possess the moral credentials to call them to repentance. Why should a woman's protection from sexual violence constitute a death sentence?

Inspired by their faith, Michael and Bolanle, the brave martyrs, looked at the horde of barking dogs and were not afraid to walk towards them. For us as Christians, while we greatly mourn their passing, their deaths are gains not losses. It was after the blood of Jesus dropped on the ground that the seeds of our redemption were sown. Today, Michael's grave stands as guard and witness at the entrance of his Seminary where he was a student. His colleagues can walk through the gates knowing they have a guardian angel. When we buried him (Feb 11th, 2020), we prayed that his killers will not go free. He has interceded for us. He now stands as a metaphor, a rallying point for us to walk towards the barking dogs of our time. Both he and Bolanle, as well as Leah Sharibu, who refused to renounce her Christian faith and remains in captivity, are metaphors for the suffering Church in Africa. Their testimony and witness represent the spiritual oxygen that our lungs so badly need today. Together with the Ugandan martyrs, St. Bakhita, Blessed Isidore Bakanja and many others marked with the scars of torture for their faith, they are the bearers of promise and hope for the Church in our Continent. Their example should serve as a rallying point for our young men and women in

Africa. Hopefully, they will inspire a new generation of defenders of the Gospel in a sick and troubled Continent. With them ahead of us, let us rise and walk with courage towards the barking dogs to uphold Christ's Gospel of Love." (End of Quote)

Sounds very much like The Rev. Al Sharpton at George Floyd's funeral services, as he had done in several other such services in lamentation of wickedness in high places and murder in the hands of the State. Actually, it will be very helpful to hear more from this thoughtful, evocative, deep, and knowledgeable Bishop. Note that the almajiri refers to the human flotsam, the millions of children carelessly sired and casually abandoned on the streets of the mostly-Muslim North of Nigeria, tools of violence and election rigging, while the mallams are their Islamic priests:

"Both the mallam and his almajiri live a life of surrender and sacrifice. The life of the mallam was a noble vocation. He abandoned the comfort of owning a house, a herd of cattle, other property and the pursuit of wealth in exchange for serving God. The community entrusted their children to him for spiritual nourishment and guidance. So, as Phil Collins asked: What happened on the road to Heaven?

Yes, you are right, the title for this article draws inspiration from Phil Collins' song titled, "What Happened On the Way To Heaven?" The almajiri and his spiritual father, the mallam, are now the poster persons of all that is negative in the face of Islam in northern Nigeria. The life of the almajiri is supposed to be a spiritual journey of nurturing and knowledge acquisition, guided by a mallam, his spiritual foster father. Today, all of this is now besmirched. In his song, Phil Collins asked: 'How can something so good go so bad? How can something so right go so wrong?' In other words, was Almajiri supposed to have ended up as a liability to the religion?

The almajiri has become a scapegoat for the multiple sins of the Nigerian state, in general, and the Muslim Umma, in particular. I have decided to add my voice to this debate in a slightly different context. As usual, as of now, the northern elite will do what they do best: Hide in the sands of self-deception, knowing that this will blow over and soon, no one will remember it. The governors indicted themselves when they said that it was time to act because the almajiri had outlived his usefulness. At least they have admitted their complicity and the fact that the almajiri system had always been a tool for political and economic forms of transaction. Here is my thesis: With regards to his condition today, the almajiri is an object, not a subject; is a victim, not a perpetrator; one sinned against, rather than a sinner.

Many readers will already be familiar with the word, 'scapegoat'. It derives from the Jewish ritual of atonement, when the priest places his hands on the head of a goat and confesses and loads the sins of the people of Israel on it as the burden bearer. At the end of the prayer, the goat is released to run into the wilderness with the sins of the entire nation. Everyone goes home and celebrates in peace because their sins have been transferred to the goat, which has escaped with their sins! Here is how.

Today, the almajiri and his mallam are in the dock and the charges are being read out to them. The children are charged with the following crimes: Being dirty and unkempt, miscreants, delinquents, nuisances to society, petty thieves, prospective Boko Haram recruits, and for being a stigma and an assault on our collective social sense of decency. Their mallam is charged with many sins including: Child abuse, abduction, human trafficking, exploitation, physical abuse, enslavement, etc. So, we identify the mallam and his almajiri more by their crimes than their names. They are spoken about and not spoken to.

In the media reports, no one bothers to give them a voice of their own. They do not speak for themselves. If they had a chance, for example, they might say: Everyone calls me, Almajiri. No one has asked me my name. We are in the millions but have only one name. I have no name. I have no father. I have no mother. I have no home. I have no town. I have no tribe. I have no address. The streets are my home. I do not know if I have brothers or sisters. I am an almajiri. No one knows if I have feelings. No one has ever asked me what I want to be in life. I live for today and for the sake of Allah. I have no tomorrow, except Allah gives me one. Tomorrow is in the hands of Allah.

In all of this conversation, there has been a lot of muckraking, excavation of age-old stereotypes and the peeling off layers of prejudice. However, very little attention has been paid to the deeper issues of why almajiranci (i.e., the act of being an almajiri) has persisted. We have treated the almajiri as a sociological category and the result is that focus and attention have been on the social cost of almajirci on the society. They have been presented as a dislocation of the social fabric of our society. This plays to our social comfort, making the almajiri guilty of inclusion in our social space of bourgeoisie comfort. The almajiri are seen as nuisances and their begging bowls, torn rags, mucus-dripping faces and their weather-beaten lips, charred by hunger and pain, assault our social comfort. We clear them off the streets when some foreign guests (read white folks), are coming to town. Before elections, they are preserved as vote banks, and during elections, they are lined up and their votes are used as barter.

What if we paused and looked at the almajiri from a theological category of analysis? I have no qualification for addressing this issue, but the theological evidence might sober us a bit. The word 'almajiri' itself comes from the Arabic word, 'Al-Muhajir.' It was a very prestigious nomenclature because it was used to describe those who had the rare privilege of having migrated from any place to Medina during the lifetime of the Prophet. It further derives from the word, 'Hajara', which means a migrant. In this case, to be called an almajiri as almost akin to being a special Muslim! So, an almajiri was associated with spiritual knowledge, piety, courage and sacrifice.

Many Christians might be quite surprised to note that Almajiri is not strange to us. First, the issue of the transmission of faith is one of the primary obligations of every good Jew. Moses warned the people to 'Engrave these words of mine in your heart and your soul, brand them on your hand and keep them before your eyes. Teach them to your children. Speak of them when you are in your house and when you travel, when you lie down and when you rise (Dt. 11: 18-19).' From time immemorial, the catechist in the Catholic Church has been the primary transmitter of the faith to children. So, the Muslims have their mallam while we Christians have our catechist, transmitters of the faith to our children.

At birth, the first words a Muslim utters to a child is, 'God is great, there is no god but Allah.' When the Prophet placed knowledge at the heart of the religion, this knowledge centred around the Qu'ran. Those who handed their children to the mallam did not do so out of malice, as it is being presented by the elites today. In the Islamic tradition, the mallam was a privileged and treasured part of the spiritual web of his society. He was the repository of knowledge, and along with that came the respect, the Albarka that every Muslim craved for. He was a pathway, a light, a source of transmission of values so treasured that the search for the essence of Islamic life began with him. The mallam was, therefore, a spiritual conveyor belt for a very special blessing for the community, the guarantor of the continuation of faith. So, no sacrifice was too much for any parent to make in order for his child to acquire this knowledge, a guarantor to salvation. When they handed their children to the mallam, they did not see him as a slave master. The almajiri of today is not different from Samuel, whose parents had placed him in the care of Eli, the priest! (1 Sam. 3:7).

He was there to be tutored in the paths of God. Both the mallam and his almajiri live a life of surrender and sacrifice. The life of the mallam was a noble vocation. He abandoned the comfort of owning a house, a herd of cattle, other property and the pursuit of wealth in exchange for serving God. The community entrusted their children to him for spiritual nourishment and guidance. So, as Phil Collins asked: What happened on the road to Heaven? In reality, the average Christian can relate to the idea of the mallam and his band of almajiris, who seek closeness to God by following and studying under him. The life of Jesus Christ was not too different from the life of the mallam today. For the Apostles, following Jesus, their Lord and Master, the Rabbi, was a form of almajiranci. Indeed, we Christians use the word almajiri for apostle/disciple of Jesus Christ. Like the mallam, Jesus and His Disciples lived off the goodwill of the community. Jesus said: The son of man had nowhere to lay his head (Lk 9:58). When the disciples of John asked for his residential address, Jesus said, Come and see (Jn. 1: 38). At the end of His life, after His almajiris had been tutored, He gave them the great commission, to preach the gospel to all the ends of the earth (Mk. 16:15).

The challenge for the Muslim umma in northern Nigeria is to answer the question, 'where did all this go wrong?' 'Where was the almajiri supposed to go at the completion of his studies?' 'Was there a career path?' 'How and why did the mallam and his almajiri, a much-treasured part of Islamic history, deteriorate to the status of the scum of the earth?' I do not have the answers to these questions, but I wish to raise a few issues for the attention of the northern Muslim ummah.

First, the northern Muslim ummah must accept full responsibility and see the almajiri as part of the huge baggage of their failure to prepare for a future for their people. They left their people in the lurch as the modern state emerged, providing no further rung on the ladder of progress for the almajiri as part of the future for their children. With both he and his mallam left behind in the cave of ignorance about the modern state, they grew to fear life outside the cave. They have remained trapped in time. The new world of modernity was presented as a contaminant to the purity of Islamic knowledge. So, while the modern elite equipped themselves and their children with the armour of Western education, the mallam and his almajiri were left behind in the twilight zone of ignorance, fear, anxiety, disorientation and discomfiture, treating those outside with veiled contempt. To be sure, we can blame British colonialism for sowing the seeds for the social dislocation of the fabric of Islamic society in northern Nigeria. However, it is tragic that successive governments at the federal and state levels have not been able to wrestle with this problem and time has not been able to heal this fracture.

A chasm of prejudice grew between Western education and the Islamic education of the almajiri. In an opinion article written long ago, Mahmud Jega referred to a song sung by non-school going children: Yan makarantan boko, Ba karatu, ba sallah, Ba'a biyar hanyan Allah, sai zagin Mallam (Children of western schools, You don't study, you don't pray, you don't follow God's path. You only abuse the mallam/teacher). By not providing a bridgehead, the northern Muslim elite sowed the seeds for disaster that has continued to loom for huge generations of children with almost no future.

Secondly, in fairness, the Sardauna did extraordinarily well in addressing the challenges of his time, with such limited human and material resources. He proved to be a master at trying to manage the transition from an Islamic feudal society to a modern state across such a vast land. He made some push to enable Islam to cope with the challenges of the time by setting up programmes on adult education. He also set up the Jama'atu Nasril Islam (JNI) to regulate and co-ordinate the various Muslim groups in the north. I think someone took his eyes off the ball and the result is the rather deregulated environment that we have today.

Thirdly, the issue of whether poor Muslims will continue to donate their children to strangers in trust to pursue spiritual knowledge should not be left to the victims to decide. There is no political will to restrain the mallam today, even if he is guilty of some of the charges of child abuse because they are often the same persons to whom the same political and bureaucratic elite turn to as marabouts in the night, when they seek to extend their political or economic fortunes.

Fourth, it is impossible to see the fate of the mallam and the almajiri outside the loop of the decay that has gripped the north. Poverty, destitution and hopelessness hang in the air and the sheer numbers are intimidating. In terms of population, if we put all the almajiris together today and accept that we are dealing with over 13 million children, we are dealing with the equivalent of the populations of Abia, Ekiti, Kwara, Yobe, Taraba, Bayelsa, and Gombe (States). Resolving the almajiri crisis will require political resolve, a commodity that is almost totally absent in the calculation of the governing elite in the region. The fate of the mallam and almajiri will hang in a balance for a long time and may consume the region as the numbers overwhelm us all. Yesterday's almajiri could graduate to become today's Boko Haram commander and foot soldier or turn to other crimes. With their main theatre of operation being northern Nigeria, it is easy to see why apocalypse may not be too far if something urgent is not done. The northern governors have spoken, but I am not alone in doubting that anything will be done. As usual, we shall await the fire next time. For now, I leave the reader with John Pepper Clark's sobering civil war Poem, "Casualties". He might as well have been referring to the Almajiri when he said:

"The casualties are not only those who started
A fire and now cannot put out. Thousands
Are burning that have no say in the matter.
The casualties are not only those who are escaping.
The shattered shall become prisoners in
A fortress of falling walls." End of Quote

Looking at Africa very closely, the Islamic terrorist activities take place in those countries, or sections of particular countries, geographically close to the Middle East. Where Christians and Muslims have some parity in numbers, it is usually the Muslims who cause most of the mass violence. These are the facts.

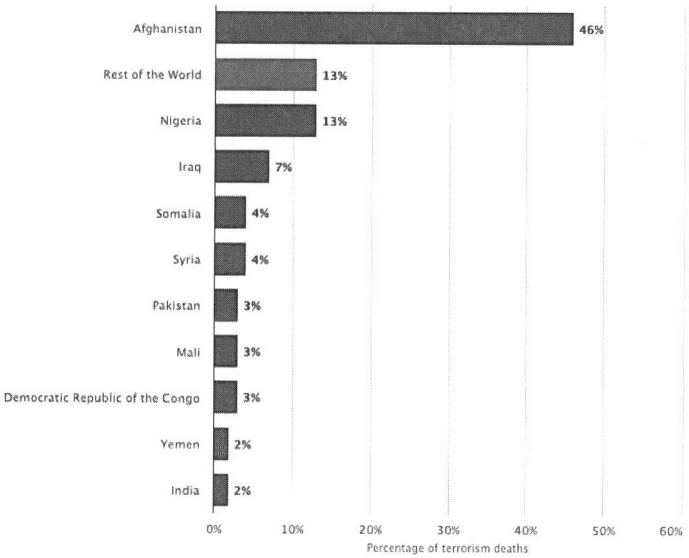

Global Terrorism Split by number of casualties, 2018. *Source: Statista*

According to the Global Terrorism Index, the most fatal terrorist attacks in 2015 took place in the following countries; the pattern has largely remained consistent since then.

#	Date	Country	City	Group	Deaths	Injuries	Description
1	9/4/2015	IRAQ	QAIM	ISIL	300	—	Assailants executed 300 civilians in Qaim, in the Al Anbar governorate.
2	21/5/2015	SYRIA	PALMYRA	ISIL	280	—	Assailants executed at least 280 people, including civilians, government employees and Syrian Armed Forces soldiers.
3	28/9/2015	AFGHANISTAN	KUNDUZ	TALIBAN	240	296	Assailants raided Kunduz, storming the prison and releasing more than 500 inmates. At least 240 people were killed in this attack.
4	25/4/2015	NIGER	KARAMGA	BOKO HARAM	230	9	Assailants attacked a military base and residential areas which killed at least 46 soldiers, 28 civilians and 156 assailants.
5	31/10/2015	EGYPT	UNKNOWN	SINAI PROVINCE OF THE ISLAMIC STATE	224	—	An explosive device detonated on a Kogalymavia passenger flight which caused it to crash in North Sinai killing all 224 on board.
6	23/4/2015	SYRIA	ISHTABRAQ	ANSAR AL-DIN FRONT	200	—	Assailants killed at least 200 civilians, and abducted at least 100 government soldiers, militia fighters, and their families.
7	13/8/2015	NIGERIA	KUKUWA-GARI	BOKO HARAM	174	—	Assailants opened fire on residents in Kukuwa-Gari village. Villagers were killed by gunfire or drowning in a nearby river, killing at least 174 people.
8	25/6/15	SYRIA	KOBANI	ISIL	174	201	Assailants detonated an explosives-laden vehicle near the Syrian Border Police, then stormed the town and detonated two more explosives-laden vehicles, resulting in 74 deaths.
9	2/4/2015	KENYA	GARISSA	AL-SHABAAB	154	104	Assailants armed with grenades and firearms attacked students at Garissa University College, executing non-Muslim students, killing at least 154.
10	9/4/2015	CAMEROON	FOTOKOL	BOKO HARAM	144	—	Assailants attacked residents, soldiers and buildings including mosques in Fotokol town, killing 144.

Source: Global Terrorism Index 2016, Institute for Economics and Peace

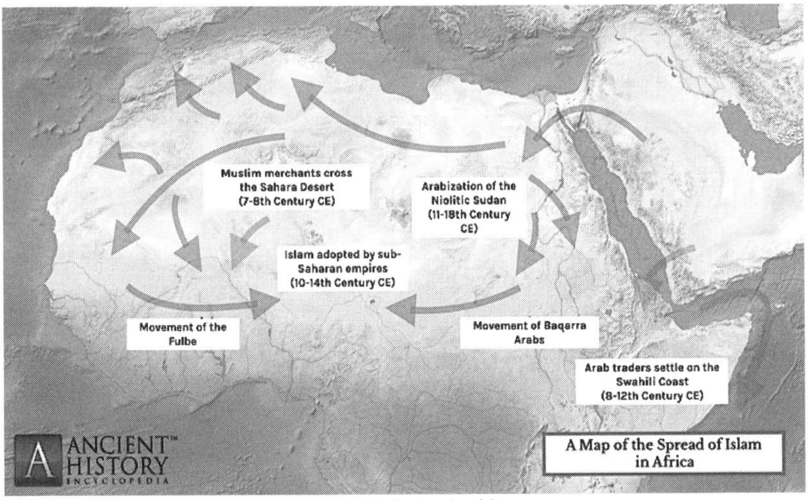

The Spread of Islam in Africa
by Mark Cartwright (CC BY-NC-SA)

And, these are precisely the parts of Africa that have Islamic-related violence, aimed at forcefully converting non-Muslims, denying them their right to worship otherwise, and to arrogantly impose their will on native peoples, while simultaneously sacking them from their ancestral lands. This is largely the picture of Africa's problem with mass violence. The proximity to the volatile Middle East has become the Continent's albatross in many respects.

Number of attacks with more than ten fatalities, 1970–2018

There have been 11 far-right attacks that have killed at least ten people.

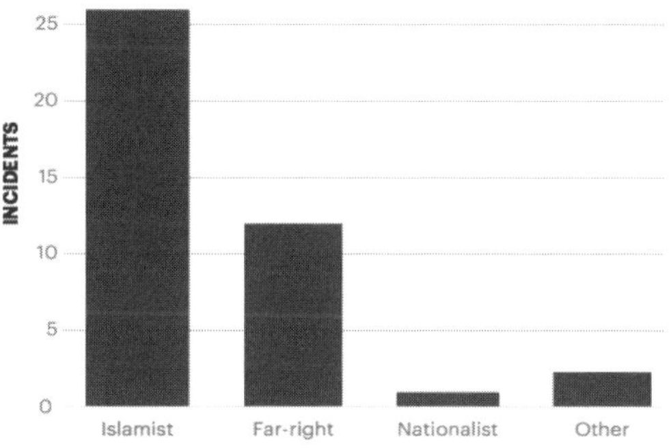

Source: START GTD, IEP Calculations

Outlook – Comparing International & Domestic Terrorism Threat to the U.S.

Terrorism Category	International Jihadists		Domestic White Nationalists	
Factor / Era	Before 2016	2016 – Present	Before 2016	2016 – Present
Does the extremist movement have designated targets? (Who)	Yes, High Profile, Symbolic targets, Event Anniversaries (U.S., Europe, Israel, Shia at times)	Yes, High Profile, Symbolic targets, Event Anniversaries (U.S., West, Israel, Shia at times)	Amorphous (Sporadic Attacks on Minorities)	***Yes*** (African-American, Jewish, Muslim Places of Worship; Local attacks on minorities)
Does the extremist movement have access to designated targets for committing an attack? (Where)	Limited	Limited	Yes	Yes
Is the extremist movement operationally capable of striking its targets? (How)	Rarely in U.S.	Less so since Islamic State's decline	Yes	Yes
Are the extremists motivated to commit violence in pursuit of their cause? (Willing)	Yes	Less so since Islamic State's decline	Rarely	***Yes***

Source: C. Watts (Foreign Policy Research Institute)

Figure 1

Terrorist Attack Spectrum – Directed, Networked, & Inspired

Terrorist Attack Category	Directed	Networked	Inspired
Category Description	Attacks planned, staffed, resourced, and designated by a terror group • Less frequent • More capable • Most Dangerous	Attacks executed by affiliated cells, trained cadre, former fighters. Varying degrees of coordination with terror group's central leadership • Frequency indicative of terror network strength • Mixed capability	Attacks perpetrated by individuals/cells inspired by extremist ideology, no formal connections to terror group. Self-funded, self-equipped, Perpetrator selects targets • Higher frequency • Lower capability, on average • Highly dangerous at times, Amateurish failures other times
International Jihadist Terrorism (Top Down Growth- Directed, Networked, Inspired)	Al Qaeda & Islamic State execute attacks, 9/11 in U.S., 7/7 in London, many others	Former foreign fighters from Afghanistan & Iraq/Affiliates join brand, execute attacks regionally & locally. Heavy at times in Europe, S. Asia, North Africa, Middle East	Social media & Internet inspired individuals conduct local attacks on designated targets & targets of opportunity. Known as Homegrown Violent Extremists in U.S.
White Nationalist Terrorism (Bottom Up Growth- Inspired, Networked, Directed)	No named group at present, may emerge if successful attacks are unchallenged, state sponsorship emerges	Successful attacks & resulting discussions increase online networking leading to physical associations, larger scale congregations, increasing complexity & frequency of attacks.	Social media inspired individuals attack places of worship, minority groups in their local area. Broadcast attacks & manifestos to like-minded communities via Internet.

Source: C. Watts (Foreign Policy Research Institute)

Figure 2

It is a sobering realization that both violent Islamic terrorists and white supremacist terrorists have historically and contemporaneously done just the same thing: kill people who do not belong to their group, stoke the embers of illiberalism, export violence, expand and dispossess those they regard as unbelievers through violence, and generally abuse the courtesies of good reception accorded them anywhere. Cowards and losers, both!!! With this realization, one begins to wonder why one will keep calling the other "terrorists" while taking the unearned moral high ground of being the moral conscience of the world. In the US, for example, both the FBI and the Southern Poverty Law Center affirm that white supremacists pose a higher domestic terrorism threat than Islamic terrorists. It is significant that the Trump Administration has refused to tag these deformed haters as terrorists. The terms "freedom fighter" and "terrorist" seem to be situational and contextual in a world of fluid aggregate morality. If the pulverized blacks of America were to systemically and vigorously resist the centuries-old and continuing carnage against them, for example, the convenient beneficial moralists would tag them as terrorists. How about respecting the dignity of all human persons and applying the law equally among all, to mitigate the risk of such "terrorist" attacks?

Judaism assumes the chosenness of the religious Jews by God, their God. Accordingly, Judaism does not have global proselytizing ambitions, because the status of chosenness thrives on exclusivity. If everyone is suddenly chosen, then their uniqueness, as assumed, ceases to be of import. That dilutes the brand. It is for this reason that gold is more expensive than sand, for example, even if we call the latter silicon. This exclusive nationalism of Judaism also united an embattled ethnic group - religious and unbelieving alike. How can one God ordain the contradictory viewpoints of these three Abrahamic Religions and still decree, as stated by all, the exclusive superiority and universal application of each one? How about other Religions? Or, are there other gods or Gods, each focusing on particular people? Is it all a man-made construct? It is puzzling if Christianity would have had its current character if it were purely a religion of the Levant, without the injection of Roman imprimatur and subsequent European expansion into the world?

Lest this work be misinterpreted and/ or the salience of the message misunderstood, there is no attempt to categorize any demographic in a uniform manner. The same way that the deplorable terroristic actions of some Muslims on 9-11 and around the world have caused some introspection and collective image problems for Muslims around the world (people accuse them of acquiescence, of ignoring what is being done in the name of their Religion, or not condemning the atrocious activities of the few among them); it is perfectly legitimate to interrogate why the majority of the (European) Christians in America allowed slavery, Jim Crow, and other apartheid policies to last for as long as they did. Indeed, while many Muslims could plead a fear of violence against themselves and their families if they speak out against Islamic terrorists or Islam itself, who are the Europeans afraid of offending by demanding universal dignity for all humans?

After the Supreme Court Ruling on Brown vs The Board of Education officially desegregated schools across the United States, regular folks protested vehemently from the university city of Boston to the prairies of Kansas. In the summer of 1958, just sixty-two years ago, a young black man, Clennon King, attempted to enter the graduate program in History at the University of Mississippi. No African-American had ever applied to the university before then, and the white power structure resisted vigorously. When King arrived for enrollment, Governor J.P. Coleman, members of the State Highway Patrol, and several plainclothes officers awaited him. After forcibly removing King from the registration area, state authorities carried him off to jail. Two doctors promptly declared him insane (for daring to seek admission into a university) and drafted him off to the state asylum for psychiatric patients, where he was held for two weeks; his younger brother, a civil rights lawyer, C.B. King, subsequently secured his release.

In 2020, various State Assemblies still enact legislations that have the effect of dividing the country along racial lines, and reopen the wounds of the past, which barely healed. We also recall the "Redlining" policy, whereby the Federal Housing Authority (FHA), other government Agencies, the private sector, and Banks specifically denied services and loans to majority-black neighborhoods across America, which worsened their poverty rates, made it impossible for them to buy homes or transfer generational wealth, increased Security problems, and ensured their continued qualification for stigmatization and discrimination, even as other neighborhoods received attention and other people's home equities grew -- widening the wealth gap between whites and blacks. When this failed, several neighborhoods had Deeds with language that expressly excluded non-Caucasians from buying homes there.

The casual taking of the lives of minorities (mostly black men) by the Police and private citizens, without consequences -- mostly over relatively inconsequential transgressions or no transgression at all, like selling loose cigarettes on the street or jogging in your neighborhood, is yet another major stain on the US; in a world of instant global dissemination of information, the world remains permanently tuned to the gory details, asinine justifications, cover-ups, pats on the back, and related graphic images on account of these killings. The frequency of these murders, and their handling, tarnish America's image around the world, with multiple implications including the disinclination to assist the US on Intelligence and Policy issues; redirection of investment funds to other countries, difficulty of American diplomats and officials to gain public trust overseas and maximize America's Soft Power potentials, privileged foreigners sending their kids to schools outside the US and buying their foreign homes elsewhere, waning support for US position on multilateral platforms, and the possible endangerment of US Government personnel and citizens around the world.

Since the subject of this book transcends systemic injustice, brutality, and the hypocritical application of religious precepts, it would suffice to mention the names of the more recent victims as follows: Emmett Till, Rodney King, Trayvon Martin, Michael Brown, Jordan Davis, Eric Garner, Freddie Gray, Amadou Diallo, Alton Sterling, Terence Crutcher, Sam Dubose, Walter Scott, Tamir Rice, Akai Gurley, and Philando Castile.

A white man, Adam Purinton, 53, of Olathe, Kansas, was sentenced to life in prison for the unprovoked Feb. 22, 2017 shooting at a local bar which targeted Indian immigrants. He killed Srinivas Kuchibhotla, 32, who had stopped at the bar with a coworker, Alok Madasani, for drinks after work. Madasani, also 32, was wounded.

A white Oregonian, James Lamb, 53, was charged with "attempted murder, two counts of a bias crime, assault, burglary, strangulation, menacing and criminal mischief", for allegedly breaking into the motel office where a 70-year-old Indian woman, Meena Puri, worked and beating her aggressively with no provocation whatsoever.

In February 2015, a 57-year-old grandfather from India, Sureshbhai Patel, who was visiting his engineer-son in Madison, Alabama, was accosted and seriously assaulted by three policemen while taking a walk in his son's neighborhood, as a result of which he became partially-paralyzed. A neighbor had called the Police on him, describing him as a "skinny black man wearing a toboggan [sic]." You see, he was not dressed the way all of mankind should dress, and also did not speak the world's only language. The team led by Officer Eric Parker slammed him to the ground when he could not respond in English language. Officer Parker was tried by the State and the Federal Government, and then reinstated in the Force, owing mostly to a jury mistrial on the first civil rights violations charge. Ten white men on the jury voted to acquit him while two black women voted to convict him.

In the past few months alone, we have had a few unfortunate incidents that involved the loss of lives in most of the cases. What is particularly illuminating is how the cases have been handled differently:

1. While making an arrest on May 25, 2020 for a possible case of forgery, as alleged, a white Minnesota Police Officer Derek Chauvin choked an unarmed black man, George Floyd, to death, even as the latter did not resist arrest and had been handcuffed in broad daylight. Three other Police Officers (Thomas Lane, Tou Thao, and J. Alexander Kueng) played varying roles or, at least, did not intervene with their colleague as he willfully asphyxiated this man in front of the public, even as the victim kept pleading that he could not breathe for over eight minutes (a la Eric Garner of New York). This same grossly-inconsiderate, savage, ignorant and intemperate Derek Chauvin had quite a history on the Force. A grocery store had alleged that George Floyd was paying for an item with a counterfeit $20 note. Are we sure he knew it was a counterfeit note? Even if the charge of forgery was proven, it is very unlikely that death would be the penalty, yet this man is dead. This murder was captured on video, which has been watched on billions of cell phones around the world. The work done by US diplomats and private citizens to build goodwill for the country around the world is seriously blunted by the searing images on that video clip, especially given the several other such cases in the past. The world cannot unsee what it has seen.

   Some glimmer of redemption lies in the fact that Mayor Jacob Frey, a Reform Jew, promptly fired the four Officers, as the public and the world await the next steps, including their arraignment for murder or yet another pat on the back. Mayor Frey also acknowledged that if Mr. Floyd was a white man, he wouldn't be dead over this matter.

   The protesters have also been largely very racially-diverse mostly among the young ones, which is encouraging too. This gives some hope that many of our young people clearly understand that there is a vast difference between being non-racist and being anti-racist. The protests have also been taking place in all the major cities of the world and have been sustained for weeks after the murder. If George Floyd, a muscular and athletic man standing at six feet six inches, were to fight with Derek Chauvin in a steel cage, we all know who will be dead in less than eight minutes, forty-six seconds, exactly how long it took this sad and depraved individual to asphyxiate and kill Floyd simply because the government gave him a uniform, a badge, and an official gun -- status and paraphernalia that Floyd respected at his peril. Why is it difficult for the Evangelical Community to condemn evident evil and demand the full application of the Law in this and other cases? Rather, some of them focus exclusively on condemning the ensuing protests (one deplores the looting and destruction of property too) as being anarchistic, yet did not find their voices to condemn heavily-armed protesters who took over the State Capitol in Lansing, Michigan, a few weeks prior, over the Governor's extension of the pandemic-related lockdown. In that case, it became an expression of their fundamental human rights.

The entire world sees through this shameful duplicity, and America is worse off for it. Must politics and race drive all considerations? As Bishop Talbert Swan put it "Calling a Black POTUS married for 25 years to 1 wife with 2 children, no mistresses, affairs or scandals, 'the antichrist' but a white POTUS married thrice, 5 kids by 3 women, mistresses, affairs & scandals, 'God's anointed,' proves your religion is white supremacy." No decency, respect for human life, and the truth? Meanwhile, the killer and his three accomplices remained at home, three days after the murder, which is not how other killers are treated; the principal, Derek Chauvin, was finally arrested four days after the murder, while the other Officers have neither been arrested nor charged with any crime as at the time of writing. The world has also seen the shenanigans that attended the Autopsy Report of this case. While the County Medical Examiner had written that everything else but the pressure on Mr. Floyd's neck by the Police caused his death, he reversed himself only when independent pathologists issued a contradictory and valid Report specifically and unambiguously attributing the cause of death to the asphyxiation caused by the Police Officers. How many previous Autopsy Reports had this County Medical Examiner rigged?

2. A young black man, Ahmaud Arbery, was waylaid and hunted down near Brunswick, South Georgia, by a white father-and-son team, Gregory and Travis McMichael. The twenty-five-year-old young man was merely jogging in his neighborhood. While this murder occurred in February 2020, the public did not become aware of it until May, three months later, because a video shot by a witness became publicly available. The tag team that took this man's life was finally arrested and charged with murder, as was the videographer, who seemed to know more than he originally volunteered to investigators. If not for the video that emerged, perhaps no charges would have been brought, or lies would have been heaped on the dead victim, since the dead do not bear witness.

   It is instructive that the man who shot the video started receiving threats from some members of the community for releasing the video, even as he claimed that he did so to exonerate the McMichaels, and not to implicate them. The public learnt during the arraignment of the killers in court that there was also audio-visual evidence that they used racial expletives on Mr. Arbery even after killing him. The State of Georgia does not have Hate Crime Laws...

3. A 17 year-old black boy, Andrein Green, was shot and killed by a white home-owner in Sanford, Florida (the same town where Trayvon Martin was killed twelve years earlier by one George Zimmerman, for doing absolutely nothing, yet Zimmerman is free and remains unapologetic!), because the boy was reliably involved in a car break-in in the home owner's place. No charges were brought against the shooter since he was at home. Car-breaking or any crime at all is condemnable and should attract the commensurate level of punishment from the judicial system, but is "Stand Your Ground" a cure-all remedy that exonerates the killer, notwithstanding the specific circumstances? Proportionality and escalation mechanisms remain relevant considerations before kinetic engagements. One supports the death penalty for a criminal or assailant who takes someone's life during an attack or robbery. One also supports a homeowner shooting an armed intruder in one's home, regardless of color.
4. How about the young, black, female Emergency Medical Technician (EMT), Breonna Taylor, who was killed by the Police in her sleep while at home in Louisville, Kentucky, in March 2020? Plain-clothed Police Officers (who were white) chose to enforce a Search Warrant (for drugs) on the young woman's home about 1 a.m. (one o'clock in the morning). With no uniforms on, creating reasonable doubts, and worried about an armed home invasion, Breonna's boyfriend, who had a licence to bear firearms, stood his ground and apparently opened fire to scare the assumed attackers away, whereupon the Police team exhausted their magazines on the apartment, killing the young female EMT who was actively involved in saving lives during the Covid-19 pandemic. No charges were brought against any of the Police Officers while the dead woman's boyfriend was arrested and initially charged with the attempted murder of a Police Officer, a charge that is possibly being dropped as we write. Stand Your Ground did not seem to matter in this case. Couldn't the search warrant be served during the day, or the Police announce themselves properly by wearing uniforms late at night? Despite the fact that eight Police bullets killed this woman, the Incident Report read that there were no injuries. No Police Officer has been charged for her death; they are still on their beats as at the time of writing -- until the next incident takes place. The so-called 'No-Knock' warrants have finally been banned in the State, but Breonna Taylor was killed at home. No drug was found.
5. A white 35-year-old amputee military veteran, former Marine, and Middle School teacher, Joshua Stewart Burks, accidentally killed a young white boy, Troy Ellis, 11, who was on a hunting trip with his father in Alabama. Mr. Stewart was promptly charged with "reckless manslaughter", even as he remains thoroughly penitent for his mistake, which led to the unfortunate incident.

6. On May 25, 2020, an enthusiastic and experienced middle-aged bird watcher, who happened to be black, Christian Cooper, asked a young white woman, Amy Cooper (no relation), to leash her dog, per the rules, at Central Park, New York. The woman quickly carried out her threat by calling the Police and alleging she was being threatened by "an African-American man." Mr. Cooper graduated from Harvard University, where he was the President of the Ornithological Society in the 1980s (so he actually knows one or two things about birds). He is also a board member of the New York City Audubon Society, where he "promotes conservation of New York City's outdoor spaces and inclusion of all people." He is an accomplished editor and writer, who had also worked on epic titles under the Marvel Comics staple. He is presently a Biomedical Editor at Health Science Communications. On this auspicious day, he was also using his pair of Swarovski binoculars to watch birds (these binoculars typically start from $2,000 a pair), his favorite pastime of about forty years. This profile is important. Mercifully, Mr. Cooper captured the entire dialogue on video and the intervening Police Officers did not respond aggressively, otherwise this could very easily have led to the innocent man's death, as has happened to many others; this case ended well. Ms. Cooper has since been fired by her employers, and she has also publicly apologized for her conduct. The danger is that she reflexively and naturally "knew" that her word would always be accepted by the Police against the protestations of an innocent black man. History is on her side.
7. Mr. Archie Williams, a black man, was wrongly imprisoned for 37 years over a rape case. New evidence in 2019 completely absolved him, having been in prison since 1982. There are many cases like his, involving all races but predominantly black men in America. Mr. Williams gained some positive attention only recently through the stellar performance he put up during a competitive TV talent show.
8. In July 2017, two Police Officers in Minnesota responded to a midnight 911 call by an Australian-American woman, Justine Damond, who reported a possible assault on a woman in an alley behind her own house. After searching the location and finding no evidence of a crime being committed, one of the Officers, a Somalian-American, Mohammed Noor, shot and killed Ms. Damond when she appeared beside the driver's side of the patrol vehicle. There was simply no reason for that gunshot, though some have ascribed it to panic, poor training, or a mistake. Ms. Damond should be alive to this day. Officer Noor was charged with third-degree murder and second-degree manslaughter and was convicted on both charges.

   After the verdict, the Somali-American Police Association alleged racial bias in the conviction; perhaps, they were motivated in their assumption

> by public statements made by the then Republican member of Congress representing Minnesota, Ms. Michele Bachman, who had asked: "Was Noor acting like the Muslim religious police, maintaining strict adherence to keeping women's bodies covered when he shot Justine? Was he acting from a cultural instinct?" Ms. Bachmann added that Minnesota was no longer a "well-ordered society and a high-functioning population like it was in the 1960s"; an era of white privilege and exclusion/ oppression of all others, one may add, and emphatically stated that Officer Noor was an "affirmative-action hire by the hijab-wearing Mayor of Minneapolis, Betsy Hodges." Mr. Noor started a 12 and a half-year prison sentence in 2019, while the City settled with the Damond family for $20 million, one of the highest amounts in history related to Police killing. If only other cases were vigorously prosecuted and concluded in the same manner.

The points being made here include: the instinctive and habitual biases and stereotypes that inform policy, Police action, the response of the society, etc., need to be fully acknowledged as grave social ills. This is not a debate on Gun Rights or any of the polarizing topics that divide America, but a vigorous push for an intrinsic fidelity to the upholding of the dignity and life of all mankind, as good and bad people abound in all demographics. It is also a false narrative to say that the demand for justice on such glaring and willful murder cases means we do not appreciate our Police Officers. This is actually a very unintelligent, unhelpful, and insensitive position to assume. When people say that Black Lives Matter, of course, this does not mean that Blue or Red or Violet colors don't matter. This is not an 'either' 'or' affair, as all lives do matter. They are merely calling attention to the overwhelming preponderance of evidence confirming the casual killing of black people in America by the Police, often with no commensurate penalty, if any at all. In any case, white and Police lives have mattered forever; it is about time that other lives mattered as well, and not in negation of white and blue lives.

While all of this was going on, the Mayor of Petal, Mississippi, Hal Marx, tweeted "If you can talk, you can breathe; think about that before rushing to judgment. #thinblueline."(**Figure 9)* Apart from the crass insensitivity of this public statement, the problem, you see, is that Mr. Marx can't even breathe. This thing, this morbidly-obese waste of space, a gluttonous pig, a whalish mass of protozoa, a massive monument to mandibular indiscipline, this grisly and grizzly slab of pork, this inflated balloon struggling with a lethal combination of bile and mucal secretion, this oaf who is guaranteed to pollute mother earth in very short order, actually thinks he is entitled to life while an innocent man can be casually murdered for doing nothing...since no knee can exert sufficient pressure on Mr. Marx's 60-inch neck, it will be nice to see his response if a crane is placed on his tree-trunk of a neck for 8 minutes, 46 seconds. What people say in public is only a fraction of what they think and what they share with confederates privately…

All men and women of goodwill appreciate the risks that our Police Officers expose themselves to on a daily basis on our behalf. Without their brave work, the society will become extremely dangerous, so we salute them profoundly. This appreciation is not a blanket immunity for their few bad eggs to kill unarmed human beings (of any color, but mostly blacks in this case) without consequences. The recurring incidence of killings without accountability should give the Fraternal Order of the Police and District Attorneys serious concerns; protection of one's members and colleagues should not be unconditional, as these recalcitrant killers tarnish the image of the majority of the Law Enforcement Community, and indeed, of the entire country. Condemning the cheap, cowardly, and extra-judicial killing of Eric Garner or George Floyd (which was done in broad daylight and is well-documented and witnessed by billions around the world) only enhances the integrity and credibility of the Law Enforcement Community.

On a related note, one continues to wonder why a country that collects and aggregates a lot of intrusive personal data, refuses to maintain a national database of Police atrocities and implicated officers, leaving this at the local level. This makes it possible for unprofessional misconduct to remain hidden; at worst, if an Officer is fired, another Police Department hires him or her without having access to relevant track history. It is also baffling that the National Rifle Association (NRA) retains a chokehold on mostly Republican politicians and Congress members, thereby ensuring that there is no national or even State Registry of all the guns in the land.

The Small Arms Survey estimates that, among US civilians, there are over 393 million guns, yielding an average of 120.5 guns for every 100 residents, out of a total population of 330 million people (including children, the sick, elderly, anti-gun activists, and those who do not own guns, so there is really a concentration of guns in the hands of owners). By law, you must register your car, motorbike, and other basic properties, but do not have to register all your guns -- especially in those parts which assume that the word 'heritage' is held in a monopoly by them.

When people express outrage that manifest instances of ignorant racist bigotry abound in the modern era, the question is: at what time should it have been right to dehumanize and kill other humans because you hate them or assume an inherent but false superiority? In the wake of NASCAR's belated ban of the Confederate Flag at its events, some shameless people have attempted to intimidate them. At a racing event in Alabama recently, these losers, these rubbish people flew the forever-condemned symbol of hate atop the arena, placed a noose in the garage of the only black NASCAR driver, encamped outside the track selling an assortment of hate symbols, and maintained a long convoy of vehicles waving this same flag. Their shamelessness truly knows no limit. One almost feels pity for them over their irredeemable ignorance and warped reasoning, but for their diabolism and conceit.

Defending the indefensible only casts serious doubts on the moral fiber, character, and professionalism of such defenders; people are smart enough to recognize willful murder when they see it. Bad cops should not define the good cops who are in the vast majority. Rightly or wrongly, people all over the world regard these killers and their protectors/ enablers as the enforcement arm of the KKK and other such malevolent Movements. We should be grateful that African-Americans are limiting their demand to equal treatment for all humans, and not revenge for centuries of unspeakable cruelty, physical liquidation, systemic dehumanization, psychological trauma, socio-cultural alienation, and economic ruination visited upon them by America, for one shudders to think of what would have happened to the United States if they had set up their own equivalent of the KKK -- given the ease of access to weapons in the country. Would America have achieved all that it has if every street was dominated by serious racial violence all these centuries, decades, and years? For a people not demanding retroactive justice or seeking revenge, the injury of continued perpetration of systemic injustice against them becomes raw and searing.

Even when America has forever treated blacks harshly, poorly, and most unfairly, they have continued to embrace the country. When they could not even vote and still faced systemic discrimination across the country, they fought in America's foreign wars, getting killed and injured (WWI, WWII, Vietnam). The Tuskegee Airmen are a good example. These committed black US fighters were discriminated against by white Officers and men, even as they all faced a common enemy. The arrogance and impunity with which the legitimate concerns of the African-American people are treated constitute a considerable stain on the moral fiber of this country, and hold the portents for serious societal decay.

As the Atlantic magazine wrote on Mr. Floyd's murder, "the indifference to Floyd's life is a clause in America's racial contract, in that the Officers did not see Floyd's life as one they were bound to serve and protect, and did not expect to be punished for failing to do so." One may add, for taking his life with casual indifference…The immediate past President of the United States, Mr. Barack Obama, strongly condemned the murder and the fact that death in Police custody is becoming normal for blacks. He also wrote that "But it falls on all of us, regardless of our race or station -- including the majority of men and women in law enforcement who take pride in doing their tough job the right way, every day -- to work together to create a 'new normal' in which the legacy of bigotry and unequal treatment no longer infects our institutions or our hearts", adding that "we have to remember that for millions of Americans, being treated differently on account of race is tragically, painfully, maddeningly 'normal' -- whether it's while dealing with the health care system, or interacting with the criminal justice system, or jogging down the street, or just watching birds in a park."

The former Vice-President and presumptive presidential nominee of the Democratic Party in the 2020 elections, Joe Biden, condemned Floyd's murder in very strong terms, related it to several similar cases in the past, and paraphrased Martin Luther King when he both noted and condemned the "appalling silence of good people." He also added that: "our complacency and silence make us complicit." Former First Lady, Michelle Obama said: "I am exhausted by a heartbreak that never seems to stop." The South-African-born comedian and television host, Trevor Host, suggested that: "Police in America are looting black bodies." Since the domestic and global publics viewed the recent cases cited above, more video clips have been released showing the Police killing black and Latino men recently in Texas, New Jersey, Oklahoma, and New Mexico States, with the black victim in Texas repeating what has become a deafening and worrisome chant for black men when they are about to be murdered by the Police: "I can't breathe."

In the Tulsa, Oklahoma case which took place in May, 2019 (a year ago), the audio-visuals from the incident show the black man, Derrick Scott, 42, who had been restrained by three white Police Officers, begging them for his medication and repeating that he could not breathe. Officer Jared Tipton's audible reply was "I don't care". The man died, and the three Officers are still on their beats a full year later. A suspect internal Review Document absolved them from blame or complicity in Mr. Scott's death, which brings up the point: why should the Police or their affiliates, the District Attorneys, investigate themselves? An independent and balanced Review Board should handle cases like this, for transparency and confidence; anything else is a negation of due process; an abuse of office; a total sham.

Former President George W. Bush issued a statement condemning systemic racism and the continued killing of African-Americans by the Police in America. In his words, "it remains a shocking failure that many African Americans, especially young African-American men, are harassed and threatened in their own country. It is a strength when protesters, protected by responsible law enforcement, march for a better future. This tragedy — in a long series of similar tragedies — raises a long overdue question: How do we end systemic racism in our society? The only way to see ourselves in a true light is to listen to the voices of so many who are hurting and grieving. Those who set out to silence those voices do not understand the meaning of America — or how it becomes a better place. America's greatest challenge has long been to unite people of very different backgrounds into a single nation of justice and opportunity. The doctrine and habits of racial superiority, which once nearly split our country, still threaten our Union. The answers to American problems are found by living up to American ideals — to the fundamental truth that all human beings are created equal and endowed by God with certain rights..."

Former President Jimmy Carter added his voice in condemning the endless cycle of entrenched racism in America, attacking "the tragic racial injustices and consequent backlash across our nation in recent weeks. Our hearts are with the victims' families and all who feel hopeless in the face of pervasive racial discrimination and outright cruelty. We all must shine a spotlight on the immorality of racial discrimination. But violence, whether spontaneous or consciously incited, is not a solution. As a white male of the South, I know all too well the impact of segregation and injustice to African-Americans. As a politician, I felt a responsibility to bring equity to my state and our country. In my 1971 inaugural address as Georgia's governor, I said: "The time for racial discrimination is over." With great sorrow and disappointment, I repeat those words today, nearly five decades later. Dehumanizing people debases us all; humanity is beautifully and almost infinitely diverse. The bonds of our common humanity must overcome the divisiveness of our fears and prejudices." He added that: "silence can be as deadly as violence. People of power, privilege, and moral conscience must stand up and say "no more" to a racially discriminatory police and justice system, immoral economic disparities between whites and blacks, and government actions that undermine our unified democracy. We are responsible for creating a world of peace, and equality for ourselves and future generations. We need a government as good as its people, and we are better than this."

Four days after George Floyd's burial and with the related protests still going on across the United States and the world, another black man, 27-year-old Rayshard Brooks, was killed by another white policeman, this time in Atlanta, for allegedly being drunk and sleeping IN HIS OWN CAR on the driveway of a local Wendy restaurant. Apparently, someone called the Police over this; forty minutes later, Mr. Brooks was shot dead from the back while fleeing from the Police. Early clips show him having a respectful conversation with the two white Police Officers who approached him; subsequently, they maintained that he was not sober enough to keep driving, then some altercation led to him struggling with the Officers who wanted to use a taser on him; he snatched the taser and started running away, pointing the taser towards one of the Officers as he fled. The response was to shoot him dead and the murderer could be heard clearly saying "I got him", and then kicked the body of the man he had just killed from the back; all of this over sleeping in one's car! A man who was visibly running away posed no threat to the Policemen, yet they shot him from the back and killed him. He could have been given a court summon, he could have been detained for the night, but not killed over this matter. What level of intoxication variance was involved? Does this attract the death penalty? The Atlanta Police Chief resigned immediately, the killer-Officer was fired, his colleague was placed on administrative leave, while the riots intensified.

Two other video clips have gone viral, showing that our Police can actually de-escalate when they choose to. In the first one, a white man who had just committed a double-murder was arrested by the Police; while on the floor, he asked for water and the Police quickly gave him a cold bottle of water while explaining to him that they needed to handcuff and take him to their station. In the second clip, another white man who was inside his car fought with two Police Officers for over four minutes while refusing to be dragged out. When they finally succeeded in pulling him out, he wrestled with them in the muddy waters for another two minutes, whereupon he snatched one of their batons and hit the Officers viciously with the baton, jumped into the Police cruiser and drove off. Through all of this, no taser was used, and bullets were not pumped into the Police vehicle he had stolen from them. It is contrasts like these which offend people's sensitivities and lead to the charge of a systemic murder of black people by the Police in America. Imagine for a moment that a black man snatched an Officer's baton, hit him violently with it, and then fled in the Officers' vehicle. Of course, the entire bullet clip would have been emptied. In this case also, no reinforcement or SWAT team was radioed in to "take care of business."

Since some people, for whatever reasons, see no reason to hold our Police Officers accountable (like other citizens) when they apply excessive and unwarranted force leading to death, a new absurd normal we are asked to live with, could we then ask for proportional representation in the profiles of those to be killed without consequences? Could we please achieve parity by killing people along the ethnic split of the country?

One shudders to think if these same people would maintain their current views if this epidemic of Police killings involved the converse profile: black Officers killing innocent and unarmed white men and women, boys and girls, with mostly no accountability? When the Minneapolis murderer, Chauvin, had his hand in his pocket while casually killing another human being slowly, who was he auditioning for? Which group was he trying to impress? The bunch of fools in New Jersey who proudly re-enacted Floyd's murder as a taunt to conscientious citizens who were protesting this gruesome act?

Since the Police Officers have finally been charged in Minneapolis, why do they consider it necessary to fight for their own lives by defending themselves in court? Indeed, what defense can they really put up? Ultimately, all lives should matter, and the deepening arrogance of infallibility and of being above the law attached to the Police, seriously threatens the social cohesion of the country. America's stature around the world is also seriously eroded. The energetic and enduring protests convey a deep message that something is definitely wrong, even as some people still play the ostrich. The arrogant threat to use the Military and the National Guard to contain the protests invokes images of the Tiananmen Square massacre in China. Truly sad.

Never one to disappoint in his recurring race-baiting, indecency, unpresidential comportment, divisiveness, insensitivity, sadism, and appeal to his fellow "Nationalists", the incumbent US President, Mr. Donald J. Trump, after a perfunctory reference to the Minnesota murder, stoked further anger and division when his tweet focused more on the protesters, looters, and arsonists, calling them "THUGS" and invoking past racial codes for official violence against blacks, when he threatened to deploy the Military to Minnesota, adding that "when the looting starts, the shooting starts." Twitter immediately flagged his comments for flouting their policies because they "glorified violence." This was the second time in a week that Twitter had rebuked the President of the United States for his comments, the first time being for lies about the integrity of the mail-in voting process. No person in his or her right mind will condone the violence, looting, and arson that have accompanied the protests, but a fundamental point to remember is that, before George Floyd was casually killed by Officer Derek Chauvin and his colleagues, no one was protesting, looting, and burning down assets on the streets of Minnesota or elsewhere. When some White House Officials and their media allies keep emphasizing the need for 'Law and Order' or recycle their characterization of ANTIFA as a terrorist organization, people clearly understand what they mean.

Nostalgic times of State-orchestrated and executed brutality against minorities, especially blacks. Apart from egregious Police actions in America, one recalls the 1960 Sharpeville massacre of unarmed black protesters by the South African Police, which called global attention to the horrors of white settler minority rule (mostly Dutch, German, and British). Sixty-nine people were killed in the presence of photographers and journalists.

Media and telephonic technologies have advanced significantly since then, and the world shall yet see how President Trump achieves his oppressive and value-less 'Law and Order.' The best way to guarantee Law and Order in the society is to treat all lives as equal; if the State cannot guarantee this, and individuals recourse to self-help, it will be a grave travesty to see the United States, the assumed Shining City upon a Hill, regress into a Hobbesian society.

Those implicated in diversionary and self-serving criminal activities during the protests should be duly charged to court for their actions, but is it too much to also demand that the instigators of the breakdown of law and order, the men who took another's life without provocation, also be charged with murder and the process handled with diligence and transparency, unlike in the past? A Republican Strategist and former Speechwriter for President George W. Bush, David Frum, has asserted in the Atlantic, that President Trump is the looter-in-chief, for the ways in which public funds have been channeled to his private businesses since he became President, a development for which other Presidents would have been removed from office but for the pliant and conniving members of his Party in Congress, a group that has remained largely silent in the wake of the recurring loss of lives at the hands of the Police in America.

George F. Will, one of America's most prominent conservative columnists, writes about Trump and The Republican Party: "this low-rent Lear raging on his Twitter-heath has proven that the phrase malignant buffoon is not an oxymoron." "Senate Republicans must be routed, as condign punishment for the Vichyite collaboration, leaving the Republican remnant to wonder: Was it sensible to sacrifice dignity, such as it ever was, and to shed principles, if convictions so easily jettisoned could be dignified as principles, for ...what? Praying people should pray, and all others should hope: May I never crave anything as much as these people crave membership in the world's most risible deliberative body." Anne Applebaum's great article in the 'Atlantic', "History will judge the Complicit", is recommended reading on the duplicitous and unprincipled complicity of the Republican Congressional members in America's decline under Trump. You can read the incisive article through this link: *https://www.anneapplebaum.com/2020/06/01/history-will-judge-the-complicit/*

As Senator Cory Booker of New Jersey reminds us, peace is not just the absence of violence, but the presence of justice. The former RNC Chairman, who happens to be black, Michael Steele, said that: "Trump does not believe in the Ideals of this country." The Senator from Vermont and former Democratic

Presidential Candidate, Bernie Sanders, also condemned Mr. Floyd's murder and the structural racism in America in very strong terms and also advocated for both comprehensive Law Enforcement Reforms and Police Accountability, while the actor, George Clooney wrote that "racism is our pandemic, and in 400 years, we have yet to find a vaccine." Former Defense Secretary in the Trump Administration and well-respected retired four-star General, James Mathis, strongly criticized his former boss, President Trump, for the latter's divisiveness and lack of maturity. In his words, "Donald Trump is the first president in my lifetime who does not try to unite the American people—does not even pretend to try. Instead he tries to divide us ...we are witnessing the consequences of three years of this deliberate effort. We are witnessing the consequences of three years without mature leadership. We can unite without him, drawing on the strengths inherent in our civil society. This will not be easy, as the past few days have shown, but we owe it to our fellow citizens; to past generations that bled to defend our promise; and to our children." Since General Mathis spoke, he has been supported by a formidable team of retired Chairmen of the Joint Chiefs of Staff, former Directors of the CIA and NSA, former Chief of Staff to President Trump (John Kelly, who retired as a 4-star General), and several others.

It must be stated that, when some people hearken to the "good old days" or Making America Great Again, those days were not good or great for all. On June 4, 2020, exactly on the day that the first Memorial Service for the murdered George Floyd was being held in Minnesota, the US Senator from Kentucky, Rand Paul, used subterfuge and semantics on the floor of the US Senate to block the passage of an Anti-Lynching Bill (from this time going forward) which had been passed by the House of Representatives. He proceeded to educate two of the three serving African-American US Senators that he knew the difference between the meaning of lynching and the wordings of the Bill, which he claimed were too loose. What if the law were to take retroactive effect? Galen machine guns and personal armored tanks would have been deployed in exercise of "our second Amendment rights." -- for, we have the right to kill any group of people without responsibility. Perhaps also, a part of this proud heritage is the infamous 1857 Supreme Court ruling in the Dred Scott case for freedom wherein the then Chief Justice of the United States, Roger Taney, wrote the majority opinion which stated, *inter alia*, that Mr. Scott, a black man, had no rights which any white man was bound to respect and that he must be treated as chattel? Could all of this just be what is euphemistically and proudly called being a Conservative in America?

Indeed, one does not know if it is a coincidence that the UN 2018 statue of the Very Distinguished Nelson Mandela, the former President of South Africa, a

Prisoner of Conscience for 27 years under the atrocious apartheid regime in his own native land, one of the most respected and iconic global personalities of the past century, has him with raised hands, almost telling the New York and American Police "don't shoot me." Hahahahaha.

Late Nelson Rolilhalha Mandela. Revered Anti-apartheid activist and former President of South Africa.
Source : www.news.cn

With kooks like William F. Buckley, Patrick Buchanan, as well as the overrated Foxian frondeur and rubble as the Archangels of this movement, there is no need to look beyond the surface to understand the bigotry, ignorance, sense of entitlement, hate, and racist crap that define and unite them. These otherwise unemployable people are deeply surprised to be given a platform from which to spew lies, ignorance, and hatred; hollow and miserable entities throwing punches much above what their intelligence and limited worldview prepared them for. That they have an audience speaks to the depth (or shallowness) of knowledge, independent thinking, and overall deformity among this horde. We have all witnessed the barbarity, the beheadings of innocent people by ISIS terrorists; pray, what is the difference between their behavior and the litany of wickedness, the official lynchings that pervade this "land of the free"? What moral right have we got to condemn beastial killings elsewhere? Indeed, did America ever really have the moral superiority to judge others, to attack and bomb others, given her own sustained and systemic violence, killings, and oppression of minorities -- the very same "crimes against humanity" for which we have invaded other lands?

Vestiges of wickedness and entitlement abound in various forms: oversized monuments to slaveholders and Confederate Officers are in public buildings and parks across the country -- including the Capitol; Mississippi State has the Confederate symbol on its State flag; the Southern Baptist Church (SBC) leader, J.D. Greer, is presently considering the retirement of the so-called Broadus gavel in their church; this gavel, which belonged to Mr. Broadus, a slave owner and auctioneer, had been in use in the SBC since 1872, and was used to rally Baptists to support the Confederate Army which fought and lost a war over their "right to own slaves and (their) way of life." Of all the symbols in the world, this particular gavel was the only selection this church could make, for almost two hundred years; the US Navy just announced a plan, (in 2020, in the wake of the massive protests over George Floyd's killing) that they would ban Confederate flags and insignia on their warships, submarines, offices, and bases; several major Military Bases in the country are still named after Confederate Generals -- a development that President Trump has vowed to retain and which he has declared to be non-negotiable; etc., etc.

In an utmost and telling demonstration of invested and ineradicable racist bigotry, triumphalism over evil conduct, callousness, insensitivity, chronic arrogance, and sheer foolishness, Mr. Trump has announced that he will hold his first political rally since the Covid-19 general lockdown on June 19th, 2020, in Tulsa Oklahoma. One would imagine that a national leader would not openly stoke racial divide and glorify or celebrate bigotry, but no depth is too low for this gingerly creature. That date, called Juneteenth, marks the exact 99th anniversary of the Tulsa Massacre, a drawn-out orgy of extremely violent carnage against blacks by the KKK, other whites, and the National Guard. Wikipedia describes it as "the single worst incident of racial violence in American History." By the time it was over many weeks later, hundreds of blacks had been killed, several thousand injured, and the entire community, which they had methodically and patiently built, was burnt to the ground.

Facing serious discrimination from whites, these blacks had decided to build their own community with schools, hospitals, shopping mall, infrastructure, parks, etc., hence offending the same whites who believed that blacks were incapable of building modern cities and running their own affairs. Part of the offense was that, having built an inclusive community for themselves, blacks were now recycling their money among themselves, instead of spending most of it in white stores and establishments -- places where they were derided and expressly unwanted. The section of the city that was destroyed with bombs and other incendiary materials was fondly called the Black Wall Street. Not a single person was held culpable for this. To make their material losses even worse, the Insurance companies to whom they had paid premiums for many years simply interpreted what was obvious and evident arson as riot and absolved themselves from any responsibility to compensate the victims. A people so thoroughly dispossessed and mistreated had no money to engage lawyers; they simply started rebuilding afresh.

The History Channel writes that 'the massacre, which began on May 31, 1921 and left hundreds of black residents dead and 1,000 houses destroyed, often overshadows the history of the venerable black enclave itself. Greenwood District, with a population of 10,000 at the time, had thrived as the epicenter of African-American business and culture, particularly on bustling Greenwood Avenue, commonly known as Black Wall Street." 99 years later, just over two weeks since the willful murder of yet another black man by a Police Officer in Minneapolis -- which threw the entire country and the world into turmoil that subsists to this day, the president of the United States, who has not seen the need for urgent Law Enforcement and Policing Reforms in the country, is proceeding to Tulsa, simply to mock the victims, burnish his credentials of bigotry and ignorance, reward and motivate racial bigots and white nationalists, as well as rally to the perpetrators of arson whose loyalty to him is mostly based on pigmentation and common hatred of "the other."

One of the three serving African-American US Senators, Ms. Kamala Harris, wrote that this planned trip " isn't just a wink to white supremacists—he's throwing them a welcome home party." Truly sad for America. Sad. No speech in Tulsa on Juneteenth will reverse years of racial bigotry and ignorance by Mr. Trump or obfuscate the real purpose of his visit.

The putative Emperor has just announced that he will shift the Tulsa Rally by a day, and we are all supposed to be very grateful. A national leader would be concerned about having tens of thousands of people in one venue during a period of a highly contagious pandemic that has already killed over 110,000 Americans to date; not this particular individual. Rather, his campaign got all intending attendees to accept disclaimers and waive their right to sue the presidential candidate or his campaign if they contract Covid:19 at the rally. It reminds one of the public remarks made by the then-candidate Trump in 2016, wherein he urged all registered voters already diagnosed with terminal ailments to hold out and vote for him, then die, and the nation would be grateful to them. You see, he is the nation. Very cruel; extreme narcissism on display. A recurring pattern.

The images, flag, and symbols of the Confederacy/ deep South (**Figures 10 and 11)*, which fought a Civil War over their "right to own human beings" have remained permanent fixtures at Mr. Trump's events and rallies. It is noteworthy that his opponent at the forthcoming 2020 presidential elections, former Vice-President Joe Biden, has expressly condemned these images and banned them from his rallies. Mr. Biden also supports the renaming of monuments that honor Confederate slave owners and military officers, including Military Training facilities like Forts Benning, Hood, and Bragg.

As the eminent African-American Sociologist, Pan-Africanist, Civil Rights Leader, Writer, and Author, the first African to earn a doctorate degree at Harvard, Dr. W.E. B. DuBois, had written in 1928 pertaining to these monuments, and, in particular, the veneration of the Confederate Leader, Robert Lee:

March 1928

Each year on the 19th of January there is renewed effort to canonize Robert E. Lee, the great confederate general. His personal comeliness, his aristocratic birth and his military prowess all call for the verdict of greatness and genius. But one thing—one terrible fact—militates against this and that is the inescapable truth that Robert E. Lee led a bloody war to perpetuate human slavery. Copperheads like the New York Times may magisterially declare: "of course, he never fought for slavery". Well, for what did he fight? State rights? Nonsense. The South cared only for State Rights as a weapon to defend slavery". If nationalism had been a stronger defense of the slave system than particularism, the South would have been as nationalist in 1861 as it had been in 1812.

No. People do not go to war for abstract theories of government. They fight for property and privilege and that was what Virginia fought for in the Civil War. And Lee followed Virginia. He followed Virginia not because he particularly loved slavery (although he certainly did not hate it), but because he did not have the moral courage to stand against his family and his clan, Lee hesitated and hung his head in shame because he was asked to lead armies against human progress and Christian decency and did not dare refuse. He surrendered not to Grant, but to Negro Emancipation.

Today we can best perpetuate his memory and his nobler traits, not by falsifying his moral debacle, but by explaining it to the young white South. What Lee did in 1861, other Lees are doing in 1928. They lack the moral courage to stand up for justice to the Negro because of the overwhelming public opinion of their social environment. Their fathers in the past have condoned lynching and mob violence, just as today they acquiesce in the disfranchisement of educated and worthy black citizens, provide wretchedly inadequate public schools for Negro children and endorse a public treatment of sickness, poverty and crime which disgraces civilization.

It is the punishment of the South that its Robert Lees and Jefferson Davises will always be tall, handsome and well-born. That their courage will be physical and not moral, That their leadership will be weak compliance with public opinion and never costly and unswerving revolt for justice and right. It is ridiculous to seek to excuse Robert Lee as the most formidable agency this nation ever raised to make 4 million human beings goods instead of men. Either he knew what slavery meant when he helped maim and murder thousands in its defense, or he did not. If he did not he was a fool, If he did, Robert Lee was a traitor and a rebel—not indeed to his country, but to humanity and humanity's God.

Let's look at the words of the U.S. National Anthem (since 1931), as well as the national song, 'God Bless America':

National Anthem:	**'God Bless America':**
Oh, say can you see, By the dawn's early light, What so proudly we hailed At the twilight's last gleaming? Whose broad stripes and bright stars, Through the perilous fight, O'er the ramparts we watched, Were so gallantly streaming? And the rockets' red glare, The bombs bursting in air, Gave proof through the night That our flag was still there. O say, does that star-spangled Banner yet wave O'er the land of the free And the home of the brave?	God bless America, land that I love Stand beside her and guide her Through the night with the light from above From the mountains to the prairies To the oceans white with foam God bless America, my home sweet home God bless America, land that I love Stand beside her and guide her Through the night with the light from above From the mountains to the prairies To the oceans white with foam God bless America, my home sweet home From the mountains to the prairies To the oceans white with foam God bless America, my home sweet home God bless America, my home sweet home

Credit: LyricFind

The violence began on May 31, 1921 and left hundreds of black residents dead and more than 1,000 houses and businesses destroyed.
Oklahoma Historical Society/Getty Images

Apart from the cruelty and socio-economic apartheid, as reflected in the so-called Black Codes, sometimes called Black Laws, for example, white people across America operated a system (as recently as 1922, less than a hundred years ago!) that issued licenses to whites to hunt down and kill black people during their so-called Open Season. A sample licence from Missouri is rendered below:

STATE OF MISSOURI
NIGGER HUNTING LICENSE
THIS CERTIFIES THAT ____
Address ____ Sex ____ Wt. ____
City ____ Age ____ Ht. ____
Eyes ____ Hair ____
Having paid the license fee is hereby licensed to hunt & kill NIGGERS during the open season hereof in Missouri. This license must be carried on person when hunting NIGGERS & gives the holder permission to hunt day or night, with or without dogs.
Issued at ____ Missouri, this ____
day of ____ 20 ____
Signed By ____ County Clerk or Warden
Signature of Licensee ____
SEASON OPENS JAN. 1 - CLOSES DEC. 31

MISSOURI
1 2 3 4 5 6 7 8 9 10 11 12 13
Name ____
City ____
Signature ____
18 19 20 21 22 23 24 25 26 27 28 29 30 31
TAG GOOD FOR ANY NIGGERS

Source : @MariaChapelleN. Posted on August 2nd 2015

As written in Wikipedia, The Black Codes, sometimes called Black Laws, were laws governing the conduct of African Americans (free blacks). The best known of them were passed in 1865 and 1866 by Southern states, after the American Civil War, in order to restrict African Americans' freedom, and to compel them to work for low wages. Even after they had lost the Civil War, which was fought over their claimed right to enslave other human beings, they instituted oppressive laws and measures against blacks, including hunting them down as game. And these were all devoted Christians!!! Devoted to evil. It must be a wonder to these fellows why African-Americans and Native Indians were able to forgive them, live mostly peacefully with them, and even pray to the God or god of a Religion that clearly excluded and dehumanized them...

Though Mr. Trump has been president for just over three years, his open racism dates back to at least fifty years, based on available evidence. In the early 1970s, for example, Mr. Donald Trump, his father Fred, and their company Trump Management, were sued by the Justice Department for racial discrimination against blacks in their properties; they systematically refused to rent out their properties in New York to qualified black and Puerto Rican prospects based on their color. In 2017, the FBI released a nearly 400-page Report on their investigations into the matter. Josh Gerstein of Politico posted the Report in his article on the same subject. In 1975, Trump and his father entered into a Consent Decree with the Government, wherein they did not admit guilt, but undertook to implement measures in their company to prevent discrimination on the basis of demographics. For many years before he became President, the German-American Mr. Donald Trump spearheaded the lie and malicious declaration that the Kenyan-Irish American 44th President of the United States, Mr. Barack Obama, was not born in the United States.

The so-called Birther Movement was built around delegitimizing Mr. Obama because his father was from Kenya, and, therefore, he was not qualified to be the President of the US, though this former president was actually born in the US. Barack Obama graduated from Columbia University and the Harvard Law School. We understand that Mr. Trump attended the University of Pennsylvania, though a lot of unresolved speculations and opacity surround his academic status, as well as his financial dealings. His niece, Dr. Mary Trump, a Clinical Psychologist, has just informed the world in her new book that Mr. Donald Trump got a certain Joe Shapiro to write the SAT examination which fetched him the Penn admission, and that her uncle, Mr. Trump, embraces cheating as a way of life. One is but only quoting a niece, who also has a Ph.D. in Psychology. The Tea Party, which sprang up during the Obama Presidency and aligned with the Birther Movement, was an outright Racist Movement, which pretended to be interested in laissez faire policies. Since Mr. Obama served out his two terms -- much to their disappointment and surprise, we have not heard anything again about the Tea Party.

In 1989, five black and one Hispanic teenagers were charged with assault, robbery, riot, rape, sexual abuse, and attempted murder over a rather grave, sadistic, and unconscionable attack on a white female jogger at Central Park, New York. While the youngsters pleaded their innocence and the entire country was outraged over the incident, Mr. Donald Trump, as a private citizen, placed full-page advertisements in New York newspapers asking for the boys to be executed. Their trial proceeded apace, and they were sentenced to various prison terms; they served between seven and thirteen years before a convicted murderer and serial rapist confessed that he was the one who had attacked this lady back in 1989. His DNA matched the forensic samples perfectly, whereupon the convicted 'Central Park Five' were released and their conviction quashed. They were released in 2002 and settled with the City of New York for a total of $41 million in 2014; they also sued the State of New York, which settled with them for $3.9 million. Despite all of this, Mr. Trump has refused to accept that he was wrong, and still sees no need to apologize to these men and their families. What if they were sentenced to death and executed before the proof of their innocence was established? Apart from his open racist comments and denigration of minorities, President Trump glorifies, motivates, and encourages so-called White Supremacists, with there "being good people on both sides", "our heritage being under assault", etc.

It might be useful to use basic arithmetic to address the obsession that Mr. Trump and his ideological soulmates have with ANTIFA. Minus Minus (Anti) Fascism = Plus or Positive or Pro Fascism; - (- Fascism) = Fascism. In essence, ANTIFA stands for Anti-Fascism; whoever is against ANTIFA is promoting Fascism. The problem with ANTIFA is that it dares to challenge Fascism in America; it dares to use the same means and tools to push back against Fascism. Fascism must be allowed a free rein for there to be peace. Whoever resists fascism becomes the terrorist and the enemy to be crushed. Everyone must meekly accept race-based cruelty that never goes punished. Indeed. It is encouraging that, while condemning the acts of violence and looting that attended the protests over George Floyd's murder, scores of former senior Defense Officials publicly criticized President Trump for trying to politicize the US Military by attempting to deploy them against Americans. The link to their public statement is provided herewith: *https://www.businessinsider.com/89-former-defense-officials-speak-out-against-trumps-protest-response-2020-6?utm_source=copy-link&utm_medium=referral&utm_content=topbar*

Other respectable people like the former Chairman of the Joint Chiefs of Staff and Secretary of State, General Colin Powell, and former Republican Presidential Nominee (2012) and serving US Senator from Utah, Mitt Romney, added their voices as well, with the latter joining the protesters in Washington D.C.

Some people, in condemning the violence that has accompanied the protests, made the valid point that arson and looting will not bring back George Floyd; but neither did all the bombs the US dropped in Iraq and Afghanistan as well as all the deaths, injuries, and destruction, reverse 9-11 or even the incorrect charge that Iraq had stockpiles of WMD. Four days after the incident, and after all the protests, violence, and losses, Derek Chauvin has finally been arrested and charged with third-degree murder and manslaughter for his direct role in the death of George Floyd. The world watches keenly to see how this process is pursued, and how the other three implicated Officers will be treated. In a remarkable departure from the past, and in a symbolic gesture of solidarity, some Police Officers across the country knelt and matched with protesters, who quickly embraced them. Beyond these welcome developments, a fundamental reorientation and systemic reversal of injustice in the Laws,

Practices, Charging Procedures, and Prosecutorial Action are urgently needed, aimed at ensuring equity for all. Let bad people be tried according to the Law (regardless of color), not willfully killed without consequences. Bad cops are still citizens and must not have immunity from personal responsibility.

In a society that values human lives as worthy and as hosting the Divine Spark, it is worrisome that these unnecessary killings do not outrage the entire country, but only segments thereof. The revulsion should not be a matter of color, not a black or white matter, but of conscience, right or wrong, our shared humanity, and common decency; maybe it is not so common after all. Like all the Holy Books admonish both believers and unbelievers alike, we should do unto others as we want them to do unto us. If people who casually, and for no justifiable reason, extinguish another person's life or subject another to grave indignity, together with the enablers, bystanders, and rationalizers, would want the same things done to them in equal measure, most people will have profound respect for them for their consistency. As it is, though, it does appear as if they will prefer different treatments for different people, then develop reasons to justify their actions or inactions, all with a straight face....we shall leave this matter for now, until we get together again in the next few weeks to condemn yet another willful murder with impunity; to assure the bereaved families that our thoughts and prayers are with them, a recurring cliché. It is instructive and disappointing that Dr. Martin Luther King's letter to his fellow Clergy from the Birmingham, Alabama prison on June 12, 1963, remains relevant today in 2020. This significant contribution to Liberation Theology can be read in detail through this link, thanks to Stanford University: *http://okra.stanford.edu/transcription/document_images/undecided/630416-019.pdf*

This is what the world sees, and that is not the full story about America, and should not be. All these cases have made it possible, for example, for the notoriously brutal Chinese dictatorship to issue a Statement condemning the treatment of minorities by the US Government, and also cited the looting and violence that have attended the Floyd-related protests in all the fifty states. And, yet, Americans are truly the most generous people in the world. The US Government, billionaires, Churches, Charities, and regular citizens give much more in international philanthropy than any other society.

When foreign nations are struck by natural disasters, Americans rally in support; when America faces its own challenges, the world largely sends in rhetorical forms of solidarity, leaving the hard work and expenses for Americans themselves. Several American billionaires led by Bill Gates and Warren Buffet pledged to give away the bulk of their wealth to uplift the poor and to solve common problems for mankind. The Bill and Melinda Gates

Foundation underwrites public health bills around the world and is very active in finding a solution for the Covid-19 pandemic that currently cripples humanity. American churches and citizens also support some of the poorest communities around the world, mostly women and children not known to them. The donations to American Colleges by the rich make it possible for brilliant but indigent kids to attend world-class Institutions at massively-discounted fees or even free of charge. These are all very commendable, which is why one wonders why the same people cannot find their voices in unison to loudly and publicly condemn the manifestations of systemic injustice and oppression that are all around them; ultimately, America's global reputation on race relations affects them as individuals. This bipolar dimension to the American persona confounds one immensely, especially given how outspoken Americans generally are.

While, of course, it is not everyone who directly promulgates, enforces, and adjudicates on discriminatory and inherently unjust laws, sufficient numbers of people have not been sufficiently outraged, to cause their nullification and reversal. In the March 1936 German parliamentary elections/ a single-issue referendum, which witnessed an unprecedented turnout of 99% of eligible voters, an overwhelming majority voted in favor of granting the Nazis their request to militarily occupy the Rhineland and also have a single-party list for their Parliament, the Reichstag, comprising exclusively Nazi members and their sympathizers. This was the first German election held after the enactment of the Nuremberg Laws, which had removed citizenship rights (including the right to vote) from Jews and other ethnic minorities. The Enabling Act of 1936, which legally, officially, and openly granted dictatorial powers to Hitler's Government, followed; this was nine whole years before WWII started. During the 1938 election, again actually a single-issue referendum to obtain legal backing for the recent annexation of Austria and the composition of the 813-member National Assembly by Nazis and their closest allies, a 99.5% turnout was achieved, 98.8% of whom voted yes on the ballot, knowing full well what the portents were. This was a year before WWII started.

What if, just what if this same majority voted against the Nazis and pointedly refused to empower the villainous Nazis, cooperate with them, or comply with their vile laws and edicts? Just what if??? What if they did not casually look the other way or even report on their Jewish neighbors and friends? What if they did not derisively taunt and dishonor the Jews, some of whose families had lived continuously in Germany and Central Europe for centuries and contributed significantly towards the growth of their countries? Or, was it their country, as History disputes? History would have been different, you see. When the world makes comments about the sub-optimal development and utilization of available resources across the Continent of Africa, that is not meant to imply or affirm that all 1.3 billion Africans are complicit in the gross mis-governance that is pervasive in their fifty-four countries.

What objective observers wonder is why so many otherwise brilliant, resourceful, educated, intelligent, cosmopolitan, confident, and energetic people would allow their Continent to be perennially ruled by successive generations of lootocrats, victims of chronic myopia, divisive elements, and generally a bunch of individuals sorely lacking in both character and confidence; demi-gods who gladly pulverize their nations for personal gain, and conspire with ruthless foreign (European, Indian, Lebanese, American, and, lately, Chinese) businesses to hold their Continent from developing at pace with the rest of the world, while shipping the proceeds of their corruption back to foreign lands. Individually, many Africans acquit themselves academically, behaviorally, and professionally across the world, but the collective performance of the Continent belies this fact. As individuals, each African pays some price for the virtual failure of their Continent.

Why are they unable to form the critical mass to drive positive change in their countries of birth; on their Continent? One may legitimately ask why perhaps the highest concentration of African talent is outside Africa? Why is the pull of emigration (or escape) as strong as it is? Why can't Africans stay back in their countries, confront their corrupt and inept leaders, and re-write the profile of the Continent from that of want, disease, waste, aid, and corruption? Why does the elite group on the African Continent (elite defined as access to wealth in this case, thus accommodating some of the very corrupt and compromised in both their private and public sectors) spend billions of dollars each year outside Africa on medical tourism, school fees for their pampered children, mortgages and taxes on their foreign homes and assets, as well as on sundry Western luxury items? Why is it taken for granted that good schools and hospitals cannot germinate on their soil? But it was not always this way, as the infrastructure levels and public goods standards in the years immediately after independence in the 1960s were much higher than the current levels. What has been the value, the purpose, the end of their political independence, then? This **dependent independence** is an oxymoron.

Accordingly, no one can, in good conscience, justifiably censor any analyst who challenges any group to rise in unison against evil, wherever seen. Honest commentators chronicle actuality; the job of ensuring positive commentaries is that of the silent majority that must insist on positive behavior. With all the migration flows throughout history, complex and widening linkages, as well as changing norms, what is identity?

Identity is a complex subject. What determines one's identity? Ancestry? Socialization? Education? Gender? Sexual Preference? Religion? Political Views? Travel and Exposure? Immigration Experience? Language? Interests? Or a combination thereof? We will leave the finer definition and arguments to Sociologists and Cultural Anthropologists; one thing is clear, though: ancestry plays a significant role in one's identity and sense of self. Identity cannot exist *tabula rasa*; it is always contextualized and situated within a sociological and anthropological framework. Since this work is an interrogation of the concepts of political independence and sovereignty, it will be in order to also consider these concepts on the individual and group levels, not just at the national level. The truth is that very rich or very educated people of different races feel more connected to other very rich and educated people of other races than they do to the poor and illiterate who happen to share their grade of melanin; so, why all the obsession with skin color?

Donald Trump, Barack Obama, Queen Elizabeth of England, Wiktoria in Poland, the poor beggar in Calcutta India, the cab driver in Nairobi, the Sumo wrestler in Japan, the Sultan or Sheik in the Middle East, the poor kid in Sao Paulo's *favelas*, the Aborigine in Australia, the tailor in Shenzhen, the billionaire and pauper, the marginalized Muslim and Orthodox Jewish women (considered only good enough for conjugal pleasure and procreation by insecure and misogynistic male bullies, unlike their God's actual plan for them), etc., all share 99.9% identical DNA, and all of them share 99% of their DNA with chimpanzees. Talking about Orthodox Jews, it remains a wonder why their men have to pray to their God each day in gratitude because He (always a He in these matters!) "has not made me a woman." And, yet, all that entitles them to this assumption of superiority to women is a wasted piece or bushy beard they did not order, pay for, or achieve, mere and automatic attachments to their gender, that's all. The convenient exclusivity of the *tzizit* and *kippah* is just that, man-made, and confers no organic superiority on these entitled men over women.

All those race warriors are just 1% different from chimpanzees. Go figure that ...

The markers of differentiation that we see are both natural and man-made, but the fundamental qualification, the ingredient of humanity, unites us all. Being tall or short, smart or dull, rich or poor, fat or slim, calm or tempestuous, hardworking or lazy, honest or dishonest, white or black, has absolutely nothing to do with your DNA profile, which is 99.9% identical with that of seven billion others. The so-called Race Supremacists should be humbled by the knowledge that they share 99% of their DNA signature with chimpanzees; if they deny this, then they are not even qualified as human beings. Why all the carnage in human history on the basis of racial discrimination? Identity is far more complex than how bright or dark you are, but this truth is not commonly shared, hence all the problems we experience.

In the modern world, it is understandable that, for several reasons, mostly economic, political, cultural, and historical, many people are unable to live in their ancestral lands, but this fact does not, or should not, vitiate the pull of the hearth. It is for this reason that the Irish proudly celebrate St. Patrick's Day in America; Jews observe their cultural and religious festivals; German--Americans and their beer-loving friends (many of us!!!) mark the *Oktoberfest*; and the Chinese celebrate their traditional New Year even if it comes towards the end of the Gregorian Year, etc., etc. For the Africans in America, whose families have been in the country for centuries, the difficulty of directly tracing where precisely they came from in Africa is understood, given the very wicked intervention of both humanity and history. Recent (voluntary) immigrants from Africa do not have this problem, and should never strive to have it, or to get lost in the convenient miasma of the American narrative…a narrative that seeks to perjure them as a group. For the African-Americans, broadly-speaking, not Ghanaian-Americans or Senegalese-Americans or Egyptian-Americans or Kenyan-Americans, but those with centuries of injurious memory about the American experience, there is an urgent imperative to symbolically and boldly restore their collective dignity and personal independence.

It is trite that people name what they own or "own"; we name our dogs, boats, children, houses, and other appurtenances of acquisition. The power to name has a metaphysical connotation of superiority, of being the grantor of identity to the named. It is in this context that it is worrisome that these African-Americans continue to bear the names they were given by those who dehumanized and oppressed them. I submit that, though slavery, then apartheid, have officially ended in America, the retention of these slave names detracts from the ultimate dignity, spiritual restoration, and independence of those bearing them. For, how can you explain that a black man or woman bears Washington, Jefferson, Carroll, Hancock, McNabb, or Lee, as a last name, or as a name at all in 2020? Since you can bear this name of all names, would it not be much more empowering and freeing to bear an African name, even if you do not know the full meaning presently? Indeed, instead of a profoundly ridiculous name like Tiger Woods, it is better to bear Rotimi Mandela or Salif Chaka, or even any of the creative mixes of vowels and consonants that define the African-American.

Indeed, with the advancements in genealogy testing, those who can afford it in this community should be able to trace their ancestral roots in Africa, and adopt names from those parts, or assume pan-African profiles, in total rejection of the residue of slavery that they live with on a daily basis through their current names. While a good number of African-Americans have overcome significant obstacles to achieve considerable success especially in Sports, Music, Entertainment, and Culture, the majority of their communities remain endemically poor and lacking in both direction and hope. These successful ones should recognize their strategic mandate to fund, provide leadership for, and own, the current phase of the continuing Civil Rights struggle, namely, the rapid and widespread rejection of these names with the lingering taste of oppression and "belonging to another", as well as the massive education of black kids across the country, and opening up opportunities to them beyond hip hop, sports, and gang warfare.

Oprah Winfrey, Lebron James, Magic Johnson, Lionel Richie, Tyler Perry, Vernon Jordan, Al Sharpton, and all others with the platform and means should lead by example, and fund this new phase of the struggle, in partnership with the Black Churches, NAACP, National Action Network, and credible Charities. I suggest that the eminent Harvard Professor of African and African-American Studies, an accomplished Researcher and Documentarian, Henry Louis Gates Jr., the distinguished Philosopher and Public Intellectual, Professor Cornel West, and the former President/CEO of NAACP, the brilliant lawyer Cornell Williams West, for example, should know better than to retain these names. They are role models for many and should set the tone towards reclaiming their identity and dignity. Indeed, a strategic partnership with the African Union or the thinking members of that Body should be *apropos*.

A name change just requires a visit to the Courthouse, but its resonance and implications are powerful. With education and new empowerment, the crime rate among blacks will drop, the family unit will be strengthened in their community, kids will stop having kids, and positive ambition will replace a life of hopelessness -- all to the benefit of the larger society. Indeed, they should emulate the confidence, ambition, and academic laurels of recent black immigrants to the United States, especially Nigerians (notably from the Igbo, Yoruba, and minority ethnic groups of Southern Nigeria), who are, by far, the most educated immigrant group, the immigrant demographic with the highest percentage of graduate degrees in America, the dominant minority group in all the top Colleges in the US, and who out-perform native-born Americans across all the academic parameters per capita. Those who can afford it should also visit Africa, to have that indescribable spiritual experience that philosophers of old called "a natal connection", also observe the considerable freedom people take for granted, as well as see the vast pool of black men and women who are doing extremely well in their various professions without any psychological or racial obstacles. Such trips will rejuvenate people's sense of intrinsic worth and broaden their horizon and confidence as they navigate the complexities of the American journey.

The future challenges of the world will involve creative solutions, a good consequence of good education. In ancient Rome, gladiators filled the coliseums, but were soon forgotten or dead, and replaced by yet another batch of gladiators. Combative sports and optimization of giantship should not be the only careers available to a people, especially given the hyper-competition and attrition rate. Young kids should aspire to be teachers, lawyers, administrators, scientists, diplomats, police chiefs, doctors, architects, writers, journalists, cellists, and engineers. Excelling in these two new areas of the Civil Rights Movement will yield enduring and powerful outcomes much beyond the transcience of the "lambo", "ice", "b....", and "Roly."

It was Maslow, in his "Theory of Human Motivation" who theorized in 1943, that human needs are in a hierarchy starting from the basic and reflexive needs to more sophisticated and enlightened needs like safety, through love and belonging, and esteem, until they peak at self-actualization. The genuine adoption and internalization of the overarching African cultural precepts of *Maslaha* (the complex positive roles played by social and cultural networks) and *Ubuntu Ngumuntu Ngabantu* (I am, because we are; since we are, therefore I am) will be recommended to the African-American community.

As we dissect the concept of Identity even further, perhaps, we should look at two men who have had the singular distinction of becoming US Presidents: Number 44, Barack Obama, and Number 45, Donald Trump (the incumbent). Both were born in the United States and had parents or grandparents from different countries, 44 being of both Kenyan and Irish ancestry, while 45 is of German and Scottish lineage. In essence, therefore, Obama is as much a Kenyan as he is Irish, yet, some individuals and groups have made careers out of portraying his Kenyan roots as some degrading, negative and unqualifying matter. No mention is ever made by these same people of the 50% Irish blood in him, or the fact that his father graduated with an M.A. in Economics from Harvard in 1965. What is the pedigree of these individuals who deign to malign others, those who are better than them?

Discounting the politics of the two presidents -- since one cannot embrace every aspect of their politics -- is it even debatable that our immediate past president, B. H. Obama, carried himself with uncommon dignity, and discharged this high office without scandal, ill repute, intemperance, inconsistency, untrustworthiness, unseriousness, extreme narcissism, ignorance, persistent lies, and unpresidential mien? The very opposite of Mr. Obama's carriage and respect for the office, has been our daily experience since January 2017. At least, these should not be debatable. If you do not accept my assessment, perhaps you may want to ask Messrs Fintan O'Toole and Michael Stevenson, eminent Irish and British writers, for their own opinions.

So, the stupidity and hollowness of anti-miscegenation become bare yet again (should the love between a man and a woman of whatever races even have a special term?) the German-Scottish American President is simply no match for his Kenyan-Irish American predecessor, or is there a doubt? All the race "theories" and assumptions are just illiterate and bigoted projections wrongly and mischievously cast as facts. Individual talent, character, responsibility, humanity, and temperance have nothing to do with race, but may have more to do with upbringing, indoctrination, and deliberate choices. Good and bad people; bright and dull people; hard-working and lazy people; healthy and unhealthy people; etc., abound in every religion, race, and country. Getting all to see this obvious fact remains a fundamental challenge of mankind.

It must be acknowledged that this tendency towards deracination, towards the obliteration of one's identity and essence is not limited to the Africans who have lived in America for centuries. Their brethren, who never left Africa, who were never traded as chattel, who have consistently drunk from the fountain of freedom and independence except for the unwelcome and unsolicited interjections of colonists and Abrahamic religionists, have also largely forfeited their own indigenous names, as they compete with one another to adopt colonial, Jewish, Christian, and Islamic names. There are more Jameses, Matthews, Johns, Isahs, Muhammeds (all the iterations), Abubakars, Marys, Elizabeths, and Aishas in Africa than in Europe, in Israel, and the Arab world.

As a matter of fact, while African Muslims proudly bear Muhammed, Mohammed, and Muhammadu, after their prophet, their Christian counterparts consider it sacrilegious to name anyone Jesus, even as this name is quite common in Brazil, Portugal, and across South America. Have these African people bothered to ask themselves why no Israeli, Arab, European, or European-American, bears Rotimi, Ikechukwu, Edet, Fatou, Makena, Zawadi, Kasyoka, Absko, Kwesi, Kojo, Priye, or Osaretin? While their Africanness is an ineradicable component of their identity, their adoption of the foreign religions of Christianity and Islam (by whatever means) represents a tangential, recent, and negotiable element of that identity. A coincidence or the consequence of man-made history does not imply, denote, or mean inevitability, metaphysical kinship, or evidence of inexorable causality. These Africans will soon start bearing Chinese names, at this rate…

To "belong", or to guarantee a place in heaven, many now bear both first and last names introduced by their relatively new foreign religion. Indeed, part of the ritual of life in Africa starts with the Christian and Muslim priest baptizing and naming the new-born child, as if Africa had no prior names and experience. For, Africa had names that bore witness to their concept of God. Among the Igbos of Nigeria, every name that has "Chi" or "Chukwu" in it references God; among the Yoruba of West Africa, names with "Olu(wa)", "Ele", are in adoration of the Almighty God. So, why lose your concept of God where you are powerful for another's where you remain inferior?

While most commentaries about slavery, colonialism, and the genocide against native peoples have usually been restricted to just calling the perpetrators Europeans or citing their nationality, it is crucial to render the full account. It was the Catholic Church which issued the Laws and Charters for colonialism and violent attacks on non-Europeans, provided the theoretical justification for White Supremacy as a basis for Europeans/ Christians to murder, pillage, rape, and exploit non-Europeans, rationalized all these actions provided that tributes and taxes were paid to the Church, and also assuaged the few disturbed consciences of the European killers and rapists during their confessorial rituals. Until the Protestant Reformation of the 16th century, the Catholic Church had been the only Christian denomination in Europe and around the world for centuries, a power they grossly abused, consolidated, and employed in convenient despotism. Specifically, Pope Alexander VI issued his Papal Bull in 1493 which contained the so-called Doctrine of Discovery; this provided the spiritual, political, and legal justification for Christians (who were all Europeans) to colonize and seize land anywhere in the world not inhabited by Christians, and to employ whatever means necessary to establish their control as the inheritors of God's universal bounties. Specific Charters to Monarchs were derived from this Doctrine, as well as other Church teachings and edicts.

The first code of legal racism had been applied against Jews in Spain. Over a half of the Spanish Jews (Sephardic Jews) had been forced to convert to Catholicism (they were called *conversos*), and, yet, they were discriminated against especially as they prospered. Their ethnic origin, color, and the circumstances of Jesus' death, were always held against them, with deprivations and violence usually accompanying the resentment. It was the official Catholic doctrine that the assumed individual and group act(s) of deicide could not be mitigated or reversed by their conversion and baptism which were obtained through coercion. The "purity of blood" concept was introduced for the first time, and the term "race" became significant for the first time ever. As Jeffrey Gorsky writes, "on June 5, 1449, Sarmiento issued the *Sentencia-Estatuto*, the first set of racial exclusion laws in modern history. It barred *conversos*, regardless of whether or not they were sincere Christians, from holding private or public office or receiving land from the church benefices unless they could prove four generations of Christian affiliation." The success with the race-based extortions from Jews motivated worldwide ambitions. History has since been repeated in many forms several times since then.

As at 1400, there was no concept of White Supremacy; societies lived in silos around the world, satisfied with their organic systems. The few who lived outside their homeland, like Jews, experienced discrimination but this was not codified until later on in the century. With the development of long-distance sailing and the musket in Europe, and armed with the knowledge of distant lands, the Catholic Church which wielded absolute authority on the Continent, granted a Holy (more like unholy) Charter to King Henry the Navigator of Portugal to attack East Indies and expropriate all the resources of the place, enslave, dominate, and "otherwise engage in any and all measures that you deem necessary." The export of European greed, mass violence against "others", White Supremacy, and their correlates had started. The Portuguese Monarch mandated or licensed Bartolomeu Dias, Diogo Cao, Vasco da Gama, Ferdinand Magellan, Pedro Alvares Cabral, etc., to embark on these missions, with the standard tax of 20% on all proceeds returned to the King, who shared the same with the Church. The first set of Portuguese sailors got to Africa in 1455, while the first Portuguese slave ship berthed in Brazil in 1526. This project also involved recruiting the renowned Flemish cartographer (modern-day Belgium), Mercato, in their propaganda efforts which deliberately distorted the locations of the various Continents simply to make Europe the center of the universe, depicted an exaggerated profile of parts of the world under the control of the Holy Roman Empire, while shrinking the actual sizes of other locations on the world map and globe. His *Orbis Imago* is an example of these lies, which were woven to give the European an inflated sense of his importance and about the assumed inevitability of his role in the world. These early visitors came under different guises: merchant-adventurers (read pirates), explorers, missionaries, and administrators.

While *en route* the Indies, they got to the Cape of Good Hope just beneath modern-day South Africa, and, from there, proceeded further into the vast African Continent where the contact was denominated in sorrow, tears, and blood for the locals. Some of them stopped in the present Madagascar, which had historically been used as a stop in oceanic travels from Europe to India since 1527. Based on the new wealth that accrued from this "expedition" (with no consideration for the human cost, after all Africans were not human beings but beasts, according to the Catholic formulation, which gained quick resonance across Europe), Portugal became a rich nation, spending enormously on infrastructure, to the envy of other European Monarchies. With the codification of the template for the exploitation, rape, murder, and systemic dehumanization of "natives" outside Europe, and buoyed by the considerable returns from the first "expedition", the Pope issued another Charter, this time to Spain, to explore the New World (America) and repeat the very successful model they had executed in Africa.

When England got into the business of exporting massive violence, greed, systemic oppression, and displacement to distant lands, it took the crown from other European nations, hence the contours of contemporary global history. It is well conceivable that Germany would have done much better than their cousins, the English, in this odious business, but for the losses they suffered in various wars, especially WWI and WWII, as a result of which their external "possessions" and programs were clipped through imposed Treaties from the victors. The rest, as they say, is history. This illuminating clarification of historical facts is very important as we deal with multiple manifestations of European greed, racism, sense of entitlement, and violence on both retail and corporate levels. Greed, expropriation, and violent domination lie at the core of the White Supremacy programs. The Catholic Church was the precursor of it all, simple. To justify the carnage and systemic pillage that accompanied the introduction of both the European religion and political systems, the owners of the land were routinely characterized as savages who needed to be converted or killed. The violence depicted on the etching below, dating back to the 19th century, is emblematic of that mindset:

Civilization vanquishing barbarism, engraving, Gustave Doré, Paris, 1855

Priest with negro children. *Source: scholarblogs.emory.edu*

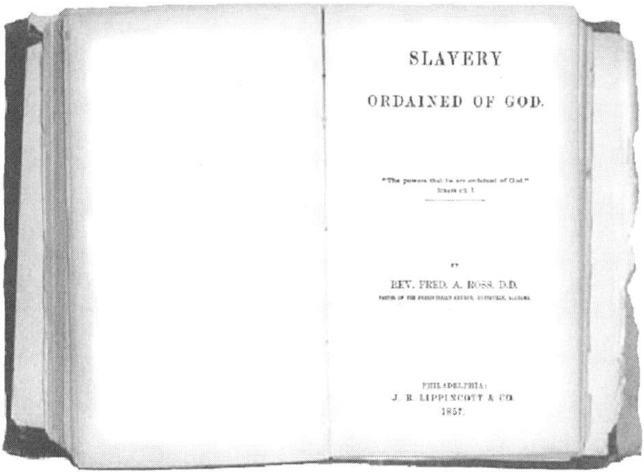

Slavery Ordained of God – 1857 – an example of many articles using religion to justify slavery

Credit: cited in racialequitytools.org

As Dan Koje instructs us extensively, during slavery, it was illegal for Africans to read any book other than the Bible. Anyone caught reading philosophy, science, governance, history, economics or any other genre of literature, faced the death penalty. Why was this so? The evil slave masters understood that thc Bible was a tool to limit the thinking of black Africans and to keep them perpetually subservient. They knew that to keep them in servitude they had to make them accept their lot as the will of God and have them thinking about the end of days, thus keeping them in perpetual servitude. They sold the falsity of heavenly peace and reward to their victims, even as these victims were routinely exploited and killed for present gain. They refused to give them anything good but they gave them Christianity and the Bible, a heavily-redacted and rigged Bible which emphasized only the acceptance of oppression -- as every situation is described in that compilation by different authors.

Over five hundred years later, the descendants of the slaves who were whipped, tortured, raped and murdered, together with their free relatives in Africa and around the world, still confess implicit confidence in the same Bible (a book hurriedly put together by Emperor Constantine in 325 AD when he decreed Christianity - an infusion of Roman paganism, Greek and Egyptian mythology) as the new State religion and his troops would violently convert most of the world's populations to this newly formed Order by force and through violence.

The Bible was central to the success of the trans-Atlantic slavery. Slaves were first baptized and letters (signifying their new names such as John, Peter, Isaac and other Christian names) engraved with hot metal on their backs - this was even before they learnt English. While in chains, blood dripping from all over their bodies, they recited the Nicean creed, not knowing the meaning. Verses like Ephesians 6:5: "Slaves, obey your earthly masters with respect and fear, and with sincerity of heart, just as you would obey Christ." lent divine credence to the predicament of slaves and consigned them to perpetual slavery. Revolting against the oppressors was a direct rejection of God - so they were made to believe.

Today, many Africans know the Bible from the beginning to the end but they know little about themselves or ideas that can improve their lives. They can feel Jesus in their spirits and they are absolutely sure that Christianity is the only true religion. They are waiting for an apocalyptic climax to humanity where a blue eyed, blonde-haired Caucasian savior would appear from the sky at the sound of a trumpet, to save them from debilitating poverty, a dysfunctional system, diseases and corrosive imbecility. 500 years later, Africans are still languishing in profuse ignorance. When they are not busy voluntarily expanding the frontiers of Christianity, they embrace the religion of their other oppressor and slave dealer, the Arabs. Islam and Christianity are growing more in Africa than elsewhere around the world -- with poverty, lack of self-esteem, and pervasive violence to show for the perpetual contestation for expansion. Who did this to them? Why can't this habit be broken? Simply pathetic, in one's view.

Koje quotes the late scholar Dr. Henrik Clark as follows: "To control a people, you must first control what they think about themselves and how they regard their history and culture. And when your conqueror makes you ashamed of your culture and history, he needs no prison walls and chains to hold you." Brigit Katz wrote in the Smithsonian Institution Magazine that the so-called Slave Bible, which was published in London in 1807, was heavily redacted to serve the evil purpose of slavery and to also condition the victims. "A typical Protestant edition of the Bible contains 66 books, a Roman Catholic version has 73 books and an Eastern Orthodox translation contains 78 books," "By comparison, the astoundingly reduced Slave Bible contains only parts of 14 books." Gone was Jeremiah 22:13: "Woe unto him that buildeth his house by unrighteousness, and his chambers by wrong; that useth his neighbor's service without wages and giveth him not for his work." Exodus 21:16—"And he that stealeth a man, and selleth him, or if he be found in his hand, he shall surely be put to death"—was also excised. All references to the Jewish revolt and exodus from Egypt were removed, and these victims were not allowed to read anything else other than this propaganda material, non-compliance being punishable by death. Other credible authorities have also confirmed these facts. Has there been any accounting, atonement, genuine apology, or restitution? It is the absence of these, and reward for the continuing cruelty against blacks in America, that pose the greatest threat to America's moral leadership in the world.

When the blacks of America finally got access to the full Bible, you would think that their response would be that of revulsion and a total rejection of the Creed used to kill and dehumanize them. No, they deepened their faith and sang "Amazing Grace" with amazing sonority, vibrancy, surrender, creativity, and artistry. A few of them embraced that other oppressive religion, Islam, which posed as their liberating refuge.

By contrast, the writer personally knows some Jews who would never buy any German vehicle, notwithstanding the quality and performance. There are also some Jewish Investment Bankers and Wall Street Traders who, out of conscientious objection and principle, would not trade in stocks of those companies that collaborated with Nazi Germany, including but not limited to VW, AUDI, Mercedes-Benz, Thyssen-Krupp, Messerschmidt, Porsche, IG Farben, Allianz, Siemens, Deutsche Bank, Nestle, Bayer, Steyr, BASF, Ford, Coca-Cola, IBM, AEG, successor-companies to Topf, etc., etc. This is entirely their prerogative and is perfectly understandable, in one's view. In fact, some of these individuals would not buy any attire made by Hugo Boss or Boss, because this Fashion House was the official tailor to the Nazis. Wikipedia writes that, in 1931, Hugo Boss became a member of the Nazi Party, receiving the membership number 508 889, and a sponsoring member (*"Förderndes Mitglied"*) of the killer group, the *Schutzstaffel* (SS).

Even as we exhaustively analyze the condition of the blacks who were forcefully removed to America and elsewhere, what explains the lack of confidence by the 1.3 billion Africans on the African Continent, people who never experienced the wickedness of slavery? Why can't they provide a protective shield for their kith and kin who are evidently embattled and threatened, even 400 years later, in America? When will the strategic handshake between Africans on the mother-Continent and Africans elsewhere (especially in America) take place? Why can't they resolve to run their countries and Continent in a way that will enhance the status of all black people everywhere in the world, especially the blacks of America? Why has their political independence meant nothing to them?

Why is their **independence dependent** on handouts and dictation from outside their Continent, even as they have very rich reserves of both human and natural resources, as well as immense skills and talents that are lost to the same region(s) of oppression? Why do they even presently sabotage the independence and integrity of their nations and Continent? If the blacks of America were as violent and assertive as our Middle Eastern brothers and sisters, would America know peace? Would the wickedness persist? Would internal subversion and mass violence not have crippled this throne of evil? These reflections inform the essence of this effort, **Dependent Independence**.

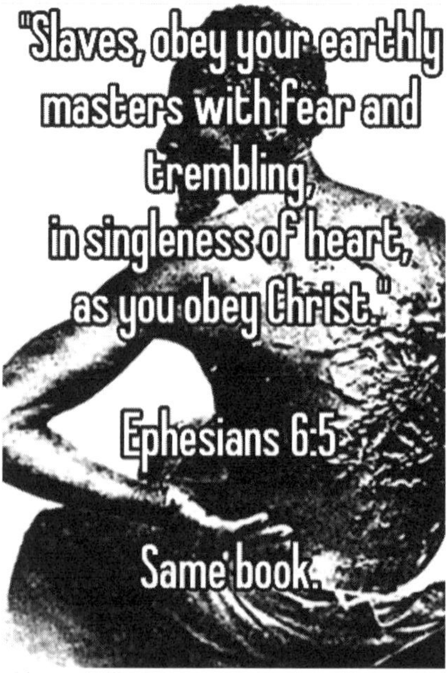
"Slaves, obey your earthly masters with fear and trembling, in singleness of heart, as you obey Christ."
Ephesians 6:5
Same book.

This picture and other disturbing ones like it appeared for the first time in "Uncle Tom's Cabin" a book published by Harriet Beecher - Stowe in the 1850s. *Source : Abraham Lincoln Presidential Library and Museum.*

The following 1883 letter which the accomplished genocidaire, King Leopold II of Belgium, wrote to Belgian Catholic Priests as they proceeded to the Congo

-- preceding the brutal killing of over fifteen million Congolese people by Belgian soldiers and officials at the direction of their monarch -- is captured in full in "Biafra: The Horrors of War; The Story of a Child Soldier", by Dr. Okey Anueyiagu:

"Reverends, Fathers and Dear Compatriots:

The task that is given to fulfill is very delicate and requires much tact. You will go certainly to evangelize, but your evangelization must inspire above all Belgium interests. Your principal objective in our mission in the Congo is never to teach the savages to know God, this they know already. They speak and submit to a Mungu, one Nzambi, one Nzakomba, and what else I don't know. They know that to kill, to sleep with someone else's wife, to lie and to insult is bad. Have courage to admit it; you are not going to teach them what they know already. Your essential role is to facilitate the task of administrators and industrials, which means you will go to interpret the gospel in the way it will be the best to protect your interests in that part of the world. For these things, you have to keep watch on disinteresting our savages from the richness that is plenty [in their underground. To avoid that they get interested in it and make you murderous] competition and dream one day to overthrow you.

Your knowledge of the gospel will allow you to find texts ordering, and encouraging your followers to love poverty, like "Happier are the poor because they will inherit heaven" and, "It's very difficult for the rich to enter the kingdom of God." You have to detach from them and make them disrespect everything which gives courage to affront us. I make reference to their Mystic System and their war fetish-warfare protection-which they pretend not to want to abandon, and you must do everything in your power to make it disappear.

Your action will be directed essentially to the younger ones, for they won't revolt when the recommendation of the priest is contradictory to their parent's teachings. The children have to learn to obey what the missionary recommends, who is the father of their soul. You must singularly insist on their total submission and obedience, avoid developing the spirit in the schools, teach students to read and not to reason. There, dear patriots, are some of the principles that you must apply. You will find many other books, which will be given to you at the end of this conference. Evangelize the savages so that they stay forever in submission to the white colonialists, so they never revolt against the restraints they are undergoing. Recite every day- "Happy are those who are weeping because the kingdom of God is for them."

Convert always the blacks by using the whip. Keep their women in nine months of submission to work freely for us. Force them to pay you in sign of recognition-goats, chicken or eggs-every time you visit their villages.

And make sure that savages never become rich. Sing every day that it's impossible for the rich to enter heaven. Make them pay tax each week at Sunday mass. Use the money supposed for the poor, to build flourishing business centers. Institute a confessional system, which allows you to be good detectives denouncing any black that has a different consciousness contrary to that of the decision-maker. Teach the savages to forget their heroes and to adore only ours. Never present a chair to a black that comes to visit you. Don't give him more than one cigarette. Never invite him for dinner even if he gives you a chicken every time you arrive at his house." End of Quote

In the wake of the global protests that attended the murder of George Floyd by the Police in Minneapolis, symbols of racism and oppression have been destroyed or forcefully pulled down by protesters around the world. In Belgium, monuments celebrating this animal, Leopold II, were damaged and defaced, whereupon his descendant, the so-called Prince Laurent, the "cursed prince" as he is called, took umbrage and reminded Belgians that Leopold built parks and gardens for them -- obviously, with blood money. This wastrel, this unemployed and unemployable leech, this waste of reproductive juices, this scion of infamy, this shameless maggot, then made his foolish point that Leopold, his ancestor, never "made people suffer" in the twenty-eight years he ran the Congo as a personal property until 1908 -- during which he murdered 15 million people and had many millions others amputated, because he "never visited the Congo."

How fatuous and farcical !!! But Hitler never visited Auschwitz, Bergen-Belsen, Buchenwald, Dachau, and the other centers of horrible and unspeakable crimes against humanity. This Laurent the buffoon who lives off the bloody proceeds of the "massive investments" in Real Estate, the major Oil Companies, Chemicals companies, and other recipients of blood money, is incapable of basic shame and decency. To deepen the arrogance and hurt, King Philippe of Belgium, a cousin to the implicated butcher, wrote a letter to President Felix A. T. Tshilombo of the Democratic Republic of Congo (DRC), wherein he recommended the need "to further strengthen our ties and develop an even more fruitful friendship", adding that "we must be able to talk about our long common history in all truth and serenity." He wrote casually about the "suffering and humiliation" which they caused the Congolese, emphasizing, instead, that "our history is made of common achievements but has also experienced painful episodes. During the period of the Congo Free State, acts of violence and cruelty were committed, which still weigh on our collective memory." Indeed!!! One continues to wonder how these Saxe-Coburg Gotha, Hapsburg and Hohenzollern families of Germany continue to populate and run the monarchies of Belgium, the United Kingdom, Denmark, Luxemburg, Liechtenstein, Holland, and Norway up to the present moment.

To reference Fela yet again, "Colonial Mentality ..." As a matter of fact, Fela's lyrics should be rendered in full as follows:

Colo-mentality
He be say you be colonial man
You don be slave man before
Them don release you now
But you never release yourself
I say you fit never release yourself
Colo-mentality
He be say you be colonial man
You don be slave man before
Them don release you now
But you never release yourself
He be so
He be so them dey do, them dey overdo
All the things them dey do (He be so!)
He be so them dey do, them think dey say
Them better pass them brothers
No be so? (He be so!)
The thing wey black no good
Na foreign things them dey like
No be so? (He be so!)
Them go turn air condition
And close them country away
No be so? (He be so!)
Them Judge him go put white wig
And jail him brothers away
No be so? (He be so!)
Them go proud of them name
And put them slave name for head
No be so? (He be so!)
Colo-mentality now make you hear me now
Colo-mentality!
Mr. Ransome you make you hear
Mr. Williams you make you hear
Mr. Allia you make you hear
Mr. Mohammed you make you hear
Mr. Anglican you make you hear
Mr. Bishop you make you hear
Mr. Catholic you make you hear
Mr. Muslim you make you hear
Na Africa we dey o make you hear
Na Africa we dey o make you hear
Colo-mentality hear
Colo-mentality hear
Mr. Ransome you make you hear
Mr. Ransome you make you hear
Na Africa we dey o make you hear
Na Africa we dey o make you hear
Colo-mentality hear
Colo-mentality hear
Colo-mentality!

It is significant, and indeed will be a good Doctoral Dissertation Topic, to trace and analyze why Africans in Africa, in the Americas (all the way to Brazil), in Europe (including Portugal), and in the Caribbean, as well as the native peoples of the modern Latin America, are the only formerly-colonized peoples who willingly and enthusiastically surrender their names and identity, to adopt the names of the foreigners in large numbers. The Chinese, Indians, Singaporeans, Malaysians, Arabs, etc., were colonized, but they bear their own names and cherish their identities. The British colonists renamed Mumbai to Bombay; once they left, proud Indians reverted the name to its original Mumbai; despite the long British abusive and exploitative control over Indian political, social, and economic life, how many people bear English names there? The name of the country 'Nigeria' was chosen by Flora Shaw, wife to the British terrorist usurper, Frederick Lugard, (elevated to a Lord in Britain!), who integrated the Northern and Southern Protectorates of the country. Over a hundred years later, the citizens have not considered a conscious decision on their national identity.

A major seaport in the country, a major city in the oil-producing region of the country, Port-Harcourt, is still named after a pedophilic racist, his pedophilia being gender-neutral. At least two major roads in Lagos, Nigeria are still named after the racist colonists, Bourdillon and Osborne. Whoever can pronounce the following names or expect others to pronounce them correctly can surely pronounce all African names: Arnold Schwarzenegger, Sokratis Papastathopoulos, Saoirse Ronan, Pyotr Ilyich Tchaikovsky, Mia Wasikowska, Zach Galifianakis, Gina Lollobrigida, Kepa Arrizabalaga, César Azpilicueta, Bastian Schweinsteiger,Tomasz Kuszczak, and Wojciech Szczęsny.

You name what you own or "own."

The great Danish philosopher, Søren Kierkegaard wrote that there are two ways to be fooled: a, by believing what is not true, and b, refusing to believe what is true. The greatest achievement of a propaganda effort is when the targeted audience needs no further persuasion, but willfully acts and behaves as you would desire.

An extensive detour, no doubt. Let's get back on track….

Well, Hitler adopted or hijacked Hegel's "force within history", which Nietzsche slightly modified as "Will to Power", as being applicable to German people, and used it to justify both the *lebensraum* and the full invasion into Continental Europe. In the idyllic blonde State, the police power of the State has responsibility for preventing poverty and the "rabble" class; this is not the job of private charity. Hegel wrote that: "poverty and the rabble mentality are systematic products of civil society." In the German State of his dreams, human beings, as rational and thinking beings, are not free until they successfully pursue ends and goals larger than their private good, or any other person's private goal. Even in this construct, it must be noted that the ultimate end of the society is the delivery of certain public goods.

Continuing with the separate State for "pure" Germans, Hegel states that the highest individual freedom is membership in the State; the highest consciousness of freedom is the consciousness of this membership, which he calls "political disposition" or "patriotism" -- which will not involve any heroism or extraordinary sacrifices on behalf of the mythical and exclusionary State. It will involve a normal life, with the State (for him, the preference will be a Constitutional Monarchy, actually) as the ultimate end, blind to atrocities committed against "others" to enrich and nourish the State. For him, the State "is the absolute power on earth", as well as the driver of world history. The needs of the State must take precedence over individual needs because "the State has the highest right in relation to individuals, whose highest duty is to be members of the State." Indeed!!!

This absolutism derives from the rationality of the State, which he elegantly and vacuously interprets as "unity and interpretation of universality and individuality." Actually, a lot of hot air!!! Continuing with the verbiage, he declares that the State systematically unifies individual goals, and is the "actuality of concrete freedom." More gas!!! The biggest problem remains transposing this mindset to other societies or in their interactions with non-Germans, a tendency that is somewhat lost in the fluid gun culture of the United States, the hijack and abuse of the genuine patriotic fervor in the country, as well as the hugging of the Confederate Flag and hero worship of "our Founding Fathers"; the presence of Nazi insignia in those gatherings exposes the particular impulse of some of these sad and angry individuals. *Heil Hitler* and the *Swastika* in 21st century America? Yes !!!

True to his agenda of a closed State, and without negating the purpose of the State, actually our main focus, he writes that: "patriotism is the consciousness that my substantial and particular interest is preserved and contained in the interest and end of an other (the State) and in the latter's relation to me as an individual."…. "as a result, this ceases to be an other for me, and in my consciousness of this, I am free." It should be much easier than this to make a statement, especially if it is the truth and does not have loaded therein some subjugation of "others."

He says that, as abnormal as wars are, occasional wars are inevitable. Some analysts have suggested that Hegel was not really absolutist, reactionary, or totalitarian in impulse, but the sympathetic response is for them to read him again without tinted glasses or screens of convenience. He defended excluding women from public life, as did the Greek philosophers who didn't know much really; Hegel also promoted denying significant segments of the society from political participation. While some have mentioned that, since he was hardly cited in Nazi literature, he could not have influenced that murderous ideology, the response should be a rigorous focus on substantive correlations, not on linguistic or declarative affirmations. He also wrote that: "when God gives someone an office, He gives him sense." He clearly gave Hitler a lot of sense...

What is interesting is how some grown men and women would see as all humans are conceived naturally in the same way (discounting the improvements of Science, which all can also access), the human blood for all races and income brackets is red (crimson) in color (never mind the weird conception and propagandistic profile of that leeching class, with their assumed blue blood, no doubt), the same desires and inclinations, the same vulnerability to the Covid:19 pandemic, and the guaranteed submission to death by all, and still believe that their kind is innately superior to the other. In what sense really, when the fact of humanity is being interrogated, without its external appurtenances, many of which were achieved through bloodshed and greed? When poor performers assume the vicarious identity of achievers who look like them, does this make all members of that slice of the human race superlative achievers? Is there any race without its own achievers, without its own full spectrum of humanity? Is it still possible to treat human beings as individuals, and stop hiding under the banner of groupthink and group identity, to dehumanize and discriminate?

Are some of these individuals aware of the considerable contributions of early Chinese people to the world? How do they interpret the unprecedented and phenomenal economic and infrastructural achievements that China has recorded since it embraced a regulated form of capitalism in 1989 under their great leader, Deng Xiaoping? Even without political liberalism or the much-touted Western Democracy, China is the second largest economy in the world (with 17% of the global GDP), a major military power, produces more Ph.D.s. in Science, Technology and Math than the rest of the world put together, is a lender to the United States, lifted hundreds of millions of their citizens from poverty to extreme wealth or the middle class, manufactures for the world, spends more money overseas than the rest of the world, has some of the best public infrastructure in the world, etc., etc., all in just about thirty years. If this had ever been done in human history, I would like to be instructed, but it has never been. They are not Europeans.

Are these bigots also aware that Africa gave the world Mathematics, Medicine, Architecture, Writing, Agriculture, Textiles, Metallurgy, Art, Language, Coffee, the Calendar, etc. In the modern era, if you have a cell phone, the chance that the cobalt powering it is from the Democratic Republic of Congo is extremely high, as this very resource-rich country produces 60% of the world's cobalt, a critical component of your phone. They also have copper, gold, and other vital materials, even as the benefits of their natural endowment are never felt by the citizens due to the corrosive, exploitative, divisive, and violent activities of foreign usurpers, originally all Europeans and European-Americans, but now, involving some competition from the Chinese – together with shameless local collaborators. How do we begin to account for the significant contributions of Africans, Arabs, Indians, and native citizens of the Americas to what is gleefully and generally regarded as the achievements of European countries, and, especially, these United States? These contributions are in all the fields, one may add.

As it pertains to Africa, though, it must be said that the vast majority of their leadership in recent history and contemporary times, has remained an assemblage of reprobates, thieves, visionless pretenders to the throne, shameless potentates, incompetent seat-warmers, and unworthy inheritors of an otherwise noble pedigree. Even Ethiopia, that great land of both historical and mystical significance, that land of proud and resourceful people which was never colonized by any foreign country or power, has decided to be notionally colonized, in the 21st century, by China.

Immanuel Kant (1724 - 1804)

A refreshing change, as we shall now study the works of a decent German philosopher, Immanuel Kant. We shall distill the relevant elements of the Kantian Doctrine from his 1785 work, "Groundwork for The Metaphysics of Morals", and particularly rely on the able translation and analysis undertaken by Allen W. Wood, as well as the seminal papers by Shelly Kagan, Marcia Baron, and J.B. Schneewind. For, you see, Immanuel Kant was truly one of the philosophical greats of all time. This deep and prolific thinker impacted mankind significantly with the profundity of his thoughts, which covered a wide range, from Metaphysics to Epistemology to Moral Philosophy to Political Philosophy to Aesthetics, all the way to Cosmogony. He wrote copiously as well.

The dry and elevated ideas of this substantial human being, make the penetration of his mind, the interpretation of his ideas, particularly challenging, hence our deepest gratitude to the Kantian Scholars referenced above. Kant gave the world the concept of Transcendental Idealism, wherein space, time, and causation are, but, mere sensibilities whose nature is unknowable. He synthesized modern rationalism with empiricism, and formulated what he called "Critical Philosophy" which rested on the tripod of Critique of Reason, Critique of Practical Reason, as well as Critique of the Power of Judgment. He is best known for his supreme standard of morality, the "Categorical Imperative", which, for him, is a rationally necessary and unconditional standard of morality, to which all humans most conform, whatever the desires, inclinations, and preferences to the contrary. This great man, who got his first Ph.D. in 1755, and the second one in 1770, was born in Konigsberg in the then East Prussia, near the Baltic Sea, far removed from the German heartland; his hometown has since been renamed Kaliningrad and is presently in Russia, a consequences of the geopolitical fluidity, adjustments and realities in that Region of the world.

Since our interest is (mercifully) narrowly focused on his Political and Moral Philosophy, we should immediately consider the Second Formulation of his Moral Law, that is, the Formula of Humanity as End in Itself: "Act so that you use humanity, as much in your person, as in the person of every other, always at the same time as end and never merely as means." His Third Formula, which is the Formula of the Realm of Ends, is: "Act in accordance with maxims of a universally legislative member, for a merely possible realm of ends." For him, only a *good will* can put gifts of nature (understanding, wit, power of judgment, power, wealth, honor, courage, resoluteness, persistence, temperament, etc.) to good use, otherwise, they can be misapplied, thereby making them extremely evil and harmful.

By this formulation, Kant is obviously instructing us on the need for restraint, temperance, and conduct in the overall interest of the polity, rather than giving free rein to our natural instincts. Here, he departs significantly from Nietzsche and Hegel. For Kant, good character is indispensable; "a *good will* to correct their influence on the mind", because power, wealth, and status can lead to arrogance. He advocates for moderation, self-control, and sober reflection as the defining essence of a person, her worth, but the principles of a *good will* are needed to purpose these ingredients and attributes to positive ends; here, "good" must be good in itself, and not made good by its achievements. His reference is to the intrinsic and unconditional full worth, and not the utilitarian value of "good" conduct, and this is guided by the Categorical Imperative, a principle of Reason, which is valid for, and binding on, all. Kant, like other philosophers before him, especially the Greeks, admits that character is difficult to cultivate or maintain, and must involve the constant repressing of natural instincts. In this regard, duty is "without any other motive of vanity or utility to self." Humans, but especially leaders, should act, not by inclination, but from duty, because "the moral worth of the action lies not in the effect to be expected from it, thus also not in any principle of action which needs to get its motive from this expected benefit."

Noting "the fragility and impurity of human nature", as exemplified in the Lutheran translation of Genesis 6:5, "And God saw the wickedness of man was great in the earth, and that every imagination of the thoughts of his heart was only evil continually", Kant emphasized further the need for refinement and character, guided by principles and Will; but a positive and moderated Will nonetheless, not Nietzsche's "Will To Power." The Kantian Will is a "faculty of choosing ONLY that which reason, independently of inclination, recognizes as practically necessary." This Will must, therefore, accord with Reason, and not hypothesis; it must have the "command" of reason, as he put it. Yet, another elegant way of introducing his Categorical Imperative. The referenced action "is objectively necessary without reference to any aim, that is, without any other end"; this kind of action is simply an apodictically practical principle; without attachments, but pure and necessary in its own right.

Proceeding further, Kant writes that: "whoever wills the end, also wills (insofar as reason has decisive influence on his actions), the means that are indispensably necessary to it that are in his control." Philosophical elocution!!! It is important to underscore the point that Kant made the fundamental assumption that human beings are rational beings (*mundus intelligibilis*) whose actions, whose morality, will be predicated on the autonomy of their Will, directed towards the ineluctable Imperative of Reason. Freedom, for him, is the quality of the Will of all rational beings, and reason distinguishes humans from other beings (animals) and things. While his optimistic perception of humanity is noted with appreciation, historical realities belie this optimism.

In Kant's considered view, "interest" is that through which reason becomes practical, that is, the Cause determining the Will. Only humans can take an interest in something; other creatures, without reason, only feel sensible or sensory impulses. When reason is directed by the Categorical Imperative for all, there is growth, security, order, and an abundance of public goods for all. A bit idealistic, one may add. Both St. Thomas Aquinas (in his *Summa Theologiae*) and Kant agree that morality involves the Law. For the former, this is mostly the Natural Law, written in the heart/ conscience--put there by God. For Kant, our reason gives us the Law; every member of the society both legislates the Law and obeys it. He departs from Orthodoxy when he insists that morality is a human creation, owing directly to our rationality....

Both paraphrasing and quoting extensively from Kant, duty is not a matter of "affection", but of commitment. "One acts from duty not by virtue of doing what is right because one wants to do what is right; rather, one does what is right because rightness makes a claim on one. One recognizes that one should." When we engage in "moral deliberation", and in recognition of the equal worth of all rational human beings, we take into consideration the welfare of others, as well as our own. This intention, this guidance by an over-arching (Categorical) Imperative is at the core of his disagreement with Utilitarian thinkers like Bentham and John Stuart Mill. It is significant and disappointing that, with all his assumed enlightenment and emphasis on him, Mill was a racial bigot. Mill wrote that 'Despotism is a legitimate mode of government in dealing with barbarians, provided the end be their improvement.' referring to all non-Europeans as barbarians."

In particular, John Rawls disagreed with Kant's position because it ignores "the distinction between persons." He also had fundamental issues with all humans having "a single prudential reasoner or benevolent despot", however categorized or defined.

Early Christians like St. Paul, and, subsequently, Pufendorf, theorized that morality consisted in the obedience to Law, God's Law no doubt. Law is the command of a Superior, and only God's commands can establish morality for all humans. Using this model, God cannot be constrained by morality because God has no superior. Given the attributes assigned to this Divine Being, the chances of a tyrannical God become very slim. Is this really the case? Is God always gentle and tolerant? The eternal damnation for "sinners", the specter of hellfire; the destruction of the world over Adam's seemingly minor transgression of disobedience, would point to a less-than-restrained or tempered God. It is significant that Kant placed the leader above the law and the members of the civic society; he preferred Monarchy.

It might be useful to quickly juxtapose Kant's formulation on morality against that of David Hume, the eminent Scottish Empiricist, philosopher and contemporary of his. Hume's idea that morality had nothing to do with God was a very radical idea at their time. He wrote that morality was causally-determined in a causally-determined nature; humans are just animals, with no special status or dignity from the rest. He went further by suggesting that religious people conceived of a supra-natural spiritual world -- which humans must be a part of -- to show that they were different from other animals. In essence, man's hubris created religion. In conclusion, Hume states that our moral knowledge entitles us to assume that we are made in God's image.

Kant rejects Hume's position and asserts that we are not merely naturally beings, like animals, and that morality shows our Free Will, which animals lack, being that they are merely driven by natural reflexes and automaticity. When appetite is invested "with an opinion of attaining", this becomes hope, which animals cannot articulate. The same appetite, without such an opinion, causes despair, aversion, and inspires an opinion of hurt and fear from the object. He further instructs that no other living creature has the seed of religion or the capacity to be religious, this being yet another distinguishing feature of humanity.

It is remarkable that Kant, like several other philosophers, traces the religious fervor to the fear of death and the ignorance of causes; the fear of the unknown made worse by man's hubris. Without seeing the cause, man settles for an invisible force or "power agent", which he calls The Omnipotent, One God, First Cause, First Mover, or the First and Eternal Cause of all Things. Essentially, for him, the gods, which started out as ghosts (called *imagines* and *umbrae* in Latin) were created by human fear. Underlying this position is a fundamental assumption of the validity of the Creation narrative; the only problem is that Evolution has been proven, while the former remains powerful and relevant only on account of the abundant psychological and mythical investments in it by vast sections of humanity.

It is logically impossible to reconcile Creation and Evolution, especially when the logical progression gets to the first atoms and particles. In developing the structure of religion, according to Kant, people simply project the elements of their ideal relationships with other humans: in the form of gifts, petitions, gratitude, submission of body, sober behavior and consideration. In other words, therefore, the elements and seeds of religion are: opinion of ghosts, ignorance of first and second causes, devotion towards what we fear (including death), ceremonies, and reliance on the scariest declarations of the prognostics in our midst, who, one might add, do not defer their reward to a later time, or to the post-mortem stage. These precepts also condition men to lean towards obedience, laws, peace, charity, and civil society, which is a totality of what earthly kings require of their subjects. The partnership of heaven and earth is made whole with priests ostensibly representing heaven, while the monarch is the manifest human king. The Ambassadors of Heaven -- they, being human as well, with worldly needs and inclinations -- demand full obedience and patronage, in exchange for the salvation of believers' souls after death. Kant clearly understood the useful role which religion plays in civic order and concord.

While we undertake the dynamics and structure of political, social, and economic systems, as we are doing, a discussion of the trigger-thoughts, which coalesced over time to produce them, becomes essential. Religion is an integral part of every society, so it is necessary to analyze the views of the dominant thinkers on this critical subject. Moral Philosophy, a major component of which derives from Religion, provides the theoretical foundation and principled reinforcement for the value placed on human life, the notional understanding of the intrinsic equality of all humans, the political rights (and duties) which are driven by this understanding, how the State treats the weak, infirm, or poor in the society, the acceptable norms and taboos of governance, treatment of the elderly, accountability matrix, all the way to Immigration policies.

He reminds us that men have worshipped all sorts of objects historically, and ascribed divinity to natural phenomena and regular occurrences like accidents, time, night, day, peace, love, contention, virtue, losses, honor, health, fever, and the like, which they prayed for, or against. He wrote that "there was nothing which a poet could introduce as a person in his poem which they did not make either a god or devil", with "pretended experience" and "pretended revelation" co-mingling with superstitions that he traced to the reliance on the priests of Delphi, Delos, Ammon, and other famous oracles, for their prosperity, safety, soul-security, and the like. He writes further that the priests dish out "ambiguous and senseless answers"; ambiguous by design (to own the event both ways), and absurd, for deliberateness, shock, and acceptance due to the audacious incredulity.

In his words, "so easy are men to be drawn to believe anything from such men as have gotten credit with them; and can, with gentleness and dexterity, take hold of their fear and ignorance"; in other words, the credibility invested in religious leaders empowers them to speak authoritatively on subjects that confound mankind, especially the fear of death, adversities, as well as the ignorance of metaphysical and cosmological subjects.

Without confidence in these priests, their viewpoints, rendered as immutable and authentic divine truths, will not be believed, accepted, or taken seriously. Confidence!!! He writes further that "the first founders and legislators of religion, whose ends were to keep the people in obedience and peace, have in all places taken care: to imprint in their minds a belief that those precepts which they gave concerning religion might not be thought to proceed from their own device, but from the dictates of some god or other spirit, or else that they themselves were of a higher nature than mere mortals…."

It bears reading Kant even further in his own words, as follows: "Mahomet/ Mohammed, to set up his new religion, pretended to have conferences with the Holy Ghost in form of a dove; they have had a care to make it believed that the same things were displeasing to the gods which were forbidden by the laws; to prescribe ceremonies, supplications, sacrifices, and festivals by which they were to believe that the anger of the gods might be appeased, and that ill success in war, great contagions of sickness, earthquakes, and each man's private misery came from the anger of the gods; and their anger from the neglect of their worship, or the forgetting or mistaking some point of the ceremony required."

For him, this template helps avoid a mutiny against the governors (leaders) by making the masses blame themselves for their misfortunes, rather than holding their leaders responsible and accountable. The masses must be kept busy with perpetual guilt, pomp, ceremony, and public games in honor of the gods. Like other philosophers who have "dared" to apply some basic wisdom to the entire Construct, Kant highlights the incongruity of the concept of "The Chosen Ones." For him, God must be assumed to be the King of the whole earth; choosing one tribe as his favorites will be identical to a General in command of the whole Army, who chooses a Regiment or Company of his own; "that which taketh away the reputation of wisdom in him that formeth a religion, or added to it when it is already formed, is the enjoining of a belief of contradictories: for both parts of a contradiction cannot possibly be true, and, therefore, to enjoin the belief of them is an argument of ignorance, which detects the author in that, and discredits him in all things else he shall propound as from revelation supernatural: which revelation a man may indeed have of many things above, but of nothing against natural reason."

Reading some of these great philosophers in their words, conveys their message better than any paraphrasing can possibly achieve; Kant instructs further when he writes "that which men reap benefit by to themselves, they are thought to do for their own sakes, and not for the love of others." Believers need to see miracles and pageantry, in order to retain their faith, so this is contrived for them. In the Catholic Church of Kant's time (and moderated somewhat through contemporary times due to challenges from without, and not any altruistic decision or revelatory mandate), some of these were in the form of crowning monarchs, excommunication, imposed penance, deposition of kings (for example, Childeric of France, who was deposed by Pope Zachary when popes still had both the ultimate ecclesiastical and mundane powers -- powers that they serially abused until the countervailing forces of history and the Enlightenment pushed back), clergy being above the jurisdiction of the King, imposition of vales of purgatory, all of this because "dominion over other men was necessary for their own preservation."

This deep thinker of the Enlightenment Era further observes that the three causes of quarrel among humans, deriving from their nature, are: competition (invade for gain), diffidence (invade for safety), and glory (invade for reputation and admiration). When men are not bound by a common power, which binds all of them in awe, they are in a state of war against one another. In this state, they rely on their own individual strengths for security. There is no Industry or Investment, as there is no point when there is continual fear, danger of violent death, and the life of man is solitary, poor, nasty, brutish, and short, to reference Hobbes. "To this war of every man against every man, ... nothing can be unjust." The notions of right and wrong; justice and injustice; have no place in this dangerous polity. Where there is no common power, there is no law; where there is no law, no injustice. "Force and fraud are, in a war, the two cardinal virtues." Many societies around the world can still relate to this observation and reality, explaining their poor outcomes in the delivery of public goods to their citizens.

The same impetus for religion keeps coming back in Kant's work, namely, the fear of death, "desire of such things as are necessary for commodious living", as well as a hope, by their longing, to obtain them. In his words, the law of nature (*jus naturale*) is the liberty each man has to use his own power as he will himself for the preservation of his own nature, that is, his life, and doing anything, in his own judgment and reason, he considers apt for this end. In this construct, peace involves a surrender of the rights of nature by all men, which only enlightened self-interest can yield. This Right is laid aside, either by simply renouncing it, or by transferring it to another (a potentate) -- in expectation of some right reciprocally transferred to himself, or for some other good he hoped for; in other words, the signs of a Contract can be expressed or by inference. The mutual transferring of rights is called a Contract, which connotes Trust, Faith, and an obligatory Covenant. It is remarkable how this position coheres with Rousseau's on the formal foundation and *raison d'être* of a political society; the entire focus of this work, as well as the evaluation thereof.

A breach of the peace in this context could involve, for example, the arrogant desiring of more than one's share. It must be noted, though, that given Kant's understanding of human nature and his resultant circumspection, he urges that each person delays and withholds this surrender of Rights until others have surrendered theirs; the problems with this are numerous, but not relevant to our central argument. Referencing Hobbes, Kant writes that the condition of nature is a condition of war among men, and that the transfer of Rights to a Common Power, must entail that Power being invested with the right and power to compel performance and compliance by all, in return for the delivery of discrete and common public goods by that inheritor of the aggregate pool of Rights. For him, "the bonds of words are too weak to bridle men's ambition, avarice, anger, and other passions, without the fear of some coercive power." The Right of the Government, so formed, includes collecting levies for collective security, public administration, etc. To make covenants with brute beasts is impossible, he informs further. Paraphrasing him, to covenant is an act of the Will; an act and the last act, of deliberation. To promise that which is impossible is not to covenant. Men can be freed from their Covenant either by performing on it ("the natural end of obligation", or by being forgiven ("the restitution of liberty").

Demonstrating a clear understanding of human nature, Kant writes that men will naturally prefer to pursue wealth, glory, command, and sensual pleasure, unless constrained by a Force or Power beyond the individual, but this Force or Power must be equitable, fair, responsive, and efficient in delivering common benefits, services, and goods. Fear is the most potent passion for all men, he writes. Going back to the formulation that found resonance among many German and Enlightenment philosophers, Kant instructs us that Religion is the fear of invisible spirits (which are remote), while Civil Society involves the fear of legal vengeance for transgressions (which is direct and guaranteed), but both still involve fear of something. Human beings are restrained from pursuing their "natural" passions by terror of some punishment greater than the benefit from breaching their Covenant. This fear and justice must be balanced, consistent, and transparent. Covenants without the sword and effective protection for all, are impotent words.

This coercive power is domiciled in the Commonwealth made up of "enlightened" individuals, that is, those who can reason for themselves; men that think themselves equal (drawing from the Law of Nature wherein they can harm one another), will not enter into conditions of peace except on conditions of equality. The response to Kant should be: how about the cruel and unequal treatment that was meted out to serfs and people conscripted, shackled, and exploited for physical labor - - who were called slaves, even as slavery was never their natural condition, and that this condition was imposed by their fellow humans? For, slavery persisted in one form or another in Kant's Europe and European-controlled reaches of the world, even as those severely-maltreated and dehumanized people were always free in their parts of the world, where every one of their kith and kin remained entirely free -- a status that was yet again assaulted by the incursion, indeed the invasion, of Europeans into their own space and native land.

The public goods desired or demanded by any group bound by this Social Contract will be contingent on certain values that are common to humans, *sui generis*, for example, freedom, private space, private ownership of economic resources; services and goods that reflect their stage of development and technology; as well as the peculiar requirements deriving from their environment, culture, and norms. In all of this, the human tendency towards intemperance seems to be played down, even as it is a dominant and consequential manifestation of our imperfection. He writes further that "Moral Philosophy is nothing else but the science of what is good and evil in the conversation and society of mankind"; in other words, the Science of Virtue and Evil.

The concept of the legal and civic person (an extension of the actual/ physical person) had been given the most eloquent definition by Cicero in his statement that *unus sustineo tres personas: mei, adversa rii, et judicis*, which can be translated into English to mean "I bear three persons: my own, my adversary's, and the judge's." The civic person is an artificial person, yet deserving of, and granted, specific Rights and dignity, as a member of the political society. "A multitude of men are made one person when they are by one man, or one person, represented; so that it be done with the consent of every one of that multitude in particular ...unity cannot otherwise be understood in multitude."

They are bound by artificial chains called civil laws. Since everyone cannot rule, for there to be peace, and since the political society is formed for the preservation of the members seeking to avoid the miserable conditions of the state of nature (in which every man is in a state of war against every man), a mechanism must be worked out to achieve majority rule; that is a Commonwealth formed on the basis of the majority preferences, as objectively and transparently determined. If and when this is not done, the recourse would be to the natural state where justice, moderation, equity, and mercy will be absent.

In the Commonwealth or political society so formed, the members have the right to expect security from injury caused by one another, and from outsiders; Law Enforcement, Judicial System, Homeland Security, Border Security, Defense, Protection of Global Interests, etc. The members also recognize the need for a continuous government, to avoid a slippage or reversion to the dangerous and unstable state of nature. Man's nature continues to be a challenge, however, given the recurring inclination towards competition for honor and dignity, as well as their envy and hatred towards one another. This great thinker has continued to affect mankind centuries after his death. Mihan and Anca Badescu, in their very useful compendium, The Origin and Evolution of Civil Society, attributed the Wilsonian thinking that guided the Versailles Treaty of 1918 -- by which the First World War was settled, as having been considerably influenced by Kant. Quoting them directly as they paraphrased him, they wrote:

"The conditions of a perpetual peace among peoples would be achievable through a number of international and internal measures. Thus:

- no peace treaties must contain the hidden germs of a future war;
- no autonomous State, large or small, can ever be and by any means (inheritance, exchange, purchase, donation) passed on to the patrimony of another;
- permanent armies must be suppressed with time;
- State debts that are related to the foreign trade of States should be avoided;
- no State must forcefully interfere with the governance and organization of another;
- no State, in war with another, must allow for hostility so serious that it makes impossible the confidence in a future peace;
- political organization in any State must be republican (constitutional);
- international law must be based on a federalization of free States;
- the right to international citizenship must be limited by the conditions of universal hospitality."

Though Man enters into this Commonwealth (*Civitas*) or political society as a rational being, and out of his enlightened self-interest, this same reason occasionally becomes a problem, especially when the untrammeled passions of humanity cannot be effectively reconciled with the rational civic obligations.

The Commonwealth connotes an artificial eternity of civic life; the right of succession beyond one potentate. Invoking Hobbes once more, Kant describes the leader so invested with the collective mandate to govern, and to discharge the joint mandate of the civic society, earning the sustained loyalty and cooperation of the members of the political society/ the citizens, in our common parlance, only by governing in a judicious and transparent manner, while providing the requisite public goods.

Peace, delivery of public goods, and common defense were particularly crucial in an era of impermanence and conflict. In the absence thereof, the mandate becomes invalid, *ipso facto*.

This reminds one of the standard Aragonese Oath in the 16th century upon receiving a new King:

"We, who are worth as much as you, take you as our king, provided that you preserve our laws and liberties, and if not, not."

Clearly, there was a correlation between privilege and service, between leadership and accountability, between assumed powers and the actuality of its origins ...... unlike the experience of vast sections of the world in the past couple of decades, even with political independence and nominal sovereignty. In the Kantian thesis, sovereignty by institution (which could loosely be interpreted as democracy presently), involved voluntary covenanting. "The sovereign is invested with a lot of powers; he acts for us who gave him the power and always."

This Leviathan is not a Generalissimo, over and above other civic participants. Kant believed in Monarchy, though, even as he assumed that Monarchy, Democracy, and Aristocracy could not be split since, for him, the sovereign power was indivisible. It would appear that a few societies have effectively adopted this precept effectively in the modern era, while the predominant impulse is to, rightly, delineate and minimize the powers concentrated in an individual, for the identified reasons of man's (woman's) carnal and defective nature. Power corrupts, and absolute power corrupts absolutely, the sage instructed us...

It has to be noted that where public and private interests are most closely aligned, the society is most advanced. We shall be explicating this point further down in this narrative. Kant did not recommend Democracy as a form of government, because of the identifiable problems we have seen with its assumed practice in vast sections of the world that pretend to be democratic.

He distinguished the concept of service (*servire*) from savings (*servare*) for a vital reason. For him, a crime becomes a sin consisting in the commitment by deed or word of that which is forbidden by the Law, or the omission of what it has commanded, "so that every crime is a sin, but not every sin is a crime." Where Law ceases, sin ceases.

Having been instructed by Kant and Hobbes, we should proceed to that other eminent and influential philosopher, John Locke.

John Locke (1632-1704)

Physician, philosopher, empiricist, Father of Liberalism, economist, and psychologist, this distinguished English man of ideas, was heavily influenced in his empiricism by Francis Bacon, while he influenced later thinkers like Voltaire, Rousseau, as well as movements like the American Revolution and the eventual Declaration of Independence. He made significant contributions to Political Philosophy, Epistemology, Economics, and Psychology. His Theory of Mind is generally recognized, for example, as the beginning of the conceptions of identity and the self, and provided a significant divergence from the prevailing Catholic Orthodoxy, which located the person within the larger social construct. This bold deviation provided subsequent thrusts for the Rights of the Person, the French Revolution, and the modified interpretations of those rights as we now have them. He enrolled at Oxford University in 1652 and disagreed with Cartesianism by insisting on the *tabula rasa* format of the human mind and that everything we know is from learned experiences. Descartes insisted on our essence being defined by the fact that we could think; *Cogito Ergo Sum.*

Locke emphatically condemned slavery as a vile and miserable practice. We shall be looking at his "Two Treatises on Government", for instructions on the purpose of governments. He writes that "government is for the preservation of every man's right and property, by saving him from the violence or injury of others, is for the good of the governed; the government wages violence only against common enemies, and to force the people to observe the positive laws of nature, for the public good." He does not accept any Divine Right of Kings. For him, "political power … is the right to make laws, with penalties of death, and, consequently, all less penalties for the regulating and preserving of property, and of employing the force of the community in the execution of such laws and in the defense of the Commonwealth from common injury, and all this only for the public good" … not personal goods. For Locke, power derives from the natural state of perfect freedom in which all men can order their actions, dispose of their possessions as they think fit, within the bounds of the law of Nature, without asking leave or depending upon the will of any other man. "A state of equality without subordination or subjugation." Reciprocal love sustains the fabric of the society. Idealism …

Natural Reason directs the laws and canons; in this state, there is liberty without license. No abuses or excesses. Being equal and independent, no one ought to harm another in his life, health, liberty, or possessions. In his affirmation of the Creation Story, Locke writes that all men are the workmanship of "One Wise Maker" -- infinitely wise, omnipotent, and sovereign. No human is made for another human's uses, in his strong condemnation of serfdom and slavery. In his ideal society, punishment is meted out when someone has taken another's life or has denied freedom to another. Justice should serve for reparation and restraint/ deterrence. The applicable punishment must match the offence, and restitution must be made to the victim. When someone runs afoul of the law of nature, that person declares himself to live by another rule other than that of reason and common equality, which constitute God's measure for men.

He writes further that every offence that can be committed in a state of nature, may, in the state of nature, also be punished equally in a Commonwealth. Men remain in their state of nature until they give their **consent** to become members of some political society. Members quit their natural executive power, and surrender it to the community, which becomes the umpire for all. The civil/ political society is thus invested with the power to enact transgressions for offences. From this state of nature, the Commonwealth is formed, which has Executive, Judicial, and Legislative powers. Government has no other end/ purpose except the preservation of property. Men give their consent and form political societies, to enable the peaceable and secure enjoyment of their properties. For Locke, majority rule or consent is expressed as the Will of the Commonwealth. This majority rule is not democracy, but simply an independent community/*civitas*.

The legislative power is the first duty of a Commonwealth; this supreme power is also sacred. This supremacy does not imply arbitrariness, as the power is limited to the public good of the society. They cannot take the citizens' property, or rule by arbitrary decrees or improvised legislation. For multiple reasons, Locke prescribes a part-time legislature. To this effect, he wrote, and we quote extensively, that "because the laws which are constantly to be executed, and whose force is always to continue, may be made in a little time, therefore, there is no need that the legislative should be always in being, not having always business to do. And because it may be too great temptation to human frailty, apt to grasp power, for the same persons who have the power of making laws to also have in their hands the power to execute them, whereby they may exempt themselves from obedience to the laws they make, and suit the law, both in its making and execution, to their own private advantage, and thereby come to have a distinct interest from the rest of the community, contrary to the end of society and government...."

The evident experience in various "democracies", which diverge completely from this prescriptive norm, underscore the prescience of this great thinker. He clearly understood human nature. The need for an Executive is to separate powers and avoid the risk of concentration of governmental powers in the same hands; we also need to maintain the continuity of government and execution of the laws made by a part-time legislature. If there is a gang-up or a lack of oversight, however, the reason for this dichotomy is defeated, and the costs attached thereto simply wasted. This incestuous relationship between the two arms of government is the recipe for corruption, at the expense of the larger society. The experience in most countries points to the observance of this strict bifurcation more in the breach than compliance, with the result that the delivery of public goods recedes in the order of priorities, and personal enrichment, mutual support and protection, as well as overall corruption replace the objective principles of governance. Legislators become legislooters. Locke also warned about legislative despotism arising from the lack of accountability to the larger society or Commonwealth.

While we must applaud Locke's foresight and institutional mechanisms to check the tendency towards absolutism, it is fair to observe that he could not have anticipated the utter helplessness of the members of the Commonwealth in modern societies. When he, therefore, writes that "in all states and conditions, the true remedy of force without authority is to oppose force to it", he clearly did not anticipate the desperate clinging to power, the prone to abuse, the corruption of State Security Forces, and the grave risk borne by citizens who oppose or protest against these self-serving government officials, especially in weak and failing States. They simply unleash the Military and Police on hapless citizens, because these deluded people assume they are the State, and must never be opposed. A slave has a right to resist his yoke, to the point of killing his oppressor. "He who makes an attempt to enslave me thereby puts himself into a state of war with me"; that person seeks to take everything else, including my life, since freedom is the foundation of everything else. While we accept his definition of tyranny as the exercise of power beyond right, which nobody can have a right to, our contemporary experience and observation in vast sections of the world clearly point to the people in government abandoning the public goods, to focus on their "private and separate advantages -- ambition, greed, revenge, covetousness, and other irregular passions."

Locke quotes King James as follows: " whereas the proud and ambitious tyrant thinks that his kingdom and people are only ordained for satisfaction of his desires and unreasonable appetites, the righteous and just king does, by the contrary, acknowledge himself to be ordained for the procuring of the wealth and property of his people...." Well, Locke did not anticipate the brigade of insensitive looters, little fellows with Messiah Complex, and primitive reflexes who are at the helm of significant sections of the world, especially in Africa, the Middle East, Latin America, Russia, North Korea, and other tyrannical systems. While China has clearly delivered on tangible public goods for their teeming population, State Absolutism remains in place.

The state of slavery, in his view, is a state of war continued between a conqueror and a captive. "God, in His own judgment, decided that man should not be alone, so, by putting man under strong obligations of necessity, convenience, and inclination, drives man into a society." Enslaving man negates from this Divine Plan. Locke advocated for religious tolerance, and, like Pufendorf, St. Augustine, St. Aquinas, and Grotius, believed in the Natural Law. In the state of nature, for him, peace, goodwill, mutual assistance, and preservation, are guaranteed, or should be guaranteed. The problem in the society arises when the "inconstant, uncertain, unknown, and arbitrary will of man" is not checked or controlled positively. In Locke's view, God is an infinitely Wise Maker (a Creator).

When he suggests that a government could be dissolved through civil disobedience, we can see some naiveté, reading his thoughts in the modern era. This subject actually raises the fundamental question: Is it ever right to disobey the Government? Let's assess this in detail. The government represents the State, which, in turn, usually comprises various peoples or nations who have come together for the attainment of general peace and the furthering of united or common goals. The contrarian theory on the formation of the State focuses generally on the initial state of war that preceded the formation of the State, this State being formed to prevent further "wars." Locke, Engels, and Hobbes had varying concepts of this central theory. D.D. Raphael says that: "the State rests on a Social Contract, on Consent, represents the general will, secures justice, and pursues the general interest." On his part, man has to obey the laws of the State. An anonymous source writes that "the body politic, therefore, is also a moral being possessed of a will; and this general will, which tends always to the preservation and welfare of the whole and of every part, and is the source of the laws, constitutes for all members of the State in their relations to one another and to it, the rule of what is just or unjust." This shows that the State decides what constitutes justice or injustice, and this is codified in laws and conventions. A basic assumption of justice is that all men have equal rights. Law then becomes the aggregate of principles, procedures, institutions, and practices, which guide a State in the management of communal relations.

Certain conflicts cannot be resolved without the assistance of the government. Law and justice safeguard the process, which the government serves. Given the existence of law, the force of legal sanctions produces the distinction between the lawbreaker and he who does not come into conflict with any legal rule. Conformism in this sense is rewarded with the absence of punishment.

This position presupposes that the government has the authority to legislate for all persons, and that a particular government has jurisdiction within a specific geographical space.

In an ideal situation, the government has to guarantee the agreed personal and property rights of the citizens, and also provide public goods, as objectively defined. In richer and more developed States, there is even the right to security in the event of unemployment (as demonstrated during this pandemic in societies like the United States, the United Kingdom, Japan, Germany, and France), sickness, disability, old age, or other circumstances that impair the person's ability to earn an income, or a good income due to circumstances beyond the person's control. While compulsory education up until High School prevails in developed societies, in vast sections of the world, the foremost need is to achieve literacy at all.

When some people argue against disobeying the State, they generally assume that the State fulfills its obligations to its citizens, and also in a fair and just manner. When this is the case, it becomes incumbent on the citizens to reciprocate accordingly. The subscription or obedience to one code of law is assumed to foster unity and help in minimizing the incidence of conflict. From this prism, the primary purpose of establishing the State, which is to discontinue the war that characterized the state of nature in which everyone was the master, is defeated by a regression towards uncontrollable conflict. In the state of nature, the conflicts could not be resolved by mutual efforts because there was no central basis for judging what was right or wrong. Again, proponents of an absolute obedience to the State suggest that, given the circumstances of its emergence, the State should have what Gerald Cohen calls "legitimate power", that is, power backed by authority. Members of a State sacrifice their individual rights for a higher goal -- cessation of "war." This position affirms, without any apportionment of corollary responsibility to the Government, that it is indefensible to disobey the government for the SOLE reason that one's "selfish" interest has not been satisfied. We are told that personal discomfiture, on its own, is not important, and that it is the general interest that matters.

Some people have to make laws while others obey. Since the possibility of a direct divine intervention in our political life is impossible, a select group of men and women has to constitute our government. This "absolute obedience" School insists that we should ensure that the process that produces the government is unassailable, so that obedience to State laws is non-negotiable. Well, practical reality belies this idealistic posturing, so the conclusion of unconditional and absolute obedience cannot stand. Any dissatisfied person should seek recourse or remedy in the courts, we are told, but the real corrupting feature of governments is ignored. When the Executive, for example, appoints members of the Judiciary, the environment and incentive for collusion and favoritism are thus created. We learn further that there can be no offence without a law (whether written or unwritten). This School further posits that people give either express or tacit consent to the government, as constituted. The Principle of the Rule of Law, which incorporates the notions of supremacy of the law, equality before the law, impartiality, the unethical nature of one trying one's case, etc., is also cited in furtherance of this position, while ignoring the several and common examples in breach thereof. We are told that the government manifests its intentions in its laws. At the foundation of this thesis is the idea that, while the government guarantees the rights of its citizens, it reserves the right to curtail the same when the interest of the majority is threatened.

The government, we are further told, could also interfere with fundamental human rights in periods of emergency (for example, in war situations or during aggravated political uprisings), and as a result of the conviction of a person by constituted law courts, for the violation of State laws. Here, the principle of "Desert" -- by which people get what they deserve -- is also used to support the proposition of no dissent. The fact, however, is that reality debunks these idealistic presentations of governments, or, at least, most of them around the world. There are several instances to this effect, in which case, it has no right of recipience if one is to adopt the contrarian but realistic view. In the under-developed countries, for example, the majority of the citizens struggle to exist; they struggle with poverty, lack of housing, poor sanitary conditions, lack of potable water, public health, security of lives and property; as well as qualitative education. It may be a factor that the resources are inadequate, but the fact remains that the government has not satisfied its own part of the bargain. When the real facts of wastage and corruption are considered, the non-performance becomes even more inexcusable.

The Principle of Rule of Law extols the virtue of equality in all its facets. A cursory review reveals that this construct is largely utopian. There is something particularly disingenuous, for example, in the Greek, European, and American societies of old, wherein the obedience of all to the law was expected and demanded, even as they stratified some human beings outside the baseline of political rights. Was it, therefore, ethical and proper to expect such marginalized and oppressed people to still obey the laws? I would say NO!!! Furthermore, when a government, however constituted, proceeds to convert the instruments of the State to private and corrupt end, or embarks on egregious acts of discrimination and injustice against a group (for example, deploying revenues generated from their Region exclusively or disproportionately towards the development of favored Regions, entrenched discrimination on the basis of ethnicity, race, religion, or politics in appointments, benefits, and infrastructure), such a government must forfeit its expectation of a universal obedience to its laws. Objective fairness is a cardinal element of Statecraft and Law; in its absence, the oppressed and marginalized must feel free to withdraw from the government and stop obeying its unjust laws. Any obedience so obtained is through coercion, and this is not sustainable. Governance by coercion exerts a major burden on the essential fabric, cohesion, and health of the State. Citizenship cannot be forced but must remain voluntary. Is it right to obey laws made by a powerful, privileged, and rich few, especially if those laws are oppressive? NO!!!

Engels writes that the State "seemingly stands above society", and that, while professing neutrality, the State is actually used to protect and project the interests of the powerful, to the detriment of the powerless. Such a government should not expect absolute compliance with its laws. Political obligation entails an element of constraint, and when this constraint is founded on the fear of consequences of actions, these obligations cannot be said to be merely voluntary. The minority (so-called elite) subjugates the majority in the name of false ideals. The government arrogates to itself the power of near-omniscience. The government is composed of, and controlled by, by persons who belong to the Ruling Class, and who have a vested interest in the perpetuation of the status quo. Opposition is stifled, the powerless are bureaucratically and subtly debarred from making any lasting political impact on the fabric of the State.

In one's view, any "normal situation" that is based on fundamental injustice needs to be upturned and challenged. To the extent that agencies of the government are used to pursue these repressive policies, the citizens are right in disobeying the government.

What is right is not necessarily what is legal. The law is made by the powerful, and is likely, therefore, to punish non-compliance with their law. The fact that people do not question State laws often is due to a few factors: fear of reprisals by the State, lack of mobilization, disagreement on the premise/s for the protest, compromise of some opinion leaders by the government, etc. Are the more privileged necessarily the conformists? No. The fact is that they have the means to literally stand above the law and, therefore, are hardly prosecuted for offences, which earn the less-privileged different penalties. Furthermore, the extenuating contrivances which insulate some from the application of the Law are duly noted, including the absolute immunity granted Monarchs like the Queen of England; Diplomatic Immunity; and variants of legislative, executive, and judicial immunity which several modern States have conferred on their most senior officials. With all these exemptions, do we still have equality before the law, especially when these same senior officials, with access to classified State secrets, State resources, the power of unchecked patronage, budgeting and borrowing powers, plus the self-imposed burden of funding extensive private, political networks, actually commit the "most senior" forms of harm against the State, or, at least, have the means to do so.

The State has universal and compulsory jurisdiction within restricted boundaries. Man does not choose where he is born but is assumed to be born with certain inalienable rights which include freedom of speech and of movement. Except for conscious and voluntary migration decisions, if we stick to the traditional model of people living in their native land, since the fact of this belonging was never voluntary from birth, is it fair to expect a reflexive compulsory obedience to all the lands of that land, even when they are evidently unjust and injurious to one?

Closely related to this consideration are the ideas of Tacit and Express Consent. Express Consent can only be given by naturalized citizens. Since natural-born citizens do not voluntarily enter into any contract of citizenship with the State or government, the latter has no right to impose its laws on the former. Thrasymachus and Hume agreed that the State arose from the acquisition of the monopoly of force by a few people. Such people imposed their Will on the masses, and, with time, obtained legitimacy by consent. Given the fact that one did not voluntarily enter into any "contract" of this sort, one should technically be free to disobey certain laws of the government that one finds reprehensible. Admittedly, this proposition could lead to anarchy if all and sundry decide not to obey different laws based on their choices or for no reason at all, but then some of the corruptive and abusive conduct of some government officials could also very easily lead to anarchy. What is the cure for divisive, unjust, self-serving government policies and laws in this context?

In a democracy, any law without the valid vote of a majority of the electorate or of its representatives may be disobeyed by a citizen. By the very fact of neglecting the majority vote, the essence of democracy is defeated, and all corollary expectations must be nullified thereto. Democracy seeks to uphold the will of the numerical majority of eligible voters, as objectively and transparently determined. Rigging elections thus becomes a clear negation of this precept. There is an inherent flaw in this "majority rule", because the majority may simply be wrong or ignorant or clannish or dangerously partisan or visionless, or all, as is the case in many so-called democracies across the world, but the majority decision and choice must be respected until structural issues are freely resolved within the polity.

An eminent international lawyer, Brierly, writes that "law is not just because it is binding, it is binding because it is just." Justice has often been taken to mean "fairness." However, though the two are synonymous terms, they do not connote "equality", as there are times when it is fair or just to give unequal parts of a thing to different people or groups of people. Some theorists have argued that civic equality is utopian because there are instances of inequality in every other area of life, for example, talents, abilities, height, and other such differentiators. A. J. Smith has even suggested that: "inequality among men is a rich source of much that is evil, but also of everything that is good." This sounds like the convenient position of the privileged, and clearly misses the point that the civic equality of all humans (denied in practice for too long in history, and still denied women and some minorities around the world to this day) is derived from their intrinsic worth and value as (common and equal) human beings, and does not preclude natural distinctions in life. Any government that enacts laws based on principles canvassed by Smith and his entourage, should expect the citizens to exercise their absolute duty of disobedience to those laws.

A basic tenet of justice is that it must not only be done but must also be seen to be done. The concept of punishment for infractions of the law in this context is not fundamentally an exercise in sadism but is designed as a deterrent to others. Where the law causes a man, in certain cases, to cease to be a person but a thing, there is no justice. Where no limit is set to the power of the State over those who break its laws (especially unjust laws), the whole legal framework should be overthrown and discarded.

It may also be proper for people to disobey the laws or decrees of a government, for example, by going on strike when the government introduces certain measures that will greatly depress the standard of living of the people. When the government, for example, implores the citizens to make sacrifices during an economic downturn, but the same government officials and their families continue to engage in waste and lifestyles of ostentation, the requested sacrifices should cease forthwith. The government has powerful means at its disposal in the effort to diminish human suffering and assist humans in their quest for identity and fulfillment. If the government does not channel its powers in a positive way, the citizens are perfectly in order if they question the laws and policies of such a State. Having surrendered their rights and fealty to such a State, the minimum they should get in return is the provision of economic and public goods – compatible with their aggregate national resources, as well the reaffirmation of their individual and common identity.

When taxes (expansively defined, not just the paycheck reduction and corporate payments, but including all the compulsory and involuntary expenses that citizens incur in providing the services that the State has failed to provide, as well as the multiplier impact on general prices due to high import and excise duties and tariffs), are collected but stolen or misapplied by the government, the people should be in order to withdraw loyalty and obedience from such a government. When we say that the government should guarantee the rights of its citizens, rights that are still regarded to be inalienable, we enable the government in its arrogation of powers to itself, in legislating for all. By this, the government (comprising imperfect men and women) has already set itself above the law. Its functionaries are given privileges and powers, which are denied the generality of the people. When this power is used to orchestrate an organized suppression of the people, vindictively, or for self-aggrandizing schemes, the people should disobey all such laws. Escaping the reaches of the law in this context should be in order.

People can only be said to have acted rightly or wrongly if they have acted voluntarily -- without duress -- and in the knowledge of laid-down rules and regulations. When they obey State laws out of a fear of the consequences of disobedience, it may not be proper to say they have acted rightly. They have merely acquiesced in the law. There is no doubt that societies need laws and the accompanying Law Enforcement Agencies. This structure is predicated on too many assumptions of nobility in the intentions and conduct of the people discharging the awesome powers of the State. We need to evaluate if State power should derive from its coercive powers or the noble examples of its leaders, the latter sustained by the will and general approval of the people, freely given and articulated. When such a Will and approval is not granted by the people, they should not be punished for disobeying the government. Almost circular, but you get the idea…

In summary, since a Utopian State is unattainable for the very fact of its utopianism, effective mechanisms of dissent must be retained by the citizens, to keep their governments in check, especially when all the Arms are in collusion, rather than being checks on one another, as originally designed. This power of disobedience, which may not be legally right (based on the convenient laws of the powerful) is a potent force recommended to poorly-served States in particular. To the extent that the government ceases to perform its obligations to the citizens, such citizens should not feel compelled or obligated to obey the laws of such a corrupt and insensitive government. This brings back memories of the conditions for granting Fealty to the Aragonian Monarchs of Old. If not… not…

After this discussion on whether or not it is ever right to disobey a government, and the conditions thereto, it will be useful to go back yet again, way, way back to the classical Greek period, and dissect the relevant political thoughts of his eminence, Plato. For some of these concepts were given their earliest coherent formulation in the Greek cities of antiquity.

Plato (428-348 B.C)

Out of a very rich philosophical tradition that produced hundreds of brilliant thinkers in ancient Greece, including Heraclitus, Thales, Democritus, Epicurus, Pythagoras, Alcibiades, Zeno, Parminedes, Anaximander, and Chrysanthius, it is generally agreed that the greatest Greek philosophers were Socrates, Plato, and Aristotle. Socrates trained Plato, while the latter taught Aristotle. These ancient thinkers also gave the world the earliest philosophical schools, formed on the basis of convergent and identical thinking. Plato bequeathed to mankind, coherent philosophical ideas in Political Philosophy, Epistemology, Metaphysics, Theology (centuries before Christianity and Islam), Cosmology, Aesthetics, Logic, Mathematics, and the Philosophy of Language, even as his thoughts were no doubt a reflection of the social norms and level of understanding during his time. This qualification is made to caution readers and analysts from taking what otherwise profound thinkers like Plato wrote as being beyond criticism and condemnation, where necessary. Plato and his generation did not give us the Holy Grail. They were still human, after all. He was from an aristocratic family, having descended on his father's side from the god, Poseidon, and on the mother's side from the great lawgiver, Solon. Plato founded the Academy, generally regarded as the ancestor to Western universities, in the 380s. This profound thinker was so dedicated to his mission that he never got married. By the way, Heraclitus, Descartes, Spinoza, Leibniz, Kant, and Schopenhauer equally forsook marriage in their pursuit of Philosophy.

Plato's major thoughts on Political Philosophy, our current interest, are captured in "The Republic." Like Cicero, Thomas Aquinas (the Angelic Doctor), Hobbes, and Rousseau after him, Plato emphasized Virtue as the cardinal quality that a leader must have. The ingredients are temperance or modesty, piety, courage, justice, and wisdom, the last being the most difficult to attain and may indeed take a lifetime without achieving it. S/he who is ruled by lawless attitudes is, in reality, leading a miserable life full of disorder, regret, poverty of the soul, insatiability, and fear, he instructs us. A truly miserable existence, drawing from "unlimited attitudes that demand more satisfaction than a person can achieve." For him, every human soul has three parts: reason, spirit, and piety. He acknowledged the imperfection of man, which he called "the weakness of will" (*Akrasia* in Greek). In his postulation, the world is divided into philosophers, honor-lovers, and money-lovers. When the last two are combined in the leadership, the society is in trouble. He emphasized that what is rational is actual, and what is actual is rational.

It is reasonable to state that, even though he acknowledged "appetite's corrupting power", Plato had an idealistic construct of the human being, an unrealistic assessment of human nature --Idealistic Utopianism. He did not favor Communism, though he acknowledged that our living well depended on others and the larger society or culture. He dwelt extensively on Forms like Beauty, Justice, and Equality, and sought a harmony among our reason, spirit, and appetite.

Jean Jacques Rousseau (1712-1778)

This Swiss and French Enlightenment philosopher had a profound impact on political systems as we know them presently. He made significant contributions to Political Philosophy, Music, Education, Literature, and Autobiography, and also introduced or refined the thinking on enduring concepts like sovereignty, public opinion, civil religion, and Social Contract. Rousseau was also a pivotal inspiration to the Jacobin Clubs, which provided the theoretical framework and guidance for the French Revolution, a critical epoch in the evolution of Western Thought, which has continued to have a significant impact on political and social systems worldwide in the 21st century.

For him, sovereignty is the "power to make laws", and this power must reside with the citizens who engage in "Direct Democracy", and not mediated through Representative Assemblies. This sovereignty is different from the government, which, for him, is the magistrate that executes the decisions of the sovereign. Rousseau was influenced by Hobbes, though his formulation of the Social Contract differed in substance from the Hobbesian template. He was friendly with Diderot, who was one of the greatest thinkers of the French Revolution period, and also knew Voltaire, the other eminence of the Revolution. He influenced Dewey, Schiller, Goethe, and Herder. The Founding Fathers of the United States, as they are called, drew considerable inspiration from Rousseau as well. For, how do you become the founder of an existing and populated land? By imposing a political system that shackled others while excluding the owners of the land? For Rousseau, human beings are good by nature, but are rendered corrupt by society. "Men are wicked, but man is good." We may need to ask him: is it not individuals who make up a society?

It is the aggregation of individual impulses that constitute the social norms and group behavior. There is no entity that is called "society" without the constitutive elements, the individual building blocks. Pursuing this further and to shut down this defective idea, if people are naturally all good, how then can the society, which they comprise, corrupt them? He recognizes a natural tendency towards self-preservation/ self-love (*amour de soi*), compassion (*pitie*), as vital elements in the multi-stage development of the human race from primitive conditions to a very modern society. It is not morality that drives this evolution, but the need for survival. It is significant how various philosophers make just about the same points about the animalistic and cruel nature of man "in a state of nature", and how their enlightened self-interest has been responsible for their surrender of their natural rights, in order to be safe from others. Are they really safe? Are people in the dangerous parts of the world really safe? Was George Floyd safe in America in 2020?

Freedom, according to Rousseau, is the ability to transcend only appetites and impulses, and embrace reason while finding new and better ways to satisfy needs. All of this leads to self-consciousness, rationality, and morality. Sadly, the real outcomes are deception, dependence, oppression, and domination. He sees *amour propre* (love of self, mostly sexual attractiveness); the competition among humans for sex appeal to others, as the source of the evil and conflict in the society.

The desire to be recognized as being superior to others (not just to be loved) leads to anger when this recognition is not forthcoming, and people would often try to exact it by whatever means, including cheating, injustice and violence. Properly handled by all, they could have a Social Contract; an *accord concordiale* among defective and destructive individuals.

The central thesis of Rousseau's Political Philosophy is that a State can only be legitimate if it is guided by the "general will" of its members; he calls this "*Volonte Generale*", an idea shared with Diderot, Montesquieu, and Malebranche. The Social Contract, in his view, essentially tries to reconcile the freedom of the individual *vis a vis* the authority of the State. Hobbes simply saw it as a mechanism to escape from the state of nature where life was short, brutish, and nasty. He recognizes that humans need other humans. Relying on Locke, and anticipating Marx, he theorized that the society is essentially a class structure where the common interests of the rich and powerful -- captured in unequal and exploitative social relations now protected by law and State power -- result in the unfreedom and subordination of the poor and weak.

This weak class, mortally afraid of the Hobbesian alternative (of the very dangerous state of nature and mutual war), consent to this arrangement, without paying heed to the structural injustice against them. In vast sections of the world, the question must be asked: have people really escaped from the risks and dangers of the Hobbesian state of nature? The simple answer is no, and we shall be exploring this further down this journey. In the absence of conditions that make citizen-legislators to make laws which reflect their common interests, that State is illegitimate, according to Rousseau. He also insists on the equal application of the law among all citizens, which we know to be mostly utopian and unreflective of our lived experiences even four hundred years later. He recommends impartial laws that are also not intrusive. In reality, however, with economic disparity, sub-national loyalties, deep societal cleavages, corruption, differences in lifestyles and occupations, as well as cultural diversities, this utopian ideal cannot be achieved.

He instructs us that political failure could be due to: ignorance and the society not being virtuous enough, so people refuse or fail to accept the requisite restrictions on their conduct -- meant for the public good. In addition, when there are factions or deep divisions in a society, but one of those factions can impose its will on the entire State, political failure is the natural result. The fragility of States is accentuated by factional abuse; mutual suspicion and lack of faith in the State are direct consequences. With this, the zeal to contribute maximally towards the development of the State is drastically reduced, because the unjust structure of the State ensures that all the gains of the State go to only tribal, religious, fraternal, party, and factional members, however and wherever the contributions were generated. Good laws make for good citizens, according to Rousseau and common sense, which is not common in actuality. The opening words of his Social Contract are "Man is born free but is everywhere in chains. Those who think themselves the masters of others are indeed greater slaves than they." Humans, for him, are different from animals "in that they can have the capacity for choice; the ability to act against mere instinct and inclination." This makes moral action possible; "a mechanism of the senses."

Renunciation of freedom is contrary to human nature; to do so in favor of another's authority is to "deprive one's actions of all morality." He categorized freedom into three: natural, civil, and moral, and also rejected representative government. In the latter instance, he departs from the Hobbesian notion of the legislative powers being invested in a group or individual who, then, acts with the authority of the people while ruling over them. Rousseau regards this structure as a form of slavery, moral decline, and loss of virtue. Like other Enlightenment philosophers, Rousseau criticized the Atlantic slave trade in direct and categorical terms, which is an indication of his moral strength and principles.

His preferred form of government was actually Elective Aristocracy, elected on merit. He promoted Deism as the civil religion of the State, as well as religious pluralism and tolerance, ideas that influenced the Political Documents of the United States in the 18th century. Drawing from Locke, he insists on the inability or unworthiness of the Sovereign to examine the private beliefs of citizens. This was a remarkable departure from centuries of the Catholic involvement in, and regulation of, both public and private affairs. A very bold position to take in that age, for which he paid dearly, regularly hounded, his residency permits revoked, and his having to live in different European countries as a vagrant and at the mercy of moody potentates.

This reminds one of the ostracism that Spinoza, a Sephardic Jew, experienced from the Dutch Jewish community (who fled Portugal due to the persecution of Jews in the 16th and 17th centuries) for daring to ask questions and have his own independent thoughts. He imbibed some ideas that were regarded as heretical at the time, and also made his own reflections known, which deeply offended the Jewish community, leading to his excommunication in 1656 (regarded then as the worst punishment possible) at the ripe old age of twenty-three. As recently as 2012, the arrogant and messianic successors to a calcified, unreflective, and static tradition still refused to lift or reverse the so-called ex-communication 350 years after it was magisterially issued, and 335 years after the great man died and was buried. Such impudent assumptions ....an indication of the god complex, deep-seated wickedness and inflexibility that lie at the core of some of these Religions. What exactly did Spinoza do, which multiple generations of Jewish leaders, playing God, could not reverse 350 years later, even in the face of the clear justification for Spinoza's prescient ideas?

For, you see, he dared to adopt the following positions, which threatened the ignorance and falsehood of the religious orthodoxy of his time, and possibly persisting until the present moment, even as these individuals take advantage of the creations of Science, Rationality, and Inquiry:

- Galileo, who had urged for the peaceful coexistence of Science and Religion in 1615
- Rene Descartes, who insisted that first we know ourselves and only then God (1637). After all, for Descartes, *Cogito Ergo Sum*, (I think, therefore, I am).
- Milton, who vigorously advocated for wide-ranging free speech and religious privilege as far back as 1644.

Building on these, plus his profound intellect and original thinking, Spinoza made the following points known, which deeply offended Jewish priests, men who, like other messianic professionals and beneficiaries of the religious construct, assume perfection and that they are God themselves:

- Religion is an organized superstition

- The Bible should be treated as a work of human literature "instead of rashly accepting commentaries for Divine documents"
- Prophets were merely imaginative and charismatic individuals who inspired others to exalt them
- There is nothing like miracles. Nature is paramount, and it chooses when to act according to known patterns or outside of patterns, which some people interpret as miracles, to their benefit. He wrote that "the power of prophecy implies not a peculiarly perfect mind, but a peculiarly vivid imagination"
- Jews are not God's specially chosen people, nor are there any chosen people for that matter. To this end, he also wrote that: "Every man's true happiness and blessedness consist solely in the enjoyment of what is good, not in the pride that he alone is enjoying it, to the exclusion of others. He who thinks himself the more blessed because he is enjoying benefits which others are not, or because he is more blessed or more fortunate than his fellows, is ignorant of true happiness and blessedness, and the joy which he feels is either childish or envious and malicious."

Based on these, the leaders of the Talmud Torah in front of the ark of the Torah in the Synagogue of the Houtgracht (for more efficacy of the curse, no doubt!!!), in their infinite, absolute, and unquestioning wisdom, in exercise of their self-arrogated powers to destroy others in life and after death, excommunicated one of their own in the following words, and have sustained this very wicked and conceited, foolish, and impotent position 350 years later:

"By decree of the angels and by the command of the holy men, we excommunicate, expel, curse and damn Baruch de Espinoza, with the consent of God, Blessed be He, and with the consent of the entire holy congregation, and in front of these holy scrolls with the 613 precepts which are written therein; cursing him with the excommunication with which Joshua banned Jericho and with the curse which Elisha cursed the boys and with all the castigations which are written in the Book of the Law. Cursed be he by day and cursed be he by night; cursed be he when he lies down and cursed be he when he rises up. Cursed be he when he goes out and cursed be he when he comes in. The Lord will not spare him, but then the anger of the Lord and his jealousy shall smoke against that man, and all the curses that are written in this book shall lie upon him, and the Lord shall blot out his name from under heaven. And the Lord shall separate him unto evil out of all the tribes of Israel, according to all the curses of the covenant that are written in this book of the law. But you that cleave unto the Lord your God are alive every one of you this day."

The proclamation of the excommunication concludes with the following famous lines of the actual warning:

"That no one should communicate with him neither in writing nor accord him any favor nor stay with him under the same roof nor within four cubits in his vicinity; nor shall he read any treatise composed or written by him."

Such arrogance!!! Such malice!!! Such irreligiosity!!! Such stupidity!!! Such nonsense!!! Empty words meant to impress only themselves and intimidate the foolish!!!

Thankfully, Spinoza's legacy has remained positive through history, and will continue to instruct mankind into the future; that is the guaranteed heaven and reward that matters to him, no doubt. Very much unlike the forgotten names and unmarked graves of his self-appointed judges and their 2012 successors....

Of the fellows who assumed they could destroy him because they are the gatekeepers of "heaven", those who can judge others on God's behalf or who regard themselves as God, one may ask: why do some of these religions insist on authoritarianism, reflexive rigidity and banishment of questions, as well as violence in deed and word for those who "dare" to ask basic questions or exercise the free will and rationality which the Divine Being bestowed on mankind? Why, for example, does Islam hold members in check through violence? Why do they expand through violence? Why is it the duty of every Muslim to hunt down and kill any Muslim who decides not to remain a Muslim, perhaps simply the religion of his or her parents? Why all the barbarity and cruelty by little, sadistic, and insecure fellows, who must lord it over others? Why the deep obsession with regulating the woman's body as a cardinal pillar of a religion? These women are from the same source as men, and intrinsically worthy human beings, with the inalienable rights of choice, speech, and all the freedoms. These women are our mothers, sisters, wives, cousins, daughters, colleagues, etc.

Anyhow, let's conclude on Rousseau. His civil religion (Deism) sits on these planks: the existence of a supreme being; the afterlife; the just will prosper; and the wicked will suffer. Well, our experience through history has not validated this lofty postulation; indeed, the wicked seem to have done much better than the meek and just. He heavily influenced Immanuel Kant, particularly in his Categorical Imperative. He also influenced John Rawls' "Theory of Justice."

Thank you very much, Jean-Jacques Rousseau, for all that you did for the world of accountability, decency, human dignity, and rationality.

We will need to consider the views of a totally different kind of human being, an inveterate manipulator, an amoral Strategist, a completely ruthless palace schemer, a man enamored of the intrigues and privileges of access to power. We are talking about Niccolo Machiavelli, perhaps the equivalent of the modern National Security Advisor to the Ruler of Florence, Italy. He was a philosopher, diplomat, and writer.

Niccolo Machiavelli (1469-1527)

Since our environment has an influence on our worldview and dispositions, it will be helpful to briefly give the socio-political context that molded Machiavelli's views. Influenced by Cicero, Plato, Aristotle, Dante, Leonardo da Vinci, Polybius, Thucydides, and Plutarch, Machiavelli lived in an era of serious political turbulence. Popes waged wars to expand their control over Italian Republics and City-States; France, Spain, and the Holy Roman Empire contested militarily against one another geared towards expanding regional control and influence. Political and Military Alliances were very fluid, and power centers shifted at will. Machiavelli closely observed the very ruthless and successful state-building tactics employed by Cesare Borgia (1475 -- 1507), and his father, Pope Alexander VI, yes, his father -- as the official celibacy of Catholic Church priests was not forbidden then. In fact, while it had been practised on and off since the 12th century, priestly celibacy became part of the Catholic Canon Law only in 1917. I digress. Apart from their military success and consolidation of Italian provinces under the Papal control, the Pope and his son also used the defense of Church interests as an alibi for their acquisitive project.

Machiavelli also closely studied the successful stratagems of King Louis XII of France. Niccolo Machiavelli's military successes lasted until the Medicis regained power, with the active military support of Spain and Pope Julius II. Displaced, imprisoned, tortured, unemployed and banished out of Florence, he took an early compulsory retirement when he produced his main works and political treatises in the form of "The Prince", and "Discourses on Livy", principally as private notes to the Ruler, as a way to curry favor with the Medicis, who totally ignored him. The "Prince" was published and became generally available after his death.

He is reputed as one of the earliest theorists of the political ideology that is presently called Classical Realism, as well as Republicanism. He took an instrumental view of power and its means, and totally focused on survival and maintaining power at all costs. He bifurcated the public and private forms of morality (which the leader must understand) and insisted that the Ruler must never be constrained (in his or her Statecraft) by the requirements of private morality and guilt. The end justifies the means; what matters to him is just the result, however procured. For Machiavelli, the Ruler must carefully nurture a good reputation even as this must be incompatible with the actions taken by the same Ruler to maintain power. Violence, fraud, bribe, lies, deceit, and other unscrupulous means must be available to, and used by, the Ruler, to achieve the desired goals (personal goals mostly). He counsels that it is better for a Ruler to be feared than to be generally loved.

He writes that "men do harm, either from fear or hate", and that good laws follow good arms; both are needed in a society and must be scrupulously and carefully controlled by the Ruler. He advises against relying on mercenaries and auxiliaries (*condottieri*), as their loyalty is superficial, fluid, transferable, and rooted simply in money. It is best to recruit your own citizens into the Army, as they have a stake in the prosecution of wars.

To this end, he writes that: "nothing is so infirm and unstable as the fame of power which does not rest upon one's own strength." The Prince (or Ruler) must always prepare for war, for "he who lets go what is done, for that which ought to be done learns his ruin rather than his preservation." The leader must use political expediency and "evil" to survive and expand, if need be. While the Ruler must not be truly religious, s/he must encourage the citizens to be very religious, as that helps conform them to the desired Order. The Prince must appear to be full of pity, loyalty, faith, humanity, religious piety, and also very open and accessible, when, in fact, he must never be any of these, to avoid ruination. Indeed, he says that the Prince must be both a beast and a man (the fox and lion being his favorite animals, for their qualities of wiliness and ferociousness).

Machiavelli emphasizes that most people are not good, so the Ruler must learn to be bad and to do bad things when necessary. The Ruler must be cunning not to lose fame/ reputation, while doing "bad" things, when necessary. S/he must have a reputation as a liberal without being one. This way, the ruler can over-tax the people to fund the habits of liberalism, without stoking the anger of the people. Humans easily forget past favors and acts of generosity, so they appreciate the unexpected giving of a "stingy" Prince.

If you give them things regularly, they begin to take those things for granted, their gratitude reduces or disappears, and they either ask for more or join the Ruler's enemies and competitors who promise to give more. For domestic stability, whenever possible, the Ruler should avoid over-taxing the people. He should also avoid general poverty, being despised, and make adequate arrangements to defend himself preferably without new taxes, but with new taxes if inevitable, but this must be disguised in its presentation to the public. Under no circumstance should the Prince dilute his security, at least, not to avoid impoverishing the masses. He must avoid being hated, ridiculed, and despised by the people. It is much safer to be feared than to be loved, if one must choose, because human beings are generally ungrateful, fickle, hypocritical, cowardly, and disloyal especially when you need them, or they are subjected to little pressure (including the threat of pain or financial ruin). They are also liars and lovers of gain. Machiavelli urges the Prince not to place value on the words uttered by people, "because men are less cautious about one who has made himself loved than one who has made himself feared, for love is maintained by a chain of obligations which, because of men's wickedness, is broken on every occasion of their own utility and choosing; but fear is maintained by a dread of punishment which never abandons them and which is not controlled by them." Be feared but not hated.

In rounding up with Machiavelli, it will be useful to end with some of his more popular quotes:

Men judge generally more by the eye than by the hand, for everyone can see and few can feel.

Everyone sees what you appear to be, few really know what you are.

It is better to be feared than loved, if you cannot be both.

Politics have no relation to morals.

Never was anything great achieved without danger.

The first method for estimating the intelligence of a ruler is to look at the men he has around him.

One who deceives will always find those who allow themselves to be deceived.

He who wishes to be obeyed must know how to command.

Where the willingness is great, the difficulties cannot be great.

If an injury has to be done to a man, it should be so severe that his vengeance need not be feared.

The promise given was a necessity of the past: the word broken is a necessity of the present.

He influenced Thomas Cromwell, King Henry VIII, Francis Bacon, Spinoza, Rousseau, Adam Smith, Descartes, Montesquieu, Hume, Hobbes, Antonio Gramsci, Stalin, and many of the Founding Fathers of the United States of America (not of the land!). On his tomb in Florence is the following elegy: *TANTO NOMINI NULLUM PAR ELOGIUM* (So great a name has no adequate praise). In reality, Machiavelli most likely influenced a good number of leaders -- political, ecclesiastical, business, just any sector, but an open identification with this complex, immoral, and immortal Florentian might not, indeed will not, do their reputation much credit. This, in itself, this obfuscation, this lie, to maintain a much-needed positive external and public reputation, is actually a tribute to Machiavelli by these silent but powerful acolytes of his.

Adam Smith (1723-1790)

This great Scottish economist, philosopher, and writer left an indelible mark on Economic Thought and Development Studies. He enrolled at the University of Glasgow at fourteen; upon graduation, he proceeded to Balliol College, Oxford University, for further studies. This very substantial man gave the world refined thoughts on concepts like Absolute Advantage, Free Market, Division of Labor, and the Invisible Hand, ideas that have continued to impact Economics almost three hundred years later. On account of his pioneering thoughts on core Economics topics, as well as the enduring impact of these ideas, he has earned the accolades attached to him, namely, The Father of Economics, as well as the Father of Capitalism. His published books include "The Theory of Moral Sentiments" and "An Inquiry into the Nature and Causes of the Wealth of Nations", simply called "The Wealth of Nations", -- his most significant work. Smith collaborated with David Hume.

Smith applied the then emerging rational mindset to his analysis of economic issues. It was becoming increasingly possible, during his time, to hold individuals and nations responsible for their economic outcomes, instead of a surrender to some inviolate mythical predestination. Actions and decisions were now regarded as having consequences. This was a radical departure from centuries of passive orthodoxy and reflexive acceptance of economic developments as the manifestations of the divine mood. These Rational and Enlightenment Thinkers truly empowered mankind and freed us all from superstition and the abnegation of human responsibility for our lives. Adam Smith's ideas, especially Division of Labor, Free Market, and Capitalism, greatly impacted the Industrial Revolution, which expanded productivity, enhanced wealth on both individual and corporate levels in an unprecedented manner, matched psychology with economics, and greatly boosted productivity and the overall wealth of nations. Matched with contemporary empowering ideas in politics and individual rights, this was an epochal stage in the development of mankind and society.

While on the economics page, we might as well mention one of the greatest influences in economic thought, F.A. Hayek (1899 -- 1992). This philosopher and economist impacted Law, Economics, Psychology, and Political Science. With two Doctorates in Law and Political Science from University of Vienna in 1921 and 1923 respectively, Hayek is generally regarded as the Father of Classical Liberalism. He eloquently articulated the nexus among economics, as well as social and institutional phenomena. In his *magnum opus*, 'The Road to Serfdom', which he wrote after reading Alexis Tocqueville's 'Road to Servitude', he invoked the Invisible Hand, an automatic logic that guides economic behavior once the right decisions have been made. Hayek also advocated for the State to support those individuals who, due to no fault of theirs, fall into indigence. This complex man and long-serving professor at both the London School of Economics and the University of Chicago won a Nobel Prize in Economics for his writings on how prices convey economic information. He received the highest national awards in the UK and the USA and was a close friend and collaborator of the great philosopher of science, Karl Popper.

Abstracts

Hopefully, the cursory review of these few representative philosophical ideas, has demonstrated the vast spectrum of thoughts on the structure and governance principles of human societies; philosophy, at the end of the day, is about humans. Cosmogony and Metaphysics, for example, while dealing with the logic of the universe and the post-life possibilities, still consider man's place in those investigations. Ethics, Political Philosophy, Philosophy of Religion, Philosophy of Science, Philosophy of Language, Aesthetics, and Logic, etc., deal entirely with the human sphere.

Ideas have consequences. Ultimately, the values and principles that underpin laws, mores, norms, taboos, State policies, treatment of the weak and poor in the society, socio-economic policies, Foreign Policy posture, etc., etc., are manifestations of philosophy. While philosophy can be, and is indeed, mostly abstract in its development and raw form, its impact is tangible and physical. An aggressive philosophy leads to wars, with consequences that are counted in dead bodies, economic ruin, poverty, lack of basic materials, and considerable physical destruction. If you regard all humans as being intrinsically worthy and equal to you, there are practices that you do not engage in, for example, slavery, predatory colonialism, Jim Crow Laws, disenfranchisement based on race and gender, etc. Cordiality and civic peace are consequences of a healthy respect for others.

While the various thinkers have given us the benefit of their ideas, agreeing on occasion, disagreeing vehemently most times, and using different words to essentially say the same things, there are certain themes and ideas that remain consistent in man's quest for sociality and political organizing, from the prehistoric times to the modern society. Some of these include: humans recognize the need not to operate in absolute silos; they form social and political societies for their mutual benefits and the minimization of one-on-one predation; the delivery of the public goods enhances the health of political societies; humans have an intrinsic need for justice and equity; the nature of public goods and the complexity of the socio-political systems are never static; the abuse of public trust destroys faith in the system; public office is a sacred trust and involves the suppression of human passions and imperfections; virtue is mentioned in several places as the ideal, even as the defective nature of man is also recognized; some of the theorists focused on the denigration and control of others while others advanced the universality of human impulses; some were parochial while others were global in their thinking; these writers gave us a peek view into their ethical formations; some emphasized the inexorability of assumed natural laws while others empowered the human person; some favored monarchies while some others promoted some mass participation in the choice of governmental models, some invoked invisible forces as a basis for them to dominate others while some others insisted on the sovereignty of mankind; some preferred surrender to magic while a few others demanded rationality, etc.

What remains is to advance further into evaluating how these disparate ideas impacted history, politics, economics, and social structures in the past five centuries or so. Actually, before we do that, for the purposes of balance, we should consider the Bolshevik Revolution of 1917 and Karl Marx, especially their views on equality and the impact that the Revolution had on 20th century History. A monolithic economic viewpoint will not be a strong pedestal to stand on. Indeed, the second largest economy in the world, China, is still led by a Communist Party, a contradiction that is significant in its novelty and success. In fact, China has a higher GDP (PPP) than the US; $25.4 trillion vs $20.5 trillion. Given the significant impact that the Marxist-Leninist Thought had on vast sections of the world in the last century, it is only appropriate that we delve into their theory, however delusory it might be. Indeed, since the concept of equality pervades all moral and political philosophy, we should particularly assess the Marxist theory of equality and the related concepts. While the core tenets of Marxism are fairly understood by analysts and philosophers, there is considerable disagreement in the interpretation of the doctrinal sub-elements, perhaps due to the vagueness of the language in the original texts. Marx's repetitiveness does not help matters; we shall endeavor to capture the salience of his maze-like theories in their various forms. Indeed, this is a good juncture to commence the assessment of political and economic systems, starting with the Revolution that started it all.

The Bolshevik "Revolution" of 1917 in Russia was arguably the most significant development of the 20th century. It is reasonable to assume that, without this upheaval, there would have been no Communism, no Fascism, no World War Two, no Cold War, and none of the massive killings that attended these epochal periods in the past century. Given the subsisting impact of the Bolshevik "Revolution", and especially the continuing threat from a rich China and a resurgent Russia, it is too hasty to proclaim the end of history, even as it is clear that the philosophical content of Communism, or lack thereof, will remain its Achilles' Heel. It is important, however, to immediately state that the attachment of the term "Revolution" to the cataclysmic events of October 1917, would be yielding to the massive propaganda of the Soviet, then Russian, Establishment. Unlike the genuine revolution of February, 1917, which led to the abdication of the Tsar and the establishment of the Provisional Government led by Kerensky, the October event was, in reality, a *coup d'etat*, in that it did not have the element of spontaneity; it was not orchestrated by the majority of the population; and was indeed spearheaded by a small team of conspirators led by Vladimir Lenin. When the term "revolution" is used to describe the Bolshevik uprising during the course of this analysis, it must be understood as meaning a putsch.

It took these plotters three years of civil war and indiscriminate terror to subdue the majority of the population. It was carried out, in deference to the democratic conventions of the age, with a feigned show of mass participation; in reality, it had no semblance of mass engagement. According to Professor Richard Pipes, "it introduced into revolutionary action methods more appropriate to warfare than to politics." The Bolshevik coup was executed in two phases: from April to July, Lenin attempted to seize power in Petrograd by inspiring street demonstrations backed by armed force, with the intent towards escalation into a massive revolt that would eventuate in the initial transfer of power to the soviets, and immediately thereafter, to his party.

This plan failed, and almost led to the destruction of the Bolshevik Party. During the intervening period leading up to October 1917 (when their next attempt was finally successful) and while Lenin was hiding from the Police in Finland, Trotsky employed a different strategy that de-emphasized street demonstrations. Rather, he disguised preparations for their coup behind the façade of a spurious and illegitimate Congress of Soviets, while relying on their armed thugs to seize the nerve centers of the government. In name, power was seized temporarily on behalf of the soviets (the people) but in reality, permanently and for the benefit of the Bolshevik Party. Trotsky duly acknowledged the conspiratorial nature of their plot when he confirmed in his History of the Russian Revolution (L.Trotskii, *Istoriia Russkoi Revoliutsii*, Vol. II, pt. 2 (Berlin, 1933) that, at most, 25,000 people participated in the events of October 1917 in Petrograd, when the population of the city was over 2 million and the country had a population of over 150 million. He further underscored the brutality of their approach when he affirmed as follows: "We shall not enter into the kingdom of Socialism in white gloves on a polished floor." What an ideology that must be sustained by blood!!!

The French Sociologist, Gustave Le Bon, had, in 1895, written in '*La Psychologie des Foules*' or "Crowd Psychology", that, on joining a crowd, men lose their individuality, dissolving it in a collective personality with its own distinct psychology. Its main characteristic is a lowered capacity for logical reasoning and a corollary rise in the sense of "invincible power". Feeling all-powerful, crowds demand action, a yearning that leaves them open to manipulation. For Le Bon, "crowds are in a state of expectant attention which renders suggestion easy." They are especially vulnerable to suggestions of violence by exhortations of idealistic states like "freedom, democracy, and socialism". It was this psychology that the unscrupulous manipulators in the Bolshevik Party exploited maximally.

Writing in his book aptly titled '*Coup D'etat: A Practical Handbook*', Edward Luttwak enumerates the conditions conducive to a *coup d'etat* as follows: an unpopular or weak regime, widespread discontent, a focused and ruthless conspiring team, seizure of the arteries of governance and utility services, leadership-followership dislocation, passivity of the population, declining social and economic conditions, concentration of real political power in a few hands, substantial independence of the polity (to ensure a low likelihood of foreign intervention against the *coup d'etat*), control and manipulation of the mass media, etc., etc.

Russia of 1917 provided an enabling environment for this violent overthrow of the Government by a conspiring few. What was not anticipated was the overall and progressive ramification of that intervention. Lenin's formulation to the effect that the Intelligentsia were the only ones who could instigate revolutionary change, is at the core of his deviation from the Marxist doctrine both of the inevitability of the Socialist regime as well as the catholicity of its authorship. In this, he agrees with Joseph Schumpeter who suggests that: "social discontent is not enough to produce a revolution." While it is difficult to locate a specific event as being the trigger for the so-called revolution, it is valid to articulate the following as contributing to the environment that enabled the putsch: the unpopularity of the WW1, the impotence of the "autocratic" Monarch as evidenced by the plethora of concessions extracted from him, resurgent Nationalism against the backdrop of losses in the Crimean War and the Russo-Japanese War in the twilight of the preceding century, the tension arising from the reluctance of the Tsar to share political power with an increasingly-educated and rich segment of the society, the role of the German Intelligence Service which funded Lenin in order for him to withdraw Russia from the war in line with the *Zimmerwald-Kiental* position, the engagement of Russian troops in overseas theaters, thus making them unavailable for quelling the ensuing riots at home, the Tsar's lack of will to remain in power at all cost, etc.

It must be noted that Russia's role in WW1 was a *Realpolitik* stratagem aimed at blunting the *Schlieffen* Plan, by which Germany planned to crush France before Russia fully mobilized in order to prevent Germany fighting on two fronts. Germany had always had expansionist plans towards Russia, principally for her abundant resources, physical size, and population. Moreover, the divergence of their positions in the Balkans made the prospects of a kinetic engagement almost inevitable, in the aftermath of Archduke Ferdinand's assassination. The aggregate costs of the prolonged war further dampened morale in Russia, depleted resources and manpower, and also yielded the enabling platform for exploitation by domestic anarchists like Lenin and his cohorts.

While Tsar Nicholas obviously lacked a desperate fixation on power, he remained mindful of his historic duty to transfer the Empire to his son in due course, as had been the tradition with many generations of the Romanovs. He had said: "I shall never, under any circumstances, agree to a representative form of government because I consider it harmful to the people whom God has entrusted to my care." This reference to a Divine source of Authority further alienated the educated elite, who insisted on the sovereignty of the people, a position that Lenin would exploit. The Monarch's initial resort to force, especially during the Bloody Sunday, substantially altered the benign reputation of the Tsar, even as his subsequent capitulation under pressure (e.g. the October Manifesto which was, *ipso facto*, the recognition of Constitutionalism that negated the extant Autocracy) eroded his stature. The loss of fear and awe for the Monarch and the Royal Institution, inspired incipient resistance to Public Order and emboldened anarchists. In addition, the absence of civic sense and patriotism exposed the tenuous fabric of the Russian State; a State held together by force, and not by intrinsic and consensual arrangements. It was the State that made Russia a country, and not vice versa.

The Tsarist Russia was essentially patrimonial, wherein sovereignty and ownership of the Empire were subsumed under the Tsar. This patrimonial structure was characterized by: monopoly of political authority; monopoly on economic matters; the ruler was entitled to unlimited services from his people while there was no sense of individual or group rights. All the inhabitants and the resources contained within the geographical space were the property of the Crown; there was also monopoly on public information. When compared with European Democracies, the latter's feudal history equipped them with a progressive history of the Monarch sharing power in some form with others. The Tsarist Russia, which was more mechanically than organically structured, was therefore sustained by the civil service, security police, the gentry, the army, and the Orthodox Church (which was financially dependent on the State!).

It is significant that even the Church was under the direct control of the Monarch, with preference accorded to ethnic Russians over Poles, Ukrainians, and natives of the Near Abroad (however well-assimilated into the Russian culture that the latter might be). Russia represented the first case where two Police Systems were run by a State/Empire: one to protect the interests of the State (as narrowly defined by the Crown) and also the State from its citizens; and the other to protect the citizens from one another. This was the origin of the Police State (*Polizeistaat*), which the *Okhrana, Cheka*, OGPU, KGB, and their other incarnations fostered. All the identified pillars of the Empire owed their existence and absolute fealty to the person of the Monarch, at whose pleasure they functioned. There was no objective and over-arching source of Authority outside of the Monarch. The concept of the Rule of Law (*Rechtsstaat*) was particularly lacking in Russia's civic formulation. The agitation for the overthrow of this structure, therefore, generated several polarities in form and approach. In addition, the rapid growth of Russia's economy in the latter part of the nineteenth century, together with the growing number of educated people (influenced by developments in France) ensured a challenge to patrimonial conservatism.

Lenin thought of revolution in international terms, and especially aspired to export the Socialist revolution to Germany and England, the two countries that he regarded far more highly than his native Russia. The approach was to gain power by guile, and then sustain it by massive terror. It is relevant to identify the factors that ensured that the Bolsheviks, even though numerically and financially inferior to the Mensheviks and Social Revolutionaries, were the Party that effectively emerged triumphant in the fluid and dangerous political climate that pervaded in Russia when the Provisional Government was inaugurated. It was only the Bolsheviks who refused to join the Government, thus developing a persona as the only alternative to the status quo, which the other parties lost due to their patriotic participation in the Provisional Government. Furthermore, the Bolsheviks were more ruthless and ardent in their pursuit of power than the bigger parties. In addition, given Lenin's lack of love for his country (as demonstrated by his earlier and subsisting treasonable collaboration with Germany during a war between both countries) as well as his consuming selfishness which did not enable any thought for the possible consequences of the decimation of Russia, the Bolsheviks were not restrained in the tactics to be employed towards gaining power.

In his pretence of seeking to entrench democracy in Russia, Lenin had actually defined a democratic state in a meeting with his close lieutenants as "an organization for the systematic use of violence by one class against the other, by one part of the population against the other." He and his type were permanently obsessed with the who-whom paradigm, that is "who is doing what to whom?" To compound matters, the other parties were reluctant to crush the Bolsheviks due to a distorted calculation of unmitigated consequences arising therefrom. The lack of concern for Russia equally led the Bolsheviks to make a wide range of promises to different segments of the society, in the knowledge that all those commitments were to be breached immediately upon achieving their single purpose of attaining power.

Posing as the representatives of the people, the Bolsheviks launched a massive nationalistic propaganda operation against the soldiers who could have been deployed against them, to the effect of psychologically disarming the soldiers against being used by the "rotten capitalist class" against committing a "pogrom" against their own people.

The so-called Kornilov affair further widened the gulf between the Kerensky-led Provisional Government and the military. The naiveté of, and lack of determination by, the contending parties for power thus ensured that the Bolsheviks were not stopped immediately they manifested their agenda for the country. Even the Bolshevik convocation of an illegal and unrepresentative Congress ostensibly on behalf of the entire soviet, was allowed to stand. It was at this Congress that the Bolsheviks, purporting to represent the people, dissolved the Parliament and Government, and then proceeded to enforce these decisions by force (yet unchallenged). The foregoing position clearly demonstrates that there was nothing inevitable about the Bolshevik Revolution, contrary to the mainstream position of Russian writers who have unfortunately influenced some American commentators. The presentation of the Bolshevik upheaval in ethereal toga by successive beneficiaries of the so-called Revolution is, therefore, a propagandistic formulation aimed both at expiating their collective guilt over the accompanying atrocities and in reifying the source of their mandate.

It is instructive that, from historical times, Russian Tsars and Communist leaders had not derived their mandate from the people. Rather, the Tsar (or Communist Leader, subsequently) is regarded as owning the country and its people, while there is no corresponding expectation of accountability on the part of this Omnipotent and Omniscient Leader. The difference between the monarchist era and the Communist (and post-Communist) period lies in the fact of the concentration of all powers in the Tsar while the latter forms depict a quasi-power-sharing arrangement among a tiny, conspiring team (with the military and Security Police duly represented, to ensure the repression and elimination of "counter-revolutionaries").

In further demonstration of the fraudulence of the claims of legitimacy and mass appeal of their putsch, Lenin issued a statement to Russians immediately after seizing the reins of power in which he stated, *inter alia* that " ... the task for which the people have been struggling – the immediate offer of a democratic peace, the abolition of landlord property in land, worker control over production, the creation of a Soviet Government – this task is assured. Long live the Revolution of Workers, Soldiers, and Peasants! …" Even while the Bolsheviks were still absorbing the relative ease with which they overthrew the system, they were already proclaiming "the Worldwide Socialist Revolution." This messianic usurpation and aggregation of powers and the interests of the majority is at the center of Communist philosophy.

The hollowness of the claim is eminently demonstrated by the lack of democracy, as well as the grave atrocities against the people, over the past century of this bizarre experimentation. The poverty of thought and sincerity inherent in this device made the employment of State repression and unwholesome practices as instruments of regime-perpetuation inevitable. None of the promises made (separate Nation-States for the various nationalities, land for the peasantry, etc., etc.) could be fulfilled once power was seized. The need to check the expected violent reaction provided further impetus for the terror and fear tactics employed to achieve the consolidation of their power. The process of consolidation involved a systematic elimination of all real and perceived opposition; incapacitation of the Orthodox Church; sporadic killings for the fear effect; closure of the political space to ensure that only the Bolsheviks wielded power and opinion in the land; confiscation of assets and nationalization of same; entrenchment of a Command Economy; all of this, while excluding the same people in whose name they claimed to rule!!!

The so-called Decrees of Peace and Land were promulgated by fiat. As is typical, the key offices in the country were allocated among the major puschists, notably, Lenin, Trotsky, Rykov, Krasin, Oppokov, Stalin, and Nogin. The roles of various elements of the military in this insurrection should be the subject of another analysis. The expansion of the "Revolution" beyond Petrograd to Moscow and other major cities was achieved with the active collusion of the military and involved the killing of all resistance forces. Lenin weighed the various scenarios before choosing to lead the Party, rather than the Government; this was informed by his internationalist agenda and the need to preside over this expanded audience, rather than be limited to a national territory. In any case, the Party was immediately invested with Executive and Legislative powers, as well as the power to appoint judicial officials, in a non-official entity called the "ruling party." As Professor Pipes argues in "The Unknown Lenin", the idea of a "one-party State" is a contradiction in terms as a "party" is necessarily indicative of the existence of "others" which, together, make the whole. In the absence of this plurality, therefore, it is counter-intuitive to use the term, One Party State.

Given the over-arching role of the Party, we could use a "dual state" to describe the amorphous construct. Deriving from Jacobin origins, this exclusive club became the only vehicle for participation in political activities, while membership was contingent on ideological "purity" and other undefined criteria. The schism over the exclusion of other parties from governance was resolved in Lenin's favor due to the reliance on the vicious tactics employed by Stalin and Dzerzhinsky. The need to free themselves from accountability to the people, or to other Institutions outside the Party, reinforced the need for extreme measures, including killing off the opposition, banishing "lucky" opponents/ "dissidents" to Siberian concentration camps and sanatoriums, mass transfers of populations, uprooting the vestiges of the old system, conversion of the soviets into pliant tools of the new ruthless power elite, etc. The origins of totalitarianism were being developed. The façade of holding power in trust for the people was abandoned early on, once there was reasonable confidence that power had been consolidated. While specific numbers are impossible to arrive at, it is generally agreed that several millions were killed during this phase of the Regime. Apart from targeted killings, there were pogroms as well, perpetrated against Jews and other minority ethnic groups.

The progressive development of the cult of Leninism and the internecine battles among these impostors continued for the next couple of years. Several political shenanigans aimed at achieving facile legitimacy were implemented even as brutality remained the valid guarantor of their usurpation. According to Pipes, "the system of government which the Bolsheviks set in place within two weeks of the October coup marked a reversion to the autocratic regime that had ruled Russia before 1905: they simply wiped out the twelve intervening years of Constitutionalism." The final vanquish of the Octobrists, Union of the Russian People, and Nationalists – leading to their dissolution – marked the final entrenchment of political monopoly in Russia. Free rein was finally given to impunity, rascality, messianic conduct, terror as a Directive Principle of State Policy, and belligerence. The Romanovs, who had been banished to Siberia, were promptly killed so that, as Trotsky said, "…the severity of this punishment showed everyone that we would continue to fight on mercilessly, stopping at nothing. The execution of the Tsar's family was needed not only to frighten, horrify, and instill a sense of hopelessness in the enemy but also to shake up our own ranks, to show that there was no retreating, that ahead lay either total victory or total doom…"

By escalating violence, nationalizing all businesses, taking control over all land and resources, maintaining a monopoly of the mass media which they controlled, abrogating all forms of competition, and emasculating all forces of dissent, the Bolsheviks gradually entrenched themselves in the polity, and imposed Communism as the ideology of the country, even as they employed both overt and covert means to achieve its foreign propagation. The Communist International (Comintern) was the vehicle for coordinating the foreign arms of the Communist Movement, with the Central Committee of the Communist Party of the Soviet Union providing both ideological and strategic direction. With the realignments that attended WWII, and especially the Soviet suzerainty over Eastern European countries, Communism was equally imposed on those countries by force. While one acknowledges the success of the Soviet Union in spreading this Ideology over vast sections of the globe, the poverty of Communism as a viable Political and Economic Philosophy has been demonstrated by: the unresolved conflict between its avowed inevitability and its imposition by force; the US, which is the epitome of capitalist success, has not automatically "graduated" into a Socialist State and never will; Communist leaders replaced the bourgeoisie they were fighting; Communism fails to understand human nature and is particularly ill-equipped to explain the role that incentives for entrepreneurship and innovation play in enhancing productivity and enterprise; the Command Economy has proved a colossal failure since the collapse of this system in Soviet Union itself; the Communist theory was always modified to explain/ rationalize new circumstances, thus showing its hollowness; in addition, the lack of emphasis on the human person, as opposed to parties, classes, states, and masses, is a fundamental demonstration of the inadequacy of Communism to explain human action.

In reality, the Communist postulation that all historical events are determined by social conflicts, was not borne out by the circumstances surrounding the Bolshevik *coup d'etat*, as well as the collapse of the Communist system in Soviet Union. In both cases, there was no class warfare as theorized by Communists. The vacuity of the Communist superstructure thus required sustenance by massive force and unbecoming propaganda, lest the truth be discovered. While the factors relevant to the success of the Bolshevik putsch have been identified and briefly discussed above, it is apposite at this stage to analyze the impact of this epochal development on world history. While the war largely aided Lenin's ascension to power, and German "War Socialism" gave him his initial economic policy, the very fact that Lenin and his group succeeded in imposing their Will on a strategic State like Russia provided an impetus to other people determined to emulate this example in other lands. The underlying moral relativism and absolutization of power as well as thought-control appealed to their type in other countries, hence the dramatic growth in the incidence of *coups d'etat* and all other forms of dictatorship. The example of unquestioned impunity was too difficult to resist. Fascism (in Germany, Italy, etc.) were early manifestations, while the inclination and audacity to defy or suspend local Laws and Constitutions, International Laws, and Treaties remain abiding sources of inspiration for dictators and predator-States across the world to this day. Irredentist and revanchist policies are examples.

The employment of the Bolshevik means of repression: concentration camps, arrests, prisons, killings, etc., has been imbibed by wielders of power with a fundamental distaste for liberal values. Paul Johnson writes that, "If Leninism begot the fascism of Mussolini, it was Stalinism which made possible the Nazi Leviathan." This is a reference to the egregious escalation in killings when Stalin took over leadership on Lenin's death. It has been suggested that a minimum of 30 million people were killed by their own Government in one form or the other within the first half-century of Communist rule in Russia. Marxist scholar, Leszek Kolakowski, described the killings in the Communist era as: "probably the most massive warlike operation ever conducted by a State against its own citizens in history… the whole Party became an organization of torturers and oppressors. No one was innocent, and all Communists were accomplices in the coercion of society, thus the Party acquired a new species of moral unity and embarked on a course from which there was no turning back." The competition for power assumed a very dangerous dimension under Stalin as well, with his liquidation of all rivals to the position, notably, Bukharin, Beria, etc., while Trotsky was tracked down and killed in his exile home in Mexico. This is a template for succession dynamics in many countries, aligning with the Hobbesian formula of "a perpetual and restless desire for power after power, that ceaseth only in death."

The mutuality of influence between the Nazi Germany and Leninist-Stalinist Russia deserves closer scrutiny and analysis. The same treatment should be extended to the influence Russia had on China, Cambodia, Vietnam, and a cross section of Africa, countries united by the sheer brutality and indecency of their political processes. Furthermore, the Russian example projected mass killings like genocide into an instrument of Statecraft. The pogroms carried out against Jews, Armenians, Igbos, Tutsis, Darfuris, and other oppressed people all over the world owe their intrinsic inspiration to the Bolshevik Revolution. This significant historical experience essentially negated the fundamental Judeo-Christian precept of individual responsibility and guilt for actions and imposed a construct of group responsibility fostered and sustained by hate and prejudice. Bolsheviks sired totalitarianism in all its forms.

The Communist System was exported by force, guile, Intelligence operations, propaganda, bare-faced lies, manipulation, and an overall negation of civility. Given the diametrically-conflicting ethos in the United States, for example, it took the Venona Transcripts and divisions among the ranks of the members of the Communist Party of the USA (CPUSA) for the US Government and society to understand the existence, scope and nature of the sustained espionage operations maintained against the US, which was a wartime-ally and benefactor! The involvement of high-ranking US officials in traitorous conduct on behalf of USSR and in pursuit of nebulous peace remains the subject of passionate discourse in the US until this date. At the peak of Communism, over half of the global population was under the remote influence of successive generations of the ruthless squad in Moscow.

Bolsheviks also systematized the Police State in modern history, with the resultant implications for loss of lives, invasion and loss of privacy, abuse of power, xenophobia leading to intense surveillance of foreigners, breakdown of trust levels among people, infiltration of other innocuous Institutions, blackmail by the State, repression of the human spirit and the capacity for innovation, etc., etc. China, Warsaw Pact States, Burma/ Myanmar, East Germany, Cuba, etc., relied extensively on USSR for guidance in this area. While propaganda in its various forms has been part of human civilization from antiquity, the Russian Communists raised this to a new art form. They incorporated outright lies and unscrupulous, yet advanced, forms of deception into their Statecraft. The adoption of Union of Soviet Socialist Republics (USSR) as the new name of the country by the Bolsheviks/ Communists was an early indication of the central role that propaganda would play in State affairs. The speed with which the USSR unraveled, with constituent parts choosing to form independent States, confirms that there was never a Union of Soviet Socialist Republics. The erstwhile colonies in the Near Abroad were held hostage under the former arrangement. Again, the moral relativism of the Bolshevik doctrine cohered completely with this propagandistic mindset, and no price was considered too high to pay in propagating the position of the new ruling class in Russia. As earlier mentioned, the international arm of Communism was largely sustained by propaganda. Hitler and Mussolini built on this in mobilizing their people to action during WWII.

Given the moral flexibility of the power elite in Russia, a sustained subscription to a policy position, or the reliance on transparent negotiation to achieve diplomatic outcomes would have been too much to expect of them. In this regard, fidelity to

Causes was never considered important or useful. It was this orientation that saw Russia conniving with Germany to subvert both the Genoa Treaty and the Versailles Treaty, crafted a Defense Treaty with Germany, and then teaming up with the Allied Powers to defeat the same Germany -- simply because Germany attacked them in Operation Barbarossa from June 1941. The Treaty of Rapallo was initiated exactly to achieve this objective, with the consequence that WWII became a guaranteed historical epoch waiting to happen.

The Cold War that lasted half a century (some argue it is still on) was a direct derivative of the Bolshevik "Revolution". The Cold War entailed strategic polarities and an intensive arms competition between the US/ NATO and USSR/WARSAW PACT, from the conventional to the strategic. Apart from proxy wars that were fought in different parts of the world (Korea, Vietnam, Angola, etc.), the two Super Powers did not engage in direct confrontation once the Cuban Missile Crisis was resolved. However, the global tension remained very high, while the rivalry between the two Blocs was protracted. Since Vladimir Putin became the Russian President, his singular mission has remained a de facto restoration of the Soviet-era geopolitical influence and geographical expansion. In many ways, the election of Donald Trump as the US President in 2016 is generally regarded by sophisticated analysts as, perhaps, the highest Intelligence success achieved by Russia in over a century. Until the collapse of the Soviet Union and her satellite control over Pact countries, there was palpable anxiety regarding the possible outcome of the bipolar competition. On a positive note, however, this competition inspired phenomenal developments in Science and Technology.

Personality cultism, backed with untrammeled power, was a defining feature of Bolshevism. In the past century, replications and reinforcements of this pattern have been seen in different parts of the world, with the typical negative implications for the citizens, freedom of speech, political freedom, succession dynamics, minority rights, and the overall health of the political system. The reverence of the Leader and the attachment of Omniscience to the Totalitarian, are necessarily counter to transparency, Rule of Law, Checks and Balances, Civil Rights, robust political systems, electoral integrity, accountability, and the release of the entrepreneurial spark. Again, the Police and Intelligence Organizations are repressive, discriminatory, and intrusive, while the surveillance of citizens and foreigners is routine. This is part of the legacy of Bolshevism/ Marxism/ Communism.

A further impact of Bolshevism is the rising spate of atavistic nationalism, which has led to various wars, regional conflicts, re-drawing of maps, and the incubation of potential conflicts. Passionate nationalism has also led to instances of genocide in the Balkans, Rwanda, etc. In all, the greatest lesson of the Bolshevik "Revolution" was the passivity of the people and Institutions that could have stopped it before it manifested. The world continues to pay a major price for this miscalculation and lack of determination, a century afterwards. The human tendency towards oppression and abuse needs to be checked and restrained because the medium and long-term implications of seemingly-innocuous actions could be very catastrophic, like in the case under review. The assassination of Archduke Ferdinand led to WW1, and the abdication of Tsar Nicholas II leading to the overthrow of the Kerensky-led Provisional Government by a group of bloodthirsty, conniving, and unscrupulous thugs, completely altered the course of history in the past hundred years. What next??????

Having developed the socio-political context within which the Marx-Engels Doctrines were propagated, we may now delve into their treatise on equality. For, the notional (civic) equality of all humans, especially those eligible for universal suffrage, is at the very core of political liberalism, and indeed of most of the political formulations. For, if you regard others as your equals, you will not put them up for sale, sell or buy them; annihilate them in genocidal greed over their land and resources; deign to colonize them and destroy their lives; refuse to attend the same schools with them; loot and corner all the public resources meant for enhancing the public good; devise means to efficientize their industrial and systematic elimination; kill them and expect that there shall be no consequences, etc. So, indeed, the concept of equality is a cardinal precept of both Moral and Political Philosophy. All the 'isms' are meant to obfuscate what the writers actually think about other humans; what they think about the fundamental and intrinsic equality of all human beings. That's all...

Perhaps, some further commentary is necessary here. With the perpetration, perpetuation, and amplification of the horrible evil against black people in Europe and America by European-Americans, it is difficult, if not impossible, to avoid accounting for these acute acts of wickedness and plain evil. The forced enslavement, casual killings, forced uprooting from their homes, work without economic payment, dehumanization, nullification of identity, permanent separation of families, psychological trauma, forced name changes, cross-generational loss of esteem, legalized wickedness and exclusion, systemic impoverishment, treating an individual as 3/5th of a person, denial of basic dignity and human rights, etc., etc., cannot be casually brushed aside especially when, to this day, some people openly rub salt on an open wound by seeking a return to these inglorious and unjust practices. Their clamor, which remains deeply offensive to all decent people, is symptomatic of their severe moral pathologies.

In the dystopian and morbid ranking such as this is, this aggregation of wickedness spanning four centuries, and continuing, exceeds multiple fold the despicable and evil holocaust by Germans, as well as their Eastern and Central European collaborators, against Jews. With the Jews, there was a start date and an end date, as horrific as the killings were. Tens of millions of blacks have also been killed by these same European people, together with the other deprivations and indignities, even as these persist on a reduced scale to the present era without responsibility.

When the holocaust against Jews is usually discussed, people typically assume that six million Jews were killed by only Germans; this is far from the truth. While the Germans ran Concentration Camps in conquered Poland, for example, there were enthusiastic locals in various European countries who butchered the Jews in their communities, often with minimal or no Nazi goading.

The following table, which the National Holocaust Museum in Washington D.C., has updated recently, provides a chilling proof of this fact. 58% of all the Jews in Europe had been systematically killed by the time WWII ended in 1945. They were killed just for being Jews!!!

Country	Pre-war Jewish Population	Estimated Murdered
Albania	200	unknown
Austria	185,000	65,500
Belgium	90,000	25,000
Bulgaria	50,000	unknown
Czechoslovakia	709,000	590,000
Denmark	7,500	80
Estonia	4,500	1,000
France	315,000	74,000
Germany	237,000	165,000
Greece	72,000	69,000
Hungary	825,000	560,000
Italy	100,000	8,000
Latvia	93,500	70,000
Lithuania	153,000	130,000
Luxembourg	4,000	1,200
Netherlands	140,000	100,000
Norway	1,800	760
Poland	3,350,000	3,000,000
Romania	1,070,000	480,000
Soviet Union	3,030,000	1,340,000
Yugoslavia	203,500	164,500
Total:	**10,641,800**	**6,844,040**

Source: National Holocaust Museum

To be sure, 5.7 million non-Jewish Soviet citizens; 3 million non-Jewish prisoners-of-war; 300,000 Serbians; 250,000 people with disabilities and confined to Institutions; 300,000 Roma (gypsies), as well as another 100,000 people comprising Jehovah's Witnesses, homosexuals, and German political opponents were also murdered.

The term "equality" has philosophical, economic, sociological, and political dimensions. In analyzing the Marxist theory of equality, one has to recognize the fact that it is involved in an asymmetry with economics; in fact, the Marxist model builds on the economic development of the society. Given the close connection discernible among the various economic terms, especially as employed by Marx, one runs the risk of repeating oneself, though in different expressions. This points to the general organicism, which one detects in Marx's works. The best way to explicate their conception of equality is to compare it with Rawls' contrarian theory on the same subject. Marx considers equality as a relation between collectivities (or classes) and not between individuals. This holistic approach informs why Marxism adopts the method of Structuralism-Functionalism, as opposed to Methodological Individualism.

For Marx, capitalism subverts the moral autonomy of individuals, and there is no basis for the supposition that categorization of people into fixed classes is inevitable. A form of social stratification exists, but this will not approximate to the fixity and determinism, which accompany class-division. How about social mobility, one may ask? Marx accepts "unequal right" as a means to the attainment of equality. Labor is alienated under capitalist conditions of private ownership of the means of production, and its transcendence and abolition under Communism. In the capitalist system, man's productive interchange with nature defines him. Man and his labor are stripped of their human essence in this system, which is based on private property and production for exchange and profit. The worker is seen as a commodity, and, therefore, has a "price" fixed on him or her. Marx writes that: "in political economy, labor occurs in the form of wage-earning activity."

When production is not taking place, man is of no relevance whatever. Division of Labor will become a less important feature of economic relations in this formulation. In fact, a system that will ensure the multi-specialization of the people will be substituted for it, thus extinguishing the injustice and inequality, which are basic features of the Division of Labor. The eradication of socio-economic classes will have the added advantage of correcting the inequity in the society, as the prior relations of exploitation give birth to a relation of basic equality.

Alienation under capitalist conditions consists of the "class" and "division" of labor; the product of the worker's labor is alienated from him for the sole reason that he does not own the means of production; rather, the capitalists do. "…labor is the essence of private property…," yet it does not appropriate its own result. The exploitation of the Proletariat also takes the form of the appropriation of surplus value by the Bourgeoisie. Marx assumes that there is perfect competition; private property; the commodities produced have exchange value; and the capitalists aim at maximizing profits. Commodity is divided into two: use-value and exchange-value. Labor determines the latter while the former is intrinsic in the commodity. This system is unjust because of its exploitative nature; its subjection of the Proletariat to perpetual dependence. The underlying assumption is that the Principle of Desert should be applied, so that people get what is commensurate with their productive efforts.

Labor determines value; labor is, therefore, what is really exchanged when commodity-exchange takes place. This is the Labor Theory of Law. The contradiction between labor and capital -- due to ownership, or lack of, the means of production -- leads to polarization between the two classes. The appropriation of the surplus value (by a few people) gives Capitalism its distinctive feature. This trend of exploitation becomes relevant to the consideration of equality for the reason that we should treat all persons with equal moral respect, and should act in ways that ensure the existence of equal moral respect, and also act in ways that ensure the existence of equal and fair opportunity for all. The Capitalist System is "closed," hence it thrives on inequality. Justice requires the ingredients of notional equality and fairness. For Marx, a fair distribution only applies to a situation where the "instruments of labor are common property, and the total labor is cooperatively regulated" -- Communism. This formula does not, however, connote that all persons must or should get equal shares. Marx recognizes "justified inequality."

In his formulation, labor becomes the standard by which equality is determined. The differences among men are natural. Marx also recognizes the need to provide for those who can contribute little or nothing to the total product: the aged, infirm, children, etc. It is in this light that he gives his definition for equal and fair distribution as "from each according to his ability; to each according to his needs." This will only obtain in a situation where there is both social production and social appropriation; where there is a central authority, which regulates all activities, in fact a Communist State. It is also characterized by collective ownership of the means of production, plus classlessness, and "statelessness." Capitalism descended from feudalism. Its basic features include private ownership of the means of production, existence of rival classes, State exploitation of labor, etc. Marx posits that the ultimate stage in the history of man is Communism.

It is characterized by the absence of alienation and exploitation, the absence of Division of Labor, of classes, therefore, of class struggle. The attainment of this utopian state does not take a universal, rigid approach. Rather, specific features of each society are considered, and do determine, whether or not all the other stages will manifest in this process; if so, the duration of each stage.

This is the Marxist response to the charge that the Ideology is unduly rigid and deterministic. As Abbott wrote, "Communism in all its forms assumes in man a virtue which he does not possess, and fails to furnish that stimulus, which is essential, not only to the production of the greatest wealth, but to the development of the best character. If the present industrial system were overturned by a revolution, and the people were to become owners in common of the commonwealth, the result would be a derangement of the industrial organization which would bring immeasurable suffering, accompanied with gross injustice, upon all classes of the community."

Under Communism, the leadership has the responsibility of radicalizing (educating) the Proletariat. It is significant to note that Communism inspired movements like Liberation Theology, which focused on reaffirming the dignity and freedom of oppressed people. The fundamental principles here are: recognition of the injustice in the world, the recognition of people's ability and capacity to positively determine their situation, the need for the oppressed people themselves to participate actively in this endeavor, the idyllic nature of the destination in each case, need to employ violence as a means to the achievement of the objectives, and the recognition of the fact that reactionary forces will frustrate their efforts. However, the elite, who "conscientize" the people, must discard all traces of bourgeoisie inclination, and must bring "real education elements" along with them (espousing Socialist ideals). This is all in an attempt to overthrow a regime of inequality and exploitation. Man's socialness is given expression in the fact of class struggle. This antagonism takes place on the corporate level. The existence of classes is social, but class struggle is political. In his Paper, "Class and Justice", Kai Nielsen, a Marxist Scholar, claims that he does not represent Marxists in his advocacy for "Radical Egalitarianism."

Engels writes in 'Anti-Duhring' that "the real content of the proletarian demand for equality is the demand for the abolition of classes; a demand for equality which goes beyond that of necessity and passes into absurdity." It must be stressed that neither Engels nor Marx adopted Nielsen's exact term which means every person should be "treated exactly alike in all respects." It might be useful to characterize Nielsen's "Radical Egalitarianism" as follows: upon the fulfillment of required conditions of relative abundance, classlessness, Democracy, Socialism, sentimentality and rationality of individuals, each person must have a right to equal freedom and opportunities. Having stressed the need for "equal moral autonomy" and "self-respect", he asserts that the classlessness of a society is not empirically impossible. Indeed, he recognizes the disparities in the status of the constituent members of a society, without giving approval, express or tacit, to the exploitation of one class over another.

Our knowledge of social reality will confirm the impossibility of having absolute equality in the world.

It is Marx's view that an impassioned analysis of the social reality will yield a realization of the fact that there is no such thing as generic equality. Difference in quality is a formidable justification for the unequal rights allotted to different men in our existential situation. The absence of "moral equality" among men spreads to the general sphere of equality itself. One sees in Marx-Engels an allusion to the clamor for equality among men based solely on their "humanity", their very essence. Even as both men reject religion, this construct is closely related to the religious structure wherein the Transcendental Essence has imbued all humans, as creations of the Transcendent, with the divine-spark (which is equally allocated to respective persons), and that this "fact" underscores God's intention for equality among men. One's religious conviction will determine one's receptibility or otherwise to this position, but our task here is a philosophical interrogation, where rationality and logic are the cardinal tools. Since philosophy seeks logic and proof, a demand for evidential rigor will not work in the ecclesiastical formulation, as circularity is no proof.

Committed Marxists often contend, after Engels, that equality, as presently understood, is a bourgeoisie ploy to complete the alienation of workers. Human labor thus becomes the standard by which things are exchanged. Man becomes a commodity, and labor represents the extent of his dehumanization. What the "class of exploiters" seems to ignore is that its agitation to be placed at par with the feudal lords when capitalism was emerging, has become counter-productive. The bourgeoisie has unwittingly sensitized the Proletariat to the need for equality and freedom, as well as the resoluteness, self-confidence, and actual practice, for the realization of these objectives. However, a point of divergence arises when the oppressed class, in an attempt to rewrite history, sets out with a program that will have the consequence of the abolition of all classes. The logic of this is that classes must exist prior to class struggle; in order to solve the combined problems of economic exploitation and political domination, we have to trace these instances of social disequilibrium to their very origins, in this case -- classes. This optimism *vis a vis* the ultimate decimation of the class struggle, is yet another pointer to the utopian content of Marxism. For as long as we have humans on earth, stratification in one form or the other shall remain.

Marx writes that "all history starts with class struggle", the implication of which is that societies without classes or class struggle have no history, which will be inconsistent with historical realities. Moreover, the emergence, or otherwise, of classes, is a function of the mode of production in a particular society, and there is no necessity about this relationship (at least, going by the Marxian doctrine). A further point often ignored by some writers is that, for Marx, classes emerged only during the slavery stage in the historical development of society. Prior to this stage was communalism -- which was classless, yet historical in the sense that it existed in space and time, and was of relevance to real human beings, not constructs.

Liberty cannot exist without equality; capitalism is incompatible with equality, as this will have a negative impact on the structure of the society -- determined by a few powerful oppressors. The ruling class in any society exerts its will on the people through several media. Given the above premises, it is only logical to infer that liberty cannot actually thrive under capitalism (since liberty equates with freedom achieved by all, and which is accessible to all as a matter of right).

Marxists conceive of classes in relation to the ownership of the means of production, as diametrically opposed to the conventional conception, which is basically political and social in nature. They are interested in the differences among social groups in terms of income, prestige, or authority, as well as the conditions which lead to these disparities. The import of the concern is derived from the fact that these variations bear significantly on one's life prospects; people should not be made to suffer for what they did not initiate, hence the need to solve the problem from source.

Marxists do not subscribe to the thesis that classes are inevitable; however, a contradiction seems to arise when they then suggest that classes and Capitalism must be extinguished for the attainment of Communism. In other words, it is what exists that can be abolished. They may respond that their theory is descriptive, and not basically prescriptive (though predictive), and that the existence of classes does not prove the inevitability of same. Marx will justify a tolerable degree of inequality for purposes of expediency. He seeks to remove "...morally irrelevant inequalities, inequalities in the primary social goods, or in basic common goods..." With this objective achieved, personal and collective domination would be substantially diminished. Justice and equality are only attainable in a self-governing society.

As a prelude to the French Revolution of 1798, Rousseau had written that "man is born free, and everywhere, he is in chains"; this thinking greatly influenced the Marxist Doctrine, but it must be stressed that there is no assumed "natural" right of all men to be treated exactly alike. Rather, men are born free and equal only in respect of their imprescriptible rights of freedom, property, security, and resistance of oppression. Social distinctions of some sort are bound to exist, but these do not subvert any "natural" right to absolute equality, which Marxists never recognized in the first place. Plato and Aristotle suggest that "a just distribution, in general, is an unequal one", thus there are rights in respect of which men are unequal. This should not mean the desirability of such identified inequality; rather, Marxists only seek to describe the social relations as they are in our existential situation, and to offer solutions which will lead to the radical equalization of all facets of that existence. We must stress, though, that it is the benefits to persons, not allocations of resources as such, that are meant to be made equal, so that unequal distribution would be required to equalize benefits in cases of unequal need. The assumption here is that distribution according to merit will not be an adequate criterion. Human beings have a right to their wellbeing, as well as an equal right to the means of wealth (noting the conditions). From this, one could further identify the implied principle to be that distribution should be so done as to ensure general equality at its highest attainable level.

Given men's sensitivities to honor and dishonor, when merit is made the measure of their human dignity, their own sense of dignity tends to be distorted. If they are talented and successful, praise misdirected from their achievements to their person will foster the illusion that they are superior human beings, and they may claim, on moral grounds, a privileged status for their own wellbeing. Conversely, if low achievement stocks are taken as parameters of personal worth, which have no iota of plausibility whatsoever, then they are human inferiors of others, and their emotions and aspirations are inferior to those of others. Marx's ingenuity is laid bare by his perception of the whole from the point of view of an even more comprehensive totality (that of a great historical process). He had a particular fondness for Economics, having related virtually all his topics to it. His analysis of Capitalism was influenced by: a. the technological fact of large accumulation of industrial capital, leading inevitably to the factory system, b. the social fact that this capital (that is, the instrument of production) was alienated from the workers who actually produced, and controlled by a separate class of owners.

The combined facts of the non-ownership of means of production by the Proletariat, together with the equation of human labor with commodities, are good indices of the inequality of the Capitalist System. For Marx, no one chooses to be poor, or, at least, not to have enough resources for the satisfaction of his basic needs. Conflicts become pronounced between the two classes when the bourgeoisie begins to witness a "falling rate of profit", as a result of which they increase their rate of exploitation of the Proletariat in order to make more profits, or, at least, maintain the present profit margin. The injustice of this practice is given expression in the fact that the Capitalists least consider the interests of the workers, nor do they pay the workers wages that could be adjudged commensurate with their labor input. Seeking maximum profits, capitalists create artificial job scarcity, so that desperate workers accept even lower wages and worse conditions of service than they would accept otherwise. The exploitation of the resultant surplus labor is yet another manifestation of this exploitative dynamic which widens the inequality.

Marx recognizes that the owners of the means of production also constitute the ruling class, so that they have the State Apparatus at their disposal for the crushing of all dissent, as well as stifling voices which could be identified as disseminating obstructive criticism. The long-term fall in profits, as machinery grows relative to labor, is the main problem for capital. Each boom will be weaker, as a result of which the capitalists transfer their exploitation into other societies, thereby increasing the number of their "victims." This is the seed of Imperialism; this international dimension to the capitalist impulse propels the Marxian charge to workers worldwide to unite. A fundamental assumption made by Marx was that all wealth was created by labor (not necessarily just manual labor); he also understood that different wages could be paid to different kinds of labor. For him, technology leads to both growth in the economy (benefit for the capitalists) and unemployment (due to the gradual displacement of labor by machines). To avoid concentrating enormous wealth and power in a few hands, Socialists would want to make the distribution of resources a social concern instead. Inherited wealth and status also worsen the inequality and must be discouraged. For them, inequalities of wealth are essentially expressions of the basic differences in accessing opportunities. How about talent, energy level, networks, location, experience, luck, enterprise, risk appetite, etc.?

In our modern economic system, fiscal policies could also favor some while substantially disadvantaging others. The granting of discretionary waivers and tax breaks, as well as the treatment of Capital Gain (not as an income), for example, could very easily distort outcomes for different players. Exploiting the loopholes in the Tax Code also widens the inequality band and could be a function of access to good education or the means to pay for professional advisory services, which a majority will be unable to possess. Marxists adhere to an "objective theory" of class-determination, that is, they assume that some objective (in the sense of being anti-subjective, accessible to all, outside us as persons) criteria which determine our class affiliations, e.g. the economic factor. Forms and conditions of production thus become the basic determinants of the class structure and class attitudes, e.g. ownership, or otherwise, of the means of production.

This is predicated on certain assumptions: productive relations and Division of Labor should be largely undifferentiated, so that the society is easily categorized into definite groups, each possessing an unambiguous relation to the means of production. The critique of this assumption is that, in modern times, there are service occupations or careers, which are not related in any direct way to the physical means of production.

Technology has also increased the number of skills a person may now have; labor may not constitute a clear-cut class, especially also with increasing globalization and international outsourcing. The society has become greatly differentiated, so that human (interpersonal) relations are now mediated. Another assumption of the thesis is two-pronged: there is a "scarcity economy" in which the Proletariat only seek to satisfy their subsistence needs while the capitalists are in perpetual fear of the possible violent uprising that will culminate in their dispossession of what they regard as their own. From a group prism, cumulative beneficiaries of systemic injustice always resist statutory adjustments that seek to compensate the excluded and marginalized while ultimately enthroning merit.

The interacting triad of education, style, and occupational status is a more important emblem of social inequality than income, hence the failure of income-redistribution to diminish class-consciousness. Marxists need to broaden their theory beyond the merely economic. Social distress and need are products, not solely of primary poverty, or an absolute lack of means, but also, and in fact significantly, of other more subtle and varied causes which operate far above the subsistence level. Any primary poverty which remains must take the first priority in a Marxist-led society. Social equality is directed at ending or relieving this social distress. They dismiss the Subjective Theory of Class because of its implication that individuals, by self-evaluation, can select which classes they wish to belong to, in which case the term "class" loses its meaning. "Class' becomes useful only in collectivity; man is a social being; though subjective evaluations of class are vital to an awareness of which classes we actually belong to, there has to be an objective determination of this. Moreover, "subjectivism" is relative to individuals, and there is no way we can even know definitively what a person's internal workings are.

Absolute equality is simply impossible; not even class-consciousness can be totally eliminated. The highest that could be achieved is the abolition of formal "units" called classes, as well as perennial and formalized class struggles. The degree of vertical mobility has an impact on the progress which can be made in this regard. The greater the mobility, the greater the degree of social equality, plus free socialization. In modern society, it is not sufficient to expect the restoration of equality by making the rich less rich in order to make the poor slightly less poor. There are extraneous factors that demand consideration, for example, there is now a large Middle Class, which is between the proletariat and the bourgeoisie, so that it becomes very difficult to isolate either the bourgeoisie or the proletariat, strictly speaking.

The enthronement of social equality will lead to the diminution of social antagonism, and the avoidance of social waste. When Adam Smith writes that "the affluence of the rich excites the envy of the poor, who are often driven by want, and prompted by envy to invalidate his possession", he should be told that contrasts in wealth profiles, when isolated, do not now seem to cause general resentment. Non-pecuniary inequalities (which lead to differential wealth in the first place) are of greater significance and excite the more resentment and repudiation. Coming from the premise that the inequality in the society is man-made, Marx seeks a human solution to the "problem" as well. He recognizes that the beneficiaries of the system will seek to perpetuate their hegemony over the oppressed, especially since the former also command the instruments of coercion. Based on this, Marx recommends a violent struggle to overthrow the "system of oppression." To be specific, he writes that the specific features of socio-economic inequality and exploitation should be studied in order to determine the appropriateness, or otherwise, of the recourse to violence as a means in this balancing struggle. In other words, he does not rule out the possibility of achieving social equality and the abolition of exploitation -- private appropriation of socially-produced labor resources -- through non-violent means. It may be added that a non-violent revolution sounds like a contradiction in terms; an oxymoron.

This Marxist Doctrine has inspired resistance struggles and movements by all oppressed people around the world, with their unified goal being their emancipation from the yoke of oppression and mass slavery. The abiding humanism which characterizes Classical Marxism is given expression here, but the central nullifying charge of naiveté and non-recognition of disparate talents/ capacities remains valid. Moreover, any attempt to impose equality (in theory) will negatively impact output, reduce living standards, adversely affect the incentive to innovate and work hard, depress the volume of savings, and lead to economic inefficiency as the effort-reward dynamic will become distorted. Social mobility must be available to all, thus curing some of the economic disparities. In the absence of such flexibility and movement, the impulse towards the violent demolition of the extant structure becomes desirable. Social mobility strengthens the society's leadership by placing emphasis on excellence, not mediocrity and entitlement or inherited social status and networks. A Socialist traces large-scale inequalities to inherited capital, not to the distribution of earned incomes, thus s/he recommends upturning the entire structure. It must be stated that the reality is far more nuanced than this linear assessment and convenient categorization.

In any case, any notional theoretical equality will not lead inevitably to a better society, as there is more to life than just money. This is not to say that we need apodictic certainty about the future to be concerned about the present. An essential feature of our humanity is the finitude of our knowledge; when we add our rationality, there cannot be any absolutism about the certainty of our predictions about the future. Additionally, how do we know what the future will yield unless we bring that future into the present, that is, unless we act, acting being a present and current undertaking? Fair treatment, not equality, should be a sufficient barometer in calibrating human outcomes.

While the Marxist demand for equality is a tenet of Utilitarianism, it must be underscored that Utilitarianism is not the sole motivating factor in social distribution as such. Rather, there are times it even becomes imperative -- for matters of expediency -- for the ruling class to initiate a program that could approximate to a semblance of social distribution, thus emphasis is usually on non-economic value-considerations, and not simply on a conception of an "equal" society. Let's attempt some rhetorical questions: is it the case that greater equality will be accompanied by a cultural loss? Whose culture? Do the tenets of modern political systems, that is, free opportunities for all citizens, universal suffrage, democracy, really support or assume absolute equality in all respects? This writer personally thinks not.

Power and Will are conflicting criteria by which power and equality are determined. While Marxism is concerned with collectivity, it does not neglect the importance of the individual. For Marx, the material life of the individual, which depends on other factors apart from their Will, is the real basis of the State. When this material life is subverted, it then becomes necessary to change it from source; invariably, this means change in a larger context, the State. It is significant that Marx criticizes Utilitarianism as being basically bourgeoisie in content, and as not being adequate for the enthronement of social equality; it is mostly for this reason that he rejects Political Economy. It is a central thesis of Marxism that demand influences production; one realizes that the amount of time put into production has no necessary connection with its usefulness and value. Social relations are closely related to the mode of production, as was witnessed at the various stages of historical development.

It might be useful to sensitize John Rawls' central contrarian arguments against the Marxist Doctrine on equality. The theme of all contrarian theories of justice is that the State and its citizens are engaged in a contract; each party has to honor its obligation to the other in order to ensure the continued validity of this contract relationship. Rawls assumes that people exist in a cooperative enterprise, and that the success of this enterprise depends on the general obedience to its rules by the members; and that the enterprise complies with the principles of justice. The fact that a person benefits from his participation in this enterprise is exactly the reason why he should obey the rules of this small social unit; this *prima facie* obligation is owed to one's co-members who make it possible for one to derive the aforementioned gains. It is an obligation of "fair play;" justice as fairness.

Rawls' thesis revolves around the inevitability of classes in the society, and juridical considerations necessarily incorporate this feature. This coheres with the capitalist system, characterized as it is by class division and a move towards more industrialization, among other things. This class dichotomy has its attendant implications for the varying levels of opportunity which members of a society have. Rawls does not see this as detracting from social equality in any way, which is truly odd, unless he is but a bourgeoisie writing to propagate his political beliefs, namely capitalism and the exploitation of the many by the few. For him, justice is to be attained by a redistribution of income in which the expectations of the less fortunate members of the society are maximized in a manner that will tally with the precepts of fair equality of opportunity and equal liberty. He seems to be arguing from both sides actually, but a deeper reflection will show more nuance than otherwise implied.

Marxism is both a rejection of both Utilitarianism and "Justice as Fairness." Rawls rejects Utilitarianism because, for him, it is possible to "consider the interests of everyone alike even when doing so will not produce the greatest utility." It is debatable if this truly departs from the theory it seems to reject, since the satisfaction of the general interest implies the maximization of utility. Furthermore, it is possible to be a member of the privileged class and yet abhor the inequality of the social system. In all, Marxism is more egalitarian than Rawls' theories, and Marxists demonstrate a more convincing impact of the consequences of socio-economic and political inequalities than Rawls does. Rawls's theory specifies the "proper role of government, its purpose, and limits." For his theory to germinate, members of the society -- a mental construct -- must be ignorant of their personal characteristics, talents, and their situation in the society: a veil of ignorance must cover them. The advantage of this general ignorance is that people will then fight to minimize their misfortunes and will make no bogus claims to varying degrees of right, hence they will act in ways which will promote and enhance the equal distribution of all social values. This equal liberty is hypothetical, it must be noted. It is difficult at this stage to know who was more utopian: Marx or Rawls.

The term "Justice as fairness" is derived from the assumption of original fairness (given the veil of ignorance) among men. It is a matter for debate if Utilitarianism is the economic model which will be adopted in this "innocent" and "pure" society, especially as the members perceive one another as being equals. What is then the need to act in ways that will add to the benefit of others, while impliedly denying oneself? If this sacrifice is made, then the original position of equality and fairness is thereby subverted. Rawls criticizes Utilitarianism because of its conflict with the notion of reciprocity which is a basic feature of a society. Part of what it takes for there to be a society is that there are many persons, not just one person, and such people agree to coexist by relinquishing their individual powers (in the Rawlsian formulation, the need for this does not arise because the "veil of ignorance" already takes care of that). For Rawls, the only pieces of information which the members have are related to the fundamentals of human society, as well as the "fact" that their society is built on the altar of justice.

However, the problem there is that it is unlikely, to say the least, that human beings occupying a historical context will be ignorant of so many things as Rawls assumes. His defence might be a reference to his earlier claim that his entire Construct is hypothetical, not a reflection of what obtains spatio-temporally. Nevertheless, if the "contracting parties' are this ignorant, what justification do we then have to characterize their relation as a form of contract? Contracts are entered into by willing and rational persons who have a proper understanding of all the (contract) terms, their rights and obligations, as well as the contents and implications. It is difficult to sustain his central arguments: the equal right of all persons to equal basic liberties, and the conditions under which social inequalities can be justified, on this basis.

Rawls' assumption about the altruism of man -- either express or implied -- is misplaced when the selfish nature of human beings is put in sharp focus. Though he recognizes the *prima facie* obligation of fair play, he does not seem to be fully aware of its limitations. Going by his characterization, there will a difficulty in determining when individuals have an obligation to obey the rules of their society, for example, if A has an obligation of reciprocity to obey the rules (in order to please B who earlier acted in a way from which A benefited), and his compliance with such rules neither benefits B nor does his disobedience harm the community, it is almost impossible to decipher how fairness to B is an indication that A must comply with the rules. Furthermore, Rawls' consideration is limited to an undifferentiated social system where human relations have not become sophisticated; this clearly shows the inadequacy of his schema for juridical considerations or determinations in the modern society which is characterized by mediated personal relations, increased mobility, considerable advancements in Science, Technology, Transportation, Communication, and even in Law.

Individuals make up a society, as it does not exist *ex nihilo* (out of nothing or on its own), so that its satisfaction of the members' needs is an indirect way of saying that those people satisfy their own needs. Rawls' assumption of absolute cooperation by the members of a society is not supported by experience, otherwise, the world will not have its preponderance of problems. Kai Nielsen criticizes Rawls' Paper, "Class and Justice", by saying that Rawls has not demonstrated a proper understanding of what classes are, and what a classless society would be like, hence Rawls' basic assumption that classes are inevitable remains a misnomer. Marxism does not assume this inevitability. Rawls seems to ignore the fact that even when a society is "well-ordered", variations in men's status will also obtain. By implication, Rawls is saying that a capitalist society, which thrives on exploitation and the institutionalization of division, is a "just" system. Some objectivity would have aided his analysis.

Furthermore, his "egalitarian" doctrine, which is supposed to apply to a society divided by classes, is limited in that it fails to anticipate the possibility of a classless society. Since classes determine the inequalities in the society, one can assume that the differences in opportunity among men are not unjust, since they are "inevitable." In this case, however, it must be stated that an extreme form of determinism is being embraced by Rawls. While Marxists find it difficult to concede the possibility of a socialist revolution degenerating into a new form of a structured and exploitative system, it is safe to remind them that this has already come to fruition. While Marx seems to have an unlimited faith in man's ability to know what is in his best interest, the reality, however, is that we often act out of ignorance; at times, man is self-destructive, and can also be manipulated by other men. The problems that an excessive devotion to revolutionary goals will lead to are: extreme self-confidence, exclusiveness, suspicion, and intolerance towards other points of view.

Marx writes that, in order to achieve justice and equality, individual circumstances, conditions, and specificities should be taken into consideration. One then wonders why he does not perceive the same weakness (of using equal standards for unequal people) in the principle of distribution according to need, which he embraces.

Even if we concede (for the purposes of argumentation) that distribution according to the products of labor is merely idyllic, redistribution will still be necessary because some unjustified social differences, which would lead to injustice and inequality, would still remain. Based on this, it is difficult to assume that any free and fair equality of opportunity shared by all men, is an indication of equality among men. In Marxism, therefore, we fail to see any definiteness as to what elements constitute equality. Accordingly, Marx and Marxists would have done well to provide substantiation on whether or not the totality of the ends of the ends of Socialism -- equality, justice, and freedom, add up to a consistent social trend, involving the use of State Power, and the eventual disappearance of the State. It is conceivable that the resolution of the conflict existing between two classes with varying and opposing economic interests will culminate in a State Apparatus which is not really controlled by either of the two, so that the State is not merely a reflection of the economic arrangement of the society.

Regarding alienation, Marxists need to enlighten us: is there any relation between alienation and the actual ownership of the means of production, or is it just a consequence of the improvement in productive forces, and in the organization of business concerns? Both capital and labor are vital to the production process. It is only in an undifferentiated society, with a minimal level of production and at general economic infancy, that the worker alone can determine both the conditions on which the labor-power is used, as well as the use to which means of production are put. Capitalism, in this context, then becomes a system which is characterized by large employment of capital in production. At this stage, the division between capital and labor is inevitable, WHOEVER might be the owner of the means of production. Here, there is an intricate sub-division of labor, as well as a huge labor force.

There is a need for a central organization which decides who gets what, mode and conditions of employment, and the use to which labor should be put. There is a need for a definite hierarchy in the production process. It is not expected that strategic decisions should be taken at mass-meetings (attended by all and sundry), as this is not only cumbersome but also time-consuming and ineffective. Going by this characterization of capitalism, then there is no absolutely Communist or Capitalist country. The crucial point is not really ownership, but the size of the production activity. Even in modern capitalist economies, ownership is gradually being divorced from effective control (with the introduction of shareholding). While the pattern of ownership influences the decisions taken, it does not SOLELY determine these.

Class-stratification could be in more or less concentration in a capitalist or collectivist system. Even when classes have been formally extinguished in Socialist societies, a new breed of leaders emerges either from the hitherto middle or upper middle-class, and they constitute the ruling elite. Yet again, it becomes clear that there is no equality, strictly speaking (including free and equal opportunity) even in Socialist Systems. Factual examples from the former Soviet Union and the Chinese State underscore this point. There is no necessity about the conclusion that when the State expropriates all industries, there will be no class which exerts its will on the people. Indeed, that is exactly what the Politburo does.

The degree of exploitation does not depend solely on the mode of ownership of the means of production. In the modern State, this is determined by the fiscal policy of the government, and by managerial decisions with respect to the disposal of profits. A Socialist country can theoretically extract as much surplus value (via taxation) as a Capitalist country can. In any case, it is not the means of ownership that exclusively determines the distribution of personal income. It is feasible that income distribution will undergo large changes without a comparable variation in ownership. Marx does not tell us why the price mechanism (that is, demand and supply) should be of no relevance to a Collectivist Economy.

The status of the worker is not necessarily higher in a Socialist, than in a Mixed or Capitalist economy, nor is it inevitable that wages and the rate of growth of the economy must be higher in a collectivist, rather than in a privately-owned, economy. As a matter of fact, the most successful economies adopt Capitalism, e.g. the US, Japan, Germany, China (with its capitalist economic system and totalitarian Communist political system, a successful hybrid, one may add), etc. What should be considered include: the degree to which new management is autocratic or democratic, the extent of joint consultation (labor-capital relations), as well as the freedom of the workers to engage in industrial action when Management policies are rationally deemed unfair and exploitative. A Socialist Economy rates poorly in these areas.

As a matter of fact, a Socialist economic system also has some features of Capitalism, including: Executives are paid salaries, Management is different from Labor and is always superior to Labor, etc. Exploitation and "class-consciousness" are, therefore, elements of the Collectivist economy. Professor Haberler, in criticizing the Marxist Economic Theory in his Paper, "Marxist Economics in Retrospect and Prospect", suggests that Marx's "systematic predictions have not worked out, and his Economics is unworkable in practice."

For Marx, once the struggle between the two classes over income ceases, there will then be a Dictatorship of the Proletariat, and the abolition of classes. Even though classes have been formally abolished, it is logical to expect that the members of the defunct classes will retain their class-consciousness, in which case what really obtains is a reversal of roles. Does Marx support class-domination only insofar as the Proletariat constitutes the dominant group? How then would the former bourgeoisie react to this dispossession? How do they get their income in the current situation? Perhaps, they are all to be killed, as indeed the Bolsheviks did in 1917.

Marx states that demand influences production, yet he affirms that the Capitalists own the means of production. Would the latter produce things which would benefit the masses, especially given the antagonism existing between the two classes, and with the exercise of authority by the majority Proletariat? Perhaps, the dispossession takes care of this? The sophisticated Marxist may say that the Labor Theory of Value may not explain actual prices, but rather that it can, and does, explain the "laws of motion of a Capitalist society", that is, why the system is unfair, unstable, and has a short life-span (Haberler).

The Marxist assumption that capital is barren is obviously misplaced, in the light of contemporary realities. For them, it is only labor which has value, therefore, labor should appropriate all profits (products). If this position were the valid case, then one would expect that the higher the amount spent by a company on salaries and allowances, and the less it spends on the acquisition of machinery and technology, for example, the more profitable such a company should be. Again, this assumed relationship is observed more in the breach than in conformity. Mechanized production leads to the Division of Labor which is time-saving, efficient, and maximum production-oriented. It also leads to a reduction in unit prices as a result of economies of scale. These combine to make the product very competitive, and, consequently, *ceteris paribus*, profits will increase. Advances in Science and Technology have made human labor increasingly irrelevant or of less value to the production process, yet prices continue to soar.

Marx may reply that he did not write for this age; even at that, he earlier acknowledged the commencement of mechanized production during his time. The basic mistake in his formulation was the failure to consider human nature, as well as to consider the results of the improvements in the quality of capital, as evident in the rise in productivity. Unemployment is not necessary for a society or company to show high profit, and to keep showing it. All that is needed really is a constant infusion of productive new ideas. In reality, and with the benefit of hindsight, all political systems and programs that promise to create societies without strata and classes, a harmonious community of comrades who are all equal in rank, are severely utopian and dangerous, being, in actuality, merely a veil for the rule of terror by a new class, the more desperate and pernicious class. The movement towards fairness and justice in a society should not be misunderstood as a call for equality; the balancing of forces and resources among individuals and nations only seeks objective fairness, respect, consideration, and dignity at its essential core.

In concluding the section on Moral and Political Philosophy, it would be useful to summarize the lessons learnt in the inimitable words of Mihai and Anca Badescu, as follows:

- Ethical and social life is based on the spirit of preservation of the human being; just reason, necessary to find the just, fair law without resorting to a universal instinct, is sufficient to give a foundation to the law (Hobbes);
- Society is merely a suppression of the state of nature, that is to say of the state of war, by establishing a force large enough to suppress the natural selfishness of the individual (Hobbes);
- Freedom is limited by the State power which people must obey unconditionally (Spinoza);
- The State dominates the citizens because it is stronger. It itself cannot impose limits on conscience, thinking; but not from a legal or rational but a material impossibility, because thinking is inherently incoercible, therefore consciousness is free because it is impossible to be violated (Spinoza);
- The distinction between "inherent" and "acquired" rights must be made: the former are the isolated man's own before he becomes "associated," the other are rights that add to men as they belong to a society, family and State (Pufendorf);
- Man is pushed to associate, by social instinct, and this instinct is considered as a derivation of interest (Pufendorf);
- The powers of the State emanate from the nation through a restriction of individual rights and precisely in order to guarantee the right to life, to freedom, to property (Locke);
- The law must take into account the nature, the factors influencing human life, the material and spiritual states through which people go (Montesquieu);
- There is no freedom outside of the law, no place for anyone to escape the rule of law; even in the state of nature man is free only through the mediation of the laws of nature that govern everything (Rousseau);
- The Social Contract is that ideal form of association in which membership in a political group does not destroy the freedom of individuals (Rousseau);
- A people must always be master of their destinies, and can change their laws at any time, even the good ones (Rousseau);

- The contract is the ideal legal basis of the State; it must be organized, based on the recognition of human rights or as a synthesis of human freedom (Kant);
- Civil society is an economic reality: it is based on the selfish and antagonistic interests of individuals, their needs and their way of organization (Hegel);
- The State is the synthesis between family, based on love and feelings, and civil society, based on antagonism of economic interests (Hegel);
- The State is the union of the ideal and of the real; it is the reunion of freedom and necessity (Schelling);
- To every people, civil law always has well-defined particular features, as well as customs, morals, political organization (Savigny);
- Purpose is the driving force of the world; there is no purposeless action (Jhering);
- State, the sole constraint holder, is the sole source of the law; the constraint exercised by the State is the absolute criterion of the law (Jhering);
- The law is the condition of the moral existence of the person, the defense of the right means the moral preservation of the person (Jhering).

We shall now proceed to assess the impact of these thoughts on the political, economic, and social systems in Europe and across the world, with serious mixed implications for different peoples. Ideas do indeed have consequences.

IV

The Impact of Ideas: How Philosophy Influenced Political, Economic, and Social Systems

It should be clear by now that, at the core of Philosophy, is the deployment of reason in designing and regulating human society, as well as interpreting man's relationship with the Cosmos. Even when we consider Metaphysics, it is still about man's place in the universe, as well as the relationship between man and the supra-rational elements, including death. Logic, Political Philosophy, Ethics, Philosophy of Science, Aesthetics, Philosophy of Religion, and indeed, all the other branches of Philosophy clearly revolve around humanity. From this fundamental perspective, it is unrealistic to expect that Philosophy or Social Science in general can be value-free. Every philosophical position is loaded with value equities. It is actually for this same fact that no philosophical position should be treated as the Holy Grail and precluded from thorough analysis. All those views were propagated by imperfect humans with their own prejudices and perspectives on the contemporary issues of their time. Indeed, philosophy plays a significant role in determining the *weltanschauung* (the aggregate worldview) of a society. With all our views, we are all philosophers…

Some scholars have suggested that this value-investment is "evidence" that Philosophy and the Social Sciences are inferior to the Natural Sciences, which have no value component. As mentioned earlier, Philosophy is about humans; its various branches deal with various aspects of human life from a rational perspective. Being animate, rational, and conscious entities, human beings employ value considerations in most things they do. These values differ from person to person as a result of differences in levels of morality, environment, experiences, cultural background, educational attainment, etc., among men. The "terrorist" and the "freedom fighter" could employ exactly the same means in prosecuting their objectives, while their nomenclature changes depending on the person who is identifying them. To use the common parlance, one man's meat becomes another's poison. While we acknowledge man's imperfections, Philosophy instructs us that there is an objective Truth, and objective Morality, which we can only attain and maintain by leading virtuous lives; by consistently choosing the Harder Right instead of the Easier Wrong. A rigorous fidelity to the precepts of the Golden Rule: "Do unto others as you wish them to do unto you", equips us with the character to embrace Objective, not Situational, Morality at all times.

Max Weber writes that there should be a value-free Social Science (including Philosophy in this context), and that Social Scientists must interrogate the reasons which inform the actions of men but should not try to approve or disapprove these reasons or the resultant actions. J.S. Mill says that the Social Sciences are inexact sciences because they lack the capacity for precise predictions, and also because of their value-laden nature. Human nature easily debunks these postulations. Even if we cannot predict human behavior with certainty, we should be content to understand such behavior, and this is only possible by the indispensability of "values" in Social Scientific and Philosophical inquiries. Both the philosopher's behavior and the one s/he is studying are instances of human behavior. Very often, the observer becomes a part of the observed. The "socialness' of a situation is derived from the "system of ideas' or "mode of living" of either the observer or the observed. Observation, interpretation, and explanation are all informed by value considerations. Human actions have meaning and are purposive.

They are aimed at attaining certain ends or "values', be they intentionally, by force of habit, or due to unreflective involvement. In other words, there is a reason or motive for virtually every human action -- even when these are not consciously acknowledged -- while we speak of causal explanations in Natural Science. Such motives are manifested in actions, policies, rules, regulations, laws, etc., which we understand through the values we hold. The philosopher has to employ '*verstehen*' (interpretive understanding) in her studies. She has to literally enter into the life of her object of study, digging very deep into the influences that have molded the individual. The analyst employs "value" in her selection of problems, in the determination of the contents of her conclusion, in the verification of facts, as well as in the assessment of evidence. The prevalence of the value-concept in the Social Sciences and Philosophy does not necessarily mean that these subjects cannot be objective, though the ingrained values color the approach towards objective standards as well as the results of the Social Sciences.

It was objectively evil and wrong to sell and buy other human beings, yet this persisted for centuries, rationalized by the perpetrators and beneficiaries even as they exported their religion around the world. Taking another person's life without cause is wrong, yet it happens routinely without consequences depending on who kills and who is killed. It is theoretically possible that a Social Scientist can "purge" herself of her own values and preconceptions while conducting an analysis. In this case, she is only concerned with the value/s of her object of study. Here, some form of objectivity could be assumed, but values are still involved, nevertheless. If the analyst is unable to detach fully, the conclusion is usually tainted, facts could be distorted, or the analyst simply demonstrates a total incapacity to deal with the analysis. The truth, however, is that the analyst approaches her mandate from a baseline of acquired knowledge or normative values. No two persons are exactly the same; therefore, it will be unrealistic to expect all members of a group to have exactly the same values and attitudes on all issues at all times. Having said that, there are certain dispositions and traits that are pervasive in particular demographics.

The task of justification in a Rational Enterprise is to show how the subjective conditions of thought and of our conditioned sensibility impair objective inquiry and validation, and not merely to achieve subjective proof. Normative statements are standard and normal components in the assessment of societal trends, and these are driven by values. The philosophical ideas we have highlighted in the preceding section had real-life consequences for human beings and cannot be analyzed strictly as abstract concepts. The codification of racism into a coherent structure, for example, led to slavery, colonialism, genocidal activities, and the dehumanization of "the other." Here, ingrained values had enduring and grave consequences for vast sections of mankind.

The Separation of Church and State, as well as the eventual emphasis on the individual as deserving of fundamental rights, inspired Revolutions and affected political systems to this day. Implicit and explicit value-premises about desired goals must, therefore, be treated with the serious attention that they deserve because, to be trite, ideas and values do have material effects. What will be undertaken immediately hereunder is a cursory synopsis of the evolution of the concepts of political independence and sovereignty in the past five hundred odd years, as well as how the preceding philosophical thoughts influenced or inspired significant social, political, and economic developments in Europe and, subsequently, around the world to the present period in history.

The Peace of Westphalia of 1648 was a pivotal development in the political development of old Europe, as it marked the emergence of the modern State.

The thirty-year war (1618 -- 1648) was a sustained and major clash between traditional and modern political Orders; between religion (Catholic Church) and Secularism, which had the fundamental objective of settling the question of political authority. Gross writes that this "represents the majestic portal which leads from the old into the new world." From this moment going forward, the era of what Mowat calls the "age of scientific and political curiosity, of investigation, of the assertion of the freedom of thought and will" was ushered in.

In the preceding Medieval Era, political jurisdictions overlapped; power was decentralized, and subjects often owed allegiances/ taxes to multiple authority figures; authority was derived from personal ties, inspired by religious fervor. The Catholic Church was engaged, at that time, in a bipolar relationship that entailed both a struggle for domination and collaboration with the Holy Roman Empire. The key drivers of this relationship included mutual dependency, Kings acting as "Defenders of the Faith", and the Pope relying on royal support to remain in power. It must be stated that the Catholic Church was vehemently opposed to the overthrow of the *Ancien Regime* in which it was the First Estate of the Realm; it opposed what it considered as Liberalism, namely, individuals being granted fundamental rights and citizens deciding their collective political outcomes, rather than relying absolutely on the imposed worldview and terms of the Monarchs and the Church.

Indeed, Pope Pius IX, in his Syllabus, wrote that "Curst be he who says that the Roman Pontiff can and ought to reconcile himself and come to terms with progress, liberalism and modern civilization." Nelsen and Guth write that Pius IX, in the Papal Syllabus of Errors (1864), condemned religious toleration, secular philosophy, the sovereignty of the people, secular public education, separation of Church and State, and divorce, refusing to "reconcile himself to, and agree with, progress, liberalism, and civilization as lately introduced." The Syllabus of 1864 condemned "all modern movements and tendencies", while imposing a gag on believers, in what Mowat calls "the assertion of sheer intellectual tyranny." As he further writes, "it was a denial of the right of the individual mind to seek out truth -- the ultimate basis of all intellectual, moral and material progress. It was a proclamation that man must give up his curiosity-- his invincible curiosity which makes him man -- and become forever intellectually submissive." It must be acknowledged that, shocked at this claim of the Papal Infallibility and extreme conservatism, Austria revoked the existing Concordat with the Vatican, thereby denying the Catholic Church of special rights in Austria and across its areas of influence.

It is concerning to the non-invested reader and analyst that, despite these vocalized and unambiguous positions of the Head of The Catholic Church against the progressive tenets and ambition of the French Revolution, for example, a relatively-new School has emerged in Theology which seeks to ascribe ultimate credit for the Enlightenment Period to the Catholic Church itself. This is quite some audacious cheekiness, in one's view. Their Doctrine is called Catholic Enlightenment, and posits that since, for example, the Catholic Church made "contributions to the abolition of torture, the deterrence of violent religious outbursts, the ending of the Inquisition, the prohibition of witch hunts", as well as what they boldly claim to be "the move towards more religious freedom, tolerance, and freedom of speech, all of which helped to civilize Europe", the Catholic Church must be recognized as the historical and philosophical inspiration for the Enlightenment. We are also told that the Pietism, which inspired "optimism about the potential of human nature" -- the foundation for Rational Thinking and Progressive Politics -- came from Catholicism and the Judeo-Christian tradition, hence the Enlightenment cannot be divorced from Catholicism.

There is no doubt that Catholicism made significant contributions to Europe in the areas of Philosophy, Theology, Statecraft, Letters, Science, Arts, Architecture, Aesthetics, Culture, Pageantry, and Diplomacy; what is indisputable, however, is that the Catholic Institution was vehemently against freedom and choice for individuals. Indeed, the Catholic Church saw itself as the Guide and Master of Mankind, with Europe, of course, being the center of the universe. As reflected in Capone's "Catholics and Europe During The 19th Century", the preference was what an anonymous voice called the "Social Monarchy of Jesus Christ" (*Le catholicisme ou la barbarie*, 1854). Undivided, absolute, unquestioning, illiberal papal monarchy, one may add. The insistence on taking all the credit for all the advancements in Europe emanates from this primary mindset.

This is quite a lot to accept and seems to the layman as an attempt at revisionism. The ordinary man on the street will like to trust what the Pope says: his declarations and efforts against the empowerment of the individual, the transfer of power and sovereignty to the citizens, the separation of Church and State, the preference for Papal Despotism, etc., are evident enough. Over forty thousand people were killed during the French Revolution, which was, in reality, a Revolution against the ultra-conservative Orthodoxy, which favored the Catholic Church, Monarchs, and Aristocracy.

It is telling that theorists of this new Catholic Enlightenment like Ulrich L. Lehner and Michael Printy, for example, acknowledge that the so-called

Enlightenment sought by thinkers of the Catholic Faith needed to accept that unlimited reason would lead to anarchy, and that the "sacred doctrine and hierarchy" must be sacrosanct. Suggestions within the Faith are different from a holistic and fundamental reordering of the society. They further inform us that: "religion presupposes a civil society that is brought to perfection within it." The preference is that the Catholic Church must determine and regulate whatever developments and changes that take place within the society, with the Church doctrines and hierarchy imposed on, or applicable, to all, with the Eminences of the Church retaining an uncontested magisterial and imperial perch in the hierarchy of the society. They must solely interpret sacred books, make rules for the society, confer or withdraw status, determine the curriculum in schools, engage in Diplomacy and make binding treaties, define and enforce the boundaries of discourse, administer taxes and levies, impose their preferred norms and practices on the society, grudgingly share power with monarchs, completely exclude independent-minded individuals except those powerful enough to threaten their Order, etc. This is what they regard as Enlightenment. And these are our fellow men (because they also excluded women from their *sanctus sanctorum*) laying claims to these powers because they claim to have a monopoly on the management of the Soul, that part which has never been seen or proven.

Plongeron writes, for example, that the in-house Catholics seeking slight changes "sought an enlightened and rational Obedience and Faith (*obsequium rationabile*)." The identified Catholic Reformers (for that was just what they were) might have suggested slight adjustments in liturgy and rituals within the boundaries of inherited and accepted Orthodoxy. Of course, reformers must believe in the system, and can only cause cosmetic or essential changes without affecting the core fundamentals of the system. That is exactly the point; the real Enlightenment needed to overthrow all of that and empower individuals to think for themselves in just any way they pleased, rather than retain the man-made Order that empowered a few, while limiting and oppressing the majority. With the Enlightenment, there were no limits, so these latter-day circuitous formulations do not hold much water. The Catholic Church vigorously fought against the Enlightenment Era and lost out, which forced it to subsequently enter into *Concordats* with evil creatures like Mussolini and Hitler, just to remain relevant; this epochal development of the actual Enlightenment released mankind from mental shackles and enabled boundless thinking, for which the world remains grateful. Fundamental Human Rights, the concept of Sovereignty, and Universal Adult Suffrage, for example, would not have been possible if the Catholic Church had the power to stop them.

The Reformation Movement (Martin Luther), the new control of monarchs over their local Church (as exemplified in England under King Henry VIII -- thanks, Anne Boleyn), the Enlightenment Philosophers, and the French Revolution, freed humanity from bondage. In any case, as earlier cited, any monopoly of power held by the Church, or indeed any fraternity of humans however clad and presented, poses considerable risk for the world, especially for those considered to be outside the natural family of the Creed or Ideology. The Catholic Church was not always a catalyst or bearer of good tidings for all of the human race; if it proudly asserts its role as the incubator of the unified European identity and culture, it must also accept its other roles which had a major deleterious impact across the world. Any portrayal to the contrary is not a valid reflection of historical facts. It might be useful to render the terms of the Dogma of Papal Infallibility in full, to highlight how it stood in contradistinction to the Movement towards rationality, inquiry, debate, and scientific discovery:

"Accordingly we, faithfully adhering to the tradition which goes back to the origin of Christianity, for the glory of the Savior, for the exaltation of the Catholic religion and the salvation of Christian peoples, we with the approval of the Sacred Council teach and define that it is a dogma divinely revealed, that when the Roman Pontiff speaks *ex cathedra*, that is, when discharging the office of the Shepherd and Doctor of all Christians, in virtue of his supreme apostolic authority he defines a doctrine to be held by the Universal Church concerning faith or morals, he enjoys (by divine assistance promised to him in the blessed Peter) that infallibility by which the Divine Redeemer wished His Church to be instructed in the definition of doctrine concerning faith or morals; and therefore such definitions of the Roman Pontiff are irreformable of themselves, and not by virtue of the consent of the Church."

Quoting directly from Mowat's informative and comprehensive analysis, Cavour was probably right when he said that there was no more certain truth in the world than the impossibility of reforming the temporal power of the Pope. Yet Cavour was confident of being able to solve the Roman Question and, shortly before his death, told a friend that he hoped to be able "to sign, on the Capitol, another religious peace which would have as grand results for the future of human society as the Peace of Westphalia."

The concepts of Sovereignty and Authority became intertwined in the 17th century. Jean Bodin, who was the main theorist of the modern idea of sovereignty, defined it as "absolute and perpetual authority of a State." Sovereignty entails the ultimate authority of a ruler over a given territory, which could not be compromised by outside influences, including the Catholic

Church. This was a revolutionary concept at the time. In this absolute formulation of sovereignty, there was nothing above the State to set any limit on State behavior, not even a higher Moral Law; State sovereignty continued after the life or displacement of its leaders. For the first time, sovereignty became and remained an attribute of State Power, regardless of changes of leadership. The State now had its own enduring character and notional inevitability, at least in Europe. It must be observed that one form of absolutism was exchanged for another; the various political units and militias across the new geographical space called a State were conquered militarily into submission, to achieve the desired centralization of authority.

In the Leviathan, Thomas Hobbes wrote that the State should wield its power over its members through a ruler (or assembly) and "direct their actions for the common benefit." For him, these common benefits were mostly actions that benefited the State. Hugo Grotius was a pioneer in the field that has metamorphosed into International Law, to regulate the relations between and among States. He characterized this as *De Jure Belli as Pacis* (1625) -- Society of States acting together for their common good. He also wrote that the international community should be guided by common ideas regarding legitimate State behavior. He recommended Laws founded on religious notions of morality which States were obliged to respect through "mutual consent", and which, hopefully, would restrict them from provoking international conflicts. He was particularly seeking an end to the armed conflicts that had substantially devastated Europe during his time. Just how idealistic and naive this great Jurist was, would be demonstrated after his time....

The Industrial Revolution was achieved owing to certain preceding triggers. J. Salwyn, Shotwell Schapiro, and James T. -- Ed., writing on "The Industrial Revolution" in The Modern and Contemporary European History (1815 -- 1836), identified some of these factors as follows: the so-called discovery of America (for, it always existed and was inhabited by the local population!), the re-emergence of China on the international scene, a hitherto unthinkable volume of raw materials became available (in America's case, on the backs of black slave labor); the prevailing manufacturing processes could not speedily and efficiently convert this new stock of raw materials into finished goods, thus creating a serious incentive for innovation; the precious metals (especially gold and silver) from Continental America inspired the gradual replacement of Barter Trade with the Money Economy, thereby easing the process of international trade. Capital became fluid and could be transported easily; modern banks also sprang up with their gold and silver reserves as well as a coherent credit system needed for large commercial transactions; while joint-stock corporations had developed in the 17th century especially through the (British) East India companies, the new availability of huge capital outlays enabled volume transactions on scales that were hitherto impossible to contemplate; and the navigation of the Atlantic and Pacific oceans expanded global trade volumes, thereby ushering in the era of modern world-wide commerce.

As the preeminent power in the world at the time, England benefited the most from these developments, and, indeed, hosted the Industrial Revolution. Paraphrasing the writers, capital, labor, and natural resources are the core requirements for industrial development. With an abundance of iron and coal, and other resources from its vast colonial empire, England was the undoubted global leader of the time. Having also displaced the Dutch and French in accessing foreign resources, she had a substantial reserve of capital for investment. The Commercial Revolution also dampened the power of the Guild System, which still held sway on the Continent, inadvertently strengthening the merchants. Joint-stock companies replaced the Guild System in England, and the guaranteed access to both raw materials (from the colonies) and an expanded market, inspired a marked improvement in the quality of available banking services as well as the extended tenor for the repayment of loans.

Applying machinery on an industrial scale to the production of clothing from cotton (grown and processed by black labor), this enhanced production and led to improvements and further innovations in tooling and machine-production. Cotton had replaced wool and linen as the default materials for making clothes in England. It will be useful to know if this pivotal contribution of forced black labor to the Industrial Revolution, wealth of England and the US, as well as the radical changes in the social and economic structures of the world, has been duly acknowledged, albeit retroactively. In the old manufacturing system, which revolved around families and catered to local markets, "there was no overproduction, no great fluctuation of price, no panics, and no great unemployment because the goods made were staple articles for a limited and definitely known market. Such luxuries as were in demand were importations from the East for the use of the wealthy few," according to the authors. With industrialization, however, the simplicity of the production process had given way to an impersonal manufacturing process, which introduced scale, speed, efficiency, and new markets for exploitation.

The hand labor gave way to machine production; producing for the immediate local community was replaced with production for distant and invisible markets; risk was introduced to replace the "Domestic System" that was run by households; speculative production replaced certainty, with the positive implications for margins. Machinery represents the ultimate expression of man's domination of the universe, according to Salwyn, et al, and this is a valid point. With the factory system, expanded production, large workforce, and specialization, the internal functions of a modern-day Corporation were being incubated, namely, Human Resources, Finance, Manufacturing and Operations, Research and Development, IT, Strategic Planning, Sales and Marketing, etc. The Organogram and various functions were refined with time and with the increasing sophistication of the society. With the pioneering revolutionary advances in transportation and communication, man had begun to dominate both time and space. With the latter also, the world had progressively shrunk into a "global village" and the isolated existence of prehistoric and medieval times had begun to recede permanently. The interconnectedness of the world had commenced in earnest, never to cease.

The notable early areas where machines made a difference, and generated considerable wealth for England were cotton, steam engine, steel, military technology, communication, electricity, and transportation technology. With the steam engine, for example, man exerted his Will over nature "independently of geography, of climate, of wind, of tide, of current", a truly revolutionary stage in man's history. The Age of Steel replaced the Age of Wood and Stone, with significant and enduring ramifications for mankind. The empowering confidence from these achievements released further creativity and amplified the message of the Enlightenment philosophers who emphasized reason, inquiry, and pursuit of knowledge, rather than a reflexive surrender to superstition and acceptance of finitude in man's capacity to solve his problems, however complex. This tradition has been built on in geometric proportions to this day. The can-do spirit and acceptance of responsibility for one's life and experiential outcomes, cohered completely with the Enlightenment Mindset.

It was exactly this progress, one may add, that the Catholic Church was stoutly against, as they sought to retain a monopoly on all knowledge, rather than the democratization of same and the achievement of significant results without the endorsement of the Church. As the writers eloquently testified, "by harnessing Nature, great engineering enterprises became possible. Lofty mountains like the Alps were tunneled; suspension bridges spanned wide rivers; oceans were connected by great canals like the Suez and Panama; the Continents of Europe and Asia were united by the trans-Siberian railway; ancient rivers like the Nile were made entirely navigable. Nothing seemed to bar the progress of man, who removed with the utmost ease obstacles on land and water that once appeared insuperable." One may add, the confidence to explore outer space centuries later, to manufacture and fly the plane, in addition to other feats across board followed, once fear, superstition, and mental shackles were removed.

The Napoleonic War was the catalyst for the export of the Industrial Revolution to Continental Europe, after the failure of initial protective policies. In the "new country", the United States of America, while the Industrial Revolution started in the 18th century, it accelerated after the Civil War in the 19th century. The introduction of the Industrial Revolution to Africa and Asia took an exploitative form, with very dire consequences for the peoples of those Continents, as well as their environment, to this day. With the Industrial Revolution in Europe, significant changes were made to population density levels, internal migration from the villages to new towns and cities near the factories for opportunities, as well as to urban and regional planning. Modern cities had emerged. The new Industrial Order had direct effects on Law, Construction, Banking and Finance, the structure of government, Trade Unionism and Labor Rights, Customs and Excise Administration, Regulatory Framework for different sectors, longevity indices, lifestyles and interests, income distribution, as well as a rapid growth in the middle class together with their new demands on government, etc., etc. The new Industrial Capitalists, together with the burgeoning middle class, progressively toppled the entitled aristocracy and landed gentry, with translated implications for governance, freedom, and the political culture. Sports, for example, developed exponentially from the Industrial Revolution, as the new labor and the emerging middle class had time for leisure, which was channeled towards creating sporting activities. Before this time, people got all their exercise through endless manual labor as serfs in Europe.

It must be noted that the conditions under which labor worked during this period were unhealthy, undignified, and even dangerous, causing J.S. Mill, as cited in the referenced Paper, to write that it was questionable "if all the mechanical inventions yet made have lightened the day's toil of any human being. They have enabled a greater population to live the same life of drudgery and imprisonment, and an increased number of manufacturers and others to make large fortunes. They have increased the comforts of the middle classes. But they have not yet begun to effect those great changes in human destiny which it is in their nature and in their futurity to accomplish."

The freedom to offer and accept the conditions of engagement during the Industrial Revolution did not mitigate or cure the human predilection for exploitation of the weak. Lyman Abbot had instructed us that "any organization or society which, allowing men to work, still fails adequately to remunerate their work, fails adequately and rightfully to adjust the relations between the workers, and takes so much for the one class that it leaves practically nothing for the other class, or leaves them but a mere pittance and bare subsistence, is an unjust organization or society." In fact, the central thesis of his Paper on Industrial Rights is best rendered directly by him as follows: "The right of every man to work, and the right of every man to the product of his work, are fundamental rights. There is enough to be done, and the world is fruitful enough, to make it possible for every man, in the present stage of civilization, to earn enough to support himself, his wife, and his children in comfort. Any organization, political or industrial, capitalistic or laborers', which impugns this right, prevents this work, or takes from the laborer the product of his industry, whether it be industry of the brain or industry of the muscles, without adequate compensation is unjust. The first industrial duty of society is to protect every man in his right to labor and in his ownership of the fruits of his labor."

For him also, the concentration of wealth in a few hands has serious deleterious consequences for the society; it depresses aggregate demand on which the economy thrives. In his elegant words, "what causes hard times is not over-supply, but under-demand." As the society gets more sophisticated, it actually fosters more mutual dependency among its members; oligopoly threatens and corrupts the integrity of the political system, just as Alexis Tocqueville had observed in the mid 19th century as the greatest domestic threat that could face the United States; the dichotomy between the 'haves' and 'have-nots' engenders class suspicions and warfare, which threaten the very fabric of the society; lastly, the bifurcation of the society along economic lines leads to a second generation of the "idle rich' which takes to gambling, excessive drinking, and licentiousness, while the next generation of the dispossessed and poor, on assuming that there are no realistic opportunities for them, stop striving and become virtually dependent on charity.

This makes them particularly predisposed to antisocial and dangerous behavior. In Abbott's words written in 1901, they "begin to listen to the man who says, "The world owes you a living;" and when a man has begun to think that the world owes him a living he has taken the first step toward getting his living by foul means if he cannot get it by fair. So out of the great working class the poor are recruited, and out of the poor the paupers, and out of the paupers the tramps, and out of the tramps the thieves, and out of the thieves the robbers." For him, therefore, the concentration of wealth leads first to material, second to political, third to industrial, and then lastly to moral evil. In his idealistic formulation, the solution lies in a more balanced distribution of wealth which does not mean taking from the rich to give to the poor, but making it possible for labor to own capital, that is "labor ceases to be a commodity to be hired, and becomes itself the hirer of capital; in other words, until, in lieu of money employing men, men employ money" -- his Democracy of Industry.

Under the previous Serfdom, the Landed Gentry even had some obligations towards their serfs, but under the new regime, capitalists mostly limited their "obligation" to paying the paltry wages, and nothing more. The displacement of human labor gave artisans very few options but to seek employment in such sub-optimal conditions as this, even competing among themselves for these jobs. It may also be noted that several laborers who could not find new jobs and could no longer survive on their prior artisanal craft in the face of the new competition posed by industrialization, emigrated to America, to seek new opportunities.

So also did over two million, five hundred thousand of the Irish poor who were fleeing the Great Irish (Potato) Famine of 1845 to 1849 -- that killed over a million. These new immigrants to America settled mostly in "New England" all the way to Delaware, hence the strong Irish-American population in places like Boston, Delaware, New York, New Hampshire, and Connecticut to this day. From "New England", some of these new immigrants resettled in the Midwest and across their new country. America and Immigration are Siamese twins, you see? While most of the descendants of these early settlers are responsible members of the US society and contribute maximally to the country they know and love, some of them now claim exclusive and primordial ownership of the country, even as their progenitors landed on American shores penniless, with no documentation, and completely destitute.

It might be added here that over a million Germans escaped from their country to the US between 1845 and 1855, due to the acute economic problems, riots, rebellion, and revolution (of 1848); they settled mostly in Ohio, Minnesota, Pennsylvania, and the Midwest states of Wisconsin, Kansas, Nebraska, Indiana, Michigan, the Dakotas, etc. In fact, the capital of North Dakota State is Bismark, named after Otto von Bismark (1815 -- 1898), Germany's first Chancellor, a conservative politician and statesman generally credited with unifying Germany in the 19th century, specifically in 1871. The capital of the neighboring South Dakota State is Pierre, an iconic French name. The capital of the State of Kentucky (actually called the Commonwealth of Kentucky) is Frankfort (the 'o' differentiating it from the spelling of the mother city, Frankfurt, in Germany). You also have towns named Frankfort in Indiana and Nebraska States. There is a beautiful suburban town named Germantown in Montgomery County, Maryland, as well as another Germantown in Indiana.

Presently, with over fifty million US citizens identifying as having German ancestry, they are the single most populous ethnic group in America, with over a million Americans having varying levels of fluency in the German language. Public reporting has confirmed that, in some predominant German-American enclaves, German language is the lingua franca and Community protocols debar "others" from buying property in their midst. In Holmes County, Ohio, for example, over half of the residents speak German at home. This ethnic concentration also explains why Milwaukee, Wisconsin, has more breweries than any other city in the US.

Poles immigrated in large numbers to the US in the 19th and early 20th centuries, to work mostly in the milling and slaughterhouse industries, and settled mostly in Illinois and the neighboring States of the upper Midwest, hence their large numbers (in the Chicago Police, for example) in those parts of America. Between 1880 and 1924, especially between 1900 and 1910, over four million Italians emigrated to the US, to escape the excruciating poverty in the Southern Italy and Sicily Regions. They settled mostly in New York, Chicago, Philadelphia, Chicago, and Boston. Americans of Italian ancestry constitute the fifth most-populous ethnic demographic in the country. It bears emphasizing also that, in relative terms, recent immigrants to the US (since the early 70s, when the apartheid policies in the US started thawing) from Africa, the Middle East, India, and from around the world, are far more educated, sophisticated, accomplished, resourceful, and knowledgeable than these early immigrants from Continental Europe. Could some of the social tension in the land owe to these evident truths? Again, while the majority of these European-Americans are law-abiding and decent Americans, some of them have transferred the hatred of Old Europe to these United States, the New World, defending "blood and soil", and refusing "to be replaced" -- in another's land!!!

When all these immigrants from Europe converged in America, they decided to create a unifying identity to distinguish them from Native Indians and blacks, hence the creation of the "white" color for humans. As written in (Kivel, 1996), "the category 'white' was created as a political construct that was used as an organizing tool to unite Europeans in order to consolidate strength, increasing their ability to maintain control and dominance over the Native Americans and African slaves, which in many places outnumbered Europeans. 'Whiteness' is a constantly shifting boundary separating those who are entitled to have certain privileges from those whose exploitation and vulnerability to violence is justified by their not being white." We learn from other experts (writing in racial equality tools.org) that "not everybody has been considered white at the same time. Irish, Jews, Italians for example went through a process of becoming white. This was a process of assimilation that required certain cultural losses in order to gain white privilege and power. Some people who may have been considered white where they once lived (South America for example) when they moved to the U.S., were then considered Latino by white society." To complete the narrative, we learn that the common term "people of color" is quite loaded with meaning, being "not a term that refers to a real biological or scientific distinction between people. People of color in the U.S. share the common experience of being targeted and oppressed by racism." And yet, this term is casually employed to this day by both the beneficiaries and victims of a melanin-structured society.

As referenced earlier, one of the positive outcomes of the Industrial Revolution was the new emphasis on the Individual; the ethos of Individualism, rather than collectivism and group identification. Hard work, access to capital, innovation, and creativity could dramatically transform one's life. As Salwyn, Schapiro, and James write, "the Individualists were also believers in the doctrines of liberty and equality, which they desired to see applied to political, religious, and intellectual affairs on the principle of equal rights to all and special privileges to none. They became staunch advocates of freedom of speech, equality of all classes before the law, religious toleration, and extension of the suffrage."

By lending their new wealth and numbers to the clamor for democracy, the capitalists and new labor gradually reversed the systems of entitlement and exclusion and brought the "abstract and theoretical" concept of democracy to real life. The ideas of nationalism and unification of standards also benefited from the Industrial Revolution. With inter-Continental travel and migration now made possible by the advancements in transportation and communication, the migration of ideas also spread, as did the concept of internationalism, with the requisite regulatory protocols. People were no longer living in rural silos. Amongst others, these ideas found eloquent expression in the writings of Adam Smith, Malthus, and J.S. Mill. The improvements in transportation and communication also exposed them to identical thoughts and movements across the canal in France and all through the Continent.

Before the Industrial Revolution, developments were mostly slow and unnoticed, except when they had to do with military conquests, plagues, or natural disasters like earthquakes. Now, people could feel the accelerated impact of development and consequential change for the very first time in human history. It is not an exaggeration, in one's view, to affirm that the Industrial Revolution represents the single most significant developmental epoch in the long history of the human race. It provided the irreversible foundation for the subsequent geometric and quantum leaps in all fields of endeavor.

The French Revolution of the late 18th century was also another major political development inspired by the Enlightenment Philosophers, notably Montesquieu, Descartes, Robespierre, Voltaire, and Rousseau, building on the cumulative ideas of their predecessors. Like all major historical developments, this Revolution did not take place overnight; the contending factors and operating context slowly but surely built up until the denouement. The defining political achievements of this Revolution included: the idea that the State should be governed by the popular will of the people, not the whims of a ruler; the locus of authority/sovereignty transferred from the ruler to the ruled; demands for citizen equality/freedom within the State and its recognized legitimacy spilled over into the State's external relations; Draft Declaration on the Rights of Nations (1795) - which introduced changes in the State-Society power relations that mirrored the trends in interstate relations; and States had right to independence from, and equality with, other States (Nincic 1970, 4).

The conception of the society as being fixed began to unravel with the Industrial Revolution, the new wealth of the capitalist class, the democratization of comfort among the emerging middle class, their demand for active and dignified involvement in the political and social processes, as well as the triumph of rationality and inquiry, which characterized the Enlightenment Period. With the new confidence deriving from man's subduing of nature, plus their new wealth, the new bourgeoisie class began to see the world and their society as progressive and dynamic. Scientists and Philosophers had demonstrated that nature ran on immutable laws, which could be discerned through reason. While Montesquieu described the divine right of kings as irrational, Voltaire attached the same badge of irrationality to both the Church and its clergy. For Rousseau, class inequalities had no basis in rationality. As Carlton J.H. Hayes wrote, "Beccaria taught that arbitrary or cruel interference with personal liberty is not in accordance with the dictates of nature or reason."

Everything could now be questioned and assessed on the basis of its innate rationality, or lack thereof. This was the operating environment that preceded and enabled the French Revolution. As to be expected, reactionary and beneficial Powers vigorously resisted these "seditious and blasphemous" ideas. These two radical ideas were the core elements of the French Revolution, which started in 1789, with profound and enduring implications for political systems, economic structures, and social dynamics in Europe and around the world in the past two hundred and fifty odd years. Significantly, the social mobility and empowerment of the individual person went counter to the traditional assumption perpetuated by the Catholic Church and Aristocracy that people were born into particular social classes as a part of God's Plan, and that querying those "Divine Placements" or seeking to emerge out of them would be blasphemous. The popular expression during the pre-Revolution era in Europe was that a man's class was "a station to which God had called him."

Writing in "The Political and Social History of Modern Europe", Hayes instructs us that Philosophy enabled the disposition for the rejection of the Old Order, since it was deemed incompetent and ill-suited for the new realities. Progressively, the Divine Right of Kings was replaced with Democracy, while class distinctions were abandoned in favor of social equality. Given the grave abuses to which successive French monarchs had subjected the people, the cumulative resentment and social tension between the classes could only find expression in a revolution, not any reform. Given the coalition of forces that increasingly favored outspokenness, the absolute divine-right monarchy was degraded to a limited monarchy in 1789, while the rights of the individual were articulated for the first time. In 1792, the monarchy was further transformed, this time into a Republic, and the first-ever crack at modern democracy was attempted in France.

While no two countries or milieus are exactly the same, in evaluating the vulnerability or otherwise of their society to a violent revolution, there are key drivers that are uniformly present: the alienation of the leadership from the people plus the insensitivity and injustice of the social, economic, and political policies and actions; the role of the middle class, if it exists; the state of the economy as felt by the poor person; the aspiration index of the society; the character and management of religious and ethnic differences as well as historical factors; equality or otherwise before the law; the articulation of the aggregate position of the peasants, poor, and artisans; as well as foreign interests. It needs to be emphasized that it is not every breakdown of law and order that is a revolution, but every revolution involves a breakdown of law and order. Protests, criminal activities, mob action, and riots, however widespread and sustained, do not constitute a revolution if there are no significant and determinate political goals being pursued for enactment.

The tenacity of purpose of the revolutionaries, character of King Louis XVI, the arrogance of Queen Antoinette, the hunger in France from a poor harvest and a devastating winter, resilience, defiance of authority, and unity of the oppressed class, combined to determine the trajectory of the Revolution, as well as its eventual success. As is perceptible, it is impossible to determine *a priori* what the trajectory of events would be once the clamor for change starts. By imposing a limited monarchy in the early days of the Revolution, the new National Assembly effectively became the repository of the sovereignty of France, as well as the bona fide representatives of the people. By legally destroying serfdom and feudalism, the National Assembly signposted and commenced a definite march towards social equality.

Drawing inspiration from England's *Magna Carta* of 1215 (plus its Bill of Rights) and the American Declaration of Independence, the Revolutionaries enacted the "Declaration of the Rights of Man and of the Citizen", which drew on Rousseau's thoughts, and was also influenced by the cumulative empowering philosophies of the Enlightenment Era. Some of its enduring Articles are as follows: "Men are born and remain free and equal in rights." The rights of man are "liberty, property, security, and resistance to oppression." "Law is the expression of the general will. Every citizen has a right to participate personally, or through his representative, in its formation. It must be the same for all." "No person shall be accused, arrested, or imprisoned except in the cases and according to the forms prescribed by law." "Religious toleration, freedom of speech, and liberty of the press are affirmed. The people are to control the finances, and to the people all officials of the State are responsible." Thus was born the concept of public opinion. These were truly revolutionary statements for the time; their accord with decency and the human spirit is demonstrated by their enduring impact and aspirational status in various societies to this day.

Given the serious financial issues which preceded the Revolution, and which continued during its pendency, the new National Assembly, on realizing that the Catholic Church owned at least a fifth of all the lands in France, seized these vast parcels of land which they used as security to enable the issuance of paper currency, while the State paid fixed salaries to the Clergy. With the "Civil Constitution of the Clergy" also, the much-diminished cadre of bishops and clergy was made a civil body, elected by the people, and divorced from Vatican sovereign control, while the State took up the payment of their salaries. All the clergy were also compelled to swear an oath to the new "Civil Constitution of the Clergy", to the shock and eternal grief of the Pope. He threatened the clergy with excommunication if they complied, while the State threatened to stop paying the salaries of those clergymen who disobeyed the decree, and also imprison them. As in the *Ancien Regime*, the interests of the entitled nobility and that of the Church were the same, diametrically opposed to both the national interest of France and the redeeming preferences of its marginalized and oppressed poor.

Citing Maier, Nelsen and Guth surmised as follows: "The Revolution of 1789 ranks next to Constantine's conversion and the Reformation in its impact on the Catholic Church. The French Revolution and the subsequent changes it wrought in the nineteenth century had three major effects on the European Catholic Church. First, it overthrew the national churches. The overthrow was violent and thorough in France. The privileges of the church, at least those associated with feudal traditions, were swept away with the aristocracy.

Church property was nationalized. Priests were forced to take an oath of loyalty to a new church constitution. And, for the first time since Diocletian, European rulers persecuted the church as an enemy of the State. Second, the Revolution first threatened then eliminated the last vestiges of papal temporal authority. Napoleon ordered the Papal States absorbed into the French Empire in 1809, thus unifying Italy under French control.

The Papal States were restored to the Pope after Napoleon's defeat, but liberal ideas took hold in Italy and undermined the Pontiff's legitimacy resulting in a second temporary loss of the Papal States in 1848. The unification of Italy in 1870 finally ended the Pope's temporal reign, but his nineteenth-century political travails, ironically, only served to raise his stature among Europe's Catholics. Lastly, the Revolution created a democratic ethos antithetical to the hierarchical culture of the Church. Sovereignty now rested with citizens not monarchs; the rights of the ruled trumped the rights of traditional rulers. The monarchical church was the cultural antithesis of the new liberal polity and reacted with some vehemence to the changed environment."

The Constitution of 1791 provided for a clear separation of powers among the Legislature, Executive, and Judiciary, as brilliantly articulated by Montesquieu. While the enduring slogan of the French Revolution, Liberté, égalité, fraternité (Political Liberty, Social Equality, and Brotherhood or Shared National Ethos or Mission) has remained very popular, what is hardly remembered is that considerable bloodshed also defined the Revolution, especially during the consolidation stage, when Revolutionary France was faced with both local and foreign threats, and combinations thereof. The Reign of Terror took at least forty-one thousand lives, extinguished mostly by the guillotine. In all, the contributions of that Revolution to the emancipation of mankind across the world, are worthy of our acknowledgment and gratitude. Particular mention must be made of Mirabeau, Sieyes, Lafayette, Marat, Danton, Carnot, and Robespierre.

In many respects, while the Industrial Revolution transformed the physical and material conditions of the world, the French Revolution changed the world in psychic, psychological, political, and social terms. Many of the rights and terms which people take for granted in the current era trace their practical roots to the French Revolution and were procured through blood. Some of these include modern and inclusive Democracy, universal suffrage, Separation of Powers, one person-one vote, rule by majority, Checks and Balances, Republicanism, abrogation of Monarchical Rule and Entitled Classes, the sovereignty of the people, etc., etc. Our objective experience is that most of these precepts are observed more in the breach than in conformance.

In Immanuel Kant's "Perpetual Peace" of 1795, he implied the right of States to non-intervention by other States. By this, no State had the right to interfere in the internal affairs of another. His major motivation for this position was the assumption that, with all States subscribing to this condition, there would be peaceful relations among European States. Again, how so naive… as borne out by subsequent history.

For our historical excursion into the origins and progressive dynamics of Sovereignty, we shall rely particularly on Ramos for guidance as we develop our framework for this segment of the journey. Her instructive work, "Changing Norms Through Actions: The Evolution of Sovereignty" is particularly summoned as a companion, as she very ably synthesized and analyzed seminal thoughts by other experts on the subject, in addition to her original insights. The concept of State Sovereignty has had a mixed but significant impact on both European and global political systems over the last four centuries. Some of the elements include: Sovereignty became the dominant guiding principle of international relations; it has become associated with the right to wage war; States continue to hold an absolute and unlimited idea of sovereignty; State behavior became progressively based on this version of sovereignty, rather than natural, moral, or religious tenets; national identity became formalized; the regulations and protocols for protecting sovereign territorial spaces became rigorous, etc.

There were some other consequences as well. Politis wrote that: "the dogma of illimited sovereignty killed the theory of the just war"; the dominant justification for violating another State's sovereignty was a historical claim to territory; for example, France reclaimed Nice & Savoy from Italy; France & Germany battled for the right to the Alsace-Lorraine Region (Hill 1976, 41-43); etc. Through the Concordat of 1801, Napoleon Bonaparte healed the schism in the Catholic Church in France, thereby unifying the country. It must be noted that the Holy Roman Empire was fast losing its influence; as Warren writes, the German defeat of the Austro-Hungarian Empire at Königgrätz in 1866, which wrested power over German-speaking Mitteleuropa finally represented the death knell for the Holy Roman Empire; the defeat of France in the Franco-Prussian War of 1870/1871 and the final unification of Germany assured that State impulses would henceforth be more dominant than nostalgic feelings about Empire.

Under the Peace of Westphalia, defeated States were allowed their existence as independent sovereign States (though some territory may have been taken). The end result of the Napoleonic Wars (1803-1815) was the reinforcement of State sovereignty, emphasized in political negotiations at the Congress of

Vienna (1815). The Congress also provided legitimacy to the principle that historical claims justified retaking of territory (Hill 1976, 39). In reality, State sovereignty was a concept of geographically limited application as, in reality, it applied only to European States and was completely ignored during the colonization of Africa, "Latin" America, and the Indian subcontinent. In those cases, power became the "ability to set the rules", and indigenous populations were not considered as residing within "States."

Given this self-serving formulation, and drawing from the both the doctrines of the Catholic Church and the writings of racist European thinkers, this new European State model was defined as being foreign to these indigenous peoples who never asked for it and who were perfectly satisfied with their lives and political systems before the European colonizers invaded their ancestral lands, arguing that the international rules of sovereignty did not apply to these innocent people and, therefore, they were not entitled to the protections and rights reserved for members of European States. There is a lot to untangle here: why did Europeans assume that their formula must work for all? Why did they feel entitled to "civilizing" people who were content with their own systems? Why use their new norms to evaluate others? Approbating and Reprobating… why mix all of this self-assigned "messianic" mission with the willful exploitation of the resources of those distant lands, genocide, and forceful conversion to their religion and ethos? Why the obsessive interest in taking over other people's land and resources, displacing or killing them, and generally disrupting or ending their lifestyle as they knew it? All of this derived from Philosophy.

We should, at this juncture, throw some light on the Berlin Conference of 1884 - 1885, which was called by the first German Chancellor, Otto von Bismarck. In order to "peacefully" (among themselves) exploit the resources of Africa among themselves, European Powers met in Berlin to allot sections of the resource-rich Continent among themselves, without any thought for the owners and occupants of the lands. Portugal was already active in Angola and along the great Congo River, while England had staked her interest mostly in East and West Africa, engaged in escalating rivalry with France in the latter part of the Continent. The participants were representatives of Austria-Hungary, Belgium, Denmark, France, the United Kingdom, Italy, the Netherlands, Portugal, Russia, Spain, Sweden-Norway (a Union until 1905), the Ottoman Empire, and the United States. Though the United States of America was represented at the Conference, she did not sign the so-called Berlin Act of February 1885, which ratified their decisions. The result was that, by World War One, 90% of Africa was under European exploitative occupation, from 10% forty or so years earlier in the late 1870s. As captured by Mowat, the Conference was expected to "settle the principles on which the division of the Continent should be based, " and thus avoid constant danger of collision over the future delimitation of territories." Sit back for a moment and attempt to discern the full import of this enterprise: Europeans met in Europe to decide how to carve up Africa among themselves without friction among themselves but maximum violence and dehumanization for the locals, buoyed by their access to superior weapons, the propagandistic weapon of Christianity, and the messianic condescension of "bringing civilization to the Dark Continent."

Berlin Conference *Source: www.wikipedia.org*

The Conference of thieves representing rapacious States -- for that was what it was -- established what Patrick Gathara called "the rules for the conquest and partition of Africa, in the process legitimizing the ideas of Africa as a playground for outsiders, its mineral wealth as a resource for the outside world not for Africans and its fate as a matter not to be left to Africans." At the very beginning, their priorities were as follows: "The Powers are in the presence of three interests: That of the commercial and industrial nations, which a common necessity compels to the research of new outlets. That of the States and of the Powers summoned to exercise over the regions of the Congo an authority, which will have burdens corresponding to their rights. And, lastly, that which some generous voices have already commended to your solicitude - the interests of the native populations." As Gathara put it, they also resolutely refused to consider the question of sovereignty, and the legitimacy or otherwise of laying claim to someone else's land and resources. One may add, the issues of morality and decency ... Thou shall not covet, they preached in their Bible, which was an accompanying tool of oppression and deceit, when the Hard Power proved unsustainable or when there were not enough bullets ...these duplicitous nations even claimed that the Conference was partly formed to stop slavery, an evil institution that they started and benefited enormously from.

With the Principle of Effectivity, which formed a fulcrum of the Agreements reached at the Conference, they proceeded to swiftly occupy the Continent, eliminating whoever stood in their way, while converting those who were willing to embrace the new ways while deprecating theirs. With the reward-punishment mechanism they instituted, it was a question of time before most people on the Continent embraced the European God, norms, ways, worldview, and culture, while losing a real sense of self. The only competition for Europeans remained that between their God and the Arabian God, Allah.

Gathara wrote further that just before the Conference ended, the Lagos (Nigeria) Observer newspaper declared that "the world had, perhaps, never witnessed a robbery on so large a scale." and that six years later, the editor of another Lagos newspaper, while comparing the Berlin Conference to the Slave Trade, wrote that: "A forcible possession of our land has taken the place of a forcible possession of our person." Theodore Holly, the first black Protestant Episcopal Bishop in the US, is also quoted as condemning the delegates who had "come together to enact into law, national rapine, robbery and murder." As very eloquently and correctly written in the article, "that first-ever International Conference on Africa established a template for how the world deals with the Continent. Today, Africa is still seen primarily as a source for raw materials for the outside world and an arena for them to compete over. Conferences about the Continent are rarely held on the Continent itself and rarely care about the views of ordinary Africans." The convenient (for Europeans) delineation and fragmentation of the Continent leading up to political independence had embedded in it, the seeds of conflict which have continued to germinate in the post-independence era. The same Europeans, who planted these seeds, then unconscionably and arrogantly use pejorative terms to describe the resultant fragility and conflicts on the African Continent. The most remarkable and insulting part of it all is that these same European thieves presented their mission in Africa as "the burden of the white man" which involved the onerous duty of managing the "Three C's of Colonialism: Civilization, Christianity, and Commerce." Indeed!!!

One may also note that the intractable problems in the Middle East can be traced directly to how the European Powers handled the unraveling of the Ottoman Empire, as well as their cumulative interventions in the Region. The Guardian wrote in 2014: "Iraq was formed by merging three Ottoman provinces - dominated respectively by Shias, Sunnis and Kurds. It was also cut off from Kuwait – the genesis of trouble later. Its king was a Hashemite from the Arabian Peninsula who had been thrown out of Syria, so was the king of neighboring Jordan, created by a stroke of Winston Churchill's pen after a boozy lunch in Cairo in 1921. Lebanon was split off from "Greater Syria" as a home for the Christians whose support would strengthen French influence. The biggest losers of the postwar lottery in the Middle East were the Kurds." The oil politics, support of dictators, weaponization of Islam by some of the Regional Powers, and the imbalance in the Israeli-Palestinian Question would come later.

As captured in Rudyard Kipling's words at the time,

"To seek another's profit
And work another's gain
Take up the White Man's burden—
And reap his old reward:
The blame of those ye better
The hate of those ye guard—
The cry of hosts ye humour
(Ah slowly) to the light:
"Why brought ye us from bondage,
"Our loved Egyptian night?"

As we are instructed by the eminent scholars at Emory University, the interpretation of these words are as follows: "The idea of the White Man's Burden was to better ("seek another's profit") an ostensibly backward people (anyone who was not white). The lines following this initial declaration reveal the prevailing attitude with regards to how such a civilizing mission would proceed. Kipling bemoans that the African people will come "slowly to the light" and would lament their release from "bondage." In essence, Kipling believed that these non-white racial groups were so backward that they would be unable to comprehend the benefits of Europeanization. It was Kipling's belief that Africans must be pulled toward the "light" in order to see the error of their, in his view, savage nature."

It is noteworthy that all this arrogance, warped morality, and triumphalism were moderated by the same man when Britain bore the brunt of the German War Machine during World War One; at that time in 1915, he wrote that "However the world pretends to divide itself, there are only two divisions in the world today – human beings and Germans." Exactly the same duplicitous manner in which Frau Frieda Fischer of Lohndorf, Germany said in 1919 that: "I like the American soldier individually but do not like the nation as a whole. America entered the war for what money she could get out of it." What drove Germany's and Europe's foray into Africa and elsewhere if not for the material things they set out to gain from those places -- through horrible means, one may add?

Going back to the pre-WW1 era, however, this ingrained mindset led to the development of theories of race superiority and inferiority based on Pseudo

Science. When human beings have to deal with their evil acts and hypocrisy, they typically adopt evasive stratagems in order not to confront the discomfort arising from the truth, their duplicity, and the wickedness of their action. One of these escape mechanisms is Rationalization, which Wikipedia characterizes as follows: "Rationalization encourages irrational or unacceptable behavior, motives, or feelings and often involves *ad hoc* hypothesizing. This process ranges from fully conscious (e.g. to present an external defense against ridicule from others) to mostly unconscious (e.g. to create a block against internal feelings of guilt or shame). People rationalize for various reasons—sometimes when we think we know ourselves better than we do (Introspection Illusion). Rationalization may differentiate the original deterministic explanation of the behavior or feeling in question."

We also know from Cognitive Science and Social Psychology that people dealing with internal conflicts and guilt usually seek recourse in the following: Denialism, Cognitive Inertia, Displacement, Doublethink, Illusory Superiority, Intellectualization (where thinking is used to avoid feeling), Minimization, Motivated Reasoning, Psychological Projection, Psychological Repression, Reaction Formation, Regression, Self-deception, What If ism, Victim-blaming, Splitting, and Spin or Propaganda. They just need to shift the blame from themselves, feel justified in their evil ways, and sleep well at night. A rapist blames the woman for dressing in a way that "led to the rape." It is never about the perpetrator of evil; the victim always causes it. This is the impetus for all race-related crimes against humanity; if "others" accept the station we have assigned to them, then there will be eternal peace….

Building on this, as we learn from "The Philosophy of Colonization: Civilization, Christianity, and Commerce", the idea of civilization was "the triumph and development of reason, not only in the constitutional, political, and administrative domains, but in the moral, religious, and intellectual spheres… the essence of French achievements compared to the uncivilized world of savages, slaves, and barbarians." People's right to be different was interpreted as evidence of inferiority and savagery, thus the need for European "salvation and redemption." Yes indeed! Kipling's "Take up the White Man's burden, The savage wars of peace—Fill full the mouth of Famine and bid the sickness cease", thus provided the theoretical justification for the conversion and exploitation of Africans and all other non-European peoples on the basis of the Christianity-based Anglo-Saxon norms.

As eloquently written in the cited Paper, Kipling's "Your new-caught sullen peoples, Half-devil and half-child" refer to the European belief that Africans were heathens, resigned to live a life of savagery. "Furthermore, European Missionaries called upon the tenets of Christianity to spread what they believed was a just and compassionate doctrine. In practice they were used to degrade the culture and society of the African people. Under the pretense of humanitarian theology, European powers strategically implemented Christianity as a divisive imperialistic tool." The monk, Daniel Kumler Flickinger, is quoted as having written in his memoirs regarding Ethiopians that "The only reason why our theological views are not as foolish and corrupting as theirs, and that we are not believers in witchcraft, devil-worship, and a thousand other foolish things, is simply because the light of Heaven shines upon us." Justification had to be built for the violence, exploitation, and deceit that accompanied colonialism.

The NewAfrican writes that: "the theory that all the peoples of Europe belonged to one white race which originated in the Caucasus (hence the term Caucasian) was first postulated at the turn of the 19th century by a German professor of ethnology, Johann Blumenbach. His color-coded classification of races – white, brown, yellow, black and red – was later refined by a French ethnologist, Joseph Arthur de Gobineau, to include a complete racial hierarchy with white-skinned people of European origin at the top. Such pseudo-scientific theories were widely accepted at the time and motivated Britons like David Livingstone to feel they had a duty to 'civilize' Africa."

This also explains why Jesus, a Palestinian with olive skin, had to become "white" once Europeans took over the religion that was founded in his name. The angels are also white while the devil is black with horns. Linguistically also, blackmail, black sheep of the family, blacklist, connote negativity and objects to be feared, as do all suggestions of 'darkness'. The only consolation for Africans, as Robert Mugabe put it, is that the tissue paper is still white in color.

Furthermore, "the Conference came at the end of 400 years during which Europeans and Arabs had considered Africans as sub-human, fit to be treated as chattel in a slave trade that severely dissipated the physical and mental energies of the Africans and destroyed their economic base. The Continent was at its weakest, its strongest sons and daughters having been shipped to foreign lands for 400 continuous years to provide slave labor that developed Europe, America and other lands. Thus, by carving up Africa for themselves, the "superior race" felt they were only performing a duty that superiority imposed on them." This is a significant point that has hardly been considered: if millions of the strongest African men and women had not been forcefully sold into slavery by Europeans and Arabs (with some local collaborators, one may add) over a 400-year period, would the Scramble and Partition of Africa have been possible? Would there have been a concerted resistance to the arrogant usurpation, the criminal exploitation, the inorganic mergers that formed new States, as well as the imposition of European systems and religion?

Relying further on the Emory scholarblogs, we learn that an English buccaneer, who had been expelled by local Ugandans made a strong case for his government to support predators like himself in the following words: "It is sufficient to reiterate here that, as long as our policy is one of free trade, we are compelled to seek new markets; To allow other nations to develop new fields, and to refuse to do so ourselves, is to go backward; We owe to the instincts of colonial expansion of our ancestors those vast and noble dependencies which are our pride and the outlets of our trade today; and we are accountable to posterity that opportunities which now present themselves of extending the sphere of our industrial enterprise are not neglected." The backdrop was the industrialization of England, the "loss" of the Americas, and the need for raw materials at all costs. As Rotimi Sankore wrote in the NewAfrican, however, "the partition of Africa must not be seen as an isolated event. It was a continuation of previous policies of European exploitation and flowed naturally from the 400 years of transatlantic slavery. Having provided the wealth that created the basis for the Industrial Revolution in Europe, transatlantic slavery had outlived its main usefulness. The industries needed raw materials, and these were to be found in Africa. To prevent hostilities breaking out over the control of Africa's resources, the Berlin Conference was held to carve up Africa and its resources" (**Figures 12 and 13)*.

Pre-the Berlin Conference, the normative African identity was based on fluid cultural, linguistic, tribal, marital, and social parameters. The "logic of nationality, geography, language, culture, and other unifying factors" was totally ignored in forming the artificial countries that presently dot the African landscape, according to the NewAfrican Magazine. With the formal delineation of States which did not consider these fundamentals, and which lumped together incompatible groups while fragmenting others across different States, the problems of the Continent have remained seemingly intractable. Mark Rosenberg quotes Harm J.de Bli who wrote that: "The Berlin Conference was Africa's undoing in more ways than one. The colonial powers superimposed their domains on the African Continent. By the time independence returned to Africa in 1950, the realm had acquired a legacy of political fragmentation that could neither be eliminated nor made to operate satisfactorily." As Adam Hochschild is paraphrased, when they first arrived in Congo, the Portuguese met a thriving African Kingdom. "Despite the contempt for Kongo culture," "the Portuguese grudgingly recognized in the Kingdom a sophisticated and well-developed State – the leading one on the west coast of Central Africa. It was an imperial Federation, of two or three million people, covering an area roughly 30,000 square miles, some of which lie today in several countries after the Europeans [drew] arbitrary border lines across Africa in 1885." Ultimately, Africans themselves need to make the necessary determinations and adjustments to foster and preserve enduring peace among them. No outsiders can do this for them, as their intentions and objectives are not altruistic, to be charitable.

As written in Mowat's "Concert of Europe", all signatories undertook in Article 6 " to watch over the preservation of the native tribes, and to care for the improvement of the conditions of their moral and material well-being, and to help in suppressing slavery, and especially the Slave Trade." Freedom of conscience was " guaranteed to the natives, no less than to subjects and to foreigners." In addition, any Power acquiring new territory or assuming a protectorate " shall accompany the respective act with a notification thereof, addressed to the other Signatory Powers of the present Act, in order to enable them, if need be, to make good any claims of their own " (Article 34). Furthermore, "any occupation of African coastal territory must be effective: " The Signatory Powers of the present Act recognize the obligation to ensure the establishment of authority in the regions occupied by them of the African Continent sufficient to protect existing rights, and, as the case may be, freedom of trade and transit under the conditions agreed upon." In all of these remote deliberations and the resultant Communique, no mention was made of the African owners of the lands, or of the need to negotiate any Agreement with them. Kill them, convert them to Christianity, disparage their values and Institutions, deracinate them, inspire and carefully nurture an ingrained loss of pride in their norms and the pursuit of European benchmarks, standards and philosophies, which expressly exclude them. How patronizing!!!

In West Africa, the British company, Royal Niger Company, was already active in the palm and groundnut trades, patterned exactly after the exploitative model of the East India Company, which had served the British very well. While the post-Conference phase was presented as being predicated on Commerce among European States, the seeds of colonialism had been sown. King Leopold of Belgium, for example, took over 900,000 square miles of the resource-rich Congo, killing over fifteen million innocent Congolese citizens in their homeland, as he plundered their natural resource endowments which this German-Belgian thug used both to enrich himself and to develop Belgium. As we learn from ShareAlike, between the Franco-Prussian War and World War I, Europe added almost 9 million square miles—one-fifth of the land area of the globe—to its overseas colonial possessions. The Congo was even ratified as Leopold's personal property at the Berlin Conference of 1884 -- 1885 and designated as the Congo Free State. Free indeed.

As one analyst is cited in NewAfrican: "In a display of diplomatic virtuosity, Leopold had the Conference agree not to a transfer of the Congo to one of his many philanthropic shell organizations, nor even to his care in his capacity as King of the Belgians, but simply to himself. He became sole ruler of a population that Stanley had estimated at 30 million people, without constitution, without international supervision, without ever having been to the Congo himself, and without more than a tiny handful of his new subjects having heard of him." As has been recalled, two months after the Conference, a US Navy vessel, the Lancaster, appeared at the mouth of the Congo River and fired a 21-gun salute in honor of [the Congo Free State's] blue flag with the gold star. This German-Belgian brute, Leopold, enabled by the German Chancellor, Otto von Bismarck, had just been awarded a colony 80 times the size of Belgium, his empire.

As enumerated by NewAfrican, at 905,355 square miles in size, this brute had just been allotted a major chunk of Africa that was as large as the following 13 European countries put together: Britain, France, Belgium, Ireland, Netherlands, Denmark, Portugal, Switzerland, Germany, Spain, Italy, Armenia and Albania! That is how large DRCongo is. And it was only the third-largest country in Africa, the Continent that, thanks to the Berlin Conference, became a colony of principally five European nations: Britain, France, Portugal, Italy, Germany and Spain. Has there been any accounting to date? Has the accompanying genocide been given wide publicity in the world? No!!! It might be useful to mention at this point that the animal, Leopold, was greatly assisted by a so-called African explorer, a Welshman who had settled in New Orleans, USA, since 1859, Henry Morton Stanley -- a man with quite a pedigree.

A housemaid, Betsy Parry, had a son on 28 January 1841, whose birth she registered at the local church in Denhigh, Wales, under the name, "John Rowlands, Bastard", for Betsy was not sure whose son she had borne. As it turned out, she wouldn't be sure of the paternity of the four other children she had after John. Locals generally assumed that John was the biological child of a local drunkard, John Rowlands, who died of delirium tremens, an acute alcoholic condition. Embarrassed by his background, John Rowlands, Bastard, changed his name at various times to Morley, Morelake, and Moreland, before completely changing his identity to metamorphose into Henry Morton Stanley when he had relocated to New Orleans.

Based on his "accomplishments" in Africa, he was knighted in Britain and subsequently elected to Parliament. One is surprised he did not live long enough to become a Lord. This biographical sketch is only brought up to highlight the discrepancy between this man's family circumstances and the accepted orthodoxy of the era (driven by Religion), and not to pass any judgment whatsoever. The Resume that qualified one for British knighthood and parliamentary seat is also to be noted: "delivery" of Africa in the service of the Crown.

Congo is generally believed to be among the top three countries in the world with the highest reserves of precious resources; perhaps, in a perverse way, this accounts for the chronic poverty of a majority of her citizens, the ceaseless violence, and the predatory practices of the West and China in that bewitched country. The country has immense reserves of crude oil, copper, cobalt, gold, tantalum, tin, diamond, germanium, palladium, and several others, as well as abundant coffee and timber.

European Exploration of Africa: Routes of European explorers in Africa to 1853.

Provided by Wikimedia Commons. No known copyright

As summarized by Rosenberg, after the Conference, the Continent was remotely carved up as follows, without regard for the cultural, linguistic, and relational patterns, which the indigenes had used to maintain their boundaries and borders:

"Great Britain desired a Cape-to-Cairo collection of colonies and almost succeeded through their control of Egypt, Sudan (Anglo-Egyptian Sudan), Uganda, Kenya (British East Africa), South Africa, and Zambia, Zimbabwe (Rhodesia), and Botswana. The British also controlled Nigeria and Ghana (Gold Coast).

France took much of western Africa, from Mauritania to Chad (French West Africa), as well as Gabon and the Republic of Congo (French Equatorial Africa).

Belgium and King Leopold II controlled the Democratic Republic of Congo (Belgian Congo), after killing half of their population.

Portugal took Mozambique in the East and Angola in the West

Italy's holdings were Somalia (Italian Somaliland) and a portion of Ethiopia.

Germany took Namibia (German Southwest Africa) and Tanzania (German East Africa).

Spain claimed the smallest territory, which was Equatorial Guinea (Rio Muni)."

In the early 20th Century - the concept of sovereignty underwent some fundamental changes due to World War 1, the war that George F. Kennan famously and aptly described as "the original catastrophe of the 20th century" (in reality, a European War pompously called a World War!) compelling States to think about how to prevent future wars. The level of destruction, volume of death and displacement, as well as the depth of the dislocation across Europe as a consequence of the Austrian Archduke Franz Carl Ludwig Joseph Ferdinand's assassination " shattered a fundamental confidence of European self-understanding and investment in its own intellectual, political, and artistic heritage", in the words of Nicolas de Warren. Such an intemperate management of an assassination of one man, however hoisted on the man-made structure of entitlement and exploitation, exposed the carnality and savagery of the European persona. Given the gains of the Enlightenment Period, it was assumed that the era of crude violence was over in Europe, but this war belied these lofty assumptions.

As captured in Professor Warren's essay, "WW1, Philosophy, and Europe", the American writer Henry James, residing in England, wrote in 1915 that:

"The plunge of civilization into this abyss of blood and darkness by the wanton feat of two infamous autocrats is a thing that so gives away the whole long age during which we have supposed the world to be, with whatever abatement, gradually bettering, that to have to take it all now for what the treacherous years were all the while really making for and meaning is too tragic for any words." This war led to the fall of four great imperial dynasties which were in Germany, Russia, Austria-Hungary, and Turkey – (the Ottoman Empire); it also resulted in the Bolshevik Revolution in Russia, the decline of aristocracies, and the emergence of nation-states as the dominant unit of the global political architecture. It would take another half a century before the artificial African countries would have their political independence.

The Atlantic Magazine wrote that: "two million German soldiers died, along with about 1 million British troops, counting those from the colonies and dominions. Proportionately higher losses were suffered in Russia, Serbia, and Ottoman Turkey, where a war of 20th-century firepower was fought under 19th-century sanitary conditions." There was no discrimination between soldiers and civilian targets. Europe's first genocide of the 20th century was also orchestrated about this time, when Turkey murdered over one million Armenians. Chemical warfare was employed on a large scale for the first time in human history (though not legally sanctioned). Chlorine, phosgene, and mustard gas were loaded into a quarter (25%) of all the shells that were launched on the western front of the war. When Nazis subsequently deployed Zyklon B in the concentration camps during World War II, they were building on the ignoble experience gained during WWI. Ultimately, over five million of the men who died in the war had no marked or identifiable graves.

In many ways also, the post-war British shenanigans in the Middle East largely account for the enduring polarities in that Region to this day. As the magazine reflected it, 'in 1915, the British High Commissioner in Egypt promised the keeper of the holy sites in Mecca independence for Arabs in return for their participation in fighting the Ottoman empire. Two years later, Britain's Balfour Declaration promised Zionists the opposite: a Jewish homeland in Palestine. And these incompatible promises were complicated even more by the secret Sykes-Picot Agreement in 1916, which divided the post-Ottoman Middle East between French and British spheres of influence and drew arbitrary borders—in Iraq, for instance—that have caused instability and conflict ever since." What is also largely ignored, as Jay Winter reminds us, is that the Japanese, having contributed significantly towards the Allied defeat of Germany during WWI, demanded racial equality among the victors, but President Woodrow Wilson of the United States, a confirmed racist bigot himself, was convinced that any accession to Japan on this point would not be accepted by the deeply-racist American South, which would make his Party lose elections.

Instead, he contrived for Japan to control the Shandong province (previously under German control) of a then much-weaker China, thus setting the stage for the subsequent industrial-scale rape of Chinese women, brutalization of the Chinese persona, and the enduring enmity between Japan and China up until this moment. In World War II, Japan could no longer trust the Allied Forces, and chose to align with Nazi Germany and Italy. It was the massive protest by the Chinese against this Japanese usurpation, staged at the Tiananmen Gate in Beijing under the auspices of the May 4th Movement, that led to the Chinese

Communist Party. In many ways, therefore, Woodrow Wilson was the remote founder of the Chinese Communist Party. Figure that out…

And…they still called it the Great War! The War to End All Wars...

Indeed, even amidst "the destruction of civilization in the First World War", some theorists have suggested that the war led to the emergence of aesthetic and literary modernism, according to Warren, because "modernism is our art; it is the one art that responds to the scenario of our Chaos." This is very laughable, because subsumed in this is the strong belief that only Europe can give the world "civilization", even in their chaos. As Warren concludes in his brilliant philosophical review of WW1, "can we still philosophically imagine Europe after Europe? Ironically, the one-hundred year commemorations of the "war to end all wars" that will now dominate the cultural memory of Europe today fails to recognize its own act of remembrance of the Great War as a mourning for a Europe that has passed from the scene of history, leaving in its wake the fullness of a nostalgia and the emptiness of a symbol."

US President Woodrow Wilson's Fourteen Points (1918) Speech advanced the idea of an international political body that would mediate conflicts among States, so that States would never experience the devastation of war again. The Speech also asserted the right to self-determination; groups within a State were recognized as having the freedom to govern themselves, if they so chose. The League of Nations (precursor to the United Nations) was established as an intergovernmental organization, but without any mention of self-determination in its Covenant. Its principal roles included the task of enforcing minority-protection treaties, as well as providing an international mechanism for holding States accountable.

However, it proved too weak and timid to confront violating States. Hitler's New Order, for example, was a clear breach of the Protocols of the League of Nations, as were his other activities as Chancellor, which clearly breached the terms of the Versailles Treaty of 1919 by which Germany surrendered after losing World War 1. (Von Frentz 1999; Fink 2004). By this, the movement toward limiting sovereignty had officially begun, but it was not carried out in practice; the lack of early containment led to Germany's aggressive postures towards the Sudetenland, Czech Republic, and Poland, which triggered off World War II of 1939 to 1945.

This most devastating war inspired a rethinking of the legitimate rights of States as well as their corresponding obligations, leading to the establishment of the United Nations (UN) as a Body outside of States that could hold States accountable and set standards for State behavior. The UN included more countries than the League of Nations; all the major Powers committed to collective security and created Laws that reached into the jurisdiction of States to protect minorities and human rights (Philpott 1997). Furthermore, leaders would now be held accountable for domestic actions. This arrangement had the fundamental defect of having no independent means by which to enforce the core principles of the UN Charter.

The UN acknowledged the right to nonintervention of States while declaring a set of universal human rights (Nincic 1970). This ambiguity allowed States to justify their actions via absolute sovereignty with little incentive to comply with International Law when it contradicted national interests, as interpreted by the local leaders, who might indeed be engaging in egregious repressive conduct against their political opponents and minorities. Under the UN System, if the five permanent members of the UN Security Council (UNSC) agree that a threat to international peace and security exists, then, maybe, the problem will be addressed. In this case, the UNSC could serve as an enforcement mechanism and ultimate interpreter of the UN Charter. The idea was to achieve what Sellars characterized as protection from one another, "while being locked together in a mutually beneficial embrace." In reality, we have seen how geopolitical considerations and competing interests among the UNSC members have consistently denied this vital Organ of a unified voice on critical political and military issues around the world. While, for example, the Geneva Convention on the Law of Treaties makes clear that a party to a Treaty may not rely on the provisions of its internal law as a justification for failing to enforce a Treaty, ensuring compliance requires more than *uberrimae fidei* -- good faith. The lack of will to force compliance in such cases nullifies the essence of such Treaties.

The clash of ideologies led to the accelerated unraveling of the Coalition that was built between the Allied Forces and the then Soviet Union, to defeat Nazi Germany in World War II. The ensuing Cold War led to a freeze on developments in State sovereignty; the rivalry between the US and the then Soviet Union rendered the UN ineffective; the competition between Communism (Soviet Bloc) and Democratic Capitalism (the West led by the US) affected virtually every Continent as spheres of influence were sought, protected, and subverted in this kinetic and non-kinetic struggle. In recruiting and sustaining allies, both sides overlooked human rights abuses, used third-party States to fight proxy wars, considerable resources were channeled towards an arms race to the detriment of social spending, international issues were neglected, including environmental degradation, global hunger, disease, etc. With the collapse of the Soviet Union in 1990, the UNSC became deadlocked, as the veto power granted each of the five permanent members became a significant clog in the unification of response to global threats. Even the definition of such threats does not enjoy a common interpretation for the reasons cited earlier.

As Professor Jason Mazzone of the University of Illinois, Urbana-Champaign, writes in his Paper, "The Rise and Fall of Human Rights: A Sceptical Account of Multilevel Governance", "Multilevel governance has a single ambition: uniformity. It aims to articulate a set of governing principles and apply-impose-them throughout the entire global system." He argues that this project ends up actually diminishing values and rights, and that, instead, local structures are best placed to guarantee and protect these rights. He likens this to a vast and diversified school system in which, he says, a multilevel system seeking universal rights risks producing "perversely, a uniform mediocrity." On this point, he needs to untangle and delineate some of the embedded assumptions, for a rigorous analysis of his postulation to be effectively undertaken.

While the bulk of his referenced Paper dwelt on the new British accommodation of absent witnesses in court trials, in conformity to European Conventions and Protocols, a development that he forcefully and convincingly argues to detract from the historical requirement of confronting one's accusers in court, one's observation is limited to his comments on the standardization of certain rights in the United States. As history and contemporary developments confirm, if the discretion was left to Alabama, Mississippi, Arkansas, Georgia, and several (mostly "praying" States) to determine what rights should be available to whom, they would still have Legal Codes that protect some while dehumanizing others in a most egregious manner. After all, they fought a Civil War just for that…

The US Human Rights and Foreign Policy pamphlet of 1978, which dwelt extensively on fundamental human rights, quoted a Greek play as follows: When Sophocles' heroine, Antigone, cries out to the autocratic King Creon: 'all your strength is weakness itself against the immortal unrecorded laws of God', she makes a deeply revolutionary assertion. There are laws, she claims, higher than the laws made by any king; as an individual she has certain rights under those higher laws; and kings and armies — while they may violate her rights by force — can never cancel them or take them away.

The irony of America's experience with these Rights for some was hardly reflected in the lofty ideals canvassed in the document. Indeed, as captured in "The Rise and Rise of Human Rights: Drafting the Universal Declaration", by Kirsten Sellars, quoting Isaiah Berlin, "Condorcet had already remarked that the notion of individual rights was absent from the legal conceptions of the

Romans and Greeks; this seems to hold equally of the Jewish, Chinese, and all other ancient civilizations that have since come to light. The domination of this ideal has been the exception rather than the rule, even in the recent history of the West." She aligns with Elaine Pagels' interpretation of the cited Sophocles' treatise as being applicable to "blood loyalty among family members", and not extended to humanity in general.

Sellars quotes Harlan Cleveland (on human rights) as follows: "In the long history of civilization, they have to be listed as 'new business.' The old business was rights conferred or arrogated – granted by God, if that could be arranged, but if necessary seized by force and maintained by claims of superiority on account of rank, race, early arrival or self-anointed citizenship ... Not inalienable rights but the alienation of rights was the rule." This is the history of mankind.

She then traces the concept of human rights to the Enlightenment Period in Europe when reason began to displace religion and the ideals of freedom and social equality gained dominance. Again, this excluded non-Europeans who, it must be stated, had their own freedom intact and who were not obligated to accept the hierarchical Eurocentric worldview that favored Europeans and excluded or maligned "the other."

As a consequence of the French Revolution, the French Parliament passed the Universal Declaration of the Rights of Man and the Citizen, a major document that epitomized and celebrated the gains of the Enlightenment. As noted in the referenced Paper, the Declaration started with: "The representatives of the French people ... believing that the ignorance, neglect, or contempt of the rights of man are the sole cause of public calamities and of the corruption of governments, have determined and set forth in a solemn declaration the natural, unalienable, and sacred rights of man", with the very first article being that "Men are born and remain free and equal in rights." From this moment, people (Europeans, one may add) were defined, at least in theory, — "by their common claim to freedom and equality, rather than by their allotted place in a God-given social hierarchy." If only they stayed forth in Europe and did not seek to invade other lands, whose peoples they regarded as inferior and not deserving of the same rights and consideration, and whose "God-given" resources were rapaciously and permanently expropriated at great human and sociological toll.

For Sellars, the impetus for the modern Human Rights Movement was the carnage perpetrated by the Nazis at their Concentration Camps. There was a need for a new Global Disposition that would replace the Old Order (based on the Balance of Power and Racial Superiority), which had failed to rein in Hitler and Mussolini. Protecting human dignity was regarded as the counterpoint to the devastating impact of Fascism and all forms of military dictatorship; there was an urgent need to respond vigorously to the "barbarous acts, which have outraged the conscience of mankind." When US President Franklin Roosevelt declared in 1941 that he sought "a world founded upon four essential human freedoms: freedom of expression and worship, and freedom from want and fear" predicated on the assumption that "Freedom means the supremacy of human rights everywhere", the United States did not contemporaneously reflect these ideals in its Domestic Laws and Policies, to put it mildly. As Hitchcock put it rather succinctly," the great powers designing the postwar architecture could gladly invoke their desire to protect human rights because they did not have to worry about an erosion of their State sovereignty, and could perpetuate-for example-racial discrimination in the United States, repressive colonial regimes in the British and French empire, and persecution of national minorities inside the Soviet Union...." Providing water, basic security, and segregated education were regarded as State protection of human rights in America.

According to Hitchcock, "the Soviet conception of human rights was not one based on the universal qualities of the human person: rather, rights were socially constructed, embedded in a particular political system, and could never be detached from the political context." This mindset viewed the US model with deep suspicion -- even as it was mostly in breach of universal standards -- because it did not emphasize the overarching role of the State (the Communist State in this context). He instructs us further that the 1977 Soviet Constitution, promulgated under Brezhnev, insisted that rights were guaranteed only for those who fulfilled their duties to the State.

The concepts of Economic Liberalism and Collective Security, which followed this policy philosophy, were reflected in the Doctrines of the post-WW2 International Organizations. With the First Article of the UN stating that "All human beings are born free and equal in dignity and rights. They are endowed with reason and conscience and should act towards one another in a spirit of brotherhood," it was assumed that the era of global wars was finally over and that peace would reign supreme. This optimism was buoyed by the first article of the Preamble as well, which read that "freedom, justice and peace" are based on 'the equal and inalienable rights of all members of the human family." With the new emphasis on Human Rights, unaddressed issues included how the supranational Institutions, notably the UN, would ensure national compliance with the precepts without contravening the assumptions of sovereignty, or when it would be appropriate to modify the assumptions of hard sovereignty in order to protect minority rights or the human rights of oppressed citizens. This fluidity has continued to bend on the arc of force, not collective rationality or agreement.

William I. Hitchcock takes the view that:" sovereignty and national interest have continued to be the currency of world politics in the past century…", and that the interests of Great Powers sustain the emphasis on Human Rights as a cardinal feature of international engagements. Human Rights pose a threat to the concepts of sovereignty and national interest, as defined by various competing States. The "responsibility to protect", which is usually mediated through international organizations, is, substance over form, an extension of the complexities of International Politics, and not necessarily a rigid or moralistic fidelity to the ethos of protecting human rights, hence all the "paradox and hypocrisy" that abound in this sphere. It is clear that the term "Human Rights" is used by Great Powers in a convenient and utilitarian manner, so political societies and nations worldwide are strongly advised to resolve their internal problems through political and peaceful means, as any deterioration towards large-scale violence may simply be ignored if their "human rights" do not mean much to the major Powers at that particular time. The Igbos of Nigeria, Tutsis of Rwanda, and black owners of South Africa found this out the hard way, as did the Kosovar Albanians in Srebrenica; indeed, Syrian civilians have been butchered in their hundreds of thousands by the Assad Regime, buoyed and protected by Russia, thus deflecting any concerted global exercise of the so-called "responsibility to protect." The Kurds were casually left to fallow by the US under President Trump, after decades of being solid Regional partners to America. No one protected the victims in those cases.

A corollary consideration when analyzing Sovereignty is that, with the increasing interconnectedness of the world (as the Covid-19 pandemic has demonstrated with universal impact and global scare), the failure of particular States and Regions also has consequences for other parts of the world, in terms of migration flows, terrorism, depression of the aggregate human experience, remittance flows, etc. As the eminent British diplomat, Robert Cooper, wrote in his 2003 book, "The Breaking of Nations: Order and Chaos in the Twenty-First Century", "the difficulty is that as borders become more open—itself a consequence of a foreign policy that has brought a long period of peace—the impact of developments abroad increases. Foreign competition, the illegal trade in drugs, illegal immigration and ... opportunities for international terrorism multiply. These challenges on the home front have their origin in problems abroad: wars and failed States captured by corrupt or criminal interests. All require foreign policy solutions. In war, foreigners arrive in violent and obvious ways; in peace, their arrival is less dramatic and their presence less obtrusive, but the effects can be just as far-reaching..."

As paraphrased in K.J. Keith (Cambridge Law Journal), the Friendly Relations Declaration which was adopted by consensus by the United Nations General Assembly on the 25th anniversary of the United Nations at the end of 1970, adopted the notional equality of sovereign States, even against the backdrop of the vast and exclusive veto powers of the Security Council. Quoted directly, all States enjoy sovereign equality. They have equal rights and duties and are equal members of the international community, notwithstanding differences of an economic, social, political or other nature. In particular, sovereign equality includes the following elements:

(a) States are juridically equal; (b) each State enjoys the rights inherent in full sovereignty; (c) each State has the duty to respect the personality of other States; (d) the territorial integrity and political independence of the State are inviolable; (e) each State has the right freely to choose and develop its political, social, economic and cultural systems; (f) each State has the duty to comply fully and in good faith with its international obligations and to live in peace with the other States.

This recognition should come with specific and enforceable responsibilities, in one's view. It would seem that, for most countries, the concept of sovereignty is understood only to mean their absolute control of developments within their physical territories, without a matching undertaking on obligations towards the provision of public goods, protection of the rights of their citizens, and the transparent inculcation of the accepted political norms earned through blood and toil over centuries. For dictators and leaders of failed and failing States, in particular, political independence and sovereignty entitle them to appropriate the country's entire budget, be above the Law, kill their political opponents, perpetuate themselves in power, fly the flags (pennants) of their countries domestically and at diplomatic meetings overseas, be protected by the State, live in secluded Palaces, and display all other negative and State-destructive tendencies including cronyism and nepotism.

There is no translation of sovereignty to mean the provision of potable water across their country or locality, quality and affordable education at all levels, quality healthcare, security of lives and property, reliable Citizenship Data, electricity, business-friendly taxation regime, sanitary conditions, etc., etc. For them, it is all about self, which negates the long journey, as articulated throughout this work, towards political independence and sovereignty. Indeed, as the Report of the International Commission on Intervention and State

Sovereignty (ICISS), chaired by the eminent former Australian Foreign Minister, Professor Gareth Evans, stated: "sovereignty is more than just a functional principle of international relations. For many States and peoples, it is also a recognition of their equal worth and dignity, a protection of their unique identities and their national freedom, and an affirmation of their right to shape and determine their own destiny." In this, as earlier mentioned, there is not a mention of the consequential responsibilities and obligations of political independence and sovereignty.

With the UN General Assembly ratifying this Report in 2005, thereby affirming the concept of the "Responsibility to Protect", the idea of hard sovereignty has been altered when "mass atrocity crimes" are being committed against a people within a State. Sovereignty, in the modern era, is not a licence to kill your own people. As Evans instructs us, the objective is to decisively put an end to "mass atrocity crimes: the murder, torture, rape, starvation, expulsion, destruction of property and life opportunities of others for no other reason than their race, ethnicity, religion, nationality, class, or ideology." This builds on the Geneva Convention of 1948, but with a more pointed and graduated framework of action in dilution of hard sovereignty and in defence of vulnerable minorities wherever they may be. Hopefully, the fluidity of Great Power Politics will allow a consensus response in critical situations, otherwise, unilateral action will be defensible in the face of contrived inaction. In this regard, the world has failed the Syrian population from Assad's bestiality, which has claimed over 200,000 lives, with Russia's active support and protection.

The US, which would have acted swiftly and vigorously, is currently led by a President, the one who routinely mocks everyone about their looks and addresses every perceived slight; the one who could not take being called "morbidly obese", a "petulant child", generally described as a "man-child", and who, for whatever reasons, is grossly enamored or afraid of Russia. China has never stood for human rights anywhere, in order not to invite attention to its own glaring human rights abuses. Indeed, the former Chinese President, Jiang Zemin, in his strident condemnation of the premium placed on human rights over (hard or absolute) sovereignty, had said that: "dialogue and cooperation in the field of human rights must be conducted on the basis of respect for State sovereignty." He also said that: "without sovereignty, there will be no human rights to speak of." Indeed!!! Any wonder that they had the Tiananmen Square massacre, have continued to oppress the Uighur minority, and also align with murderous dictators across Africa.

Under President George W. Bush, the Secretary of State, Dr. Condoleeza Rice, faced with the egregious abuses of minorities within their own countries, wrote that the concept of sovereignty needed to move “from mere State control to civil and global responsibility." As quoted in Ramos, the UK was also in alignment with this central principle, with their then Prime Minister, Tony Blair, commenting that “international terrorism post-9/11 and the spread of weapons of mass destruction require a further redefinition of the rights of a nation-state."

In summary, the long and checkered journey that led to the formation of modern States compels the rigorous correlation of privilege with responsibility, to avoid the unraveling of these States. In those countries and regions with historical and structural challenges, the fact of their political independence and sovereignty equips them with all they need to resolve their issues amicably or peacefully agree to restructure or dissolve their union.

We shall now evaluate State performance, which is a central thesis of this book. How have (especially newly independent States) performed on the provision of public goods to their people and to the global community, in full affirmation of their sovereignty? Is Political **Independence independent** or **dependent**?

V

State Performance

It is significant that the major political developments of the past century or so have revolved around the State; these include industrialization, decolonization, and political independence. In the external exercise of their sovereignty, States are notionally equal to other States (we know this to be untrue in reality), and not superior in any form. They are simply independent at this point, the textbook teaches. The fundamental assumption is that States are formed to provide public goods within their territories, even as they also perform those international duties and obligations generally expected of States in the modern era. As Naomi Chazan (ed.) traces in "Irredentism and International Politics" and quoted by Carment, the global system has witnessed four major thrusts for State-formation, arising from the collapse of empires, namely: South America in the 19th century (the Spanish Empire); Europe after WWI (Russia, Austria-Hungary, Ottoman Turkey); Asia and Africa after WWII (Belgium, Holland, France, Britain and Portugal) and Central Asia and Eastern Europe in the late 1980s (the Soviet Union)."

Oliver P. Richmond's "Failed State-building" will also be a good guide at this point.

He writes that a State "implies a dominant, impersonal, rational, centralized and unified authority, control of the means of violence, and management of inequality and stratification. It requires a legitimate authority structure that can wield military and disciplinary power, and that has the flexibility to respond to changing demands for progress as well as to external pressures." This State avoids the creation of rents, in his formulation. He departs from the traditional paradigm when he recognizes the classic definition as being too rigid in an increasingly fluid world with several cross-border activities, and that this model simply reflects the progressive development on European History, which may not apply to all societies. It would seem to one that, since all human activities and interactions are ultimately resolved within a territorial space, it is crucial to retain the accepted norms of sovereign responsibility for definite parcels of land, for proper accountability. The international and rapid nature of online commerce and banking, for example, should not obviate the need for sovereign accountability.

The primary impetus for the modern State was to achieve a departure from the prior European architecture of Power-driven units, which bred several wars; while Security is generally agreed as a fundamental responsibility of the State, it must also have proven capacity in delivering other public services, including, but not limited to, environmental protection, taxation and tariff, foreign affairs, stable markets, institutions, cohesion, utilities, rule of law, development, education, healthcare, etc. to its citizens. Indeed, the Millennium Development Goals cite public services and poverty reduction as crucial State functions. As paraphrased in the referenced work, the US Agency for International Development (USAID) insists that: "governance should be addressed in order to increase the local legitimacy of government, with enhanced security, democracy promotion, reform of institutions and development as its targets." The IMF and World Bank Systems share identical goals and visions for States, which have become, in the modern era, the organizing units for (theoretically) spreading the rewards of proper governance across the planet, regardless of the political system in each country.

The State functions best when it has a decentralized power structure, strong participation in civic matters by the citizens, governance is based on rationality and fairness, discrimination of any demographic/ constitutive unit is absent and discouraged, and there are no limits to legitimate aspirations by all. Divisive policies and willful abuses of the Rule of Law weaken the fabric of the State considerably. It has been observed, for example, that in weak States with natural resources, the central function of those States has been to protect the abusive interests of the elite in those countries. Nigeria, Angola, DRCongo, and Venezuela, are good examples. The predatory elite class in those societies comes from politics, government, culture, religion, business, Media, Military and Security Services, as well as their foreign collaborators. Unless and until there is a fundamental (often violent) shift, these individuals are usually above the Law unless they threaten group interest, voice independent opinions, or align with the wrong factions, in which case the entire apparatus of the State is often deployed to destroy those aberrant individuals, often to the applause of the perennially-underserved majority.

In States such as above, the elite consensus is not usually development-oriented, but geared towards rapacious and primitive accumulation with impunity. There is often no critical mass amongst this class to entrench or pursue a positive national agenda. Changes in such societies are often accompanied by substantial bloodshed. Citing the 1997 World Bank Report, Dr. Richmond recognizes the importance for States to deal "with poverty, marginalization, the vulnerable, decentralization, unemployment and public services in an equitable manner for ordinary citizens, so that the State and the people are closely connected." For him also, the OECD maintains that "State building rests on three pillars: core functions of State structures; legitimacy and accountability; and the market." Performance by the State on its core functions as identified above enhances its legitimacy in the eyes of its citizens, as well as from the global audience. Conversely, State failure lays it bare to contestation for space and authority by warlords, terrorists, and criminal gangs. The enormity of the threats posed by these failed States is reflected in the fact that on page one of the National Security Strategy of the United States, it is written, *inter alia*, that "America is now threatened less by conquering States than [...] by failing ones." This recognition and the related commitment of resources, as well as the strategic dimensioning of its scope, have been amplified significantly in the ensuing years.

For Richmond, some of the causes of State failure include: unresolved pre and post-colonial issues, neo-patrimonialism, resource-curse, being clientelistic, shadow State status, denial of human rights, engaging in, or ignoring, ethnic cleansing, together with other factors. One may add corruption, weak Rule of Law, nepotism as the operating principle of governance, discriminatory practices against Regions or peoples, inequity in fiscal policies (generation of, and access to public revenue), regression of meritocracy, etc. "Such States are seen as failing, collapsed or predatory, neither meeting cosmopolitan standards nor providing for local, regional or global security or access to global markets and resources." Furthermore, "a quasi- state, in which parallel structures and informal systems compete in distributing resources, perpetuates ethnic inequalities." This is very profound indeed.

As captured in "Failed State-building", the World Bank assesses State weakness on the basis of governance performance, the rule of law, governance effectiveness, corruption and human rights. It is refreshing to note that some responsibility for failed or failing States is correctly apportioned to Western countries (one may add China) by this author, some of the often-ignored triggers being, in his view, "historical processes, including colonialism, global inequality, powerful strategic interests, displacement, immigration, settlement and other external forces." For him also, the linear transposition of Northern Hemispheric norms in global developmental assessments, does not take into consideration operative local realities, contexts, and nuances. While this is true, one may respectfully add that the provision of basic public goods should have no conditionalities or be based on one's place in the Hemisphere. Indeed, uncharitable analysts might attribute conclusions to the contrary to some ingrained racism and paternalism, which is not the case here. His fundamental respect for varied local customs and social structures is clearly evident, even as he urges for a reconsideration of the assumption that one cap (Northern Hemispheric, Western) can fit all. For, what do potable water, electricity, security, health care, etc., in 2020 have to do with your location or Region in the world?

It is for exactly this same reason that one finds it difficult to accept the excuses generated by failed and failing States on their performance even as the elite in those societies continue to loot their countries and enjoy uncommon perks of office without excuses. Charles Alao states that the origins of State failure in Africa can be found in colonialism, which brought people of different ethnic, political and religious identities together to form States, before commencing the vital task of forging a common sense of citizenship. Furthermore, the integration of the economies of these African States into the Western Capitalist framework at a time they were not ready, considerably accounts for their fragility, according to this argument. While some concessions could be made regarding these "causes", it must be stated that there is no inevitable causality about these relationships. Visionary and selfless leadership would have inspired national cohesion and the delivery of public goods to the citizens.

The concentration of these failed and failing States in Africa should be a cause for concern to their leaders and citizens, rather than the perpetual recourse to rear-view excuse generation even as their current practices and engagements with China, for example, perpetuate their depressing profile. In addition, no one will stop any leader who cuts out corruption and waste, then deploys creative and transparent Statecraft towards providing potable water, quality education, security, electricity, capacity for research and innovation, world-class infrastructure, etc., to the citizens. Rather, we find a proliferation of incompetence, a glorification of corruption and cronyism, low ambition and esteem, clannishness and divisiveness, as well as an abiding fixation with self-interest, across the Continent. Individual and group authoritarianism defines the political landscape of Africa, with personal ego and selfish interest defining most official decisions. The Rule of Law, when evenly and equitably applied, will also unite diverse societies; in this case, diversity easily becomes a source of strength.

It is also rather optimistic to posit that State failure necessarily leads to a positive reset. With the collapse of a State, all options are on the table, including perpetual warfare. Accordingly, one does not share the position that leaves the possible interpretation that State collapse is almost a necessary or natural condition before development and stability can be achieved. As captured in Lemay-Hebert's "The Bifurcation of the Two Worlds", Mehler and Ribaux state that 'the collapse of States in crisis need not be prevented, since a "better State" cannot emerge until that collapse has taken place." Similarly, for Eisenstadt, 'collapse, far from being an anomaly, both in the real world and in social evolutionary theory, presents in dramatic form not the end of social institutions, but almost always the beginning of new ones'. One will submit that it is possible for a State to make progress without the catastrophic experience and disruption of State failure.

In the elegant words of Dr. Richmond, "because the structural, sociological and anthropological traditions of State formation have been ignored, many post- conflict States are not constructed on the basis of local needs or identities at all. Rather, they operate on the basis of maintaining a disciplinary distance between local and elite or international actors." While it is debatable that the structure of the global system fosters the dependency of the post-colonial States on external Blocs and Institutions, it remains difficult for one to accept that as a valid excuse for a visionary and competent leader from one of those countries not to serve her citizens diligently. We have seen, for example, what Lee Kuan Yew was able to achieve in Singapore, as well as the early encouraging steps by Paul Kagame in Rwanda in the aftermath of their genocide of 1994. For leaders without character, integrity, capacity, and vision, the identified spectacle of the inflexible alignment of national programs with international elite and institutional preferences, not the requirements and priorities of the local population, becomes the norm as they increasingly seek their validation and legitimacy from outside. In one's view, however, the responsibility still resides domestically. It is evident that the alienation of local leaders from their own people, in an expansive and absolute interpretation of their own powers, is a significant contribution to both underdevelopment and consequential State failure. Lemay-Hebert paraphrases Arendt as theorizing that: "power becomes the essence of political action and the center of political thought when separated from the political community which it should serve."

A School of Thought posits that a majority of the States that emerged after the colonial era, were essentially sustained by the crumbs that attended their alignment with either the West or the Soviet Union during the Cold War decades. Michael Ignatieff wrote in his "Blood and Belonging", that "huge sections of the world's population have won the right of self-determination on the cruelest possible terms: they have been simply left to fend for themselves. Not surprisingly, their nation-states are collapsing." This somewhat patronizing assessment should ordinarily be a rallying point for such States to take the necessary policy steps to avoid the projected pitfalls, but they seem satisfied with the negative prognosis. These States also do not clearly understand that the concept of Absolute Sovereignty has become outmoded, replaced by a Contingent form of Sovereignty, wherein the eligibility to retain a State's legitimate sovereignty is contingent on that State's performance for its people on objective indices, as well as on its responsible membership of the International Community.

State failure creates an enabling environment for the manifestation of various forms of violent extremism. With the incapacity to deal with conflict, which is a defining attribute of failed States, these non-State actors continue to pose existential and enduring threats to Failed and failing States. By extension, the Regions experience fragility, thereby expanding the base of ungoverned areas around the world. It is ironic that these States also have significant population increases, with citizenship data remaining unreliable and borders largely porous. With the toxic mix of Islam and poverty, as we are experiencing in large sections of Africa and the Middle East, these areas continue to pose a serious threat to the global ecosystem. State health can be assessed at a glance based on the capacity for political action, legitimacy, and authority. Carment analyzed these dynamics very capably in his related work, and further identified illicit gun flows, child soldiers, black market activity and AIDS-problems as symptoms of "State weakness and human insecurity." One may add a few more indicators as follows: capital flight, declining volume of medium to long-term investment funds, upsurge in religious activities, deepening cleavages among the constituent units, accelerated inflation, erosion of investor confidence, anomie, distrust of political leadership, increasing violation and denial of citizenship rights by Security Forces, overall danger involved in basic commute, and worsening corruption.

Placing Nation-States on a developmental spectrum, he characterized States as "'strong", 'weak', 'failed' and 'collapsed'", with some States never achieving the status of 'strong'," moving instead from 'weak' at independence to 'failed' and, in extreme cases, to 'collapsed'. Others may linger on as 'weak' States for years and even decades. Others remain strong." He cites Somalia, Congo, Liberia, Sierra-Leone, and Bosnia, as instances of failed States; one may add a much longer list to this snapshot of State failure, especially if we consider the defining signs of State failure which he captured as follows, upon reliance on other cited analyses on the subject: "States weaken and fail when they are unable to provide basic functions for their citizens. The economy weakens. Education and health care are non-existent. Physical infrastructure breaks down. Crime and violence escalate out of control."

These conditions generate opposition groups, which often turn to armed insurrection. More often than not, 'the weapons of choice are small arms, light weapons and explosives because they are cheap, plentiful, durable, easily transported and simple to use'. These conflicts create huge population shifts and refugee crises, long-term food shortages, failing economies, and the death of large numbers of civilians from disease, starvation and direct conflict." Countries like Iraq, Afghanistan, Chad, Central African Republic, Zimbabwe, and Pakistan immediately come to mind, even as a much longer list hovers presently in the "failing States" region. Indeed, the citizens of most African, Latin American, Middle East, and Indian subcontinent countries can easily relate to these banners of State failure. For the World Bank, these fragile States are characterized by "a debilitating combination of weak governance, policies and institutions."

Drawing from Dearth's work, he affirms that: "State collapse begins when the central State starts to deteriorate, leading to the fractionalization of society, with loyalties shifting from the State to traditional communities that seem to offer better protection." This involves three primary steps towards the final delinquency: "institutions fail to provide adequate services to the population; improperly channeled ethnic, social and ideological competition erodes the effectiveness of these weak Institutions even more. Finally, the cumulative effects of poverty, over-population, rural flight and rapid urbanization, as well as environmental degradation, overwhelm the weak State to the point of collapse." Since State failure has consequences, he draws from Vernon Hewitt who suggests that: "high levels of domestic instability limit a State's ability to act authoritatively within the international community, limit its ability to act on domestic society with any legitimacy, and to deliver socio-economic packages aimed at bringing about widespread industrialization." As should be clear by now, group favoritism and protection, apart from seriously threatening the fabric of a State, also fundamentally weakens the Social Contract among the constituent units, hence the reversion to a State of Nature as it were.

The Fund for Peace further instructs us that the following are also core features of failed States: the loss of territory or the capacity to wield the legitimate powers of coercion as a monopoly; the absence of legitimacy to make collective decisions; the inability to provide reasonable levels of public services/ goods. These effectively delegitimize the State, as the much-dreaded Hobbesian State emerges. In a useful compilation published by Thomasina Lester on Slideplayer.com, the primary causes of State failure are identified to be: artificial borders deriving from colonialism, low levels of development, attainment of political independence when the States were not "ready" for the demands of modern governance; failed attempts to build a national identity, especially due to group favoritism and alienation; incompetent governance arising from patronage, corruption, and autocracy; extreme poverty and crippling national debt stock misapplied or stolen by the leaders; end of Cold War support to client States; non-resolution of outstanding national issues; as well as greed and grievance. Carment comments, drawing from Gurr and Duvall, that "greater social justice within nations in the distribution of economic goods and political autonomy is the most potent path to social peace."

With this self-evident truth, why do these failed States keep blaming others for their outcomes, rather than reversing course and institutionalizing progressive programs in an inclusive and equitable manner for all their citizens? In resource-rich countries, for example, the aggressive exploitation of natural resources located in one Region for the revenue sustenance of the entire country -- without differential benefits for the particular Region -- is bound to erode public confidence and faith in the system. When the proceeds of these resources are managed rather exclusively by people from other Regions, who devise all means possible to favor their non-contributory Regions, the ingredients for disaggregation and State fragility are sown, possibly forever. Sub-national identities then become stronger than the national consciousness. As Carment put it, "both the trust required for a contract and the legitimacy needed for a stable hierarchy will be elusive when ascriptive and exclusive identification holds sway in a society."

Some of these poorly-governed territories also act as major drug hubs, hence the deepening violence, corruption, and weak systems (**Figure 14).*

Stefan Wolff makes the strong case that State failure actually occurs in clusters, in Regions, thus the analytical framework must necessarily consider this, rather than fixating on individual States. For him also, the term "fragile States" is now generally accepted as describing "a range of phenomena associated with State weakness and failure, including State collapse, loss of territorial control, low administrative capacity, political instability, neo-patrimonial politics, conflict, and repressive polities." A cursory glance at the regional maps (**Figures 15, 16, and 17)* of the implicated States buttresses his central thesis; specifically, the clusters of countries in the Great Horn of Africa, West Africa, the Caucasus in Central and South Asia, as well as the agglomeration of failed States in South America. Relying on other experts on the subject of State failure, Wolff writes that "military capability, enduring patterns of amity and enmity between State and non-State actors, sets of transnational conflicts forming mutually-reinforcing linkages and including military, political, economic, and social networks at the regional level with links to the global level, trans-border movements of politically-organized and regionally-concentrated groups contesting the legitimacy of existing borders, and transnational political mobilization", all highlight the regional dimension of State failure.

As it pertains to Africa, we cannot over-emphasize the contributions of the West towards the fragility and non-performance of most of the countries on the Continent. Europe controlled and ran 90% of the Continent after WWI, and only reluctantly "granted" political independence to these artificially-constructed States from the 50s to 60s owing largely to the existential competition with the Soviet Union during the Cold War. The vigorous and ruthless efforts by both sides to expand their areas of influence led to the Vietnam War, Korean War, overthrow and assassination of charismatic and nationalistic African leaders like Congo's Prime Minister Patrice Lumumba (by the CIA), support of Independence Movements by the Soviets, suborning of the national interests by the erstwhile colonial powers, overt and covert manipulation of these young States in a neo-colonialist structure, alignment of the educational, economic, political, military, and cultural policies and orientation of these new countries with the West, etc.

In Lumumba's case, his sin was to have dared to envision true independence for his Congolese people, without any demand for proper retroactive accountability for the large-scale holocaust against his people by Belgium as well as the massive expropriation of their resources. On their Independence Day in 1960, he had declared in a speech (witnessed by King Baudoin of Belgium) that "we are going to show the world what the black man can do when he works in freedom, and we are going to make of the Congo the center of the sun's radiance for all of Africa. We are going to keep watch over the lands of our country so that they truly profit her children. We are going to restore ancient laws and make new ones which will be just and noble… And for all that, dear fellow countrymen, be sure that we will count not only on our enormous strength and immense riches but on the assistance of numerous foreign countries whose collaboration we will accept if it is offered freely and with no attempt to impose on us an alien culture of no matter what nature...The Congo's independence marks a decisive step towards the liberation of the entire African Continent." He was assassinated within six months by the US, Belgium, and misdirected local allies or stooges.

The US and South Africa, in particular, played a destabilizing role in Angola. When the MPLA won the presidential election, the US supported a sustained armed insurgency waged by a self-declared anti-communist, Jonas Savimbi of the UNITA group. The US spent over $250 million arming, training, and supporting Savimbi, with a White House meeting even held between President Ronald Reagan and this common thug (whom Reagan called a freedom fighter). The destruction that attended the long war inspired a declaration by UNESCO that Angola was the worst place in the world to grow up as a child. Fortunately, the Cold War ended and Savimbi was also assassinated in 2002, giving Angola an opportunity to rebuild. Sadly, the oil curse afflicted them, leading to President Eduardo dos Santos being in power from 1979 to 2017, fostering a deep culture of cronyism, sit-tight syndrome, nepotism, and corruption in this resource-rich country. This once-powerful president now lives in exile in Barcelona, Spain, as does his eldest and favorite child, Isabel, who was assessed by Forbes to be worth over $2 billion in 2013 -- with no visible and verifiable evidence of the sources of this wealth. One can surmise that the political psychologists and profilers at Langley clearly got it wrong by ignoring this man's love for lucre simply because he aligned with Moscow during the Cold War; otherwise, they might just have backed the "right" horse… as they did the vile, murderous, and uber-corrupt Mobutu Sese Seiko in Zaire.

When these Western countries aligned with specific local power merchants or ethnic groups, the result was always large-scale brutality against the people, and a fundamental alienation of those new potentates from their fellow citizens, a phenomenon that persists to this day. Political office has become a cult in Africa, an access to considerable wealth and power accumulated on the backs of the citizens and nullification of the entire essence of governance. The new power elite, which replaced European colonialists, has become even more cruel and corrupt than the foreigners; competition for membership into this protected class of ruthless operatives is what passes for elections in most of Africa. Ascendancy on the ladder of impudence, insensitivity, and corruption is predicated on one's performance (to political godfathers) while on the lower rungs of the prebendal system of patronage, while the entire network exists and expands for mutual protection (politicians, the Military and Security Services, Traditional Rulers, pliant Private Sector Executives, senior journalists and Media Moguls, Religious Leaders, the Judiciary, etc.) These individuals are simply above the law, and have no appreciation of any civic obligation to their people. A few bright stars are emerging on the African Continent, for example, the visionary, focused, and determined Rwandan Strongman, Paul Kagame, as well as the lucid articulation of an ambitious national development program by Ghana's President Nana Akufo-Addo.

Ultimately, Africans themselves will have to determine their own outcomes, but they will do well to seriously consider the sage words of Ghana's first President, Kwame Nkrumah, a pan-Africanist, who said that: "It is clear we must find an African solution to our problems, and that this can only be found in African unity. Divided we are weak; united, Africa could become one of the greatest forces for good in the world." Suspected by the West of harboring Socialist views, he was overthrown in a violent military coup in 1966 while on a foreign trip. As Benjamin Talton writes in his 'The Challenge of Decolonization in Africa', "There are debates about the forces behind the coup that overthrew him in February 1966, but there is strong evidence from the State Department Archives that the United States was interested in removing him from power and that they worked to manipulate the international cocoa price to fuel dissatisfaction with his regime."

As written in Wikipedia, in 1978, John Stockwell, former Chief of the Angola Task Force of the CIA, wrote that agents at the CIA's Accra Station "maintained intimate contact with the plotters as a coup was hatched." Afterward, "inside CIA Headquarters, the Accra Station was given full, if unofficial credit for the eventual coup. ...None of this was adequately reflected in the agency's written records." Later the same year, Seymour Hersh of the New York Times, citing "firsthand intelligence sources," defended Stockwell's account, claiming that: "many CIA operatives in Africa considered the agency's role in the overthrow of Mr. Nkrumah to have been pivotal." Wikipedia added that these claims have never been verified, as should be expected in clandestine operations of that nature, if they were to take place. Nkrumah never returned alive to Ghana but lived in perpetual apprehension as an exile in Conakry, Guinea, dying of prostate cancer in Romania in 1972.

Another pioneering visionary African leader was President Julius Nyerere of Tanzania, fondly called Mwalimu (teacher) by his fellow citizens. While it is debatable if his Ujamaa or African Socialism would have stood the test of time, it is noteworthy that he understood early on that political independence and sovereignty must count for something, and that Africans needed to chart their own course based on their own realities. He warned against the reliance on aid and external borrowings, writing that: "it is stupid to rely on money as the major instrument of development when we know only too well that our country is poor. It is equally stupid, indeed it is even more stupid, for us to imagine that we shall rid ourselves of our poverty through foreign financial assistance rather than our own financial resources … from now on, we shall stand upright and walk forward on our feet rather than look at this problem upside down. Industries will come and money will come, but their foundation is the people and their hard work, especially in agriculture. This is the meaning of self-reliance." This is true Independence, not **Dependent Independence**.

As Frantz Fanon wrote in 1964: "Every former colony has a particular way of achieving independence. Every new sovereign State finds itself practically under the obligation of maintaining definite and deferential relations with the former oppressor." On the Cold War, he added that: "this competitive strategy of Western nations, moreover, enters into the vaster framework of the policy of the two blocs, which for ten years has held a definite menace of atomic disintegration suspended over the world. And it is surely not purely by chance that the hand or the eye of Moscow is discovered, in an almost stereotypical way, behind each demand for national independence, put forth by a colonial people."

Adopting the UK's DfID's definition, he describes fragile States as "those where the government cannot or will not deliver core functions to the majority of its people, including the poor. The most important functions of the State for poverty reduction are territorial control, safety and security, capacity to manage public resources, delivery of basic services, and the ability to protect and support the ways in which the poorest people sustain themselves."

Wolff makes the revolutionary assertion that the status of failure should not be attached to States on account of their inability to deliver on certain ends and public services but should rather involve understanding their failure to secure the means that are necessary to deliver on those ends or public goods. He offers us his translation of the Weberian thesis to advance what he describes as "empirical sovereignty" as follows: "Sociologically, [...] the State cannot be defined in terms of its ends. There is scarcely any task that some political association has not taken in hand, and there is no task that one could say has always been exclusive and peculiar to those associations, which are designated as political ones: today the State, or historically, those associations which have been the predecessors of the modern State. Ultimately, one can define the modern State sociologically only in terms of the specific means peculiar to it, [...] namely, the use of physical force, (...) a State is a human community that (successfully) claims the monopoly of the legitimate use of physical force within a given territory."

In this context, State Failure reflects a contestation for power, and could potentially involve some circuitous argumentation especially in those States that wasted or corruptly degraded their capacity to deliver public goods. Furthermore, this minimalist definition without an ethical dimension, focusing strictly on the "monopolistic use of force within a territory" seems cut out for irresponsible and egoistic brutes who acquire power by whatever means, to satisfy their large egos, repress their own people, and see no civil obligation to attach optimal performance to their positions. In the modern world, this is hardly sustainable, and indeed provides a fertile basis for considerable social dislocation, economic stagnation or ruination, as well as possible State failure. Power should be premised on legitimacy, and legitimacy must be earned and freely given, not stolen.

It is troubling to evaluate State performance purely on the basis of its capacity, or otherwise, to exercise its "legitimate monopoly" on the use of force within its defined territory. This militaristic formulation negates the significant motivations for the formation of the State, apart from its mutual Security elements. Human societies have developed way too much to be strictly assessed based on violence -- however couched. In any case, some States operate efficiently and transparently within their limited means, and still manage to work for all. It is, therefore, not the quantum of means that determines the service offering. Statesmanship, vision, character, and a developed civic culture will trump resource curse among malcontents, for example.

Wolff makes a significant point by recognizing the contribution of environmental factors to State failure. For him, landlocked States that depend on neighbors for trade access to the seas, "riparian States" which share water resources, and States with dependency on pipelines for either energy supplies or transit-related revenues, are particularly fragile and vulnerable to failure.

Wolff's analytical framework bears rendition as originally developed by him:

	State Structures and Actors	Non-state Structures and Actors	'Issues'
Local	• local elites/leaders, authorities and representatives of the central government • institutional arrangements (including distribution of political power and judicial practices) • socio-economic structures (including resource allocation/ distribution)	• locally resident communities/ethnic groups/religious groups and their elites/leaders • locally operating NGOs, rebel forces, private sector interest groups, and criminals • demographic settlement patterns	
National	• national elites/leaders, central government, • institutional arrangements (including distribution of political power and judicial practices) • socio-economic structures (including resource allocation/ distribution)	• communities/ethnic groups/religious groups and their elites/leaders • state-wide operating NGOs, rebel forces, private sector interest groups, and criminals • demographic settlement patterns	• environmental degradation • resource scarcity • energy security • food security • communicable diseases
Regional	• neighbouring states and their institutions • regional powers, and regional IOs, as well as their respective elites/leaders; • structures of political and economic cooperation	• cross-border/ transnational networks (ethnic, religious, civil society, business, organised crime, rebel groups, etc.) and their elites/leaders • demographic settlement patterns	
Global	• powerful states and IOs of global reach and impact and their elites/leaders	• INGOs, diaspora groups, international organised crime networks, and TNCs, as well as their respective elites/leaders	

Table 2. *The levels-of-analysis approach to the study of state failure*

Source: Wolff, Stefan & Dursun-Ozkanca, Oya. (2012). Regional and International Conflict Regulation: Diplomatic, Economic and Military Interventions.

If we employ Graf's template for evaluating the health of various States, we find yet again that the concentration of failed and failing States can be found in the identified Regions of the world. His dimensions of State capacity are as follows: 'the State's capacity to claim the monopoly of the legitimate use of force; to generate sufficient revenue to finance its operations; to effectively administer its operations; to regulate civil society through the provision of public goods; and to command legitimacy.' On their part, Rice and Patrick writing under the banner of the Brookings Institution in 2008 defined weak States as those States that "lack the essential capacity and/or will to fulfill four sets of critical government responsibilities: fostering an environment conducive to sustainable and equitable economic growth; establishing and maintaining legitimate, transparent, and accountable political institutions; securing their populations from violent conflict and controlling their territory; and meeting the basic human needs of their population."

In the interconnected world we live in, the provision of public goods and services within a defined territory should be reasonably taken for granted; the growing demand and requirement of Responsible Sovereignty is what Inge Kaul characterizes as "States' external responsibility to ensure that other nations are not being unduly harmed by spillovers from their jurisdiction that they could reasonably be expected to internalize." While jurisdictional exclusivity can still be assumed, sovereignty, in the modern world, cannot be strictly and classically defined or interpreted as the freedom from "legal subordination to any other authority." Irresponsible and beggarly conduct by nations both depress their stature and enhance the likelihood and incentive for the international community to directly intervene in their internal affairs. Respect is earned in the modern world, and not unconditionally conferred. As Kaul correctly put it, "States would need to act more as intermediaries between external and domestic policy demands, and less like conventional Westphalian nation States. They would need to take the outside world into account when formulating national policies and defining national interests."

Going further, Kaul delineates public goods into peace and security, health and health care, financial stability, environmental sustainability, norms and standards for traded goods, straddling fish stocks, the ozone layer, the atmosphere, an international migration regime, a knowledge and technology framework, communication and transport networks, the World Wide Web, the universalization of human rights norms, as well as globalizing markets.

Smith's schematic on the various services and goods will be helpful here:

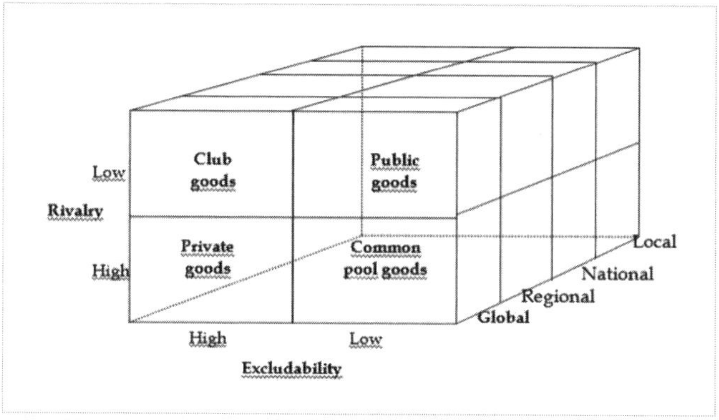

Figure 1.

Private, club, common and public goods,Source: Smith, 2004

As Bernur Ersoy writes, "a private good is the opposite of a public good. Private goods are excludable and rivalrous. For example, a cup of coffee is a private good, and the coffee's owner can exclude other users from using it, and when it has been used, it cannot be consumed again." For him also, the examples of Global Public Goods (GPGs) include information, environmental sustainability, disease prevention, political, economic and social stability, and transportation networks, as well as international communication. As these examples point out, GPGs can be both tangible (e.g., infrastructure or the environment) and intangible (e.g., social, economic or political stability). In this realm, he is dealing with the international community, not merely the responsibilities of States within their sovereign space. Referencing Kaul, he submits that GPGs are public goods that do not "obey" national borders, and some of them are naturally global; furthermore, "GPGs satisfy the needs of present generations without putting into question the needs of future generations."

Local public goods:	National public goods:	Regional public goods:	GPGs:
Street signs or Street safety	National electoral system	Early-warning systems for tsunamis	Global warming
Law and order	National health system	The management of river basins	Peace and security

Source: Kaul, quoted in Ersol, Globalization and Global Public Goods

Those interested in reading further on this subject will get good guidance from Stiglitz, Kaul, Cook and Sachs, Ferguson, Ferroni, and Stansfield.

State Performance: Parameters of Assessment

While the ethical concern about the environment is a relatively recent development, the primary focus and objective principle of all governance mechanisms from prehistoric times through antiquity to the current era, has always been the human person. In this section, we shall rely mostly on credible statistical data and pointed summaries, to emphasize the impact of State policies on the human experience within territories. In essence, we shall be using the global score sheets to assess State performance. In the prior sections of this work, we have attempted to explicate the various theories and concepts that guide governance; it is time to evaluate the consequences of poor governance, corruption, waste, lack of vision, elite profligacy, sub-optimal investment in human capacity development, weak societal cohesion, insecurity, inclement business environment, and the other pathologies that afflict under-developed countries, all of which are politically independent and sovereign, one may add. These consequences and outcomes are not abstract or theoretical to the victims, but real and daily experiences. The time for Philosophy is over; now, we must evaluate its impact on people's lives. The wider the base of the chronically poor, the less competitive the entire country will be in the global environment.

The opening chapter of the UNDP Human Development Index (HDI) Reports has the following words: "The HDI was created to emphasize that people and their capabilities should be the ultimate criteria for assessing the development of a country, not economic growth alone. The HDI can also be used to question national policy choices, asking how two countries with the same level of GNI per capita can end up with different human development outcomes. These contrasts can stimulate debate about government policy priorities. The Human Development Index (HDI) is a summary measure of average achievement in key dimensions of human development: a long and healthy life, being knowledgeable and having a decent standard of living. The HDI is the geometric mean of normalized indices for each of the three dimensions."

The UNDP model is summarized as follows:

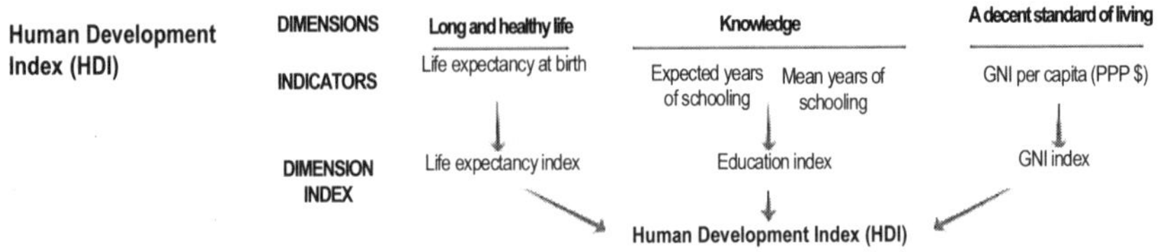

Credit: UNDP HDI Reports

From available UNDP data (**Figures 18,19, and 20*), it is evident that 94 million multi-dimensionally poor people live in upper-middle-income countries, where the sub-national incidence of multidimensional poverty ranges from 0 percent to 69.9 percent; 792 million multi-dimensionally poor live in lower-middle-income countries, where the sub-national incidence of multidimensional poverty ranges from 0 percent to 86.7 percent, while 440 million multi-dimensionally poor people live in low-income countries, where the sub-national incidence of multidimensional poverty ranges from 0.2 percent to 99.4 percent.

Furthermore, while other Regions of the world have some instances of income inequality, it is significant that 84.5% of all the multi-dimensionally poor people in the world live in Africa and South Asia.

The breakdown of the UNDP Report further highlights the fact that children are the most impacted in the most vulnerable poverty capitals of the world. As is evident, disaggregating the global MPI by age reveals inequality across age groups. Children under age 18 bear the greatest burden of multi-dimensional poverty. This section spotlights the 2 billion children—1.1 billion of whom are under age 10—living in the 101 countries covered by the global MPI. Half of multi-dimensionally poor people are children, and a third are children under age 10.

Of the 1.3 billion people who are multi-dimensionally poor, 663 million are children—and 428 million of them (32.3 percent) are under age 10. One adult in six is multi-dimensionally poor, compared with one child in three. While 17.5 percent of adults in the countries covered by the MPI are multi-dimensionally poor, the incidence of multidimensional poverty among children is 33.8 percent. Over 85 percent of multi-dimensionally poor children live in South Asia and Sub-Saharan Africa, split roughly equally between both regions. Some 63.5 percent of children in Sub- Saharan Africa are multi-dimensionally poor—the highest incidence among all developing regions. In Burkina Faso, Chad, Ethiopia, Niger and South Sudan, 90 percent or more of children under age 10 are multi-dimensionally poor. Children are more likely than adults to be multi-dimensionally poor and deprived in all indicators. A higher proportion of children than of adults are multi-dimensionally poor and deprived in every one of the MPI indicators, and the youngest children bear the greatest burden of State delinquency.

In South Asia the percentage of school-age children who are multidimensionally poor and out of school varies by country

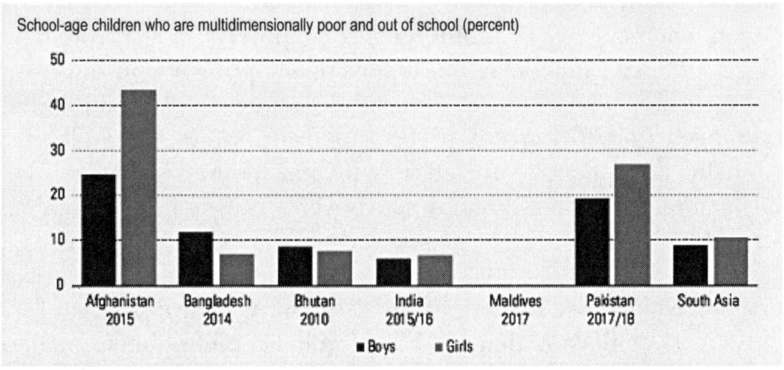

Note: Out-of-school children are school-age children who do not attend school through grade 8.
Source: Alkire, Ul Haq and Alim 2019.

According to the UNDP, of Ethiopia's 102 million inhabitants, 85.5 million are multi-dimensionally poor, meaning that the country has more multi-dimensionally poor people than the total population of Germany—and more multi-dimensionally poor people than any of the 101 countries covered by the Multi-dimensionally Poor Index (MPI) except India and Nigeria. Over half the population is multi-dimensionally poor and has a malnourished person in the household, and half is multi-dimensionally poor and lives in a household in which no one has completed six years of schooling. For the poorest countries, the human experience is worsened by overpopulation, especially in those countries with significant Muslim numbers and rigid cultural patterns. The Koran permits every Muslim man who can afford the responsibilities and who can be fair among all his wives, to marry up to four wives at a time, with the flexibility (under the *Talaq B'ida* or repudiation: أنا أطلقك ، فأطلقك ، وأطلقك) to divorce and replace any of the wives merely by saying "I divorce you" three times. The divorce modalities also include *khul* (mutual divorce), judicial divorce, and oaths, but the ease of the *talaq* option, in particular, gives men license to treat women poorly, in some cases, just to satisfy their carnal desires. The net result is that one man may actually marry more than four wives in his lifetime, and have children by them all, with the children regarded as "blessings from Allah." This practice contributes significantly to the debasement of womanhood and the reckless production of children that cannot be taken care of, thus complicating and deepening the aggregate poverty profile in the implicated countries, with the related security and socio-political implications.

According to the UNDP Africa Human Development Report of 2016 (**Figure 21)*, gender inequality costs sub-Saharan Africa an average of $US 95 billion a year, peaking at US $105 billion in 2014– or six percent of the region's GDP – seriously hampering the Continent's efforts for inclusive human development and economic growth. For a Region that faces multiple challenges, this self-imposed loss is particularly worrisome and indicative of the wrong economic choices. Remedial steps must include addressing "the contradiction between legal provisions and practice in gender laws; breaking down harmful social norms and transforming discriminatory institutional settings; and securing women's economic, social and political participation." While some appreciable progress has been made in women's education, especially in the more liberal parts of Africa, a lot more work must be done to optimize the full potentials of African women, enhance their contributions to the national and regional economies, and nullify historical gender-based barriers. Some of the identified areas of focus are "health deprivations and economic barriers due to such factors as early age marriage, sexual and physical violence, and the continued unacceptable high incidence of maternal mortality." It must be added that the more traditional societies still prioritize giving opportunities (including education) to their male children, to the detriment of the entire society. As the World Economic Forum (WEF) noted in 2014, "...because women account for one-half of a country's potential talent base, a nation's competitiveness in the long term depends significantly on whether and how it educates and utilizes its women." I personally won't use the word 'utilize' in this context. 'Engages', 'empowers', 'economic inclusiveness', etc., will be better.

The traditional roles assigned women in various parts of Africa do not incentivize their exposure to empowering Western norms and skills; this needs urgent attention as well. Women and girls are particularly vulnerable in Africa's numerous wars, conflicts, mass movements, dislocations, and violent clashes. It is observed that the predominantly Christian and elite-Muslim families which enable the best education locally and across the world for their daughters, are, occasionally, regarded as disrupting cultural norms. For the elite Muslims who train their own daughters, there is no commensurate urgency and focus in training the daughters of the poor, as the life of privilege in traditional Islamic societies thrives on the enduring ignorance of the majority, who should be kept satisfied with acquiring only Islamic knowledge. The terrorist organization, Boko Haram, derives its name from the colloquial "book haram", that is, Western education is a taboo. They attack and destroy schools, kidnap and rape girls who dare to attend such schools, including Leah Sharibu, who has remained in the captivity of her Islamic kidnappers (ISWAP) since February 2018.

The point must be made that Africa has complexities and differences on Continental, national, and even sub-national levels, so it will be unhelpful and faulty to attempt a linear analytical approach in assessing the dynamics within the Continent. With 54 countries and over 1.3 billion people, Africa is the world's second largest and second most populous Continent, after Asia, and is about 12 million square miles in size. It is also one of the most nuanced Continents in the world, with religion (Christianity, Islam, Traditional Religion, Syncretism), Culture, Language, History, Geography, Traditional occupations, Values, and other slices of identity ensuring their intrinsic diversity. Within the same country, for example, religious forms may inhibit certain practices and choices, but the same taboos are wholeheartedly embraced in other parts of the country.

This is one of the deficiencies of Statistics, as it seeks averages and not particularities. When it is broadly stated that a lot of African women are not educated, the several millions who have attained the highest levels of education across the world are hardly captured in the matrix because of the density of the majority. When the poverty index is high, the tens of millions who live in super-affluence do not make much dent on the numbers. Admittedly, one of the common features across board is the gross inequality between the rich and the poor, but the traditional social safety nets mitigate the harsh conditions of the endemically poor. It is typical for rich Africans to support poorer relatives and non-relatives alike in a structured manner; the numerous events and parties on the Continent also ensure that most people can find food to eat, for Africans like their lavish weddings, burial ceremonies, child-naming ceremonies, Thanksgiving, and just any "provocation" to host grand events, even on borrowed funds (which are generally recouped through gifts and "spraying" of cash).

An analyst interested in understanding the Continent and its people must, thereby, pay close attention to the similarities and dissimilarities, the historical factors which affect current dynamics, the linguistic and marital affinities which bind ethnic groups, the mutual suspicion and hatred which are rife among groups in each country, and the recurring yearning by all Africans for better governance and representation. Any attempt to transpose Western templates and norms will yield sub-optimal results. There is not much, for example, in terms of pension and social safety nets funded by the governments but providing for one's indigent relatives and for the larger community is an expected responsibility of the more successful ones.

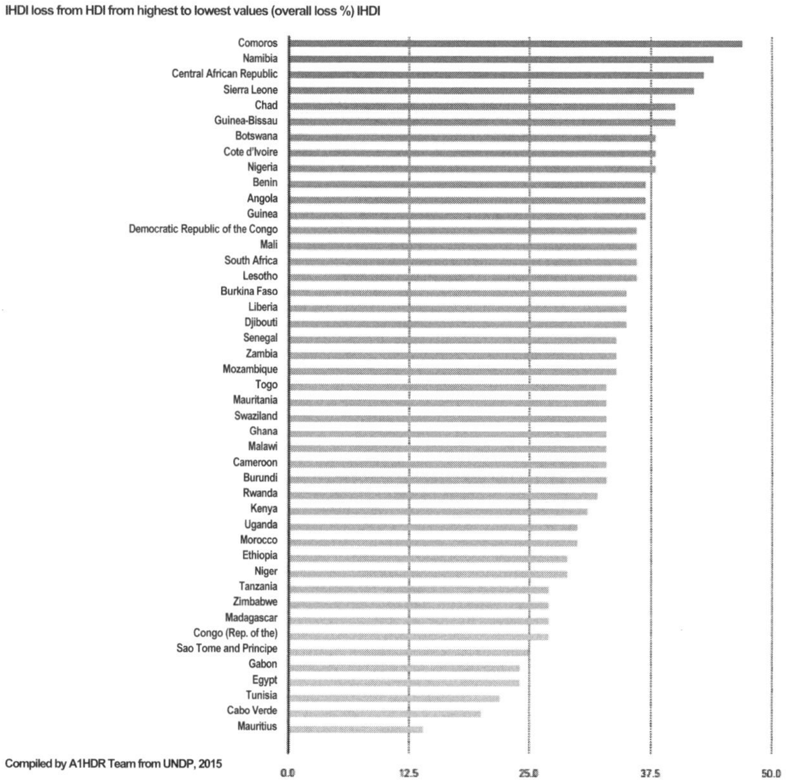

Yet, an abysmal profile across board. Nature seems to reward African women with slightly more years than their men, though -- across the relatively low longevity baseline in the Region (*Figure 23)*. A lot of factors contribute to this, including the excessive stress their men are exposed to in their bid to be the sole or dominant providers in their households, and the observation that children generally take better care of their mothers than their fathers in old age. Empowering women will extend either party's life span, thereby democratizing longevity. Work alone, die alone. In any case, men are advised to save for their old age, in order to avoid disappointments:

UNDP data also state that: "in Sub-Saharan Africa there are on average 39 primary school pupils per teacher, followed by South Asia with 35 pupils per teacher. But in OECD countries, East Asia and the Pacific, and Europe and Central Asia, there is an average of one teacher for every 16-18 primary school pupils. And, while in OECD countries and East Asia and the Pacific there are on average 29 and 28 physicians for every 10,000 people respectively, in South Asia there are only eight, and in Sub-Saharan Africa not even two."

While it is evident that extreme poverty and overall low human development indices abound in every region of the world (*Figure 24)*, especially Africa, Latin

America, and South Asia, we shall adopt the statistical modality of density/ concentration in our remaining effort. From this prism, we shall focus more on Africa as we proceed towards the conclusion of this journey, which started eons ago with our paleontological origins. It is fitting that, since man's journey started in Africa (not with Adam and Eve in the Middle East, as is the popular and profitable legend), we should conclude the journey with the Continent as well, as homage to our origins. Actually, Africa's dubious reputation as the host of the highest number of failed and failing States, is of more import than any obsession with ancestral worship. The fact that 90% of the countries on the Continent also gained political independence as modern nation-States in the last 60 years, provides a further impetus to query how their independence and sovereignty have impacted performance and overall development. Has their aggregate independence been truly independent, or has it been dependent on externalities? **Independent Independence** or **Dependent Independence**?

While countries like Venezuela, El Salvador, Colombia, India, Bangladesh, and several others have some of the same pathologies as most African countries (resource curse, corruption, wide disparities in income, unresolved local dynamics, etc.), our interest is on the density of these problems, and Africa, sadly, comes first here. As we proceed, therefore, it shall be useful to evaluate how the internalization and practice of the precepts of governance and accountability - which took a very long time to develop - (as, hopefully, one has demonstrated) have been executed in Africa, *sui generis*. References to other Regions, going forward, shall be for the purpose of comparison and referencing. Our entire focus through the end of the book will be on Africa, that mother-Continent whose potentials only remain perennially potential. For, one would have thought that political independence and transfer of authority back to the locals would engender accelerated development. Is it enough to keep blaming the colonialists sixty odd years later when the various political players now have the sovereignty of their thoughts, development plans, and overall orientation? They even have the sovereign power to dissolve unworkable and imposed structures of irresoluble incompatibility without shooting wars, or to renegotiate the parameters of their artificial unions, if they so please. It is entirely up to them to take full responsibility for their actions, inactions, and outcomes. No more excuses whatsoever.

It should be of concern to all Africans that, following a consistent pattern, the 2018 UNDP Human Development Index (HDI) Report has Norway, Switzerland, Australia, Ireland and Germany leading the ranking of 189 countries and territories, while Niger, the Central African Republic, South Sudan, Chad and Burundi (all African countries) have the lowest scores in the HDI's measurement of national achievements in health, education and income. This becomes especially problematic against the profligate lifestyle, insensitivity, and wholesale corruption that define the disposition of most, if not all, African leaders at all levels. For them, access to power is access to unbecoming wealth, privileges, and immunity from accountability. In many respects, these local leaders or dealers have been worse for their respective countries than were the erstwhile European colonizers; a sad but honest admission to make. In many cases also, these shameless people are, due to greed and corruption, replacing the condemnable European colonization with emerging and ferocious Chinese colonization.

What was the purpose of their independence, one may then ask?

A Continent that scares most of her best brains away; fails to dignify all black people around the world; looks elsewhere as her citizens take perilous risks on deserts and seas to seek asylum elsewhere; embraces brain drain as a badge of honor; loses its cultural strength and vibrancy through the unfiltered ingestion of everything foreign; refuses to envision and do the necessary hard work to lift their status and the living experiences of their people; has no shame in having Europeans and the Chinese replace electric bulbs and maintain the gardens in their Presidential Complexes; cannot optimize their huge population and resources in planning for manufacturing, services, policies, trade, tariff, and other common standards; readily exports ill-gotten wealth to Europe, America, the Middle East, and core Asia due to their lack of confidence in the continued viability of their own countries; a Continent with no single city that has comprehensive public water supply; a Continent where Ph.Ds. in all fields are fairly common but locals do not construct bridges and highways; a Continent where egos are larger than the massive Continent with nothing to show for all the pomposity; leaders and followers with zero fidelity to the requirements and principles of accountable governance and delivery of public goods; a Continent where lives are transformed overnight owing to political positions and connections; where traffic is regarded as a part of the topography;

A Continent where low group ambition is pervasive with people being satisfied with mediocrity; a Continent of superfluous religiosity and chronic corruption; a place where even well-intentioned private sector players must appease the gods of inefficiency and corruption in the public sector, to thrive; competition to belong is rife; agents and cronies of the ruling class permanently seek to censor public comments and to stifle critical opinions; a place filled with merchants of influence and very wealthy people with no visible means of livelihood and whose employees are limited to drivers, cooks, and Security guards -- with zero productivity; a Continent where providing your entire spectrum of utilities is evidence of success; a Continent without functional libraries and deep appreciation for intellectualism; no bookstore thrives; a place where the imminent expression of "arrival" is wearing an expensive wristwatch (real or fake); where it is a requirement to have Security contacts for protection from the guaranteed problems with the Police and sundry Agencies -- a typical phenomenon; an environment where it is virtually impossible for someone to drive from one town to another in a nice car without Police escort; a Continent where both public officials and private citizens gauge and demonstrate their "power" by their high impunity index; a place where looters and their acolytes prove their success by the length and quality (of the cars) of their convoys and their privatization of Security Forces as personal thugs and bag-carriers; where having wailing siren on your arrival is a sign of "arrival"; where goats are transformed into lions overnight and erstwhile criminals and drug peddlers make State Policy; a Continent that trivializes human life even as they chant "black lives matter" more than Americans; a Continental leadership with zero understanding of the requirements of the Social Contract; a people with no demonstrable capacity for shame due to their strategic failure; an environment with sundry Ph.D. holders (sub-standard and substantial alike) with zero translation into independent national capacity;

A Continent where thousands of sundry experts in Ministries of Agriculture rely on Israeli citrus farmers for guidance; presidents and senior government officials feel no shame in seeking medical attention overseas, after stealing the funds meant for their national hospitals; the currency of the francophone countries - the CFA is still tied to the French Francs while France is still allowed to get away with usurious impositions sixty years after official colonialism ended; external countries summon their presidents to foreign capitals to discuss Africa; a challenged world is not looking up to the Continent for solutions to the Covid:19 pandemic; regular electricity supply is still a mirage in 2020; there is no shame in the absence of efficient and safe intra-Continental flights thereby causing people to fly from one African country to London, Paris, or Dubai first before proceeding to another African country; government officials, their families and cronies, as well as their private sector emulators and fronts fill out first and business class cabins on international flights before major airlines sell seats in the economy cabin; one's children cannot attend the same public schools attended by one; their understanding of elitism and intellectual distinction subsists in attending overpriced short-term classes at Harvard and buying the biggest Alumni rings at the gift store; both stark illiterates and otherwise educated people feel insecure until they attach a fake Dr. to their names -- with all those appellations translating into zero aggregate development; there are arguably more Mercedes G Wagons of all specifications in Lagos and Abuja, Nigeria, than in the whole of Germany and Europe put together; indeed, Africa has far more bullet-proof vehicles than any other Continent in the world -- mostly assigned to thieving government officials who have failed to solve insecurity, while the privately-rich or politically-connected constitute the balance of these patrons; a vast space with a ratio of religious (Muslim and Christian) centers of worship to factories at a minimum of 2,000:1. Even with the proliferation of these mosques and churches of all hues, there is no holistic transformative behavior, as is reflected in the dire conditions of the majority on the Continent;

A Continent that imports more Japanese SUVs than any other for its government officials without demanding the establishment of Toyota Assembly Plants all over the Continent or the transfer of automotive technology; a people who gladly import toothpicks and pencils; a Continent where a significant section still callously subjects girls to genital mutilation; a shameless group that permits some pedophiles to marry young girls (citing Islamic authority), thus making the Continent the global hub for obstetric fistula; people who learnt nothing from their past and are actively parceling out large acreages of land to Chinese entities; a people who only think about self and not the group or national interest; where everyone in government is addressed as Your Excellency (excellent crooks), Distinguished (by infamy), and Honorable (actually dishonorable); societies that celebrate and reward political criminals and ass lickers while punishing decent people; a space with government officials who place newspaper advertisements when they pay the miserable salaries of government workers several months in arrears, even while these local colonizers feel entitled to disproportionate compensation and sundry avenues for stealing public revenue;

A Continent where political leaders pile up external loans for their future generations (even signing Loan Agreements written in Chinese language, we are told) with nothing to show for those debts; in fact, people who have no basic understanding and acceptance of the concept of the public good -- the very essence and raison d'être for political societies in the first place. What was the purpose of their political independence, then? With the widespread popularity of football (soccer in America), the related abundant talent on the African Continent, as well as the significant representation in all the major European and Asian Leagues by African players, one wonders why there is no significant League in Africa. A systematic approach would identify, train, nurture, and retain most of the talent on the Continent, forging sporting and cultural links, attracting huge advertisement funds, creating jobs, and projecting a respectable and friendly image to the world. The same applies to basketball, with all the giants that are all over the Continent, especially in Senegal, Rwanda, Mali, and Gambia. Alliances with the US NBA and NFL would be a good way to start, or they simply grow organically and compete with the rest of the world. Why are the people so eager to consume everything foreign, even when they are the ones providing the "foreign" entertainment?

The President of Madagascar recently claimed that they had a herbal remedy for Covid:19, but refused to submit this concoction to basic empirical investigation. He also refused to claim the billions of dollars awaiting whoever finds the actual cure for this pandemic, because he is only selling snake oil. The Director of one of the useless Government Agencies in Nigeria, the so-called Raw Materials Research and Development Council, recently announced to their Parliament that the greatest achievement they had recorded in over thirty years was producing a machine that blends pepper and condiments for the local beef delicacy called *kilishi*. This, after wasting or stealing hundreds of millions of dollars over the decades!!! And the idiot is still in that office … because of clannish reasons. Yet, this same country has highly qualified Scientists, Researchers, and sundry experts, who are mostly contributing in rarefied fields in Europe and America. This, at a time when the world is advancing research in Artificial Intelligence, Robotics, Cloud Computing, 3D printing, Telemedicine, Quantum Computing, and Big Data.

The point being made is not that every country has the human and natural resources to be a First World country, but the absence of corruption, waste, inefficiency, nepotism, and sub-optimal thinking will lead to the optimization of whatever resources that are available. The primitive accumulation of the collective patrimony, the misallocation of resources, the celebration of mediocrity and mendacity, the comfort with little things, the perpetual freeze of mental sagacity, the lack of confidence in the long-term viability of their own countries, the fraudulence in political structures that remains unaddressed, the elevation of sub-national cleavages over national and Continental identities, the marginalization of significant productive segments of the society, the personalization of power and demand for cultic followership, the subversion of State and Security Institutions, and the design of policies around personal benefits instead of the public good, combine to ensure the outcomes that are so very prevalent across the Continent.

The citizens of the countries know the thieves and oppressors, but feel completely powerless to confront them, finding expression only through the vibrancy and vehemence which the anonymity of the social media platforms provides. It is recognized that the fractious internal cleavages also detract from the unified response required to exterminate this blight on an otherwise very rich Continent, but the people themselves must just seize the moment and reclaim both their dignity and the potentials of their Continent. Excuses will no longer suffice.

Singapore produces merely about 20,000 barrels of crude oil daily (number 78 on the list of oil-producing countries), but is a major hub for oil sales and has a network of sophisticated refineries; it is also in the top five of every list of the major global financial centers -- with the rest being New York, London, Shanghai, Frankfurt and Hong Kong. After initially joining Malaysia in its independence from Britain in 1963, Singapore was forced to pull out and attain its own independence in 1965 --- after the bulk of African countries had attained theirs. The tremendous success achieved by China, Japan, Hong Kong, Taiwan, and Vietnam, for example, inspires confidence in Asian people wherever they may be in the world. It must be noted that, whereas Western Oil Majors operate in Africa and cause considerable environmental damage in their operating areas, they mostly do not make long-term investments by way of building and operating refineries. In Singapore, however, they are held to very strict environmental standards, which they comply with; Total, ConocoPhillips, ExxonMobil, Shell, and Chevron all operate refineries in Singapore -- a very minor oil producer. This says a lot about investor confidence, absence of corruption, patriotism of national leaders and Oil Regulators, as well as respect for host-countries.

Though the Middle East Region is the origin and base of Islam, countries like the UAE, Oman, Qatar, and Bahrain have infrastructure standards that can match or exceed European and American standards. The other Middle Eastern country, Israel, the origin and center of Judaism, is a world leader in Research, Defense Technology, Medicine, IT, and Agriculture. Why can't African countries that practise the subsidiary elements of the Abrahamic Religions develop their Continent as well? Why can't the deserts of Africa be transformed like Abu Dhabi and Dubai have been totally changed in less than three decades? Why can't the Muslims of Mali, Nigeria, Niger Republic, Chad, and elsewhere be as ambitious and patriotic as the Muslims of the Middle East? Why the shameless rush to Dubai for pleasure and investments instead of building their own Dubais? Why can't proud African people choose a life of real independence; a life of equality and not that of aid and dependence? Can their **independence** finally be truly **independent**?

The international ecosystem does not assume exclusivity of national capacities or absolute self-dependence, but respectable nations deploy optimal policies and apply their full potentials and resources to enhance the areas in which they have comparative advantages. This way, their dependence on external parties is limited to those areas in which they do not have comparative advantage. When this dependence becomes absolute -- loans, brain drain, healthcare, construction, policies, excessive imports, culture, religion, basic planning, sanitation, urban renewal, etc., etc., there is justifiable reason to query the performance of those

States that interpret sovereignty as the exclusive power to rape and pillage within a hard defined piece of geography, and not a call to duty; a projection and manifestation of the collective ambition, dignity, and vision of a people.

The choice for African people (not their leaders) is clear: behave like some of their progenitors who either cooperated with Arabs and Europeans during the Slave Trade or failed to resist; and those who, on an individual basis, achieve excellence in their chosen fields across the world. This pool of excellence needs to be aggregated and the forces of light need to push aggressively against the forces of evil and primitivity, if Africans, indeed all black people, are to be seriously respected as a group in the comity of nations. Young Africans need to draw inspiration from some of the following individuals who were and are Africans: Richard Spikes invented the automatic gear system in cars which the entire world uses; Alexander Miles invented the open and close mechanism on elevator doors; the cooling vans and trucks which enable the transportation of refrigerated food items were invented by Frederick James; the modern letterbox used across the United States was pioneered by Phillip Downing who also had 61 patents to his name; the traffic lights, as we know them today, were designed by Garrett Morgan; the communication between two distant train stations was made possible by Granville Woods, who also developed the egg incubator. He had 50 patents to his name. Otis Boykin improved the pacemaker and he had 26 patents to his name. If not for slavery and the brutal negation of their identities, this sample of noble men might have been called Olufemi, Chege, Kwame, Diallo, or Rolihlahla.

In the modern era, we have people like the eminent Harvard-trained lawyer, Investment Banker, Goldman Sachs Director since 2012, and Founding Chairman/ Managing Director of Global Infrastructure Partners (owners of London Gatwick and Edinburgh Airports, Ports of Melbourne and Brisbane and other major assets), Adebayo Ogunlesi; and Phillip Emeagwali -- whose pioneering work in supercomputing produced the then fastest computer in the world (1989) which could process 3.1 billion calculations per second, and the updated versions of which are still used in weather forecasting and global warming assessments to this day. They can also draw inspiration from the fact that Steve Jobs of the Apple fame was a Syrian (who took the Jobs last name of his very kind American adoptive parents), so excellence can germinate anywhere. His biological father's name is Abdul Fattah Jandali. The concern should be as follows: why was it possible for these eminent men (and the female counterparts not presently listed) to achieve such great excellence, in some cases, as dehumanized individuals, only outside Africa?

What is it about Africa that deplores excellence and stifles creativity? This is a question that only Africans themselves can answer. Both the descendants of slaves and the voluntary immigrants in the West, will prefer that they could optimize their full potentials back at home, in mother Africa, surrounded by love and breathing the air of organic freedom while walking on the soil of their ancestors. No complete person entirely enjoys the experience of involuntary or voluntary dislocation. What can be done to incubate new models of excellence on the Continent? This clarion call becomes even more urgent with the rise of racial bigotry in Europe and America, with Africans forever being the victims of derogation and race-based violence, often due to ignorance and foolishness, but still facts measured in deaths, loss of limbs, and economic deprivation. Permanently looking through the rear-view mirror should not replace the urgent need to look at life through the much-wider windshield in front.

As should be fairly obvious to anyone who has endured the rigor of reading this book from the beginning to this moment, no one else will develop Africa but Africans themselves. Do they expect Mr. Trump, descendants of Leopold of Belgium, Nietzsche, and Hegel, to wish them well? It is in the interest of many parts of the world to perpetuate the falsity about the black man's incapacity to run his own affairs, for that provides some moral salving, some theoretical justification for all the horrible things they have done to Africa and Africans, and which, by acquiescence, modern-day Africans allow to be done to them both by outsiders and their own local oppressors who lack conscience and a sense of history. A hundred years from now, the current status symbol attached to the acquisition of the citizenship of European and American countries will replace the forceful conscription of labor that slavery represented, together with the loss of culture, language, and identity. All of this contribution to societies that may remain bigoted along racial lines; a structure that perennially disrespects even the brightest and most upright African. Africans should develop Africa for and by them and derive joy and fulfillment from their strategic response to centuries of cruelty, exploitation, and disrespect against them. Local perpetrators are even worse than external enemies.

Thinking people should be very concerned about the endless profusion of negativity out of the Continent, and the loss of their best brains to Europe and America, with the consequential impact on their languages and cultures as the future generations of these *émigrés* lose their wholesome identities. Objective data from the Global Terrorism Index (GTI) also confirms that the concentration of terrorism-related deaths take place in failed and failing States (**Figures 25, 26, and 27*).

Even without the emotionally tangled problems of the Middle East, Africa has become a Region of death and instability. The reporting on international affairs follows the same Eurocentric patterns of paternalism towards Africa, even for the most objective people who may not be aware of their subliminal biases and sociological conditioning. In this regard, just in the same way that Arabs have *Al Jazeera* and the Chinese have their CGTN, why can't Africans have their own media stations, which present balanced narratives on the Continent? Would private sector investors be enabled or stifled? For, Africans definitely do not live on trees, Africa is not one country, Africans do not have monkeys and lions as neighbors, and the level of opulence available to wealthy Africans is unsurpassed anywhere else except, perhaps, in the Arabian Palaces. That is exactly the problem: the disparity between the haves and have-nots, and the inability to present a balanced narrative to the connected world. Control of the African narrative is critical in the modern age. With all the violence in the US and UK, for example (including religion-inspired and race-based ones), their media houses have never described both countries as terrorist States. The classification would be different if other countries were involved; that is the power of the media.

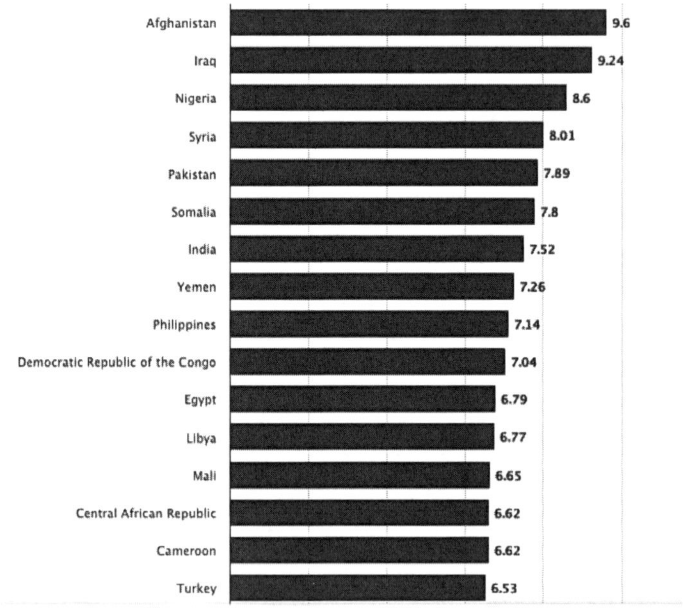

Top terrorist countries as at 2018. *Credit: Statista*

A profile of the most active terrorist groups in the world in 2017 shows African groups, including the Fulani extremists of West Africa who do not self-identify as terrorists, well-represented. Indeed, since the Fulanis intensified their attacks on Nigerian communities in recent years, their ranking on this list of infamy has gone up by several notches. While Afghanistan remains the terrorism capital of the world, quite a few African countries are accelerating their credentials as terrorist

States. Without Security, there can be no development or peace. The Nigerian Government under Buhari, a Fulani Muslim, has proved extremely incompetent or unwilling to vanquish these killers and their Boko Haram counterparts, hence the seriously degraded security profile of the country. This failure has been so bad that otherwise very clannish organizations like the Northern Elders Forum and the Arewa Consultative Forum -- incubators, perpetrators, defenders, and beneficiaries of the feudalistic patronage system and primitive networks that afflict Nigeria (hitherto Buhari's staunch supporters) have come out publicly to deplore the Government's inaction.

According to the GTI, the terrorist group, Boko Haram, has, "since 2009, been responsible for thousands of deaths throughout the Lake Chad Basin Region of West Africa. The Salafi -Jihadi insurgency has led to 35,000 combat-related deaths and 18,000 deaths from terrorism since 2011, mainly in Nigeria. The group is most active in the north-eastern Nigerian State of Borno but has also perpetrated attacks in Burkina Faso and Cameroon." While several Nigerian soldiers have been killed by these terrorists, the Buhari Administration has what it regards as a rehabilitation program for captured Boko Haram terrorists, wherein they undergo some training, are given some money, and let back into the society while some are absorbed into the Army -- much to the consternation of objective analysts. The recidivism rate has remained extremely high in a country with unreliable citizenship records, while many of these "resettled" terrorists use their new Intelligence about the Nigerian Army and improved weapons skills, to boost the lethality of their terrorist organization. Some have also been suspected of partnering with the protected Fulani terrorists who are on a murderous rampage all over the country.

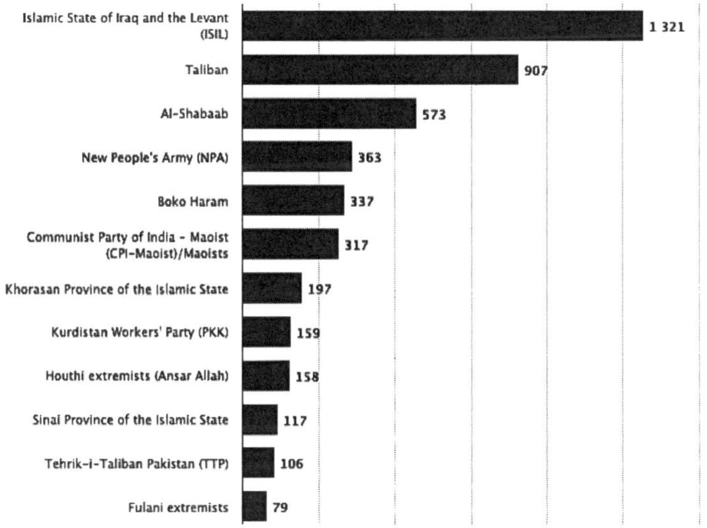

Most active perpetrator groups worldwide in 2017, based on number of attacks. *Credit: Statista*

The Global Terrorism Index Report for 2019 writes in its Executive Summary that: "conflict remains the primary driver of terrorism, with over 95 per cent of deaths from terrorism occurring in countries already in conflict. When combined with countries with high levels of political terror, the number jumps to over 99 percent. Political terror involves extra-judicial killings, torture and imprisonment without trial. The ten countries with the highest impact of terrorism are all engaged in at least one armed conflict." It adds that, other than Afghanistan, only three other countries recorded a substantial increase in deaths from terrorism in 2018: Nigeria, Mali, and Mozambique. Each of these countries recorded more than 100 additional deaths. We are further informed by this respectable Report that "the primary driver of the increase in terrorism in the (sub-Saharan) Region was a rise in terrorist activity in Nigeria, which was attributed to Fulani extremists. Of the 13 groups or movements that recorded more than 100 deaths, six are primarily active within sub-Saharan Africa."

Some of the key trends from the same Report should worry Africans (and other implicated Regions): "Between 2002 and 2018, South Asia, Middle East and North Africa (MENA) and sub-Saharan Africa accounted for 93 per cent of all deaths from terrorism. The largest number was recorded in MENA, with more than 93,700 fatalities; Terrorism is also correlated with the intensity of conflict. There is a strong correlation between the number of battle deaths per year in a conflict country, and the number of terrorist attacks in the same year." (**Figures 28 and 29)* While it is difficult or impossible for every section of a country to experience terrorism, or for every citizen to face personal vulnerability to terrorist attacks, perception matters. The citizens of each country are usually lumped together by foreigners, have the same currency, they share the same passport -- with challenges in getting consular benefits, and internal dependencies in trade, agriculture, and manufacturing are seriously affected by terrorism in any part thereof.

Out of the ten countries which accounted for 87% of all the terrorism-related deaths in 2018, five are in Africa, namely, Nigeria, Chad, Burkina Faso, Mali, and Mozambique. Again, that recurring exemplar of absolute State failure, Afghanistan, led by a wide margin on the chart. The Global Terrorism Index scores for the most implicated countries are as follows: Afghanistan (1st, 9.603); Iraq (2nd, 9.241); Nigeria (3rd, 8.597); Syria (4th, 8.006); Pakistan (5th, 7.889); Somalia (6th, 7.800); India (7th, 7.518); and Yemen (8th, 7.259). A common feature in all these terrorist attacks is the fact that they were all perpetrated by adherents of the "religion of peace", Islam, using, not the Koran or *Hadith*, but semi-automatic weapons and bombs. However fringe their views, they claim to seek an imposition of the Islamic Caliphate wherever and whenever they strike innocent people. Nigeria has no business being on this list, but for the unchecked activities of the Islamic terrorist elements, which blight over 170 million Christians, traditional worshippers, and non-terrorist Muslims alike.

Context is everything, though. Nigeria, with a population of between 180 million and 220 million people (depending on whom you ask, and the purpose of the inquiry -- tax? allocating resources based on assumed numbers? elections? --, since no reliable census has been held in the country for over fifty years, despite billions of dollars wasted and stolen on census operations), cannot be compared with a much smaller country with, say, 10 million people and who are mostly or all Christians. The number of Muslims in a country (especially the vulnerable illiterate and poor), the porosity or otherwise of the national borders, the predominant religion of the countries with which a State shares borders, etc., all affect the terrorist profile of that country.

According to the Report, and this bears extensive referencing, "in Nigeria, terrorist activity is dominated by Fulani extremists and Boko Haram. Together, they account for 78 per cent of terror-related incidents and 86 per cent of deaths from terrorism. The Fulani extremists do not constitute a single terrorist group. Certain deaths within the ongoing conflict between pastoralists and the nomadic Fulani have been categorized as terrorism and attributed to extremist elements within the Fulani. This categorization is reflective of terrorism used as a tactic within an ongoing conflict. There are an estimated 14 million Fulani in Nigeria, with substantial populations also in Guinea, Senegal, Mali, and Cameroon. It is almost certain that the recent escalation in violence and deaths caused by Fulanis in Nigeria are due to their alignment with their ethnic kith and kin, with extensive terrorist experience in Mali, plus tacit encouragement by Nigerian Administration officials. We refer here to that extremist Islamic group called the *Front de Libèration du Macina (FLM)*. In 2018, Fulani extremists were responsible for the majority of terror-related deaths in Nigeria at 1,158 fatalities. Terror-related deaths and incidents attributed to Fulani extremists increased by 261 and 308 per cent respectively from the prior year. Of 297 attacks by Fulani extremists, over 200 were armed assaults. Over 84 per cent of these armed assaults targeted civilians."

One may add that these civilians were all murdered in their ancestral homes and on their subsistence farms by Fulani terrorists masquerading as pastoralists, with the declared objective of sacking communities through violence and taking over: These killers openly display AK-47 rifles and are never arrested by Security Forces.

Terrorism also adversely affects the economy, as evidenced by the following statistics:

Top ten countries for economic cost of terrorism as a percentage of GDP, 2018

The countries with the highest economic impacts of terrorism are all suffering from ongoing conflict.

Country	% of GDP	GTI 2019 Rank
Afghanistan	19.4%	1
Iraq	3.9%	2
Nigeria	2.7%	3
Central African Republic	1.6%	14
Syria	1.6%	4
Mali	1.4%	13
Libya	1.2%	12
Somalia	1.1%	6
South Sudan	0.8%	17
Yemen	0.6%	8

Source: START GTD, IEP Calculations

Economic impact of terrorism by region, $US billions, 2018

REGION	ECONOMIC IMPACT OF TERRORISM (US$ BILLIONS)	REGIONAL ECONOMIC IMPACT AS PERCENTAGE OF THE GLOBAL TOTAL
sub-Saharan Africa	12.17	37%
Middle East and North Africa	11.9	36%
South Asia	5.87	18%
Asia-Pacific	1.22	4%
Europe	0.6	2%
South America	0.59	2%
North America	0.49	1%
Russia and Eurasia	0.23	0.7%
Central America and the Caribbean	0.12	0.4%

Source: IEP

Relying on quantifiable parameters alone, IEP assesses that the total global economic impact of violence was $14.1 trillion in 2018, or 11.2 percent of global GDP. As the Report acknowledges, this profile is conservative because "it does not take into account the costs of counterterrorism or countering violent extremism, or the impact of diverting public resources to security expenditure away from other government activities. It does not calculate any of the longer-term economic implications of terrorism from reduced tourism, business activity, production and investment." With the African GDP estimated at $2.58 trillion (Nominal; 2020); and $6.36 trillion (PPP); 2017), the sheer impact of violence on economic performance becomes clearer.

As further written, "violence arising from terrorism and the fear of terrorism creates significant economic disruptions. Fear of terrorism alters economic behavior, primarily by changing investment and consumption patterns as well as diverting public and private resources away from productive activities and towards protective measures. Terrorism and the fear of terrorism also generate significant welfare losses in the form of productivity shortfalls, foregone earnings and distorted expenditure - all of which affect the price of goods and services." They also identify the indirect costs of terrorism to include adverse effects on: Trade, Financial Market, Tourism and Foreign Direct Investment (FDI).

HOW IS LIFE?

It should be clear by now that, for the vast majority of the people on the African Continent, life is not good at all. While the Continent is estimated to have 140,000 millionaires (in US Dollars), the truth is that the actual number is much higher than this. The several thieves in the public services, Military, Police, Customs, the favored girlfriends and concubines, Parliamentarians, and sundry executive leeches, who have no visible means of income to justify their global assets and lifestyles, are not captured in this profile, for they have no need for such recognition and exposure. If we estimate that there are 1 million USD millionaires in Africa, that is still one of the highest concentrations of wealth in the world, since the Continent has a population of 1.3 billion people (and growing).

It is a telling fact that at least 70% of these "rich" people can trace their money directly to the governments in one form or another: as government officials who stole directly, favored contractors who stole with their patrons and partners in government, beneficiaries of concessions and tax waivers from government for which they paid bribe, spouses and children of government officials who pursue business interests funded with corruption funds, fronts for government officials, and business partners of thieves in government. In the absence of a developed middle class, you are either rich or poor in Africa. The poor depend on rich relatives for survival, thus worsening their outcomes in life and providing, in a perverse way, a further incentive for the privileged to keep stealing, without any limits or conscience. The failure of State infrastructure also entails the provision of one's electricity, water, security, etc., while maintaining a network of doctors in Europe, the US, and Asia.

In the latter regard, the Covid-related travel restrictions have ensured that a good number of these leeches have died on African soil during this pandemic. The net result is also that the genuinely rich professionals and business owners come under severe pressure from their numerous poor relatives, even as they are usually the targets of common crimes, armed robberies, kidnap for ransom, and assassination. The government officials, having cornered all the Security personnel to their private use, expose hard-working professionals and business owners to extreme personal risk as the group of successful people whom the poor can easily access and attack. This group also bears the brunt of government policy instability, discretionary impunity, arbitrariness, crippling bureaucracy and inefficiency, as well as multiple taxation. Those who are so inclined among them, also "buy" the services of armed government security forces, thereby further depleting the number of Security personnel available to serve the public. A self-reinforcing cartel is thus created and sustained, especially in those countries where access to personal arms is strictly prohibited (to avoid an insurrection against the ultra-corrupt and alienated local oppressors in government); Police Chiefs assign armed police escorts to rich people, who then pay them personally for the "service". Add the fleet of bullet-proof cars, as well as pilot vehicles with siren and LED Security lights, then the profile of an African big man is complete. Now, they can bully other road users, intimidate their neighbors and relatives, and be regarded highly in the society.

The intercourse among these elements of the local population is responsible for Africa's problems. Feeding and pampering this cohort is the entire premise of governance across the Continent, while the citizens are held down by violence or threat of violence. This partly explains why, on virtually all the parameters of assessment, African countries fare poorly on the delivery of public goods to their people. The Organization for Economic Cooperation and Development (OECD) issues regular Reports on State and Regional performance in the following areas: Education, Housing, Income, Jobs, Environment, Individual Freedom, Political Stability, Personal Safety, Ease of Doing Business, Predictable Government Policies and Regulations, Stability of Currency Strength, Environmental Quality, Job Security, Civic Engagement, Health, Life Satisfaction, Safety, and Work-Balance. Together with the usual culprits in South Asia and Latin America, African countries provide a depressing cluster of non-performance along these criteria.

In a rigorous Study jointly undertaken by the BAV Group and the esteemed Wharton Business School of the University of Pennsylvania, employing 65 variables, the countries that were ranked the highest in the world on the aggregate quality of the human experience were: Switzerland at no. 1; Canada at 2; Japan at 3; Germany at 4; Australia at 5; UK at 6; USA at 7; Sweden at 8; Netherlands at 9; and Norway at 10. Conversely, on another set of data, the countries with the worst living experiences for the majority include: Guinea, Niger, Nigeria, Angola, Yemen, Cameroun, Sudan, Mali, Chad, Congo, Central Africa, Iraq, and Afghanistan. Of course, these are averages, but the absence of any African country on the 'good list' is a clarion call to duty. Personal wealth and comfort will continue to be a burden until the majority can be lifted out of poverty and their quality of life drastically enhanced. Alternatively, even the richest, most sophisticated, and best-educated citizens of "shithole" countries will be regarded and treated in shitty ways by foreign embassies and non-Africans.

The World Population Review defines the Social Progress Imperative as "the capacity of society to meet the basic human needs of its citizens, establish the building blocks that allow citizens and communities to enhance and sustain the quality of their lives, and create the conditions for all individuals to reach their full potential." It rests on the tripod of Basic Human Needs (health care, sanitation, and shelter); Foundations of Wellbeing (life expectancy and access to education and technology), and Opportunity (personal rights, freedom of choice, and general tolerance). Obviously, having access to potable water, general security, electricity, quality education, good-paying jobs, leisure, freedom, healthy aspirations, respectful treatment by their government, accountable governance, good roads, equipped hospitals and qualified manpower, efficient and multi-modal transportation systems, etc., etc. have no religious, ethnic, or social markers. These are HUMAN needs in the modern world.

As the distinguished Harvard Scholar and Sinologist, Ezra Vogel, wrote in his biography of the phenomenal Founder of modern China, Deng Xiaoping, societies that are serious about development typically transfer the efficiencies, corporate culture, and habits of their private sector to the public sector. In paraphrasing Akio Morita, the co-founder of Sony Corporation, who observed certain dynamics in various countries as he built factories, "countries without modern industry tend to preserve inefficient bureaucracies -- but once modern industry introduces new standards of efficiency, those standards begin to spill over into governments." Deng insisted that the notoriously over-staffed and inefficient Communist Chinese government offices adopt these proven standards of efficiency which their private sector pioneered in Guangdong and Shanghai in 1989. The rest, as they say, is history. The miracle of China's economic success in just a few decades -- even without democracy and a liberal political space -- is a testament to the power of vision, character, self-confidence, and hard work. African countries need their own Deng Xiaopings and Lee Kuan Yews. Would nepotism, corruption, divisiveness, clannishness, myopia, surrender of both personal and national destinies to invisible and impotent forces, selfishness, and ego, allow this to happen? Which country would set the pace, and redeem the sick Continent, an adult that still feeds through feeding bottles?

Apart from the residual profile of the hitherto-apartheid South Africa, the Quality of Life profile for the majority of Africans remains absent on the global stage, according to the World Population Review (**Figure 30*).

Performance across both the WHO Millennium Development Goals (MDGs) and UN's Sustainable Development Goals (SDGs), yield about the same profile of delinquency: eradicate extreme poverty; reduce child mortality; improve maternal health; ensure environmental sustainability; and develop a global partnership for development (MDGs) on the one hand and no poverty; zero hunger; quality education; gender equality; affordable and clean energy; decent work and economic growth; reduced inequalities; sustainable cities and communities; climate action; life below water (aquatic life); peace, justice, and strong Institutions; Partnerships; and Life on Land (SDGs) on the other hand. According to the UN High Commission for Refugees (UNHCR), Africa, together with sections of the Middle East, generates most of the number of internally displaced people, apart from the refugees seeking succor far away from home.

The UNHCR Report states that countries with high levels of new internal displacement include Somalia (602,700), Nigeria (581,700), Cameroon (514,500), Afghanistan (343,300), DRC (322,000), Central African Republic (266,400), Yemen (264,300), Syria (256,700), the Philippines (212,600), Iraq (150,200), Colombia (118,100), Mali (82,100), Niger (51,800), Burkina Faso (44,700), Libya (33,200) and Congo (30,200). This is yet another indication of fragility and incipient State collapse. While it is true that 20% of the 2.1 million global asylum applications in 2018 were from citizens of the Bolivian Republic of Venezuela, the Middle East and Africa also contributed significantly. While, in 2017, there were 8.5 million internally displaced people within their own countries, this number dropped to 5.4 million in 2018. The profile of the major recipient countries for new asylum applications in 2018 is as follows:

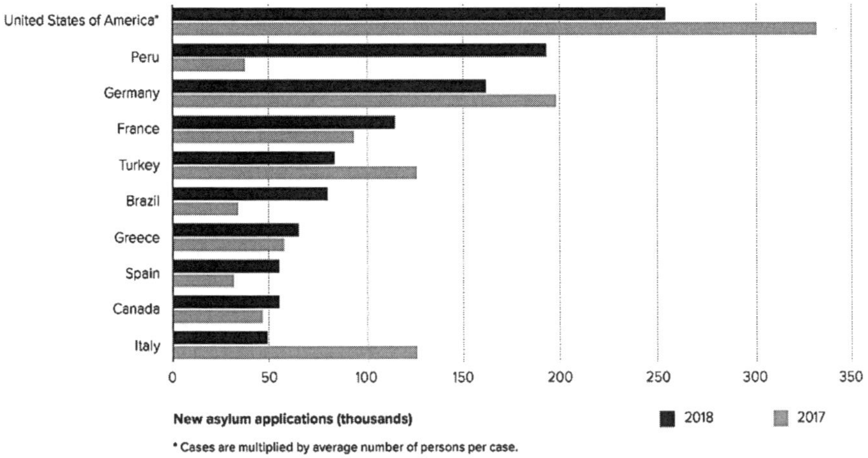

Credit: UNHCR. Not inclusive of visa overstays.

Other notable contributors to the global asylum application profile include Afghanistan, the Democratic Republic of Congo, Syria, Iraq, El Salvador, Eritrea, Honduras, and Pakistan. Conflicts and violence continue to be the main drivers of both the IDP and asylum numbers. A significant percentage is comprised of women, as well as unaccompanied and separated children. 3.9 million people reported at national borders as being Stateless. It must be stressed that these pressures on other countries inflame and energize the latent nationalistic fervor and resistance in those countries, exploited by local demagogues and which coalesce the local populations against "intruders" -- with the consequences that are only too obvious. Already, there have been instances in rural Germany where Muslim refugees from Syria and Yemen, once they had recovered from acute malnourishment, stabbed women and girls dressed in swimsuits at communal swimming pools built and funded by Germans for Germans going back several centuries and decades. Some of these attackers have justified their violence against their local hosts on the grounds that "Allah forbids women to dress in that manner", and that the sale of pork meat must be outlawed in the communities according to their Islamic dictates and preferences. Pork that Germans have eaten and relished for centuries; a way to pay them back for taking in these refugees when the refugees' rich ethnic and religious relatives did not accommodate them in the Middle East…

Let us look at some sobering sample objective data and wonder what exactly African leaders have been doing since their political independence. What exactly entitles them to the pomp and pageantry with which they carry on? Their understanding of political independence and sovereignty seems to be limited to mounting their countries' flags on their luxury fleet, living in massive palaces funded by the State, maintaining a fleet of presidential aircraft, junketing all over the world in shameless and unmerited opulence, buying prized real estate and stashing ill-gotten wealth overseas, deepening systemic failure, planting their children in expensive cities around the world; stealing their collective patrimony, as well as jailing and killing Opposition members and critics.

Employing the two World Bank extreme poverty stanzas of $1.90 and $3.25 to $5.50 daily, Burkina Faso has 45% of its population of 20 million living below this poverty line (World Food Program); Egypt - 27.8% (CIA World Factbook); Malawi - 50% (World Bank, 2017); Liberia - 50.9%); Mali - 42.7%); South Africa - 79% (DW); Nigeria - 82 million people (a minimum of 41% of its citizens if we accept their artificial population of 200 million). Nigeria has earned the dubious distinction of becoming the poverty capital of the world (in absolute numbers), replacing a much more populous India; Zimbabwe - 72% of their people live below the poverty line (CIA), while their late civilian dictator, Robert Mugabe, his family, and their partners live/d in extreme affluence; Tanzania - 90% of the population can afford less than $45 on housing per month (Habitat for Humanity); Togo - 47% live below the poverty line (World Bank), etc., etc. Out of Ghana's 14m urban population, 5.5 million live in slums, with 10 to 20 persons sharing single rooms (African Research Institute, 2016); these slums match places like Makoko, Ajegunle, Mushin, and other such locations in Lagos, Nigeria, as well as other towns in the country. Indeed, there are 24.4 million homeless people in Nigeria (UNHCR) with over 4 million Lagos residents living in informal housing, just to be charitable; two-thirds of the people who inhabit Liberia's capital, Monrovia, live in unplanned and slum communities; South Africa's acute housing shortages and homelessness are due to severe disparities in income, 28% unemployment rate, excessive urbanization, and the unresolved consequences of the evil apartheid regime which ended officially in 1994 (CIA World Factbook). This is indeed a very poor Report Card and a negation of the promise of independence.

It should also be of importance to Africans to know how they fare in the following areas: the world population is presently 7.8 billion people (and Africa is growing geometrically with no opportunities and services to support this growth); despite the severe reversals caused by the Covid:19 pandemic, the global GDP as at June, 2020 is $41.3 trillion (how much has Africa contributed?); there are 4.6 billion internet users in the world (adjusting for babies, toddlers, and all others who cannot reasonably access the internet); an average of 12.84 billion emails are sent globally each day, and there are also 360 million Google searches each day; 1.23 million new books have been published around the world in 2020 as at mid-June; there are at least 843 million severely undernourished people in the world; there are over 1 billion people with no access to a safe drinking water source; 780 million cigarettes are smoked globally on a daily basis, with 2.3 million smoking-related deaths this year (and we are just half-way gone); there were 1.8 million new HIV/AIDS cases around the world in 2018; 1.3 million died from road accidents globally in the same year, with 20m to 50 million people injured in road accidents the same year; there is one doctor for 417 persons in the Americas, 293 persons in Europe, 1,239 persons in South East Asia, and 3,324 for Africa. The availability of modern healthcare infrastructure is also heavily skewed against Africa.

When it comes to public debts and capacity to service the debts, Africa has the most depressing cluster in the world (**Figure 31)* -- with nothing to show for the loans, the future of their children has been mortgaged, and people with access to political power have mostly diverted these funds. If we use air freight as an indicator of commercial activity, again, Africa is equally absent (**Figure 32).* And, yet, when it comes to the burden of dealing with the Customs, Africa, yet again, has a very unimpressive record (**Figure 33*), owing to inefficiency and corruption. In terms of rail infrastructure per kilometer, again, Africa performs very poorly, despite the billions of dollars that their governments claim to have spent on this vital sector (**Figure 34).* When it comes to the Corruption Perception Index, Africa still has a problem as a very corrupt Continent (**Figure 35).*

According to the World Bank, "Until the 1990s, more than half of the World's poor lived in East Asia and the Pacific, and about fewer than 1 in 5 were in Sub-Saharan Africa. By 2015, the relationship had flipped, with over half of the world's poor living in Sub-Saharan Africa and just 6 percent in East Asia and Pacific. Due to high population growth and slower declines in poverty rates, the total number of poor in Sub-Saharan Africa is not falling significantly. In East Asia and the Pacific, slower population growth and rapid declines in poverty rates have reduced the number of poor from more than one billion in 1981 to just above 45 million in 2015. Meanwhile, South Asia has been home to about one third of the global poor throughout the past three decades and the remaining regions combined account for less than 10 percent of the world's poor." The uncontrolled population explosion in African countries is not just depressing the aggregate living experience for the people, but also both affecting their Development Indices and the prospects for violence.

The International Energy Agency (IEA) Electricity Access Report for 2018 states that "of the 674 million people still without access to electricity, 90% live in sub-Saharan Africa." This Report actually assumes that the balance of 700 million Africans have access to constant electricity, which is simply not the case. For most Africans, regular power outages, extended blackouts over days and weeks, alternative power sources like generators, power batteries called inverters, solar infrastructure, or simply no power, are very common experiences. The provision of these alternatives costs them significant amounts in equipment and fueling, exposes them to fire incidents, contributes significantly to carcinogenic emissions, steeply increases the cost of doing business or of just being alive in the very temperate and humid region; it also enables the sustenance of the complex (and unnecessary) regulatory framework plus the consequential corruption in the energy/ electricity sector. Satellite images taken at night above Europe and Africa (*Figure 36*) depict an African continent that is largely lacking in electricity infrastructure, even as private generating sets and other ancillary devices account for the flickers of light on the continent.

The International Labor Organization (ILO), while recognizing the extensive size and dynamics of the Informal Sector in Africa, still returns a depressing unemployment and under-employment profile on the Continent. While the bulk of the population (60% to 65%) is below 25 years old -- a considerable pool of productive resources --, they are simply unable to find jobs or to employ themselves optimally. The several millions who are pumped into the labor market each year from African and foreign universities, teachers' training colleges, as well as trade schools, only complicate and worsen the experience for the majority. In this situation, the very few jobs are usually not obtained on merit but on the basis of family networks, patronage, sexual favors, or nepotism. Furthermore, this worsens the security profile of the Continent, especially in the face of endemic, brazen, and visible corruption by government officials and their families.

Their lives of ostentation belie the experience of their fellow citizens, fueling widespread resentment. The hopelessness also drives the brain drain to other parts of the world and the overall desperation by young people to escape from the Continent. It was Cicero who wrote that: "Anyone who breaks an oath is worse than infidel." African leaders have, in the main, continued to be worse than infidels. There is recognition of the fact that, while politicians worry about the next election, Statesmen worry about the next generation. Emile de Girardin instructs us that: "to govern is to foresee." No one is seeing or foreseeing presently in Africa.

IMF data demonstrate a Continent that is becoming largely aid-dependent, with the Current Account, Capital Account, and Financial Account Net for virtually all the countries, in the negative. While the productive base of most of these countries continues to degrade, borrowed funds are serviced with virtually all the internally generated revenues, thereby deepening and worsening the medium to long-term outlook for the Continent. Investible funds are drying up, and governments use all their money to service ballooning bureaucracies and government officials, as well as to meet interest obligations on their burgeoning loans -- with principal repayment, default, activation of default clauses including seizure of strategic national assets and re-colonization -- pushed to future Administrations. The cycle of aid dependency and state delinquency nullifies the essence of these countries' political independence. **Dependent Independence** cannot be the same as **Independent Independence.**

Phew!!! It has been quite a journey; thanks for coming along. We need to gradually end it, to avoid depression, boredom, fatigue, or to start the decline from the saturation point towards the zone of negative marginal utility. What remains, if you pardon me, would be some exegesis on some relevant concepts, and we will truly be done.

It will be useful, in my view, to summarize why Africa should matter to the world. The Continent and its citizens should not be viewed as beggars, for the story is far more complex than that. Linearity and analytical laziness will fail one in this very complex Region. The Continent needs to empower the thinking and decent members of their population, if any changes will be achieved, otherwise, sub-Saharan Africa will repeat the mistakes of the past, this time on a much larger scale and with dire consequences both for its people and the entire world, in an increasingly connected universe.

Some theorists, mostly out of ignorance and racial jingoism, haughtily affirm that Africans can never govern themselves due to embedded or organic limitations and the stage of their "cultural" development. The picture on the Continent, as highlighted above, will seem to support this position, but you also have clusters of State non-performance around the world. Even in the West, the assumed beacon of excellence, we have acute issues of racial hatred, income disparity, homelessness, corruption, elite conspiracies, subversion of democratic principles, and Trumpism. Taking the United States under Mr. Trump, for example, we have seen persistent and undisguised forms of corruption (nepotism, lack of transparency in the disbursement of over $500 billion of the Stimulus Package, war on Inspectors-General and oversight, war on Institutions which form the bedrock of American Democracy, subversion of the Rule of Law by interjecting presidential power into judicial processes, refusal to accept the Checks and Balances that strengthen the American system, solicitation of foreign help in elections, hurried elevation of unqualified or stained individuals to the High Judicial Bench, refusal to disclose the President's tax records, etc.).

In all of this, Mr. Trump is aided and abetted by people who should constitutionally check him, including the financial machinist at Treasury; the crude, humpty dumpty, and pompous villager, a nobody who celebrates his surprise at being elevated to run Langley and State by stuffing a limitless number of sausages through all his orifices. This impostor in Kissinger, Jim Baker, Condoleeza Rice, Hillary Clinton, and John Kerry's Office Suite?; the sorely-unqualified pretender and Resume-booster whose rat-hole on the cliff of decency remains infested as he desecrates the DNI Office; the conniving and ever-eager one who creates legal magic for the naked emperor barring any sense of personal or professional decency -- an enforcer of sorts; the self-hating and insecure one at HUD with particular dexterity in cracking skulls; Abraham Lincoln's sleazy elementary school classmate at Commerce; froggy Mitch; crazy Cruz; grammy Lizzy; Rubic Macko; the little Cotton boy who, together with his entire family, must be enslaved by Africans as a "necessary evil"; all the Republican Senators and House of Representative members (except Mitt Romney; Providence keep him), including those who threaten us with possible independence and integrity only to genuflect at the critical moments and relish their enduring pastime of licking the substantial ass of the gingerly Imperium, only to recover partially and threaten yet another round of freedom and repeat the lack of character, sense of history, and decency which our Republican confederates have rightly earned. We must not forget the enthusiastic and arrogant cheerleaders and operatives who only recover their voices once they are fired. Together, these individuals have succeeded in exposing the underbelly of the United States. And this is not happening in Africa, as we may agree. It will be useful to address one of those writers, Adda Bruemmer Bozeman, who is picked to represent her fraternity.

Since colonialism and apartheid were significant periods in the African History, it will be useful to adopt Frantz Fanon's response to these developments, as the aggregate views of the Continent. This is especially useful, given the easy recourse of failed Continental leaders to the blights of slavery, colonialism, and apartheid for their manifest incapacity or unwillingness to govern responsibly.

Democracy is generally touted as the be-all, the medicine that cures all political and societal problems, regardless of the Region and local peculiarities. Interrogating the success or failure of Democracy in Nigeria, indeed its suitability as a development model in that country, will be insightful. Nigeria is chosen for many reasons: its large population, its diversity, complex history, the energy level of the people, their GDP which is the highest on the Continent, they are easily the most educated Africans, their significant diaspora contributions and numbers, the acute dissimilarities in experience between the rich and poor, Nigerians are very confident people, the defective political recruitment structures, the intensifying ethnic and religious cleavages, the strategic positioning and dashed hope to be the central source of pride for all black people and Africans around the world, the disastrous failure with governance, the invidious role of their military, and just the massive disappointment that the country represents.

While Egypt would have been considered for assessment, its lukewarm African identity disqualifies it as a standard African nation, for the majority-Muslim population seeks its validation and identity in the Muslim-Arab world and not down south towards the core of Africa, to the disadvantage of its minority Coptic Christian population.

A recurring theme is China's role in Africa. Are they re-colonizing the Continent, after the sad spectacle of European colonization? How does their propagandistic fidelity to hard sovereignty and non-intervention cohere with their aggregate strategy on the Continent? Is China truly a "fellow" 3rd world country as the countries of Africa? Why do most African leaders love the Chinese, and are increasingly detaching from the US and Europe?

For a lot of Africans experiencing internal subversion and violence, some or all of which is State-sponsored and/or State-ignored, when they are not turning the other cheek while being slaughtered and displaced by determined killers, there is an idealistic yearning and expectation that the world would come to their rescue. Well, I simply do not believe this to be the case; the UN Responsibility to Protect is an impotent mechanism. We shall fully explore how the world responded to the Rwandan genocide by the Hutus against the Tutsis in 1994, which spilled over into Burundi. Over a million people were butchered by their erstwhile friends, colleagues, and neighbors, in less than 100 days while the world stood akimbo. The holocaust by the rest of Nigeria against Igbos between 1966 and January, 1970 -- in which over 3 million Igbo people were killed -- was far worse given the direct complicity of Britain and Russia on the side of Nigeria against the hapless Igbo victims, their position inspired by the greed for the crude oil located in Igbo land and the neighboring Niger Delta Region -- but coveted by other Nigerians without this resource. Egypt also provided Air Force pilots who dropped bombs mostly on Igbo civilians, women, and children. A recently declassified document shows how the British Labor Government under Harold Wilson collaborated with Nigeria in the massacre against Igbos/Biafrans, for the purpose of protecting its oil interests.

The link is provided herewith: *https://consortiumnews.com/2020/04/30/how-britains-labour-govt-facilitated-massacre-of-biafrans-in-nigeria-to-protect-its-oil-interests/*

While Britain was doing all of this, the sons of their upper-crust families were also bullying and taunting a young Igbo boy, Dillibe Onyeama, who was attending one of the most prestigious boys' secondary schools in England, Eton. Since its founding in 1440, Eton has produced over twenty British Prime Ministers, including the current Turkish-British Prime Minister, Boris Johnson (who strives very hard to hide the Turkish part of his roots). Sons of the Royal Family and sundry aristocracy also attend Eton. When Dillibe graduated from the school in 1969, he was the first black student ever to do so. In 1972, he narrated the persistent racist taunts, insults, and caricatures he endured throughout his stay at Eton in a book, whereupon the school officially banned him from ever visiting Eton again. Some background is useful here: Dillibe's father, Charles D. Onyeama, was an eminent Nigerian and international jurist who was a Justice of Nigeria's Supreme Court from 1964 until the civil war started three years later. Between 1967 and 1976, he was a Judge at the International Court of Justice, The Hague, Netherlands, and a Judge of the World Bank Administrative Tribunal between 1982 and 1990. Onyeama Senior graduated from both University of London and Oxford University.

Dillibe's younger brother, Geoffrey, who is currently Nigeria's Foreign Affairs Minister, graduated from Columbia University with a B.A. (Honors) degree in 1977. Over the next seven years, he also earned a B.A. in Law from Cambridge, an LL.M from the London School of Economics, and an M.A. in Law from Cambridge University. He was also admitted to the Grey's Inn in 1981 and was the Deputy Director-General of the World Intellectual Property Organization in Geneva for many years before his current appointment in 2015. As impressive as this family profile is, it is actually not unique or uncommon in Nigeria and across Africa. Despite all of this, boys whose admission into Eton was mostly owed to generational wealth acquired through immoral and nefarious practices in African countries, India, and elsewhere, felt that they could bully an innocent kid, a young man of solid pedigree, a dedicated student, a rising star, and an African Prince, based purely on race and nothing else. The school caused him a double jeopardy by punishing him for speaking out. Well, almost fifty years later, and amidst the global protests over George Floyd's killing and the plight of America's black population, the Headmaster of Eton has issued a public apology to Dillibe and rescinded their ban. The boys of 1969 and before have since made policies as men at senior levels in the UK, driven by deep and ignorant racist prejudices. See *https://www.bbc.com/news/world-africa-53139325*

While the Nigerian genocide is a bit distant from memory (for others, not the Igbos), the more recent Rwandan experience will be evaluated, in the hope that oppressed people will learn to take their destiny in their own hands and not wait for foreigners to rescue them. Apart from racism and a lack of strategic stake, the serious economic challenges caused by the drawn-out and unabating Covid-19 pandemic as well as the debilitating trade-offs and paralysis at the UN Security Council, will ensure that the internal problems in any African country will be resolved only through meaningful dialogue or extreme violence among themselves, with various non-Continental nations and entities queuing up to supply weapons at high margins. Syria is another good example, but Rwandan explication should suffice. It is impossible to see a U.S. President (discount Trump) who would stake her/his political fortunes on convincing an Iowa, Montana, or Ohio mother to send her only son in the US Military to take a risk on behalf of some African women and children. While the UN might mean well, it has no military force, it is a massive and inefficient bureaucracy, it is not self-funding, and the concentration of powers in the hands of the permanent members of the Security Council, should impose some sobriety among Africans. Illusions, exuberant idealism, willful ignorance, and self-deceit are dangerous in the geopolitical realities we live in and may not change soon. The wrong calculations will lead to a river of human blood on the Continent -- yet again.

Humans operate within a cultural milieu defined and explained by their history, religion, values, ambitions, self-perception, attitude towards others, economics, worldview, language, race, shared historical experiences and ways of thinking, attachment to a particular physical space, education and overall knowledge base, as well as their moral code. It is axiomatic that there is no uniform culture among the disparate peoples of the world. Accordingly, while it is romantic to expect that all instances of kindness, innocence, good gesture, good faith, altruism, and consideration, would elicit varying levels of symmetric reciprocity, reality and experience confirm otherwise.

Once we are done with this assessment, the postscript will follow, and we are done, leaving the references and bibliography for researchers.

VI

Case Studies

Why Africa Still Matters

From a rational standpoint, Africa is a very significant Continent for multiple reasons. In many ways also, their relative under-performance presents a huge opportunity for countries that will engage with them on the basis of mutual respect and benefit. The African street is understandably alienated from their leaders at all levels, owing to the sustained profligacy and outright fraudulence of the latter. Any outsider intent on adding strategic value to the Continent (not as a favor, an aid package, or a loan, but as a long-term investment) must consciously cultivate the people and reject the temptation to align with their local oppressors, who, in any case, come and go.

Some of the immediate opportunities include: a young and vibrant population; abundant natural resources (which must now be exploited in an ethical manner, as the locals have grown militant towards exploitative undertakings),1.3 billion people and the related population-driven demand, opportunity to influence the cultures, Africans in different Regions are fluent in English, French, and Portuguese. Indeed, there are more English-speaking people in Africa than in Europe (most of these 700 million African speakers of the English language have a high proficiency in the language, with the highest concentrations in Nigeria- 80 million; South Africa - 58 m; Kenya - 52 m; and Egypt - 28m), 60% of this huge Continent is younger than 25, remote minimization of threats, their love of foreign people and norms will generate a vast reserve of goodwill if they are treated with respect and not condescension, the world needs to pay very close attention to Chinese activities on the Continent and contest that space with them in an ethical manner. Most Africans are bilingual or trilingual, huge opportunities for Media and cultural penetration. Alliances with the vibrant and successful African Film Industry (notably Nollywood in Nigeria) is yet another opportunity. Synergies and partnerships will enhance standards in acting, film editing, videography, technical aspects, costume, stage construction, production, etc.

Tyler Perry decided to think out of the box, do the necessary hard work, he defied all the odds, he refused to be patronized by the Hollywood moguls, and he has remained very successful in this field. Is there anything stopping African entrepreneurs (not the governments, please) from partnering with him and upgrading the standards of the Movie Industry in Africa, while forging closer links with the African-American community as well? Africans themselves will like to foster an African Identity that resists the corrosive Arab/ Muslim influence and the deleterious aspects of Western influence. There are over a hundred African cities with well over 10 million consumers each. With an urbanization rate that is projected to exceed 50% in 2030, there are great opportunities for housing, utilities, education, health, security applications, as well as lifestyle products and services.

There are also considerable opportunities to mechanize agriculture, and invest in agricultural extension services, especially in packaging, preservation, and crop yield technologies. Kenya, for example, already ships tulips and rose flowers around the world, while some mechanized farms in northern Nigeria were supplying citrus and fruits to Europe before the security condition in the Region impacted access.

We shall rely extensively on Michael I. Tripp's articulation of relevant data. Some of the threats and issues, which are both isolated and linked, will include: Terrorism in some parts which will require trusted local guidance, public health issues, risk of State collapse and mob action ensuing, proliferation of small arms in some countries, population explosion and congestion in inhabited areas, the food insecurity in some areas which drives violence, drought in some countries, vast swathes of ungoverned territories, etc. Sub-Saharan Africa has 16% of the world's population and only 2% of the global GDP, which creates an enormous opportunity, especially as the world is seriously considering breaking the Supply Chain monopoly currently residing with China. Africans are quick, ambitious, and proud to provide for their families through their labor, and not handouts. What Africa needs are partners who will stay for the long haul, empowering the people directly, and helping to reverse some of the debilitating definers of the Continent.

The low and medium-intensity forms of violence in different parts of the Continent have not always been there. Most of the countries did not wage violent struggles for their political independence. Some of the triggers of mass violence in the region include: ego clashes among African big men which then involve their ethnic groups and nominal religions, unresolved issues of cohesion and internal justice, Islamic terrorism and the continuing ambition to expand the territories under Islam, irrational ethnic hatred, and the zero-sum competition for a perpetually-shrinking national cake. The result is that, in many parts of the Continent, you have a coalition of the angry, brainwashed, illiterate, and poor. With the ease of access to light arms principally from Libya, Liberia, Congo, China, Ukraine, Turkey, and Sierra Leone, the security profile has continued to deteriorate.

This is accentuated by the absence or unreliability of citizenship records; porous borders; the presence of the Hausas and Fulanis in over ten countries, with kinship protection and loyalties assuming trans-national dimensions (to the disadvantage of those ethnic groups bound to specific countries); poor governance has alienated the majority of the citizens and led to extreme poverty -- opportunities for recruitment into malevolent groups - criminal gangs or terrorist groups; illiteracy and Islam remain a toxic and dangerous chemical formula; we will keep referring to the unresolved issues of nationhood; ethnic rivalry that routinely assumes a religious coloration as well; the lack of a vigorous and Continent-wide response to terrorism since it started in the Region; sub-optimal patrol of the coastal waters thus leading to the high incidence of oil bunkering and fostering of water-based militia operations; as well as the sustained sense of entitlement by a segment of the society and the intimidation of others, which produce resentment and resistance.

Further contributors to the degrading Security climate include politics by other means (election-rigging, military intimidation, etc.) which alienate people from their governments and induce them to zero-sum calculations; Resource Curse -- fragile States, and the hyper-competition for access to State resources; Weak Rule of Law and just too many sacred cows generating a very high aggregate Impunity Index; Weak Institutions and the perception that the coercive devices of governance are meant for the weak, poor, and for vindictive purposes; attempts at intimidating the elected and constituted government, to extract concessions in resource allocation, assurances of protection for past transgressions, or to enhance the group's negotiating position in a fractured entity; historical, religious, and religious affinity of many of the countries with the cauldron of the world, thc Middle East; malevolent activities of some Muslim countries in the Middle East -- funding *madrasas*, promoting Islamic extremism, pushing for the adoption of Sharia and building mosques, China's role especially in the illegal mining business and the proliferation of weapons, etc.;

The influence of the Middle East also manifests in different forms: repression of women, since the status of Arab women in the current era is worse than that of European women a hundred years ago; conquest or conversion mentality leading to justified resistance and violence; declining emphasis on research and rigor, as over 300 million Arabs publish fewer scientific materials than 6 million Israelis, for example; and relatively-tiny Greece publishes more books than the entire Arab world. A very influential Jihadist Text written by Abdullah Azzam 'Join the Caravan' expressly directs Muslims that "The sin is not lifted off the necks of the Muslims as long as any area of land which was once Muslim remains in the hands of the Disbelievers, and none are saved from sin except those who perform jihad." This has since been extended to include any land they covet. When this charge is fed to unfortunate, illiterate and poor Muslim kids, it becomes clear why they go berserk with violence against innocent people. Everything is resolved through jihad and violence, and not dialogue or negotiation. Understanding this is critical for non-Muslims so that they drop their veil of self-deception.

Azzam further writes and assures any of these killers that: "he is forgiven with the first spurt of his blood; he sees his place in Heaven; he is clothed with the garment of Faith; he is wed with seventy-virgins from the beautiful *Houris* In Heaven; he is saved from the punishment of the Grave; on his head is placed a crown of dignity…and he is granted intercession for seventy people of his household." This is all they need to go insane and kill innocents, over the silly and patently-unverifiable and false assurances made to them. This ensures that the economy remains barren as little or no productive activity takes place, the normal outlets for young people to express themselves socially (nightclubs, bars, cinemas, parks, sports, shopping, visits to museums, mixing with the opposite sex, etc.) are completely banned or discouraged through violence, to ensure their undivided ingestion of toxicity in form of religious instruction, while the wealthy and their children are, at best, only nominal Muslims with no candidacy for terrorism or heavenly virgins.

Tripp makes the significant observation that, shorn of normal socialization and adolescent behavior, 67% of the boys suffer from depression, there is an absence of a way to feel powerful, no freedom to assemble, they are deprived of female companionship and not socialized to what women want, thus producing some seriously angry, malformed, and vulnerable young men, exploitable in the service of clever manipulators. With no rational solution in sight for the normal problems of being alive in a functioning society, no other vision of the future other than the Caliphate is ingrained. There is no regard or consideration for policies, as death is what is offered, and martyrdom, not victory or creative solutions, becomes the desire of abused and poisoned minds. This is the only way they feel powerful in what Lawrence Wright calls "Radical Utopianism." To manage the repressed social development and anger, and in the absence of the structured process that formal education requires, these unfortunate human beings are encouraged to marry very young, have many children as "Allah Wills", thereby creating multiple problems for the society and ensuring a multi-generational pool of malcontents to recruit from; an endless cycle and threat to all.

Even as some of the following countries have majority-Christian or animist populations, they have continued to experience terrorist attacks from local Muslims or their confederates in the Region: Somalia, Kenya, Eritrea, Tanzania, Mali, Libya, Nigeria, Tunisia, and Chad, while the Central African Republic (CAR), Niger, Sudan, DRC, and Algeria, remain vulnerable to these bad actors. The displacement of ISIS and Al Qaeda from the Middle East has also impacted the security profile of Africa; these malcontents, together with the remnants of the Gaddafi Regime in Libya, provide weapons and training to franchisees across the Region. If more States fail in the Region, that vast swathe of land could easily replace Afghanistan (plus some sections of Pakistan) and become the incubatory ground from which to export terrorism to the world; the time to checkmate this portent is now. The distance of the southern part of Africa from the Middle East, for example, largely insulates it from this form of violence, thus further validating the thesis of the toxic impact of Radical Islam on the African Continent.

It is also noteworthy that Africa has some strategic choke points along the Mediterranean, Red Sea, and Gulf of Aden, abutting Egypt and Yemen. Significant maritime traffic navigates those waters. Given the irresolute Strategy on Africa by the West (there is also deep suspicion towards the West on the Continent given past and current realities), China is filling the strategic void thus created, with serious implications for all. When the world looks at Africa, it also has to consider its significant diaspora population, with significant backwards remittances to the Continent and opportunity to influence public opinion in their new countries. Nigerians, Ghanaians, Egyptians, and Kenyans, in particular, have large numbers of immigrants in Europe and America, with Nigerian-born medical doctors in the US numbering almost eleven thousand (according to US Records), Nigerians being the most educated immigrant group in the United States, as well as the immigrant sub-set with the highest number of advanced degrees in the country-- skills that are lost to their motherland and Continent.

While it is standard for bearers of a national passport to be categorized together, the truth is that deep differences exist among these demographics. The ethnic groups boosting Nigeria's academic profile in Europe and America, for example, are mostly Yorubas, Igbos, and the ethnic groups of the Niger

Delta (Edo, Itsekiri, Uhrobo, Ishan, Afemai, etc.) This category also seeks opportunities overseas for professional development after their studies, while the few Hausas and Fulanis who attend foreign Colleges, typically rush back to Nigeria after completion, to take up senior government positions and appointments in an endless cycle of cronyism and entitlement; a system that structurally excludes the brightest and the best (because of the parts of the country they come from), who are invariably lost to other countries.

In crafting national strategies on how to engage with Africa, therefore, nations must be clear-eyed about their expectations and the dynamics. It is very helpful to be guided by reliable and knowledgeable experts, and to remember that no single template applies in every corner of this vast and complex Continent or even within countries. Ultimately, however, in recognition of the inter-relatedness of the modern world, the countries outside Africa need to pay very close attention to this dynamic region. If we employ Ersoy's definition of globalization as "the broadened access to knowledge, communications, trade, and, together with these, new possibilities for human development," we need to show more than a cursory interest in what happens on the Continent, and also develop the capacity for long-term, not episodic, engagements. Understanding Africa, as every other region, starts with an attitude of humility, openness, and respect. What is different is not necessarily better or worse, for it is those normative judgments of superiority and inferiority that have caused a lot of problems throughout history. Citing Stansfield, Ersoy also writes that: "this unheard-of mutual connection and mutual dependence among societies also presents shared risks."

As it pertains to Policy, therefore, nations need to review the parameters for Direct Air Travel to their countries based on the Risk Profiles of originating countries in Africa; intensify collection activities against implicated local individuals and demographics given the increasing diversification and risk of internal subversion, hold Chiefs of State personally responsible for terrorist emanations from their sovereign territories, extend the focus on the Middle and Near East to the northern, eastern, and western parts of Africa, promote and encourage the strengthening of Institutions and Public Accountability/Governance, match Intel with Consular Services, then subvert and weaken terrorist States or the identified official and private sponsors and enablers of terrorism within fragile States. The majority of the people will applaud that.

It is also important to show respect (not tolerance) for local realities and values, e.g. LGBTQ (the consonants just keep growing) issues. For multiple reasons that have nothing to do with Islam or Christianity, over 95% (to be conservative) of all Africans cannot understand same-sex activities and the various iterations of Identity that have developed from this. While they may not and should not necessarily advocate violence against people with such preferences, Africans also seriously resent the vigorous push to force them to accept what has become the norm in the West. Most Africans think that this advocacy recruits, converts, and rewards otherwise "straight" individuals who "come out." They do not, in any way, feel inadequate to any country or Region for holding this position.

And, yes, they still call gifted and talented female thespians 'actresses' and people of the female gender who engage in edifying conduct remain 'heroines,' not 'heroes.' The fact of acknowledgment of the two genders does not in any way diminish the quality of work done by our women, or indeed the equality of both sexes. In many ways, the masculinization of all terms and appellations is sexist in its core. A woman can be a great actress, not an actor; an African man does not have to join the Negritude Movement to prove that he is black… we know women when we see them. Africans also do not call people who love their dogs "dog parents", nor do they recognize boyfriends and girlfriends as couples.

The consensus opinion on the Continent is that it is deeply insulting to equate racial equality and the need to reverse systemic wickedness against blacks with what they regard as an alien and strange sexual preference or identity. When the form goes beyond homosexuality and proceeds to rarefied areas like transgender protocols and all, you lose all Africans. At the very least, this dominant position needs to be handled carefully and with respect. The West has no right to impose its preferences around the world, especially given the justified suspicion with which they are viewed all over the world. Heterosexual forms like polygamy, which are perfectly normal and practised in Africa and the Middle East, are outlawed in the West. Why then should same sex "marriages" and practices be imposed on these Regions? When will polygamy become legal in the UK and the USA? Indeed, Africans generally suggest that the West easily respects the cultural norms and religious practices of the Middle East, but arrogantly and casually seeks to bully Africans; this is causing deep resentment. As mentioned earlier, other growing areas include: Cultural Diplomacy opportunities, Religion, Education, Films, Music, Fashion, Technology, Lifestyle, Leveraging the database of African students who studied in one's country for multiple purposes, etc.

The rest of the world can also help to identify and prop up deserving role models on the Continent while aligning with the citizens to expose, shame, and punish corrupt officials and their cronies - while demanding the channeling of retrieved funds from Western banks towards specific transparent projects. The world can also boost capacity on the Continent by partnering with relevant entrepreneurs and agencies to enhance skills and facilitate Exchange Programs. Imagine making clothes (jeans, t-shirts, etc.), shoes, and other consumables for 1.3 billion people right there on the Continent, while engaging in backward integration to grow and optimize the raw materials. Building materials for the numerous private and public projects provide another great opportunity. The deepening of the Financial Services Industry through FINTECH, and in sundry Service sectors like tourism, publishing, media, tourism, communications, and others, yearns for robust attention as well. The emphasis on natural resources alone must begin to be de-emphasized, while the extraction of the abundant physical resources should be done with ethical responsibility -- not the way European, American, and Chinese companies alike have performed, to the detriment of the people.

Adda von Bruemmer Bozeman Barkhuus on Africa

Dr. Bozeman uses sociological tools to attempt an explanation of the varied developmental profiles of the different peoples of the World. She essentially uses a Eurocentric paradigm as a basis for evaluating other Regions, and concludes that, given several factors, the strict universal application of the term "State" has substantially nullified the essence of this political nomenclature as some of the Regions of the world do not inherently have the capacity to fulfill the intrinsic conditions and assumptions attached to the term from a Western perspective.

She says Africans have a certain pull towards their past which is mired in violence, and that the traditional code of conduct in Africa is incompatible with the "Western" ideas of liberty, self-determination, democracy, and development. She uses her example of the interaction between King Alfonso of Belgium and the Kongolese people some three hundred years ago, to make rather sweeping statements regarding contemporary developments about Africans. For the avoidance of doubt, the Western World clearly introduced some very positive values and precepts across the world; this is not adequate, however, to embark on the sweeping condemnation of a people who, for the most part, equally suffered the direct and indirect effects of the unwritten aspects of colonialism and forced amalgamation of incompatibles in various countries.

The evaluation of other societies on the European model obviously retains some form of paternalistic condescension and fails to identify the positive strains of life in those societies. While there is great room for improvement, it is not true that other societies did not have some semblance of democracy, for example. The African society has evolved considerably over time but, even in its purest form, there were clear structures of Public Administration. These might not have been codified or exported to other cultures; these limitations do not limit their intrinsic elements. The Igbo people of Nigeria, for example, practised Democracy before the US was formed as a country. Rejecting the absolute monarchical forms that defined other major Empires like the Benin Kingdom, the Yoruba of West Africa (Ife, Oyo, and Egun), as well as the Hausa and Fulani of West Africa, etc., Igbos ran a flat system that emphasized collective administration and responsibility.

They also empowered women before that became the norm in the West, definitely before even Caucasian women could vote in America. The markets were the exclusive preserve of the womenfolk, while they also had a structural representation, by right, through their various societies (like the Otu Odu), in public administration. Women of a certain age were also treated as men (as in most societies, insecure and entitled men always design the pecking order to favor them). While practising communalism, the Igbos also emphasized and rewarded private excellence; the merits of excellence only became recognized when applied to collective goals and objectives, and not exclusively towards personal consumption and ego massage. In the current era, the unique and very successful Igbo trade apprenticeship or mentorship system has been regarded as the largest informal business incubation system in the world, involving over $14 billion annually and meriting a Case Study from the Harvard Business School and TED Talk Sessions.

This system largely enabled Igbos to recover from the a most-devastating civil war waged against them in Nigeria, and to quickly become the ethnic group with the highest per capita and democratically-held (broadest-based) wealth in the country. While their systematic exclusion from the Central Government and levers of economic patronage have resulted in not being able to steal from the government in consolidated amounts like the favored ethnic groups, they have focused mostly on Commerce and have channeled their entrepreneurial acumen and cultural support systems to spread wealth among a wide pool. The Igbo people who steal in government -- like their confederate thieves from the other parts of the country -- at the federal, state, and local government areas -- do not steal for the ethnic group, but for themselves and their families, but the Igbo domination of Commerce in the country has helped spread wealth among those disconnected from government patronage and stealing opportunities.

This structure made it impossible for the British colonialists to practise the Indirect Rule, as they did through the autocratic Fulani and Hausa rulers in Northern Nigeria, and in some respect through the Obas in Yorubaland and Edo Kingdom. The colonists empowered Warrant Chiefs and appointed District Officers in Igboland, for effective exploitation of the people to take place -- a level of involvement they detested.

Dr. Bozeman proceeds to conclude that Islam encourages terror because "shari'ah and jihad are not bound by Western systems of secular constitutional law…" Again, while the manifestations of extremism in any form must be condemned at all times (be it Nazism, Communism, or religious fanaticism), it is too convenient to make these broad characterizations. One certainly shares her view that the contradictions between Christian Europe and the Islamic Middle East represent the most potent sources of tension in the world presently. I would like the West, for example, to insist on reciprocal treatment and for Citizenship Rights, especially in the UK, to be drastically revisited in line with the real risks of homegrown insurgency. Muslim countries should allow foreigners and people of other Faiths to practice their religions in the Middle East, the same way Muslims demand freedom of worship in the West.

Having made this point, the West must equally accept its responsibility for its direct and indirect roles in the present conditions in the Middle East.

She treats Africa as an exotic anomaly, and proceeds all through to sensitize developments on the Continent against Occidental norms. This convenient approximation necessarily makes the "other" less than the "center"; Africans, Chinese, Japanese, or Arab people could do the same to Europeans or European-Americans and propound "theories" on the basis of Europeans' inability to dance to the African 'gbedu' talking drums, for example. If the Levantine or Western God wanted all human societies and cultures to be the same, hopefully this God would have been able to achieve that. Bozeman sees conflicts in Africa as being normal developments arising from their cultural past, while conflicts in Europe are driven by disagreements on written and formal agreements. For her, the "subsisting superstitions and non-literacy" drive political developments on the Continent, manifesting in the preference for immediate results and rewards rather than deferred gratification and a common ethos. She also writes that Africa is a timeless sphere, where modernization, industrialization, and independence have had no impact, citing what she calls the "primitiveness" of modern Africans.

This is patently false. While the selfishness of African leaders, *sui generis*, is acknowledged, the deficiency of this assumption is that the identified issues are not exclusive to Africa. In Western Europe, the norm pre-the Industrial Revolution, was for workers to plan for the immediate rather than an extended timeframe. Production volumes, income levels, and improved conditions of service had not begun to be implemented. Our hunter-gatherer ancestors behaved exactly this way until storage, preservation, and security processes were introduced into their society. The reality is that people can only save when they have produced enough food, made enough money, and taken care of their immediate needs. While multiple factors account for the fate of the majority on the African Continent -- including the direct and indirect actions of the European people -- it is rather too sweeping and false to conclude in the way that Bozeman has done; this remains the major failing of the cultural analysis of politics. Life in Africa is an entire spectrum of experience, as it is in all other societies. It is also simplistic and lazy to use the same analytical framework to interpret the experiences of 1.3 billion people.

She also locates the broad discretionary powers exercised by African leaders in the cultural system that produced these leaders in the first place, so that a modern-day President believes that s/he is, and behaves like, a traditional ruler, with no recognition for any checks on her/his powers, and simply no understanding of the institutional and structural requirements of checks and balances in the modern political system. While these manifestations are clearly evident across Africa, which is a major problem, there is a great difficulty in assigning this pathology exclusively to Africa or to its cultural past. The Rulers in the Middle East fare much worse than African leaders in their toleration of dissent and the duty of responsible accountability. The German-President of the United States, a man of European descent who should embody all the excellent civic virtues idealized and propagated by Dr. Bozeman, wishes he could trade places with African, Arab, and Chinese leaders, to give full expression to his inherent tyrannical disposition. The residual capacity of America's strong Institutions, including a vibrant and professional Media, is the ONLY guardrail stopping this man from his full dictatorial manifestations. It becomes very clear, therefore, that, in all societies occupied and run by human beings, strong Institutions and a robust Rule of Law are critical ingredients to check the tempting slide towards absolutism, societal decay, elite conspiracy, alienation of the citizens, and negation of civic virtues. This is not peculiar to Africa.

It must be noted that Dr. Bozeman, who was born in Latvia in 1908, but taught for several decades at Sarah Lawrence College in the US, most likely could not entirely strip herself of the pervasive ignorance about other parts of the world and the resultant Eurocentrism, which was needed to justify a lot of predatory conduct in those other parts. Otherwise, how could an analyst who lived through WWI and WWII, and who obviously knew about all the tempestuous wars of Europe in the preceding century, choose Africa as the epicenter of her analysis on conflicts? Obviously, she was driven by other impulses. While she conveniently dropped the 'von' from her name when she lived in the US, she was the daughter of Baron Leon Charles von Bruemmer and Baroness Anna von Bruemmer, of Baltic German descent. Bozeman's father was an officer in the Tsarist Guarde Regiment and a Marshal of Nobility of the Russian province of Vitebak.

As Gary Remer writes on Bozeman: "Her tone is condescending, not objective, which detracts from her credibility as an African analyst, independent of the intellectual quality of her arguments … The conclusions she arrives at, based on her cultural assumptions, perpetuate certain stereotypical images of Africa, and often border on racism." In all, Dr. Bozeman has raised issues, which demand more focus and analysis. She is willing, for example, to recognize China, India, Japan, etc., as approximating the Western requirements of Statehood, even though these countries equally have fundamental differences with the West and have had their fair share of violence and terror which we thought were exclusive to Africa and the Middle East! Africans need to do better and to seize their narrative.

On a final note, if Bozeman accuses Africans of being steeped in their cultures, what is she steeped in? Was it not her culture, her family circumstances, her situation as a Germanic woman born in Latvia to a family of privilege, that informed her perspectives and condescending views on non-Europeans and notably Africans? Was this also not why, following Hegel, she wrote about "the paramountcy of conflict in life, the legitimacy of hatred in human relations, and the essentialness of war for the security and well-being of society," and also assumed that every society must have a monolithic population when she defined Statecraft as "the sum total of human dispositions, doctrines, policies, institutions, processes, and operations, that are designed to assure the governance, security, and survival of a politically unified group?"

Africans, and only Africans themselves, need to decide if the historical, current, and future narrative about their Continent will follow a seemingly inexorable pattern of non-performance and destitution. They need to decide for themselves if they will continue to accept excuses from their rulers and if the convenient stoking of divisions along ethnic and (foreign) religious lines will continue to cause strife among them and inhibit the realization of their full potentials. They need to determine if people like Dr. Adda von Bruemmer Bozeman Barkhuus and other people aligned with her views, will continue to define the African Continent in the condescending manner that they do. Is the following image what Africans themselves want to perpetuate, several decades after their political independence?

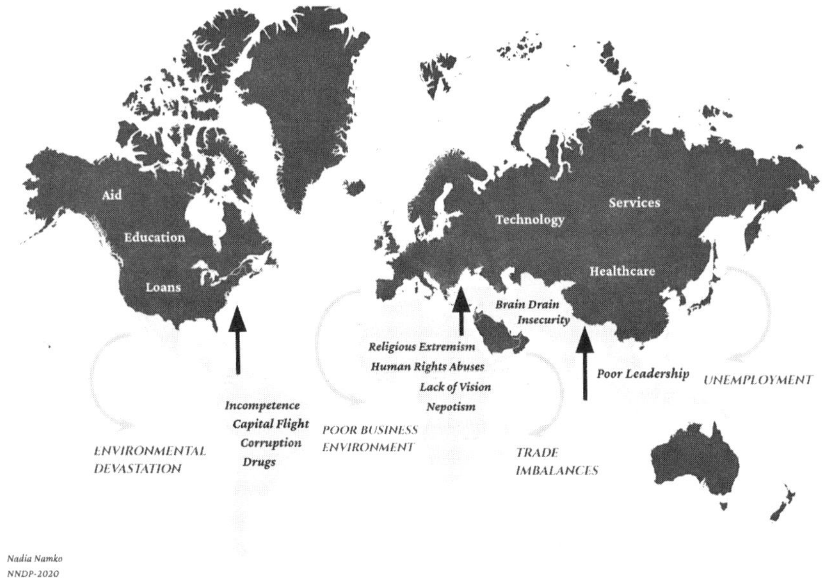

Indeed, are Africans happy to be perennially lumped together with South America and South-East Asia in the indelible imagery below? Their fate and outcomes are not fixed and permanent; the right policy choices will yield a different outcome from this profile:

Nadia Namko
NNBC-2020

Frantz Fanon on Racism and Apartheid

While the apartheid regime in South Africa finally ended officially in 1994 and the majority black political party, the African National Congress, has produced every president since then through democratic processes, a brief commentary on that era is apposite, especially through the prism of the eminent Scholar, Franz Fanon, for we are still evaluating the ideas of equality, State performance, inclusiveness, political independence, and the delivery of public goods.

Fanon is both a moralist and humanist. This fact is portrayed in his analysis of both pre- colonial and post-colonial Africa, especially with regard to the exploitation and degradation to which Africans have been put on their own Continent mainly because of the color of their skin. For Fanon, racism, apartheid, and colonialism are engaged in a very close relationship, and the problems experienced by the so-called independent Africans are traced to events that preceded their attainment of flag Independence. For, the truth is that no white South African arrived there through the immigration instruments by which non-Europeans become citizens of European countries. They imposed themselves and operated a race-based system against the owners of the land, a system that was sustained through violence and deep oppression.

Originally, African societies were classless in nature, and communalism was the predominant way of life. Men derived their humanity from their socialness, as no man lived in isolation of others. All this changed with the colonization of the Continent. Individualism and classes were introduced; the desire to satisfy personal interests, even at the expense of the collective interest, became normal, so to speak. Colonialism was accompanied by virtual slavery, deceit, exploitation, racial discrimination, as well as the erosion of people's history and cultural values. In Fanon's work, we learn that Africans had an apparatus by which they repelled alien rule. It then becomes logical to infer that it was either that the apparatus was not strong enough to resist Europeans or that the greed, ignorance, and emotionality of the then leaders all contributed to ensure a somewhat-easy penetration of Africa by the European fortune seekers. This becomes especially relevant today as we evaluate the conduct of the current African leaders.

The over-glamorization of Africa's past is faulty, in that there were aspects of that past which were not conducive to the overall growth of the society. Perhaps, it is not right to judge the practices of that epoch by modern standards. However, for Fanon, the Europeans installed themselves in Africa through violence, and relegated the indigenes to the level of mere objects. The entire societal arrangement was designed to ensure a perpetuation of this subjugation. Mineral resources were tapped and taken to Europe for the development of that Continent, while those who were directly involved in the mining of these minerals - Africans, were reduced to the level of mere existence. There was no compensation to them for the fact that the minerals were obtained from their natural habitat.

This divisive and morally reprehensible practice was informed by the conviction of the colonizers that they were both genetically and materially superior to blacks; this constitutes the racial element of colonialism. They felt that the practice of colonialism, by which they raped Africa's soil and subverted the humanity of African ancestors, was a “burden unto themselves”; a burden that they killed for and with no invitation! Yes indeed! Our knowledge of human nature negates any claim they may have to altruism. With time, some indigenes of the colonized places were incorporated into the machine of oppression; these people, out of selfishness, betrayed the trust of their people, and acted in ways that tended to institutionalize the socio – politico -economic domination by Europeans over Africans.

Walter Rodney, in his seminal work, ‘How Europe Underdeveloped Africa,’ cuts an identical picture of exploitation. Europeans applied violence to all instances of rebellion. It is perhaps important to note that the European taskmasters succeeded in their scheme largely because of their higher level of organization, their ruthlessness, their formal education, religion, superior weaponry, as well as the active collaboration of some natives. To “prove” their claim as per the inferiority of the black race, Europeans advanced spurious theories, which pointed to the incomplete development of some physiological features of the black race. Their anthropologists claimed that Africa had no history and that Africans were the missing link between ape and man. It is not surprising that these stay-at-home investigators were able to influence Africans. Their success lay mainly with the facts that they controlled the propaganda machine and they were able to effect the cultural alienation of the African person through psychological violence.

Religion (Christianity) contributed largely to this success by exhortation to its new African adherents that passive resignation was the wish of God, as “the kingdom of God belongs to the meek and gentle.” The result of this was the general lack of awareness which pervaded Africa and the benign tolerance of man's inhumanity to man. However, when the peak of the tolerance level had been reached, coupled with a re-interpretation of the Gospel, men began to reject Orthodoxy and to recognize their inherent capacity for change. The era of Providential Determinism was over, and the cloud of deceit evaporated. This reawakening could be traced to the adoption of Western education as well as the recognition of the irreconcilable differences between God's design for man and the *status quo ante*.

The sequel to this realization was the search for a means by which the situation could be reversed, or at least minimized. It came to be accepted that violence was the only viable option in this regard. This mode: violence: was controlled and directed by the elite in order to prevent its abuse. Only violence can match violence. Fanon says that: "no attempt must be made to encase man for it is in his Destiny to be set free." The combination of critical consciousness – 'conscientization' and violent action -- is then employed to fight the violent oppressors with a view to the realization of man's inalienable rights to self-determination. With the success of this program, political and economic control of the society should revert to the indigenous population.

Fanon recognizes the significant role which language plays in the process of colonization. He is particularly concerned about the set of people who take over from the alien oppressors. This latter group must not be replaced by those who are "whiter than the whites"; that is, the internal collaborators. Rather, there should be a replacement of politics based on resource distribution and ethnicity with politics of service and resource creation, patriotism, and Continental vision. It is his contention that it is only Socialism that can serve this desired need. Socialists accept all the formal tenets of formal, political democracy but they also insist that democracy should be extended to incorporate the control of the economy. This is borne out of the view that there is no democracy *sui generis*; rather, we have either 'bourgeoisie democracy' or 'popular (proletariat) democracy', the criterion for distinction being who owns what in the society? The State should control the means of production in order to prevent exploitation. Fanon and Cabral have a lot of things in common; they both operate from within the Marxist context and recognize the inevitability of the employment of violence in any genuine liberation struggle.

Fanon criticizes the rhetorical commitment to the ideas of social justice, equality and freedom, which some people manifest. For him, commitment must involve identification with the oppressed people in their struggle to become liberated. It is obvious that Fanon takes the concrete historical context or reality seriously. The fact of violent exploitation is to be repelled through violent action, not through dialogue or appeals to the conscience of the violent oppressors. It is difficult, in fact impossible, to prick the conscience of the oppressors when their own self-interest is involved.

A true liberating struggle must start with the people after this conscientization; they must participate directly in it and must pursue their objective collectively, not individually. This is because there is unity in strength, and they are the joint victims of exploitation. Fanon's credibility as a commentator on racism and apartheid derives from the fact that he experienced discriminatory practices as a result of his color. He is not merely empathizing with the oppressed people but is one of them. There are features which are common to all instances of oppression or colonization, (perhaps with minor variations), namely, racial content, arrogance emanating from a conviction of the superiority of the oppressors over the oppressed, exploitation, and the general under-development of the colonized people and their place. However, violence plays a "cleansing and purifying" role, as well as gives psychological satisfaction. Through violence, the oppressed people assert their humanity (thus debunking the claim of their oppressors). A new man and a new society are generated.

Fanon has influenced the orthodox trend in post-independence African political experience and has also brought the application of Dependency Theories to bear on the analysis of political processes in contemporary Africa. The colonialists, together with their chosen successors, felt, and still feel, uncomfortable with his work, hence their strident efforts at halting its circulation. However, Fanon does not tell us how the radicalization of the different strata of the society is to be achieved so as to form a coherent whole.

Colonialism is not progressive; it is "rapacious, exploitative, and disruptive of people's history." It is "violence in its natural state." Together with Cesare, he identifies Nazism and Fascism as having internal manifestations of the philosophy of colonization. It is worthy of note that the post-war Germany has publicly apologized to Jews worldwide for the heinous crimes committed against them during the Nazi period. It stands to reason then that Europeans should at the very minimum publicly apologize for the atrocities they committed on African soil. Fanon's purpose is to aid the dis-alienation of the African person who is "a slave of his appearance." He does not discourage racial contact *per se* but abhors the form it takes in the colonial context. It is exactly this factor that distinguishes colonial rule from other kinds of racial contact.

Fanon could be criticized for overlooking the fact that there are other races apart from white and black. In the Caribbean countries, his backyard, you find different castes that do not fit into this broad categorization. He ignores the possibility of there being gray between white and black. His neglect of the salient role played by attitude in the analysis of race relations is equally conspicuous. Moreover, he tends to think that all the members of a race hold identical views all of the time. A relevant refutation of this line of thought in the South African situation is the fact that some white South Africans worked in active collaboration with the black majority in the effort to overthrow apartheid and install a truly multi-racial society with all its attendant positive implications.

It may appear as if Fanon is not certain about the sense in which the term 'violence' is to be used. However, the reality is that he extols defensive violence and condemned the violence employed by the colonizers because the former has a freedom-content while the latter stifles all forms of liberation. According to L. Adele Jinadu's characterization of violence in Fanon's work, it is the "praxis of decolonization and freedom of self-realization." Fanon identifies three forms of violence: physical, structural, and psychological. He owes his theory of psychological violence to Sartre but goes beyond him when he (Fanon) asserts that the black man is over-determined both from inside and outside. His categorization of violence into groups or different kinds plays a heuristic role especially the relation between physical and psychological violence. His emphasis on violence depicts his knowledge of the reality of our existence; it will be idealistic and naïve to suppose that violence does not exist when we are surrounded by it every day to this moment.

However, his classification of violence does not distinguish violent behavior from non-violent conduct, for example instances of civil disobedience could generate examples of physical violence, yet they may not involve as much physical harm as armed resistance. Psychological violence is used in the cultural alienation of a people. Language is used in communicating a society's shared morality and way of life from generation to generation, so it affects thoughts and human action. The implications are that one's identity is closely related to one's language and language is central to one's psychological character. Fanon's assumption that, when members of the colonized race accept and imbibe the colonizer's language, they necessarily become alienated from their primary culture, is false indeed.

It is desirable, if not necessary, that the colonizer's language be understood by the colonized so that the latter will be able to halt further deceit, grasp the workings of colonialism, interpret classified materials, etc. It is not enough to pretend that the colonizers do not exist or that they do not affect the indigenous society by their practices. Moreover, the people who mastered this alien language may do so in order to advance their lot in life. Invariably, the alien language becomes the lingua franca and the language of officialdom because of the many reasons arising from the possible choice of an indigenous language. In the modern world, being multilingual enhances one's chances of advancement. There is no wishing away the fact that English, French,

German, etc. are some of the most widely spoken languages in the world as presently constituted. Africans speak them all, and very well too.

A clear manifestation of this is found in Africa where the countries have adopted the languages of their former colonists as the official languages of the independent countries. It is possible that such "neutral" languages were introduced to aid communication among indigenes in a multilingual society, and to facilitate communication between them and outsiders, so why not learn them? One finds it important to stress that there are other factors apart from the mastery of the foreign language, which lead to cultural alienation. This understanding of a foreign language would just be an imitation and extra benefit, not a total acceptance of foreign values and the corollary rejection of one's language and culture. In the first place, certain 'objective' conditions, for example race, make one's mastery of a foreign language inadequate for admission into the colonizer's world, as Africans who tried to join certain Freemasonry Lodges in London and Paris found out to their dismay. Language cannot be the cause of culture, since it expresses such a culture. Culture precedes language, which is a part of it. Fanon then comes up with the 'Linguistic Relativity Theory."

Given the realities of the modern times -- a period characterized by great advances in Science, Technology, Medicine, increased mobility etc., it will seem obvious that Africans' embrace of European languages enables them to easily fit into the larger International family and to articulate their views in the major languages of the world, though there was no good intention at the introduction of these languages. There is no doubt that European languages have gained global applicability because of the fact of colonization; it is one's view that prospective leaders should not be disqualified mainly because of their fluency in European languages. Rather, we should be concerned with other factors, for example, their commitment to general welfare, personal qualities, performance, prudence, integrity, etc.

Fanon suggests that liberation involves more than the conception of the term but extends to the removal of the structure of social, economic, political, and cultural restrictions placed on the colonized people; restrictions which limit their opportunities and choices. He differentiates between true and false forms of liberation. True liberation is obtained through struggle by the oppressed themselves whereas false liberation is handed down by the colonizer, and, therefore, can never be complete. Revolution, for him, is a continuing process by which the horizon of man's opportunities is consciously and deliberately widened; it is not accidental or a matter of fate. His call for the creation of a "new man" has a universal scope applicable to all oppressed people everywhere in the world.

He argues that genuine liberation is only achieved when the colonizer decides that his interest would be better served with the dissolution of the repressive system of colonization.

Fanon has to tell us how we can know the exact point at which the "new man" is created. Is it ever too late to create him? It is not clear what features this "new man" will have. What justification is there for our assumption that a "new man" is necessarily a "better man" as we have seen with the post-independence group of African leaders who replaced colonialists? Fanon may reply that we do not need to see a new man before we can conceptualize him; in other words, this is done *a priori*. The problem with this is that we can never be sure *a priori* that the "new man" will be better than the "present man". If all we have are concepts, then we should look for some other form of justification since we can conceive of things that are not related to the world, as we know it. Religion is a good example here, with the elaborate narrative about the unproven, unprovable, and abstract soul, a Construct that drives the entire enterprise.

Fanon's pragmatism is celebrated in his recommendation of violence as a solution for ills inflicted violently; in other words, non-violent means might have been appropriate if the situation had demanded it. Whenever Fanon seems to be in an equivocation regarding violence, the issue can be resolved by distinguishing Fanon the Political Sociologist from Fanon the Moralist or Ideologist. He takes relative situations seriously and does not extrapolate from one situation to another. Violence leads to the regeneration of man, and this is a "psychological reorientation towards social and political relations"; it is an attitudinal change.

Much unlike what Fanon posits, people can achieve freedom without struggling for it, and yet appreciate it, so that there is nothing necessary about this relationship. How does one determine that violence is the only means left? What guarantee of success is there? He may call these academic distractions, then say that the issue of whether violence actually leads to liberation is different from whether resorting to violence is necessary or not. He has to tell us if the use of force is really the cause of the changes in consciousness. If not, then what is? From the observation of changes in attitude in individuals during revolutions, we cannot draw an inference concerning the futuristic nature and structure of the socio-politico-economic system that will emerge. Our experience with the Bolsheviks in Russia is instructive here. It has been argued by some people that, perhaps if resources were not scarce, it would be unnecessary to use race as a criterion of access by whatever means to these resources, but that can only be a matter of conjecture. The human mind is complex, and we also need to deal with our reality as we have it, not as we would prefer it. Man's nature is fundamentally inscrutable, and there is great difficulty and folly in trying to dimension it exactly.

One could also respond that other criteria like merit, input, political expediency, etc. should be used not race. A natural quality like one's color should not be used against one. Admittedly, this remains prescriptive with no conclusive correlation with actuality. People should be judged by what they have been able to do with their lives in terms of individual achievements as well as by the quality of their hearts. Fanon sees reality from the Marxian perspective.

Like Marxists, he sees violence as a structural necessity; he and Marxists also agree that violence is a defensive mechanism, and it always accompanies revolution. However, while Fanon suggests a decentralization of power, Marxists advocate for a centralization of power. I think that what Fanon does is not to reject Marxism-Leninism as such, but rather he modifies it. He is even criticized by Marxists for not differentiating between types of proletariat. It is important to add that he rejects the Marxian idea of an international class solidarity, as well as Historical Materialism. His criticism of the African middle class is due to the latter's inaction in the face of the oppression of their people, their virtual alignment in the subjugation of the masses, and their perpetuation of European values. His characterization of the proletariat as being "pampered" is misplaced when the cost of living in the cities is considered, together with the uncertainty that features in their daily lives.

Fanon's thesis in this regard will only be valid if he compares the proletariat with the peasantry in the rural areas. Moreover, he is wrong in assuming that the national bourgeoisie class is always colluding with the alien bourgeoisie. There are cases where members of the aristocratic class demonstrate utter contempt for the machinations of the Imperialist. Fanon's view is that classes came with colonization; a logical conclusion from this is that, without colonization, there would have been no classes in Africa, but Ethiopia and Liberia, which were not colonized, have socio-economic classes, so that colonialism is neither a necessary nor a sufficient condition for the emergence of classes, that is, Africa's incorporation into the International Capitalist Order. Fanon's work has been criticized for not being systematic and coherent; his recommendation of violence has been criticized as immoral and against the Will of God.

The response will be that Fanon does not claim to be systematic; therefore, the charge of not being systematic is misguided. With relation to violence, it is rather odd that the critics see nothing wrong in the present situation of wholesale violence perpetrated against Africans by other races and their resources pillaged but pick issues with a recommendation to respond in kind out of an affirmation of dignity. It is only when the same actions are directed against the oppressors that God's Will becomes relevant. Moreover, a few instances where violence is not cleansing are not enough for an entire refutation of Fanon's thesis. He does not, strictly speaking, say the violence originated with colonialism; rather he highlights the fact that it gave strength to colonialism. Humans should stop speaking for God, or, at least, try to be balanced and consistent in their morality.

To the charge that he did not give the formula by which Socialism could be established in Africa, one may reply that, perhaps, if he had lived longer, he would have done this. This brilliant psychiatrist and political philosopher died at 36. It is to his credit that he did pioneering work on the following subjects: racism and colonialism, the link among culture, ideology and modernization, class analysis of African politics, and Pan-Africanism. His treatment of racism is closely tied to his analysis of colonialism, and by extension, apartheid, though he never used this term. Apartheid and slavery shared some features in common: belief in the superiority of one race over another, the exploitation of the labor of the oppressed, etc.

Here, the color of one's skin determines one's progress. "You are rich because you are white and white because you are rich." It was through the Sharpeville massacre that the outside world first became aware of the apartheid system in South Africa. In terms of logic, the apartheid regime remained evil by the facts of its oppression of the owners of the land as well as by the denial of opportunities for advancement to them. The further trouble with the system was that it turned the immigrant white race into demigods with the indigenous population performing all the menial jobs. The blacks had a ceiling placed on their achievements, solely because of their color even in their own country!!! It was rather contradictory that the regime did not recognize the universal franchise of the black people; all modern political systems are built on the principles of universal suffrage, freedom, equal opportunities, and rights for all persons and citizens, etc. South Africa lacked all these. It was equally ironic and very telling that, just like the various Christian denominations in the United States, the white Afrikaner Reformed Church which should have preached and practised universal love and brotherhood of mankind, contributed significantly to the enthronement and maintenance of apartheid in South Africa for a century. Are these the people who will admit black people to their heaven that is not seen when they have clearly demonstrated repeatedly how they regard blacks: the evidence that is clear? Their God is simply not a God for black people. It is their manipulative creation to hoodwink the gullible.

The African National Congress (ANC), having been convinced that a non-violent approach will yield no positive dividend, had to resort to guerrilla warfare as well as other forms of violence: sabotage, terrorism and open revolution. The ANC did not seek the reversal of positions between whites and blacks, rather it advocated for a Polity that would recognize the diversity and equality of races in South Africa. Again, Europeans would not have taken all these indignities from other races in Europe or their new extension, America. Their resorting to violence vindicates Fanon's thesis. The apartheid system has been interpreted by some people, not along racial lines, but in terms of its capitalist nature, namely that it was a replacement of slavery by which the International Capitalist Centers sought to perpetuate their exploitation of Africans. However, any interpretation of apartheid that does not consider its racial foundation will not be plausible. Indeed, it will be fraudulent and puerile.

The whole structure of the society was designed to serve only the interests of whites; violent repression was commonplace. What was practised in South Africa was internal colonialism. The apartheid system was morally reprehensible and should be condemned by all men and women of conscience; it was because of this that the anti-apartheid movement gained a lot of international support, though nothing concrete was done to overthrow the system for the longest time. Most African countries, especially Nigeria, which spearheaded this endeavor, did not have the necessary political and economic clout to terminate the cancer of apartheid, but Nigeria privatized some British companies as a response to Britain's vigorous support for the minority race-based regime in South Africa. Nigeria also took in many of the ANC members, and funded some of the activities of the ANC. A white South African Member of Parliament, talking about the usual states of emergency in that country said then that: "we must accept that the minority regime would not be able to govern without the very wide powers afforded it by these states of emergency." People actually know when they are usurpers.

The minority apartheid regime was characterized by intransigence and repression at home, as well as provocative forays into neighboring countries like Angola (aligned with the US under Reagan in their cuddling of Jonas Savimbi) and Namibia. Its self-evident arrogance arises from the fact that it counted on the active support of the developed countries of the world -- notably the US, UK, Germany, Netherlands, and very sadly, the State of Israel supplied them with weapons, crowd-control machinery, and nuclear skills; a people who had known oppression and holocaust at the hands of the ancestral kith and kin of these same killers and oppressors!!! Moreover, South Africa had an advanced economy, sophisticated defense systems, etc., and these differentiated it from other countries in which revolutions took place at different times in history (China in 1949, Russia in 1917, and Cuba in 1959). The internal nature of this colonialism was also significant. Aggression against oppression should come typically from outside, for example, against Hitler's Germany and Mussolini's Italy.

Such an external involvement was unlikely and absent in South Africa because the countries which could genuinely effect a change were allied with the brutal minority regime. The United States of America has been involved in a lot of contradictions regarding its categorization of freedom fighters and terrorists. Its much-publicized advocacy for a "Constructive Engagement", "Negotiated and Peaceful Settlement" was just a lot of distraction for a long time. When they choose to be direct and vigorous, as in Israel and the entire Middle East, there is never any ambiguity. For a long time also, the OAU (now AU) remained at the level of rhetoric, having learnt nothing from the situation in the Middle East. Nkrumah had recommended the establishment of an African High Command, which would drive all vestiges of colonialism from Africa. With the various countries still unable to prove their worthiness for their political independence to this day, the prospects for unity and dignified engagement with the rest of the world diminish by the day. Their **Independence** remains **Dependent** on external factors.

Ultimately, Africans themselves need to make some tough decisions, agree to agree or disagree among themselves, and begin the arduous, necessary, and critically urgent work of reversing their collective destiny and fortune as a people, not as individuals.

Nigeria, Democracy, and State Performance: An Assessment of Wasted Opportunities

"Nigeria is not a nation. It is a mere geographical expression. There are no 'Nigerians' in the same sense as there are 'English,' 'Welsh,' or 'French,' The word 'Nigeria' is a mere distinctive appellation to distinguish those who live within the boundaries of Nigeria and those who do not." - Chief Obafemi Awolowo, 1947.

"It is better for us and many admirers abroad that we should disintegrate in peace and not in pieces. Should the politicians fail to heed the warning, then I will venture the prediction that the experience of the Democratic Republic of Congo will be a child's play if it ever comes to our turn to play such a tragic role" - Dr Nnamdi Azikiwe, 1964.

"Since 1914 the British Government has been trying to make Nigeria into one country, but the Nigerian people themselves are historically different in their backgrounds, in their religious beliefs and customs and do not show themselves any signs of willingness to unite ... Nigerian unity is only a British invention" – Alhaji Sir Abubakar Tafawa Balewa, 1948.

Some interpretation is necessary here. Chief Obafemi Awolowo, a British-trained lawyer, from the Yoruba ethnic group, political philosopher, author, and Nigerian statesman, was one of the most prominent politicians pre-independence and thereafter, emerging as the first premier of the Western Region. He is generally regarded as having been an excellent manager of resources as well as a visionary leader for the Western Region, and as someone who understood very clearly that the country called Nigeria lacked the fundamental elements to succeed as a nation; he, therefore, focused on his Region, where he is still mostly revered to this day decades after his death. Conversely, he is mostly regarded by non-Yoruba people in Nigeria as a parochial leader, who did not work towards national unity. His statement above paraphrases Count Metternich's "geographical expression" in referring to the disparate units that constituted the Italian peninsula; the good thing is that they all came together to form the modern Italian Republic, a unity that still fundamentally eludes Nigeria in spirit and essence. Awolowo has also been described as "the best president Nigeria never had." And will never have in its current Construct, one may quickly add.

Dr. Nnamdi Azikiwe, US-trained political scientist, statesman, an Igbo man, and Nigeria's first president (mostly ceremonial in a Parliamentary System, as was then practised at independence in 1960 through 1966), was also an accomplished journalist, author of many books, political philosopher, orator, and owner of newspapers across Nigeria and Ghana. He used his vast media, political, and social networks to agitate with others for Nigeria's independence.

Together with Kwame Nkrumah, Sedar Senghor of Senegal, Ahmed Sekou Toure of Guinea, Emperor Haile Selassie of Ethiopia, Marcus Garvey, W.E. B. DuBois, Julius Nyerere of Tanzania, and Félix Houphouët-Boigny of Ivory Coast (now Côte d'Ivoire) they were the driving force behind the Pan-African Movement, which focused on reversing the horrid consequences of slavery, racism, colonialism, and neo-colonialism on Africans.

They inspired people like Malcolm X, Bob Marley, and the Civil Rights Activists in the United States, who drew inspiration from the robust intellectual and principled response to these race-based policies from Africans. Dr. Nnamdi Azikiwe was an internationalist in an era of ethnic consolidation among his peers, an orientation which is presently regarded as naivete on his part. Before Nigeria's independence, he was a fervent believer in the unity of the country, a view that was moderated in a few short years (as evidenced above) due to his observations and experiences. He saw the unity of the country as a *sine qua non* in his larger mission of uniting the entire Continent with his fellow pan-Africanists.

Alhaji Sir Abubakar Tafawa Balewa, educated at Barewa College and the Institute of Education of UCL, London, was Nigeria's first prime minister and representative of the Northern Region. He was a mild-mannered politician and statesman whose primary loyalty was to the Premier of the Northern Region, Alhaji Ahmadu Bello. Tafawa Balewa was of the minority Gere tribe but had a half-Fulani mother. The PM role was considered inferior at the time by Ahmadu Bello, who chose to remain as a Regional Head in Kaduna. Bello was a Fulani man, a migrant minority ethnic group in northern Nigeria which had, through a very brutal jihad led by Uthman Dan Fodio from Futa Jallon, Guinea, in 1804, sacked the leaders of the vastly more populous Hausas and imposed Fulanis as Emirs. Having displaced and dismantled the Hausa political structure, it became easy for the Fulanis to impose their Will on the numerous fragmented ethnic groups in the northern parts of the country, even as they adopted Hausa as the lingua franca for the North. The term 'Hausa-Fulani' is, therefore, simply an oxymoron as there is no ethnic group so called.

Admittedly, inter-marriages occur between the two groups, but the linguistic and cultural connotation of the term is a non-starter. To this day, every Emir in the North is a Fulani Muslim, even where they are vastly outnumbered, while the declared ambition is to replicate the same structure all over Nigeria by violence, displaying and killing whoever resists. They claim that the British colonists interrupted their jihad by over a hundred years. The resistance to this obvious agenda by indigenous populations across the Middle Belt and the South, threatens the very survival of the country. As at the time of Nigeria's independence, Bello preferred to consolidate the Fulani hegemony across the core North and the Middle Belt rather than be a Prime Minister at the center of the country. Apart from about 25% of Yorubas who are Muslim (moderate, not violent, accommodating, unlike the extremists up North), the entire South West, South East (Igbos), Niger Delta (South South) and over 70% of the Middle Belt are Christians. The concentration of Muslims in Nigeria is in the core northern states near the Niger and Chad borders, a fact with some implications for the country.

When, in March 1953, Anthony Enahoro raised a motion for Nigeria to become independent in 1956, the North vigorously resisted and threatened to secede from Nigeria. Having, for decades since the amalgamation of the northern and southern protectorates by Britain in 1914, refused to embrace Western education on the same scale as the South, they declared their unpreparedness for independence. Awolowo threatened that, if the North proceeded with the secession, his Region, with access to the Atlantic Ocean and the ports - would block the North from utilizing those ports for exporting their groundnuts to Europe. The North generated most of its revenue at the time from their popular groundnut pyramids as well as textiles.

Since the discovery of crude oil in the South and the control of the oil industry and national government by the Fulanis and Hausas, the groundnut pyramids have since disappeared while all eyes are now on oil and gas proceeds. Bello insisted that the suggested year of independence be changed from a certain '1956' to the uncertain 'as soon as practicable'. As it is, the country became independent on October 1, 1960. Bello said further in 1953 that: "it is true that we politicians always delight in talking loosely about the unity of Nigeria. Sixty years ago, there was no country called Nigeria. What is now Nigeria consisted of a number of large and small communities all of which were different in their outlooks and beliefs. The advent of the British and that of Western education has not materially altered the situation and the many and varied communities have not knit themselves into a composite unit."

The then British Governor-General in Nigeria, Macpherson, in a memo back to London, wrote that: "if Nigeria splits, it will not be into two or three parts, but into many fragments." The British Authorities persuaded their Fulani clients to rescind their decision, promising them that the then capital of the country, Lagos, would be officially excised from the Western Region, and made a federal territory, to assuage the concerns about blockade. The North is entirely landlocked. The then British Minister of the Colonies, Mr. Lyttleton described "Hausa-Fulanis" as "Muslims and warriors, with the dignity, courtly manners, high bearing and conservative outlook which democracy has not yet debased." He also described Yorubas and Igbos as people "with higher education, but lower manners and inferior fighting value, somewhat intoxicated with nationalism, though loyal to the British connection at least so long as it suits them."

In his memo to the British Cabinet on the matter, Lyttleton wrote that:

"the north with their deep but already somewhat shaken trust in the British and distrust of their 'brothers' in the West and East fear that greater autonomy now suggested for regions will lead to the West seceding when it suits them, especially as the West incorporates Lagos, at once the commercial and political capital and only effective outlet to the sea for the trade and commerce of the North... The North now insist on Lagos being a federal area under separate administration to safeguard it from becoming a Yoruba preserve and to make sure their access to the sea remains open... We cannot let the North down. They are more than half the population, more attached to the British and more trustful of the colonial service than the other two...if my colleagues agree, I shall state that we have decided to excise Lagos from the West... to act otherwise would be to alienate our [northern] friends, probably drive them into secession, to cast aside our responsibilities and to leave a dismembered Nigeria to settle its own differences perhaps with the spear."

Britain proved its loyalty to its northern "friends" in the genocide and Civil War against Igbos between 1966 and 1970.

The above context largely explains contemporary dynamics in that blighted country up until the current era. We should perhaps set out some basic parameters for understanding the country:

- The Fulani oligarchical and feudal system has been successfully imposed on the majority Hausas and minority ethnic groups in the North since Uthman Dan-Fodio's 1804 Jihad.
- The Fulanis, who are 100% Muslims, are forever on an expansionist mission, buoyed by their previous success and a Messianic arrogance.
- There are many minority ethnic groups in the core North and in the Middle Belt who are Christians, but they are under permanent violent assault, the objective being their liquidation, conversion, and/or occupancy of their territory, to achieve a 100% pure Muslim territory up North, and possibly all over the country.
- The North contributes nothing to the federal purse but feels entitled to control the Oil Industry (the main revenue and foreign currency generator), the Customs, the entire Security Services, key administrative ministries and agencies, and all the "lucrative" government offices. The North is not known for entrepreneurship and business risk-taking, choosing to serve

mostly in the federal government, where they end up much richer than business people.

- Igbos and the entire oil-rich Niger-Delta (South-South Region) are 100% Christian and highly educated and resourceful. They do not get their due in the country and feel justifiably alienated from the system.
- The Yorubas of the South-West are highly educated and resourceful; they choose when to cooperate with the North and when to seek alliances with the rest of the country that feels marginalized and under-represented. Their primary strategic goal seems to always ensure that Igbo people do not advance politically at the center, even if this means the Yorubas playing second fiddle to the Fulanis. While neither the Igbos nor any group for that matter have ever attacked the Yorubas, they consort with the Fulanis who actually attacked them. A renegade Yoruba Chief, Afonja, was betrayed and killed by Fulani jihadists in 1824, as a result of which the minority-settler Fulanis installed and have maintained an Emir of Ilorin ever since. Ilorin is a Yoruba town populated and dominated by the Yoruba, but they have not found it worthy 200 years later to take back their town, withdraw the recognition accorded the Emir of Ilorin as the Ruler of the town, or, at least, appoint their own Oba (Ruler) in parallel to this imposition, but they generally get riled up by the legal business and real estate transactions of Igbo people in Yoruba land, all bound by contracts by free parties. The day that the Yorubas and Igbos team up in honesty, trust, and mutual respect will be the beginning either of the restoration of the country's full destiny or its disintegration.
- While there are over 250 distinct ethnic groups in the country, the dominant ones are the Yorubas, Igbos, and Hausas (based on numbers, but the deceptive term 'Hausa-Fulani' if we consider influence). The other tier would be the Ijaws and Edos of the oil-rich Niger Delta, Kanuris of the North-East, and Tivs of the Middle Belt. Managing the complexities of the various identities has remained a challenge due largely to nepotism, corruption, abuse of the coercive powers of government in protecting "one's own" and punishing "others." The absence of a vigorous Rule of Law is also a major challenge, thereby replicating "Big Man's" Rules across the entire country.
- It is only the Igbos who feel confident enough to make considerable fixed investments in real estate and other assets outside their Region; other peoples are entirely clannish in their investments, even as they have no difficulty in acquiring properties in the UK, USA, UAE, and elsewhere. Commute into and within Igboland remains oppressive due to the sheer number of exploitative Federal Security checkpoints that litter their landscape. A road trip from Lagos to Onitsha, for example (about 160 miles) has well over a hundred checkpoints; the same intensity is found all over the East, with discretionary levies and bribes openly taken and people detained at will, expensive vehicles seized, auctioned,

and reassigned to people outside the Region, etc., etc. Most of these Officers (Army, Police, State Security, etc.) hail from other Regions) and generally extort commuters and abuse authority. This is yet another source of discontent in the country, as no other part of the country is treated that same way.

- History and contemporary realities do instruct that the fragile unity of the country is sustained by the deep hatred of the rest of the country towards Igbos; a fact borne out by their collective slaughter of over 3 million Igbos between 1966 and 1970, their systematic impoverishment of Igbos after the civil war in 1970, the seizure of Igbo properties in different parts of the country to this day, and the targeted physical attacks on Igbos especially in the core North in the intervening years. Igbo enterprise and readiness to develop other Regions where they reside also presents them for systematic hatred in Lagos, Western Nigeria, by the Yorubas, and in the core North.
- While the country is purportedly a federation, it has always been run as a unitary State (since the days of military rule and their centralization of power), with the Center wielding extraordinary powers and encroaching into minor and concurrent areas that should fall within the jurisdictions of the federating states and the counties. There is no state or county police, for example, with the Center deploying Security Officers all over the country -- an inefficient structure that is also abused during elections, for example.
- Apart from Olusegun Obasanjo (1999-2007), Goodluck Jonathan (2010-2015), and, perhaps, Shehu Shagari (1979-1983), no other Nigerian president or military dictator has been able to effectively project and maintain a unifying national identity that trumps ethnicity and religion.

With your permission, before we trace and assess the role of democracy in Nigeria's woeful developmental outcomes, indeed if that is the correct political and developmental model for the country, allow me to quote extensively from the Nigerian philosopher and public commentator, Dr. Douglas Anele, in his assessment of the Civil War which the rest of the country fought against Igbos between 1967 and 1970, the residues of which still threaten the fabric of the country:

"Liters of ink have been spent by historians, academics, and other interested parties to explain both the remote and immediate causes of the war. But the truth, which most members of the sybaritic ruling class in Nigeria have stubbornly refused to take seriously, is that Nigeria was created by Britain primarily to bolster her economic interests. British colonial imperialists were certainly not interested in working as equal partners with the various peoples they brought together for the optimum development of the country they named Nigeria.

Instead, they were keen to harness the impressive human and natural resources in the new geopolitical amalgam to build a stronger and resilient economy back home as dictated by white supremacist logic and the imperatives of colonialism. This implies that the continued existence of Nigeria is a clear endorsement by Nigerians of British imperialist designs and their failure to outgrow the template cobbled together by Lord Lugard and the avaricious colonial establishment in the dying days of the 19th century and the beginning of the 20th....

Now, British colonial administrators and prominent Nigerian politicians across the country during the nationalist agitation for independence knew that forging a truly united nation from the multiple ethnic nationalities of Nigeria was a very difficult task. The most formidable was how the north with its rustic conservative emirate system based on Islamic theocracy could be blended seamlessly with the largely variegated Christian communities in the south. Different outcomes of indirect rule in the three major regions of Nigeria ought to have indicated to the British that Project Nigeria would be an unstable proposition right from the start, but they were blinded by the huge economic benefits from exploiting the country through the amalgamation of the "southern lady of means" and the "promising well-conducted youth" or northern Nigeria.

As Max Siollun, a perceptive writer on Nigerian history who sometimes obscures truth in a bizarre quest for "neutrality" observes, "Nigeria [is] so ethnically, religiously and linguistically complex that even some of its leading politicians initially doubted it could constitute a real country." I have written severally in this column about how British officials connived with conservative Muslim northern politicians to ensure that the north held on to political power at the centre after independence, especially through manipulating census figures and elections to give northern region demographic superiority and political advantage over the south.

Unfortunately, Dr. Nnamdi Azikiwe played into the hands of both the British and the north by working hard to create a centralised Nigeria. Dr. Azikiwe's naivety stemmed from two sources. One, he thought that given the meritorious preeminent position of Ndigbo in key areas of the new Nigeria, the people can hold their own in a united country where merit and excellence prevailed in public life and determined who gets what at all levels of governance. Two, he envisaged that, as the leading Pan-Nigeria nationalist it was more prestigious to preside over a bigger Nigerian nation than to lead a much smaller geographical space called the eastern region. With the benefit of hindsight, Dr. Azikiwe was gravely mistaken to think that leading members of the northern establishment shared the same liberal democratic principles that he imbibed as an Igbo and from his studies in the United States.

More specifically, Alhaji Ahmadu Bello, Sir Abubakar Tafawa Balewa, and most leading northern politicians were core Muslims; and since the Koran and the Hadith are radioactive to the principles of liberal democracy, the great Zik of Africa failed to notice the perilous implications of working together with political juggernauts from the north when he entered into alliance with the Northern Peoples Congress (NPC) to form a coalition government in 1960.

Let me put it this way: Muslims can deny it till the end of time, but the two most important Islamic literature unabashedly advocate an ideal authoritarian theocracy or caliphate which is incompatible with the principles of liberal democracy and human rights as they are understood today. There are accounts from few prominent Igbo and Yoruba commentators, each blaming Chief Obafemi Awolowo and Azikiwe respectively for failure of the National Council of Nigerian Citizens (NCNC) and Action Group (AG) to provide a united front at independence, which would have automatically left the NPC out in the cold.

The most plausible conclusion that can be distilled from these accounts is that the two respected politicians squandered a great opportunity because given their solid intellectual background and liberal democratic orientation they ought to have put aside their personal differences and worked together. That failure, with the consequent unrelenting northern push for dominance despite the region's economic stagnation and yawning educational disadvantages, when compared to the south, can be counted as one of the remote causes of the Biafran war." End of Quote.

From the foregoing, a few things become very clear: the seeds of disunity were sown from the time before independence when incompatible peoples and worldviews were casually lumped together; the citizens of the newly-independent State have been simply unable to design a workable format for their union on the basis of equity, mutual respect, and balance; the issues of indigeneship and citizenship have remained unresolved sixty years hence and are indeed intensifying; a section assumes that a structure of inequity can last forever; the Islamic Feudalism that predominates in the Fulani-run North is fundamentally and irreversibly incompatible with the understanding of liberal democracy, Western education, competition, merit, social progress, and *laissez faire* capitalism which most of the Middle Belt and all of the South embrace; the lack of creative space for Southerners is mostly responsible for the considerable brain drain from their population -- to the benefit of Europe and the United States; some displaced people recourse to "digital" crime to survive and to prove that they have also "arrived" like the thieves in power; the inability to develop and sustain a national identity permanently inhibits the full potentials of the country and perennially ensures the fragility of the State; State failure has cascaded the entire system (like metastasized cancerous tumor) with thieves emerging at all strata of government; the structure of connections driving progress cannot be resolved with an ethos of transparent reward for excellence; and the fatalism of the Islamic social architecture is intrinsically and diametrically opposed to a system where a poor but talented person can rise and prosper without connections and based purely on merit and talent.

It is safe, therefore, to affirm, though sadly, that Nigeria, in its current structure and form, is a fraud and cannot work. The necessary honest dialogue to resolve the identified limitations in the system has never held and is not likely to hold. In the absence thereof, therefore, the State will continue to decline and may, indeed, implode either along manageable lines or into utter chaos, with significant grave implications for the people, the Region, and the entire world. This assessment is not made easily, happily, or casually, but is informed by a hard-nosed, objective, and unsentimental instruction from History, Geopolitics, Philosophy, Political Science, Sociology, and National Security.

Official Nigeria is also simply a criminal enterprise, which nullifies and blemishes the people who seek an honest living through creativity, tenacity, enterprise, and alignment with global best practice. Nigeria has millions of innocent and hard-working people who can hold their own against the best anywhere in the world -- as they prove when overseas, but their national system stifles, punishes, and kills innovation and excellence. Nigeria is a mystery hidden in a maze and wrapped in a conundrum—a sovereign amoeba (*Figure 37*)!!!

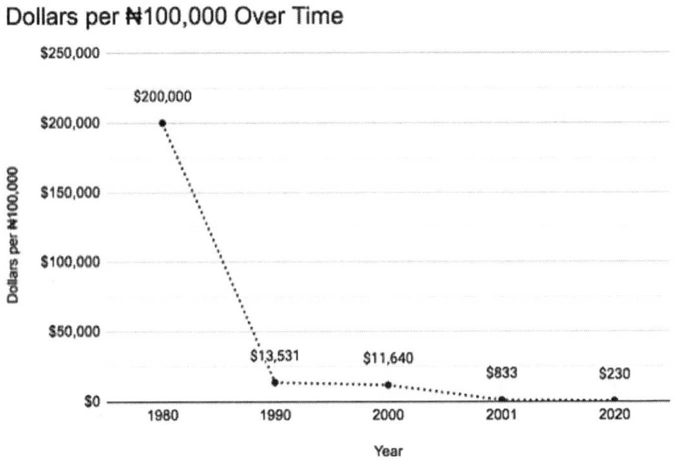

National Currency (Naira) Erosion vs the $. *Credit: Nadia Namko*

This currency erosion chart summarizes Nigeria's deplorable performance in graphic terms. The steep devaluation of the national currency, the Naira, is reflective of the loss of potential and national purpose in the country. Whereas N100,000 exchanged for US$200,000 in 1980, the same amount in Naira presently exchanges for a mere sum of $230. This has had obvious direct consequences for citizens and companies, especially the vast majority without access to public resources or the declining private sector opportunities: jobs, capital formation, quality of life, home ownership, family stability, absence of leisure, declining life expectancy figures, absence of reward for educational achievements, frustration, security and social problems, societal fissures, the increasing anger towards those who "have made it" including the innocent professionals and business people who have achieved financial success in spite of the government, mounting pressure to escape from the country, the recourse by the morally-agnostic to cyber and other crimes, business failures, etc., etc.

As a clear demonstration of the manifest incompetence and economic illiteracy of the Buhari Administration in the country, for example, the Naira to Dollar exchange rate in February 2020 (4 months ago) was N360:$; for the past month, it has been oscillating in the range of N460: $; a 28% devaluation in just three to four months, with no prospects of either abatement or recovery. When Mr. Buhari was sworn in as Nigeria's President for his first term in May 2015, the exchange rate was N220: $. The national currency has been devalued by over 100% in just 5 years, with the obvious implications. The erosion of currency value continues...

In other countries, this would have inspired massive protests, but Nigerians are too busy hating along religious and economic lines to galvanize their energy against a failed Government (whose family members and officials still live in opulence and also obtain foreign currencies at massively subsidized rates!) Enough said.

In evaluating whether or not the seeds of true democracy can germinate on the Nigerian soil, it will be helpful to quickly refresh our memory on the salient aspects of Political Philosophy, and conduct a cursory comparison with the United States, the country whose Constitution and political structures Nigeria has adopted in form, though not in practice. Philosophy remains relevant to all human activities; we shall limit the philosophical discourse in this section to what the cited thinkers said about democracy. We will also try and determine if democracy is transplantable, and if it is the best form of government for all the countries of the world, whether the critical underlying ingredients are present or not. Indeed, is democracy the only route towards providing the optimal pool of public goods while respecting the civil rights and dignity of man, all in affirmation of the eligibility of that society for political independence and sovereignty?

If a society cannot function as a modern State, with responsibility towards its citizens and the international community, should there be consequences? and what should those be? Some of the aforementioned themes will recur in the analysis hereunder. Democracy, in its prescriptive and ideal form, remains the best form of government ever formulated by man. The corruption of its essence, owing to man's imperfection, contextual nuances and factors, as well as the absence of restraining devices, has continued to generate considerable debate. While social, economic, and cultural factors definitely impact the variant of democracy practised in a society, routes to the ideal form of democracy, or its approximation, will necessarily also reflect local dynamics and realities. Democracy's innate alignment with the human spirit is responsible for its functional exploitation by many political actors who, nevertheless, project the profile of dictators. We need to highlight and analyze the weighty factors that presently account for Nigeria's suboptimal democratic experience. Democracy is currently used interchangeably with Good Governance, and this is adopted herein.

It is one's considered view that, while local factors limit the potentials for a wholesale export of a democratic experience from one society to another, the corollary requirement of good governance is universally acknowledged. In this regard, therefore, the institution of the fundamental pillars of democracy and the minimization of the corrupting factors, should combine to produce a successful Democracy. Drawing from this perspective, therefore, the dissimilarities in historical and political experience among States are not adequate to explain or justify their inability to imbibe the democratic ethos.

Theoretical Excursion

While the roots of universal modern democracy can be traced to Classical Antiquity and the cumulative political experience of the Western Tradition, it must be stated *ab initio* that, in strict terms, this classical variant did not meet the essential requirements of universal suffrage and equality. In addition, the *Gemeinschaft* of those societies, and the small pool of citizens (owing to disenfranchisement and civic hierarchy), are incompatible with the diversity and scale of the contemporary democratic experience. Democracy, in its current form, is a reflection of the American political evolution. The minimum ingredients of democracy are, therefore: general and free elections; freedom of expression; Rule of Law (not of Man); and Equality; while the concepts of the inalienability of human rights, human dignity, plurality of thought and options, and the resultant creative tension, are adjunct but critical elements of democracy. We will proceed by tracing the sources of democracy, as currently practised in the United States, which is the best exemplar of modern democracy. Since a comprehensive review is beyond our current focus, representative interventions will be briefly analyzed, for their cumulative impact on how the Western Society is presently organized. Some points have been deliberately repeated, both for emphasis on their criticality, and to highlight the import of their realized potentiality.

Plato recognized the need for justice in a properly governed polity. He wrote in 'Politics' that: "...in establishing our city, we are not looking to make any one group in it outstandingly happy, but to make the whole city so as far as possible. For we thought that we would be most likely to find justice in such a city, and injustice, by contrast, in the one that is governed worst…"

While he did not prescribe universal parameters of justice, he underscored the general salience of the core essentials. While aligning with the Socratic formulation on the qualifications of the leaders of the *polis or* political unit/ society, Plato further urges temperance and moderation – the equivalent of Aristotle's "middling sort of life".

While Aristotle has high civil standards for electors – "choosing correctly is the work of those who know" --, he nevertheless underscored that Laws, not man, should be authoritative for all. The political good is justice, and this is the common advantage. For him, justice is held by all to be a common affirmation of equality. The Aristotelian template is discounted by its prescription of a permanent cadre of leaders, and for his limited recognition of the applicability of civic participation by all adults. In some respects, his exclusionary writings could provide a philosophical basis for the subsequent disenfranchisement of sections of the society in many countries. His recognition of human imperfections and passions (arrogance, fear, contempt, pre-eminence, disproportionate growth, electioneering, underestimation of others, neglect of small things, and dissimilarity) as limiting factors in public governance, therefore, makes it difficult to understand his other positions on permanent rulership and a hierarchical society. For him, the ruler has the exclusive virtue of prudence, hence the prescription of permanence in office; history has since nullified the extreme optimism immanent in this position.

He further writes that "… those regimes which look to the common advantage are correct regimes according to what is unqualifiedly just, while those which look only to the advantage of the rulers are errant, and are all deviations from the correct regimes; for they involve mastery, but the city is a partnership of free persons…" Including slaves, women, and foreigners who have no civic stature whatsoever and "do not share in happiness and in living in accordance with intentional choice …"!!! The risk of adopting Aristotle's position *in toto* is that the perpetuation of vices by leaders lacking in virtues would be the norm. His subsequent emphasis on the Rule of Law does not provide adequate mitigation for this risk. His variant of democracy remains, however, the most moderate political system out of the available options, with tyranny being the worst along the spectrum.

Aristotle proceeds to recognize various forms of Democracy:

- The type based on equality; the law here states that there is equality when the poor are no more pre-eminent than the rich, and neither have authority, but both are treated as similar.
- The form wherein offices are filled on the basis of assessments, but this is open to abuse and manipulation by those who possess the money to share.

- The type of democracy wherein all citizens of unquestioned descent participate but the law rules. Where the law does not rule, there is no regime.
- When all have a part in the offices provided only they are citizens, but the law remains supreme. Here, the best citizens preside, and not the popular leader.
- The majority has authority and not the law. Here, decrees are authoritative, and not the law. This model applies mostly to charismatic leaders. In this regard, the manifestation of tyranny and monarchical rule becomes a recurring tendency.

For Aristotle, the minimum defining attributes of Democracy are: the majority having authority, as well as freedom. Civic equality connotes that whatever the multitude resolves is authoritative and binding, while freedom and equality involve doing what one wants to do. The citizens, all being free, consider themselves to be equal simply. He notes that homogeneity conduces to accepted equality and resultant harmony and suggests that dissimilarity of stock can only result in nominal equality when the law (as freely negotiated and accepted) is pre-eminent and binding on all. Again, his complicated theses on citizenship and leadership make it difficult to attempt a direct transposition of his views to contemporary circumstances, but the essential message is noted.

Overall, the Greek conception of democracy was in many ways more extreme than the contemporary model; for instance, Aristotle says that to elect magistrates is oligarchic, while it is democratic to appoint them by lot.

St. Thomas Aquinas, the greatest of the Scholastic Philosophers, used his balanced analytical method to demonstrate the compatibility of human political systems with the Natural Law. After "proving" the existence of God in his seminal and influential work, *Summa Theologiae*, he emphasized the criticality of aligning human organizing principles with the eternal Laws. God is good, and in His own goodness; He is the good of every good. He is intelligent, and His act of intelligence is His essence. He understands by His essence and understands Himself perfectly. There is free Will in God; a reason can be assigned for His volition, but not a cause. While emphasizing God's Absolutes, and the human connectedness to Him on account of the Divine Spark in all humans, the "angelic doctor" instructed us about the higher calling involved in political leadership, which, necessarily, resembles our relationship with the Transcendent. Considerations other than, and beyond, self, therefore, essentially constitute the core of civic responsibility and custodianship. This revolutionary dimension amplified the moral component of leadership, and the consequential imperatives of fidelity to the common cause, accountability to both man and God, humility, and an overarching commitment to the public good.

The Thomistic position is that Divine Providence does not exclude evil, contingency, free will, chance, or luck; evil comes through second causes and is not derived from the nature of God. Since we will all confront/ face God after our physical sojourn, according to this theory, Aquinas adopts a teleological paradigm when he suggests that Man, tending towards God (who is the End of all things), should continually strive to overcome carnality and all manifestations of passion (pride, honor, glory, wealth, worldly power, etc.) as these are not the ultimate end in themselves. In accordance with Divine Law, we should love God and, by extension, our neighbors. Drawing on Augustinian teachings, Aquinas writes that, by committing mortal sin, man forfeits the last end to all eternity and, therefore, deserves eternal punishment. A significant contribution made by Aquinas to Western Moral Tradition was his adaptation of Aristotle's Philosophy to Christian dogma. The progressive impact of this intervention continues to be seen in the values, political systems, and in the expectations of conduct among public office holders.

Thomas Hobbes (1588 – 1779), writing in his '*Leviathan*,' departs from the Platonic assumption that reason was innate in the Rulers; for him, reason is developed through a rigorous search. Projecting this to his Political Philosophy, he, therefore, suggests that people would, out of self-interest, introduce some Order in the society in order to relegate the maintenance of the status quo anarchical situation in which life is "short, nasty, and brutish." It is significant, however, that he recommends a Monarchy rather than Democracy, as the best system of government, but invests the citizenry with the right of self-defense even against a Monarch. This balancing formula would gradually lead to the diminution of the Rights of Kings, as well as inform Montesquieu's later postulation of Checks and Balances. For Hobbes, a man has no duty to a sovereign who has not the power to protect him, thereby sowing the early seeds of the mutuality of responsibilities between the State and the Citizen, which would subsequently be expanded and encapsulated in the Social Contract.

Proceeding from a different paradigm but achieving the same philosophical conclusion as Hobbes, Russell Kirk writes in his Opus that: "the Ten Commandments (the Decalogue) are not a set of harsh prohibitions imposed by an arbitrary tribal deity. Instead, they are liberating rules that enable a people to diminish the tyranny of sin; that teach a people how to live with one another and in relation with God, how to restrain violence and fraud, how to know justice and to raise themselves above the level of predatory animals." In its bare essence, that is what both democracy and good governance aim to achieve.

It must be stated, however, that the Hobbesian fixation on the National Interest involves the erroneous assumption that all the citizens (monarchy and commoners alike) have a common interest, with the result that the progressive consequences of positive tension in the society are devalued; furthermore, Hobbes has been cited by contemporary Statesmen who would rather violate civil liberties "in the National Interest". This is possibly on account of his thesis that authority is given to the ruler, and not just loaned to her/ him, and that individual Wills are given up in favor of the single sovereign Will. In addition, the projection of the assumed permanence of anarchy to the international environment ignores the critical role of diplomacy and other non-kinetic tools of Statecraft in advancing the National Interest (instead of a reflexive recourse to wars).

Among the Modern Philosophers, Locke retains a prime position for the direct impact of his thoughts on the Western Political arrangements. In his 'Treatises On Government', he criticizes hereditary power, thereby providing critical philosophical support for the subsequent rejection of Monarchy (and the supposed Divine Rights of Kings), as well as sowing the seeds for the French and American Revolutions. Locke emphasizes the injustice of primogeniture, which is unavoidable if inheritance is to be the basis of monarchy. He also theorized on the essentialness of freedom, as well as the need for binding Contracts between the people and their leaders. The ideas of laissez-faire and the rights of man were thus substantially inspired. The Declaration of Independence of the United States reads in part that, "… but though this (state of nature) be a state of liberty, yet it is not a state of licence: though man in that state has an uncontrollable liberty to dispose of his person or possessions, yet he has not liberty to destroy himself, or so much as any creature in his possession, but where some nobler use than its bare preservation calls for it. The state of nature has a law of nature to govern it, which obliges every one: and reason, which is that law, teaches all mankind, who will but consult it, that being equal and independent, no one ought to harm another in his life, health, liberty, or possessions." (for we are all God's property).

Locke's revolutionary position regarding the contractual basis/ origin of civil governance equally emphasized the place of responsibility in civic conduct, rather than the casual and convenient reference of all matters to the Divine Realm. This release also inspired some major developments in Science, Research, Economics, and overall human development. Under the Social Contract, however, the Government must have a right to exact obedience, this right being contingent on its discharge of its own duties. If not, not… This concept could be traced to medieval Scholastics like William of Ockham who theorized that the State's power derived from the people's Will.

Rousseau's book: 'Social Contract', (1762) equally dealt extensively on this. Locke concluded that people join in the Social Contract not simply out of fear but in accordance with REASON, and not only for personal protection but for mutual benefit. Accordingly, any resultant tyranny should be opposed by all. A society's social contract is not Holy Grail and should be re-written to remedy an abuse of power. A casual interpretation of Locke's recognition of the State's rights to exact obedience could also be regarded as a basis for tyranny, while conveniently ignoring the implicit responsibilities. In order to specifically dilute the risk of concentration, Locke splits the powers of government among competing but complementary Institutions which act as checks on one another, even while insisting that the public good must be objectively defined by the majority.

Locke considerably influenced the Founding Fathers of the United States. The independence of the Executive, Judiciary, and Legislature is a derivative of his thinking, for example. His greatest contribution lies in his postulation of a representative government that is also held accountable by the people. His was an improvement on Hobbes' position, which recognized the need for a government but seemed to leave room for power abuse in the future. It must be stressed that Locke's Political Philosophy proved inadequate to address the outcomes of the Industrial Revolution, namely, the enormous power of property, the enhanced power of the State, spikes in nationalism and alliances, etc. Globalization during our time, as well as revolutions in Media, Transport, and Technology, have further eroded the power of the single individual in favor of nations as the primary political units.

Edmund Burke (1729 – 97) was perhaps the most eloquent Conservative Theoretician. In his great work, 'Reflections on the Revolution in France', he emphasized the importance of prudence and moderation in all our undertakings, especially since "government is a contrivance of human wisdom to provide human wants. Men have a right that these wants should be provided for by this wisdom". Even in his conservatism, however, Burke did not criticize the American Revolution, as he did the French Revolution, for the reason of divergent local context in both situations, stating that "…circumstances give in reality to every political principle its distinguishing color, and discriminating effect. The circumstances are what render every civil and political scheme beneficial or noxious to mankind…" Burke also understood those national and even tribal loyalties, which are at least as important as any ideological factors in the revolutionary movement. Accordingly, this recognition of the hearth is sufficient basis for recognizing local nuances and realities when evaluating a subject even as ennobling as the entrenchment of democracy; a retention of the 'sense of habitual native dignity'.

He distinguished the American Revolution from the French Revolution in that the American revolutionaries in general held a biblical view of man and his tendency towards sin, while the French revolutionaries in the main tried to substitute for the biblical understanding an opportunistic doctrine of human goodness influenced by the philosophies of the rationalistic Enlightenment. In essence, the early Americans were more realistic about human nature than the French Revolutionaries who had an unrealistically optimistic conception of Man. Burke identified the following as the rights that were derived from the Revolution in France, and which were encapsulated in the Bill of Rights:

To choose our own governors
To cashier them for misconduct
To frame a government for ourselves

These were further movements towards the codification of the framework for democracy, as we now know it. Out of fidelity to his Conservative position, however, Burke would prefer a system of succession in England that ensured 'the peace, quiet, and security of the realm'. No tumultuous means of succeeding the monarch. For him, preserving 'a certainty in the succession thereof, the unity, peace, and tranquility of this nation doth, under God, wholly depend.' The emphasis on the protection of the Realm continues to be the Directive Principle of British Statecraft to date. The character and Institutions of the British Parliamentary System owe a tremendous debt to Burke's Political Philosophy.

Burke further defended the British Monarchy when he wrote that: "no experience has taught us that, in any other course or method than that of a hereditary crown, our liberties can be regularly perpetuated and preserved sacred as our hereditary right. An irregular, convulsive movement may be necessary to throw off an irregular, convulsive disease. But the course of succession is the healthy habit of the British Constitution…"

Burke locates religion as the basis of civil society; in effect, the duty to obey God is transferred to the relationship between the people and the Monarch. On the other hand, those entrusted with leadership must "stand in the person (presence) of God Himself, should have high and worthy notions of their function and destination, and their hope should be full of immortality… they should look beyond the praise of the vulgar and the tribulations of the moment, but to a solid, permanent existence, in the permanent part of their nature, and to a permanent fame and glory, in the example they leave as a rich inheritance to the world". This alignment of political duty to a Higher Cause is consistent with the Thomistic Doctrine. To further reinforce this position, Burke writes that " all persons possessing any portion of power ought to be strongly and awfully impressed with an idea that they act in trust; and that they are to account for their conduct in that trust to the one great master, author, and founder of society". When leaders abuse their trust, they are either cut off by a rebellion of their people, or they remain subject to Divine Judgment. This identification of accountability to a Higher Being is expected to rein in some of man's excesses and passions.

It must be stated, however, that Burke did not advocate a perfect democracy, as we know it today; however, his emphasis on the counterpart duties of the Monarch and the people, as well as their submission to God, has substantially influenced our contemporary civic architecture. He clearly identifies society as a contract, with all the implications thereto. This partnership, the ends of which cannot be obtained in many generations is, therefore, between not only those who are living, but among those who are living, who are dead, and those who are to be born. The design of Public Policy in successful democracies is anchored on this solid philosophical foundation. Given the participation of all in this binding partnership, the world on the whole will gain by liberty, without which virtue cannot exist.

For him, the religion of most Americans was "the dissidence of dissent, and the Protestantism of the Protestant Religion, combined with the liberty of liberty"- (that is, dissent from the prerogatives of the Church of England, not from the Law).

For Burke, tyranny of any sort degrades and vitiates humanity. It is salient to mention that he regards democracy as being potentially tyrannous, hence the need to institute mechanisms for the protection of minority rights and views. While we will proceed with a more detailed analysis of the Nigerian democratic experience further down in this work, Burke seems to have foreseen the Nigerian situation when he wrote that "… one of the most decided tyrants in rolls of history, before he could venture, by bribing the members of his two servile Houses (of Parliament) with a share of the spoil, and holding out to them an eternal immunity from taxation, to demand a confirmation of his iniquitous proceedings by an act of Parliament. Had fate reserved him to our times, four technical terms would have done his business, and saved him all this trouble; he needed nothing more than one short form of incantation-- "PHILOSOPHY, LIGHT, LIBERALITY, AND THE RIGHTS OF MEN."

Edmund Burke also underscored the criticality of achieving and sustaining justice in the polity, for peace to endure. He wrote that: "justice is itself the great standing policy of civil society; and any imminent departure from it, under any circumstances, lies under the suspicion of being no policy at all." The instruction for our subsequent analysis is poignant.

It is only fitting that, after a review of Burke's position, we look briefly at Paine who maintained views that were diametrically opposed to Burke's. Paine advanced radical and revolutionary changes, and indeed provided the rhetorical impetus for the American Revolution, advancing an anti-monarchical stance and insisting on the people constituting their own government out of enlightened self-interest. For him, all hereditary succession arrangements are faulty and must be overthrown. He writes that "society in every State is a blessing, but government even in its best state is but a necessary evil; in its worst state an intolerable one; for when we suffer, or are exposed to the same miseries by a government, which we might expect in a country without a government, our calamities are heightened by reflecting that we furnish the means by which we suffer. Government, like dress, is the sign of lost innocence…"

As social and political beings, we need a government to repair the defect of moral turpitude. The emphasis on the public good, which runs through all these views, is a cardinal imperative of the formal civic systems as we now know them. The sense of despair is intensified when the ruling class impose themselves on the people, thereby dramatizing the latter's impotence. Paine regards monarchy (and all variants of hereditary rule, including dictatorships that are not amenable to the periodic renewal of mandate) as both unnatural and oppressive. He writes in 'Common Sense' that "men who look upon themselves born to reign, and others to obey, soon grow insolent; selected from the rest of mankind their minds are early poisoned by importance; and the world they act in differs so materially from the world at large, that they have but little opportunity of knowing its true interests, and when they succeed to the government, are frequently the most ignorant and unfit of any throughout the dominions".

Another major departure from Burke is Paine's negation of the importance of ancestry and fidelity to the hearth. For him, migration and settlement are natural for man, while fixation on extant structures only benefits the monarchy. "Is the power who is jealous of our prosperity and liberty, a proper power to govern us? Common Sense will tell us that the power which hath endeavored to subdue us is, of all others, the most improper to defend us." He also states emphatically that virtue is not hereditary. The undercurrent of allegiance to God, not Man, which is a vital feature of Western Political Thought, also runs through Paine's Philosophy.

Russell Kirk did an excellent job of tracing the roots of American Order in a book of the same title. In the book, he identifies some of these roots as: the Hebrew understanding of the Covenant; Hellenic philosophy; Roman Law and moral concepts; Christian doctrine; English Common Law and Parliamentary Government; Medieval Universities; the Protestant Reformation; seventeenth-century controversies in Church and State; the American colonial experience; and the eighteenth-century political speculation. Again, the reference to a Power higher than oneself is a critical component of his thesis, as indeed of the entire Western Moral Tradition. It is profoundly ironic that, while the Founding Fathers of the United States of America found inspiration in the redemptive biblical stories of freedom from slavery, they were steeped in slavery against others. The Old Testament provided further instruction regarding the justiciability of taking all steps to free oneself from all forms of dominion, while also emphasizing order/ hierarchy, man's fallibility, scholarship, etc. In many ways, therefore, the social realism of the Founding Fathers drew considerably from the Old Testament. It remains to be seen if the simultaneous duplicity involved in some of their other activities also met the standards of the Old Testament.

The choice of "IN GOD WE TRUST" as the motto of the new nation was a significant way of identifying with the Covenants God made with Noah, Abraham, Moses, and the children of Israel. The Aristotelian emphasis on moderation (his Doctrine of the Golden Mean) equally inspired the institution of checks and balances, aimed at compelling moderation and diffused power in governance. The Roman influence was mostly in the areas of Rule of Law, Virtue in Civic Life, Civic Duties, Republicanism, and Separation of Powers. Cicero wrote in his 'The Republic' that: "True Law is the Right Reason in agreement with Nature".

Broken down further, the roots of American Order can be summarized as follows:

- The exemplary life of Christ
- The Middle Ages and Scholasticism
- Reform Period (Self-Reliance, Protestantism, etc.)
- Constitution of the Church and State (private property, Bill of Rights, human equality, etc., etc.)
- Colonial era (austerity, self-reliance, isolation, and freedom)
- French Revolution/ Enlightenment (Montesquieu on Separation of Powers, Checks and Balances, Constitutionalism, ordered liberty, Rousseau, Hume, Hobbes, Burke, and indeed, the cumulative impact of the 18th century Intellectual Movement).

The manifestation of these origins can be seen in the spirit and wordings of both the Declaration of Independence and the Constitution. In fact, the United States was founded on the Western Moral Tradition, with its unique emphasis on the integration of Ethics, Rationality, and Scientific Method into the organization and management of human societies. It needs to be repeated, however, that some of the practices at the founding of this idealistic Nation did not reflect any fidelity to the otherwise noble provenance to which it laid claim. At his first inaugural Address in 1789, George Washington had referred both to American Exceptionalism and the cosmic endorsement of its founding when he wrote *inter alia* that, "…the preeminence of free government be exemplified by all the attributes which can win the affections of all its citizens and command the respect of the world since there is no truth more thoroughly established than that there exists in the economy and course of nature an indissoluble union between virtue and happiness…"

While Benjamin Franklin subsequently acknowledged the existence of tyranny in other lands, he declared that: "tyranny is so established in the rest of the world, that the prospect of an asylum in America for those who love liberty, gives general joy, and our Cause is esteemed the Cause of all mankind… We are fighting for the dignity and happiness of human nature. Glorious is it for the Americans to be called by Providence to this post of honor."

This celebratory hymn was only punctuated by the sharp contrast with the then-extant domestic social policies, which invariably questioned the common divinity of the spark in every human breast, especially when evaluated against the backdrop of Locke's reference to the "indissoluble trinity" of life, liberty, and property for all humans. Blacks and Native Indians did not feel this love…

Kirk correctly recognizes Order as the foundation of development, peace, and harmony. He writes that: "… the human condition is insufferable unless we perceive a harmony, an Order, in existence. Order is the first need of all…" Laws arise out of a Social Order; they are the general rules that make possible the tolerable functioning of an Order. For him, an Order is more important than its laws, and many aspects of any Social Order are determined by beliefs and customs, rather than being governed by Positive Laws. He quotes Richard Hooker who suggested in the sixteenth century that: "without Order, there is no living in public society, because the want thereof is the mother of confusion". In essence, we cannot live in peace with one another without recognizing some principles of Order by which to do justice. It is this Order, which developed as the Western Tradition evolved, that is at the core of the organizing principles of the Western society, including its democratic norms. He regards the American Founding Fathers as basically organizing their

Commonwealth by the Ten Commandments and the books of Leviticus and Deuteronomy, and also as drawing parallels between themselves and the people of Israel and Judah.

The good society is defined by a high degree of Order, justice, and freedom, which are founded on principles that are consensually agreed on, and which work for all. Justice cannot be enforced until a tolerable civil Social Order is attained, nor can freedom be anything better than violence until Order gives us Law. Drawing from this, therefore, it should be clear that there can be no improvement in a society except upon a solid foundation, and that foundation cannot endure unless it is progressively renewed. Western Civilization owes an enormous debt to the Hebraic formulation of Covenants and Laws, both in religious and secular manifestations of this precept.

The idea of an enduring Covenant or Compact, whether between God and people, or between people, manifested during medieval times through Christian teachings, largely informed the Social Order in Britain, and greatly influenced the early settlers in North America (who came from England, in the main). Lincoln recognized Man's Order as drawing from, and subordinate to, a Providential Order. The absence of Order, and the underlying foundation of robust systems and intrinsic fairness, is a major contributory factor for the failure of many States in our contemporary experience.

The prevalence of or, at least, the quest for, Order, which Tocqueville observed during his sojourn in the US can, therefore, be explained by reference to the various factors enumerated and discussed above. His inculcation and amplification of Royer-Collard's thesis about the inevitability of democratization was hugely influenced by his observations in the early United States. The assumption of this inevitability lies at the core of the Neo-Conservative School in the US and will deserve further attention shortly as we proceed. In drawing comparisons with the contemporary French situation, Tocqueville located the concentration of powers in the despotic State (after the Revolution) as a recipe for crisis given the elimination of the provincial and communal rights and privileges of local governments, which had once restrained and decentralized authority in the *Ancien Regime* in France.

Tocqueville also investigated federalism, localism, and especially centralism, while noting the habits and cultures of the early settlers, which conduced to democracy. His characterization of America as "the embodiment of a providentially-sponsored evolution of the democratic spirit as it replaces, in some cases for better and others for worse, the aristocratic ideals that had flourished for centuries in England and France" seems to be a direct source of inspiration for Francis Fukuyama's assertion, two centuries later, of the End of History, though the latter thesis was against the backdrop of the demise of Communism. It is debatable if history has really ended, given the realities in China, the resurgence of Russia, the threat of Islamic terrorism, the unresolved issues in the Korean Peninsula, the crippling impact of public health challenges, the continued softening of fragile States, and the growing threat of extreme politics.

Tocqueville saw America as a system where there was "equality of conditions" and where the European standards of hierarchy and deference were being rapidly replaced by new ideals of individualism and equality. Again, if we accept the minimum *desiderata* of the nominal equality of all humans, then the extant policies and prejudices in America clearly nullify this assertion. Validity can only be conferred on this assumption of equality, by a willful diminution of the humanity of a section of the American society, as it then was. That would be an egregious undertaking to embark upon...

Referencing God, Tocqueville asserted that resisting democracy would amount to resisting the will of God, since the egalitarian ideals of Christ meant that all human beings were, by nature, equal and alike.... While the concept of nominal equality dates back to the Greeks, the basis of that equality, as well as the application thereof, have remained sources of passionate dispute. The Greeks themselves rationalized slavery and excluded women from the polity while theorizing on egalitarianism; Medieval Christianity considered all humans equal in the eyes of God in one breadth but sanctioned slavery and aligned with absolutist monarchies that sat at the top of a rigid pyramid of class privileges; the Hobbesian formulation of a Social Contract accommodated the necessity of authoritarian power to ensure equal protection from the depredation of others, and Rousseau did not tolerate individual dissent from the so-called general Will. While Jefferson advocated universal education as the foundation of participatory democracy, he was opposed to political participation by women, and actually "owned" slaves who were civic non-persons.

While recognizing that the early American settlers were "inhabitants who had no common past, no shared roots, no memories, no prejudices, no routine, no common ideas, no national character, ...", he regarded these factors as being largely responsible for the absence of hierarchy in the original American society, and why democracy could be incubated in the system that was being developed by the twilight of the eighteenth century. He asserts that Americans were born equal, unlike Europeans, who had to contend with centuries-old hierarchical structures, divisions, and prejudices. It is instructive that Tocqueville's purview extended only to white males, since he justified the exclusion of women, blacks, and Native Americans, from politics. While his limited worldview is noted, he re-affirms the Greek concept of democracy, which is: people (as narrowly defined) having sovereignty over themselves and ruling themselves! The idea of the divine rights of kings, which was the norm in Europe of the time, had been replaced by the divine right of the people, "The people reign in the American political world like God over the universe." Aligning with Rousseau, he suggested that, because Americans took an active part in politics, they respected the law, which, in any case, was formulated by themselves for their mutual benefit, and not imposed on them.

Tocqueville was also impressed by the minimal role of the American government in people's lives, and then proceeded to advance historical, geographical, and ideological reasons for this. In any case, he identified Americans' love of freedom and independence as preparing them for an intrinsic suspicion of government. It is clear from this position that the vigilance of the citizenry, Civil Society, and the numerous advocacy groups in the US to this day, has a long-lasting pedigree. He suggested that the absolute sovereignty of the people led to the emergence of average people as political leaders, thereby denying the system of the services of the ablest or the most talented. This is particularly significant since a sovereign entity recognizes no authority higher than itself. Hobbes, Hugo Grotius, and others theorized on sovereignty, but the accepted definition relates to popular sovereignty, as we now know it. Tocqueville also identified the real risk of the tyranny of the majority, which he equated with the despotism of the kings, aristocrats, and the clergy, in Europe.

This tyrannical predilection strongly informed the various devices instituted to ensure proper checks and balances in the system, for example, dividing and dispersing the sovereign power with a bicameral legislature, a veto-wielding Executive and independent Judiciary, Federalism, etc. While these mechanisms could check tyrannous impulses among the majority, he was deeply worried by the scourge of public opinion. We continue to witness the effects of public opinion on Statecraft to this day. When he identifies the "spirit of association", the "spirit of locality", and the "American spirit of provincial liberty", Tocqueville shares the Burkean tradition of fidelity to the hearth. They differ when Tocqueville celebrates the Republicanism of the American people. The individualism he saw in the American ethos is also checked by the paradoxical communalism of the people, as well as their membership in various associations and their active involvement in self-governance which "draws Americans out of themselves, drawing them away from a preoccupation with private interests and turning them to shared common needs and sympathy for others…" Most importantly, their sense of religion checks excessive self-absorption and individualism.

The central place of religion in American life is juxtaposed with the seeming dichotomy between the State and Religion, even while the dominant civic standards are anchored on essential religiosity. For Tocqueville, this immersion of civics in religion is a more enduring way of preserving the role of religion in public life, rather than a recourse to vacuous piety and unhelpful orthodoxy. Indeed, Jefferson, though raised as an Anglican, espoused DEISM, which sought to eliminate the aspects of Christian thought which were contrary to REASON. He stated that the teachings of Christ were the world's greatest doctrine, but that religion had been corrupted by the Clergy. Tocqueville also understands the translation of all these elements of the dominant American character into a strong desire to excel, and especially to make money, thereby authenticating a central thesis of the nexus between Liberal Democracy and *Laissez-Faire* Economics.

Perhaps, a further exploration of this link would be useful at this stage. Private property, which is a consequential derivative of liberty, connotes the recognition of the material sphere in which individuals have some relative dominance, and the capacity and willingness to guarantee the Social Order necessary for the protection of private property and individual initiative as a whole. A political-economic Order which places a premium on the individual, rather than on the group (as in Socialism and Communism) is more likely to result in democracy. This idea will be further dissected under Michael Novak. Suffice it to render, however, that the private ownership of the means and outcome of production is crucial for the Democratic-Capitalist system, though this is not a sufficient condition for democracy. No country is democratic which does not recognize and uphold (in all forms) the right to hold private property. Indeed, Thomas Jefferson based his philosophy on a belief in NATURAL LAW and a faith in the ability of citizens to govern themselves. His vision of an American REPUBLIC based on agriculture and decentralized governmental powers resembled, and was indeed inspired by, Aristotle's ideal *polis*. Rule of Law is a natural consequence of private property; where anarchy or chaos reigns, law does not. Additionally, and most importantly, the equality of all before the law, as well as the integrity of the judicial process, are irreducible ingredients of democracy. No distinctions should be allowed on the basis of race, gender, status, religion, caste, nationality, economic class, or any other parameter whatsoever. But these early Americans conveniently ignored these…

While this position remains a theoretical rendition in most (developing) States, a further reason for adopting the US as a model of democracy is the robustness of its legal system in its totality -- a system that has not always been entirely fair to all races and which is currently under assault in the Trump Presidency. Where the notion of juridical equality is negated in a society, democracy becomes debased to the extent of that aberration. In the latter regard, it will be wrong to characterize that kind of polity as a democratic one. The rights and privileges of some people in that kind of society (including voting rights) are necessarily (at least, in practice) different from those of others, thus providing one of the unspoken/ unconscious justifications for the manipulation of the democratic process, apart from the other incentives. The notion of legal equality is, thus, critical both for democracy and for the capitalist system.

The Civil Rights, which accompany and define democracy, are also natural consequences of the emphasis on the individual, as well as the afore-mentioned discussion of the bearing of the Transcendent on our earthly undertakings and devices. These rights include: freedom of speech, freedom of the Press, freedom of religion, freedom of movement, freedom to engage in any profession or trade of one's choice, and fair adjudicative processes. The recognition of these pristine goals and conduct in approximate fulfillment of their exerting and exacting standards, are adequate confirmations of a democratic system, while the intrinsic denial of the precept, as well as departure from the identified standards in practical life, aggregate and define the absence of democracy.

The right to vote, and for the vote to count as cast, is yet an extension of this philosophical base. In fact, it is this particular right that gives democracy its name; it is derived from Greek language: *demos* (people), and *kratein* (rule). According to Tom Stoppard, **it is not the voting that is democracy; it is the counting.** In a democracy, therefore, the people rule, simply put. Political power in a democracy must, thereby, not be held for the benefit of the rulers or any clique for that matter; it is a trust, the purpose of which is to protect the interests of the citizens.

Having traced the very rich philosophical and historical pedigree of democracy, it will now be proper to discuss its structure, before proceeding to evaluate its foundation and performance in the Nigerian, nay African, context. All successful modern democracies have incorporated constitutional guarantees of individual rights and such structural devices as Separation of Powers, judicial review, and several other checks and balances. Indeed, writing in the FEDERALIST Papers (No.47), James Madison had warned that: "the accumulation of all powers legislative, executive, and judiciary in the same hands ... may justly be pronounced the very definition of tyranny." It is apposite to mention that the judicial review of legislative and executive actions, thus completing the tripod of the institutional Checks and Balances, was established, not by the Constitution, for example, but by the U.S. Supreme Court's 1803 decision in Marbury v. Madison.

Further examples of the extensive network of checks and balances in the US system include: the Congressional power of impeachment, the Senate's duty to "advise and consent" to certain Presidential appointments (in fact, to vet and approve!), the President's right to veto legislation, and Congress' ability to override that veto. The knowledge base and confidence levels of the Operators, the vigilance and enormous powers of the Civil Society, strong Rule of Law, as well as the proven efficacy of the entrenched devices, combine to assure the integrity of the system in the US. It must be recognized, even from prior commentaries in this effort, that universal adult suffrage is a relatively recent development. New Zealand was the first country to grant voting franchise to women in 1893; until the Federal Civil Rights Acts were enacted by the US Congress in the 1960s, several formal barriers were implemented in most US States to ensure the disenfranchisement of blacks and immigrants.

Given the trajectory that democracy has undertaken before arriving at its current status, it must be stated that one's reference to the term means indirect (representative) democracy wherein legislation is enacted by representatives who are elected by the citizenry, and in whose name they act. I do not refer to the numerous variants, which Theodore Gericault captured as: bourgeoisie democracy, Christian democracy, Consociational democracy, Directed (or guided) democracy, Industrial democracy, Popular Democracy (favored by Communists and other Totalitarian Regimes who pretend to represent the "popular Will", as defined by the wielders of power!), or Social democracy.

It must be stated that democracy, when properly conducted, confers authority (agreed legitimacy) upon the elected officials, rather than the mere power of coercion, which has become the norm in democratic aberrations. The need for legitimacy is crucial given the underlying assumption of the sanctity and validity of the Compact between the leaders and the led. When Plato wrote in his political dialogue, '*Crito*', that, by choosing to live in Athens and accepting its protection and the benefits it offers, one had an obligation to obey its laws, he also recognized the integrity of the process that produced the leaders as well as the embedded structures for ensuring their continuing accountability to the people.

After the Renaissance and the social dislocations in Europe arising from the Reformation, the emphasis on the individual witnessed a major surge. Society was no longer a God-given structure within which individuals were expected to fit, but a deliberate social design by rational people in which freely devised political rules and duties would guide civic behavior, indeed a rational justification for the modern State as we know it. The mutuality of responsibilities must, therefore, be recognized for the overall integrity of the system to be maintained. In the minimum, the level of representation and consent is best determined when the following questions are asked:

- Does this government represent me fairly?
- How do I give or withhold my consent for the government to act on my behalf?
- At what point is my consent sought? What triggers it off? Is the fact of being born in a country the only reason for assuming that I have given my consent?
- What if I belong to a minority position? Are there mechanisms in place to protect the minority?
- What is the overall level of integrity of the entire democratic process?

In the absence of a positive resolution of these fundamentals, what ensues is a rape of democracy and of the people.

In a robust democracy, 'the paradox of sovereignty' would typically result when the people– who are the sovereign – are now subject to a ruler who is selected by them to act as their Agent. Rousseau would prefer that the General Will acts as a restraint on the proclivity towards abuse. It is instructive, however, that his assumption of a natural state in which private property (to which he attributes all the ills of the society) would not yet have commenced. Since private property is a part of modern living, we need functioning Institutions to safeguard democracy.

Moreover, Rousseau's approach has the major problem of assuming a unanimity of human wants and desires, that is, the General Will represents the self-interest of all, and that it is the moral and political obligation of every citizen to follow the imposed self-interest. Dictators have relied on this to impose their Will on their people. Self-interest must be freely chosen and is subject to change in the light of new information or experience. How do we even reconcile the rights of the individual with the need for decisive action by the government? Again, how do we retain some form of control over the Leviathan, once created? Locke's treatise on the powers of the people to change their government by due process is the solution.

Are the wishes of individuals a wise and secure basis on which to establish government and law? Democracy is the logical outcome of civic equality. Even if we adopt Bentham's Utilitarianism, democracy remains the best form of government since it coheres with the interest of the majority -- if transparently and objectively determined. The objective value of the collective choice is not as important as the decision itself. Aristotle adopted a discriminatory citizenry ostensibly to ensure that only informed and financially secure people participated in the civic life of the polis.

Kant recommended democracy in which only people who earned their living by business or profession ought to vote. Nietzsche, on his part, completely rejected democracy as being capable of restraining the development of the Strong. It is also questionable if the periodic renewal of leadership mandate through elections does not unduly affect the quality of political decisions. Plato regarded democracy as a form of mob rule, "an unthinking majority". In any case, recent history confirms that representative democracies are mostly carefully managed and manipulated by the political class. John Stuart Mill suggested in his 'harm' principle that not every society was ready for its individual members to assume responsibility for freedom. For "backward" States, he wrote that: "… despotism is a legitimate mode of government in dealing with barbarians, provided the end be their improvement, and the means justified by actually effecting that end. Liberty, as a principle, has no application to any state of things anterior to the time when mankind have become capable of being improved by free and equal discussion…" He failed to provide the parameters for evaluating other societies, but it is safe to assume that his Eurocentric Anthropology substantially infected his worldview and imposed an irredeemable hubris. Vast sections of the world experienced civilization much earlier than Europe, but this fact has not always been acknowledged in propagandistic templates.

JS Mill must have inspired the Imperial Adventure which was portrayed in messianic terms even when the development of England was largely funded from the resources acquired in the so-called Commonwealth! What is common between England and India, Arabia, Nigeria, etc., etc.???

In his provocative book, "The Spirit of Democratic Capitalism", Michael Novak makes a very rigorous and convincing case for a nexus between democracy and economic liberalism. For him, both precepts are best enabled in an environment of trust, respect for human dignity, freedom of thought, mutuality of goodwill, plurality, disposition towards experimentation and invention, and an embedded network of checks and balances, to avert or minimize the human tendency towards abuse. He further asserts that: "the legitimacy of democracy rests upon economic growth and the pervasive optimism it generates." Societies that absolutize power and thought are poor examples of democracy and economic development. Novak situates democracy on a tripod of political, economic, and moral-cultural dimensions, and highlights the organic relationship among these elements. The emphasis on Rule of Law, as well as non-discriminatory and impersonal structures, encourages the release of human inventiveness, while ensuring the even-handed application of laws in proximate reflection of the conceptual equality of all citizens and players.

Adam Smith's "natural system of liberty" was guided by this idea as well. The active participation of the people, indeed the decision of the people, in the choice and form of their governance, is the source of the legitimacy of the government, while the inherent device of periodic elections is an abiding opportunity for self-correction by way of voting out non-performing, corrupt, or non-responsive leaders. The sanctity of the electoral process is, therefore, critical to the integrity of the democratic system.

The Founding Fathers of the United States took additional steps to reinforce this political system meant for imperfect wo/men. The bicameral legislature, three arms of government with constitutionally-guaranteed competing powers and responsibilities, the focused devolution of powers to the States, the constitutional defense against the tyranny of the majority, and the deliberate entrenchment of countervailing forces, etc., are manifestations of institutional and structural ways to optimize the inherent qualities of democracy. A detraction from, or corruption of, these elements necessarily and logically connotes the non-qualification of the end-product as democracy. To the extent that the Founding Fathers recognized that "... to secure these rights, governments are instituted among men, deriving their just powers from the consent of the governed...", the primacy of the electorate is assured, hence the requirement that the government MUST remain accountable to the governed, the source of their mandate and indeed their employers. Practised in its pure form, democracy provides both an ethical and political formula for running human societies.

Prof. Joshua Muravchik writes that: "democracy is at bottom an ethical system, in which the citizens discipline themselves to the principle that it is better to decide things by the right means than to get their own way." Fidelity to these ideals is the minimum condition for democracy to thrive. Implied therein is a spirit of compromise and negotiation, as opposed to exclusionary and absolutist zero-sum calculations. The latter scenario is the formula for predatory democracy.

Civil society plays a pivotal role in democracy; this role is reinforced by experience while the active participation of the eligible citizenry in the democratic experience provides, in a direct manner, the *raison d'être* for the qualification of the term "democracy". Each element reinforces the other in a perfect symphony. It appears quite obvious that, while local realities can, and should, impact the specific structures of democracy and the route thereto, the irreducible defining ingredients must remain inviolate for the political system to qualify as a democracy. However, experience confirms that the wholesale negation of the spirit and conditions of democracy is ignored or subverted by many so-called democratic States once a symbolic element of the instrumental process can be dramatized.

Welcome to Nigeria!

Nigeria's experience with democracy is an eloquent manifestation of this subversion. In this regard, however, it is salient to stress the point that, in especially developing countries, the voice of the vast majority is usually stifled while the oppressive, conniving, predatory but powerful few, project their selfish perspectives as the aggregate and popular views in their respective countries. Civic-republican theories of democracy posit that a robust civic culture enables effective political institutions and improved decision-making processes, thereby leading to overall development.

Putnam, Coffe, Geys, and Cusack, have respectively done extensive work in determining this linkage. It is certain that greater levels of political participation make public officials more responsive to public criticism. Putnam, in particular, insists that the relative "civicness" of a society is the "most important factor in explaining good government within its boundaries." He proceeds to identify four general features of a civic culture that influence accountability and governance: civic engagement; political equality; solidarity, trust and tolerance; as well as social structures of cooperation.

Tocqueville identified participation in civil associations as the most important dimension of a civic culture in advanced democracies. Boix and Posner equally supported this thesis by further emphasizing that the voluntary participation of the citizenry in political affairs and policy engenders trust as well as relieving authorities of "the burden of enforcing compliance." This way, public order becomes an indirect consequence of participatory engagement even while social capital is enhanced. Rice and Feldman wrote in 1997 that "an engaged, active citizenry views itself as a collection of political equals and is more likely to feel an obligation to promote the public good.... especially in homogenous societies."

It is one's considered view, however, that while their postulation might have more resonance in smaller and homogenous societies, the very fact of plurality in most modern societies does not obviate the underlying import of the participation of the citizenry in civic affairs. The United States' successful experience proves this. The question should be asked, though: why do people participate in some societies and not in others? The answer lies at the very core of democratic principles. Dr. Francis Fukuyama wrote in 1995 that higher levels of trust in a society reduce the cost of transactions, enhance the volume of market exchanges, provide an enabling environment for innovation, and eventuate in overall prosperity. The converse scenario obviously damages economic activity and constrains associational life, societal cohesion, and prosperity. A breakdown in both the vertical and horizontal dimensions of trust thus has multiple implications and could very well explain most of the unsavory developments in non-democratic systems. Low levels of mutual respect and trust typically manifest in heightened criminality levels among people. Criminality could be violent crime, political crime, abuse of office, etc.

Dewey argues that: "a public is deficient in political democracy when leaders or policies are imposed by force or unquestioningly accepted by custom or when, however selected, leaders use their positions (in public space) to pursue private ends." Democratic thought has undergone considerable evolution from the classical to the postmodern eras, and has benefited immensely from critical thinkers like Tocqueville, Mill, Hayek, and Jurgen Habermas, among many others. The progressive movement has yielded terms like liberal democracy, democracy and capitalism, classic democracy and representation, participatory democracy, democratic pragmatism and the value of democracy, deliberative democracy, radical pluralism, as well as democracy and globalization. In all of this, Dewey's point remains very valid.

The US experience with democracy is the closest approximation we can find to the ideal. While there has been a tendency for freedom to be occasionally regarded as licence, the fact of the robustness, transparency, success, predictability, and accountability of the system (until 2016, one may add rather sadly) cannot be ignored or trivialized. The efficacy of the inherent checks and balances, the literacy and political awareness levels of the citizenry, the power of the Media and Civic Society, the zero-tolerance for even minor breaches of trust and character by public officials, all combine to strengthen the democratic process. The self-correcting nature of the democratic structures further reinforces the prospects for democracy in the United States. The equal application of the Law to all (except for Policemen who kill black people or President Trump, his family and his friends -- a typical Third World phenomenon), regardless of status, is a direct affirmation of the notional equality of all citizens in the modern era, while the real independence of State Structures from political manipulation and domination by a single individual or a small group (again, until Mr. Trump became the President), nullifies the prospects for personality cultism and abuse. It also helps that living standards are very high. The success of democracy in pluralistic America confirms that plurality is not incompatible with democracy.

Against the backdrop of the continuing debate over the relative importance of the delivery of political goods (such as order, civil rights, and good governance) or economic goods for the sustenance of democracy, Michael Bratton and Peter Lewis are convinced that, even when the economic performance is poor, people's preference for democracy sustains the democratic project. In essence, economic performance has no direct bearing on the sustenance of democracy. While I disagree with their position, it should be in order to dissect their commentary further. They would appear to maintain a different position from theorists like Przeworski, Elster, Dalton, Anderson, and Larry Diamond, who have argued very robustly and convincingly, that economic performance sustains the public trust in the democratic system. In one's view, the majority of the people seek the satisfaction of their basic material needs either simultaneously with, or before, political needs. Maslow and Inglehart support this position.

Bratton and Lewis quote many authorities like Evans and Whitfield, Linz and Stepan, Hofferbert and Klingermann, etc., to support their position that "politics matter more than economics" and note "a surprisingly high degree of political support for the new political regime … despite economic hardship." One will suppose that democratic consolidation must necessarily involve both political and economic performance, and not either in exclusivity.

It is too sweeping and patronizing to suggest that, for some societies, an obsession with democratic ideals mutes the consideration of the related performance of the economy. In fact, in those very societies, the average standard of living is very low while the brazen corruption, incompetence, and impunity of the political leadership, inspire deep-seated distrust in the political system and an understandable focus on meeting basic economic needs. Democracy becomes a distant philosophical concept when the more immediate need to feed remains outstanding. Common political goods like security, justice, liberty, welfare, rule of law, etc., are as important to the human heart as the natural imperatives of satisfying human material and biological needs. Moreover, Statistics can be used to justify any position at all. Using Nigeria as a Case Study, Bratton and Lewis suggest that the demand for democracy can "readily coexist with the imperfect delivery of certain economic goods". More details are required to validate this generalization. Where did they conduct this research? What was the lot size? How representative of the society was their base of interviewees (or did they just interview Government Officials and their cronies)? What age segment(s) were polled? What was the economic status of those interviewed? In all, political and economic dividends of democracy are not mutually exclusive. Moreover, the clinical treatment and reification of "lived" experiences and reduction of same to percentages, fractions, and abstracts (e.g. standardized regression Beta coefficient, linear-additive equations, residual coefficients, sole dependent variable, explanatory efficiency, etc.) do not show a proper understanding of the nuances of every society, or of the grave disappointment Nigerians feel over the successive failure of governance (especially as reflected in their standards of living). These writers are totally wrong in their summation that "ordinary Nigerians do not draw a closer connection between the control of corruption and the construction of democracy."

Thankfully, Dr. Gizachew Tiruneh of the University of Georgia applies more rigor in his Paper titled "Towards Normal Democracy: Theory and Prediction with Special Reference to the Developing Countries". While acknowledging that no perfectly egalitarian state can ever exist, he asserts that: "the open-ended nature of democratic development is mainly a function of economic development, the political process, and external factors." He essentially shares the fundamental points made by Michael Novak in his earlier cited book, namely, that an increasingly growing middle-class plays a more active role in their political governance, the inherent tension between individual liberty and equality will not allow an equal distribution of power, modernization theory explains the link between socioeconomic and political systems, and a large middle class stabilizes the political system. He relies variously on Aristotle, Lenski, Gerhard, Seymour Martin Lipset, and Huntington to support his reasoned position that economic development reinforces democracy. The underlying liberty cuts across both streams while material comfort enhances one's connectedness with the system.

The Aristotelian formulation sought optimality in income distribution: an alignment with the upper class for its wealth and with the majority lower class for its numbers, as any rule by only the wealthy or the poor will generate considerable systemic tension. This is a further case for the expansion of the middle class, which only an effective economic policy will accomplish. In the same way that it will be intrinsically contradictory to talk about democracy in a Communist State, an environment of avoidable poverty is incompatible with the sustenance of democracy in its essential form. Democracy thrives best where education, innovation, private enterprise, and trade are encouraged. For Przeworski and Limongi, "the effect of economic development on democratic survival or stability is even more valid and stronger than its impact on transition to democracy."

Since the ideal democracy connotes an equal distribution of power, which is fundamentally impossible, some theorists have sought other names for "democracy", as we know it presently. Dahl recommended "polyarchy" or majority rule but this never gained ground. Noting the emotive appeal of the term "democracy" despite the inability to achieve equality in the distribution of power, Tiruneh defines democracy, as we practise it, as "a political procedure that allows the presence of political rights, civil liberties, and a majoritarian decision-making or voting mechanism, and which permits the continuous achievement of a more equal distribution of political power." It must be pointed out, though, that, in reality, it is the elected leaders (and not the majority electors) who make policy decisions in a democracy, with the benefit of the input of the Civic society (especially in advanced or successful democracies).

Can Democracy be Exported?

History is replete with examples of both successful and unsuccessful attempts by the US to export democracy to other lands. While the operative and instrumental elements of democracy can be exported, it will be foolhardy to expect absolute uniformity in the democratic route, form and content across the world. Local cultures, values, power dynamics, literacy levels, regard or otherwise for laws, religious pressure and content, demographics, economic performance, history, aggregate trust levels, etc., will necessarily impact the growth or impediment of democracy in each society.

The fact that a government "must be suited to the habits and genius of the people it is to govern" is further incentive for the proper understanding of those people, so that the desired outcome grows organically in their society without a patina of obvious imposition. Since the essentials of democracy cohere with human nature, the likely result is most probably different positions along the spectrum of democracy by different societies. The desire for democracy is real, but man-made obstacles would usually impede its development. Writers on both sides of the divide have argued extensively over the exportability or otherwise of democracy.

The essential political ingredients which the overwhelming majority desire in their government are: a direct reflection of the choice of the majority in electing the government, accountability of the government, transparency in governance, liberty, resultant legitimacy of the government, periodic elections for validation or correction of mandates, tenure limits, Rule of Law, recognition of their various inalienable rights, delivery of public goods in an equitable and optimal manner, etc. The Founding Fathers of the United States recognized this form of government as a theory of human nature and that "to secure these rights, governments are instituted among men, deriving their just powers from the consent of the governed." Having traced the theoretical, historical, and philosophical origins of democracy, it remains to evaluate the Nigerian democratic foundation and experience. However, before this task is undertaken, it will be helpful to quickly refresh our memory with some Continental context. One recognizes that you have been on this journey with me for a while, and some of the points might just naturally have been forgotten or lost in all the narrative.

African Continent: A Revolving Work-in Progress

The modern history of Africa can be traced to the Scramble and Partition of the Continent at the Berlin Conference of 1884, among European Powers. Following the armistice that ended the First World War in 1918, the League of Nations assigned the so-called German territories in Africa to the victorious powers as spoils of war. All of this was done remotely in Europe and without consulting with the affected people. This was underscored by the comments made by the then British Prime Minister, Mr. Salisbury (this writer chooses to not add LORD as an appellation to any mortal's name!), to the effect that "we have been giving away mountains and rivers and lakes to each other, only hindered by the small impediment that we never knew exactly where they were." Britain traded the North Sea Island of Heligoland with the Germans for Zanzibar, and parts of northern Nigeria with the French for fishing rights off Newfoundland. France exchanged parts of Cameroun with Germany in return for German recognition of the French protectorate over Algeria. At the end of the Scramble for Africa, some 10,000 African distinct political units and peoples had been amalgamated into forty European colonies and protectorates. This was enforced in Africa by treaty and conquest.

This assignation was portrayed in messianic and altruistic terms as "a sacred trust of civilization" involving the administration of African colonies until they were able to "stand on their own feet in the arduous conditions of the modern world." In essence, the colonial powers were not only to govern, but also develop the colonies (most of which were very rich in resources) into functioning members of the international system – politically and economically according to the extant capitalist model of the Nation State, not out of any declared altruism, but purely for exploitation of their resources. Such paternalism and arrogance! A natural consequence of this attitude towards

Africa was a reversal of its developmental experience, and a deliberate conditioning of the new elite class being groomed in the image of the West.

The colonial assumption of superior knowledge in all things was derived from the affirmations of the late-nineteenth century Europe, and also from the faulty assumption that Africa had no history or culture worthy of that definition until the contact with Europeans who meekly accepted the "sacred trust of civilization." The accumulation of achievements in commerce, Christianity, and military force gave Europe an inflated self-image, as buoyed even by Social Darwinism, which put Europeans at the top of the evolutionary ladder with Africans at the bottom. The colonialists deliberately "set about inventing African traditions for Africans", including the formulation of an "Imperial Monarchy" which was propagandistically invested with "theology" of the triple absolutes, namely, omniscience, omnipresence, and omnipotence.

While Africans would naturally, like all others, have adjusted their traditions when those ceased to optimize aggregate benefits, the sheer erosion of all learned habits and the imposition of a foreign personality, continue to have serious implications to this day. No tradition lasts forever anywhere. By constructing an image of Africa permanently steeped in its past, the colonialists aimed to convey the persona of a Continent living in a reconstructed moment of its past, and totally averse to all forms of progress. The employment of the term, "tribe" is a clear example of this tendency. The term has been in use since Roman times, but the Oxford English Dictionary claims that it was coined in 1886 (just two years after the Berlin Conference!), meaning "no national life, much less civilization," while only Africans are depicted as those who organize their societies along only ethnic lines. All other people have Nation-States!!! Contemporary history informs us that the tension between the Serbs and Croats, Israelis and Palestinians, the Irish and the English, are directly traceable to ethnic rivalry.

Indeed, was the holocaust by Nazi German against Jews not driven by ethnic hatred and the push for "ethnic purity?" However, these are reflected as religious and nationalist differences! When the Massai and Kikuyus engage, the Zulus and Xhosas fight, the Yorubas, Igbos, and Hausas seek to destroy one another, or the Hutus carry out genocide against Tutsis, these are regarded as the "proof" of African barbarity and lack of civilization! The imposition of only tribal identity on Africans meant that Chiefs must be found for each tribe, who would be amenable to colonial manipulation and direct control. The reinforcement of ethnic identities also engendered an "us-them" mindset with the endless rendition in bloodshed, while the new chiefs were gradually alienated from their own people without being fully accepted by the colonialists, a tendency that has been carried over to this day. This, in addition to the structural and institutional inadequacies in Africa, has contributed significantly to the pervasive culture of impunity and lack of accountability on the Continent.

Since the chiefs did not owe their mandate to the people, why should they be accountable to them??? Herein we find a fundamental negation of the essence of democracy. To complete the conditioning of the new elite, a focused program of "selective acculturation" had to be implemented, with the result that they learnt less and less about their past and country, even while these Africans gained immeasurable knowledge about "how we defeated the Spanish Armada in 1588" and how "the Gauls, our ancestors, had blue eyes." Indeed!!!

The impetus for the independence of African States can be attributed to several factors, including: the Leninist rhetorical support of all colonized people after the Bolshevik Revolution of 1917, the exposure and insight of the African soldiers who fought in WWI and WWII on behalf of the colonial powers, the new confidence of the "educated elite", as well as the conditions attached to the Marshall Plan extended to Europe by the US after WWII. Specifically, Clause Three of the Atlantic Charter negotiated between President Roosevelt and a desperate British Prime Minister Churchill stated that: "They (the British and United States governments) respect the right of all peoples to choose the form of government under which they live; and they wish to see sovereign rights and self-government restored to those who have been forcibly deprived of them."

Despite the clear terms of this provision which Churchill reluctantly signed to elicit US Lend-Lease strategic support at a time Britain was virtually bankrupt and threatened with an imminent German invasion, Churchill would return to London and proclaim that the relevant section of the Atlantic Charter only applied to the "States and Nations of Europe … under the Nazi yoke." He also stated that "I did not become his Majesty's first minister in order to preside over the liquidation of the British Empire", as if they had a right over others and their resources! Inasmuch as Roosevelt insisted on the spirit of the said Charter, it should be noted that a supplementary document sharpened and clarified the real US position, which called for "access on equal terms to the trade and to the raw material of the world", thereby evidencing motives less noble than altruism or high principle.

All of this possibly led the African delegates to the sixth Pan-African Congress in Manchester to declare that "… we are unwilling to starve any longer while doing the world's drudgery, in order to support, by our poverty and ignorance a false aristocracy and a discarded imperialism … therefore, we shall complain, appeal and arraign. We will make the world listen to the facts of our condition. We will fight in every way we can for freedom, democracy, and social betterment…" Winston Churchill, the overrated and racially-bigoted coveter, notwithstanding the glorification by latter-day inheritors of a sullied inheritance, was also a raving drunkard. He had said most notably, for example, that "I have taken more out of alcohol than alcohol has taken out of me", and also that "When I was younger, I made it a rule never to take strong drinks before lunch. It is now my rule never to do so before breakfast."

Against the backdrop of the patronizing resistance of France, Britain, and Belgium to the independence of African States, and the global bifurcation that attended the Cold War, the United Nations General Assembly declared in October 1960 that "unpreparedness should not be a pretext for delaying independence", thereby opening a floodgate of independence across Africa.

It is axiomatic that, but for the Cold War and possibly the Second World War, the independence of African States would have been very difficult in the extreme. The newly-independent States were handed over to those who had been trained by the departing Europeans; this group of emergent African leaders were, in the main, not politically, philosophically, and psychologically developed for the scale of responsibilities thrust on them in the new political system that was the norm.

In addition, they occupied buildings abandoned by colonialists, assumed the air and absolute powers of the colonial administrators, without any corresponding restraint on their powers, or even the participation of the majority in the political process. Africa's experience with democracy has, altogether, been very depressing, with the cyclicality of military interventions and poor democratic norms being the defining character.

In many respects, this new elite class was "elected" into office by their people, who saw the attractions of democracy as consisting in the prospect of having a local representative (one of their own) at the center of power – a rich and influential man (mostly men at the time) who would "capture" a share of what was available in the distant city-center and bring it home. These were products of the village, whose obligations to the new nation as a whole were, at best, only secondary (where existent at all). Over time, however, these people have been serving only themselves, as is only natural in that kind of context. The incubatory and political processes that enabled toleration, civic stature and vigilance, acceptable political behavior, and accountability, were skipped in the rush to attain independence. By 1991, only seven out of the then forty-five African States had a semblance of democracy.

It was only Botswana that held regular competitive elections (but then, Botswana is the size of a county in the US and is constituted by people of common linguistic and ancestral identity – the Tswanas). One-party rules, transformation of Heads of State into Presidents-for-Life, large-scale and pervasive corruption across board, physical annihilation of political opponents, privatization of the instruments of coercion, etc., are some of the better-known features of governance on the Continent. Access to the monopolistic control of State resources remains the overarching incentive for the competition for power, with the accompanying expectation of alignment with foreign interest groups for the exploitation of their people and resources.

In most of Africa, therefore, the pain of injustice under colonialism has been replaced by the usurpation of the levers of that injustice by locals. The injustices of the colonial system inspired nationalist movements that united diverse peoples only temporarily for the purpose of attaining independence; once this threshold was met, the festering and unresolved cleavages became manifest. The weak foundations of the artificially-constructed and imposed States unraveled along mostly ethnic lines, with the struggle for power and wealth assuming truly desperate dimensions, while national issues are unattended to, and lingering injustices remain unresolved.

The role of Africa during WWII, and subsequent history, remains under-mentioned. During the Second World War, for example, the numerous natural resources of Congo were exploited by the Belgian colonialists to sustain Belgium's independent existence as the resultant funds provided 85% of the funding for the London-based government-in-exile when Germany had over-run Belgium. African colonies contributed over 750,000 troops to the war being fought over purely European politics but was tagged the World War! Over half of this number became casualties. With German disruption of access to established sources of materials, Africa provided all the iron, zinc, tin, copper, uranium, silicon, etc. that the Allied Forces used in prosecuting the war.

These materials were simply excavated, processed, and exported to Europe as part of the fabled Commonwealth, with no payment to the owners! The rail lines that were built in Africa at this time were, therefore, for this purpose, and not for the purpose of boosting the infrastructural base of the Continent. Attempts at activities of this nature would go by other names presently. The lingering inequities of this enterprise explain some of the systemic distortions across Africa. For a lot of people in Africa, there is a lot of dishonesty and inconsistency involved when European and American citizens and countries complain about losses they incur on "sweetheart" deals and corruption solicitation schemes.

The subsequent and continuing mantra of globalization is immediately traceable to the immediate post-World War attitudes of the West. Clement Attlee, the Prime Minister, Ernest Bevin, Foreign Secretary, and Sir Clifford Cripps, Chancellor of the Exchequer, saw the development of "our" African resources as of critical importance and a major consideration in planning the recovery of Britain's shattered economy. Field Marshal Montgomery stated that British living standards should be maintained by Africa's minerals, raw materials, land, and cheap coal. It is significant that Globalization involves the intensification of economic, political, social, and cultural relations across borders (mostly among unequals), with the effect of weakening the integrity of the nation-state which had, until now, been propagated as the best unit of international relations.

When Africans have approached the IMF and the World Bank for Economic Planning Advice and Loans (even as their stolen funds are in Western Banks), the conditionalities and prescriptions have always included: devaluation of the local currency, liberalization of trade on terms favorable to Western interests, removal of subsidies, privatization and commercialization on imposed templates with low local congruence, reduction in government expenditure, wage freeze (even though Africans earn sub-survival wages), free repatriation of profits by transnational corporations, anti-strike laws (to stifle protests against abuses), removal of minimum wage laws, increased borrowing interest rates, and reduced spending on social services. How do these enable governance and the entrenchment of democracy?

It is important to immediately reflect the ignorance and conceit which characterize the mainstream depiction of Africa in the Western world. When the term "dark Continent" is used, it is not just with reference to the color of the people of Africa, but rather a propagandistic and linguistic portrayal of a Continent where all the terrible things happen, and where the darkness of humanity is immanent. Africa is not just about general poverty, lack of development, aid dependence, debt, corruption, civil wars, lack of democracy, and failed States. The truth is very far from it. The fact that ALL humanity has proven over time to be imperfect is conveniently ignored, while Africa is typically depicted as being the home place of all barbarity, where people are inherently less civilized than the rest of the world. But civilization and humanity started in Africa!

As the eminent Africologist, John Reader, renders it, that people have behaved terribly in Africa is undeniable, but this is not an exclusive African tendency. Civilization, as an expression of cultured behavior, is a very transitory feature of the human story. Civilization is not a predetermined consequence of human progress, as the Victorians believed, with Anglo-Saxons leading the way, the rest of the world following in their wake, with Africans straggling several centuries behind.

Indeed, civilization is a protective skin of enlightened self-interest that societies develop as they learn to regulate their interactions with the environment and with one another, to the long-term benefit of all. The human capacity for barbarity lies just beneath its surface, as early Greek and Thomistic philosophers recognized. If anything, humans everywhere are forever capable of doing unspeakable harm to one another when short-term exploitation takes over from long-term regulation, when the notion of accountability is set aside and the promise of the future is dimmed by the challenges of current survival. Accordingly, African, as all other, tragedies, diminish us all.

Part of the depiction of Africa is that of a Continent with an exclusivity of corruption. While corruption of various forms has definitely wrought a major damage to the Continent, the imposed leaders of Africa have ready accomplices in Governments and Corporations of the West (and, increasingly, China), while most of the ill-gotten wealth is stashed away in Western and Chinese banks, invariably never transferred to the respective families or the originating country when the depositor-tyrant dies.

The Speaker of the Ohio State Assembly, Mr. Larry Householder, was arrested a few days ago by the FBI, over a $60m bribe he allegedly received from an Energy company. Halliburton, Shell, ENI, Siemens, Julius Berger, Pfizer, and the various Oil Corporations, have been implicated in various corruption scandals across Africa. Levels of corruption have not been affected by democracy or economic liberalism. What amount of corruption competed with slavery and colonialism? Is corruption an African word? While corruption is more discreet in Asia, and mostly confined to corporate dealings or the euphemistic political lobbying in the West (until the trumpian brazenness and crudity), it is more overt in Africa, due to the absence of objective restraining mechanisms.

In the US, we have earmarks, pay-to-play politics, lobby groups, pork barrel projects, campaign contributions, Russian help in presidential elections, ponzi schemes, etc., and not corruption! Guy Arnold characterizes corruption into three forms: venal corruption – the demand for bribes and payments for services or contracts; patronage corruption – nepotism and the provision of jobs or kickbacks for supporters, and political corruption – the manipulation of elections and constitutions against the existing rule of law to perpetuate an individual's or party's hold on power. He refers Western business and venal corruption as working very closely, even as they remotely sponsor political corruption across Africa. It is clear that the inadequacy of the structures to deal with corruption in Africa, largely explains the attribution of Continental exclusivity of this problem.

The average African has as much aversion to corruption as any European or American; the direct consequences of corruption are felt daily in Africa. In the absence of specific information or other forms of empowerment, the average people are powerless to confront this menace. They require the assistance of established democracies by exposing funds laundered through their financial system, by strengthening Civil Institutions, and by reducing the haste with which they recognize the products of rigged elections/ stolen mandates. The report of the Commission on Global Governance, our Global Neighborhood, states *inter alia* that, "... vast sums that should have been in government treasuries to be spent on national objectives were siphoned off to be invested abroad. The people of these countries were effectively robbed. The great powers that supported corrupt rulers in the full knowledge of their venality must share the blame. So must the banks that help stash away ill-gotten funds and launder the money of drug dealers and other criminals...", including government criminals. By aligning with characters like Mobutu of Zaire and his several replicates on the Continent, for example, against their own people, the US and her allies effectively undermined their own moral authority in Africa, and progressively weakened their ability to influence events.

Writing in 'This House Has Fallen', Karl Maier captures the similarity between Nigeria's post-independence leaders and the colonialists in their rapaciousness. For him, the process of extracting wealth from Africa, which was the starting point of colonialism, now continues with Africans as the prime movers with the West as more passive recipients – with the majority of Africans being the losers in either scenario. While Arnold quotes Chabal and Daloz in suggesting that a little dose of corruption must exist in every system, and the operative lever being that the fruits of corruption be suitably redistributed in order to minimize the abhorrence of corruption, one has to respectfully submit that corruption, in all its forms, is intrinsically wrong.

The redistribution of stolen wealth does not vitiate its essential wrongness. While the Report further states that strengthening democracy and accountability is the antidote to corruption, and that "while there are no guarantees against corrupt practices, as so many democracies confirm, a free society with vigorous independent media and a watchful civil society raises the chances of the detection, exposure, and punishment of corruption", it must be stated that democracy and its norms must be protected in their essence and purity, and not just in form, for the applicable conditions to be relevant. In addition, enabling conditions like over-centralization, limited administrative capabilities, laxity and corruption of tax administration, privatization of the Military and Security Services, Judicial Corruption and connivance, reward-punishment matrix in a society, and authoritarianism, must also be addressed.

Nigeria: An Overview

Nigeria attained independence from Britain on October 1, 1960. In terms of physical size, Nigeria is about 1/10th the size of the United States, but with a high population density especially in the urban areas. With an indicative population of about 200 million people, making it the seventh most populous country on earth, Nigeria has at least 250 distinct languages with many more dialects. It is also the 4th largest democratic State by definition, though her Democracy Index is very low. The population is broadly split 55%: 45% between Christians and Muslims, while it is common for adherents of both faiths to combine their mainstream religion in a syncretic manner with elements of their traditional religion as well. Geographically, most of the Muslims are in the North while the South is dominated by Christians. At independence, Nigeria adopted the Parliamentary System in practice in Britain. The Regions had relative fiscal and political autonomy, even while the competition among them inspired the development programs they implemented. The Northern Region generated most of its revenue from the export of groundnuts, the West from exporting cocoa, while palm produce was the primary product in the East.

Some of Nigeria's identity politics and fractious pursuit of power are traceable to pre-independence realities. Please permit me to repeat the quotes that started this section. Nigeria's first Prime Minister, who was a prominent member of the Northern political establishment, Abubakar Tafawa Balewa, had remarked in 1948 that "Since 1914, the British government has been trying to make Nigeria into one country, but the Nigerian people themselves are historically different in their backgrounds, in their religious beliefs and customs, and do not show themselves any willingness to unite… Nigerian unity is only a British invention." In a book published in 1947, the Yoruba leader, Obafemi Awolowo, who dominated the politics of the Western region for over thirty years, wrote that: "Nigeria is not a nation. It is a mere geographical expression. There are no "Nigerians" in the same way as there are "English", "Welsh", or "French". The word "Nigerian" is merely a distinctive appellation to distinguish those who live within the boundaries of Nigeria and those who do not."

As is the case in most other African countries, Britain left the people with a very weak national identity. Large-scale national organizations did not exist before colonization because the different people had existed and functioned parallel to one another, and the first indigenous experience with this involved exercising political control over the new State post-independence! The immediate challenges should have been building a sense of community among the disparate people of the new country – instilling a sense of identity among the people in order to engender voluntary allegiance to the State, enhancement of the capacity to foster economic, social, and political development well into the future, and also the nurturing and sustenance of democracy and civil liberties. The experience, however, has been that the boundaries established by the colonialists did not recognize local realities, with the result of their unraveling after independence. Ready reference can be made to India/ Pakistan, the *pot pourri* in Nigeria, etc. The colonial legacy thus nullified the salient terms of the Versailles Treaty, which emphasized self-determination.

While the Hausas of the North had an entrenched feudal system, the Yoruba of the West practised limited government in their traditional institutions. The Igbos of the East were very republican, and yet the British merged these three, together with over two hundred and fifty minority groups on a uniform template of local kinship and assumed amity. The name of the country was even chosen by Flora Shaw, an English woman who later married Frederick Lugard, the then Chief Colonialist in Nigeria. The country became an entity in 1914, when the Northern and Southern Protectorates and Lagos were merged by fiat under a single colonial administration. The British practised Indirect Rule in the North through the Emirs, who collected tax from their people on behalf of the British, and invariably assumed a superior status on account of the colonial recognition. This formed the basis for the subsequent political devices, which resulted in literally handing over the entire country to the North at independence. At least, they could be trusted by the British to protect the interests of the departing colonial power.

In the South, however, the people resented all imposed cultures, and had to be controlled by force. The fiscal inequities involved in awarding control of resources to Northerners (especially oil and gas in the South) even as the North contributes nothing to the national treasury, is at the core of the recurring tension in the country. Another point to note about Nigeria is that the various ethnic groups are geographically-based, even as people settle outside their home-regions, for economic reasons. States are composed of largely homogenous local citizens, while all settlers (and contributors to their economy and development) are formally debarred from seeking office or public employment since they are not "indigenes". The houses they build, the tax they pay, their investments in these "other" lands, etc., attract no such discrimination. This further demonstrates some of the deep issues confronting the country. It would be similar to a situation where, for example, in the US, all German-Americans are the natives of Ohio, Irish-Americans occupy Massachusetts, and Polish-Americans are the indigenes of Chicago in exclusivity.

Immediately after independence in 1960, career in the Military was not prestigious, and did not appeal to the cadre of young men from the South who had embraced Western education. The British, who had worked with the Emirs in the North to ensure that Western education was not introduced in the Region (in order to not empower the people with ideas that would threaten the feudal system), encouraged the North to fill the military rank and file with their young men. This background of their lack of intellectual sophistication, and primordial loyalty, informed the subsequent roles they played in the political life of the young country.

The initial Officer Corps was composed mostly of educated Officers from the Southern part of the country; young men from the South, who would have staffed the rank and file, preferred to advance their studies for careers in the Diplomatic Service, Civil Service, Academia, or the Professions. Out of Nigeria's sixty years since independence, the military (either in uniform or in civilian clothes) have been in power for over forty-two years to date. Some of their longest monopolies on power include 1966-1979, 1983-1999, 1999-2007, and 2015 - date (2020 and continuing to 2023).

Consequent upon the violence that attended the 1963 and 1966 elections, the Military intervened in the political process of the country. The immediate fallouts and especially the pogrom carried out against the Igbos (of the South East -- 100% Christians) residing in the North, led to the three-year civil war, which lasted from 1967 to 1970. The attempt by the Igbos to secede from Nigeria in order to ensure their safety and protection was accordingly defeated, with the active involvement and participation of Britain, Russia, and Egypt -- at the prompting of the majority-Muslim feudal North. From a strategic standpoint, it must be stated that the discovery of oil in commercial quantities in the larger Eastern Region inspired the strident unity of effort by the other ethnic groups to reverse the secession of the Igbos. It is worthy of emphasis that, by colonial design, the vast majority of the non-commissioned Officers and, subsequently, the Officer Corps, of the Army came from the North. Apart from the three-month Ironsi regime in 1966 (he was killed by Northern Officers while serving as Head of State), the only other time a Southerner was a Military Head of State, was when General Olusegun Obasanjo, as the number two in the hierarchy, was promoted to Head of State when the incumbent, Gen. Murtala Muhammed, was assassinated in a bloody coup on February 13, 1976. Obasanjo's fulfillment of a commitment to hand over to civilians in 1979 was, therefore, more out of a sense of self-preservation than honor, contrary to popular opinion.

Nigerian Chief Executives, 1960-2009

Dates	Name	Title	Ethnicity	Cause of Departure
1960- January 1966	Tafawa Balewa	Prime Minister	Hausa-Fulani (North)	Coup (killed)
1963- January 1966	Nnamdi Azikiwe	Ceremonial President (appointed)	Igbo (East)	Coup (removed)
January – July 1966	Aguiyi Ironsi	Military Head of State	Igbo (East)—the most senior Officer in the Army	Coup (killed)
July 1966 - 1975	Yakubu Gowon	Military Head of State	Tiv/ Hausa (North): the illiterate recruits took over	Coup (removed)
1975-1976	Murtala Muhammed	Military Head of State	Hausa-Fulani (North)	Coup (killed)
1976 - 1979	Olusegun Obasanjo	Military Head of State	Yoruba (South West); 2nd in command to the assassinated Head of State	Handed power to civilian administration
1979 - 1983	Shehu Shagari	President	Hausa-Fulani (North)	Coup (removed)
1983-1985	Muhammed Buhari	Military Head of State	Hausa-Fulani (North)	Coup (removed)
1985- 1993	Ibrahim Babangida	Military Head of State	Gwari/ Hausa (North)	Forced out of office
Aug. – Nov. 1993	Ernest Shonekan	Interim Head of State (appointed by the Military)	Yoruba (Southwest)	Coup (removed)
1993 – June 1998	Sani Abacha	Military Head of State	Kanuri (North)	Died in office
June 1998 – May 1999	Abdulsalam Abubakar	Head of State	Gwari/ Hausa (North)	Handed power to military-turned civilian former Head of State
May 1999- May 2007	Olusegun Obasanjo (was also Head of State in 1976-1999)	President	Yoruba (Southwest)	Handed power after the worst election in history, and after failing to perpetuate himself in office
May, 2007 – 2010	Umar Yar'Adua; Doubtful legitimacy. Younger brother of Obasanjo's No. 2 while a Military Head of State	President	Hausa Fulani (North)	Died in office
2010 - May 2015	Goodluck E. Jonathan	President	Ijaw; owners of the oil	Lost in an election and conceded to Buhari
May 2015 - (2020)	Muhammadu Buhari, former Military Head of State	President	Fulani (North)	While he may have won his first term, the second election in 2019 was a major fraud

It is clear from this table that the preferred method of succession in Nigeria is by *coup d'etat*, while the disproportionate hold of the non-contributing North on power is a continuing source of anger among the people. Military rule and expansion of military coups are politically-driven processes. Democratically-elected governments (when the process is fool-proof) following autocratic regimes, therefore, typically combine gradualism, tactfulness, diligence, and strict adherence to democratic values in their dealings with the military, to reduce the incentive for a comeback. The assumption here is that the military and civilian political classes are different entities. When they are part of the same group, the recommended approach becomes moot. Politics in Nigeria remain a game of big money, treachery, and violence; accordingly, the retired military officers and senior civil servants who made substantial amounts through corruption during their many years in government, continue to exert enormous influence on the political system. When they are unable or unwilling to assume political office, they recruit and impose acolytes, on the condition that the State Treasury is made available to these so-called Godfathers *a la* Sicilian Mafia style.

The large-scale exploitation of oil resources and the oil boom of the early 1970s, effectively led to a major reversal in the focus, structure, and performance of the country. Oil is regarded as national patrimony! It is ironic that, while more States were created ostensibly for the devolution of power, and while the country is called The Federal Republic of Nigeria, the reality has been a reinforced unitary system, while traditional rulers (notably in the Muslim North) continue to wield disproportionate influence. Progressively, the autonomy of the erstwhile Regional economies ended, reliance on centrally-shared oil and tax revenue grew exponentially (to date), and the competition for political leadership, especially at the center, assumed very dangerous dimensions. Nigeria remains a mere formal Federalism while the reality emphasizes the centrism of the Military Structure. The strident clamor for a true Federalism by mostly the South, has not been addressed.

Access to power in Nigeria is access to unimaginable powers and wealth, without the constraints and accountability that are integral parts of the democratic system in the US, until Trump emerged. Africans understand Trump's impulses better than Americans because they have always been ruled, not governed, by Trumps. Nigeria is presently the sixth largest oil producer in the world, ranks within the first five countries with the largest gas reserves, has the second largest certified bitumen reserves in the world, and has a rich reserve of several other diverse minerals and natural resources. The quantum of corruption, inefficient allocation of resources, white-elephant projects, etc., has grown in direct proportion with the public revenue stream. Transparency International estimates that a minimum of $500 Billion of oil revenues has been siphoned or stolen by public officials since 1973. This is apart from similar treatments extended to other sources of public revenue like Customs Duties and Tax Collections. The result is that all the progress made in the immediate post-independence period has been reversed, while the impunity of the looters has effectively eroded values among the citizenry. Oil has become a curse for Nigeria. The Guardian wrote a Report on the extensive environmental damage (done by the major Oil companies like Shell, Chevron, Texaco, Exxon-Mobil, Conoco, Total, etc.) in the Niger Delta, with the result that the locals, having been denied the benefits of their resources, cannot even engage in subsistence farming and fishing as well (**Figures 38, 39, 40, and 41*). The Report can be accessed through this link: *https://www.theguardian.com/global-development/2019/dec/06/this-place-used-to-be-green-the-brutal-impact-of-oil-in-the-niger-delta*

This is worse than blood money. When your oil stock rises, this is the source. Congratulations. While primary blame resides with the oil companies that operate in this manner, final responsibility must be attached to the Nigerian (and African) government officials at federal, state, and local levels who allow this to fester with impunity -- simply because of the bribes they collect and the so-called opportunities these oil companies make available to them and their families. How is this different from slavery? Wherein lies the tangible expression of political independence and sovereignty?

Despite official propaganda and colossal amounts officially earmarked for projects, Nigeria's infrastructure in 2020 has not improved very much beyond the foundational and elementary jobs done by the military in the early 1970s. The only visible addition has been the development of Abuja as a capital city, but even that has been a major conduit for wholesale corruption. In the midst of all this looting, most Nigerians lack access to basic medical facilities, the infrastructure is collapsing, the public schools lack basic tools and do not meet even very modest standards, and have been replaced by private schools for the children of the elite, electricity supply remains grossly inefficient despite huge amounts purportedly spent on this sector over the years.

In 2009, a Federal House of Representatives Investigation revealed that the Obasanjo Administration, which left office in 2007, spent $16 Billion on a so-called Integrated Power Project (out of the excess crude oil revenue account and without Parliamentary appropriation). Visits to the indicated sites confirmed that absolutely NO work had been done even while all the local and foreign contractors were paid in full. These were surely conduits used to siphon public funds. Nigeria continues to be the largest importer of generators in the world. Nigeria's liquefied natural gas has been pre-sold for twenty years and the revenue is opaquely reflected in the Government Accounts.

Due to corruption, sabotage, and incompetence, no oil refinery has worked in Nigeria for the past twenty years. This suits the political leadership and their agents in the Oil Corporation, which export crude oil, and import refined products through fronts at huge mark-ups, foreign currency gains, and minimal supervision on volumes delivered. Nigerians are at the mercy of this cabal and queue up for several hours and days to fill their car tanks with gasoline during periods of extreme scarcity. The industrial sector has collapsed under the weight of the cost of doing business, multiple tax regimes, declining purchasing power of the majority of their addressable customer base, trade policies that encourage the dumping of inferior goods from China, and the bureaucratic dislocations that define most countries in sub-Saharan Africa. Security is a major challenge, with Government Officials, Corporate Executives, and rich private citizens privatizing the Police Force and sections of the Military for their protection. Typically, several of these Officers are attached to individual "VIPs"/ official thieves and their families, thereby ensuring a drastic reduction in the number of policemen available for routine police work. Again, converting policemen to bodyguards for the rich and "powerful" seriously affects discipline and expectations within the Force. Most Nigerians remain poor and disillusioned with the system, even while their sensibilities are daily assaulted by the raw evidence of brazen and wholesale corruption.

It is apposite to mention at this stage that, while appeals to religion and ethnicity are usually made by the power elite when they lose out in the power game, the majority of the mass clashes in Nigeria can be traced to the successful manipulation of the poor majority by the few. It is not uncommon, for example, for people who are being probed for corruption or serious security breaches to whip up group sentiments by claiming that they are being persecuted because they come from particular ethnic groups, or because of their religious faith. In reality, they do nothing for their people, and only retain the loyalty of their faith leaders (by making financial donations) for occasions like this.

It is instructive that many Nigerians are demonstrably and symbolically very religious. Official rhetoric is suffused with very familiar references to piety and the Transcendental, while the proliferation of churches and mosques is a known phenomenon. Every official meeting starts with Christian and Muslim prayers, then they settle down to the actual business of looting and wasting public funds. If no funds remain, they borrow from China or the Bretton Woods Institutions and steal the money, feeding their citizens with propaganda and intimidation. The Winners' Chapel in Otta, near Lagos, has been rated as one of the three largest places of worship in the world. The Redeemed Christian Church is presently building a mega-church that will dwarf the Winners' edifice, and they have also acquired a huge lot in Kenya for yet another cathedral, even as they have a network of branches and franchises (like McDonald) all over Nigeria, Africa, UK, and the United States. Many car bumpers in Nigeria have faith-based stickers, ostensibly protecting them from armed robbery and accidents actually caused by corruption and faith-based tranquilization and foolishness.

In the midst of all this religiosity, however, the ethical, philosophical, and social underpinnings of democracy are almost absent. Intrinsic, not symbolic, respect for others; trust; treating others as you would like them to treat you; compromise instead of zero-sum position; consistently choosing the harder right instead of the easier wrong, working towards the objective common good at all times; etc., are mostly lacking, hence the gross subversion of the system. The moral-cultural component of democracy, which Novak emphasized in his book, remains antithetical to democratic practice in its true form. This recognition is not intended to trivialize the hunger of the vast majority for genuine democracy and public accountability; this majority is too engrossed in existential challenges to bother about the form of government in practice. Both the military and civilians have failed them. A feature of Nigerian democracy is that the commanding heights of the polity are held by ex-military Officers who have become democrats by dropping their uniforms for civilian clothing; the same people responsible for Nigeria's under-development, for the massive corruption in the land, for the entrenchment of a military mindset in the polity, and the same people who killed and betrayed their course mates in *coups d'état* for career advancement, the only ones with sufficient loot to fund national political structures.

They have infected the polity with the atrocious elements of their odious pedigree: the large-scale corruption, the killings, the betrayals, the confidence of impunity having suspended the Constitution in the past without any penalty for treason coming their way, the command mentality, sheer philosophical rejection of the concept of political equality, and the lack of intellectual sophistication to appreciate the salience of democracy in its real form. These are the protectors and mandarins of Nigeria's democracy!!! When these individuals also drink from the milk of Islamic feudalism, the outcome becomes much worse. The Military typically suspend the Constitution, and dissolve political parties, which are regarded as the symbols of disunity and corruption that necessitated the military intervention in the first place. They also regard the parties as threats of social mobilization and resistance against the military imposition. Given their very limited exposure, education, and worldview – in most cases, they also rely on bureaucrats who, on their part, do not like to share power with enlightened politicians, thus perpetuating military rule.

Perhaps, the Nigerian Military subsequently internalized Ataturk's recommendation that when the military seize power, either the soldiers involved leave the Army and become politicians, or they must accelerate the process of handing over power back to the politicians. Yes, they easily remove their uniforms, and hand over to themselves. The legitimacy of opposition, as evidenced in the tolerance for criticism, opposition, and competition for political control, is a critical component of democracy. These Leviathans are not equipped to either understand this vital precept, or to ensure its entrenchment in the polity. For them, conquest is the same as electoral victory. Their civilian counterparts have learnt very quickly, with the result that politics in Nigeria remain a most dangerous game played with sub-machine guns, thugs, bombs, intimidation, arson, as well as the kidnappings of political "enemies" and their family members.

As a symptom of the deep rot in Nigeria's Oil Industry, below is a snapshot of the Financials for one of the major refineries in the countries, located in Kaduna in the northern part. Billions of Naira (the local currency) were spent on paper without generating a single cent in revenue. Despite this oil-producing country's complete dependence on imported gasoline after exporting crude oil, the refineries are still theoretically open and funded, monies that are paid to non-performing staff and also stolen. It is also revealing that, while Saudi Arabia spends $4 to produce a barrel of crude oil, Russia spends $3 barrel for the same barrel, Nigeria spends $21.2 to produce 1 barrel of crude oil. The latest OPEC Report confirms that Nigeria had a negative variance of $58.8 billion between its crude oil exports and refined gasoline import. All this layering is evident corruption, waste, and inefficiency. The net result is that, with oil prices below this high threshold of $21.2 per barrel, Nigeria permanently reports losses from oil prospecting even as individuals are billionaires in dollars. It is also scandalous that, in a country where ethnic identity remains very strong and the South is, by far, more educated than the North, the entire leadership and management of the national Oil company, with its numerous subsidiaries and branches, comprise northern Muslims from a part of the country with zero crude oil or gas. In fact, having a dark stain on one's forehead (assumed to arise from constantly hitting the forehead on the floor in Islamic supplication) seems to be a higher qualification for office in the Oil Industry and federal institutions than academic credentials and cognate experience. This is yet another generator of instability. The Regions where the oil and gas resources are located and which bear the environment brunt of the prospecting operations, do not have people with Oil Block allocations but connected people from the Yoruba West and the Hausa, Fulani, and Kanuri North have these blocks which yield them billions of dollars even as they have never visited the oil fields and do not have to.

Frustrated by the environmental disaster that attends oil exploration in Nigeria, as well as the absence of both infrastructure and opportunities in the oil-producing Region, some criminally-minded people within the Region have taken to vandalizing oil pipelines and to siphoning and selling salvaged crude oil for survival. This has led to aggressive militancy in the Region, the branching out into kidnapping, gun-running, and armed robbery, as well as the constant clashes with federal military forces deployed to ensure the constant flow of oil money to the center, which is stolen and shared on terms designed and run by yet Northern Muslims on terms that favor the non-contributing North.

It must be affirmed that Yoruba Muslims of the South-west, in the main, pose no risk to anyone, and generally adopt the enlightened cosmopolitan mien of the Yoruba nation. In the Islamic hierarchy of Nigeria, Northern Muslims do not allow Yoruba Imams to preside over their Jumat services in the nation's capital and elsewhere, forcing the Yoruba Muslims to build and run their own mosques. Divisions galore everywhere!!!

KADUNA REFINING AND PETROCHEMICAL COMPANY LIMITED
ANNUAL REPORTFOR THE YEAR ENDED 31ST DECEMBER 2018
STATEMENT OF PROFIT OR LOSS AND OTHER COMPREHENSIVE INCOME

	Note	2018 N'000	2017 N'000
Revenue	6	-	2,241,489
Direct Cost	8(a)	(24,689,718)	(92,627,209)
Gross Loss		**(24,689,718)**	**(90,385,720)**
Other Income	7	134,443	98,709
Administrative Expenses	8(b)	(39,994,585)	(21,720,200)
Operating Loss		**(64,549,860)**	**(112,007,211)**
Finance Income	10	209,514	154,233
Finance Cost	10	(616)	(39,884)
Printing & Stationery			
Telephone, Postages & Internet			
Net Finance Income		**208,898**	**114,349**
Loss Before Minimum Tax and Income Tax	9	(64,340,962)	(111,892,862)
Company Income Tax	12(a)	(13)	(2,814)
Loss Before Income Tax		**(64,340,975)**	**(111,895,676)**
Income Tax Expense	12(b)	-	-
Other Comprehensive Income, Net of Tax		-	-
Total Comprehensive Loss		**(64,340,975)**	**(111,895,676)**

The notes on pages 15 to 41 are an integral part of these financial statements

Source: NNPC KRPC Ltd. 2018 Financial Statements

Nigeria's "Democratic" Experience

While some assessment of the African political situation has been undertaken, it might be useful to ask the questions: Why should the Nigerian democratic experience be evaluated? What are the portents for Africa, and indeed the world? Nigeria is the most populous black country on earth; it has over one-fifth of the total African population, Nigeria is the sixth largest oil-producing country in the world, and has abundant reserves of natural gas, and other natural resources -- with absolutely nothing to show for all of this. She was the third largest exporter of crude oil to the US until recently at 2.3 million barrels per day. Nigeria has the highest concentration of quality manpower in sub-Saharan African, though a sustained brain drain ensures that some of the best of this manpower base is in diaspora in North America, Europe, and the Middle East. In addition, her military strength, when it mattered, had been deployed towards achieving peace in many parts of Africa and the world.

Moreover, while national realities differ, an understanding of the Nigerian condition would be a good entrée into understanding the various factors that determine outcomes across Africa. In this regard, therefore, Nigeria's prominent place in the world remains more potential than real.

Most ominously, however, a close watch over Nigeria is crucial both to understand how such a richly-blessed country has progressively slipped into a failing State, and to emphasize that it should be in our collective interest to avert the failure of that country, as the implications for the Region and the world will be quite severe in all respects. Samuel P. Huntington refers to the "Third Wave" of worldwide democratization, which ostensibly extended to Nigeria. In the particular case under reference, it would appear that democracy, when practised, has been more in form than in content. Furthermore, democracy has been employed as an economic system rather than a political system, in that it is a vehicle for accessing the national wealth, which is administered at the center. The process has failed to produce stable institutions and effective public policies, while the pervasive content remains definitely authoritarian. The legitimacy of a political system provides the foundation for a successful political process. It follows, therefore that, in the absence of this legitimacy, the political process is likely to be deficient.

A political system premised on real legitimacy can effectively make and implement policies and is best equipped to galvanize the voluntary support of the people. While the expansive notion of legitimacy could be based on tradition, ideology, citizen participation, or specific policies, the emphasis here is on that form of legitimacy freely given in free elections. The duality of responsibilities involves citizens obeying the laws of the land while the government meets its civic obligations to the people. When the latter is lacking or the basis of the legitimacy is polluted, the people have the right to resist imposition. The dialectic of this resistance and the determined imposition of the leadership will on the people by coercive means, leads to violence and the destruction of civic peace, with the resultant implications for certainty, development, and political maturation. This arises because the opposite of trust is hostility. Accordingly, democratization must necessarily involve not only the provision of competitive elections but also the minimization of the bias in interest aggregation. It has been suggested that the aspects of political culture are:

Aspects of Political Culture	Examples
System	Pride in Nation National Identity Legitimacy of government
Process	Role of citizens Perceptions of political rights
Policy	Role of government Government policy priorities

As earlier mentioned, a robust civil society boosts the democratic profile and content of a State. The role of education and economic wellbeing cannot be discounted; contemporary experience from various countries indicates the varying impact of these indices on the democratic quotient of a nation. While local factors affect the nature and quality of the democratic process in a country, the minimum conditions of its validation have assumed almost unanimous character.

In democratic systems, competitive elections empower the citizens to shape policy through their selection and rejection of key policymakers. Based on this, Almond, Powell, et al developed a matrix of Political Goods, which anchor the focus of the political leadership:

Levels of Political Goods	Classes of Goods	Contents and Examples
System Level	System maintenance	The political system is characterized by regular, stable, and predictable processes domestically and internationally.
	System adaptation	The political system adapts to environmental change and challenges.
Process Level	Participation in political inputs	The political system is open to and responds to a variety of forms of political action and speech, which may directly produce a sense of citizen dignity and efficacy
	Compliance and support	Citizens fulfill their obligations (e.g. patriotic service) to the system and comply with public law and policy
	Procedural justice	Equitable procedure (due process) and equality before the law.
	Effectiveness and efficiency	Processes have intended effects and are no more cumbersome, expensive, or intrusive than necessary
Policy level	Welfare	Growth per capita; quantity and quality of health and material goods; distributive equity
	Security	Safety of person and property; public order and national security
	Fairness	Non-discrimination in government policy; mutual recognition of individuals from ethnic, linguistic, or other groups; protection of vulnerable or disadvantaged persons
	Liberty	Freedom from regulation, protection of privacy, and respect for autonomy of other individuals, groups, and nations

General Obasanjo gained stature for handing over power to civilians in 1979, though it is arguable that his real motivation was more personal than altruistic (given that his predecessor was killed in office). His subsequent attempts as a civilian president over twenty years later, to extend his stay in office beyond the constitutional limit of two terms, define a man who acts more out of personal preferences than high principles. The 1979 Constitution prescribed the US Presidential System for Nigeria and adopted the bicameral legislature and notion of separation of powers as well. The Principle of Subsidiarity was emphasized by way of entrenched provisions for the devolution of powers to the States and Local Government Authorities. In reality, however, the retention of the coercive powers exclusively at the Center, as well as the enactment of the Land Use Decree, effectively ensured the retention of the unitary system typical of military establishments. With crude oil generating over 90% of the country's revenue, Obasanjo, as Military Head of State, promulgated this Decree, which transferred ownership of all the land in the country to the Government, for the real purpose of depriving the communities and States with oil deposits of the revenues accruing from oil.

Oil revenue mandatorily belonged to all Nigerians, even as revenues from cocoa, groundnuts, and palm produce, were exclusively spent by the generating Regions in the 1960s before the advent of oil! The distributive tension in Nigeria is worsened by the fact that other natural resources located in the Western and Northern parts of the country (gold, bitumen, bauxite, iron ore, limestone, kaolin, marble, granite, etc.) are mined privately by individuals and companies on Concession Arrangements with the local Governments, under a loose supervisory structure. These do not belong to all Nigerians!!! Another Commonwealth model! Since the oil-producing areas of the Niger Delta Region are part of the dispersed minority ethnic groupings, their political clout is severely limited. Accordingly, while oil exploration activities damage their waters and environment, Central Political Leaders from very distant parts of the country have consistently made oil policies, allocated and sold their oil, and colluded with the oil Majors to ensure the permanent under-development of the oil-producing areas and the impoverishment of their people. Pipelines were laid thousands of kilometers from the oil creeks in the thick mangroves and coastal South to the arid city of Kaduna, the political capital of the defunct Northern Region, where both a refinery and a petrochemical plant were built. Abuja, the new federal capital city, was built with oil proceeds even as the oil-producing areas remain unfit for human habitation in any century. This glaring injustice is also responsible for the tension in the country.

Larry Diamond identifies as a critical problem for Nigeria, the relationship between the economy and the State. He writes that: "stable democracy is associated with an autonomous, indigenous bourgeoisie, and inversely associated with extensive State control over the economy. In Nigeria, and throughout much of Africa, the swollen State has turned politics into a zero-sum game in which everything of value is at stake in an election, and hence candidates, communities, and parties feel compelled to win at any cost." Revenue allocation from the center is based on such very inexplicable indices as the land mass of each state (for the simple reason that the North has more land mass than the South where all the money is generated). In essence, the North used successive military regimes to entrench structures of inequity and discord in the system.

These are some of the direct causes of the agitation in the oil-producing parts of the country. It is for the same purpose of ensuring the perpetuation of inequity and opaqueness in the system that Nigeria has not had a generally accepted population census since 1963! The projected population figures are used in allocating funds out of the Federation Account, but NOT in assigning taxation or contribution! In addition, while some states in the North have introduced the Sharia Law – with ostensible connotations of rejection of the sale and consumption of alcohol, they readily partake of VAT revenues from alcohol sales in the South, and indeed sue the Federal Government when there are delays in sharing these sums! The civilian government that was inaugurated in 1979 was overthrown by the military in December 1983. The northern military Heads of State remained in power until 1999 when the current stage of the democratic development commenced. In effect, previous attempts at instilling democracy in 1963, 1966, 1983, and 1993, failed to achieve their objective.

The military conducted the 1999 elections and handed over power to General Olusegun Obasanjo (yes, the same one), who was now a "civilian", having retired from the military twenty years earlier. His "heroic" handover of power to civilians in 1979, his incarceration under General Sani Abacha over his doubtful involvement in a coup against Abacha, and his being from the same Yoruba ethnic stock as Moshood Abiola who died in detention after winning the 1993 Presidential election, all combined to generate considerable goodwill for Obasanjo. In a comical but real depiction of the Nigerian variant of democracy, after the relatively-free Presidential election of June 12, 1993 was won by Moshood Abiola, whom the superintendent Military did not wish to hand over to, the Head of State, General Ibrahim Babangida annulled the results of the election and paved the way for the appointment of a civilian interim Head of State from Abiola's ethnic group before quitting office himself.

The Interim Government was duly sacked three months later by the Military under the Chief of Army Staff, General Sani Abacha, who proceeded to set up five political parties that contested local and state elections under him three years later. These so-called parties were allowed to exist only if they refrained from any criticism of the regime, and they complied so extremely well that all five nominated the military Head of State, Abacha, as their presidential candidate! He would have contested against himself and become a civilian President if he had not died in office! Politicians who dared to voice independent views during this perfidy were killed, detained indefinitely, or chased into foreign exile. Credible international organizations assess that General Sani Abacha and his family stole over $5 billion from the Nigeria treasury before his sudden death in 1998; over $3 billion of this amount has been returned to the Nigerian Government by banks and authorities in Europe and the US over the years and, most likely, re-looted by the incumbent recipients. One of Abacha's fronts, Mr. Bagudu, is presently the Governor of Kebbi State in the North and a prominent member of the ruling party. The Lebanese Chagouri family, which was Abacha's main business partner, continues to exercise immense clout in Nigeria and to expand their network of "business partners", notably Bola Ahmed Tinubu, a former two-term Governor of the rich Lagos State, Godfather in the South-west, and a financier of the ruling party. He is generally regarded as a creative thief.

Expectations were very high that Obasanjo would deviate from the country's known path of poor performance. People overlooked the glaring electoral irregularities that produced his government in 1999, just to give him a chance to redeem the nation. To the extent that single individuals could make or wreck a nation, it was generally adjudged, after eight straight years of Obasanjo's civilian leadership, that his stewardship was mixed. He negotiated and paid off Nigeria's foreign debt completely but approximated too much personal power. He also initiated and completed substantial reforms in telecommunications, banking, and public service. He also recognized and rewarded talent from all parts of the country, constituting at all times a pan-Nigeria and merit-based Cabinet. Obasanjo was, and is, a proud Nigerian, a proud African, and an internationalist. He is completely comfortable in all parts of the country and has genuine personal friends in every state, a fact of non-tribalism, which offends his Yoruba kith and kin. It must be acknowledged that instances of cronyism in his Administration deepened the existing culture of corruption in the country.

Ultimately, his attempted subversion of the Constitution and compromise of State Institutions to serve the personal ends of tenure elongation and electoral victory "by all means" will define his legacy. All objective analysts acknowledge Mr. Obasanjo's genuine love and passion for Nigeria, as well as his earned reputation both for hard work and personal discipline, which is why it remains difficult to relate some of these pathologies to him. While section 2(b) of the 1979 Constitution states that "the security and welfare of the people shall be the primary purpose and responsibility of the government", Obasanjo's government presided over the large-scale impoverishment of the people, even while the country made hitherto-unimaginable income from spikes in oil prices. His

Administration did not add much value to the infrastructure base in eight years and exhibited a complete disregard for fiscal discipline and transparency.

He bypassed the Legislature by single-handedly operating Dedicated Crude Oil Excess Revenue Accounts which were not subject to audit; allocated and cancelled oil blocs at will; granted Duty Waivers and Import Monopolies to his cronies and family members; used the Police, Military, and Security Forces to kill, maim, and intimidate independent citizens and communities; empowered proxies to buy privatized State Companies and Utilities at give-away prices; extended his "influence" to the Stock Exchange which was co-opted into his political projects; debased all the precepts and Institutions of Democracy, including the Judiciary, by his flagrant and arrogant contempt for order and propriety; orchestrated by propaganda, wholesale bribery, and intimidation the impeachment of five Senate Presidents in eight years; protected known criminals on the condition that they would always rig elections on his behalf; etc., etc. In addition to being the President and Commander-in-Chief of the Armed Forces, he was also the Minister of Petroleum Resources and Minister of Defense!

When Nigerians talk about democracy, they remember that Obasanjo was an "elected" President. They remember how he constantly threatened the stability of the deformed and faltering federal structure; they remember the corruption, vindictiveness, massive electoral fraud, the impunity, and the fetishism of absolute control, the absolute disconnect with the citizens, the focus on buying state-of the-art Presidential jets even while the people were getting poorer in the midst of plenty; the rhetorical vacuity and puerile propaganda that convinced only Obasanjo and his cronies that their performance was stellar.

For eight years, he could not fix or build new refineries, nor repair major roads. Worst of all, he made it impossible for the people to vote him out in 2003 and, in the 2007 general elections, he ensured the scale and type of vote-rigging that even Nigerians had never seen before. After his first term, he embarked on a program of self-perpetuation in office. He reportedly spent hundreds of millions of dollars of State funds bribing federal legislators (there were media confirmations of \$1 million dollars for each of the 109 Senators, and \$750,000 for each of the 360 Members of the House of Representatives) to effect an amendment of the Constitution for the purpose of lifting the tenure limit of two terms, to enable him remain President for Life.

This was a man who had been Head of State for three years while in his thirties, Minister of Works, Chief of Staff (Supreme Headquarters),etc.,etc., and whom

Nigerians and Africans praised to high heavens because he handed power over to civilians. People also generally ignored how he was able to establish an integrated network of sophisticated farms and a university for himself when he left office as a military dictator.

The heated debate about tenure elongation stressed the polity and almost led to a military comeback. The Vice-President's insistence on the sanctity of the Constitutional provision on tenure (because of his own ambition to become the President in 2007) led to a collapse in his relationship with Obasanjo. The entire State machinery was unleashed on him, and all forms of humiliation meted out to him. He finally left the ruling People's Democratic (democratic indeed!) Party (PDP) and formed the Action Congress with other former Founders and Stalwarts who had left the PDP because of the President's ways. The Vice President contested the Presidential election in 2007 and, expectedly, lost by a wide margin to the President's candidate due to the gross manipulation of the voter registration process and the elections proper.

After his failure to secure a tenure extension, Obasanjo caused the ruling Party to amend its Constitution to require that only a former President would be the Chairman of its powerful Body of Trustees and that all elected Officials of the Party (including his successor-President) would take instructions from the Chairman, Board of Trustees, on policy issues and on appointments. Extension by subterfuge! He imposed the bulk of candidates for the Governorship and Federal Legislative elections, and guided the manipulation of the electoral process to ensure their "victory" at the polls, so that they would protect him when finally out of office. The so-called Anti-Corruption Agency, the Economic and Financial Crimes Commission (EFCC) became a ready tool in the victimization of the President's political opponents, many of whom were jailed or disqualified from holding public office, even while the most egregious acts of corruption were being perpetrated by favored people.

In all of this, State resources were deployed towards muzzling the Free Press and the Opposition Parties. The Electoral Commission members are appointed by the President, who equally supervises them. Their funding is at his pleasure, so the power of incumbency in Nigeria invariably means that the President's electoral wish is always observed. In any case, the Police Force, which is centrally controlled, is always on standby to kill protesters. Independent judges are punished as the President is the final Appointing/Recommending Authority for Federal Judicial Officers. The Nigerian Constitution grants immunity from prosecution (while in office) on the President, Vice-President, Governors, and Deputy Governors. This Immunity Clause has been grossly abused and needs to be repealed. The emerging picture is the concentration of untrammeled power in one person, as well as the absence or inefficiency of constraining checks and balances. These clearly negate the spirit of democracy.

It is very disappointing that Nigeria keeps the company of some of the poorest countries in the world per capita. Apart from the immense natural reserves, Nigeria has an impressive pool of manpower which is now mostly in the diaspora. 70% of Nigerians survive on about $1 a day.

The UNDP's Human Development Reports continue to rank Nigeria very low. Infant mortality rates remain unacceptably high – higher than figures for other countries in coastal West Africa apart from war-ravaged Liberia and Sierra-Leone. The Obasanjo Administration built a new stadium in Abuja, which cost (on paper) more than the combined budgets for health and education for 2001 and 2002. Government Officials obtain medical treatment for minor ailments in foreign lands. Nigeria earned over $250 billion in oil revenue alone during the eight years of Obasanjo's civilian government, and there is hardly anything to show for it in tangible terms. The fact of the negotiation and payout of Nigeria's debt has already been acknowledged, as we also affirm that his administration started a Savings culture, funds that were stolen and wasted by subsequent administrations.

Obasanjo never favored the multi-party system. Several years ago, he publicly stated that in his native language, Yoruba, the word for "opposition" equally means "enemy". In the run up to the 2003 and especially the 2007 elections (which he conducted), he used terms like "do or die", "PDP or nothing" in his public utterances. He attempted on many occasions to impose a one-party system on Nigeria. To be sure, the Governors emulated the President in terms of waste, corruption, non-performance, lack of accountability, and mindless oppression of the people. A particular Governor spent about 70% of his two terms of eight years overseas where he claimed he was seeking foreign investments – all the while collecting stupendous estacode allowances!

The Sharia System in operation in certain Northern States, the crippling poverty and low literacy levels of the people in those States, are a potent mix for extremist behavior and intolerance. It is not inconceivable that variants of the Al Qaeda Network, ISIS, and other terrorist groups could find the northern part of Nigeria as a safe haven. The absence of citizen and planning records, together with a reactive and incompetent Military and Security Service, further bolster the chances of this scenario. Moreover, some of the fundamental principles and practices of Islam are in direct conflict with the democratic ethos. Universal suffrage is hampered by the treatment of women;

free will is negated by messianic imposition and arrogance; the hierarchical structure of Muslim societies detracts from the political equality notion under democracy; Islam is rooted in the past and equally teaches fatalism, while democracy and capitalism are necessarily forward-looking and sustained by hope in the redeeming capacity of man to improve his position in life. The *Insha Allah* concept in Islam depresses the human capacity for invention and development. Surrender kills thinking.

The 2003 and 2007 elections witnessed the direct employment of policemen and soldiers to stop people from casting their votes in places where the ruling party was sure to lose, Nigerians and foreign observers equally witnessed deliberate logistical blunders which ensured that millions of eligible voters were not registered, ballot papers were not delivered to polling centers until after the elections, several people were killed while protesting, thugs were employed to stuff ballot boxes, thus "voting" for the citizens, some results were announced even before the votes were cast, confusion between electronic voting and manual voting, the forceful hijack of ballot boxes by armed PDP thugs and pliant policemen, the announcement of precast results which belied the fact of massive disenfranchisement, etc., etc. In many States, the announced results indicated that the number of voters exceeded the total population for the States. "Defeated" candidates sought recourse in the courts, while pro-Government Opinion Leaders implored them to accept the results "in the interest of building our nascent democracy". Local and foreign observers catalogued and announced the enormity of irregularities perpetrated during the "elections".

It is quite significant and disappointing that election-related matters are never disposed of in the courts before the "winners" are sworn in. As horrible as the profile above is, Nigeria under Buhari has become much worse. We shall shortly render a factual assessment on the worst Administration, military or civilian, that Nigeria has ever had. One never quite believed it could get as bad as it has become since 2015 under Mr. Buhari. It needs to be short because a detailed rendition will require an entire book. One is excited to be on the verge of completing work on the current book; I have also been typing for over two months and need to rest my hands. Carpal Tunnel Syndrome is not much fun, notwithstanding the quality of your compression gloves.

In essence, the usurpers of people's mandates are sworn in while the case lingers in court. Over time, the combination of fatigue, bribery of the judges, incumbency advantage, etc., decides such cases in favor of the usurping incumbents. Some of the cases from the 2003 elections were only concluded in 2006, three years into the tenure and a year to the next elections! The same pattern repeated itself in all subsequent "elections." Some "senior" Silk lawyers in the country have developed a reputation as Election Tribunal juggernauts -- bribing the right judges and making their money only once in four years following the election cycle. The April 2007 elections surpassed the infamy of the 2003 elections in all respects. Local and foreign observers unanimously judged the 2007 elections the worst ever in the world; they had no words to describe what happened under Buhari in 2019: heist? impunity? wholesale corruption of the electoral process? Active and visible involvement of the Police, Military, and Security Services in rigging the elections to favor a grossly unpopular and uber-incompetent Mr. Buhari? What do you call their so-called elections in 2019? Some of the more obvious irregularities mentioned included: using the Police and Military freely and openly to intimidate, disperse, and kill the opposition and voters while voting took place in areas where Mr. Buhari and his cronies were not popular, detention and assassination of the opposition candidates, exceeding the number of registered voters, centralized collation and reporting controlled exclusively by the Government, disqualifications of Opposition candidates, materials deliberately not supplied to opposition strongholds, underage voting in areas where Mr. Buhari was popular, clear partisanship of the Electoral Body, etc.

The Economic Community of West African States (ECOWAS), AU, EU, and observer delegations sent by non-governmental bodies in Europe and the US all agreed that the 2003, 2007, and especially the 2019 elections were a massive fraud, a charade, and a total failure. The former US Secretary of State, Madeleine Albright, who led one of the delegations in 2003, called the so-called elections "a failed process... a shame of humanity." Testimonies on subsequent elections, as cited, have been even much worse.

The Nigerian Labor Congress, Nigerian Political Science Association, Nigerian Medical Association, Nigerian Bar Association, all the Opposition Parties, as well as all other Pressure Groups and Institutions, respectively and collectively condemned the outcome of the so-called elections. In the case of the 2007 "elections", for example, given the overwhelming revulsion at the brazenness of the electoral fraud, the departing President and the perpetrator of the electoral crime, Obasanjo, finally and arrogantly suggested that the degree of irregularities did not warrant an outright cancellation of all the results! For him, "we should not be measured by European or American standards." He conveniently ignored the fact that acceptable elections had been held in Ghana, Namibia, and South Africa – all African countries. While Obasanjo sought a *mea culpa*, Mr. Buhari has continued to feel entitled to the result of his assault on democracy, spending his time picking his teeth from morning to night.

A popular and credible Public Commentator in Nigeria, Dr. Sylvester Odion-Akhaine, while also commenting on the deplorable 2007 elections which he characterized as the natural consequence of the past docility of Nigerians, also attributed same to deep structural issues, personalized rule, ethnic and religious suspicion/ crises, the absence of robust Institutions to support democracy, and an overall lack of legitimacy on the part of those exercising political power in Nigeria. While virtually all the "elected" officials for the State Legislative and Governorship, as well as Federal Legislative and Presidential elections were tainted by fraud, the "winners" assumed office while the "losers" were still in court years later.

The reward of impunity and criminality contributes significantly to voter apathy, and overall disillusionment with the political system; these are hardly the expectations of an ideal democratic system. The people do not bother to vote or participate fully in the democratic process since their votes will not count any way! Selections, not elections, are held. This creates serious legitimacy problems. When this is coupled with the chronic non-performance of the political office holders, the masses truly do not care whether the military or civilians are in power.

Mundt and Aborisade wrote that: "… many people have stopped bothering themselves with classifying African regimes as democratic or otherwise. They instead keep asking: How much do the regimes address themselves to the needs and aspirations of the people? All the noise about democracy and democratic culture are mere luxuries to the sufferers…" Once Obasanjo left power in 2007 and could no longer intimidate them, the Judiciary found the courage to reverse the elections of seventeen out of thirty-six State Governors (several months and years after the usurpers were sworn in as Governors). On February 23, 2009, the Appeal Court reversed the "election" of the PDP Governor of Ondo State in the Western part of the country, and declared the opposition candidate the actual winner in the elections which were held almost two years earlier in April 2007! Given the fact that many of the reversed cases usually proceed on time-wasting appeal to the Supreme Court, the status quo remains. In effect, the real winners are excluded from office while election riggers are protected by the State and could, indeed, end up being in office for the entire four-year tenure, with all the implications for accountability, equity, civic character, democracy-building, and reinforcement of impunity. With the limitless resources available to these impostors and electoral thieves, plus the appurtenances of offices that suddenly become theirs to "enjoy", fatalistic, compromised, and prayerful people typically urge the preferred candidate of the people to accept the theft, the subversion of the people's mandate as the "Will of God" and try the next time…

The further implications for service, policy continuity, and corruption – owing to uncertainty – are equally strong. The massively rigged Presidential Election of April 2007 was finally decided by the Supreme Court in favor of the incumbent only in December 2008, as was the even worse election of 2019. In a 4-3 decision in 2008, the Supreme Court recognized the scale of irregularities that attended the so-called elections, but the majority decided to recognize the new incumbent, Mr. Yar'adua, "in the national interest". The lack of fiscal accountability in public office intensifies the struggle for power. It is an open war in which weapons, acid, and bombs are used. Family members are killed or kidnapped for ransom when the politician becomes a hard target due to the number of armed thugs and policemen who constitute his or her bodyguard. The emphasis on the central government has been in recognition of the African saying that the fish starts rotting from the head. In reality, the corruption, nepotism, personal aggrandizement, cronyism, lies, the celebration of mediocrity, the lack of vision and ambition, reflex to settle for undemocratic compromises, recognition and cuddling of so-called Godfathers, disdain for democracy, and utter contempt for the citizens, are replicated on all the levels, thus accounting for Nigeria's continuing abysmal performance as a sovereign State.

While General Olusegun Obasanjo was the civilian President between 1999 and 2007, the Chairman of the ruling party was Col. Ahmadu Alli (rtd.); the Chairman of the Board of Trustees of the Party, Anthony Anenih, was a retired Police Commissioner; the Chief of Staff to the President was Major General Mohammed (rtd.); the Vice-President, Atiku Abubakar, was a retired senior Customs Officer; and the successive National Security Advisers, Aliyu Gusau and Sarki Mukhtar, retired as a Lt.General and Major-General respectively.

Both the Chief of Staff and the National Security Adviser were retained in their capacities by the Yar'Adua Administration bequeathed by Obasanjo, while the former Chairman of the Party was appointed Nigeria's Ambassador to South Africa. The recruitment process, the influence of money, and the patronage networks qualify Nigeria's democracy as a perfect example of what Ronald Pennock calls "The Elitist Theory of Democracy", in which: the society is broadly categorized in reality into the few who have power and the majority who do not. Only a few people allocate values for the society; the majority plays no role in Public Policy. The few are not typical of the majority; Upward status migration must be slow and open only to those who accept the elite conspiracy against the majority; The so-called elite share an agreement on the basic values of the System; Public Policy caters exclusively to elite interest, while the majority is ignored; The latter are sustained by propaganda and repression; Huge disconnect between the people and the political, economic, military, economic, traditional, media, or bureaucratic elements of the elite conspiracy.

In Nigeria's specific case, it is very unfortunate that her so-called political elite comprises, in the main, of particularly a visionless, brutal, unsophisticated and callous set of citizens who are further united by a ruthless and overwhelming propensity towards primitive accumulation. Despite everything, Obasanjo set up the Economic and Financial Crimes Commission (EFCC), to probe and prosecute cases of fraud and financial crimes in the system. The immunity of various categories of public officials ensured that no case could be brought against them while in office. In any case, EFCC turned out to be a tool for victimizing only those who disagreed with the President; this has remained the practice to date, in addition to the corruption and diversion of recovered loot carried out by the anti-corruption officials themselves. The leadership and bulk of the staff of this Agency, police officers all, are Northern Muslims, thereby adding a clannish dimension to their work, with the exposed and targeted people usually being Southerners and Northerners not aligned with the President. This pattern has since gotten much worse under Mr. Buhari. This selective approach to their work dampened the credibility of the Commission. Some of the worst offenders bankrolled the 2007 electoral "war" for the ruling PDP in lieu of future prosecution. Mr. Buhari's "elections" in 2015 and 2019 were also funded principally by known public thieves, who enjoy protection from the State for the fact of their "investment' in the President's "election."

In addition, all the big looters of the treasury are free and enjoy unfettered access to the seat of power - once they are in the President's Party. Apart from the direct implications of the massive corruption for Nigeria's continued under-development, the translation into the reward-punishment matrix of the society is dire. It is impossible to build a society of trust where Novak's "spirit of cooperation, mutuality, and common striving" can thrive. The emphasis on the collective and group dynamic cannot be expected when looters have been rewarded with their loot. The absolutization of power is responsible for the unwillingness of successive Administrations or Regimes to engender a real Free Enterprise System. Machiavelli had advised that the greatest enemies of a free government are complacent and self-interested citizens. The retention of a Statist Economy is but a reflection of the inclination towards control. Why should government officials be trusted with economic decisions when, on the average, they lack legitimacy, they lack knowledge, they have not handled political power well, and there is a real danger of concentration and compromise? While some key sectors have witnessed some private sector participation, the final control on policy is exercised by the Federal Government. Most of the multiple regulatory bodies are headed and staffed by Northern Muslims, not out of merit but mostly out of cronyism and nepotism.

Buhari's choice for Chief Justice of the Federation, Ibrahim Tanko Muhammad, is in actuality an expert in Sharia Law, and had previously advocated for the incorporation of Sharia Law into the mainstream legal tradition of the country, a tradition that was originally derived from British Common Law. This, in a country with first-grade legal minds who attended some of the best Law Schools around the world and have successfully practised Law at very high levels, unlike Mr. Muhammad. As always, the pliant Senate approved his candidacy and inflicted him on the country. The South, which is by far more educated, ends up being regulated in Communications, Stock Exchange, Agriculture, Security, Education, Healthcare, Finance, Infrastructure, etc., by people who did not necessarily compete for those positions and who have no demonstrable capacity to regulate others. This is yet another major cause of pervasive angst in the country, especially in the South, and why some of the best brains remain in diaspora. All these factors have ensured that Nigeria shares a platform with much poorer countries on the list of the countries with the lowest Per Capita Purchasing Power, lowest Human Development Indices, and all such other depressing statistics.

It is clear that mere Constitutionalism will not resolve underlying inequities and grievances. Nigeria has had nine Constitutions in all since her founding, and five since Independence, yet the objective conditions that militate against true nationhood, federalism, and genuine democracy, subsist. A constitutional document cannot succeed at papering over a lack of trust among the country's subcultures. Convenient devices like the informal rotation of offices will also not have a long-lasting effect on the resolution of underlying issues. Nigeria is currently a mere geographical expression, and not a nation-State in the strict sense of the term. However, the inherent plurality could be put to good use by the sheer force of leadership and service. Nigerians have been conditioned to NOT expect anything from their government, so very minimal and token achievements are applauded

Mancur Olson observed that: "resolute autocrats can survive even when they impose heinous amounts of suffering upon their peoples. When they are replaced, it is for other reasons (e.g., succession crises) and often by another stationary bandit." He also concludes that democracy appears under "historical conditions and dispersions of resources that make it impossible for any one leader or group to assume all power." In Nigeria's case, these conditions are very distant presently, with the economy overwhelmingly dependent on oil and State's resources, controlled directly by the regime at the Center. While the US economy is currently undergoing a meltdown, for example, and many families have lost their jobs and homes, the Government has embarked upon several stabilization and stimulus programs to cushion the impact of the economic challenges on the citizenry. That is what it should be!! African countries do not copy the two-way intercourse between the US Government and the electorate; they focus on an outmoded form of Capitalism where no benefits ever accrue to the majority. African Governments do not ever tell their citizens about the Social Security Program, the support for the unemployed and infirm, and the Social Welfare Schemes that exist in the Western World (including the US).

It is extremely difficult, if not outright impossible, for any objective assessment of the Nigerian condition to yield a positive commentary. If we adopt Ali Mazrui's template for evaluating the success or failure of a State, the evaluation must objectively be a failing grade. These criteria are: sovereign control over territory; sovereign supervision (though not necessarily ownership) of the nation's resources; effective and rational revenue extraction from the people, goods, and services; the capacity to build and maintain an adequate national infrastructure (roads, postal services, telephone systems, railways, and the like); the capacity to render such basic services as sanitation, education, housing, and health care; and the capacity for governance and the maintenance of law and order. In rounding up this section, we should undertake a further analysis of diverse evaluations of the Nigerian democratic experience.

Writing in 'The Problems and Prospects of Sustaining Democracy in Nigeria', Bamidele Ojo attributes the perennial prospects of the Nigerian democratic foundation to the eternal optimism and resilience of the people. Optimism cannot remain eternal in the face of egregious crimes against the people, while the assumed resilience is on the basis of the continuing lack of empowerment. Once this is reversed, the consequences can neither be predicted nor the *status quo* sustained. It is only a polity that is founded on responsibility, equity, and good governance that can have real prospects of voluntary peace, and not the peace of the graveyard that exists in the country presently. It is clear that "confidence" in the continuing docility and so-called resilience of the people is responsible for the level of impunity in the country.

Victor Aikhionbare suggests that Constitutionalism holds the key to the resolution of Nigeria's myriad issues. As discussed earlier, however, mere constitutionalism cannot erase or repair deep-seated and real cleavages in a polity. There is a need to objectively and realistically analyze the issues, and jointly agree implementable solutions. Constitutions are mere documents and frameworks for governance, without the Will or infrastructure for execution. Evod Mmanda emphasizes the validity of a Constitution as deriving from its implementation while its legitimacy is a function of "the way it is freely accepted by those it is targeting... the result of the way they consciously participated or were involved in making it." The current 1999 Nigerian

Constitution was hastily packaged and imposed on the country by a departing military regime headed and dominated by Northern Muslims intent on awarding unmerited and disproportionate advantages to their Region and Religion (including number of states and local government areas, criteria for sharing - never for producing or contributing - public revenue, etc.) It remains a wonder why, twenty-one years later of consistent civilian rule, the Middle Belt and the South have been unable to demand a drastic renegotiation of those terms or, indeed, to insist on the people writing their own Constitution.

Nigeria has had several Constitutions, yet the problems endure. Fundamentally, Nation-building and independence have been meaningless without a broad consensus about what the nation, the regime, institutional arrangements, and the rules of the game, should be. As a result, no government – military or civilian – has been able to develop the authority or legitimacy that would enable it to govern with the required degree of effectiveness or accountability.

Writing on Federalism, State Creation, and Ethnic Management, Adegboyega Somide affirms that State Creation along ethnic lines has failed to solve Nigeria's problems, and that a powerful ethnic pull continues to render nugatory the country's federal experiment. His conclusion is that Federalism is not the solution to the ensuing ethnic conflict, and that Nigeria does not meet the minimum conditions for a successful Federalism: desire to federate, State Autonomy in decision-making, and financial independence from the Central Government. This seems in accord with a portion of Thomas Franck's position, namely, that: there must be an ideological commitment among the constituent units to establish a Federation; Federalism must be considered an end in itself and not a means to an end; there exist historical, cultural, and linguistic sameness, and physical and economic complementarity; as well as an acknowledged need to solve ethnic imbalance or to secure independence from foreign rule. Franck's position cannot be taken in totality since the noble example of the US experience with Federalism and extreme diversity is an inspiring one. The problem with the Nigerian situation arises, in part, from the casual adoption of terms without any rigorous effort to internalize their essential ingredients, hence the country officially had a Federal Military Government under the Military, an Institution that is basically unitary. The title was, therefore, a contradiction in terms. Federalism is essentially incompatible with Authoritarianism or Military Rule.

Military Rule and its civilian offspring conveniently called a democracy in Nigeria, lack checks and balances, separation of powers, legality, Rule of Law, electoral politics, a party system, etc. Perhaps noting the grave damage done to the country by a militaristic mindset, Adeolu Osho and Layi Abegunrin posit that, in the minimum, the journey towards reclaiming the country's potentials must necessarily involve: accountability with responsibility; transparency in governance, responsiveness, principled leadership, effective checks and balances to minimize the potentials of abuse and concentration, revitalization of the economy by diversifying the revenue base and overhauling the infrastructure, entrenching true Federalism, changing the societal values, emphasizing the uniting, nor divisive factors, professionalizing the Military and Security Forces, and ensuring the real equality of all before the Law. These are all noble prescriptions, but their applicability can only be contingent on the outcome of a real National Conference. It is generally agreed that Federal Character (the Nigerian variant of Affirmative Action which tends to favor only the North!), Revenue Allocation Formula, and State Creation as tools of managing multi-ethnicity have failed woefully.

One completely aligns with Victor Okafor's view that: "gaining political office by snatching ballot boxes and by filling ballot boxes with fake votes is as unconstitutional and destructive (as stealing public money) and should be considered and treated as treasonable as seizing the reins of government with a gun." Part of the process of checking impunity must consist in the retroactive punishment of both electoral fraud and military seizure of power. It is evident that people do not kill others or snatch power by all means just to serve the public interest. Christopher Agulana writes that: "from independence until now, Nigeria has had the misfortune of having inane, jejune, and callow individuals masquerading as political leaders." It just remains to be added that the non-retribution for illegal access to power and malfeasance while in power are responsible for this sordid state of affairs.

In the same way that it is impossible for a man to get pregnant and give birth; no person can walk on the Atlantic Ocean from the UK to US; no human being is 20 ft. tall; or for Donald J. Trump to be known for empathy, integrity, presidential comportment, and protection of the national interest (not his), it is impossible for anyone to get a public sector contract in Nigeria (at all levels) without paying a bribe. The rate has progressively got worse over the years, from 10%, 20%, 50%, and simply sharing the entire contract amount with the government officials awarding the contract and entering zero performance. In many cases also, the same projects will be budgeted for in subsequent years and given the same treatment; this partly explains why these Ministries and Agencies will "settle" Parliamentarians who approve the allocations, for it is an endless and systemic abuse of office. It is also a known fact that, unless you are a senior Government Official, you cannot obtain an international passport or driver's license within the advertised time frame without paying a bribe. The evidence is in the absence of commensurate infrastructure and services across board, and the corresponding personal wealth of relevant politicians, civil servants, and their entourage.

The level of systemic corruption and sense of entitlement, shamelessness, and cruel insensitivity is so high that, for years, successive Presidents, Governors, senior Parliamentarians, County Chairmen and women, and even Ministers and sundry appointees and top civil servants take significant amounts off the system and without audit under guises like 'Security Vote', 'Entertainment Allowance', "Constituency Vote," "Out of Station Allowance," etc. The president, for example, could easily have a discretionary figure of close to $100 million annually as 'Security Vote' (not the budget for Defense or Security) apart from the absolute power to award and cancel oil contracts, major concessions and projects, or indeed to get foreign currencies by the Central Bank allocated to favored parties at subsidized exchange rates much lower than what the rest of the country pays. The reintroduction of such foreign currencies into the market creates a substantial arbitrage in a system called 'round tripping'. Another expression of corruption is excessive gifting when a prominent politician or Chief Executive of a major Government Agency (like the Oil Corporation, NNPC) marks a birthday, buries the parents, or any of their children gets married (this is becoming a pattern once the parents get into high office).

The convergence of high-profile fortune-seekers and patronage merchants at such events typically represents an assemblage of most of the perpetrators of Nigeria's endemic pathologies, and gifts in cash (Dollars), paid-for honeymoon at exotic foreign destinations, and materials run into several millions of dollars. When the daughter of a president had her wedding a few years ago, over seventy-five brand new vehicles of exotic brands were counted, apart from the expensive wristwatches, jewelry, and prime land allocations that the young couple could never have afforded in a normal lifetime. You gift the couple, then the parents who hold office. Governors, Ministers, Central Bank Governor, Heads of Government Agencies typically out-compete one another in the open and secret "eye service", that is, fawning and sycophancy -- with no explanation on how they are able to access government resources for frivolities. Their cross-fertilization and cross-contamination of ideas define the parlous state of affairs in the country.

Should the Principal lose power, no one remembers his or her birthday the next year and no one will attend his family functions, both because he is no longer relevant to them and in order to not offend the new incumbent by showing loyalty to his or her predecessor. Politicians and civil servants have also been known to grossly inflate their bank balances and asset portfolios on their mandatory Asset Declaration Forms before they get into office in anticipation of the money they will steal while in office; the subsequent acquisitions are explained away as prior assets. On those Forms, even paupers are billionaires in Naira, multi-millionaires in dollars, and Real Estate Moguls. All lies!!! When Institutions like the Central Bank, the Oil Corporation, the Intelligence Agencies, etc., need to hire new staff at all levels, no open and competitive process is adopted; rather, the Heads of those Offices visit senior Administration Officials in all the Arms of Government, influential outsiders, and their wives (typically late at night) and ask them to nominate candidates to fill the positions. This is yet another form of corruption, and perpetuates the cycle of mediocrity and patronage, while denying the country of marginalized talent.

As Nigeria's respected columnist, Dr. Chidi Amuta, eloquently put it, "a political Industry led by rascals and unenlightened power opportunists cannot be trusted to guarantee accountable and smart governance according to any Constitution." This typically produces unqualified and sub-optimal candidates who are fast-tracked through the system if their sponsor remains influential. Those without these connections simply negotiate and pay a hefty amount or the young women are asked to visit recruiters in Guest Houses or travel with them. Having been recruited this way, these individuals are not amenable to Institutional discipline and end up repeating the cycle once they become senior enough to do so. These untouchables are also the eyes and ears of their sponsors at those Agencies, identifying big contracts that must be channeled their way, destroying documents and trail if and need be, etc. The net result is a perpetuation of impunity and the exclusion of bright talents. When there are not enough Government Agencies for cronies to head, new ones are spun off, simply to have access to the till. The Nigerian Library Commission Headquarters, for example, is a skyscraper in the nation's capital, Abuja, with hundreds if not thousands of staff, and may even have branches across the country. The thing, though, is that there is no single functional public library in the country. The only libraries that there are are located in, and owned, by schools and universities. The country even has an Atomic Research Agency even as they lack basic power supply; this Agency spends the bulk of their annual budget awarding contracts for furniture, cars, salaries, renovation of properties, and "sensitization", anything and everything but Atomic Energy Research. The same thing applies to the so-called Space Research Agency. Corruption in Nigeria is systemic and pervasive; it knows no ethnicity or religion. They never fail to end all official letters (signed in red and green ink, no doubt) by "assuring the recipient of my highest regards." No creativity, no variation, just a mutuality of cronyism and self-inflation.

The reward of impunity and criminality leads to the form of patronage politics played in Nigeria, wherein Godfathers control the State due to the weakness of the institutions of governance. The results include the erosion of the rights of voters to effectively have candidates and leaders of their choice, eligible and decent people have left the political space for charlatans, the democratic culture has been uprooted, development remains in abeyance, diversion as well as a waste of state resources, unbridled militancy and violence, impoverishment of the people, etc., etc.

Part of the problem of strengthening the democratic foundation of Nigeria lies in the fact that even the major NGOs owe their allegiance to the foreign system, rather than to the Nigerian people; and the people do not understand or accept that legitimacy should derive from them as citizens. Accordingly, Nigeria seems to be trying to build democracy without democrats. The net result remains an Authoritarian State. The continuing sub-optimization of the State could very easily lead to the breeding of warlords in the oil-rich Niger Delta and Muslim terrorists in the North, since people now realize that the only effective way of accessing power is outside the established but malfunctioning democratic structures.

Democracy in Nigeria thus becomes what Dr. Nkolika Obianyo calls "a devaluation and deconstruction of democracy itself." The late Dean of the Social Sciences in Nigeria, Professor Claude Ake, wrote that: "if the Nigerian experience is any guide, Africa appears to be spawning a unique historical experience, a self-absorbed political elite with no national project whatsoever, not even an inadequate one. They are totally absorbed in the quest for absolute and eternal power. They know only their interests. It is the only morality they have and their only religion. They hear only echoes of their own voices and see only images of themselves looming to fill every space and every consciousness."

On their part, N'diaye Boubacar, Saine Abdoulaye, and Houngnikpo Mathurin, instruct in their joint work, 'Not Yet Democracy: West Africa's Slow Farewell to Authoritarianism' that the failure of the democratic experience and overall governance in West Africa can be summarized as follows:

The role of the Colonial Powers; Quality of Leadership, especially at Independence; The Military as a major Contributor to the Democratic pitfalls. Initially viewed as a symbol of National Sovereignty at the early stages of decolonization, the Military in Africa have since become the repressive arm of the Ruling Elite, with scant regard for the legitimacy of the control over the instruments of power; An urgent need to involve the people in the benefits of freedom, which the local usurpers and oppressors will not willingly accept.

While times have changed in as much as the countries are now politically independent, the clear challenge of the relationship between the elite and their people seems to have remained constant. In many ways, Africans have fared far worse after colonialism in allowing basic freedoms to their own people; etc.

It is clear that, with the increasing sophistication of the society and the revolutionary improvements in IT and Information Management, the African people will not always accept their current lot. Any strategic assessment of the Region must, therefore, note the inherent volatility, the seeming intractability of its political phenomena, and the difficulty of predicting with certainty what the future holds. In a further affirmation of the points already canvassed before now, Cyril Obi underscores the problems that Oil has created for Nigeria. Since petroleum is the fiscal basis of the Nigerian State, access to the Oil revenue has become a critical element in the reproduction of the political class and the ultimate trophy for political conquest by all means. Accordingly, the staking of claims to power and resources has intensified, resulting in the escalation of mistrust, tension, and conflict between those who control power, access, and resources (and are unwilling to share, give up, or account for, such power under any circumstances) and those to whom all access is blocked/ denied (who are made to bear the full brunt of being powerless), with severe implications for the fragility, or otherwise, of the Body Politic.

The clamor for Fiscal Federalism (derivation-based sharing), Resource Control, Niger Delta Crisis, and all forms of demand for equity, are predicated on this experience. To compound the seriousness of the grievances, ultimatums for redress by aggrieved oil communities are visited with serious State repression, in partnership with the Oil Corporations, thus sustaining a cycle of increasingly-popular protests, sabotage, kidnappings, stockpiling of weapons by militant groups from the oil-producing areas, disruption of oil exploration activities, and even more repression.

The Obasanjo Administration, for example, sent in Nigerian troops to Odi in Bayelsa State in 2000 when the local communities protested the most serious oil spill in the area, which led to some soldiers being killed. The result was the killing of over seven thousand men, women, and children, as well as the burning of all the houses in the town. This particularly radicalized the Region, with the results being felt till date. Unarmed agitators for self-determination in Igboland were mowed down by the Military under Buhari's Administration. The same Will has been absent in vanquishing the Muslim terrorists who litter the land and operate with impunity, thus inspiring rumors of official complicity, especially as it pertains to the Fulani murderers. Counterterrorism has also become a lucrative business for the Administration and Military, with billions of dollars spent to date on an effort that has not yielded much result.

While the Igbos of Nigeria constitute one of the three major ethnic groups (when you conveniently lump the Hausas and Fulanis together), contribute maximally in the development of the different States where they reside as highly-itinerant business people and professionals, contribute substantially to the aggregate State revenue base, etc., there is zero federal infrastructure and presence in the Region of over 40 million people. Some of Nigeria's crude oil also comes from this Region, yet the only Federal presence they feel is the overwhelming deployment of armed Federal Forces to extort them and brutalize their psyche. While previous Administrations paid lip service to the need to replace a much-strained pivotal bridge leading into the Region, the Buhari Administration has commenced work on this short but crucial bridge, and there is considerable gratitude to them in a country where little things impress people. But there is a catch.

While all the several Federal projects in the other Regions, especially the non-contributing North where Mr. Buhari hails from, are directly funded by the Federal Government or through loans which Igbo people will join the Yorubas, South-South oil-producing people, and sundry Southern minority states to repay, the critical bridge leading into their Region is being built under an opaque Private-Public Partnership (PPP) Program, wherein toll gates will be installed on this fundamental chokepoint to recover the amount of the "investment", making it the ONLY federal road that would be tolled in the entire country!!! If you want to impose a yoke on people, they should be able to make inputs into the costing of the project. Not in this case; the Federal Government has massively over-inflated the cost of a basic bridge which a small US town will construct without attention or fanfare and is then transferring this massive cost to people from one Region. The impudence of the Construct, the partiality of the treatment, and the arrogance of the inflated imposition, are also generating considerable anger among people from the Region, leading to a coalescing demand for self-determination. At the best of times, the current bridge handles millions of vehicles each year, with congestion experienced during festive Seasons.

The imperatives of a national bargain are, therefore, very urgent. Oil-based accumulation without conscience cannot be sustained in perpetuity. With the sustained crash in the price of oil, the rapid advancements in alternative fuel and electric cars, the considerable shale deposits in the US and Canada, as well as new emphasis on eco-friendly technologies, oil-producing countries that failed to diversify the base of their economies before now, may yet drink all their crude oil soon, with the serious security problems that will ensue. As the revenue from oil has been crashing, African countries, including Nigeria under Mr. Muhammadu Buhari, have been piling up and wasting or stealing foreign debts denominated in foreign currencies, using a disproportionate percentage of their internally generated revenue to pay the accrued interest, without repaying the principal amount. This seriously compromises their **independence,** making them even more **dependent** on external forces. The expected inability to repay will completely erode the gains of sovereignty, whatever they have been.

As far as people from the Southern part of Nigeria are concerned, the laying of oil pipelines from oil wells in the Niger Delta (South) and the transportation of crude oil to Kaduna (North – where there is no oil) for refining in the largest refinery on the African Continent built by Chiyoda of Japan– which has now conveniently been rendered comatose to enable importation of finished products (for corruption), is parallel to the colonial railroads which linked the hinterland with the shores of Nigeria at Port-Harcourt and Lagos, for the purpose of exploitation through the transportation of raw materials from the colonies to industrialized metropolitan Europe. The counterpart jobs, ancillary businesses, taxes, and skills are, accordingly, denied the people who suffer the oil and gas flares, severe ecological devastation, and other hardships that accompany oil exploration activities.

Under Mr. Buhari, this has got much worse, as his Regime is presently using borrowed funds (to be repaid by the South) to pipe natural gas from the Niger Delta through the northern part of the country, through Niger Republic to Nigeria's north, all the way across the Sahara Desert to Algeria, in a structure that is completely opaque. While public (borrowed) funds are paying for this major project, there have been rumors that the ownership resides with favored individuals close to the President. In the absence of clear information, it is difficult to determine the truth. Analysts are guided by the fact that, though entire Regions of the country are completely excluded from the antiquated and overpriced Rail program which Mr. Buhari's Administration is executing with Chinese loans and manpower, the rail network extends well into Niger Republic, a neighboring country with religious, cultural, and linguistic commonalities with the President and the Hausa/ Fulani stock.

The numerous sources of tension in Nigeria make it difficult to clearly define classes, while the elites are fragmented by ethnic-language group membership, place of origin, and institutional identity. This fact compounds the problem of achieving a broad-based consensus on issues. It becomes very difficult to create alliances among students, workers, and poor farmers, just as it is difficult to create cohesive political groupings based on high-income or high status in Nigeria. These combine to account for the limited resistance, to date, to the rapid deterioration of accountability and services by the State, but this is no guarantee of a continuing lack of resistance into the future.

Against the backdrop of the cumulative injustices in the Nigerian system, including the pogrom against the Igbos, how the Civil War was fought, the fact that Igbo people were made to forfeit all their properties in Port-Harcourt by official proclamation to date, Niger Delta issues, brazen corruption and insensitivity, failure of the State to provide the basics of modern life, various ethno-religious massacres in the North directed at Southerners and Christians (while their reaction is usually stopped by Muslim soldiers and policemen!), the persistent jihad by the Fulani terrorists, the unabating onslaught by Boko Haram against both Muslims and non-Muslims alike, the worsening economic conditions of the majority, the disproportionate role of the North in the public space, especially given their zero contribution to public coffers, other natural resources being mined privately, political issues, etc., it is clear that the time for honest discussions among Nigerians is NOW. In fact, it was yesterday. What is clear is that no country can develop optimally with the man-made systemic issues afflicting the country.

Nigeria's festering issues became manifest within two years after independence and have remained largely unresolved to this day. The necessary incubatory stage for the negotiation of relationship parameters was skipped in the rush towards so-called independence. In one's considered view, free Nigerians must hold a free and representative National Conference where ALL the current and potential sources of tension must be tabled, negotiated, and resolved. Pretending otherwise is a formula for episodic spikes in violence, which, with the declining fortune of the majority and the widening cleavages, could lead to the total collapse of the "mere geographical expression" as presently constituted.

Part of what must be resolved is the desirability, or otherwise, of the continued Union. The Native Authority System, which was operated in Northern Nigeria during the years of colonialism, for example, is derived from the political architecture of the Arab World, in which power is concentrated in the Emir, and "which places him in a position to control all appointments in the State, the relations of clientage and vassalage … which places a premium on loyalty above all other considerations, … all of these militate against and are dysfunctional in a modern bureaucratic system … of accountability, separation of powers, as well as checks and balances."

The transposition of this mindset onto the administration of the country, together with the emanation in a false sense of entitlement, account for the country's state of under-development. It is agreed that values determine behavior and the translation into the mode of governance in a System. When this is contrasted with the progressive culture of the Christian South, the frustration over the undefined terms of engagement becomes evident.

The entrenched resistance to reforms, which is part of Islamic Orthodoxy, must, therefore, be confronted for exactly what it is, or those subscribing to the status quo allowed to govern themselves. The current House cannot stand as it is; instability is an inescapable condition in the creation of a viable political Order with deep roots in injustice and is, therefore, inextricably and intimately bound up with the process of modernization and political development. Against this regard, political instability could have some positive features, as stability to preserve a decadent political Order or a corrupt regime cannot be advocated in good conscience. Stability is only preferred when it is a necessary condition for the attainment of the aggregate objectives of the State, as consensually determined. A discussion of the issues becomes urgent, to avert a recourse to attempts at passionate and kinetic resolution which, invariably, still lead to discussions. Majority of Nigerians will prefer not to participate in their political processes only through violence. To the extent that they can help overcome and integrate diverse and competing interests, Institutions matter. Otherwise, they are useless.

Nigeria's Place in the World

It does appear that, from the perspective of the West, Nigeria's strategic value lies only in energy matters. For a long time, Nigeria supplied a quarter of US crude oil requirements, especially when the uncertainties in the Middle East posed grave risk to the security of energy supplies from that volatile Region in the medium to long-term, and also when the shale deposits had not been optimized. America's disengagement from the world under Trump is creating a void on the Continent and elsewhere. As it is, China has entrenched herself in those countries by various means.

In the past, once oil flowed to the US, the White House did not exercise the leverage it had with African dictators, by aligning with the people in enthroning civility, transparency, human rights, accountability, and a culture of service. It should be necessary to ask if the concept of democracy and good governance differs across Continents. Why is the West ever ready to accept and rationalize manifest abuses of the democratic process in Africa by recognizing the emerging "Governments"? Is this an extension of the long-standing impression of Africa? Has careful thought been given to the implications for the image of the West among African people, as well as the real risk of the disruption of the energy and resource supplies, which seem to be their primary focus? Already, the sustained ruptures in the Niger Delta Region have contributed to the uncertain supply and price dynamics on the international energy market.

Most African populations are powerless before their indigenous oppressors with absolute control over the instruments of coercion. They need support and real understanding. They need empowerment. One out of every five Africans is a Nigerian. The US will reap considerable goodwill if its Public Diplomacy initiatives would include supporting the people against their oppressors, censuring public officials, exposing instances of fraud, identifying and exposing where the stolen funds are hidden all over the world. Instead, despite the manifest electoral fraud that the 2003, 2007, and 2019 elections were, the US was the first country on those occasions to congratulate Nigerians on "successful and peaceful elections". Victims of intimidation regard such laudatory encouragement of criminals as quite depressing signals from the bastion of democracy and the country that should lead by the moral force of her example.

This contributes to the problem of marketing and entrenching democracy in some of these countries. Properly run, most African countries will not require aid packages and other concessions from the world. In the event of the unraveling of Nigeria, the social, health, demographic, security, and economic implications for the sub-Region, Africa, and the world will be widespread and catastrophic for all.

So, Can Democracy Work in Nigeria?

Having discussed some of the unsavory manifestations of the democratic experience in Nigeria, it is tempting to conclude that democracy cannot survive in the country. The opposite is actually the case. Nigerians, like other human beings, yearn for self-government and for public accountability. They correctly expect their Government, which controls the lever of power and the public purse, to work for them, to enhance their living standards, to energize their entrepreneurial capabilities, to provide the infrastructure which makes life meaningful, and to lead by example. The combination of both political and economic expectations is quite natural and in order. While it is true that man does not live by bread alone, he still needs to eat some bread. Philosophy does not obviate Material Science or Biology. Nigeria is currently a mere geographical expression, and not a Nation-State in the strict sense of the term. However, the inherent plurality could be put to good use by the sheer force of leadership and service. Nigerians have been conditioned to NOT expect anything from their government, so minimal and token achievements are applauded.

Postmodern Theorists will suggest that the best formula for reinforcing democracy in a society like Nigeria would lie in de-emphasizing group (religious, social, ethnic) identities, but would rather involve treating each citizen as a person deserving of dignity on account of her/his intrinsic humanity. This is a very romantic proposition, especially in pre-industrial societies. There is nothing inherently wrong about sub-national identities. They are elevated to prominence when the collective identity conferred by common citizenship in a formal state, becomes tenuous. The polarity and tension in most under-developed States is, therefore, a reflection of the failed or failing status of their States.

Democracy is a preferred form of government for all the reasons already discussed above. Majority Rule remains preferred as it aids unity and helps the process of achieving a consensus across several divisive lines; ensures quick decision-making; affords a basis for legitimacy; is less complicated in nature as compared to other decision-making Systems, which invariably lead to problems; and also promotes stability, responsibility, and accountability in the process of governance. The prevalence and implications of the inequality of wealth, inadequate information, deep cleavages, illiteracy and ignorance, as well as the risk of producing one-party systems that limit choice and involve an autarky of sorts, must be considered in developing the details of the democratic platform in Nigeria. However, it must be stressed that kangaroo democracy is different from democracy. It is either democracy or it is not democracy. The ingredients of democracy must be sacrosanct for the political system to earn the qualification of democracy. The efficacy of the instruments of constraint on power must be objectively tested on a recurring basis, for validity, adjustments, etc.

It is very clear that some of the issues that must be addressed before real democracy can survive in Nigeria include:

- Convocation of a National Conference among all the peoples of the country where the decision to remain one country, as well as the parameters of nationhood must be freely negotiated and agreed, and the standards of public governance determined
- Retroactive Accountability Checks/ Audits (from 1970 to date)
- Institution of effective guardrails to seriously minimize, discourage and punish abuse of office
- Review of extant laws to reflect contemporary dynamics

- Overhaul of the bureaucracy
- Urgent and direct enhancement of infrastructure and services across the country, and especially in the oil-producing parts of the country.
- Serious punishment of all previous looters, as a deterrent to others, and as a symbolic communication of a deviation from the past
- Enhancement of the educational standards
- Focus on areas that generate distrust among people
- Even-handed application of laws and rules, as well as an equitable distribution of facilities
- Public exposure of abuses of office
- Leadership by example
- True Federalism
- A truly independent Judiciary and Electoral Commission
- Stable and transparent structures for the incubation of a Free Market Economy
- Aggressive efforts towards the diversification of the economy
- A sustained program of political enlightenment, to empower the citizenry
- Re-orientation and reconstitution of the Military, Police Force, and the Security Services
- Sustained efforts towards the economic emancipation of the people.
- Recovery of the ill-gotten wealth.
- Indigeneship/ Settler Issue Resolved
- A transparent Census that reflects all the slices of identity: ethnicity, religion, etc., regardless of place of domicile

The advanced countries can assist by enhancing capacities across the board and by providing information on the whereabouts of the stolen funds. Cooperation on retrieval will be key, while utilization towards national causes should be guaranteed. All of this should be done publicly. It was partly in false hopes that Mr. Buhari, a retired Major General and former Military Head of State, would lead this national redemption effort and solve Nigeria's Security problems to boot, that he was overwhelmingly elected as the Civilian President in 2015 during his fourth attempt at becoming a Civilian President, defeating the incumbent President, Goodluck Jonathan -- who conceded unlike many African leaders. Mr. Jonathan, as Vice-President in 2010, completed the presidential term of his boss, President Yar'adua, who died in Saudi Arabia after a protracted illness. Mr. Yar'adua was a decent man who had crippling health issues, which were exploited by his wife and closest civilian and military aides -- who effectively ruled the country on his behalf, completely humiliated and ostracized the Vice-President Jonathan, and looted the treasury at will.

After serving out his boss' term, Dr. Jonathan won an election in his own right -- despite the gang-up of the northern elite that was insistent on fielding a northern Muslim candidate for what would have been Mr. Yar'adua's second term. Jonathan's Administration was defined by paranoia over the persistent threats from the North (including from Mr. Buhari), maintenance of the status quo, an Administration that had a national outlook, even spread of infrastructure across the country, the ubiquity of his wife, spinelessness especially towards two female Cabinet members who epitomized corruption, one in charge of the vital Petroleum Ministry and the other presiding over the Aviation Ministry. While one of these women is now cancer-stricken and in exile in the UK (she has since transformed into a Dominican Republic national with a Diplomatic passport), the other is presently a Nigerian Senator, also granted a Diplomatic passport as a reward for her corruption.

A few years prior, the anti-corruption Agency, EFCC, had publicly displayed a pile of very expensive wristwatches and jewelry they seized when they searched the residence of the erstwhile Oil Minister; since then, nothing more has been heard about these items worth tens of millions of dollars -- of course, they have been re-looted by the policemen and women who run the Agency, and some taken to the wives of sponsors, benefactors and protectors, to ensure their retention at this "lucrative" Agency. In the case of the former Aviation Minister, credible and documented petitions against her were submitted to the anti-corruption Agency, EFCC, over her diversion of funds (running into hundreds of millions of dollars) earmarked for the renovation of airports, the comprehensive upgrade of Security equipment at all the airports, as well as the introduction of $20 Security Levy on every airline ticket for the maintenance of procured equipment, establishment of an Aviation Security Academy, and planned future replacement of those equipment, etc. She simply used part of the stolen funds and bought herself a seat as a "Distinguished" Senator, joining what has largely become a Haven of past and present lootocrats, a refuge for scoundrels, a facility where former governors retire after their uninspiring tenures, resuming their lives of predation against the State.

EFCC Operatives have since resorted to using the petition to extort money from the woman distinguished by infamy -- as is commonly known --; the Security Levy is still being collected on over 15 million passengers annually (arbitrarily jacked up to $50 per ticket) and there is no visibility on the application of the funds. What is evident is that no Aviation Security Academy was built, and inferior Security equipment was bought at less than 10% of the initial contract amount. Wives of Regional and national-level Godfathers are also assigned seats at the Senate. The Parliament of roughly 470 members -- Senate and House of Representatives -- appropriate more money to themselves than the combined national budgets for education and health care. This is apart from the fraudulent device they call Constituency Projects, as well as the open extortion and bribery that characterize their oversight function. Government Agencies and Ministries also have to bribe these reprobates to have their departmental allocations "secure" for their own looting.

Credit: *@echwalu; June 7, 2017*

Mr. Buhari's Attorney-General for five years, a particularly mediocre lawyer of insignificant professional pedigree but with the vital qualifications of being a Northern lawyer and a loyalist to the Cult of Buharism, has sustained a particular penchant for intervening on behalf of uber-corrupt officials (Northerners, no doubt) and justifying the payment of several millions of dollars as professional fees to lawyers nominated by him.

Early in July 2020, the Acting Chairman of the EFCC, Police Commissioner Ibrahim Magu, was forcefully dragged before a Special Investigative Panel to defend himself against weighty and credible allegations including: the diversion of recovered funds, assets, and real estate; buying expensive properties overseas with the proceeds of corruption; under-reporting the amounts recovered by the Agency to the tune of over $100 million in the local currency; entrenching a culture of personality cultism and cronyism at the Agency by assigning "juicy" investigations to the so-called 'Magu Boys'; using internal and external proxies to extort money from individuals under investigation and to buy seized properties at ridiculously-low prices; running an ultra-corrupt Agency; generally living way above his means, etc., etc. Unable to provide a satisfactory defense, he was summarily dismissed while the country awaited either his possible prosecution or the extension of the "soft landing" which was given to his predecessors in office. While any of these allegations should ordinarily be incompatible with the operating philosophy and operations of an anti-corruption Agency, Nigerians are not particularly too shocked, noting that the Attorney-General who is spearheading Mr. Magu's problems, is not necessarily very clean himself.

While State failure is a cumulative development that gets worse over time, Mr. Buhari has, by all standards, been the worst leader or ruler in Nigeria since their independence in 1960. It has become clear to both his supporters and adversaries alike that they were sold a dummy, as the man is thoroughly lacking in vision, ambition, integrity, energy, fairness, intellectual curiosity, and capacity to govern a plural society, or any society for that matter. He has very easily remained the most nepotistic, clannish, bigoted, and narrow-minded leader in the history of the unfortunate country. His unqualified relatives and cronies populate the high levels of the Presidency and other prestigious offices in the land through nepotism, the corruption level in the country has worsened even as the Administration retains their propaganda to the contrary, the Administration is credibly in support of the Fulani Jihad across the country given that none of the arms-toting killers has ever been apprehended or tried and the same Government is channeling State resources towards resettling the terrorists, the binge of external borrowings under Buhari threatens the survival of the country, he has proven gross incapacity to solve basic Security problems in five years despite billions of dollars expended on same -- thereby putting a question mark on his credentials and eligibility for the high military rank of Major-General, his disdain for Southerners and notably non-Muslim Igbos and oil-producing minorities is not hidden, the display of ill-gotten wealth by the children of thieves in power has assumed unusual dimensions, he has completely emasculated both the Judiciary and the Legislature, etc., etc.

During the 2019 elections, which he was billed to lose, he deployed the election commission, the military, Police, and Security Services to openly kill and maim people in Regions where he was unpopular while also making it impossible for people to vote against him. All this while, he and his backers allowed and enabled voting by nine-year-olds in the zones where Mr. Buhari was popular. The Election Monitors (US State Department, EU, AU, ECOWAS, Global NGOs, and local bodies) captured all of these in their Reports. Mr. Buhari is presently in the second year of a four-year final term. His closest associates have also been listed as the biggest players in the Oil Industry as well as the beneficiaries of a quiet differential exchange rate arbitrage regime which yields annual gains in excess of $1 billion to them. He demonstrates unseen levels of tone-deafness and insensitivity by placing Muslim Northerners at the helm of all the Security and Military Agencies, as well as other "juicy" government offices -- with the cascading monoculture and nepotism evident in all those cases. In five years, he has caused more division among the people than in the first fifty-five years of their independence, massively devalued their currency owing to gross incompetence; insecurity has worsened which affects productivity, created more Government Agencies staffed by cronies and relatives in a country already choking from an overweight bureaucracy, and sustained a binge of national debts which the country cannot ever repay -- with nothing to show for the loans. Recall that President Obasanjo left office with zero foreign debt in 2007. While Presidents Yar'adua and Jonathan started borrowing afresh, the levels were nothing compared with the binge borrowing under President Buhari. It must be emphasized that President Buhari is also the Minister of Petroleum.

Since the Covid:19 pandemic started three months ago, for example, the National Assembly headed by his lackeys, has approved the following loans for the Administration, apart from previous borrowings: $22.79 billion; $3.4 billion (IMF); $3.5 billion; and N850 billion Naira local debt. The World Bank has also just announced a $750 million loan for Nigeria's Power Sector. As always, the power issues will persist and there will be no accountability for this loan. The country's foreign debt has shot up to over $90 billion in 2020, from zero in 2007, with a declining capacity to repay plus no translation into commensurate deployment of the funds. Mr. Buhari also spends extended periods of time in the UK attending to his health without realizing the need to uplift his country's healthcare system in five years since he has been president; the pretenses about modesty and asceticism have been revealed to be hollow; he has surrendered governance and decision-making to a cabal of unelected individuals some of whom live lavishly in mansions within the Presidential Complex and are maintained by the Government. Nigeria has regressed significantly under Mr. Buhari and may indeed not recover from his assault on the fabric that was weak even at the best of times. Mr. Buhari's problem is not so much that of geriatric incapacity as it is a combination of malevolent aloofness, extended and regular periods of insentience, a profound lack of curiosity, a belated exposure as chronically incompetent, and surrender of the reins of power and the national till to unelected feudal thieves and ethnic bigots.

Former Vice-President under Obasanjo, a massive beneficiary of the prebendal State himself, now a very successful businessman, and a professional presidential aspirant, Alhaji Atiku Abubakar, was so overwhelmed by the spate of borrowings that he issued a public Statement, for which he was expectedly insulted by the Administration. His full observations entitled 'How to Pull Nigeria from the Brink" bear full rendition as follows:

"On Monday, April 27, 2020, British oil and gas giant, BP, became the latest in a growing number of energy firms to declare a massive quarterly loss. Their loss was in the region of $4.4 billion dollars. Bear in mind that this was a conglomerate that posted a $2.6 billion profit in the corresponding quarter of 2019.The challenges that are already engulfing the oil and gas sector will continue to plague that industry for at least the rest of the year, and may reach apocalyptic levels sooner than we expect. As I write this, there are hundreds of crude oil laden ships, all filled up, with nowhere to berth, and accruing daily charges of an average of $30,000. We have also seen crude oil prices plunge to record lows, to the extent that some

variants of the product have been given out for free, or worse still, producers have paid storage facilities to take their products. As at today (May 1, 2020), Nigeria is pricing its very low sulphur sweet crude at $10 per barrel, yet buyers are balking. Our sweet crude is becoming a little bitter.

I had earlier warned that Nigeria needs a Strategic Reserve to store unsold crude. Now, we have so much crude and no one to buy it, nowhere to store it, and little idea what to do with it.

Barely three years ago, I had also alerted that the "crude thinking" promoted by our dependence on crude oil will lead to a rude shock. 'If you are still talking about oil, you are in the past. As far as I am concerned, the era of oil is gone. If you want to believe it, believe it. If you do not want to believe it, you will see it. It is crude thinking to continue to talk and base development projections on crude oil', I had said at a public event in the nation's capital. We must face the fact that reliance on crude oil is failing Nigeria and other mono product economy crude oil exporters. Now is the time for Nigeria and her contemporaries to cure their addiction to sweet crude. For far too long we have grown high on our own supply, to the extent that we have neglected almost every other sector of our economy.

This present rude awakening should be seen as a blessing in disguise – a blessing that compels us to take those drastic actions that will free us from the crude oil trap. We need to diversify our economy, and yes, it is easier said than done, but that does not mean it is an impossible task. Prior to Nigeria's October 1, 1960 independence from Great Britain, not only were we a nation self-reliant in food production, but we also exported food to other countries, earning precious foreign exchange in the process. Who can forget the great groundnut pyramids in Northern Nigeria? For example, in 1957, agriculture formed a whopping 86% of our export revenue. By 1977, agricultural exports had dwindled to 6%, and today, the figure is less than 3%. How did our country go from being a net exporter of agricultural products to a net importer of food products?

How did we go from a country that could feed itself to one that desperately depends on foreign imports for survival? The answer to these questions is leadership focus. During elections, Nigerian politicians spend a significant amount of their campaign time discussing how they will manage the nation's resources. However, the fundamental difference between a leader and a manager is that while a manager focuses on managing existing resources, a leader sets out a creative vision which the country must follow to chart a course to political and socio-economic greatness.

Certainly, what is abundantly clear is that Nigeria is never going to become an industrialized nation by selling more oil, even if the oil market recovers. The lessons from Venezuela's current predicament come to mind. If oil and gas could have saved any nation, that nation would be Venezuela. Unfortunately, Venezuela is bankrupt and insolvent. Saudi Arabia, despite its huge reserves and a highly publicized listing of Saudi Aramco, is feeling the pinch and working rapidly towards its Vision 2030, which requires Saudi Arabia to diversify from its dependence on Oil. Other prudent countries facing the same predicament are doing the same. Oil economies need to learn a thing or two about economic diversification from the United Arab Emirates. Despite being a young nation, the leadership of the UAE has managed to diversify the economy of this country from an almost complete reliance on oil in the 1970s, to a country where 72% of the GDP comes from the non-oil sectors of the economy such as aviation, tourism and services sectors.

In Nigeria, our diversification should embrace agriculture as the primary sector earmarked for development, because agriculture is a low hanging fruit, is key to ensuring food subsistence, and with the recent signing of the African Continental Free Trade Area agreement (AFCTA), which favors Nigeria's economy greatly, Nigeria can take advantage of this to become an agricultural powerhouse in Africa. For example, Africa has the lowest intra-regional trade amongst the seven Continents. Indeed, 68% of Europe's trade is within the Continent. However, Africa does more trade with non-African nations than we do amongst each other. Our intra-Continental trade is an abysmal 18%. This must change and Nigeria is key to altering this sad state of affairs.

Within the Agricultural sector, the African Continent in 2014, earned $2.4 billion from the export of coffee to Europe. That sounds impressive. However, one country alone, Germany, made $3.8 billion from re-exporting Africa's coffee in 2014. This trend continued into 2015, 2016 and has not changed to date. What is it that Germany does to add value to the coffee, cocoa, and other produce that they buy from Africa that we cannot do in Nigeria? Nigeria can easily become a value-added re-exporter of African coffee to the world. Ditto for tea, cocoa, wheat, sugar cane, and other cash crops. There are none of these products that I have mentioned that Nigeria cannot either grow in commercial quantities or add value to, in the same way other industrialized economies are doing.

I should know because I am already practicing what I am advocating. I have multiple profitable farms and other businesses in the agricultural value chain. With about 60% of its land assessed as arable, I truly believe that Nigeria is capable of becoming the food basket of the rest of Africa, and in the process, it can capture a sizable portion of the $48 billion that goes towards food imports in Africa. That money should be circulating within Africa, strengthening our currencies, growing our GDPs, and enriching our people. I was in Benin Republic recently and I was informed by one of the most successful industrialists in the country that Benin buys its cement from China.

Why should a country that shares land borders with Nigeria have to import cement from China 7000 miles away, when Dangote cement is perfectly able, and I am sure willing, to provide the same product at a competitive price? Is this not what the AFCTA agreement is meant to promote? Why would Nigeria maintain an insane policy of border closures at a time it desperately needs them open to promote trade? Now is the time for Nigeria to make those hard decisions it has postponed for far too long otherwise the alternative is an apocalyptic scenario we would rather not entertain. We must, as a nation, begin to invest our resources wisely in order to maximize dividends. We must liberalize our land tenure system to make it possible and easy for some of the 27 million unemployed Nigerians to become farmers, even as sharecroppers. Last year, Ethiopia mobilized its 100 million strong population to plant 350 million trees in 12 hours (a world record). Nigeria can similarly mobilize its population of twice that number to plant billions of cash crops through the planting season. It is possible. I have repeatedly charged my farm associates to sow seeds and they have done so successfully.

When the huge opportunities of agriculture are combined with a rejuvenated manufacturing and MSMEs sectors, then a new era of sustainability and prosperity beckons for Africa. Nigeria is at the lowest point we have ever been as a nation. We have over-indulged on seemingly cheap loans and have quadrupled our foreign debt in just four years. Taking more of such loans will just sink our country deeper and deeper into a quagmire. What is certain is that we cannot continue with things the way they are now except we want to ensure an implosion of our dearly beloved nation. We must cut our coat, not according to our size, but according to our cloth. Our Presidential Air Fleet of almost 10 planes should go. Our jumbo budgets for our legislature must go. The planned $100 million renovation of our Parliament must be cancelled. We cannot be funding non-necessities with debt and not expect our economy to collapse. Our civil servants must come to the realization that Nigeria cannot sustain its size and profligacy. The same cost -saving measures must be adopted by the States and Council Governments. From henceforth, our energies, resources and focus must be on how we can diversify our economy, not on how we can increase our expenditure." End of Quote.

As we consider testimonies from objective parties, it will be useful to render in full the article written by the Managing Director of one of Nigeria's notable newspapers, 'Thisday', Mr. Eniola Bello, titled: 'Insecurity and Buhari's *Mea Culpa'*:

"Perhaps for the first time in the life of the Buhari administration, all the security chiefs jointly addressed the media Thursday last week. At the press conference, National Security Adviser Mohammed Babagana Monguno led Defence Minister Bashir Salihi Magashi; service chiefs, Gen. Abayomi Olonisakin (Chief of Defence Staff), Lt. Gen. Yusuf Tukur Buratai (Army Chief), Vice Admiral Ibok-Ete Ekwe Ibas (Naval Chief) and Air Marshal Sadique Saliu Abubakar (Air Force Chief); Inspector General of Police Mohammed Adamu;and intelligence chiefs Yusuf Magaji Bichi (Department of State Services), Ahmed Rufai Abubakar (National Intelligence Agency) and Mohammed Sani Usman (Defence Intelligence Agency) to express the president's disappointment with their failure in arresting the worsening insecurity in the country. Buhari, through Monguno, for the first time publicly chided the security chiefs in what could be described as his mea culpa, his acknowledgement of his error, while vowing not to accept any more excuses for the heightened insecurity in the country. Standing out like a sore thumb at that press conference, in a country whose peoples are overly sensitive to their ethnic, cultural and religious diversities, is the lop-sidedness in the composition of the top security chiefs, zonally. Only two – Olonisakin from Ekiti State in the southwest and Ibas from Cross River State in the south south – out of nine security chiefs are from the south. Monguno and Buratai come from Borno State, and Abubakar from Bauchi State in the northeast; Magashi,

Bichi and Usman come from Kano State, and Rufai from Katsina State in the northwest; and Adamu is from Nasarawa State in the north central. Yet, insecurity, particularly in the north, has been on the upswing in the last five years of this administration.

Boko Haram insurgents, an extremist Islamic group that Buhari had promised to decimate within three months when he first took the presidential oath in May 2015, have made scorched earth policy an article of faith in some parts of northeast, particularly Borno, kidnapping and killing and maiming and raping, and in the process turning hundreds of school girls into sex slaves. In the northwest states of Katsina and Kaduna and Sokoto and Zamfara, bandits and rustlers strike at will, leaving in their wake death, blood and tears. And in the north central states of Nasarawa and Niger and Kogi, bandits, armed robbers and kidnappers have long had a field day sowing death and destruction. The common denominator among these non-state agents of violence is that they fight for no higher purpose; they simply kill the people and burn down communities for the fun of it.

Raiding from the north down south are gun-totting herders and kidnappers on the loose, attacking farmers, destroying farmlands, raping women and killing for sport. Before now, state governors, political, religious and community leaders, and socio-cultural organisations across the southern zones had called on the security agencies to stop the killings, even cried out to the president, and long demanded the removal of the service chiefs, and their reconstitution to reflect the country's diversity, but all to no avail.

But for the recent spate of protests in Katsina, organised by the Coalition of Northern Groups; the Northern Elders' Forum's trenchant condemnation of the administration's inability to handle the reign of armed gangs; Sultan Muhammed Sa'ad Abubakar III desperately crying out from the Sokoto Sahel; and more importantly, the US denunciation of the "senseless and brazen killings of civilians", Buhari may not have had the sense of duty to call out his security chiefs. Even then, the president's yellow card to the security chiefs not a few Nigerians have said didn't go far enough; many individuals and groups have in the last two years, and rightly so, called for their removal.

Although the problem of Boko Haram insurgency, violent communal clashes, kidnappings, and insensate criminality predated this administration, the insecurity situation has deepened and widened and worsened under Buhari in the last five years. Indeed, it wouldn't be uncharitable to conclude that on the strength of his performance, or lack of it, that Buhari, with his leadership style, his policies, his utterances, his actions, no inaction, has enabled non-state actors of violence. For clarity, let us examine these one after the other. The president's leadership style for one! Bruna Martinuzzi, an author, columnist and presentation skills trainer in an article, "The 7 Most Common Leadership Styles (and How to Find Your Own)" itemises some primary leadership types as: the autocratic leader who believes he is the smartest and makes decisions without input from his team; the authoritative leader who is visionary and shows the way for others; the pacesetting leader who sets the bar high and ruthlessly pushes his team; the democratic leader who shares information with, and seeks opinion from, team members before making a decision; the coach leader who seeks to develop the talent and unlock the potentials of his team; the affiliative leader who gets up close and personal and supports the emotional needs of his team; and, the laissez-faire leader who lets his people swim with the current, and exercises the least amount of oversight.

Either by nature or nurture, Buhari's leadership style can be classified as laissez-faire, the principle of which the president himself described as belonging to everyone and no one. In other words, Buhari only knows Buhari. Is it any wonder that the president, in the last five years, could hardly be bothered with any matter that doesn't affect his election and personal enjoyment of presidential office? Writes Martinuzzi, "On the surface, a laissez-faire leader may appear to trust people to know what to do, but taken to the extreme, an uninvolved leader may end up appearing aloof. While it's beneficial to give people opportunities to spread their wings, with a total lack of direction, people may unwittingly drift in the wrong direction..." Indeed, no Nigerian leader has been as distant, and aloof, to the goings on in his government the way Buhari has been. There are too many competing and conflicting power centres. Aides create their own mini-empires and work at cross-purposes. The president is there like he's not there; there's no cohesion, no oversight, no clearinghouse, no fear of sanction for bad behaviour.

The result is self-evident. At the Presidential Villa, First Lady Aisha Buhari has been in incessant public spat with her husband's family members for control. The leadership of the ruling All Progressives Congress (APC) is in disarray. Buhari has failed to concretely deliver on the tripod of his campaign promises – tackling insecurity, fighting corruption, and reviving the economy – on the strength of which he was elected in 2015. Buhari's laissez-faire leadership style has been unhelpful in the battle against Boko Haram insurgency in the northeast and banditry in the northwest. There's no cohesion, no coordination among the armed services; the army deploys troops to insurgents' enclaves without air support, air force jets bombard Boko Haram camps without the ground troops to mop up operations. The NSA and Service Chiefs play cat and mouse games, avoid holding strategic meetings. Serial claims of killing scores of bandits, or hundreds of insurgents, or technically degrading Boko Haram become hollow with every such claim countered by indiscriminate violent attacks on innocent civilians, or bloody ambushes of soldiers in the theatre of war. Security chiefs do not seem to feel the pressure of presidential oversight perhaps because of Buhari's peculiar nonchalance.

The administration's policy of rehabilitating repentant Boko Haram members smells. A group of anarchists, in the name of Islam, take up arms against the state. They bomb and kill and rape and maim and burn down communities. Rather than bring those captured in war to justice by prosecuting them, the government rehabilitates them, some allege, even recruit them into the military, while the battle is still on as their erstwhile comrade-in-arms are killing our soldiers and burning down civilian communities. It is difficult to comprehend the woolly thinking behind this policy. It creates the impression that criminality is rewarded, and may not be unconnected, willy-nilly, with the mutation of other criminal gangs in the north west and north central. The utterances of the president and his aides also appear to enable the agents of violence. A few examples will suffice. Sometime in 2016, when the Benue State government was making efforts, through legislation and robust policy implementation, to nip in the bud the herders' bloody attack on farming communities and destruction of farmlands, Buhari had urged mourning victims of a massacre to accommodate their countrymen. The administration's then Defence Minister Mansur Dan Alli had also justified herders' violent attacks by blaming their victims for farming on cattle routes.

And presidential spokesman Femi Adesina, at the height of the controversy surrounding the opposition to the establishment of cattle colonies in every state of the federation, had appeared to explain away, if not justify, herders' violent attacks on farming communities while answering a question on the ancestral attachment to land in some parts of the country. "Ancestral attachment?," he had asked scornfully before adding, "You can only have ancestral attachment when you are alive. If you are talking about ancestral attachment, if you are dead, how does the attachment matter?" The president's communication strategy has indeed been galling. Where he should talk to the people, he talks at them, that is, when he talks at all. The presidency mistakes abuse for engagement, contempt for empathy, campaign for governance, and pettiness for statesmanship. There is an arrogance in communication that would have been laughable were Buhari's leadership not so terribly poor.

A good leader understands the need to combine two or three leadership styles, particularly when administering a country in a state of war. With his laissez-faire approach, Buhari has not served the nation well as he has failed to uphold the security (and welfare) of the people, which Section 14 (2b) of the 1999 Constitution says shall be "the primary purpose of government". The president, with his style and policies and utterances, is perhaps the single biggest cause of the deteriorating insecurity situation in the country. With a critical self-examination and a change in strategy, he could also be the solution. Having acknowledged the failure of the security chiefs, perhaps Nigerians would begin to take Buhari seriously when he appoints new service chiefs and doesn't shy away, as he is wont, from holding them responsible whenever they fail to rein in the terrorists in different guises or disguises. After all, little Chad Republic did show us recently how to deal with Boko Haram, comprehensively". End of Quote.

In a first of its kind, on Monday, June 22, 2020, the recognized non-political elders and leaders of the entire Middle Belt, South-West/Yorubas, Niger-Delta/ South-South, and South-East/ Igbos, instituted a Fifty Billion Naira lawsuit at a Federal High Court against the Buhari Administration over its persistent lopsidedness in appointments since 2015. As reported in the local media (Ikechukwu Nnochiri's article referenced): Sixteen elder statesmen and leaders of socio-cultural groups in the Southern region of Nigeria, on Monday, dragged President Muhammadu Buhari before the Federal High Court in Abuja, alleging that most appointments since the inception of his administration in 2015, were in breach of the 1999 Constitution and the Federal Character Principle.

The plaintiffs, led by Chief Edwin Clark, Chief Reuben Fasoranti, Dr. John Nnia Nwodo, Dr Pogu Bittus, Chief Ayo Adebanjo, Alaowei Bozimo, Mrs Sarah Doketri, Chief Chukwuemeka Ezeife and Air Commodore Idongesit Nkanga, alleged that the Southern region has been deliberately marginalized by the President Buhari-led government. They are praying the court to among other things, determine whether it was not "reckless and adverse to the interest of Nigeria", for President Buhari to obtain a loan facility from the Islamic Development Bank, African Development Bank, the World Bank, China, Japan, and Germany amounting to $22.7 billion (USD), for infrastructural development, only to allocate the bulk of the fund to the Northern region.

They are seeking a declaration that the loan facility purportedly for infrastructural development wherein less than 1% of the amount is to be allocated to the South East Zone of Nigeria for specific infrastructural development, violates section 16 (1) (a) (b) and S16 (2) (a) (b) (c) of the 1999 Constitution (as amended). As well as, "A declaration that the 1st Defendant's procurement of any loan which would increase Nigeria's outstanding debt by up to 30% of its GDP or which would increase its interest payment above 50% of government revenue is unconstitutional".

Other plaintiffs in the suit marked FHC/ABJ/CS/595/2020, are Senator Kofoworola Bucknor-Akerele, Prof Julie Umukoro, Elder Stephen Bangoji, Alhaji Tijani Babatunde, Mrs. Rose Obuoforibo, Mr Adakole Ijogi and Dr. Charles Nwakeaku. Aside from President Buhari, also listed as 2nd to 4th Defendants in the matter are the Attorney-General of the Federation, Clerk of National Assembly, and the Federal Character Commission. Specifically, the plaintiffs, in the suit they filed through a consortium of lawyers comprising of 10 Senior Advocates of Nigeria led by Chief Solomon Asemota, SAN, and Chief Mike Ozekhome, SAN, are further praying the court to determine:

Whether the power to appoint designated public officers including permanent secretaries, principal representatives of Nigeria abroad, which is vested in the 1st Defendant has been lawfully exercised by him since the inception of his administration from 2015 till date and Whether his actions are in breach of Sections 171(5), 814(3) (4) of the 1999 Constitution (as amended).

Whether the power to appoint Nigeria's Armed Services Chiefs, other Commanders or top officials of the respective Armed Forces Higher and High Commands' General Staff; namely the Chief of Defense Staff (CDS), Chief of Army Staff (COAS), Chief of Naval Staff (CNS) and Chief of Airforce Staff (CA8); the other statutorily established Nigerian National Security agencies or services , namely: The Inspector General of the Nigerian Police (1GP), the Directors General (DGs) of the State Security Service (SSS), National Intelligence Agency (NIA) and the Defense Intelligence Agency (DIA); the Heads of

National Security Associated Federal Government (FG) establishments, namely the Nigerian Civil Defense and Security Corps (NCDSC), Economic and Financial Crimes Commission (EFCC), the Nigerian Customs and Excise Service, the Nigerian Immigration Services (NIS), the Nigerian Correctional Services (NCS), the National Emergency Management Authority (NEMA), the National Youth Service corps (NYSC), the National Security Adviser (NSA), the Ministers of Defense, Interior, Police and the respective National Security ministries' Permanent Secretaries' which is vested in the 1st Defendant, has been lawfully exercised by the 1st Defendant since the inception of his administration and whether these appointments are in compliance with 81(2), 814(3)(4), 8217(3) of the 1999 Constitution (as amended).

They urged the court to award N50 billion against the Defendants to represent punitive, aggravated and exemplary damages to the constituents of the Plaintiffs for the illegal, wrongful discriminatory and unconstitutional acts committed by the 1st Defendant against the people of the Plaintiffs' states and geopolitical zones. Meanwhile, Justice Okon Abang has fixed July 10 to hear the case, even as he directed Chief Ozekhome, SAN, who represented the plaintiffs on Monday to serve the court processes on all the Defendants.

The thing to add is that the plaintiffs represent the Regions that produce and contribute 100% of Nigeria's public revenue from Oil and Taxation, and will also bear the brunt of repaying the piling debts used, in the main, in providing infrastructure in the North and all the way to neighboring Niger Republic. Apart from the scornful and insensitive treatment of non-Muslims and Northerners by the Buhari Government, his failure in stemming Security challenges in five years has further exacerbated the tension in the country. As a reminder, the First World War lasted for four years (1914 - 1918) while WWII lasted for six years (1939 - 1945). Nigeria has been waging a war against a rag-tag Boko Haram Islamic team of terrorists for over ten years, while the Fulani terrorists and other variants of bandits have sharply intensified their chokehold on citizens in the past five years. Mr. Buhari had sworn to crush and defeat Boko Haram within three months of assuming office. He is in his sixth year, billions of dollars have been "spent" on the Mission, and all that Nigerians get are excuses. His Administration has also allowed the Fulani onslaught against Nigerians to fester thereby grossly complicating the Security situation; yet another instance of State delinquency and incapacity to secure their sovereign space: a waste of political independence.

No ethnicity or demographic has a monopoly of talent, but nepotism and differential standards impose laziness and a sense of entitlement, thereby depressing both innate talent and competitiveness which enhance standards across board. Given the entrenched powerful interests that would resist any drastic change, and in consideration of the urgency of this imperative, the ineluctable conclusion is that the democratic structures, as at present, CANNOT produce the kind of leadership that would embark on these audacious and urgent remedial steps. No civilian product of the Old School can challenge or punish some of the entrenched potentates. As counter-intuitive as it sounds, many well-meaning Nigerians think that what is needed is a modern, modest, focused, ruthless, and committed Military Officer (with no ethnic or religious leanings) to effect the necessary adjustments, lay the necessary foundation for proper democracy and good governance, and quit the stage as a National Hero for life. Nigerians are clamoring for this solution and, in fact, pray for the liquidation of their oppressors of all hues, and the disgorging of all the stolen wealth. This may be a wrong-headed and passionate prescription informed by their anger, realization of impotence in the face of avoidable oppression, and frustration over Nigeria's squandered potentials.

One will rely on Burke who wrote in 1789 that: *"criminal means, once tolerated, are soon preferred. They present a shorter cut to the object than through the highway of the moral virtues. Justifying perfidy and murder for public benefit, public benefit would soon become the pretext, and perfidy and murder the end; until rapacity, malice, revenge, and fear more dreadful than revenge, could satiate their insatiable appetites. Such must be the consequences of losing in the splendor of these triumphs of the rights of men, all natural senses of right and wrong."*

Military interventions are not a solution to Nigeria's problems; rather, they worsen instability as every Military Administration, from experience, stifles democracy and governance, and is assessed for ethnic composition, thus fueling countercoups. The difficulty of eliciting the genuine cooperation of the individuals and segments of the Society with vested interest in the preservation of the status quo, towards a program of national transformation, is also evident. It does seem that only pressure of some sort would yield the desired outcome, but then the fragmented polity holds minimal prospects for galvanizing a nation-wide movement. Whatever happens, Nigeria needs to redefine the parameters of coexistence and governance. It is essential to reduce or extinguish outright the pervasive and all-consuming nature of State power, as well as the venality of its Institutions. The current circumstance inspired the Ghanaian Economist, George B.N. Ayittey, to write that: "the State, as usually understood, does not exist in Africa." It is the duty of all Africans to institute these States, on their terms.

Then, and only then, would Nigeria truly qualify as a democratic State. In due course, perhaps, the performance of the civic structure could begin to approach the standards of the US Democracy. Nigeria thus remains work in progress. That is sadly how bad the Nigerian situation is.

In the immortal words of William Butler Yeats,

Things fall apart; the center cannot hold;
Mere anarchy is loosed upon the world,
The blood-dimmed tide is loosed, and everywhere
The ceremony of innocence is drowned;
The best lack all conviction, while the worst
Are full of passionate intensity.

In summary, therefore, what Nigeria needs urgently is not Democracy but the restoration of Trust and a Common Purpose. Diversity is a positive factor when it is handled with sensitivity, fairness, and respect for all. In the absence thereof, diversity produces diverse feelings of alienation and widening chasms of disunity. In this environment, no form of government can deliver the public goods that constitute the very purpose of government and Statehood.

Questions that should have been asked 60 years ago still have not been asked, while the culture of corrosive corruption, divisiveness, and impunity tears at the very foundation of the country. The competition for political power and access underscores the reward incentives. If and when the foundation is restored, then we can revisit the integrity of the democratic process in the country. Hopefully, our understanding of Nigeria is better after this exposition. A great country it could be, but a great country it is not yet. Great people, fractured, ambitious, energetic, hardworking, and seemingly unable to confront their local demons, instead export their considerable skills and talents to foreign lands in their millions, while charlatans, in the main, continue to define and deface their motherland. As they wail "black lives matter", the lives of their kith and kin back home, indeed the lives, destiny, and hope of the entire black race should also matter. For, if Nigeria fails, the implications for all black people around the world will remain dire into the foreseeable future.

No other country is nearly as equipped and metaphysically-mandated as Nigeria to redeem the fate of this vital segment of humanity. If they choose to remain derelict with this mandate under their current structure, perhaps, a serious discussion about splitting the country into two, three, or four parts should proceed, without the need to shoot over this. The divergences are deep, the conflict of cultures between Western aspiration and Islamic feudalism will continue to tear at the very core of this country, there is no discernment that the beneficiaries of entitlement and corruption fully understand the damage they cause to the System, so this puzzle continues to unravel…

Given all the fake religiosity in Nigeria -- with no reflection on civic behavior, service orientation and integrity in office, the country's ingrained corrupt practices, etc., perhaps, we should end this section with the inimitable words of Kahlil Gibran as follows:

Pity the nation that is full of beliefs and empty of religion.
Pity the nation that wears a cloth it does not weave and eats a bread it does not harvest.
Pity the nation that acclaims the bully as hero, and that deems the glittering conqueror bountiful.
Pity a nation that despises a passion in its dream, yet submits in its awakening.
Pity the nation that raises not its voice save when it walks in a funeral, boasts not except among its ruins, and will rebel not save when its neck is laid between the sword and the block.
Pity the nation whose statesman is a fox, whose philosopher is a juggler, and whose art is the art of patching and mimicking
Pity the nation that welcomes its new ruler with trumpeting, and farewells him with hooting, only to welcome another with trumpeting again.
Pity the nation whose sages are dumb with years and whose strongmen are yet in the cradle.
Pity the nation divided into fragments, each fragment deeming itself a nation.

As the author was practising three great violin pieces: Williams' Schindler's List, Brahm's Violin Sonata No. 3 and Bartok's Violin Concerto No. 2, in his Kalorama, Washington, D.C., home on a restful Sunday afternoon, a close friend who had just read the section of the manuscript on Nigeria quipped that "with all the pretensions at normalcy, Nigeria is like playing the violin while the Titanic sank gradually" and also that "no amount of watering will save a tree with dead roots." As the distraction had been achieved from my solemn concentration, my friend then added further that, perhaps, "Nigeria should be euthanized and its ashes should serve as compost for a new beginning; perhaps, a cradle with genuine and sustainable promise."

Is China Recolonizing Africa?

Africa, with fifty-four countries and Island-states, remains a Continent perpetually in search of discovery and development. A Continent very rich in both human and natural resources, the level of development remains largely inconsistent with the abundant blessings of Nature, perhaps because of that very reason. While most of the Nation-States underwent varying forms of colonialism under the British, Portuguese, French, and Italians, before attaining Independence, the measure and impact of their self-governance have remained limited, on the average, to the symbolic elements of Independence like National Anthems, Flags, Governments, etc., while the corollary or logical implications for the right levels of industrial, political, economic, and social development have remained a challenge. It is in this context, therefore, that we evaluate China's resurgent interest in Africa.

China and Africa have a long history, but we shall restrict the scope of our assessment to the period starting from 1950, and especially in the past twenty years. Most African States became independent in the 1950's and 60's. After the geopolitical realignments that followed World War II, the Independence Movement spread all over Africa, ultimately leading to the loss of colonies by the erstwhile Colonial Powers, and the transfer of political power to local political elites under varying arrangements. It is significant that China competed with her ideological mate, the former USSR, in radicalizing and equipping some of the Independence Agitators in Africa. Some of their allies included Ghana's Kwame Nkrumah, Egypt's Gamal Abdel Nasser and, many years later, Robert Mugabe of Zimbabwe. China employed rhetoric to posture as an enduring ally supporting Africans in resisting the "imperialism" of the West. By the mid-1960s, 38 of the then independent African States aligned with Beijing rather than Taipei, which had relations with just 14 (and the number has consistently shrunk since then!) China currently has diplomatic relations with 52 of these countries.

With the Chinese Cultural Revolution in 1966 and the death of the extreme Ideologue, Mao Zedong, however, Sino-African relations suffered a major setback and China began to focus on its own economic development and commenced the aggressive cultivation of nations with the capacity to further that goal, irrespective of their internal ideological, political, or social systems, notably the United States, Japan, and Korea. China equally joined international financial institutions like the IMF and the World Bank. The collapse of the Soviet Union finally removed the incentive to compete with the USSR for ideological allegiance in Africa, so Africa was relegated in the scheme of things in China. However, given China's rapid emergence as an economic powerhouse in the 1990s – becoming the second largest economy in the world in very short order (displacing Japan) – and the second largest consumer of petroleum products since 2003, she had to sustain her "peaceful rise" (*heping jueqi*), by seeking out external sources for her scarce basket of natural resources to fuel this robust economy.

In addition, the current Geopolitical structure has invariably created the US as the new global hegemon; China's new economic capacity gives her the confidence to position herself as the counterforce to hegemony. She adopted the concept of "democracy in international relations" to drive this ambition. Furthermore, Africa's support for China during the aftermath of the Tiananmen Square fiasco elicited a realization of seeming commonality of human rights violations between the two entities. These considerations drive China's current interest in Africa, which hold dire consequences for Africa and the world at large.

In 1996, the value of China's trade with Africa was $4 billion; by 2004, this had grown to $29.6 billion and, in 2006, was $55.5 billion. By 2014, the high figure of $215 billion was achieved, which fell to $148 billion in 2017. The figure for the first half of 2019 was recently published, and the volume of trade was $101.86 billion (half-year). The global economic compression caused by the Covid:19 pandemic will have a significant impact on 2020 numbers. While Angola exported the most items in 2018 to China, followed by South Africa and the Democratic Republic of Congo, South Africa imported the most from China in the same year followed by Nigeria and Egypt.

China's Strategic Approach

China has employed an extensive range of strategies in "cultivating" Africa. These include: rhetoric involving the commonality of shared experiences in resisting "imperialists" and being part of the "developing countries" with common destiny; propagandization of their five principles of "peaceful existence": mutual respect for sovereignty and territorial integrity, mutual non-aggression, non-interference in internal affairs, equality and mutual benefit, and peaceful coexistence; an intensive focus on Public Diplomacy; provision of Development Funds and loans without the usual conditionalities and strictures of Western Institutions; direct investments in various sectors of the African economy; propping up malleable dictatorships; no criticism of corrupt practices and the gross abuse of human rights (perhaps given her own records); floating the suspect Forum on China-Africa Cooperation (FOCAC), China-Africa Cooperation Council (CACF), etc., etc.

China and Oil

China's business interest in Africa has grown at a phenomenal rate in the past twenty years. China's economy returned an average annual growth of 9% for twenty years until recently, leading to a deep thirst for energy and other natural resources to fuel and sustain the industrial base. The People's Republic of China (PRC), though an oil-producing nation, has been a net importer of petroleum since 1993 and has increasingly relied on Africa for this resource. China's consumption has driven up the aggregate international demand levels for oil and sustained the prices, together with the developments in the Middle East and oil-producing part of Nigeria affecting supply. Between 1995 and 2003, China's oil consumption doubled to 6.8 million bpd.

This index grew by 15% while her output rose by a mere 2%, and the 2004 levels represented a 16% growth on the prior year's figures. China has been importing about 45% of her oil requirements since 2010 due to their very active factories. With the softening of global demand for goods, this appetite for fossil fuel will drop, with implications for the exporters' economies. The US Energy Information Administration projected that China's demand for oil will increase by 130% to 12.8m bpd by 2025. At this time, it is difficult to confirm the validity of this assessment given all the vagaries that remain unsettled. However, this demand pattern will exert pressure on the supply and price of oil in the global market, though this will also be muted by the rapid advancements in electric cars and alternative sources of energy.

The Chinese Government controls the key elements of economic activities in the country; core investments are, therefore, indirectly made by the Government in furtherance of strategic goals and objectives, rather than mere immediate economic gains and/ or reaction to shareholder pressure for high returns on equity. This concept underpins the conflict between the investment strategies of China and the West. The Chinese model accommodates huge interim losses, once the medium-to-long-term national objectives are met. In realization of the real challenges it faces in the area of sourcing energy for her sustained economic growth (and possible global dominance), China has embarked on a series of deliberate investment strategies:

- Acquisition of foreign energy sources through long-term contracts and the purchase of overseas assets in the energy sector. The turbulence in the Middle East, and the domination of the West in that Region, shift the focus to Africa
- Adopting option 1 above, secures access to energy sources and positions China as a possible key player in the Oil Market in the coming years,

dictating prices and dynamics, etc. This informs the strategic choice to acquire equity, rather than enter into supply contracts/ futures.

- Diversification of the areas of engagements, for risk diffusion. This explains the network of related investments in countries as far-flung as Sudan, Angola, Nigeria, Kenya, Côte d'Ivoire, Namibia, Congo-Brazzaville, and even in Canada!
- Deployment of Chinese Security Forces to the African countries where they have invested, ostensibly as a form of military cooperation but, in reality, to secure the oil and related facilities they have invested in, to guarantee the steady supply of energy to PRC.

At this point, we should briefly introduce the conceptual framework that guides the Chinese engagement in Africa.

- A supposed policy of non-interference in the internal affairs of "sovereign" States; an amoral disposition and, indeed, partisanship by weapons supplies, in the several cases of genocide and repression afflicting Africa.
- A clinical separation of business from politics and human rights considerations. The former Director of the African Studies Section at the Chinese Academy of Social Sciences, He Wenping, had said that: "We (China) don't believe that human rights should stand above sovereignty… we have a different view on this, and African countries share our view." Former Chinese President, Li Peng, said in 1990 that: "no country is allowed to interfere in the internal affairs of the developing countries, or pursue power politics in the name of "human rights, freedom of speech, and democracy." To reinforce this position, the-then Chinese Deputy Foreign Minister, Zhou Wenzong, said that: "Business is business. We try to separate politics from business … I think the internal situation in Sudan is an internal affair", to explain China's active materiel support for, and widespread partnership with, the Government in Khartoum which was engaged in genocide in Darfur. China replaced the Western oil companies that pulled out of Sudan due to the inability of the Sudanese Government to meet the benchmarks of decency set by the West.
- China is still Sudan's biggest investor; her interests there include the largest equity stake (40%) in the National Oil Corporation, (the Greater Nile Petroleum Operating Company) three weapons manufacturing factories, and a host of other assets. While the genocide was going on, China granted the then Sudanese leader, Omar al-Bashir, an interest-free loan to be used in building a Presidential Palace. "Our relationship is truly a relationship of friendship with no strings attached or pressures or political agenda", according to al-Bashir. Of course, a Chinese company handled the contract

and bugged every inch of the place. China has consistently used her Veto Power to block UN efforts to effectively sanction Sudan over the Darfur genocide.

- Given the depth of her pocket, ultimate objectives, and indicated aversion to decency, China grants soft loans and ancillary funds to African countries without the usual delays and contingent conditions of transparency, rule of law, guarantee of human rights, development of Institutions, and democratic culture, which accompany funding from Western countries and Institutional Lenders like the World Bank and IMF. The prevailing mood among the elite ruling class across Africa finds the Western conditions too onerous and against their odious inclination towards repression, regime protection and perpetuation, narrowing of the democratic space, colossal corruption, lack of vision, and overall decadence. They, therefore, wholesomely welcome the Chinese model as a veritable alternative to "imperialistic" conditionalities and "plots to ensure Africa's continued under-development." By aligning with the reprehensible ruling class across Africa, China is invariably threatening her long-term interests in that Region, in the event of regime changes or mass uprisings.
- Ignoring the massive corruption that prevails in the Public Sector, thereby deepening her relationship with the looters. In some cases, China is complicit in the fact of corruption, thereby weakening Africa's chances of ever strengthening her structures. Conversely, China executes its own Officials back home who are implicated in corruption.

A Short Sample of Chinese Investments in Africa

- In January 2006, the State-controlled China National Offshore Oil Corporation (CNOOC) paid $2.25 billion for a 45% stake in an offshore Nigerian oilfield, which had previously been concessioned to an influential retired Nigerian Lt. General, T.Y. Danjuma, when he was in the good books of the Government in Nigeria. The Federal Government subsequently revoked the Operating License of this company, and the parties proceeded to court. He has since regained the Oil Block.
- The purchase of several refineries in Algeria at the cost of $350 million
- 40% equity stake in Sudan's Greater Nile Petroleum Operating Company. The total investment in Sudan is worth about $4 billion
- Forceful acquisition (with the active support of the Angolan Government and her Oil Monopoly, Sonangol) of the 50% equity stake in Shell Exploration and Production, Angola. This was shortly after the Chinese Export-Import Bank had extended a $2 billion line of credit to Angola,

without extensive and "humiliating" conditions. In all, China presently has over 50 Oil agreements with various African States.

- Extensive investments in countries with reserves of titanium, iron ore, gold, and other minerals. They have equally invested heavily in timber, without any replenishment or environmental plan
- Accelerated economic growth in China has adversely affected food security as farm acreages have been lost to industrialization; agricultural extension options have virtually been exhausted. Given the huge population that must be fed, as well as the likelihood of the sustenance of the loss of agricultural land to industrialization, Chinese business interest has extended to extensive agricultural and fishing investments in Gabon, Namibia, Zimbabwe, and Cape Verde, with shipping infrastructure set up for direct transfer to China. It is significant that, by investing in Agriculture and textiles in Africa, China is taking advantage of the preferential trading terms granted African countries under the African Growth and Opportunity Act (AGOA, AGOA II and AGOA III) of the United States and EU's 2000 Cotonou Agreement, while the profits go back to Mainland China.
- Several Construction projects across Africa, funded in the main with the loans and credits granted the various countries, thereby ensuring that the bulk of the money returns to China. Typically, awarding the contracts to Chinese companies is a standard condition for the loans.
- A joint coal venture, a glass factory, a ferrochrome smelting plant, and a telephone assembly plant in Zimbabwe
- Investment in human capital and building up a future generation of pro-China elite groups by sponsoring thousands of African students on scholarship programs in technical areas in China. These students spend their first two years learning Chinese language and culture.
- Various other endeavors in which over 800 Chinese companies engage all over Africa.
- Various substantial and penetrating telecoms projects and contracts through Huawei and ZTE, entities tied to Chinese Military Intelligence
- Multiple high-level visits on both sides, further cementing the relations between Africa and China

They are also very active in rolling out railway lines and in construction.

Implications for Africa

The renewed attention being paid to Africa by China is utilitarian and exploitative. In employing shortsighted strategies to achieve her aims on the

Continent, China is invariably entrenching the challenges that have been responsible for Africa's overall sub-optimization. By supporting the lack of Institutions and accountability, she is encouraging incompetence, arbitrariness, repression, and the overall privatization of the common weal. By enabling the proliferation of small arms, China is directly sponsoring various acts of crime and brigandage on the Continent. These, plus its "no interference" approach, combine to pose a serious threat to Chinese interests on the Continent over time. Would China still respect nations' sovereignty if her investments in Africa are nationalized or over-run by criminal gangs? Surely, sovereignty must have responsibilities and limits!

It is disturbing when some African Public Officers gloat about their romance with China, without looking at the larger implications of the sovereign commitments they make with regard to this unscrupulous hegemon. The argument that China is merely emulating the West, while committing her funds and "dignifying" Africa at the same time, immediately conveys the assumption of two fallacious concepts, namely:

- That the relationship between Africa and other places must essentially involve the technical exploitation of the former
- That Africa is incapable of subscribing to redeeming ethos and must, therefore, embrace China, which recognizes, respects and dignifies the essential African persona.

These two constructs remain exactly what they are: fallacies!!!

When oil-producing African countries had a windfall occasioned by the high prices of crude oil (without the necessary structures of accountability, rigor, and transparency) this led to higher levels of corruption, the execution of white elephant projects, no incentive to diversify the economy, and the deepening of the malaise commonly called "resource curse".

The implications to this day include:

- The attendant risks and issues with running mono-product economies
- Africa continues to supply only primary products without adding value, to earn more and develop her industrial base. This is the formula for perpetual under-development
- Complacency
- Unsustainable growth due to the unpredictable vagaries of Commodities Markets
- Vulnerability to future price shocks

- Currency over-valuation, which invariably weakens the local manufacturing capacity
- The absence of democracy and Human Rights will continue to influence brain drain to other lands
- The flooding of the African Continent with substandard Chinese goods equally leads to severe job losses. The cheap labor in China, together with their lack of observance of those humane employment conditions that add to the aggregate cost of production in the West, invariably make Chinese products very cheap. Even when they set up plants in Africa, Chinese companies often do not respect minimum labor, human rights, and environmental standards.
- In all, the greatest risk one sees arises from the virtual conferment of the status of an African Oil Producer on China by the nature and spirit of the oil deals she has been able to package with her African puppets.

The crash of oil prices has since softened the African economies, as anticipated.

While the injection of funds into Africa by the Chinese Government represents a window of opportunity, the absence of structures and Institutions will nullify whatever the gains that would have derived from this engagement. China's global geostrategic ambitions must necessarily connote some subscription to higher ideals and standards, and not a preoccupation with base and mercenary behavior. But again, the onus lies with nations and States that claim to be sovereign, to be politically independent, to be repulsed by the centuries-old injuries against Africans by outsiders, to just do what is right. Africa's particular history with oppression and wickedness from without should inspire a permanent sensitivity towards external manipulation or exploitation of any type. It does seem that African Rulers (for they are not leaders) have learnt nothing, and their citizens feel castrated to flush them out. Is this Africa's destiny? How long will this last? China has an extensive sprawl in Ethiopia and Eritrea, conferring virtual sovereignty to this Asian country on African soil.

Beijing's view is that countries are in a better position to define the development model that suits their individual national conditions and that she does not necessarily seek out undemocratic regimes to support. She equally makes the factual point that her adversaries in the West equally supply arms to States and entities of their choice, and that the West did not adopt better standards in dealing with Africa. China then proceeds to validate its view by its own unique development model: significant economic growth overseen by a disciplined, one-party totalitarian state with full authority, if not control, over all economic activity.

While China's example demonstrates that the democratic model is not the *sine qua non* for economic development, economic progress may be more retarded when aid and money flow into weak and failing States without systems of accountability; such funds are usually stolen or squandered if not tied to the development of institutions for good governance; Customs and tax collection; Port and Maritime Security; Law Enforcement; judicial reforms; and the delivery of healthcare and education. When these are undermined, as they are in Africa – with China's active role – the long-term development of the Region is questionable. Zimbabwe under Mugabe was a representative case. Increasing isolation and pressure from the West were frustrated by China's lifeline. China provided for Mugabe's military needs without interfering in his "internal affairs" and also praised Mugabe as "a man of great achievements, devoted to world peace, and a good friend of the Chinese people." He obviously had a lot in common with them.

The Chinese attitude towards Africa indicates that you can construct refineries, educate scientists, build new rail lines, and simultaneously engage in genocide. As a consequence, Chinese support for political and economic repression in Africa counters the latter-day liberalizing influences of Africa's traditional European and American partners.

China and Weapons in Africa

China partially strengthens her relationships with African leaders by selling weapons to them; weapons used in repressing their people. The proceeds are used to pay for the oil and natural resources she buys from them. These, together with the "strategic understanding" (namely, bribery and corruption) they have with their clients in Africa, inform the haste with which the oil patrimony of certain States has been surrendered to China by way of part-ownership. It is clear that China's aggregate oil assets in Africa, apart from her domestic reserve, exceed what some of the oil-producing African countries have. Chinese weapons supplies have led to proliferation of wars and crime on the Continent, given the relative ease of access to the weapons and the combustible state of the political, economic, religious, and social factors in many of these countries. China has sold various forms of weapons to Sudan, Equatorial Guinea, Democratic Republic of Congo, Ethiopia, Eritrea, Burundi, Nigeria, Tanzania, and Zimbabwe. In the case of Eritrea and Ethiopia, she supplied weapons worth over $1 billion to both sides during their border war from 1998 to 2000. Given the porous nature of most African borders, the linguistic, religious, and ethnic loyalties across countries, etc., weapons have been smuggled effortlessly across the Continent, leading to a serious escalation in violent crime and terrorism levels. The genocide in Darfur, Sudan, was prosecuted with Chinese weapons and even inspired the construction of three weapons factories in that country!

A natural consequence of this proliferation in poor societies is the perpetuation of strife and poverty. Many African countries are currently, *ipso facto*, failed States insofar as their capacity to exercise effective control over their entire territories is concerned, apart from the other economic, political, and social indices of assessment. Sudan, DRC, Zimbabwe, and Cote d'Ivoire are in this category, with more States becoming eligible soon; they would increasingly be unable to stop terrorist groups from establishing bases within their countries. Terrorist groups find failing States as safe havens due to the lack of capabilities, Institutions, effective Law Enforcement and Border Operations, as well as the infrastructure to check them. It is fairly trite that the greatest security threats facing the world today are not military threats from rival States, but rather trans-national risks from a variety of extremists, as well as sustained public health challenges such as we presently face.

Francis Fukuyama opined in his work, "The End of History", that: "since the end of the Cold War, weak and failing States have arguably become the single most important problem for the International Order". These States, which are no longer capable of exercising responsible sovereignty, are largely responsible for mass migration, environmental degradation, global pandemics, international crime, the proliferation of WMD, and trans-national terrorism.

It is very important that global risk assessment focuses on this issue, rather than just looking at such failed and failing States through the prism of humanitarian support only. If the flow of foreign investment towards Africa were to shrink further due to a negative risk profile, China would have invariably harmed the Continent further as the capacity to recover would become seriously jeopardized.

Redeeming Responsibility of African Leaders

While the world could have an interest in what happens on the Continent, mainly due to geostrategic reasons, Africa and her people have the primary responsibility to redeem their Continent by making the right choices. Since many of the current leaders have obviously failed the people, there must be a mechanism for removing them or nullifying their influence. Africa should develop a Policy on China and use platforms like an energized New Partnership for Africa's Development (NEPAD), with its Peer Review structures, to define minimum standards for each country. An aggressive overhaul of the political system must be undertaken to enable true democracy. The declared objectives of NEPAD are obviously threatened by China's activities on the Continent. China's exploitative style and vacuous rhetoric will only succeed only insofar as African leaders and people allow them. A structure of accountability must be instituted and rigorously implemented, even after leaders have left office. Impunity must stop on that Continent.

The West and the International Community

While the 2006 National Security Strategy of the United States declares that "Africa holds growing geo-strategic importance and is a high priority of this Administration", as it should be, given that about 25% of her oil needs were sourced at that time from Africa (apart from other precious metals), the threat to Western interests by China on the African Continent (especially China's ownership of oilfields and the widening commercial, social, and cultural advances) should elicit urgent reviews and action. The non-material connections between Africa and the West are much stronger (culture, education, music, language, lifestyle, etc.) than the Manichean relationship China has with African rulers. America's calculations should go beyond resource-sourcing, as there are other connectors, which Mr. Trump may not see. The medium-term risk assessment of the Middle East does not look too positive given unresolved and contemporary issues, so it makes strategic sense to focus more closely on the African sources of steady energy supply, young population, Romanic language skills, Western education, vibrancy, etc., especially as the world calibrates a diminution of China's global Supply Chain monopolies.... powers given by the United States. Factories, Consolidation Points, Supply Chain Centers, etc. could be established all over Africa immediately, for example.

The US and the West will do well to learn some of the very few positive aspects of the Chinese model, namely Public Diplomacy, soft elements of Statecraft, involvement in downstream and retail segments of the economy, blending with the people rather than being isolated in garrisoned barracks and unreal splendor while in Africa, a paradigm adjustment on loan terms and conditions, exposing more information to the population to foster internal resistance to corrupt leaders, a decision to make long-term commitments to the people of Africa, etc., etc.

Conclusion

Africa's capacity to benefit from the positive elements of globalization will be a function of how much individual countries end conflicts, improve governance, check corruption, and establish the Rule of Law. If this is achieved, then the current profile of FDIs would extend to other sectors other than oil. Access to State Power must stop being a passport to wealth. Prosperity will definitely reduce the level of conflict. There will be a need for the diversification of economies, together with the pursuit of value-add initiatives, to stop the export of primary products.

While genuine democracy may be difficult to entrench in many African countries, due to elite conspiracy, there is no doubt that most Africans accept democracy as the preferred norm but are frustrated by their inability to be heard. An emerging generation of leaders will include many from the private sector, who are more comfortable with democracy and the redeeming values of Liberal Economics than their predecessors and could provide a strong political impetus for democracy in the future. Leadership remains the key challenge.

China is indeed a global economic power but has neither the experience nor the capabilities in Institutional Reform. To get the right level of support and assistance, driven more by a convergence of interests than altruism, in building appropriate institutional frameworks to enhance sustainable economic growth, it appears African countries will have to look westwards or inwards preferably. In all that they do, Africans must remember their history, note their present, and envision a future driven by all the positive affirmations of political independence and sovereignty. Excuses and scape-goatism shall no longer be sufficient to explain the Continent's poor performance on the tangible measures of performance on the delivery of public goods. Perhaps, an ancient Chinese proverb will suffice in conclusion: "If you want to know your future, look into your present actions."

An Evaluation of the Peacekeeping Operation During the 1994 Rwandan Genocide

We are effectively ending this journey on a sober note with an evaluation of the peacekeeping operations during the Rwandan Genocide of 1994. We do this for multiple reasons: it tests all the theoretical assumptions of International Relations, Ethics, Political Philosophy, Sovereignty, Political Independence, Internal Capacity of Nations, Man's inherent capacity for evil, Racism, our assumed shared humanity, the dysfunction, unwillingness, or incapacity of International Organizations to respond effectively (and on time) when crimes against humanity are being committed -- especially in Africa, the role of erstwhile colonial powers, ethnicity and religion, the competing demands for resources, time, and attention, as well as the ease with which nations can easily slide into genocide. This is a clarion call to Africans and African nations; all the assumptions that the international organizations (with no military force) or foreign nations will intervene in acute Security challenges on the Continent are manifestations of naiveté. History does not support this, as we have tried to explain in the past couple of pages.

Nations have their own priorities and internal domestic political realities and calculations. Africa is at the lowest rung of most of these calculations, simple. The Arab, European, American, and Chinese activities on the Continent should provide sufficient instruction in this regard. As the Covid:19 global lockdown has shown, if African leaders and their private sector fail to build, equip, and maintain hospital systems that will address their healthcare needs, they may just never get a chance to fly out to foreign lands in an emergency. Indeed, those foreign countries could also, as is their prerogative, turn them back at the border even if they manage to fly out. Influential and otherwise powerful Africans including a President, Chiefs of Staff to Presidents, a prime minister, top politicians, business executives, and sundry members of the African elite died of multiple ailments on the Continent just because they could not, as always, access hospitals in Europe, America, the Middle East, and Asia during the pandemic. In the same vein, if particular countries or a cluster of countries collapse completely, no one can be entirely certain who the casualties would be. Current failed rulers, their enablers and defenders, as well as the beneficiaries of grand theft, systemic injustice, and corrosive leadership, should always bear this in mind. When the moment is critical, they also cannot access all the money and properties they have hidden outside Africa -- assets that will most likely be diverted by the host countries or the "trusted" Agents.

In summary, no one else but Africans will develop or secure Africa. The brain drain that is affecting Africa should concern all. The absence of services should inspire an urgent push for reversal. The density of absolute poverty and the hopelessness among the youth in most of Africa should worry Policy Makers and citizens of goodwill alike. The fractionalization that defines most of the countries can only but yield a horrible outcome for all.

While historical factors like the inconvenient combinations that constitute nations have happened, citizens should, on the basis of their independence and sovereignty, agree either to remain as one (with adjusted parameters) or to split peacefully into agreed parts that will relate harmoniously as independent States. The human desire for justice, fairness, and respect cannot be squelched by the smelly jackboots of the under-paid and increasingly partisan Police and Military. As earlier cited, there are now many ways to skin a rat. Enduring peace can only be predicated on equity, not on intimidation and injustice. The issues that cause tension are well-known in each country; it is only the nationals of those countries or other Africans who can resolve those matters. A temporary advantage by a group is not a reliable prognosis of outcomes if the entire country unravels, as human dynamics do not follow any linear pattern. In the world of asymmetric powers, anything can happen. The independence of African nations must and should mean something to them. If not, the devastation that will engulf nations and regions will have significant and irreversible implications for the recovery and reconstitution of those entities.

Even with the best of intentions also, most countries and even the UN can only offer rhetorical support and condemnation if wholesale strife ensues in any African country. The assumed 'Responsibility to Protect' is an academic concept. The pandemic has also imposed near-depression in most national economies, with governments' priorities understandably being the welfare, recovery, and security, of their own people. There is no money to spare for external commitments or fancy interventions in Africa. Indeed, widespread violence on the Continent might suit the strategic preference of some of the global actors. For a people who endured centuries of slavery, colonialism, cultural and religious alienation from their origins, cross-generational psychological trauma, persistent insults and denigration around the world, despoliation of their environment, forced dispersal around the world -- with their cousins killed and dehumanized at will where they may be presently situated, denigrated for having the full dosage of melanin which others lack, and casually discounted in the international congress of nations, one would expect much better of organic leaders exercising the rights and powers of full sovereignty, a sovereignty that was wickedly truncated, in the service of their own people and in the redemption of their kind.

The experience thus far is depressing, and the prospects for redemption are very dire. Africans cannot keep blaming others. They are ultimately responsible for their station in this cruel world. No outsider stopped African leaders from delivering on the various public goods to their people instead of simply serving themselves. No one else is responsible for the fact of their wickedness to their own people, the very low ambition, the lies and propaganda which they start believing, the sheer failure across all governance standards 60 odd years after regaining their sovereign authority. The **dependence** on externalities to intervene in what should be resoluble among sovereign people will be the ultimate manifestation of the futility and uselessness of a people's **independence**.

Enough said. Let's look at Rwanda, where the international response was absent and ineffective, as it was too during the holocaust by Nigerians against Igbos between 1967 and 1970, even as the pogrom against innocents actually started in 1966...in writing about Rwanda, it must be noted that it is not every African country that will have the blessing of a President like Paul Kagame who has substantially healed the wounds of this ugly chapter in the history of his country, forged some appreciable unity, and set the country on the path of decency, ambition, confidence, and achievement; the ingredients of true independence.

The World failed Rwandans during the 100-day genocide of 1994. By the time the genocide against the Tutsi ethnic group was over in July, 1994, over a million people had been slaughtered, with a larger number displaced and without limbs; 540,000 girls and women had been raped and butchered; one-tenth of the country's population had been wiped out using mostly crude implements like machetes, spears, and broken bottle; the triggers responsible for the centuries-old rivalry between the Hutus and Tutsis had been reinforced; the prospects for genuine reconciliation had become very distant thus raising the specter of a repeat genocide; the economy was in complete ruins; the country had been thrown back to the stone-age era; while the popular slogan, "NEVER AGAIN", had ceased to have any meaning, especially with the Darfur genocide in Sudan underway, current, and ignored. The world should be concerned that the dubious reputation of the most efficient genocide in human history was "achieved" in tiny Rwanda (smaller than the State of Vermont in the US!). What are the implications for the rest of Africa and, indeed, humanity, if a million people could be killed in a hundred days with very basic tools and weapons? How did Rwanda plunge into a genocidal impulse?

The 1994 Rwandan genocide was painstakingly planned and orchestrated, contrary to the convenient, albeit diversionary, suggestion that it was impromptu. Admittedly, the Hutus and Tutsis have never really coexisted peacefully; however, this is not a sufficient condition for the carefully planned and executed acts of genocide against the Tutsis. Again, historical reality (holocaust against the Jews, Serb cleansing of the Croat ethnic group, Saddam Hussein's genocide against the Kurdish population, Turkish cleansing of the Armenians, etc.,) confirms that genocide is not peculiar to Africa but is a threat to our collective humanity. The history of the demographic and racial polarity in Rwanda dates back to colonial times.

At the Berlin Conference of 1884, European Powers divided up the African Continent among themselves, without the input of the African people. The participating powers were: Austria-Hungary, Denmark, France, "Great" Britain, Spain, Portugal, Norway, Holland, and Sweden. The USA was equally in attendance. Africans did not participate in any capacity while factors like kinship, language, geography, trade patterns, culture, and history, did not reflect in the artificial borders that were drawn up.

This scramble and partition of the Continent led to the imposed agglomeration of peoples within artificial geographical boundaries, as well as the assumed obliteration of traditional rivalries, alliances, and world views. The newly created Rwanda was allocated to Germany, which had no interest in the new country. After Germany's defeat in the First World War, Rwanda was re-allocated to Belgium under the League of Nations Mandate.

The new colonialists met a hierarchical society in which the majority Hutu ethnic group (with over 70% of the population) was subservient to the minority Tutsis. The Tutsis constituted the elite class while the Hutus were relegated to lowly positions. This structure was communicated and reinforced in churches, schools, and folklores. Hutus were programmed to serve Tutsis in perpetuity and were propagandized to accept an innate inferiority to the Tutsis. Hutus and Tutsis are equally major population segments in neighboring Zaire and Burundi.

All Rwandans speak a common language, namely, Kinyarwanda. In this language, Hutu means "servant" or "subject" while Tutsi means "rich" and "superior". This formulation built on the fantasy of an English explorer, John Hanning Speke, who suggested that the Tutsis could trace their ancestry to Noah of the Bible, and that they migrated from Egypt through Ethiopia to Rwanda and were, accordingly, superior in all forms to the "savage" Hutus. This postulation of Tutsis as non-indigenous people entitled to permanent suzerainty over the indigenous Hutus would, with time, influence the sustained acrimony and violence between the two peoples, notwithstanding the inter-marriages and other exchanges between them. The Hamithic Hypothesis of their perceived Biblical origins inspired considerable arrogance and messiah complex in Tutsis. In 1957, the Hutus commenced a violent struggle for majority rule, and published their so-called Hutu Manifesto, seeking an end to the oppression by the minority. This new campaign threatened the privileged status and sense of entitlement of the Tutsis.

The United Nations, in 1959, concluded that the chances of a "*rapprochement* between the two races" were very slim. With the death of the Tutsi-born monarch in controversial circumstances, the Tutsis killed a prominent Hutu leader, thus setting off the very first episode of Tutsi killings, which took thousands of lives. The surviving Tutsi population scattered in many directions, with a great number fleeing to Uganda. The Belgians imposed Martial Law and embarked on major political reforms, which saw the Tutsis losing their traditional privileges. A UN fact-finding team reported that: "Nazism was being perpetrated against the Tutsis". Both the Belgians and Hutus were blamed. The team stated that, unless reconciliation was effected, the prospects for peace in Rwanda would remain grim. A Belgian device, which would have severe consequences in due course, was the depiction of people's ethnic grouping on their compulsory identification cards.

When Rwanda gained independence in July 1962, the country was already fragmented along ethnic lines, thus negating the potentials for a national identity. Political parties were formed along these lines, while competition for power was a desperate endeavor; this polarity against the backdrop of poor economic performance. The introduction of democracy and its pivotal element of adult suffrage meant that the Hutus, with the vast majority, would always produce the President in elections (especially since the electorate would always vote for one of their own). The first President, Gregoire Kayibanda, embarked on a systematic and aggressive process of entrenching Hutus in government, and generally ensuring their dominance of the country, under a Program dubbed the "Hutu Power". In the interim, the Tutsi population that had become refugees in Uganda, Burundi, and Zaire, were repelled each time they ventured to return to Rwanda, leading to their formation of the Rwandan Patriotic Front (RPF), an insurgent force aimed at their return to the country. The Tutsis were treated poorly by the neighboring countries where they had sought refuge, hence the urge to return to their homeland.

The failure of their November 1963 attempt to overthrow President Kayibanda led to the systematic elimination of over 15,000 Tutsis within Rwanda, according to estimates of the World Council of Churches. This was the second round of genocide against the Tutsis in Rwanda and was targeted mostly at their leaders. A massive propaganda effort mounted by the Hutu political class under the direction of the President incited common Hutus against their Tutsi neighbors. Bodies were mutilated and violence administered at will because the Hutu population was programmed to resist "the Tutsi plan to enslave them once again."

President Kayibanda had, in March 1963, warned Tutsi invaders from across the border with Uganda to the effect that "some of you are causing trouble for your brothers who live in a democratic Rwanda… and suppose you take the capital, Kigali, by force, how will you measure the chaos of which you will be the first victims… it will be the total end of the Tutsi race." In 1964, the then President also warned that if the Tutsis ever sought political power again in Rwanda, "the whole Tutsi race will be wiped out." Despite the global attention that was drawn to this planned extermination of a people, no punishment was meted out to the perpetrators, and there was no acknowledgment of the threat and fact of genocide. Even though the eminent British philosopher, Bertrand Russell, correctly characterized the killings as the most horrible since the holocaust, the predominant current in the West was to dismiss this act of bestiality as the "savagery of the negro". Thirty years later, the casual insensitivity with which the most recent genocide in Rwanda (in which over one million people were killed by their compatriots) was handled at all institutional levels raised issues regarding the value of the human life.

In 1972, in neighboring Burundi, the political control by the minority Tutsis was challenged in a failed coup attempt by the Hutus, leading to over 200,000 Hutus being systematically massacred. Every Hutu member of the cabinet was killed; all male Hutus above fourteen, all Hutu military officers, teachers, and administrators, were killed.

The Carnegie Endowment for Peace correctly depicted this as a genocide. The Belgian Government captured it as "a veritable genocide". The only action taken by the UN was the appointment of a Working Committee by the Commission of Human Rights in Geneva, to meet with the conniving authorities in Burundi. In the absence of individual culpability, the incentive for impunity was being reinforced. Across the border, the Hutu majority, under the vile political leadership of President Kayibanda, embarked on a large-scale program of revenge killings, aimed at "purifying" Rwanda by ridding it of the Tutsi population. So-called Public Safety Committees were set up, and official media were employed to intimidate the remaining Tutsis who had escaped death and had not gone on exile to the neighboring countries. Kayibanda was overthrown in a bloody coup led by a fellow Hutu, Juvenal Habyarimana, in 1973.

The new leader foisted a One-Party State on the country and made it compulsory for every citizen (including children) to become a member of his political party, the '*Mouvement Révolutionnaire National pour le Développement (MRND)*'. Political dissent was outlawed and severely punished. While Habyarimana made noble statements, he deepened the schism between the Hutus and Tutsis by completely marginalizing the latter from the scheme of things. He equally entrenched a very corrupt system sustained by cronyism and parochialism. His government killed whoever attempted to expose the maladministration and corruption in the system. Progressively, the quality of life of the Rwandese deteriorated further, but the repressive system ensured an imposed silence.

On October 1, 1990, elements of the insurgent RPF made an incursion into the border area between Uganda and Rwanda, killing some fifty Rwandan border guards before they were repelled by mostly French and Congolese forces assisting the Hutu administration in Kigali, the capital of Rwanda. The near success achieved by the RPF led to considerable anxiety among the ruling elite in Rwanda. This anxiety was reinforced when the RPF successfully stormed a major prison in the northern part of Rwanda on 22 January 1991, freeing all the 1,500 inmates who were mostly RPF sympathizers. The RPF had demanded the following, among other things: an end to ethnic politics and compulsory identity cards; a revamped economy; democratization of the Security Forces; and the return of Tutsis who had remained refugees in other lands since 1959. With superior experience gained in assisting Yoweri Museveni to seize power in Uganda, the RPF Forces would have overrun Rwanda but for the French and Congolese intervention. Belgium's reluctance to assist the Hutu-led government in Rwanda and the French eagerness to step in, led to the realignment of alliances, with France effectively replacing Belgium as Rwanda's core European Ally.

Belgium equally became unpopular with the cabalistic ruling class in Kigali, capital of Rwanda. With French tactical and Intelligence support, the Hutu-led leadership in Rwanda killed over 20,000 Tutsis among their population even as the few Tutsi elites were held as ransom, with the clear understanding that, if the RPF advanced any further into the country, the Tutsi elites would be killed. Simultaneously, the government exploited the panic situation to incite the Hutu majority further against the Tutsis and, invariably, divert attention from the criminal and incompetent Hutu Leadership that was exerting severe hardship on their own people. Fake artillery attacks were staged across the country; Hutus were encouraged to "arrest and deal with" Tutsis, Hutus were told through the radio and government-owned newspapers that the Tutsis were plotting to enslave and/or wipe out the Hutu population. The Tutsi population in Rwanda were called accomplices of the RPF and described as "cockroaches" that must be exterminated. Notice the dehumanization of a group to justify acts of mass violence against them. Nazis applied this against Jews, Leopold the animal used it against the Congolese, Nigerians did the same against Igbos, Europeans did it against Native Indians in America, etc. This was a contrived sense of danger aimed at power preservation for the corrupt, repressive, and abusive elements in office.

Widespread extermination of Tutsis ensued, and their houses were burnt down. As at December 1990, the Ambassadors of Germany, Belgium, France, and the Representative of the European Union (EU) in Rwanda, had warned that "the rapid deterioration of the relations between the two ethnic groups, the Hutus and the Tutsis, runs the imminent risk of terrible consequences for Rwanda and the entire Region". Again, nothing was done. At this stage, the Tutsis across the border hoped to achieve military victory to avert the assured genocide of their people within Rwanda. The French, in particular, did everything to deny them this victory. The French were motivated in their intervention by the larger consideration of a perceived competition for dominance in Africa between France and the English-speaking nations of the UK and USA. For France, therefore, if the RPF won the war, Rwanda would be lost to RPF's main backers, the English-speaking Uganda. This coalesced with the Rwandan Government's ambition to preserve their privileges at all cost.

The "Civilian Self-Defense" (*auto-defense civil*) and the local administrators appointed by the central leadership were stridently and effectively incited to regard all remaining Tutsis in Rwanda as RPF accomplices who must be eliminated in order to achieve unfettered Hutu rule. Accordingly, there were at least three years of preparation for the last genocide that eventually shocked the world. In essence, regime perpetuation was the central driver of the propaganda, fabrications, and fear mongering, which laid the foundation for the wholesale massacre of the Tutsi people by a largely unsophisticated Hutu tribe. The *inkotanyi* (a derogatory term reserved for Tutsis) was extended to moderate Hutus and all those who were reluctant to cooperate in the act of genocide. Between 1991 and 1994, it was common for roadblocks to be mounted jointly by soldiers and thugs of the sole Party, for the purpose of restricting access to theaters of slaughter even while French Military Advisers under the *Detachment d'Assistance Militaire et d'Instruction* (DAMI) from the elite corps of the French Military trained both the soldiers and these thugs jointly.

These French Military personnel were listed on the Staff Lists of the Rwandan Army. A nationwide structure was established, ostensibly for repelling the RPF Forces but, in reality, for information dissemination and effective coordination of the genocidal act against the Tutsis. The Rwandan Military, being a predominantly-Hutu Army, worked very closely with Hutu Administrators and thugs on all levels, to execute the genocide against the Tutsis. This should be of particular significance to people of the Middle Belt and the Southern parts of Nigeria, who have always had cause to doubt the impartiality and balance of the Muslim and Northern-dominated rank and file of the Nigerian Army. In cases like these, coordinated and effective self-help is the only protection from systematic genocide and dispossession.

The continuing economic woes of the country led to friction among the ruling Hutu class, thus creating the environment for bold clamors for real democracy. All the protagonists were eventually killed as "saboteurs" of the Hutu Power Project. Renewed agitation led to the creation of the roguish *Interahamwe*, a group of criminals and unemployed young men, who were placed at par with the military, with the clear mandate of killing opposition elements across the country. Military weapons were assigned to them while they were technically above the laws of the land.

This again sounds like the Fulani terrorists in Nigeria. These criminals were trained by French and Israeli Military Forces on the several ways of killing people, while they were required to work very closely with the Rwandan Military. These civilian Militia Forces progressively killed Tutsis and moderate Hutus in the three years preceding the cataclysmic genocide of 1994, in which they were the key perpetrators with the military. Another extreme Hutu group, the Zero Network (*Le Reseau Zero*), was also established and empowered by the Government, to denote the number of Tutsis the government planned to leave behind in Rwanda; zero meant none.

Public Media outlets like the Radio Rwanda, and the journal Kangura (meaning "wake others up"), were employed in the graphic incitement of the people against Tutsis. The Kangura regularly published the Hutu "Ten Commandments" including "Let us learn about the RPF and Tutsi plans and let us exterminate every last one of them", "Know that the person, whose throat you do not cut, will cut yours", etc. In the interim, the Tutsi RPF's military incursions into Rwanda finally forced the Rwandan Leadership to seek a political solution under the auspices of the then Organization of African Union (OAU). While a formal Peace Treaty was signed with RPF in Arusha, Tanzania, with definite provisions towards reconciliation, a coalition government, power sharing, and possible reintegration of the country, President Habyarimana and his lieutenants remained steadfast in subverting the Peace Process. Again, this sounds like Igbos of Nigeria under Ojukwu insisting that the Aburi Accord terms with the rest of the country be respected and implemented. Habyarimana and his group considered a coalition government as a precursor to accountability for their atrocities and maladministration; therefore, the killings and propaganda continued. Bombs were exploded within civilian areas in Kigali by the Rwandan military, and mischievously attributed to the RPF, to mobilize people against the RPF and Tutsis in general.

Given the delay in implementing the Arusha Treaty, the RPF attacked again in early 1993, reaching just twelve miles from the capital city of Kigali. This successful operation led to the intensified propaganda by the government that the Hutus should rise against all Tutsis or be killed by the advancing Tutsi RPF insurgents. The result was renewed killings while over 1,000,000 people were displaced internally out of a population of about 8,000,000. A weakened Administration was forced to concede more points to the RPF at the next round of the Arusha Talks, thus fueling further resentment among the political class. The lack of knowledge by the majority, and the exploitation of deep ethnic and religious hatred by politicians always lead to genocide. Hitler benefited from that too.

The military and the political cadre then became firmer in their determination to stop the implementation of the Peace Treaty. Rhetorical excess was employed in the Open Media in describing Tutsis, while over 600,000 machetes and thousands of grenades were imported from China and distributed openly among Hutus. 50,000 units of Kalashnikov assault rifles and over 1m pieces of ammunition were equally imported (from France, Egypt, and China) and distributed, while several members of the *Interahamwe* killer gang were hastily absorbed into the Army.

Again, so-called Boko Haram terrorists "who have repented" are being absorbed into the Nigerian Army. All of this in 1993, several months before the genocide, and nothing was done to stop the decline towards bestiality. It is instructive that Dr. Boutros Ghali managed these arms sales between Egypt and Rwanda when he was the Deputy Foreign Minister of Egypt, before becoming the UN Secretary-General. The Rwandan genocide took place under his watch as UN Secretary-General.

Another political party, the '*Coalition pour la Defense de la Republique (CDR)*' was spun off to articulate extremist Hutu doctrine and coordinate the theoretical aspects of the incitement program. The RTLM Hate Radio Station was equally established for the purpose of purveying hateful messages. The Nigerian Government under Buhari considered establishing a Radio Station for his ethnic Fulanis, funded by revenues generated in the Regions attacked by Fulanis, as "an education channel" for Fulanis. None of the other 250 ethnic groups in the country, including those actually funding and sustaining the government, qualified for this "education." Who knows, they just might have used surreptitious means and conduit funds to achieve their objective after the mass resistance to the plan. Anyhow, back to Rwanda. The President was a major shareholder, while all the other potentates were equity holders in this Radio Venture. The level of impunity reached the absurd level when individuals were denounced and sentenced to death over the air, while the distribution of arms and genocidal logistics would eventually be broadcast using these radio facilities.

A benign acknowledgement of the crime of genocide even before 1994 is underscored by the Report of the UN Special *Rapporteur* for the Commission on Human Rights for Extrajudicial, Summary, or Arbitrary Executions, Bacre Waly Ndiaye, in April 1993, wherein it was considered appropriate to use the term "genocide" in describing the systematic elimination of the Tutsis between 1990 and 1993. Many ethnic groups in Nigeria qualify presently. Accordingly, the Convention on the Prevention and Punishment of the Crime of Genocide of 1948 was applicable. Yet, nothing was done institutionally to avert the major ethnic cleansing which claimed a million lives exactly a year later. If anything, Mr. Ndiaye was warned by his bosses at the UN to refrain from using the term, "genocide", as it would impose responsibilities on all States towards its prevention and punishment.

Peacekeeping Operations

The recurring tension between Utopianism and Realism is given particular expression in the philosophical underpinnings of Peacekeeping Operations. While Utopians of the Wilsonian strain posit that the anarchical circumstances of international politics will be transformed to a condition of World Order based on the interdependence of nations and the enthronement of Collective Security, this positive assessment of human capabilities and intentions has been substantially negated in history. The Realist School theorizes that power and interest should guide the international engagements of nations, rather than idealism and faith in internal and international relations for their own sake. Realism is, thus, conservative, prudent, reliant on historical lessons, empirical, and essentially amoral.

A major proponent of Realism in the 20th century, Hans J. Morgenthau, had considered that "universal moral principles cannot be applied to the actions of States in their abstract, universal formulation, but that they must be filtered through the concrete circumstances of time and place." Morgenthau further stresses the autonomy of the political sphere, and does not consider that other considerations like economics, morality, etc., should influence political decisions. In his view, political realism does not identify the "moral aspirations of a particular nation with the moral laws that govern the universe." Nations have been known to oscillate across these two extreme positions on the spectrum. A related consideration guiding intervention would be a nation's view regarding the assumption of a shared humanity, and the civilized behavior that should guide human activities. Non-Africans have NEVER demonstrated this kinship of mankind towards Africans. In the absence of this assumption, the commitment to intervene would be seriously eroded especially when there are no obvious material or strategic advantages for the country. It is one's considered position, however, that a hybrid position is achievable, especially using the instrumentality of the United Nations.

In their very useful work, 'Contending Theories of International Relations: A Comprehensive Survey', James E. Dougherty and Robert L. Pfaltzgraff, Jr., propose the merger of international law and organization with effective power to ensure international peace, the security of nations, and the equitable settlement of disputes. The ensuing debate over the desirability and effectiveness of the United Nations, thus, becomes quite germane. How much sovereignty would nations be willing to surrender to unelected international civil servants? Is a nation defined by geography, linguistics, or kinship? Who controls the United Nations? How do we ensure that the inter-State rivalry among the Security Council members (in particular) does not impair the capacity of the UN to discharge its functions? Who sets the priorities and what are the criteria?

Sigmund Freud wrote in his 'Civilization, War, and Death' that: "so long as there are nations and empires, each prepared callously to exterminate its rival, all alike must be equipped for war." While the Freudian postulation refers to discrete nations, most casualties in recent history have arisen from internal wars and skirmishes, like the Rwandan genocide. Should the Just War Theory be applied to internal "wars"? How about slow and steady acts of genocide? These manifestations of anarchy typically lack the definitive delineations of identity and form, which characterize the traditional paradigm: known States at war, uniformed combatants, etc., etc. Nevertheless, endangered people must take their destinies in their own hands, as no one is coming to help them. Acts of genocide also develop slowly, are persistent, perpetrators are usually quite arrogant and vocal about their intentions (but foolish people choose not to believe them until it is too late), their agenda is reinforced when a religious dimension is introduced to it, and the long time-frame until full-blown genocide is usually long enough for serious people to arm themselves and take the battle to their aggressors and silent sponsors/enablers (to avoid all the bombs and bullets dropping in their own terrain) or make it impossible for the determined aggressors to operate with impunity within the defended space. Prayers and wishful thinking become impotent stratagems at this point. Fifty years after total displacement and renaming towns, the new reality is different, and the victor tells his version of historical tales. Nobody remembers justice, the dead, or the authentic history.

Applying Freud's thesis to the domestic environment could lead to the recommendation that, perhaps, the Tutsis should have armed themselves to avoid being exterminated by the Hutus. They made the mistake of relying on the United Nations to protect them. Kenneth N. Waltz aligns with Morgenthau's position that "…there is the ubiquity of evil in human action" arising from man's ineradicable lust for power and transforming "churches into political organizations … revolutions into dictatorships … love for country into imperialism…" Waltz further supports the position adopted by Niebuhr, St. Augustine, Morgenthau, and Spinoza, namely, that human nature is defective, hence the perennial prevalence of political ills and violence. From the foregoing position, it is evident that genocide was already underway in Rwanda between 1990 and 1993 (discounting the previous phases). In deploying a Peacekeeping Force, therefore, the UN should have taken due cognizance of the extant reality. Peacekeeping is different from peacemaking, as it is different from peace enforcement. Peace can be kept when the contending parties are willing to achieve it, and when an equitable settlement to the contending issues can be found. In the absence thereof, peace can only be imposed for a while. In the Rwandan case, there was neither the willingness to keep the peace nor the capacity to make it.

The United Nations hastily dispatched the 81-member UN Observer Mission Uganda-Rwanda (UNOMUR) under Canadian Major-General Romeo Dallaire in May 1993, to monitor the "observance" of the Arusha Treaty Terms by both Rwanda and the RPF. By late August, this was transformed into a 2,700-man Peace-keeping Mission without proper briefing, logistics, manpower, and political direction. The US and the UK were particularly against the Peacekeeping Operation (PKO), perhaps due to the Mogadishu (Somalia) embarrassment, which was still fresh. The US was equally concerned about the cost of the PKO, even when she had deliberately refused to pay up her dues to the UN, thereby almost crippling the Organization. The Pentagon and the Congress had a confluence of opinion against any PKO. Arguments for intervention did not find much resonance until a lukewarm approval was finally extracted, enabling the deployment of a poorly funded, constrained, and inadequate Force to Rwanda, purely for symbolic reasons (many of the troops were not even armed!). The Force was drawn from developing countries like

Ghana, Bangladesh, and Senegal, with the obvious implications for materiel, training levels, and experience. The irony is that the UN expected this sub-optimal Force to achieve remarkable successes that would reverse the abysmal peacekeeping failures in Somalia and Bosnia. The compromise UN Assistance Mission for Rwanda (UNAMIR) was created on October 5, 1993 under Resolution 872.

On October 22, 1993, the Burundian Hutu President, Melchior Ndadaye, was assassinated in an attempted coup, thus inspiring an orgy of reprisal killings against Tutsis in neighboring Rwanda. The campaign for Tutsi elimination became more strident while credibility seemed to have been lent to the propagandistic assertions of Tutsi plot to impose themselves on the Hutu majority at all cost, including killing Hutus. Within Burundi itself, when Hutus rose against Tutsis for the assassination of the President, the Tutsi-dominated Military killed over 50,000 Hutus while over 500,000 escaped to Rwanda where they narrated the experience Hutus had undergone at the hands of Tutsis and the military in Burundi.

This coalesced with the prevailing sentiments against Tutsis and made the work of the UNAMIR impossible *ab initio*. This would have been an opportunity to boost the capacity of the PKO. The direct and strident requests made by the UNAMIR Commander to UN Headquarters in New York were ignored. While eight military helicopters were provided for, none arrived; out of the twenty-two armored personnel carriers (APCs) initially planned for, only eight arrived late, with only five being serviceable without parts, tools, or manuals. The UNAMIR's Civilian Police component (CIVPOL) had only 60 members. The UNAMIR lacked basic items like telephones, desks, and chairs, while they were explicitly debarred from establishing Intelligence capabilities. In addition, they were not to fire any shot except when under direct threat. The implementation of the Arusha Peace Treaty equally became seriously threatened.

Dallaire's repeated messages to UN HQ regarding the nature and escalation of the genocide on ground did not receive any urgent or positive attention. He was emphatic about the systematic manner of the ethnic cleansing against Tutsis within Rwanda. The growing incapacity of the PKO emboldened the Hutu extremists who acted with utmost impunity. Even the transmission of indications of further escalation to UN HQ did not elicit an enhancement of capacity and adjustment of the mandate. Hutus were openly canvassing for the mass killings of Tutsis and, indeed, suggested *a priori* that if the Rwandanese President died mysteriously by any chance, the Tutsi problem would then be solved once and for all. The UN Mission was ridiculed in the Hutu Hate Media under presidential guidance and protection. The Commander was further undermined by the appointment of a former Cameroonian Foreign Minister, Jacques-Roger Booh-Booh, as the Special Representative to Rwanda, in November 1993. Mr. Booh-Booh reported directly to the UN Secretary-General, and demonstrated obvious partisanship in favor of the Rwandan Hutu leadership, thus tainting the feedback to UN HQ. It became clear, for example, that he worked actively with France to weaken and delay the Tutsi RPF Forces even while the Hutus were being trained.

A dubious attempt at partial implementation of the Arusha Treaty when Hutus had been strengthened led to the arrival of a detachment of Tutsi/RPF Forces in a designated section of Kigali, for the protection of the Tutsis who participated in the planned Coalition Government. The UN Mission lacked the means to ensure that these RPF Forces did not leave their designated location.

About this time also, President Habyarimana made a *volte face* on the core elements of the Peace Treaty which his government had earlier accepted. This led the RPF to reject outright any role for the Hutu extremist party, CDR, in the Peace Process. Technically, the Arusha Treaty was dead at this stage. The presence of RPF troops in Kigali further incensed the radical elements of the Hutu military-political elite. Volunteer informants made it clear to the UNAMIR leadership that weapons were being distributed among Hutus, while the lists of Tutsi citizens had been collated for elimination. This was relayed to New York, and there was no response. The plan to seize illegal arms dumped at various sites was not approved by UN HQ. Requests for the quick establishment of an independent radio station, to counter the Hate Messages from the government media, were also declined.

When the US was, therefore, asked to provide equipment to jam the radio stations disseminating hate, the US considered the expenditure of $7 million required for that operation too high and demanded full payment by a cash-strapped UNAMIR before activation. Of course, this was never done. In the interim, the maintenance of roadblocks by soldiers and the militia continued. The Belgian Government alerted the UN Security Council on February 21, 1994 to the effect that an urgent strengthening of UNAMIR's mandate and proper provisioning were required to enable them avert what was a guaranteed calamity. The US and UK rejected this, while the UN Secretary General (Boutros Ghali) asked the UNAMIR Commander to work closely with Rwandan Authorities – the same people orchestrating the violence!!! Frantic messages to UN HQ detailing the rapidly deteriorating security situation, the depletion of UNAMIR's meager resources, and their obvious incapacity to act, were yet ignored. A February 27 cable read as follows, "we are rapidly depleting and exhausting our resources and may, in the near future, be unable to secure the weapons secure area. Time is running out as any spark on the security side could have catastrophic consequences."

It was at this time that the US started demanding that UNAMIR should be wound down. The US arranged for its Defense Attache in Burundi to evacuate Americans working in Rwanda (working mostly at the Embassy). In the confusion, the prospects of obtaining financial, manpower, or logistical support for UNAMIR further evaporated. To compound issues, President Habyarimana, his Burundian counterpart, as well as Military and Political Chiefs from both countries, were killed in a crash involving the Rwandan Presidential jet as it made its descent into Kigali from Tanzania on April 6, 1994. It became quite clear at this stage that a major crisis would ensue. The Presidential Guard, media, political leaders, militia, ordinary Hutu citizens, and municipal authorities outperformed one another in the rape, decapitation, and elimination of Tutsis who were collectively accused of being responsible for the plane crash! Sounds like the irrational but real program of violence against Igbos across Nigeria after the January, 1966 coup (with 3 Igbo Army Officers out of the 12 major coup leaders -- Officers representing themselves and not any ethnicity), a precursor to the war against Igbos in which acts of genocide were committed against them as well – leading to 3 million people dead and the entire Igbo nation devastated and impoverished.

It is common knowledge by now that over 1 million Tutsis were killed between April 6 and July 20, 1994 when the RPF finally defeated the Rwandan Forces and claimed Kigali. Within the 100-day carnage, pregnant women were cut open; babies were killed; machetes, spears, and sharp knives were freely employed to kill Tutsis; girls and women were routinely raped and killed; houses were burnt; people were forced to dig their own graves before their heads were cut off; the streets were filled with piles of corpses; churches and hospitals were invaded where Tutsis seeking refuge and treatment were killed; mass graves were quickly dug and utilized; identity cards were used to delineate regular Tutsis who were promptly slaughtered, those who attempted to flee to neighboring countries were butchered, etc., etc. The worst manifestations of human capabilities were released in a blind orgy of hate. The Western reaction was to hastily evacuate all foreigners and leave Tutsis to their fate. Considerable steps were taken to ensure that only foreigners (mostly Europeans and Americans in this case) were rescued by well-equipped troops that flew in from France, Belgium, and the US. About 4,000 foreigners of 23 nationalities were evacuated (including their pets).

If only some of these troops had been used to quell the carnage being perpetrated by ill-equipped vampires. If only the committed UNAMIR troops were provided with the right level of logistics and support, "NEVER AGAIN" would have had a meaning. The moderate female Prime Minister, who was constitutionally required to take over the reins of government, was quickly killed with her family in the very presence of her UNAMIR "Protection Squad" that was instructed by New York to not fire a shot unless personally assaulted. Ultimately, ten Belgian soldiers were killed by Hutu elements, thus leading to a Belgian clamor for the collapse of the entire Mission. In the prevailing genocide, Hutu elements appointed an Interim Government comprising some of the vilest killers. Desperate messages to the UN HQ for urgent reinforcements, at least to save the lives of the UNAMIR Peacekeepers, were ignored or trivialized, thus leading the Commander, Romeo Dalladier, to query if he and his few men (the 450 Belgian troops had been withdrawn at this stage!) had been abandoned to die in Rwanda, and if the value of human life had any meaning to all the bureaucrats at UN and the various world capitals. Bureaucracy and narrowly defined national interest immobilized action when it was needed most. Africans should always remember this.

The unrestrained genocide against Tutsis released the RPF troops from any responsibility under the abolished Arusha Accord. They, therefore, regrouped to engage the Rwandan military and militia. UNAMIR Commanders took exceptional risk with their lives by sustaining a semblance of negotiations between the belligerent forces. The unilateral appointment of an interim Government by the Hutu killers conveyed an impression of a stabilizing polity to Western capitals and the UN, despite the factual renditions by the UNAMIR Command on ground. The genocide was still being treated clinically and in a detached way by Powers that could have stopped it. On April 11, 1994, for example (5 days into the genocide), the US Department Of Defense Under-Secretary Frank Wisner was told in a memorandum that unless both sides could return to the peace process, " a massive (hundreds of thousands of deaths) bloodbath will ensue that would likely spill over into Burundi", while the Region would be engulfed in a major refugee crisis. The report was filed away. Major-General Dallaire described this and the overall abandonment of Rwandans as "inexcusable apathy... that is completely beyond comprehension and moral acceptability." He and his remaining men were abandoned, while at the UN, "there was a void of leadership. No supplies, no reinforcement. No decisions." This could very easily repeat itself. Israelis understand this, and do not rely on luck or the convenient kindness of outsiders in their defense, given their location in the midst of existential enemies.

It is particularly disappointing that, while the Red Cross, *Medecins Sans Frontiers,* Human Watch, and a coterie of other foreign humanitarian organizations provided relief for surviving Tutsis and also called global attention to the genocide that was underway in Rwanda, the Catholic Church (to which over 70% of Rwandans adhered) had no institutional response to the carnage against its faithful. Isolated cases of mercy and heroic interventions existed, no doubt, but the Catholic Church was very detached from the entire bestiality. While the Catholic leadership in Rwanda was composed of Hutus, the Vatican should have provided a more vocal moral voice.

Despite the obvious genocidal conduct that was on, the campaign to withdraw the remaining UNAMIR Forces remained persistent. The Belgian decision to withdraw led to their strange campaign for all UN troops to leave with them. They aggressively canvassed this position at the UN. Meanwhile, the extremists became more emboldened by the discriminatory evacuations, and UNAMIR's sheer impotence.

The Hate Media were openly announcing the names and numbers of prominent Tutsis who had either been killed or were being sought, with congratulatory messages sent on air to particular units, which had done "the work" very well. Leads were equally being provided about where machetes and guns could be obtained, all on public radio!!! In spite of all of this, the UN Security Council voted on April 20, 1994 to reduce the UNAMIR Force to a residual group of 250, as a stated concession to those insisting on any role for the UN in Rwanda at all!!! For their role in inspiring UN's aiding and abetting of a genocide, Gen. Dallaire says of the French, American, and British that "No amount of their cash and aid to survivors will ever wash their hands clean of Rwandan blood." This was an extreme reaction, no doubt, since the Americans and British played no role in causing the carnage.

There was particular aversion to the acknowledgment that genocide was taking place, because of the duty and responsibility this would automatically have imposed on these countries on the basis of the provisions of the 1948 UN Protocol technically outlawing genocide. If the UN was reluctant to believe the UNAMIR Commander regarding the ethnic cleansing in Rwanda, the RPF representative in New York, Claude Dusaidi, who had waited outside the UN Security Council Chambers every day since the genocide commenced 20 days earlier in the expectation of an urgent and robust UN intervention, finally wrote the President of the Security Council, Ambassador Colin Keating, on April 26, 1994, as follows: "When the institution of the UN was created after the Second World War, one of its fundamental objectives was to see to it that what happened to the Jews in Nazi Germany would never happen again. Today, in Rwanda, we are witnessing the implementation of a carefully-planned campaign to exterminate the Tutsi ethnic group. The mass killings of Rwandan Tutsis for no other reason than their ethnicity, is genocide. The

International Community, under the Genocide Convention, is obliged to suppress and punish genocide. The perpetrators of this horrendous crime are the Presidential Guard and the MRND-CDR militia." As it turned it, this did not stir any conscience...

Despite powerful objections from the British Ambassador to the UN, a compromise Statement was issued condemning the killings but avoiding the word "genocide". The US proposed that a delegation be sent to Rwanda. Both countries then suggested that the Organization of African Unity (OAU) should anchor all future military deployments. Several other bureaucratic bottlenecks were placed on the way. The Tutsis needed much more than words and delegations. Of course, due to this casual treatment of the matter, 700,000 more people were killed over the next 80 days, giving a total of 1 million dead. In a surprising move, when the RPF were on the verge of defeating the Rwandan Army, the French quickly started canvassing for the deployment of a "Humanitarian" Force to Rwanda.

Unwilling to accommodate delays in New York, France unilaterally dispatched a contingent of their elite troops to Rwanda for the real purpose of reversing RPF military gains. The so-called Operation Turquoise operated independently of UNAMIR, and comprised over 2,500 paratroopers and French Foreign Legion, fully kitted with state-of-the-art weapons, one hundred armored vehicles, heavy mortars, helicopters, jet fighters, etc. These troops worked very closely with the Rwandan Army directly implicated in the genocide. The international media that had sustained global attention on the Bosnia Crisis, treated the Rwandan massacres rather casually. In the April 29, 1994 edition of The Guardian of London, there was a confirmation that Oxfam and UNAMIR had determined the fact of genocide in Rwanda, but the ten-paragraph story on an inside page equally emphasized that "glum pragmatism dictates that there is precious little that the international community can do to stem the fighting in Rwanda at this stage." Other journalists who witnessed the ethnic cleansing were unable to convince their editors to publish their stories. An editor told her Reporter that there was "compassion fatigue about Africa." Africans should note this.

Two months into the massacre, the world had still not reacted robustly. The Department of Peacekeeping Operations had, by now, contacted forty-four countries seeking vehicles and logistics for the troops that were available in Rwanda. Ghana, Senegal, Ethiopia, Zambia, and Nigeria were now ready to send troop reinforcements. The US under Bill Clinton provided 50 Armored Personnel Carriers stored in Turkey from the Cold War stock but insisted on a leasehold rate of $4 million and an additional $6 million for the transportation of the APCs. These rusty vehicles were delivered after the genocide had ended, and lacked machine guns, radio, tools, spare parts, and ancillary components.

Against all possible odds, the RPF finally took Kigali, the capital of Rwanda, on July 4, 1994. Members of the Interim Government, Military Leaders, Militia members, and municipal authorities involved in perpetrating the slaughter, fled the country and joined over one million, five hundred thousand Hutus in seeking refuge in deplorable conditions across the border with Zaire. Gradually, the masterminds of the genocide fled to other countries, notably Cameroon, France, and Belgium. As the RPF troops advanced, the Hutu media implored Hutus to flee the country to avoid retaliation from the Tutsi-led RPF Forces. Kigali had less than fifty thousand inhabitants when the RPF Forces arrived. Most had been killed or had fled. The exodus represented the largest instance of dislocation in modern times, and led to dire medical, nutritional, and related challenges at the Goma Camp, as elsewhere. The ensuing refugee crisis in the Central African Region was severe for many years. The French troops provided security for the refugees including the killers, while the US quickly spent $400m and dispatched 4,000 soldiers to assist in providing relief for the displaced Hutus (including the killers).

No commensurate humanitarian assistance was extended to the few Tutsis who survived the genocide inside Rwanda. After an interim period, the RPF leader, Paul Kagame, became the President of Rwanda. Many Rwandan Tutsis who were on exile have returned to their country, to join in the rehabilitation efforts, while Hutus have now become refugees in other lands. As a first measure, ethnic origin has been removed from identity cards.

While an International Tribunal was convened in Arusha, Tanzania, for the trial of the captured masterminds of the genocide, cases were handled in a very slow manner while the UN set a time limit for the sitting of the Tribunal. To the last person, all the perpetrators who were tried, refused to show contrition for the genocide. With this disposition, together with the fact that a proper reconciliation was not effected, it is only a matter of time before the Hutus on exile will take up arms against the Tutsi leadership in Rwanda, thus igniting yet another phase in the seemingly-endless killings between these two peoples – mostly a consequence of the Berlin Conference. It is hoped that the world would take proactive measures then. If the handling of the subsequent genocide in Darfur is a basis for assessment, then the prospects of a definitive resolution remain very bleak indeed. Perhaps, Mr. Kagame's leadership qualities and the economic successes that Rwanda achieves under him will finally enable full reconciliation and national unity. Just hopefully…

Conclusion

Apart from *Realpolitik* considerations that influence intervention decisions, the imperative of saving defenseless civilians is equally a fundamental incentive. While the foregoing position clearly captures the failure of a robust external intervention towards averting or mitigating the genocide against Tutsis in Rwanda, it is one's considered opinion that the bulk of the blame for this failure should be reserved for African countries. While the rest of the world could conceivably afford to ignore the carnage, the OAU (as it then was) and respective African States owed Rwandans the duty of urgent intervention and facilitation of the negotiation process towards a sustainable resolution of the underlying differences. If they required assistance from the rest of the world, that would be secondary.

The expectation of Western intervention was predicated on the assessment of their public morality, their financial and logistical capacity for swift operations, their global stature which confers leverage, their antecedent action in other parts of the world, etc. While the betrayal of these expectations was painful, it is understandable. After all, Rwanda has no crude oil -- which was in acute demand at the time. The core blame must still be reserved for Africans themselves who failed Rwandans. Their insensitivity over the genocide in Darfur and the earlier one against Igbos in Nigeria is instructive in its reinforcement of a pattern. While the arrogant manner in which the Europeans carved up Africa and established countries remains a major cause of most of the tension in African countries, Africans owe themselves the duty of having meaningful dialogues among themselves and agreeing the parameters of association within their various countries or disassembling amicably.

The problem has always been that those ethnic groups and segments disproportionately favored by colonialists are unwilling to re-negotiate the terms of existence. Rwanda can easily be replicated across Africa. While it is tempting to assume that genocide could only happen in Africa, contemporary history belies this assumption. The Holocaust against Jews in Germany and Eastern Europe, as well as the ethnic cleansing in Bosnia, did not happen in Africa. Mao, Stalin, Pol Pot, Saddam Hussein, Syria's Assad etc., were/are not Africans. The "pilgrims" in the US virtually wiped out the original Indian occupants of the land. Humanity as a whole has an evil dimension, which must be tamed or re-channeled to positive ends.

Endangered people must also rely on themselves and on themselves alone. The purported Peacekeeping Mission in Rwanda by the UN recommended a major structural and philosophical overhaul. While it is admitted that the UN does not have its own Military Force and must necessarily follow the dictates of the Security Council, an Organization run by wo/men of stature and credibility would have elicited the kind of response required during this trying period. Most of those who were killed in Rwanda could have made their own defense arrangements if not for their absolute reliance on an impotent and confused UN. The RPF, for example, could have provided Tutsis with weapons and machetes, just like the Rwandan military and government did for the Hutus, but they relied on the UN! This is a major lesson for all the endangered people across Africa and around the world.

The failure of the so-called Peacekeeping Operation is further demonstrated by the following:

- An environment of total confusion regarding the objectives, mandate, and *modus operandi* of UNAMIR. Were they supposed to enforce peace, keep an elusive peace, or what? The entire Mission was not thought through *ab initio*, hence the endless spates of indecision and leadership failure. After this, and similar failures by the UN, it is difficult to resist the suggestion that the UN should be scrapped, so that people do not have illusory expectations of help from a quasi-World Government. There was no peace to keep in Rwanda. Peace is a mutual agreement of non-aggression either achieved through laws that all sides have agreed to abide by or based on negotiated terms that satisfy all parties. Without the process of negotiation, there can be no real and enduring peace. Peacekeeping in that context will be an exercise in futility. As long as one side perceives that it holds the leverage, it will exercise it. The role of third-party intervention must be to assist belligerents to agree on a mutually acceptable compromise situation.
- An abysmal provision of logistics, manpower, equipment, and resources for the UN Forces in Rwanda
- Playing cheap politics with human lives. There was never a sense of urgency at the UN or the major world capitals all through the period of the genocide.
- The corrosive role of the dominant members of the UN aggravated the situation. The leadership and bureaucracies in those countries demonstrated an unbecoming level of insensitivity and shortsightedness. President Bill Clinton eventually apologized for their lack of response.
- All the alerts, messages, and requests for an expanded mandate and reinforcements were ignored, thereby exposing even UN troops to grave danger. The decision to withdraw and/ or reduce the number of troops at the peak of the genocide demonstrated gross incompetence, callousness, and detachment from reality.
- The corollary inability of the UNAMIR Forces to make any impact whatsoever considerably emboldened the genocidal perpetrators and diminished UN's stature.
- The inability to address the core issues in the months and years leading up to the 1994 genocide was a most shameful development. All the signs were there

regarding the imminence of a major crisis. The Nigerian situation has been brewing for many years now, and especially since 2015. Hopefully, the demographics under perennial attack will learn the necessary lessons.

- The subsequent provision for Hutu killers and refugees, without any counterpart consideration for the few surviving and more deserving Tutsis, gives an impression of partisanship, insensitivity, and foolishness.
- The UN did not use its resources to fast-track the trials of those responsible for the genocide and to apply the maximum punishment, as a possible deterrent for the future. Many years later, many of the notable killers were still free. Only very few of the masterminds were tried. The suggestion by some people that Rwandans should use their traditional justice system (old village justice system for minor cases) in resolving the genocide, fails to appreciate the gravity and scope of the crime committed especially in 1994. People must be punished for it, even as political negotiations are held.
- The Darfur genocide was not stopped with dispatch, demonstrating that the lessons of Rwanda were never learnt.

Many thanks for your time and attention. Every journey must have an end, however long it takes; even life itself has an end. We have finally come to the end of, hopefully, an evocative, thought-provoking, and insightful narrative. Ultimately, every creative work is a projection of values. It is my earnest hope that mine have come through clearly. A few people might agree entirely with the central theme of this book; a great number will definitely disagree with the work or sections thereof; some people will ignore the message and focus on the delivery mode and style; indeed, a few readers will wonder why Philosophy should be interlaced with what they regard as *ad hominem* or polemical attacks; few will just be ambivalent. That is exactly as it should be; intellectual positions reflect the great spectrum of the human experience. As Cicero instructed us over 2,000 years ago, "if we are not ashamed to think it, we should not be ashamed to say it." One has chosen to say it, since they were not ashamed to think and do it. The author has written as he has seen fit, guided by the Truth and Decency, however and whoever may be offended. No apology is considered due and none is rendered.

May you be a force for good in our very wicked and complex world. Help the weak, caution the strong, protect the marginalized, blame the oppressor, encourage and empower the disenfranchised, deflate and vanquish the evil ones among us. Thank you.

Washington, D.C.

June 22, 2020

Postscript

In the almost three months since work on this book started, there have been two most significant developments. There has been a spike in the Covid:19 infection and casualty rates both in the United States and globally. 2.43 million people have cumulatively been diagnosed with the Coronavirus in the US alone, while we have unfortunately lost 124,000 people to the pandemic-related illnesses. Globally, 9.51 million people have been diagnosed with Covid:19 to date, while 484,000 have died from it. While Public Health experts are not in agreement on whether the first wave is over and we are guaranteed a second wave, there is a unanimity of views that, with the necessary vaccine still several months away, we need to retain the safety and mitigation protocols that were mandated during the compulsory lockdowns across the world. The front page of the May 24th 2020 edition of the New York Times was a mosaic of the names of the individuals who had died from Covid:19-related causes in the US. There is also legitimate concern that the hasty re-openings in some parts of the United States and the world, might lead to a reversal of the gains we made during the lockdown. While Statistics have been rigorously maintained and the necessary lessons adapted to the treatment of new cases in the developed countries, there has sadly been a stigmatization factor attached to the illness in developing countries, thus combining with the inadequate testing, inefficient contact tracing, and sub-optimal healthcare facilities, to depress the number of reported cases in those countries.

Small businesses, corporations, governments, and international organizations continue to evaluate the evolving impact of the pandemic on social and economic activities, as well as on every sector of the economic system. Schools remain shut down globally, with no guarantee that Fall or Autumn classes will hold in person; domestic and international travels remain eroded by over 90%, with direct and indirect implications for ancillary services and sectors; major Corporations have filed for bankruptcy; 43 million Americans have filed for unemployment benefits during the pandemic, with realistic assessments of over 20% unemployment numbers projected into the medium to long-term, which will impact aggregate demand, taxes, credit card, mortgage, and sundry loan servicing; the disruption has permeated every Sector. The pandemic has remained a public health crisis, a revenue crisis, and has also triggered off serious socio-political crises.

The US Government released a Stimulus Package of $2.2 trillion targeted at vulnerable individuals and businesses, while another sum of $500 billion was earmarked for small businesses (currently enmeshed in some controversy over the transparency of the disbursement). The Government Accountability Office (GAO) of the United States has just confirmed that over a million checks (from the Stimulus Funds) with a total value of $1.4 billion were mailed to dead people. Hopefully, the funds will be fully recovered; the US Government made available the sum of $765 million to Kodak for pharmaceutical research and development. In Germany, 70% of salaries are paid to their working citizens by their government, with 600 billion Euros made available to big businesses. No rent or tax will be due until 2022; other countries and blocs have also intervened according to their capacity, to cushion the effects of the unusual pandemic, and the EU planned to spend 825 billion Euros directly, thereby raising issues about the roles of nation-States and politico-economic Blocs.

The World Bank confirmed that Nigeria had started its worst recession in forty years. For certain, certain pandemic-conditioned habits will remain with us into the foreseeable future, and fundamental adjustments will be made to the business and social culture across the world. The Q1 2020 GDP of the United States fell by 33%, the highest ever in recorded history.

Remote meetings will become popular, for example, with serious adverse effects on the demand for business or commercial real estate, or even residential real estate in expensive neighborhoods and City Centers. If you can now work zoomically from the Catskills Region of New York or West Virginia, why remain in Manhattan, for example? The pandemic has also exposed and highlighted the cumulative delinquencies that define the Third World, even as their rulers (not leaders) live in opulence. The contraction in global economic numbers, as well as the consequential steep drop in the demand for the natural resources which these countries export for survival, will worsen the social and political conditions in those countries. The legacy issues of unsustainable population numbers, acute unemployment, fractured citizenry, tsunamic disparities in income distribution, the burden of foreign currency-denominated loans, ageing or absent physical infrastructure, refusal to diversify their economic base in the years of buoyancy, the absence or inefficiency of the Rule of Law, endemic corruption, and lack of Social Trust, will only worsen their outcomes.

The poor performance of the particular countries and Regions raises new issues for the global community, apart from the immediate threats they pose to their citizens. If these countries have failed to channel the freedoms and flexibility of their sovereignty towards providing basic services to their people, how will they fare as the world gets increasingly more sophisticated? What risks do they continue to pose to the world in an increasing-connected ecosystem? What are the remedies? If a country has not provided constant electricity, potable water, standard education, and quality healthcare to their leaders and citizens, is it realistic to expect that country to handle a pandemic effectively, or deflect cyber intrusions and attacks on its national data and financial systems? According to the World Economic Forum and Zurich.com, the global risk profile will assume a multi-pronged dimension which will challenge even the most sophisticated societies, much less the failed and failing States (**Figures 42 and 43)*.

The second major development in the recent period was the widespread domestic and global revulsion over the cruel and unnecessary murder of Mr. George Floyd by policemen in Minnesota. We have exhausted discussions on the related dynamics, but people of good faith from all races and ages protested in all the 50 US States and major cities around the world for weeks on end, using the opportunity to upturn vestiges and symbols of racial injustice in their communities. Monuments to slaveholders and racial bigots were knocked down by protesters around the world, while Institutions were forced to reckon with their past. Mr. Floyd's killing, which was captured on video, was a wake-up call to the conscience of the country and the world, a global audience that had forever endured similar spectacles of white police officers casually killing black men and women, mostly without consequences. The day of reckoning had to come someday. While the Democratic Party led in the enactment of laws to hold the Police more accountable, the Trumpian Republican Party continued to play the ostrich, creating and peddling false narratives and unhelpful binaries. Sports Associations and professional bodies were forced to recognize America's despicable history of racial injustice. The New Yorker Magazine cover page of June 22, 2020, paid homage to George Floyd and all the other recent cases of Police killings of black people in America.

Prominent members of the Italian-American community have publicly criticized the demolition of Christopher Columbus monuments, regarding this as a diminution of the contribution of early Italians and Romanic people to these lands. One may ask them why we should knock down Robert Lee's effigies and leave those of the original mass killer? This same community that only gained stature and respect in America when JFK, a Catholic, became the first non-WASP US President, now seeks to stake an ancestral claim to America, however tainted and despicable that distant pedigree. Perhaps, the idea is to suggest an older claim to these bloodied lands?

The Democratic Party-led House of Representatives under Speaker Nancy Pelosi passed the George Floyd Justice in Policing Act of 2020 by 236-181 mostly along Party lines, with only three Republican members voting with all the Democrats for reforms that introduce justice in policing in America. These were Brian Fitzpatrick of Pennsylvania, Will Hurd of Texas, and Fred Upton of Michigan. 181 Republican members of the House of Representatives saw no need for accountability, humaneness, equality, and proportionality in policing and police violence, even against the backdrop of the recent killings and the widespread protests demanding immediate legislative and institutional reforms against centuries of systemic racism against blacks in America. With this investment in evil, is there any wonder then than some policemen and women across the country have taken umbrage against the long overdue need to stop their casual murder of innocent black men and women, their cracking of a senior citizen's skull in Buffalo, New York, and their overall abuse of office with impunity? If they seek a perpetuation of their brutality, their children are available for chokeholds, and they can crack their mothers' skulls as well.

Some of the brutes have mercifully since resigned. President Donald Trump has already confirmed that, if the George Floyd Bill is passed by the Senate as well (very unlikely given the Republican Party's slim majority there presently, their shameless spinelessness before this man, their utter lack of principles and recognition of their Oversight Powers as demonstrated during the Impeachment Hearings earlier this year, as well as their shared worldview with their confederate, Mr. Trump, on the structure of the American society; a hearkening to the "good old days"), he would veto the Bill.

In 2006, a black female Police Officer, Cariol Horne, stopped a fellow Police Officer (white?/Jewish) from applying a chokehold on a black suspect, David Mack, over a minor offence. After her suspension and the other disciplinary measures meted out to her, the woman was sacked by the Buffalo Police Department in 2008 for her intervention in that case, and she lost her pension since she was a few months to qualification. She had spent nineteen years on the Force and eligibility for pensions started after twenty years; nineteen wasted years!!! The perpetrator remained in the Police System while an innocent woman was sacked. Fourteen years later, thanks to George Floyd and the other recent cases, the City Council has voted to revisit her case. What if she had died in the intervening period of twelve years? Does anyone care how she and her family have survived all this while, and the psychological anguish her treatment has imposed on her? Obviously, the delinquent Officers seek a full-scale return to a culture of willful murder and impunity, but the time might just have changed a bit.

The Board of Trustees of Princeton University has just voted to remove the name of the 28th President of the United States, Woodrow Wilson, from their well-regarded School of Public Policy, due to Wilson's deep racism. He was a beneficiary and perpetrator of racism, having re-introduced racial discrimination and segregation into the federal civil service when he was the President at the turn of the last century. Wilson had been the governor of New Jersey (not Alabama, Mississippi or any of the other densities of wickedness in the South). He had also been the President of Princeton University, so he was a very educated and knowledgeable individual, yet he could not cure himself of ignorance, prejudice, sense of entitlement, and racial hatred. In the words of the Board of Trustees, "we have taken this extraordinary step because we believe that Wilson's racist thinking and policies make him an inappropriate namesake for a School whose Scholars, Students, and Alumni must be firmly committed to combating the scourge of racism in all its forms," and that "Wilson's racism was significant and consequential even by the standards of his own time." Princeton President Christopher Eisgruber added: "He (Wilson) segregated the federal civil service after it had been racially integrated for decades, thereby taking America backward in its pursuit of justice… He not only acquiesced in, but added to the persistent practice of racism in this country, a practice that continues to do harm today. Wilson's segregationist policies make him an especially inappropriate namesake for a Public Policy School. When a University names a School of Public Policy for a political leader, it inevitably suggests that the honoree is a model for students who study at the School. This searing moment in American history has made clear that Wilson's racism disqualifies him from that role. In a nation that continues to struggle with racism, this University and its School of Public and International Affairs must stand clearly and firmly for equality and justice. The School will now be known as "The Princeton School of Public and International Affairs.""

Dr. Eisgruber then concluded as follows: "Princeton honored Wilson not because of, but without regard to or perhaps even in ignorance of, his racism. That, however, is ultimately the problem. Princeton is part of an America that has too often disregarded, ignored, or excused racism, allowing the persistence of systems that discriminate against Black people. When Derek Chauvin knelt for nearly nine minutes on George Floyd's neck while bystanders recorded his cruelty, he might have assumed that the system would disregard, ignore, or excuse his conduct, as it had done in response to past complaints against him."

As to be expected, the pretender-monarch who hides his amorphous frame behind his tiny fingers, the modern-day racist US President, Mr. Donald J. Trump, has expressed displeasure over Princeton's redeeming and corrective action.

As work on these notes was being concluded, three white Police Officers: James Gilmore, Jesse Moore II, and Kevin Piner were sacked by the Wilmington, North Carolina Police Department for provocative racial slurs and threats they shared on a reviewed in-car camera feed. They were recorded saying they were bent on "slaughtering" and wiping black people off the map. They said: "We are just gonna go out and start slaughtering them", referring to black people. They also negatively characterized their black colleagues in the Police Department, criticized the Black Lives Matter Movement, and called for a civil war to be fought along racial lines. Well, some Police Departments in Alabama, Mississippi, or Arkansas may lionize them and immediately hire them to execute their mission.

The world has just become aware that, in 2019, some white police officers in Aurora, Colorado stopped a 23-year-old black man and violinist, Elijah McClain, as he walked home from a convenience store. His offence was that he wore a ski mask in the frigid temperatures of Colorado, as recommended by his doctors, owing to his anemia and the need to warm up his body. Even as he committed no crime, the Officers applied a carotid chokehold on him as he kept saying that he could not breathe; the paramedics who were invited injected him with ketamine and he went into a cardiac arrest on the way to the hospital, dying a few days later. During the memorial service in his honor at which violinists performed, three white police officers: Erica Marrero, Kyle Dittrich, and Jaron Jones, chose exactly that venue and time to re-enact the chokehold that led to the young man's death while giggling all through. They sent a picture of their foolish and morbid joke to their colleague, Jason Rosenblatt, who was among those who applied the killer-chokehold in the first place. His response was "hahahaha." Well, the Police Authorities decided to sack the first three Officers, while Mr. Rosenblatt decided to resign. They were sacked for the re-enactment, while no Officer was disciplined or fired for killing an innocent man; that is quite telling. They remained in service a year later.

Across state boundaries, in Utah, a Black man (Jeffery Ryans) who was lounging on his own porch while preparing for his shift as a train engineer, was mauled by a police dog on the instructions of a white police officer (Nickolas Pearce). Mr. Ryans had identified himself in his own home, and had complied with the Officer's requests to get on his knees and raise his hands. While the attack ensued, the Police Officer kept encouraging his dog, as he repeated "good boy!" As at now, doctors have concluded that an amputation of Mr. Ryans's leg will be necessary while Officer Pearce has merely been suspended, pending an investigation into whether the use of force was necessary.

Since we have chosen to degrade our humanity and deflect from individual responsibility for our actions by lumping people together and judging them on the basis of their melanin content and not the quality of their heart and their sense of responsibility, the next narrative will assume a familiar but unfortunate and invalid pattern. The society chooses terms like 'white', 'black', 'brown', 'people of color', etc., even as no human being is really white or black, as previously stated. Even if they were, the pejorative term 'people of color' conveniently excludes the people we regard as white even as white is obviously also a color. Some 'black' people also have less melanin than some 'white' people, but it matters not. Convenient bifurcations must be retained for a race-based social architecture; a "polite" perpetuation of racism and all its dynamics of reward and punishment.

On Monday, June 29th, 2020, a white policeman (you know what I mean by now), Sgt. Craig Johnson, was shot and killed by a white man, David Ware, during a routine traffic stop in Tulsa, Oklahoma. Sgt. Johnson's junior colleague remains in intensive care as at the time of writing. Mr. Ware escaped but was promptly tracked down, arrested and charged with first degree murder and two other felonies, namely: shooting with intent to kill and possession of a firearm after former conviction for a felony. This cowardly attack, the unprovoked and unnecessary taking of Officer Johnson's life, as well as the shooting of the other Officer, must be condemned by all people of conscience, regardless of "race." The Police do an important and risky job in our society. A family has just lost their husband, son, brother, father, uncle, nephew, and friend for no reason. The full weight of the law must be applied to get the maximum punishment for Mr. Ware, even as this will not bring back the dead. Officer Johnson might also have been among the many Police Officers doing their difficult job with decency, professionalism, balance, and restraint, without inherent biases.

The questions are: since we can all agree that this killing was wrong and must be punished, why is it difficult to agree on the same treatment for Police Officers who kill unarmed people (black or white) fleeing from them, sleeping at home, sleeping in their own cars, sitting on their porches, not resisting arrest, driving with expired licences, selling loose cigarettes, or who keep pleading that they cannot breathe while the knee of an Officer is choking them to death, etc., etc.? Would it have made any difference if Officer Johnson was killed by a "black" man? Would it have also mattered if Officer Johnson was "black", and was killed by a "white" or "black" man or woman? If Officer Johnson had been killed by a "black" man, would this have triggered off revenge killings of innocent "black" people? Is his unnecessary death not adequate to allocate responsibility where it resides (on an individual basis) and seek full legal

punishment? The speed with which his killer, Mr. Ware, was arrested and charged, is commendable; why is this difficult when Police Officers kill others for no reason? Can our moral compass remain stable and focused on the action and the individual perpetrators, seeking objective justice and equal treatment at all times? Are some lives more worthy or worthless than others? Racism is really for fools, insecure fellows, unenlightened minds, and unthinking wastrels. Rest in peace, Craig Johnson, and best wishes to your struggling colleague. Our condolences go to the Johnson family. May Ware never be a part of decent society again, as should apply to the Officers who killed George Floyd and the other victims of excessive and race-based Police brutality in America.
A few other developments worth reporting include:

President Donald J. Trump of the United States chose the period of the pandemic to withhold America's subventions to the World Health Organization (WHO), and, subsequently, to pull out of the WHO entirely, thereby leaving both a leadership and funding gap that countries like China could step in and provide, to the continuing regression of the United States. Exiting the WHO also limits the collaborative access that will be critical in detecting public health threats on time. Ego trumps all; every person and institution must bow to the insecure Emperor. As America is witnessing widespread spikes in infection rates (including the highest daily jumps since the pandemic started three months earlier) -- after the related lockdowns were lifted in many States --, Mr. Trump has made the remarkable but dangerous observation that "if we stop testing (for Covid:19), we'd have fewer cases." For a man whose grandfather, Friedrich Trump – who was born in Kallstadt, Bavaria, Germany- and died from the 1918 influenza pandemic, one would expect President Trump to be particularly sensitive to the health hazards caused by pandemics. As an aside, it may be added that, while his grandfather (Friedrich) illegally emigrated to the US in 1885 to dodge enlistment into the (Bavarian) German Army, the president's father, Frederick (the English version of Friedrich) also avoided enlisting in the US military during WWII, while our beloved president of braggadocio, Donald, also dodged being drafted for the Vietnam War like his mates. A family track record of wimpism and evasion of civic responsibilities.

The great Nigerian "man of God", Mr. Enoch Adeboye of the ubiquitous and successful Redeemed Christian Church of God (RCCG), even with the abundant information about the scope and intensity of the pandemic, magisterially declared that he had heard directly from God that "true worshippers" will be saved from coronavirus-related deaths. Apart from the non-discriminatory nature of the casualty list, one assumed that "true worshippers" would be eager to proceed to meet their God. The celebration of life, as against death, seems rather counter-intuitive. The other "man or merchant" of God, Mr. David Oyedepo, also heard from the same God that the pandemic will "end soon." Of course, 'soon' will match when Science, Rationality, and billions of dollars in Vaccine R&D investment have yielded positive results, then the scam operation in the name of God will resume fully and ferociously, to recoup what they "lost" when their sheep could not bleat cash for the next private jet in the "service of the Almighty." Mr. Oyedepo also added that: "tithing is an inescapable Covenant obligation. Prosperity, not just wealth, is impossible without tithing, because when you're not paying your tithe, you are under a financial curse." He who collects, keeps, and spends hard cash on behalf of God then closed with the hashtag: #Tithe' #Breaking limits. These fellows and their little games…

Our world involves what Inge Kaul calls a "deepening Policy Interdependence." Responsible Sovereignty is required of all States. In the absence thereof, and given the vulnerability of the entire world to such widening delinquency, what should be the remedy?

Re-colonize the countries all over again, as Boris Johnson haughtily wrote in 2012? This will not work, given all the history.
Build walls against such "shithole" countries? This will not work either, given the fluidity of our interconnectedness, the diaspora population of those countries, transportation advancements, the borderless nature of communications, news, and technology.

Since the aggregate performance of the world is seriously impacted by individual or Regional State Failure, what then is the solution? Use the instrumentalities of the UN and impose mentorships on those countries, involving their diaspora population? Practicability should always be evaluated when prescribing solutions. This will not work, for obvious reasons.

What else, then? Ideally, at the very minimum, the OECD and major countries should insist on certain minimum objective standards and performance levels, which should earn a country the continued recognition as a sovereign and independent State. In the absence thereof, membership in all international bodies should be revoked, diplomatic and consular relations severed, and the family members and entourage of the responsible State officials should be held directly responsible, with no visas or citizenship privileges extended to them anywhere outside their countries. Any country that defies these Rules should face serious consequences. What if those countries are China, Russia, and North Korea?

Our world is complex, and humanity is a maze. The world cannot suddenly shrink, after four hundred years of increasing integration. Multilateralism should be predicated on principles. The major countries need to define and decide (can they?) what the minimum standards of behavior among them should be. This utopian ideal is not supported by reality. John Ruggie defines multilateralism as "an institutional form (including norms, regimes, and formal multilateral organizations) that coordinates relations among three or more States on the basis of generalized principles of conduct", while unilateral actions are those that are taken alone, or with other States, but not in accordance with a rule-based principle, or do not involve adjustments in policy preferences. Multilateral cooperation is not a coincidental harmony of State interests, but a political bargaining process of policy adjustment. It entails some voluntary dilution of policy autonomy or discretion, premised on the calculation that the immediate or long-term gains of policy coordination are greater than the costs of the loss of policy autonomy. Absolutes hardly apply in reality.

While the US played a key role in establishing the primary International Institutions after the Second World War, charges of Unilateralism and Arrogance have been leveled against her in recent times, most especially since after the Cold War and particularly since Mr. Trump became the President in 2016. It has also been suggested that the US employed these Institutions as tools of Statecraft during the Cold War years and has since discarded them in the aftermath of that epochal era, given the beneficial Unipolarity that has since ensued. America's growing withdrawal from the world and the Institutions it created, leave a void likely to be filled by malevolent actors. This is the more reason why America needs to resolve her own internal contradictions, to retain the moral leverage to be the world's pre-eminent behemoth. If not, not...

It is significant that the character of 19th and 20th Century Empires is not feasible in contemporary times. Strong National Identities and the revolutionary impact of the Information Superhighway have largely ensured this. The growing inter-connectedness of States and peoples would entail the inescapable need for dominant States to, indeed, define, supervise, and ensure the observance of acceptable and accepted global codes of behavior, within context, rather than leaving the space for possible exploitation by negative Forces. The contingent diminution of sovereignty and rationalization of global priorities are, in the end, most beneficial to the major powers. This does not, in any way, deprive them of their relative military and economic superiority, but confers legitimacy and acceptance on their leadership and actions. The leader should be interested in preserving the status quo, and in ensuring that Sovereign Entities indeed earn the title by discharging the roles and duties which, *ipso facto*, informed the formation and increasing sophistication of both social and political societies in the first place, namely, the provision of public goods. This was why our earliest ancestors deemed it necessary and wise to avoid the Hobbesian option by forming political systems.

Even in the enlightened self-interest of the major countries, not altruism, reparative conscience, or unusual kindness, it should be a matter of grave concern that the weak States keep getting weaker. The loans and grants given to them are stolen or wasted by their rulers, to the chagrin and genuine anger of their citizens. Widespread State Failure will definitely instruct unprecedented migration (and escape) flows to safe countries, with the obvious implications. As nations play their geopolitical games, therefore, let there be a realization that, ultimately, we are all in this together. We should demand the strengthening of fragile States, to minimize the **dependence** on the richer States. Let their **independence** actually mean something. Short-term calculations will not cut it any longer. **Dependent Independence** inures to no one's benefit at the end of the day….

I am back to the C and O Canal trail to clear my head; the birds and turtles are still impervious to our panic. The natural water system and the foliage do not recognize our anxiety; this too shall pass -- hopefully. Has our "civilization" and "development" as a specie really purified us beyond the carnality and primal instincts that inspired the formation of social and political societies by our earliest ancestors in the first place, or has this "civilization" only amplified our capacity to do evil, in the name of race, even as there is only one race, the human race? I just can't breathe with all that is going on. The wickedness of man, the greed of our species, and the destructiveness of our essence are yet to alter this pristine space, even as I long for my beloved California.

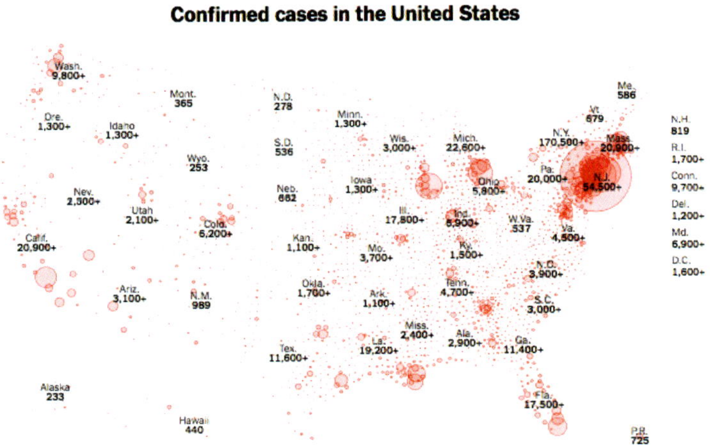

Figure 1 Covid:19 Spread Profile as at April, 2020. *Source: Johns Hopkins Health*

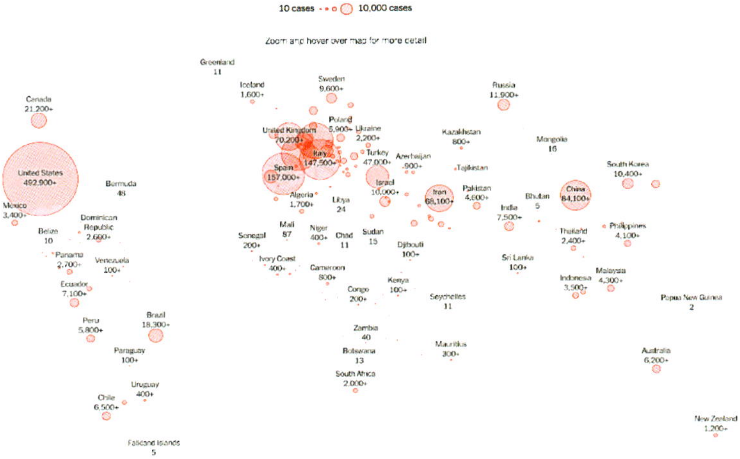

Figure 2 *Source: New York Times, April 9, 2020*

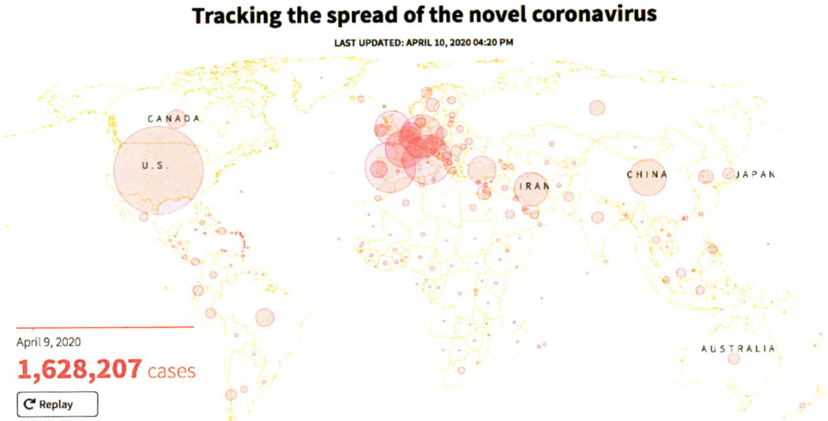

Figure 3 *Source: Reuters, April 10, 2020*

Figure 4 Religion waiting on Science *Source: @akinalabi. March 23, 2020*

Figure 5 Bye-bye Nigeria *Source : @saratu_ibrahim . April 12 2020*

Figure 6 Nigerian President Muhammadu Buhari meets Guinea Bissau's Prime Minister Umaro Embalo *Source: www.vanguardngr.com*

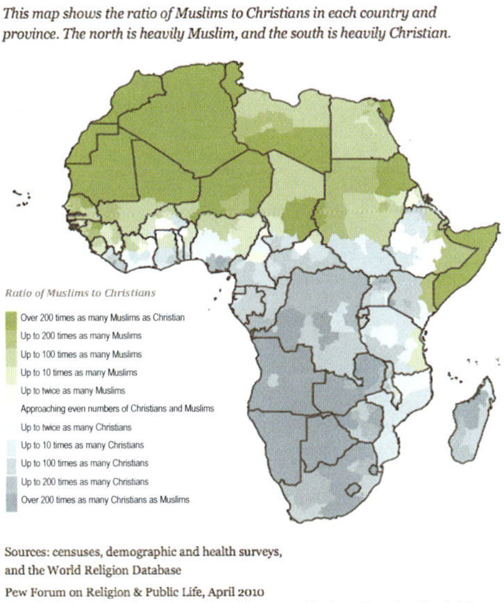

Figure 7 A strong correlation exists between Muslim population density in Africa and Islamic terrorism.

DEAR RACIST, YOUR CHILD NEEDS A PINT OF BLOOD.
CHOOSE THE WHITE ONE.

Figure 8 The folly and ignorance of racism. *Source: Klressa*

Mississippi mayor criticized for comments following death of George Floyd
Petal Mayor Hal Marx is facing criticism for his comments following the death of George Floyd. (Source: WDAM)

Figure 9 *Source: :www.metro.co.uk*

Figure 10 *Source: Politico*

Donald Trump (Getty Images/Salon)

Figure 11 Trump and the rebel flag *Source: www.politico.com*

Figure 12 Map of Africa, as conveniently drawn up at the Berlin conference. *Credit: scholarblogs.emory.edu*

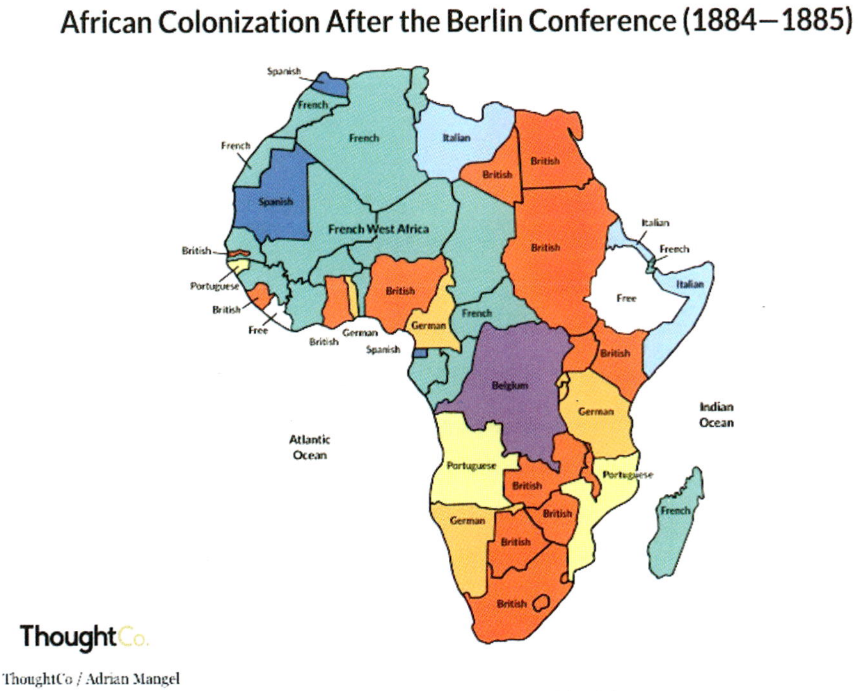

Figure 13 Colonial map of Africa *Source: ThoughtCo*

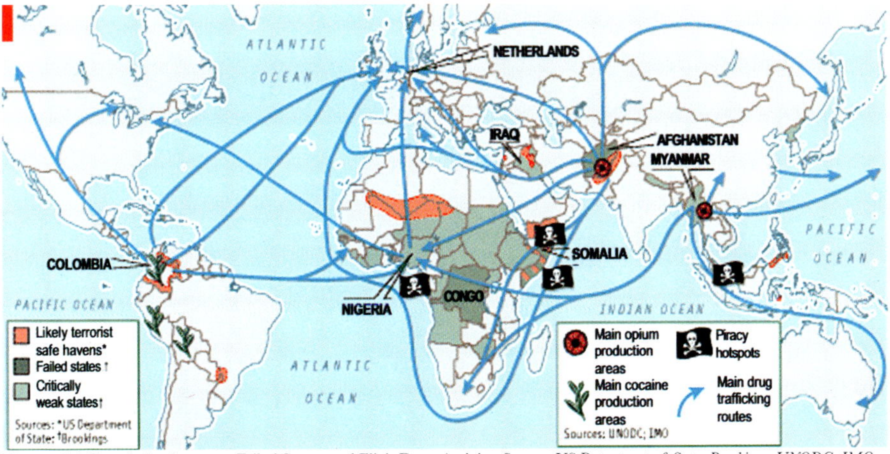

Figure 14 Correlation between Failed States and Illicit Drug Activity. *Sources: US Department of State: Brookings, UNODC, IMO*

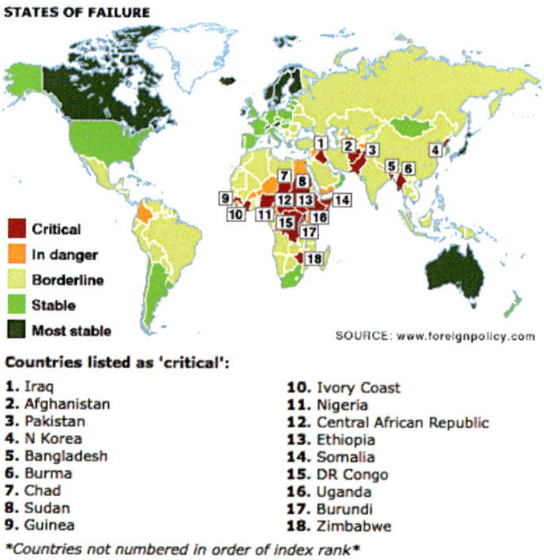

Figure 15 Failed States labeled as 'critical.' *Source: www.foreign policy.com*

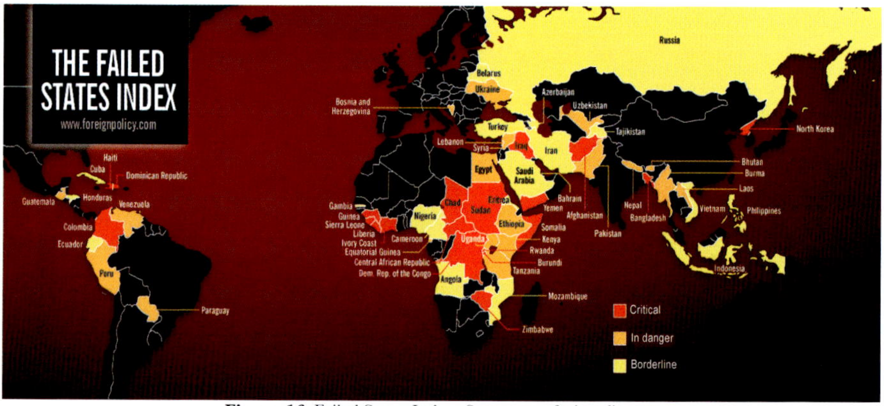

Figure 16 Failed States Index. *Source: www.foreignpolicy.com*

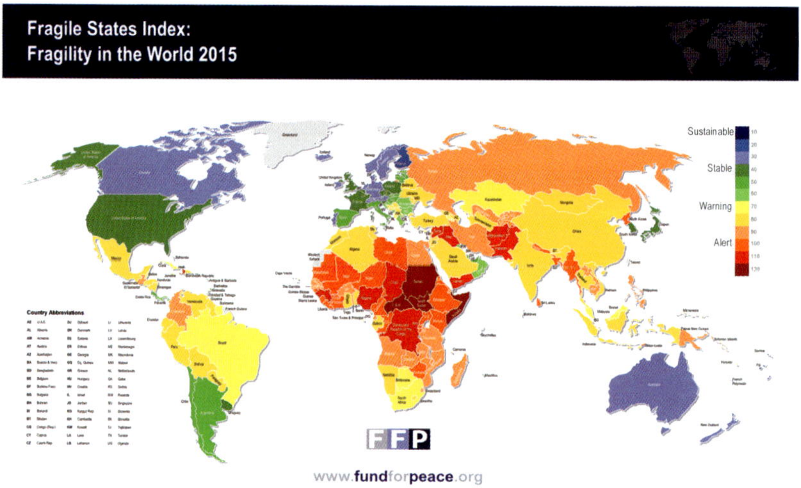

Figure 17 Fragile States Index 2015. *Source: www.fundforpeace.ord*

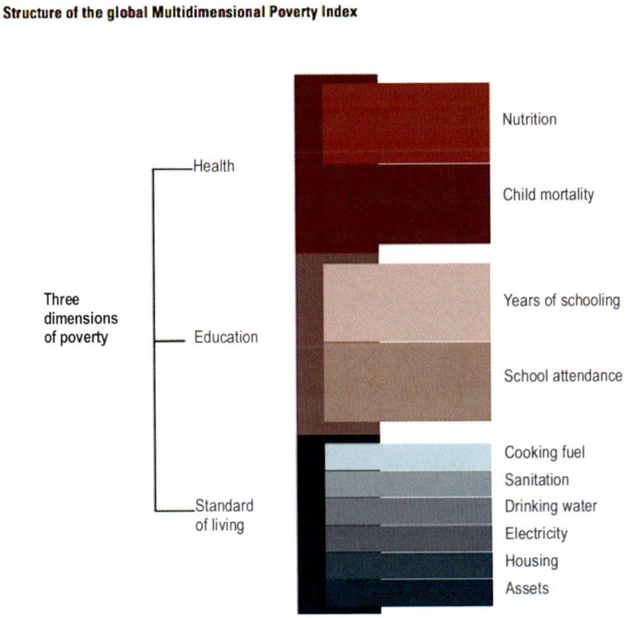

Figure 18 *Source: Oxford Poverty and Human Development Initiative 2018*

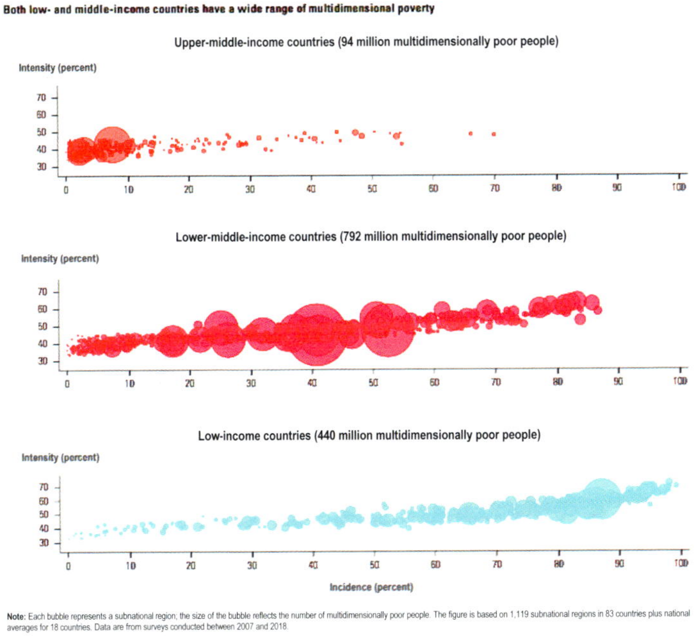

Figure 19 *Source: Akine, Kanagaratnam & Suppa (2019) based on Human Development Report Office and Oxford Poverty and Human Development initiative calculations.*

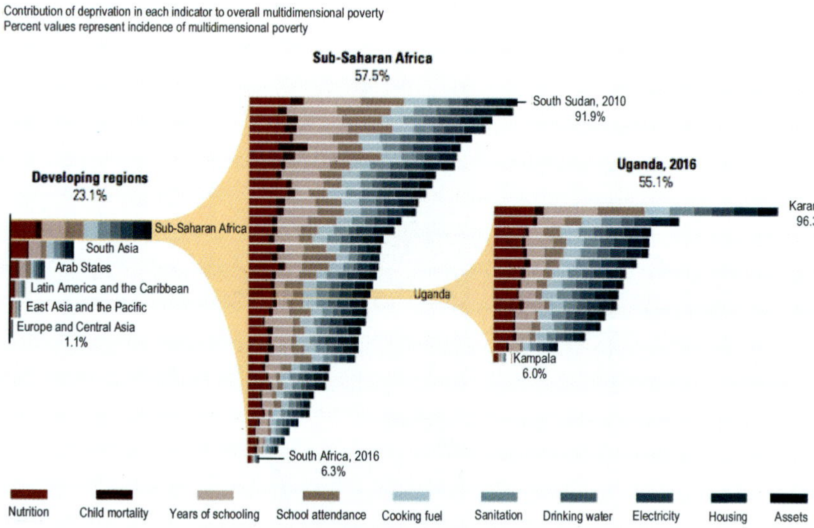

Figure 20 *Source: Akine, Kanagaratnam & Suppa (2019) based on Human Development Report Office and Oxford Poverty and Human Development initiative calculations.*

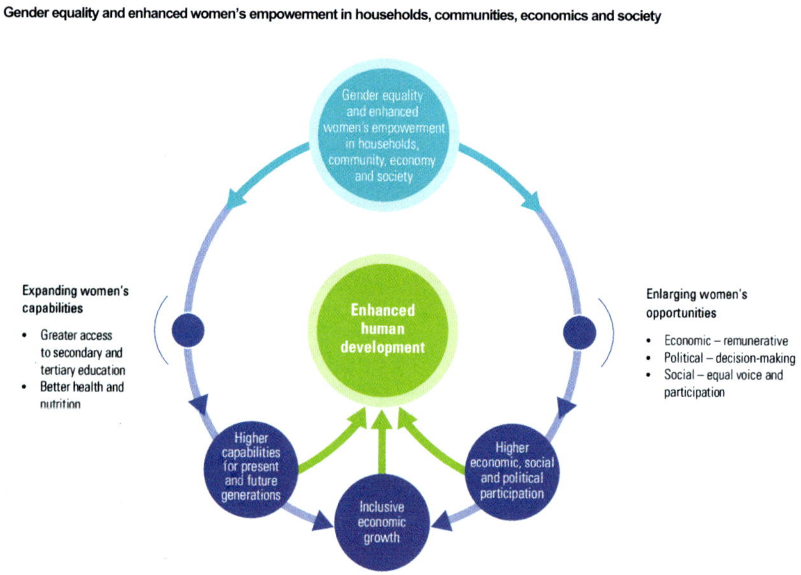

Figure 21 *Source: Contributed by Selim Jahan. Human Development Report Office (HDRO). 2016*

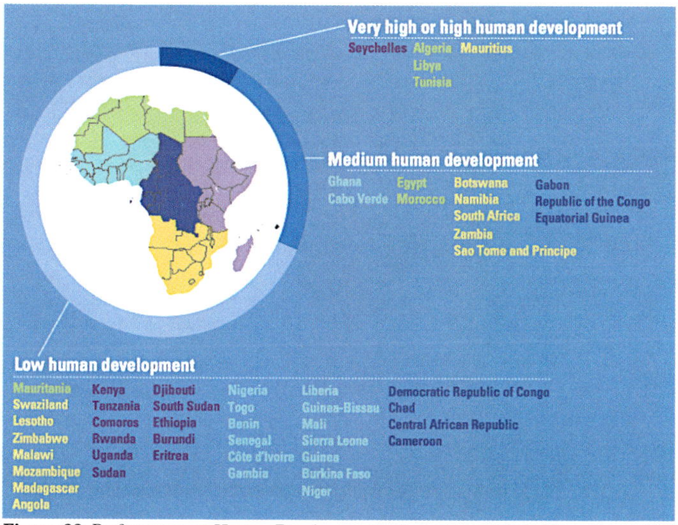

Figure 22 Performance on Human Development Indices. *Source: UNDP African Report, 2016*

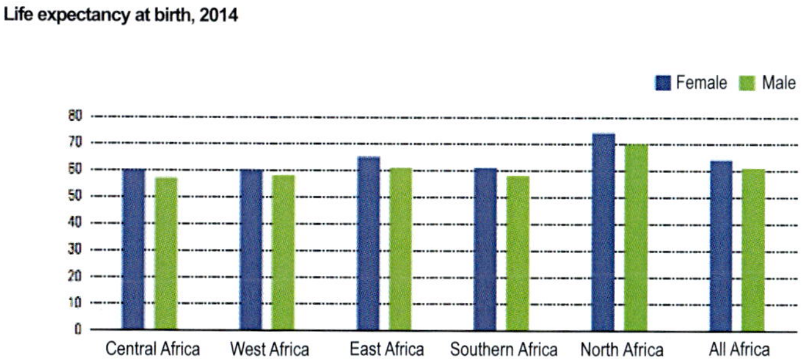

Figure 23 African life expectancy data (gender split) *Source AfHDR Team from data in ILO 2015d.*

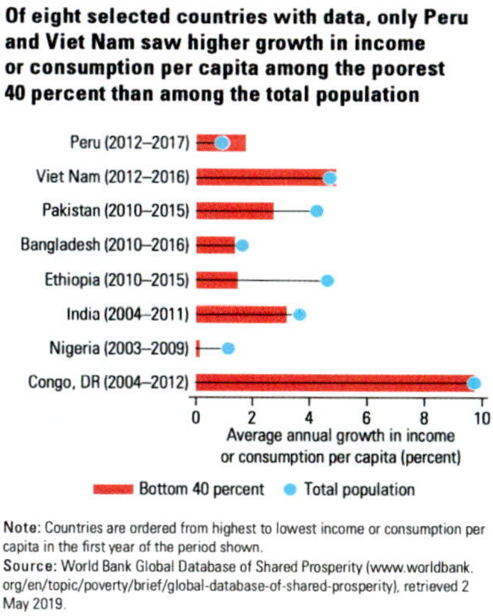

Figure 24 Income per capita for eight selected poor countries *Source: World Bank*

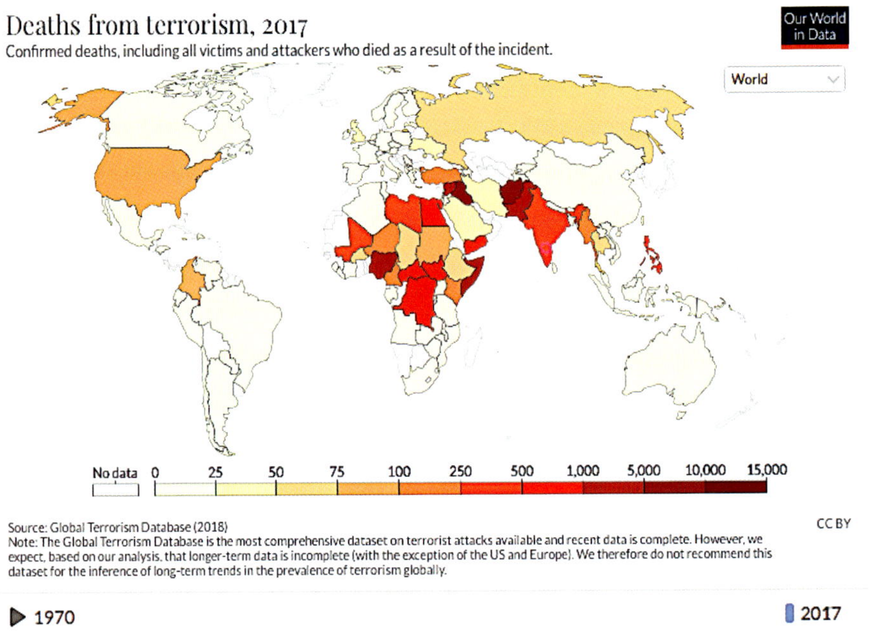
Deaths from terrorism, 2017
Confirmed deaths, including all victims and attackers who died as a result of the incident.
Our World in Data
World
No data
0
25
50
75
100
250
500
1,000
5,000
10,000
15,000
Source: Global Terrorism Database (2018)
Note: The Global Terrorism Database is the most comprehensive dataset on terrorist attacks available and recent data is complete. However, we expect, based on our analysis, that longer-term data is incomplete (with the exception of the US and Europe). We therefore do not recommend this dataset for the inference of long-term trends in the prevalence of terrorism globally.
CC BY
1970
2017

Figure 25 Most terrorism-related deaths take place in failed and failing States. *Source: Global Terrorism Database (2018)*

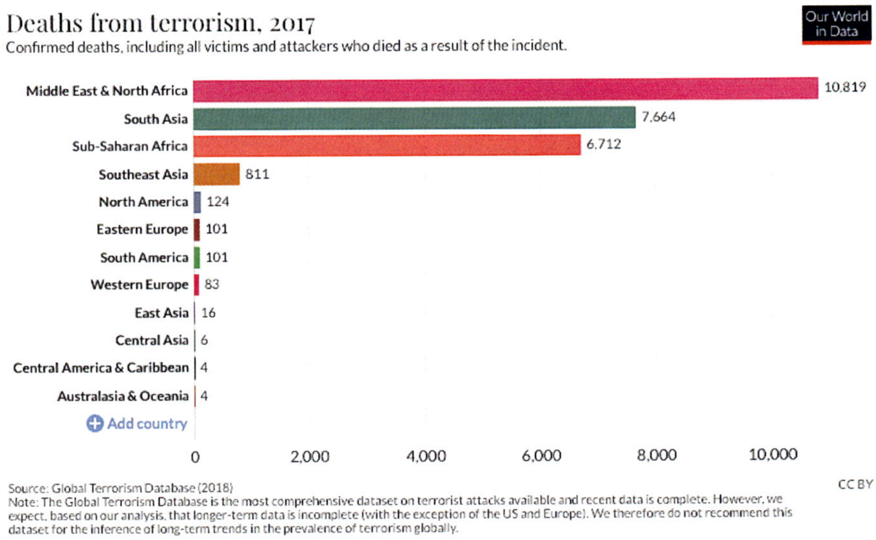
Deaths from terrorism, 2017
Confirmed deaths, including all victims and attackers who died as a result of the incident.
Our World in Data
Middle East & North Africa 10,819
South Asia 7,664
Sub-Saharan Africa 6,712
Southeast Asia 811
North America 124
Eastern Europe 101
South America 101
Western Europe 83
East Asia 16
Central Asia 6
Central America & Caribbean 4
Australasia & Oceania 4
Add country
0
2,000
4,000
6,000
8,000
10,000
Source: Global Terrorism Database (2018)
Note: The Global Terrorism Database is the most comprehensive dataset on terrorist attacks available and recent data is complete. However, we expect, based on our analysis, that longer-term data is incomplete (with the exception of the US and Europe). We therefore do not recommend this dataset for the inference of long-term trends in the prevalence of terrorism globally.
CC BY

Figure 26 Geographical density of terrorism-related deaths. *Source: Global Terrorism Database (2018)*

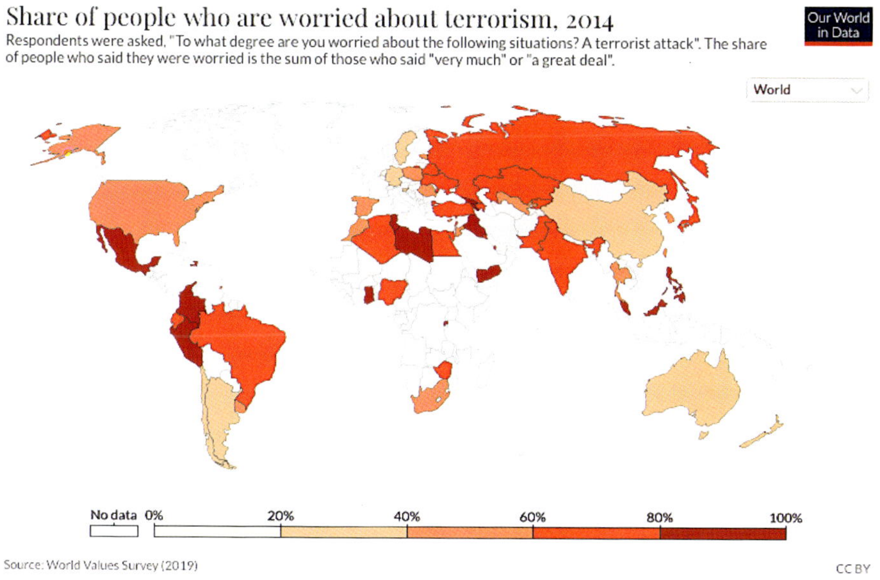
Share of people who are worried about terrorism, 2014
Respondents were asked, "To what degree are you worried about the following situations? A terrorist attack". The share of people who said they were worried is the sum of those who said "very much" or "a great deal".
Our World in Data
World
No data
0%
20%
40%
60%
80%
100%
Source: World Values Survey (2019)
CC BY

Figure 27 *Source: World Values Survey(2019)*

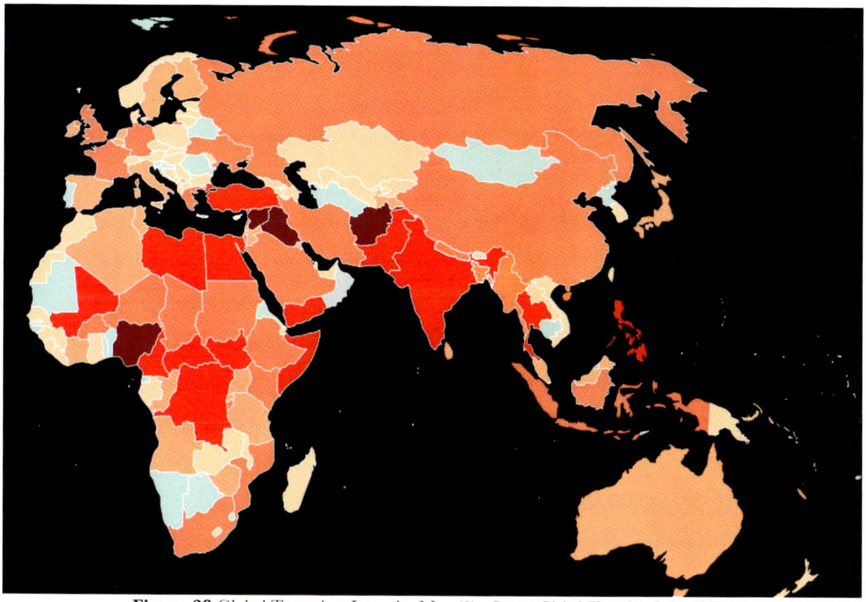

Figure 28 Global Terrorism Intensity Map (1). *Source: Global Terrorism Index* (GTI)

Figure 29 Global Terrorism Intensity Map (2). *Source: Global Terrorism Index* (GTI)

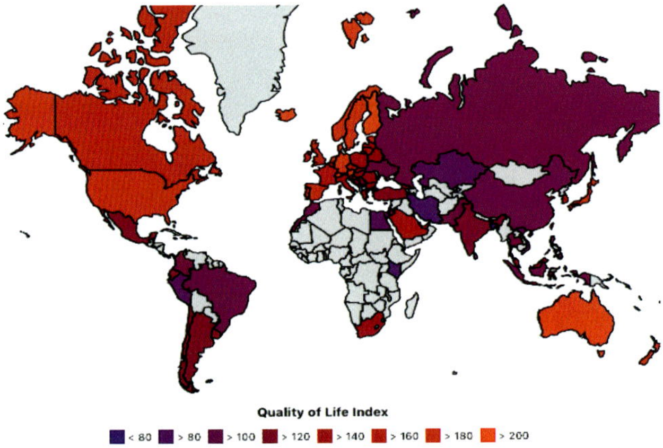

Figure 30 Apart from the residual profile of the hitherto-apartheid South Africa, Africa is clearly absent in the Quality of Life Index (for the majority). *Credit: World Population Review*

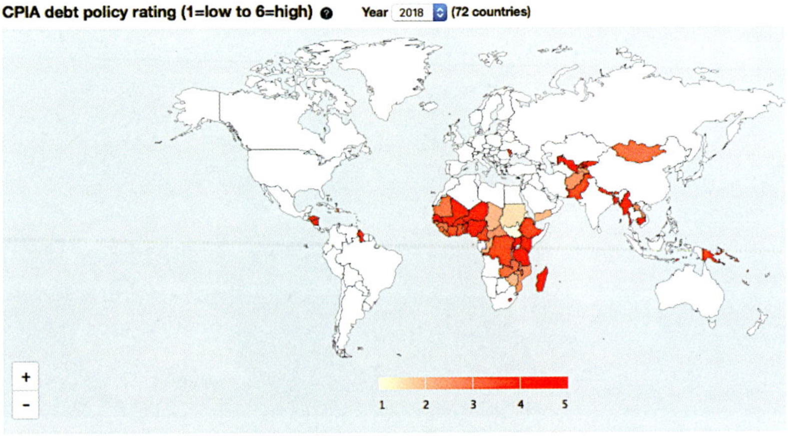

Source: World Bank (citing: World Bank Group, CPIA database (http://www.worldbank.org/ida).)

Figure 31 Concentration of Public Debt; Africa has the highest regional concentration. *Source: WorldStatistics.Org citing World Bank data*

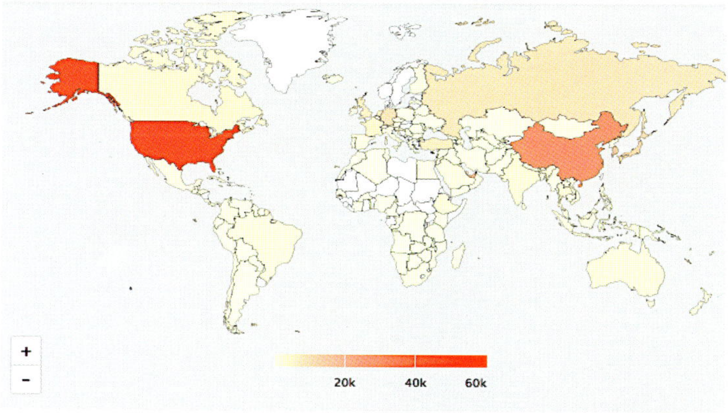

Source: World Bank (citing: International Civil Aviation Organization, Civil Aviation Statistics of the World and ICAO staff estimates.)

Figure 32 Air freight as an indicator of commercial activity; Africa is absent. *Source: World Bank*

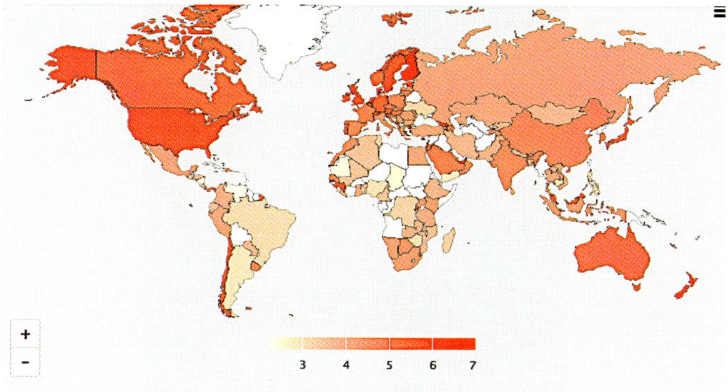

Source: World Bank (citing: World Economic Forum, Global Competiveness Report and data files.)

Figure 33 Ease of dealing with the Customs (darker colors represent better experiences with the Customs); Africa has a very unimpressive record, owing to inefficiency and corruption. *Source: World Bank*

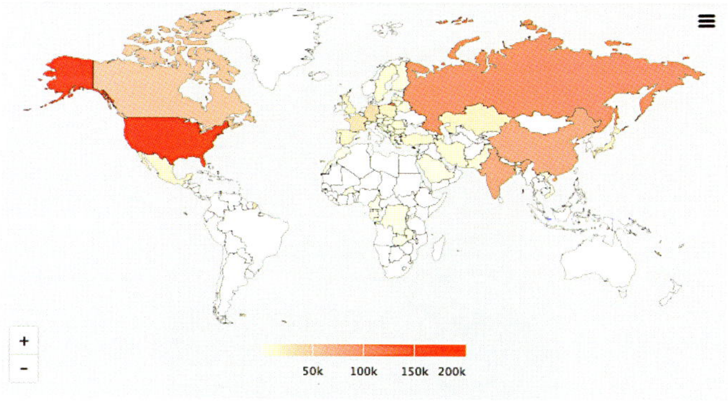

Source: World Bank (citing: World Bank, Transportation, Water, and Information and Communications Technologies Department, Transport Division.)

Figure 34 Rail infrastructure per kilometer; Africa performs very poorly, despite the billions of dollars that their governments claim to have spent on this vital sector. *Source: World Bank*

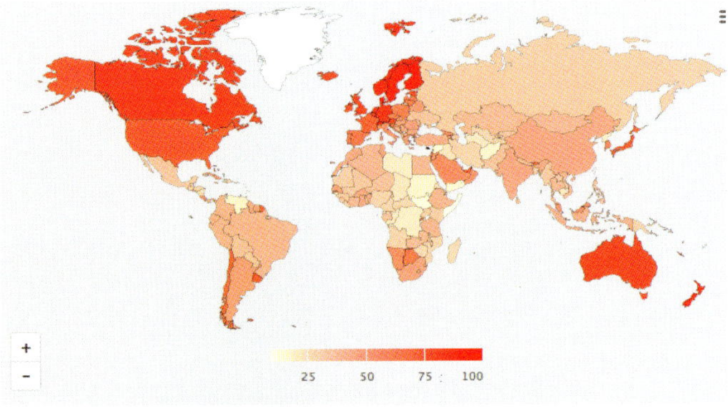

Source: TI (citing: Transparency International)

Figure 35 Corruption Perception Index (deep red connotes a high score in Transparency and Integrity, while the lighter colors align with a high Corruption Perception); Africa still has a problem as a very corrupt Continent. *Source: Transparency International*

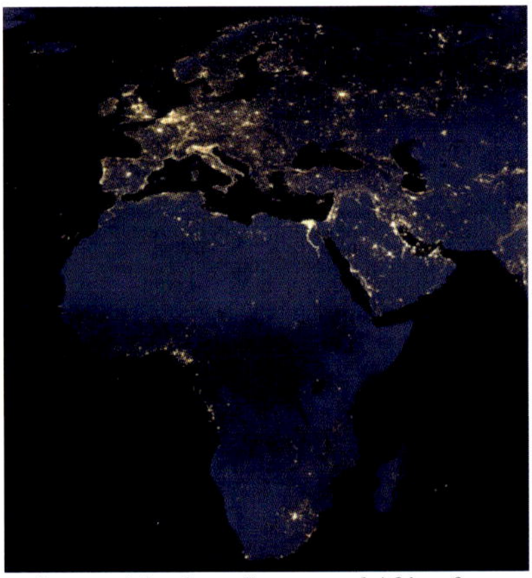

Figure 36 A satellite image taken at night above Europe and Africa, for contrast. Private generating sets contribute to the flickers of electricity seen in Africa. *Source: Geology.com*

Figure 37 The state of Nigeria *Credit: Unknown*

Figure 38 Oil spillage caused by major oil corporations in the Niger Delta region of Nigeria. *Source: Starconnect Media*

Figure 39 Utter despoliation in the Niger Delta, Nigeria. *Source: AfricanArguments.org*

There are hundreds of oil spills each year in the Niger Delta, Nigeria. Credit: Michael Uwemedimo/cmapping.net.

Figure 40

Pastor Christian Lekoya Kpandei walks through his ruined fish farm in Bodo, Nigeria, May 2011. The farm flourished before the August 2008 oil spill, but the pollution destroyed his fish farm, leaving him and his workers without a regular income. (PHOTO: Amnesty International)

Figure 41

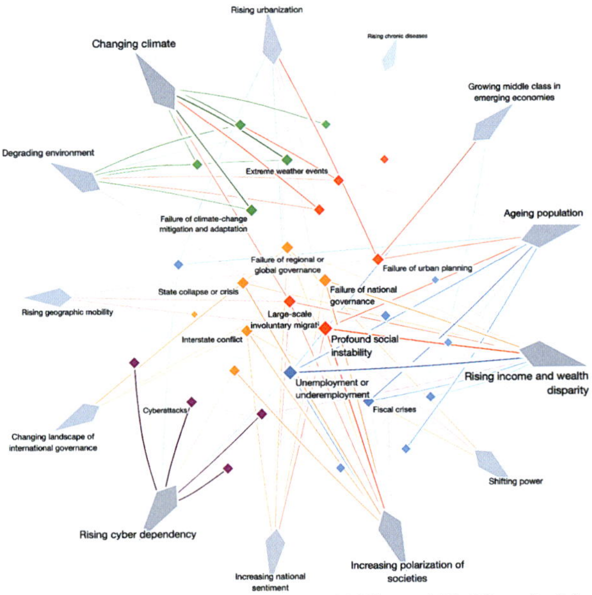

Figure 42 Interconnected map of global risk trends. How would failing and failed States fare? *Source: World Economic Forum(2019)*

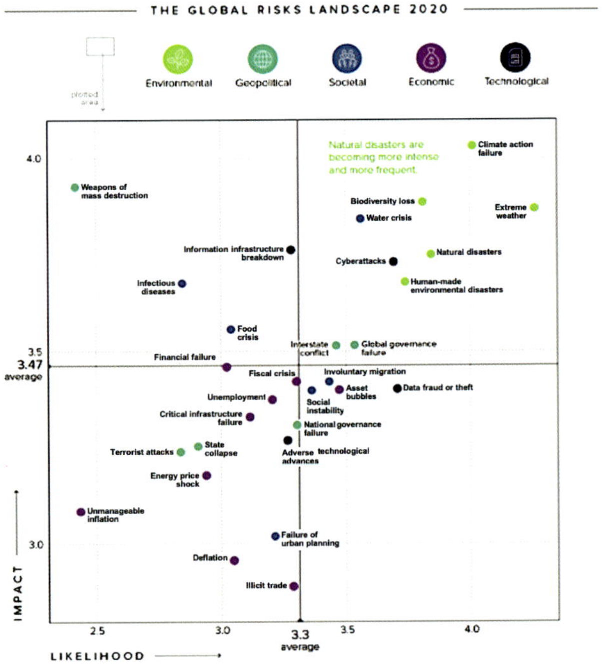

Figure 43 Global Risks Landscape(2020). Contemporary and Future Challenges of Statehood. *Source: Zurich.com*

Appreciation

Every creative process is a collective effort involving the people who provide the inspiration; those who play direct roles; those who create and sustain the proper environment for creative fecundity; those who translate one's vision into a final product; those who review and improve the work; and also those who have historically and consistently encouraged and assisted one. Since only a few members of one's network were aware of this project, the job of acknowledgment has been made much easier. I will like to thank my family and friends; you know yourselves. I am very grateful for all your love, encouragement, sacrifice, sponsorship, understanding, and facilitation over the years.

This book would not have been possible without the unique efforts and contributions of my very close friend and one of my business partners, Dr. Liu Zhang; apart from reading, critiquing, and improving the manuscript as it developed, Liu handled all the operational aspects of the development of the manuscript into a book format, even while standing in for me in our Consultancy to enable me complete the work on time. I remain deeply indebted for all the support and insights; I gained enormously from your brilliant mind, uncommon capacity, and strategic understanding of geopolitical realities.

Without my very capable and resourceful Executive and Research Assistants, I would not have been exposed to the depth and scope of relevant materials required for this effort. It helped greatly that they had both the academic and professional credentials and competence to assist in realizing this project. I am very grateful to Chantal Deshotels, M. Elias Walters, and Oyin Fernandez. You are simply the best!!!

Gratitude is in order for the enormous work done by the various professional teams who assisted all through the process: the Developmental Editors, the Copy Editors, the team of lawyers who reviewed the entire document and made invaluable inputs towards its integrity and refinement, the Copy Setting and Book Design partners and staff, etc., etc. I wish to particularly thank the very gifted and resourceful Nadia Namko for the brilliant book cover, content pagination and design, as well as the creative graphics and schematics that summarize the message of the book; Lynn Carter for all your professionalism, grace and patience during the editing process; Elisabeth Shapiro for the brilliant things you did with the various iterations of the manuscript; Bella Gregory for all your brilliance and late hours; to Ayesha Deris for your attention to detail; to Pat McIver for your excellent logistics coordination and support; to Dr. Evan Schmidt for being a tough, demanding, yet patient and balanced intellectual sparring partner; and to my young friend, neighbor, and dog-walker, Alex, who took care of my dogs while I researched and typed away. Hopefully, the pandemic will soon be over, so that you will resume your college studies, Alex.

Thank you all

C. O. Makame
2020

References & Bibliography

Section One

1. "Coronavirus Disease (COVID-19) Situation Reports." World Health Organization. World Health Organization. Accessed April 5, 2020. *https://www.who.int/emergencies/diseases/novel-coronavirus-2019/situation-reports.*
2. "Global Research on Coronavirus Disease (COVID-19)." World Health Organization. World Health Organization. Accessed March 30, 2020. *https://www.who.int/emergencies/diseases/novel-coronavirus-2019/global-research-on-novel-coronavirus-2019-ncov.*
3. COVID-19 Tracker. Accessed April 2, 2020. *https://www.bing.com/covid.*
4. Center for Systems Science and Engineering (CSSE) at Johns Hopkins University (JHU). "COVID-19 Map." COVID-19 Dashboard. Johns Hopkins Coronavirus Resource Center. Accessed March 25, 2020. *https://coronavirus.jhu.edu/map.html.*
5. "COVID-19 in the WHO African Region." World Health Organization Regional Office for Africa. Accessed March 25, 2020. *https://www.afro.who.int/health-topics/coronavirus-covid-19.*
6. JHCHS website. "Situation Reports on the Novel Coronavirus Identified in China." Johns Hopkins Center for Health Security, April 1, 2020. *https://www.centerforhealthsecurity.org/resources/COVID-19/COVID-19-SituationReports.html.*
7. "Coronavirus (COVID-19): News, Analysis and Resources." UNCTAD. Accessed May 4, 2020. *https://unctad.org/en/Pages/coronavirus.aspx.*
8. Pazarbasioglu, Ceyla. "Swift Action Can Help Developing Countries Limit Economic Harm of Coronavirus." World Bank Blogs, March 9, 2020. *https://blogs.worldbank.org/voices/swift-action-can-help-developing-countries-limit-economic-harm-coronavirus.*
9. "How the World Bank Group Is Helping Countries with COVID-19 (Coronavirus)." World Bank, April 5, 2020. *https://www.worldbank.org/en/news/factsheet/2020/02/11/how-the-world-bank-group-is-helping-countries-with-covid-19-coronavirus.*
10. Fenz, Katharina, and Homi Kharas. "A Mortality Perspective on COVID-19: Time, Location, and Age." The Future Development Blog. Brookings, April 7, 2020. *https://www.brookings.edu/blog/future-development/2020/03/23/a-mortality-perspective-on-covid-19-time-location-and-age/.*
11. "UN Launches Global Humanitarian Response Plan to COVID-19 Pandemic." UNICEF, March 25, 2020. *https://www.unicef.org/press-releases/un-launches-global-humanitarian-response-plan-covid-19-pandemic.*
12. Lancaster, Kirk, Michael Rubin, and Mira Rapp-Hooper. "What the COVID-19 Pandemic May Mean for China's Belt and Road Initiative." Council on Foreign Relations, March 17, 2020. *https://www.cfr.org/blog/what-covid-19-pandemic-may-mean-chinas-belt-and-road-initiative.*
13. Segal, Stephanie, and Dylan Gerstel. "The Global Economic Impacts of Covid-19." Center for Strategic and International Studies, March 10, 2020. *https://www.csis.org/analysis/global-economic-impacts-covid-19.*
14. Toyana, Mfuneko. "South Africa's First Coronavirus Deaths Drive Rand Lower." Edited by Barbara Lewis. Reuters. Thomson Reuters, March 27, 2020.

https://www.reuters.com/article/safrica-markets/south-africas-first-coronavirus-deaths-drive-rand-lower-idUSL8N2BK1VK.

15. Bremmer, Ian. "Why the Coronavirus May Be a Major Blow to Globalization." Time. Time, March 5, 2020. *https://time.com/5796707/coronavirus-global-economy/.*
16. Craven, Matt, Linda Liu, Mihir Mysore, Shubham Singhal, Sven Smit, and Matt Wilson. "COVID-19: Implications for Business." Edited by Mark Staples. McKinsey & Company, March 18, 2020. *https://www.mckinsey.com/business-functions/risk/our-insights/covid-19-implications-for-business.*
17. "The Impact of COVID-19 on Key African Sectors: Insight: Baker McKenzie." Insight | Baker McKenzie, March 10, 2020. *https://www.bakermckenzie.com/en/insight/publications/2020/03/the-impact-of-covid19-on-key-african-sectors.*
18. Mallapaty, Smriti. "Scientists Fear Coronavirus Spread in Countries Least Able to Contain It." Nature News. Nature Publishing Group, February 13, 2020. *https://www.nature.com/articles/d41586-020-00405-w.*
19. Hickok, Kimberly. "How Does the COVID-19 Pandemic Compare to the Last Pandemic?" LiveScience. Purch, March 18, 2020. *https://www.livescience.com/covid-19-pandemic-vs-swine-flu.html.*
20. Jane's Report | Accessed April 3, 2020. *https://www.janes.com/.*
21. Stratfor | The World's Leading Geopolitical Intelligence Platform. Accessed March 30, 2020. *https://www.stratfor.com/.*
22. "Help Us Better Understand COVID-19." Kaggle. Accessed April 13, 2020. *https://www.kaggle.com/covid19.*
23. CDC. "Coronavirus Disease 2019 (COVID-19)." Accessed April12, 2020. *https://www.coronavirus.gov/.*
24. Knopman, Debra, Krishna B. Kumar, Howard J. Shatz, Jennifer Kavanagh, and Jeffrey Hiday. "The Economic Wallop of COVID-19: Q&A with RAND Experts." RAND Corporation, March 26, 2020. *https://www.rand.org/blog/2020/03/the-economic-wallop-of-covid-19-qa-with-rand-experts.html.*
25. Kaye, Dalia Dassa. "COVID-19 Effects on Strategic Dynamics in the Middle East." RAND Corporation, March 26, 2020. *https://www.rand.org/blog/2020/03/covid-19-impacts-on-strategic-dynamics-in-the-middle.html.*
26. "Coronavirus in Africa Tracker: How Many Covid-19 Cases & Where? [Latest]." African Arguments, June 22, 2020. *https://africanarguments.org/2020/07/02/coronavirus-in-africa-tracker-how-many-cases-and-where-latest/.*
27. "Africa Is Woefully Ill-Equipped to Cope with Covid-19." The Economist. The Economist Newspaper, March 26, 2020. *https://www.economist.com/middle-east-and-africa/2020/03/26/africa-is-woefully-ill-equipped-to-cope-with-covid-19.*
28. Tadesse, Addis Getachew. "COVID-19 Death Toll in Africa Reaches 72." Anadolu Ajansı, March 26, 2020. *https://www.aa.com.tr/en/africa/covid-19-death-toll-in-africa-reaches-72/1781142.*
29. Ozturk, Talha. "COVID-19 Violation: Serbia Sentences Man to 3 Years." Anadolu Ajansı, March 27, 2020. *https://www.aa.com.tr/en/europe/covid-19-violation-serbia-sentences-man-to-3-years/1782134.*
30. Vaughan, Adam. "We Don't Know Why so Few Covid-19 Cases Have Been Reported in Africa." New Scientist, March 10, 2020. *https://www.newscientist.com/article/2236760-we-dont-know-why-so-few-covid-19-cases-have-been-reported-in-africa/.*
31. Nordling, Linda. "'A Ticking Time Bomb': Scientists Worry about Coronavirus Spread in Africa." Science Magazine, March 15, 2020. *https://www.sciencemag.org/news/2020/03/ticking-time-bomb-scientists-worry-about-coronavirus-spread-africa.*

32. Watkins, Kevin. "Africa's Race Against COVID-19." Project Syndicate, March 25, 2020. *https://www.project-syndicate.org/commentary/africa-race-against-covid19-by-kevin-watkins-2020-03.*
33. Politico Magazine. "Coronavirus Will Change the World Permanently. Here's How." POLITICO, March 19, 2020. *https://www.politico.com/news/magazine/2020/03/19/coronavirus-effect-economy-life-society-analysis-covid-135579.*
34. Harris, Karen. "Tracking the Global Impact of the Coronavirus Outbreak." Bain, April 9, 2020. *https://www.bain.com/insights/tracking-the-global-impact-of-the-coronavirus-outbreak-snap-chart/.*
35. Chen, Daphne, and Stephen J. Dubner. "The Side Effects of Social Distancing (Ep. 409)." Freakonomics, March 18, 2020. *https://freakonomics.com/podcast/covid-19-effects/.*
36. Kaplan, Robert D. "Coronavirus Ushers in the Globalization We Were Afraid Of." Bloomberg.com. Bloomberg, March 20, 2020. *https://www.bloomberg.com/opinion/articles/2020-03-20/coronavirus-ushers-in-the-globalization-we-were-afraid-of.*
37. Buchanan, Patrick J. "Will the Coronavirus Kill the New World Order?" Rasmussen Reports, March 13, 2020. *https://www.rasmussenreports.com/public_content/political_commentary/commentary_by_pat_buchanan/will_the_coronavirus_kill_the_new_world_order.*
38. Campbell, Kurt M., and Rush Doshi. "The Coronavirus Could Reshape Global Order." Foreign Affairs, March 18, 2020. *https://www.foreignaffairs.com/articles/china/2020-03-18/coronavirus-could-reshape-global-order.*
39. Korybko, Andrew. "The Coronavirus: Crown Jewel of the New World Order or Crippling Blow to Globalization?" Global Research, March 18, 2020. *https://www.globalresearch.ca/coronavirus-new-world-order-blow-globalization/5706729.*
40. Kadomtsev, Andrei. "A New World Order, or Will Globalization Survive the Coronavirus Pandemic?" Modern Diplomacy, March 17, 2020. *https://moderndiplomacy.eu/2020/03/17/a-new-world-order-or-will-globalization-survive-the-coronavirus-pandemic/.*
41. Ravelo, Jenny Lei, and Sara Jerving. "COVID-19 - a Timeline of the Coronavirus Outbreak." Devex, Accessed June 13, 2020. *https://www.devex.com/news/covid-19-a-timeline-of-the-coronavirus-outbreak-96396.*
42. Muccari, Robin, Denise Chow, and Joe Murphy. "Coronavirus Timeline: Tracking the Critical Moments of COVID-19." NBCNews.com. NBCUniversal News Group, March 10, 2020. *https://www.nbcnews.com/health/health-news/coronavirus-timeline-tracking-critical-moments-covid-19-n1154341.*
43. "WHO Coronavirus Disease (COVID-19) Dashboard." World Health Organization. Accessed May 13, 2020. *https://covid19.who.int/?gclid=EAIaIQobChMI08H7sZ6w6gIVCK_ICh26MQe8EAAYASAAEgI41fD_BwE.*
44. Nextstrain. Accessed March 10, 2020. *https://nextstrain.org/.*
45. State Action on Coronavirus (COVID-19). Accessed April 24, 2020. *https://www.ncsl.org/research/health/state-action-on-coronavirus-covid-19.aspx.*
46. "State Department: The United States Is Leading the Humanitarian and Health Assistance Response to COVID-19: Fact Sheet." U.S. Agency for International Development, May 11, 2020. *https://www.usaid.gov/news-information/fact-sheets/mar-2020-us-leading-humanitarian-and-health-assistance-response-covid-19.*
47. Bengali, Shashank. "Asian Countries Impose New Restrictions as Coronavirus Cases Come Roaring Back." Los Angeles Times. Los Angeles Times, April 2, 2020. *https://www.latimes.com/world-nation/story/2020-04-02/these-countries-seemed-to-have-tamed-the-coronavirus-its-come-roaring-back.*

48. Kitty O'Meara - "And the People Stayed Home" *https://www.oprahmag.com/entertainment/a31747557/and-the-people-stayed-home-poem-kitty-omeara-interview/*
49. Pynchon, Thomas. Gravity's Rainbow. New York: Penguin Books, 2006.
50. Beanz, Tracy. "Why Italy?" UncoverDC, March 20, 2020. *https://uncoverdc.com/2020/03/20/why-italy/.*
51. Okwonga, Musa. "The French Doctors Who Wanted to Test Vaccines on Africans and Western Medicine's Dark History." Quartz Africa. Quartz, April 10, 2020. *https://qz.com/africa/1836272/french-doctors-say-test-covid-19-vaccine-on-africans-spark-fury/.* \
52. Horowitz, Julia. "The Global Coronavirus Recession Is Beginning." CNN. Cable News Network, March 16, 2020. *https://www.cnn.com/2020/03/16/economy/global-recession-coronavirus/index.html.*

Section Two

1. Despain, David. "Early Humans Used Brain Power, Innovation and Teamwork to Dominate the Planet." Scientific American. February 27, 2010. *https://www.scientificamerican.com/article/humans-brain-power-origins/.*
2. Locke, John, and Paul E. Sigmund. The Selected Political Writings of John Locke: Texts, Background Selections, Sources, Interpretations. Longueuil, Québec: Point Par Point, 2006.
3. Barden, Garrett. (2009). Robin Lane Fox. The Classical World: an Epic History of Greece and Rome. (Penguin Books, London, 2006. Nordicum-Mediterraneum. 4.
4. Scott, Michael. Ancient Worlds: an Epic History of East and West. London: Windmill Books, 2017.
5. Hobbes, Thomas. "Leviathan." SparkNotes. Accessed April 11, 2020. *https://www.sparknotes.com/philosophy/leviathan/full-text/.*
6. Presbey, Gail M. "Leonhard Praeg: African Philosophy and the Quest for Autonomy: A Philosophical Investigation." Philosophia Africana 6, no. 1 (2003): 67+. Gale Academic OneFile. Accessed April 1, 2020.
7. Harvey, Marc. "Early Humans' Egalitarian Politics." Human Nature 25, no. 3 (2014): 299–327. *https://doi.org/10.1007/s12110-014-9203-6.*
8. Barnes, Harry Elmer. "The Natural State of Man (An Historical Resumé)." The Monist 33, no. 1 (January 1, 1923): 33–80.
9. Fukuyama, Francis. The Origins of Political Order. New York: Farrar, Straus and Giroux, 2011.
10. Green, Duncan. "How Change Happens." Oxford Scholarship Online, October 2016. *https://doi.org/ 10.1093/acprof:oso/9780198785392.001.0001.*
11. Currie, Thomas E., and Ruth Mace. "Mode and Tempo in the Evolution of Socio-Political Organization: Reconciling 'Darwinian' and 'Spencerian' Evolutionary Approaches in Anthropology." Philosophical Transactions of the Royal Society B: Biological Sciences 366, no. 1567 (2011): 1108–17. *https://doi.org/10.1098/rstb.2010.0318.*
12. Serge Svizzero & Clement A. Tisdell (2016) Economic Evolution, Diversity of Societies and Stages of Economic Development: A Critique of Theories Applied to Hunters and Gatherers and their Successors, Cogent Economics & Finance, 4:1, DOI: 10.1080/23322039.2016.1161322
13. Foley, R., & Gamble, C. (2009). The Ecology of Social Transitions in Human Evolution. Philosophical Transactions of the Royal Society of London. Series B, Biological sciences, 364(1533), 3267–3279. https://doi.org/10.1098/rstb.2009.0136
14. Shermer, Michael. "Evolution Explains Why Politics Is So Tribal." Scientific American. Scientific American, June 1, 2012. *https://www.scientificamerican.com/article/evolution-explains-why-politics-tribal/.*

15. Hawkes, K., O'Connell, J., & Blurton Jones, N. (2018). Hunter-Gatherer Studies and Human Evolution: A Very Selective Review. American Journal of Physical Anthropology, 165(4), 777–800. https://doi.org/10.1002/ajpa.23403
16. Layton, Robert. "Political and Territorial Structures Among Hunter-Gatherers." Man 21, no. 1 (1986): 18–33. *https://doi.org/10.2307/2802644.*
17. Spencer, Herbert. The Factors of Organic Evolution. Singapore: Origami Books, 2020.
18. Britton-Purdy, Jedediah. "Paleo Politics." The New Republic, November 1, 2017. *https://newrepublic.com/article/145444/paleo-politics-what-made-prehistoric-hunter-gatherers-give-freedom-civilization.*
19. Morgan, Christopher, Shannon Tushingham, Raven Garvey, Loukas Barton, and Robert Bettinger. "Hunter-Gatherer Economies in the Old World and New World." Oxford Research Encyclopedia of Environmental Science. 29 Mar. 2017; Accessed April 1, 2020. *https://oxfordre.com/environmentalscience/view/10.1093/acrefore/9780199389414.001.0001/acrefore-9780199389414-e-164.*
20. Osafo-Kwaako, Philip, and James A. Robinson. "Political Centralization in Pre-Colonial Africa." Journal of Comparative Economics 41, no. 1 (2013): 6–21. *https://doi.org/10.1016/j.jce.2013.01.003.*
21. Brown University. "Political Theory Project (PTP)." Accessed March 13, 2020. *https://www.brown.edu/academics/political-theory-project/.*
22. Cashdan, Elizabeth, Alan Barnard, M. C. Bicchieri, Charles A. Bishop, Valda Blundell, Jeffrey Ehrenreich, Mathias Guenther, et al. "Territoriality Among Human Foragers: Ecological Models and an Application to Four Bushman Groups [and Comments and Reply]." Current Anthropology 24, no. 1 (1983): 47–66. *https://doi.org/10.1086/202934.*
23. Peterson, Nicolas. "Hunter-Gatherer Territoriality: The Perspective from Australia." American Anthropologist 77, no. 1 (March 1975): 53–68. *https://doi.org/10.1525/aa.1975.77.1.02a00040.*
24. "Racial Equity Tools." Accessed May 15, 2020. https://www.racialequitytools.org/home.
25. Marean, Curtis W. "The Transition to Foraging for Dense and Predictable Resources and Its Impact on the Evolution of Modern Humans." Philosophical Transactions of the Royal Society B: Biological Sciences 371, no. 1698 (July 5, 2016). *https://doi.org/10.1098/rstb.2015.0239.*
26. Banathy, Bela H. Guided Evolution of Society: a Systems View. New York: Springer, 2011.
27. Maryanski, Alexandra, and Jonathan H. Turner. The Social Cage: Human Nature and the Evolution of Society. Stanford, CA: Stanford University Press, 1992.
28. Wilson, David Sloan. Darwin's Cathedral: Evolution, Religion, and the Nature of Society. Chicago: University of Chicago Press, 2010.
29. North, Douglass C., and Robert Paul Thomas. The Rise of the Western World: A New Economic History. Cambridge University Press, 1973.
30. Monga, Célestin, Justin Yifu Lin, and Gareth Austin. "The Economics of Colonialism in Africa." In The Oxford Handbook of Africa and Economics: Volume 1: Context and Concepts. : Oxford University Press, 2015-07-01. *https://www.oxfordhandbooks.com/view/10.1093/oxfordhb/9780199687114.001.0001/oxfordhb-9780199687114-e-4.*
31. Harari, Yuval Noah. Sapiens: A Brief History of Humankind. New York: Harper Perennial, 2018.
32. Riches, David. "Hunter-Gatherer Structural Transformations." The Journal of the Royal Anthropological Institute 1, no. 4 (1995): 679-701. Accessed April 2, 2020. doi:10.2307/3034956.
33. Scott, James C. The Art of Not Being Governed. New Haven: Yale University Press, 2011.
34. National Center for Biotechnology Information. Accessed April 16, 2020. *https://www.ncbi.nlm.nih.gov/.*

35. Renfrew, Colin. "The Archaeology of Ritual, of Cult, and of Religion." ResearchGate, January 2007. *https://www.researchgate.net/publication/303250974_The_archaeology_of_ritual_of_cult_and_of_religion.*
36. Easterly, William, and Ross Levine. "Tropics, Germs, and Crops: How Endowments Influence Economic Development." Journal of Monetary Economics 50, no. 1 (2002): 3–39. *https://doi.org/10.1016/s0304-3932(02)00200-3.*
37. Lee, Richard B., and Irven DeVore. Kalahari Hunter-Gatherers: Studies of the Kung San and Their Neighbors. Cambridge: Harvard University Press, 1976.
38. Seidler, Michael. "Pufendorf's Moral and Political Philosophy." Stanford Encyclopedia of Philosophy. September 3, 2010. *https://plato.stanford.edu/entries/pufendorf-moral/.*
39. Lavenda, Robert H., and Emily A. Schultz. Anthropology: What Does It Mean to Be Human? 4th ed. New York, NY: Oxford University Press, 2017.
40. Markoe, Glenn. Phoenician Bronze and Silver Bowls from Cyprus and the Mediterranean. 26. Vol. 26. Berkeley: University of California Press, 1985.
41. Brewer, Marilynn. Taking the Social Origins of Human Nature Seriously: Toward a More Imperialist Social Psychology (2004). Personality and Social Psychology Review: An Official Journal of the Society for Personality and Social Psychology, Inc. 8. 107-13. 10.1207/s15327957pspr0802_3.
42. Brewer, M. B. The Importance of Being We: Human Nature and Intergroup Relations. American Psychologist (2007). 62(8), 728–738. *https://doi.org/10.1037/0003-066X.62.8.728*
43. Woodburn, James. "Egalitarian Societies." Man 17, no. 3 (September 1982): 431–51. *https://doi.org/10.2307/2801707.*

Section Three
1. Birkhaeuser, Jodocus Adolph. History of the Church, From Its First Establishment to Our Own Times: Designed for the Use of Ecclesiastical Seminaries and Colleges. Forgotten Books, 2018.
2. Kealotswe, Obed N., F. Nkomazana, and James Amanze. "Christianity in Africa in the 20th Century." In Biblical Studies, Theology, Religion, and Philosophy: An Introduction for African Universities. Zapf Chancery, 2012.
3. Lehner, Ulrich L., and Michael Printy. A Companion to the Catholic Enlightenment in Europe. Leiden: Brill, 2010.
4. Capone, Alessandro. "Catholics and Europe during the Nineteenth Century." Accessed April 4, 2020. *https://ehne.fr/en/article/political-epistemology/political-models-make-europe-modern-era/catholics-and-europe-during-nineteenth-century.*
5. Dawson, Christopher. The Making of Europe: An Introduction to the History of European Unity. London: Forgotten Books, 2017.
6. Morris, William Edward and Brown, Charlotte R., "David Hume". The Stanford Encyclopedia of Philosophy. Edited by Edward N. Zalta. Summer 2020. *https://plato.stanford.edu/archives/sum2020/entries/hume/*
7. Peter, Fabienne. "Political Legitimacy". The Stanford Encyclopedia of Philosophy, Edited by Edward N. Zalta. Summer 2017. *https://plato.stanford.edu/archives/sum2017/entries/legitimacy/.*
8. Dagger, Richard and Lefkowitz, David. "Political Obligation". The Stanford Encyclopedia of Philosophy. Edited by Edward N. Zalta. Fall 2014. *https://plato.stanford.edu/archives/fall2014/entries/political-obligation/.*
9. Dovi, Suzanne. "Political Representation". The Stanford Encyclopedia of Philosophy. Edited by Edward N. Zalta. Fall 2018. *https://plato.stanford.edu/archives/fall2018/entries/political-representation/.*

10. Tanner, Norman. New Short History of the Catholic Church. Continuum International Publishing Group Ltd, 2011.
11. Johnson, Robert, and Adam Cureton. "Kant's Moral Philosophy." Stanford Encyclopedia of Philosophy. Stanford University, July 7, 2016. *https://plato.stanford.edu/entries/kant-moral/.*
12. Augustine, Gerald Groveland Walsh, and Vernon J. Bourke. City of God. Garden City, NY: Image Books, 1958.
13. Anderson, R. Lanier. Edited by Edward N. Zalta. "Friedrich Nietzsche", The Stanford Encyclopedia of Philosophy. Summer 2017. *https://plato.stanford.edu/archives/sum2017/entries/nietzsche/*
14. Newton-Smith, W. H. Rationality of Science. Taylor & Francis, 2016.
15. Friedman, Michael. "Kant, Kuhn, and the Rationality of Science." History of Philosophy of Science, 2002, 25–41. *https://doi.org/10.1007/978-94-017-1785-4_3.*
16. Nickles, Thomas. "Historicist Theories of Scientific Rationality," June 14, 2017. *https://plato.stanford.edu/entries/rationality-historicist/.*
17. Waldron, Jeremy. "The Rule of Law". The Stanford Encyclopedia of Philosophy. Edited by Edward N. Zalta. Summer 2020 Edition. *https://plato.stanford.edu/archives/sum2020/entries/rule-of-law/.*
18. Ferguson, Niall. Civilization: The West and the Rest. UK: Penguin Books, 2012.
19. Ferguson, Niall. The Square and the Tower: Networks, Hierarchies and the Struggle for Global Power. S.l. Allen Lane, 2017.
20. Ramos, Jennifer M. Changing Norms through Actions: The Evolution of Sovereignty. Oxford University Press, 2013.
21. "About Adam Smith." Accessed May 1, 2020. *https://www.adamsmith.org/about-adam-smith.*
22. Spinoza, Baruch, and Michael L. Morgan. Spinoza: Complete Works. Indianapolis: Hackett, 2002.
23. "Friedrich August Hayek." Accessed May 6, 2020. *https://www.econlib.org/library/Enc/bios/Hayek.html.*
24. "Thomas Sowell." Accessed May 14, 2020. *https://www.tsowell.com/.*
25. Dyson, R.W. Aquinas Political Writings; Cambridge Texts in the History of Political Thought. Cambridge: Cambridge Univ. Press, 2004.
26. Aristotle. "Politics " Translated by Benjamin Jowett. Accessed February 28, 2020. *https://socialsciences.mcmaster.ca/econ/ugcm/3ll3/aristotle/Politics.pdf.*
27. Kim, Sung Ho. "Max Weber," November 12, 2019. *https://plato.stanford.edu/archives/win2019/entries/weber/.*
28. Compendium: Catechism of the Catholic Church. USCCB Publishing, Catholic Church, 2006.
29. Vattel, Emer de. The Law of Nations: or, Principles of the Law of Nature, Applied to the Conduct and Affairs of Nations and Sovereigns. Translated by Joseph Chitty. Cambridge: Cambridge University Press, 2011.
30. Francisco, De Vitoria, Anthony Pagden, and Jeremy Lawrance, Editors. Political Writings: Cambridge: Cambridge University Press, 1991.
31. Miller, Jon, "Hugo Grotius", The Stanford Encyclopedia of Philosophy. Edited by Edward N. Zalta. Spring 2014. *https://plato.stanford.edu/archives/spr2014/entries/grotius.*
32. Elshtain, Jean Bethke. Just War Against Terror: The Burden of American Power in a Violent World. Basic Books, 2008.
33. Walzer, Michael. Just and Unjust Wars: A Moral Argument with Historical Illustrations. New York: Basic Books, 2015.
34. Grotius, Hugo, and A. C. Campbell. The Rights of War and Peace: Including the Law of Nature and Nations. Elibron Classics, 2005.
35. Tuck, Richard. The Rights of War and Peace: Political Thought and the International Order from Grotius to Kant. Oxford: Oxford Univ. Press, 2010.

36. Ramsey, Paul, and Stanley M. Hauerwas. The Just War: Force and Political Responsibility. Lanham: Rowman & Littlefield Publishers, 2007.
37. Warwick J. The Principles of Political Philosophy. London: Ivory Publishers,1976)
38. Brierly, J. L. The Law of Nations. New York and London: Oxford University Press, 1961.
39. Bush, George, and Brent Scowcroft. A World Transformed. New York: Knopf, 1998.
40. Marx, Karl, and Frederick Engels. "Manifesto of the Communist Party." Translated by Samuel Moore. Marxists Internet Archive. Progress Publishers. *https://www.marxists.org/archive/marx/works/1848/communist-manifesto/.*
41. Marx, Karl. Critique of the Gotha Programme. Moscow: Progress Publishers, 1970.
42. Marx, Karl, and David McLellan. "'Power as the Basis of Right.'" Essay. In *Karl Marx: Selected Writings*. Oxford: Oxford University Press, 2011.
43. Marx, Karl, and David McLellan. ""Utilitarianism."" Essay. In *Karl Marx: Selected Writings*. Oxford: Oxford University Press, 2011.
44. Marx, Karl, and David McLellan. ""Class Antagonism"' Essay. In *Karl Marx: Selected Writings*. Oxford: Oxford University Press, 2011.
45. Marx, Karl, and David McLellan. ""Method in Political Economy"' Essay. In *Karl Marx: Selected Writings*. Oxford: Oxford University Press, 2011.
46. Marx, Karl, and David McLellan. ""On Strikes"' Essay. In *Karl Marx: Selected Writings*. Oxford: Oxford University Press, 2011.
47. Arthur, John, William H. Shaw, and Kai Nielsen. "Class and Justice." Essay. In Justice and Economic Distribution. Englewood Cliffs, NJ: Prentice-Hall, 1979.
48. Arthur, John, William H. Shaw, and John Rawls. "A Theory of Justice."' Essay. In *Justice and Economic Distribution*. Englewood Cliffs, NJ: Prentice-Hall, 1979.
49. Arthur, John, William H. Shaw, and John Rawls. "The Basic Structure as Subjects" Essay. In *Justice and Economic Distribution*. Englewood Cliffs, NJ: Prentice-Hall, 1979.
50. Lukes, Steven. *Essays in Social Theory*. London: The Macmillan Press Ltd, 1977.
51. Smith, Adam. *The Wealth of Nations*. London: Methuen & Co., 1908.
52. Haberler, G. "Marxian Economics in Retrospect and Prospect." *Einheit und Vielfalt in den Sozialwissenschaften*, 1966, 69–82. *https://doi.org/10.1007/978-3-7091-7932-1_7.*
53. Lewin, Kurt. *Resolving Social Conflicts: Selected Papers on Group Dynamics*. Edited by Gertrude Weiss Lewin. 27. 2nd ed. Vol. 27. New York: Harper and Brothers, 1948.
54. Casey, William J., Herbert E. Meyer, Leo Cherne, and Jeane Jordan. Kirkpatrick. Scouting the Future: The Public Speeches of William J. Casey. Edited by Mark B. Liedl. Washington, DC: Regnery Gateway, 1989.
55. Bozeman, Adda Bruemmer. Politics and Culture in International History: from the Ancient Near East to the Opening of the Modern Age. New Brunswick: Transaction Publishers, 2004.
56. McIlwain, Charles Howard. Constitutionalism: Ancient and Modern. Indianapolis, IN: Liberty Fund, 2008.
57. Troy,Thomas F. "The 'Correct' Definition of Intelligence." Essay. In International Journal of Intelligence and Counterintelligence5, 4th ed. Vol. 5. Winter 1991-1992, n.d.
58. Lenin, Vladimir I., David Brandenberger, Catherine A. Fitzpatrick, and Richard Pipes. The Unknown Lenin: From the Secret Archive. New Haven: Yale Univ. Press, 1999.
59. Lewis, Bernard. Essay. In What Went Wrong?: the Clash between Islam and Modernity in the Middle East. New York: Harper Perennial, 2006.
60. Dornan, James E. "United States National Security Policy: 'Retrospect and Prospect.'" Essay. In United State's National Security Policy in the Decade Ahead. London: Macdonald and Jane's, 1978.
61. Pilon, Juliana Geran. "American Exceptionalism: Implications for Strategic Communication." Israel Journal of Foreign Affairs 2, no. 3 (2008): 129–40. *https://doi.org/10.1080/23739770.2008.11446337.*

62. Pilon, Juliana Geran. Why America Is Such a Hard Sell: Beyond Pride and Prejudice. Lanham: Rowman & Littlefield, 2007.
63. Dornan, James E. "The Search for Purpose in American Foreign Policy." *Intercollegiate Review* VII, no. 3 (1970): 97–110.
64. Madison, James, Gaillard Hunt, and James Brown Scott. The Debates in the Federal Convention of 1787: Which Framed the Constitution of the United States of America. Amherst, NY: Prometheus Books, 2007.
65. Kennan, George F. American Diplomacy 1900-1950. Chicago: University of Chicago Press, 1984.
66. Codevilla, Angelo M. Informing Statecraft: Intelligence for a New Century. New York: Free Press, 2006.
67. Foreign Intelligence Surveillance Act of 1978, P.L. 95-511, 25 Oct. 1978, Sec. 101, (e)
68. George, Roger Z., and James B. Bruce. "Making Analysis More Reliable: Why Epistemology Matters to Intelligence." Essay. In Analyzing Intelligence: Origins, Obstacles, and Innovation. Washington, D.C.: Georgetown University Press, 2008.
69. Heuer, Richards J. Psychology of Intelligence Analysis. Washington, D.C.: Center for the Study of Intelligence, Central Intelligence Agency, 1999.
70. Betts, Richard K. Warning Dilemmas: Normal Theory vs. Exceptional Theory. Pennsylvania, PA: Jai Press for the Foreign Policy Research Institute, 1983.
71. Lord, Carnes. The Modern Prince: What Leaders Need To Know Now. New Haven: Yale University Press, 2003.
72. "Racial Equity Tools." Accessed May 15, 2020. *https://www.racialequitytools.org/home.*
73. "Great Philosophers." InterQuest Philosophy. Oregon State University. Accessed April 19, 2020. *https://oregonstate.edu/instruct/phl201/modules/Philosophers/index.html.*
74. Insights on the Great Philosophers. Journal of National Security Law and Policy 1, no. 1 (2005).
75. McElvoy, Anne, and Markus Wolf. Man Without a Face: Communism's Greatest Spymaster. New York/Toronto: Random House, 1997.
76. Gates, Robert Michael. From the Shadows: The Ultimate Insider's Story of Five Presidents and How They Won the Cold War. New York: Simon & Schuster Paperbacks, 2006.
77. Bon, Gustave Le. The Crowd: A Study of the Popular Mind. Atlanta, GA: Cherokee Publishing Company, 1982.
78. Schumpeter, Joseph Alois. Capitalism, Socialism, and Democracy. New York: Harper Perennial Modern Classics, 2008.
79. Johnson, Paul. Modern Times: The World from the Twenties to the Nineties. New York: Perennial Classics, 2001.
80. Rummel, R. J. *Death by Government: Genocide and Mass Murder Since 1900.* Routledge, 2018.
81. Ruggie, John Gerard. Multilateralism Matters: The Theory and Praxis of an Institutional Form. New York: Columbia Univ. Press, 1993.
82. Ikenberry, G. John. "Is American Multilateralism in Decline?" Perspectives on Politics 1, no. 03 (2003): 533–50. *https://doi.org/10.1017/s1537592703000380.*
83. Kissinger, Henry. Does America Need a Foreign Policy?: Towards a New Diplomacy for the 21st Century. London: Simon & Schuster, 2001.
84. Nye, Joseph S. The Paradox of American Power. New York: Oxford University Press, 2002.
85. Cox, Ronald W. Production, Power, and World Order: Social Forces in the Making of History. New York, NY: Columbia University Press, 1987.
86. Kagan, Robert. "Power and Weakness." Hoover Institution, June 1, 2002. *https://www.hoover.org/research/power-and-weakness.*
87. Thucydides. The Peloponnesian War. Translated by Steven Lattimore. Indianapolis, IN: Hackett Publishing Company, 1998.

88. Morgenthau, Hans J. Essay. In Politics Among Nations: The Struggle for Power and Peace, 4th Ed., 98–99. New York: Alfred A. Knopf, 1967.
89. Bull, Hedley. The Anarchical Society. New York, NY: Columbia University Press, 1977.
90. Haass, Richard N. The Opportunity: America's Moment to Alter History's Course. New York, NY: PublicAffairs, 2006.
91. Kagan, Robert. "America's Crisis of Legitimacy." Foreign Affairs 83, no.(2004): 65-87. Accessed June 7, 2020. doi:10.2307/20033903.
92. Kupchan, Charles A. The End of the American Era: US Foreign Policy and the Geopolitics of the Twenty-First Century. New York: Vintage Books, 2003.
93. Reed, John. Ten Days That Shook The World. New York, NY: International Publishers, 1967.
94. Pipes, Richard. The Russian Revolution. New York: Vintage Books, 2004.
95. Dziak, John, J. Chekisty: A History of the KGB. Lexington, MA: Lexington Books, 1988.
96. Andrew, Christopher, and Vasili Mitrokhin. The World Was Going Our Way: The KGB and the Battle for the Third World. New York, NY: Basic Books, 2005.
97. Flynn, Thomas. "Jean-Paul Sartre." Edited by Edward N. Zalta, December 5, 2011. *https://plato.stanford.edu/entries/sartre/.*
98. Strauss, Leo, and Joseph Cropsey, eds. History of Political Philosophy. Chicago: Rand McNally, 1963. See the following chapters: PLATO, by Leo Strauss, pp. 7-61. ARISTOTLE, by Harry V. Jaffa, pp. 64-129. St. Augustine, by Charles N. R. McCoy, pp. 151-158. St. Thomas AQUINAS, by Charles N. R. McCoy, pp. 201-222. Thomas HOBBES, by Laurence Berns, pp. 354-377. John LOCKE, by Robert A. Goldwin, pp. 433-467. Jean-Jacques ROUSSEAU, by Allan Bloom, pp. 514-534. John Stuart MILL, by Henry M. Magid, pp. 679-695. Karl MARX, by Joseph Cropsey, pp. 697-722. Friedrich NIETZSCHE, by Werner J. Dannhauser, 724-744.
99. National Center for Biotechnology Information. Accessed June 16, 2020. *https://www.ncbi.nlm.nih.gov/.*
100. Stevenson, ~ Michael. "British Writer Pens The Best Description Of Trump I've Read," March 8, 2019. *https://thehobbledehoy.com/2019/03/08/british-writer-pens-the-best-description-of-trump-ive-read/.*
101. O'Toole, Fintan: Donald Trump Has Destroyed the Country He Promised to Make Great Again." The Irish Times, April 25, 2020. *https://www.irishtimes.com/opinion/fintan-o-toole-donald-trump-has-destroyed-the-country-he-promised-to-make-great-again-1.4235928?mode=sample&auth-failed=1&pw-origin=https%3A%2F%2Fwww.irishtimes.com%2Fopinion%2Ffintan-o-toole-donald-trump-has-destroyed-the-country-he-promised-to-make-great-again-1.4235928.*
102. Solzhenitsyn, Aleksandr. The Gulag Archipelago. Translated by H. T. Willetts. Vintage Publishers, 2002.
103. Solzhenitsyn, Aleksandr. The Red Wheel. Translated by H. T. Willetts. University of Notre-Dame Press, 2017.
104. Solzhenitsyn, Aleksandr. In the First Circle. Translated by H. T. Willetts. Harper Perennial Publishers, 2009.
105. Khlevnik Oleg V. Stalin: New Biography of a Dictator. Translated by Nora Seligman Favorov. Reprinted. New Haven: Yale University Press, 2017.
106. Radzinsky, Edvard. Stalin: The First In-Depth Biography Based on Documents from Russia's Secret Archives. Translated by H. T. Willetts. Anchor Publishers, 1997.
107. Andrew, Christopher, and Oleg Gordievsky. KGB: The Inside Story of Its Foreign Operations from Lenin to Gorbachev. Reprinted. Perennial Publishers, 1991.
108. Rayfield, Donald. Stalin And His Hangmen: The Tyrant and Those Who Killed for Him. Reprinted. Random House Trade Paperbacks, 2005.
109. Bullock, Alan. Hitler and Stalin: Parallel Lives. London: Vintage Publishers, 2019.

110. Kant, Immanuel. "Kant's Principles of Politics, Including His Essay on Perpetual Peace. A Contribution to Political Science." Translated by William Hastie. Online Library of Liberty. Accessed February 28, 2020. *https://oll.libertyfund.org/titles/kant-kants-principles-of-politics-including-his-essay-on-perpetual-peace.*
111. Wootton, David. Modern Political Thought: Readings from Machiavelli to Nietzsche. Hackett Publishing, 1996.
112. Badescu, Mihai, and Anca Badescu. "The Origin and Evolution of Civil Society." Journal of Law and Public Administration, 2018.
113. Hammond, Scott J. Classics of American Political and Constitutional Thought. Edited by Kevin R. Hardwick and Howard Lubert. Hackett Publishing, 2007.
114. Badescu, Mihai, and Anca Badescu. "The Origin and Evolution of Civil Society (II): The Concept of Civil Society as the Equivalent of the Politically Organized Society versus the Natural State of Society." Journal of Law and Public Administration, 2019.
115. Birkhaeuser, Jodocus Adolph. History of the Church, from Its First Establishment to Our Own Times: Designed for the Use of Ecclesiastical Seminaries and Colleges. Forgotten Books, 2019.
116. Green, Duncan. "How States Evolve." Essay. In How Change Happens. Oxford University Press, 2016. *https://www.oxfordscholarship.com/view/10.1093/acprof:oso/9780198785392.001.0001/acprof-9780198785392-chapter-6?print=pdf.*
117. Smith, Adam. The Wealth of Nations. Capstone, 2010.
118. "Main Page." Wikipedia. Wikimedia Foundation, March 25, 2020. *https://www.wikipedia.org/.* Sundry biographical information
119. Hayek, Friedrich. The Road to Serfdom. Createspace Independent Publishing Platform, 2015.
120. Sowell, Thomas. The Vision of the Anointed. Basic Books, 1995.
121. Weber, Max. Protestant Ethic and the Spirit of Capitalism. Translated by Talcott Parsons. Wilder Publications, 2015.
122. Locke, John, and Paul E. Sigmund. The Selected Political Writings of John Locke: Texts, Background Selections, Sources, Interpretations. Longueuil, Québec: Point Par Point, 2006.
123. Cicero, Marcus Tullius. On Duties. Edited by Miriam T. Griffin and E. M. Atkins. Cambridge University Press, 1991.
124. McInerny, Ralph, and John O'Callaghan. "Saint Thomas Aquinas," May 23, 2014. *https://plato.stanford.edu/archives/sum2018/entries/aquinas/.*
125. Nietzsche, Friedrich. On the Genealogy of Morals. Translated by Horace Barnett Samuel. New York, NY: Barnes & Noble, 2006.
126. Hegel, Georg Wilhelm Friedrich. Elements of the Philosophy of Right. Edited by Allen W. Wood. Translated by H. B. Nisbet. Cambridge University Press, 1991.
127. "Immanuel Kant - On Moral Principles." Lumen. Accessed May 2, 2020. *https://courses.lumenlearning.com/suny-classicreadings/chapter/immanuel-kant-on-moral-principles/.*
128. "Books Received." Kantian Review 25, no. 1 (2020): 165–65. doi:10.1017/S1369415419000530.
129. Callanan, John J., Melissa Merritt: Kant on Reflection and Virtue. Cambridge: Cambridge University Press, 2018 Pp. Xvi Kantian Review 25, no. 1 (2020): 149–53. doi:10.1017/S1369415419000505.
130. Davies, Luke J. "Kant on Welfare: Five Unsuccessful Defences." Kantian Review 25, no. 1 (2020): 1–25. doi:10.1017/S136941541900044X.
131. Dobe, Jennifer K. "Kant's Aesthetics and the Problem of Happiness." Kantian Review 25, no. 1 (2020): 27–51. doi:10.1017/S1369415419000451.
132. Dunn, Nicholas, Courtney D. Fugate (Ed.). Kant's Lectures on Metaphysics: A Critical Guide Cambridge: Cambridge University Press, 2019. Kantian Review 25, no. 1 (2020): 153–58. doi:10.1017/S1369415419000517.

133. Eran, Uri. "Which Emotions Should Kantians Cultivate (and Which Ones Should They Discipline)?" Kantian Review 25, no. 1 (2020): 53–76. doi:10.1017/S1369415419000463.
134. "KRV Volume 25 Issue 1 Cover and Back Matter." Kantian Review 25, no. 1 (2020): b1–b3. doi:10.1017/S1369415420000023.
135. "KRV Volume 25 Issue 1 Cover and Front Matter." Kantian Review 25, no. 1 (2020): f1–f3. doi:10.1017/S1369415420000011.
136. Landy, David. "Kant's Better-than-Terrible Argument in the Anticipations of Perception." Kantian Review 25, no. 1 (2020): 77–101. doi:10.1017/S1369415419000475.
137. Pasternack, Lawrence. "On the Alleged Augustinianism in Kant's Religion." Kantian Review 25, no. 1 (2020): 103–24. doi:10.1017/S1369415419000487.
138. Rueger, Alexander. "Kant on Feelings, Sensations and the Gap Between Rationality and Morality." Kantian Review 25, no. 1 (2020): 125–48. doi:10.1017/S1369415419000499.
139. Vanden Auweele, Dennis. "Sandra Shapshay, Reconstructing Schopenhauer's Ethics: Hope, Compassion, and Animal Welfare. Oxford: Oxford University Press, 2019. Kantian Review 25, no. 1 (2020): 158–63. doi:10.1017/S1369415419000529.
140. Kant, Immanuel, and Jonathan Bennett. "Groundwork for the Metaphysics of Morals." Early Modern Texts, July 2005. *https://www.earlymoderntexts.com/assets/pdfs/kant1785.pdf.*
141. McQuillan, J. Colin. Immanuel Kant: The Very Idea of a Critique of Pure Reason. Evanston, IL: Northwestern University Press, 2016.
142. Kant, Immanuel. Fundamental Principles of the Metaphysics of Morals. Courier Corporation, 2012.
143. Finnis, John, "Aquinas' Moral, Political, and Legal Philosophy", The Stanford Encyclopedia of Philosophy (Summer 2020 Edition). Edited by Edward N. Zalta. *https://plato.stanford.edu/archives/sum2020/entries/aquinas-moral-political/.*
144. Brown, Christopher M. "Thomas Aquinas (1224/6—1274)." Internet Encyclopedia of Philosophy. Accessed March 23, 2020. *https://www.iep.utm.edu/aquinas/.*
145. Rousseau, Jean-Jacques. The Social Contract. CreateSpace, 2014.
146. Bertram, Christopher, "Jean Jacques Rousseau", The Stanford Encyclopedia of Philosophy (Summer 2020 Edition), Edited by Edward N. Zalta. *https://plato.stanford.edu/archives/sum2020/entries/rousseau/*
147. Machiavelli Niccolò. The Prince. Translated by Rufus Goodwin. 1st ed. Dante University of America Press, 2003.
148. Zeitlin, Irving M. Rulers and Ruled: An Introduction to Classical Political Theory from Plato to the Federalists. 1st ed. Toronto: University of Toronto Press, 1997.
149. Scott, Michael. Ancient Worlds: An Epic History of East and West. UK: Hutchinson, 2016.
150. Harvard Divinity School. Religious Literacy Project. Accessed May 1, 2020. *https://rlp.hds.harvard.edu/home.*
151. Mowat, R. B. The States Of Europe. 1815-1871. A Study Of Their Domestic Development. New York, NY: Longmans, 1932.
152. John T S Madeley, Religion and the Struggle for European Union: Confessional Culture and the Limits of Integration. By Brent F. Nelsen and James L. Guth, Journal of Church and State, Volume 59, Issue 4, Autumn 2017, Pages 693–695, https://doi.org/10.1093/jcs/csx035
153. Toropin, Konstantin, Jennifer Henderson, and Leah Asmelash. "Salt Lake City Police Officer Ordered His K9 to Bite a Black Man's Leg Repeatedly, Lawyers Say, and Now It May Need to Be Amputated," August 14, 2020. *https://www.cnn.com/2020/08/13/us/salt-lake-city-pd-dog-excessive-force-trnd/index.html.*
154. Viorst, Milton, ed. "The Declaration of the Council of Pisa." Essay. In The Great Documents of Western Civilization. New York, NY: Barnes & Noble Books, 1965.

155. Hannah-Jones, Nikole. "The 1619 Project." The New York Times. The New York Times, August 14, 2019. *https://www.nytimes.com/interactive/2019/08/14/magazine/1619-america-slavery.html.*
156. Atkins, C. Justice: Myth or Reality? London: Oxford University Press, 1973.
157. Smith A.J. Fundamental Human Rights. Princeton University Press, 1972.
158. Nietzsche, Friedrich Wilhelm. 'On the Genealogy of Morality' and Other Writings. Edited by Keith Ansell-Pearson. Translated by Carol Diethe. 2nd ed. Cambridge, United Kingdom: Cambridge University Press, 2017.
159. Kirkland, Paul E. "Nietzsche's Tragic Realism." The Review of Politics 72, no. 1 (2010): 55-78. Accessed March 26, 2020. www.jstor.org/stable/25655890.
160. Nietzsche, Friedrich Wilhelm. On the Genealogy of Morality: a Polemic. Translated by Maudemarie Clark and Alan J. Swensen. Indianapolis, IN: Hackett Pub. Co, 2009.
161. Nietzsche, Friedrich. Writings of Nietzsche. Edited by Anthony Uyl. 2. Vol. 2. Independently published, 2017.
162. Keenan, Dennis King. "Nietzsche and the Eternal Return of Sacrifice." Research in Phenomenology 33, no. 1 (2003): 167–85. *https://doi.org/10.1163/15691640360699663.*
163. Apeldoorn, Laurens van, and Robin Douglass. Hobbes on Politics and Religion. Oxford: Oxford University Press, 2018.
164. Duncan, Stewart. "Hobbes on Politics and Religion." Edited by Laurens van Apeldoorn and Robin Douglass. Notre Dame Philosophical Reviews, April 14, 2019. *https://ndpr.nd.edu/news/hobbes-on-politics-and-religion/.*
165. Hobbes, Thomas. "Leviathan." SparkNotes. SparkNotes. Accessed April 11, 2020. https://www.sparknotes.com/philosophy/leviathan/full-text/.
166. Tuckness, Alex, "Locke's Political Philosophy", The Stanford Encyclopedia of Philosophy (Spring 2020 Edition). Edited by Edward N. Zalta. *https://plato.stanford.edu/archives/spr2020/entries/locke-political.*
167. Moseley, Alexander. "John Locke: Political Philosophy." Internet Encyclopedia of Philosophy. Accessed April 13, 2020. *https://www.iep.utm.edu/locke-po/.*
168. Locke, John, and Peter Laslett. Locke: Two Treatises of Government. Cambridge: Cambridge Univ. Press, 1989.
169. "Jeremy Bentham (1748-1832)." Online Guide to Ethics and Moral Philosophy, 1996. *http://caae.phil.cmu.edu/Cavalier/80130/part1/sect4/BenandMill.html.*
170. Bentham, Jeremy. Introduction to the Principles of Morals and Legislation: A New Edition, 1823. *https://www.econlib.org/library/Bentham/bnthPML.html*
171. Grier, Michelle. Edited by Edward N. Zalta. "Kant's Critique of Metaphysics". The Stanford Encyclopedia of Philosophy (Summer 2018 Edition). *https://plato.stanford.edu/archives/sum2018/entries/kant-metaphysics.*

Section Four

1. World Population Review. "Sovereign Nation 2020." Accessed March 3, 2020. *https://worldpopulationreview.com/country-rankings/sovereign-nation.*
2. Ramos, Jennifer M. Changing Norms through Actions: the Evolution of Sovereignty. Oxford: Oxford University Press, 2014.
3. Jackson, Robert. Sovereignty: The Evolution of an Idea. Cambridge: Polity Press, 2007.
4. Brown, Cynthia Stokes. "The Industrial Revolution (Article)." Khan Academy. Accessed April 3, 2020.
5. White, Matthew. "The Industrial Revolution." British Library, October 14, 2009. *https://www.bl.uk/georgian-britain/articles/the-industrial-revolution.*
6. ushistory.org. "Economic Growth and the Early Industrial Revolution." U.S. History Online Textbook. Independence Hall Association. Accessed February 19, 2020. *https://www.ushistory.org/us/22a.asp.*
7. Winch, Peter. The Idea of a Social Science and Its Relation to Philosophy. London: Routledge, 1958.

8. Smith, Patrick. "African News, Analysis and Opinion." The Africa Report.com. *https://www.theafricareport.com/.*
9. Nagel, Ernest. The Structure of Science. London: Gordon and Breach Science Publishers, 1961.
10. Laszlo, Ervin, and James Benjamin Wilbur. Human Values and Natural Science. London: Gordon and Breach Science Publishers, 1975.
11. Walters, Jonah. "A Guide to the French Revolution." Jacobin, July 14, 2015. *https://www.jacobinmag.com/2015/07/french-revolution-bastille-day-guide-jacobins-terror-bonaparte/.*
12. Popkin, Jeremy. "What Can We Learn from the French Revolution Today?" Edited by Sam Haselby. Aeon, January 20, 2020. *https://aeon.co/essays/what-can-we-learn-from-the-french-revolution-today.*
13. Schwartz, Mr. "History 151 The French Revolution: Causes, Outcomes, Conflicting Interpretations." Mount Holyoke College. Accessed June 13, 2020. *https://www.mtholyoke.edu/courses/rschwart/hist151s03/french_rev_causes_consequences.htm.*
14. "The Berlin Conference." South African History Online, May 22, 2015. *https://www.sahistory.org.za/article/berlin-conference.*
15. Gathara, Patrick. "Berlin 1884: Remembering the Conference That Divided Africa." Al Jazeera, November 15, 2019. *https://www.aljazeera.com/indepth/opinion/berlin-1884-remembering-conference-divided-africa-191115110808625.html.*
16. Rosenberg, Matt. "The Berlin Conference to Divide Africa." ThoughtCo, June 30, 2019. *https://www.thoughtco.com/berlin-conference-1884-1885-divide-africa-1433556.*
17. "The Berlin Conference." Lumen Boundless World History. *https://courses.lumenlearning.com/boundless-worldhistory/chapter/the-berlin-conference/.*
18. "The Philosophy of Colonialism: Civilization, Christianity, and Commerce." Violence in Twentieth Century Africa. Accessed May 5, 2020. *https://scholarblogs.emory.edu/violenceinafrica/sample-page/the-philosophy-of-colonialism-civilization-christianity-and-commerce/.*
19. New African. "On This Day! Carving up Africa...133 Years of the Berlin Conference and Their Licence to Colonise." New African Magazine, February 26, 2018. *https://newafricanmagazine.com/16411/.*
20. Winter, Jay. "How the Great War Shaped the World." The Atlantic. Accessed March 28, 2020. *https://www.theatlantic.com/magazine/archive/2014/08/how-the-great-war-shaped-the-world/373468/.*
21. Thornton, John Kelly. Africa and Africans in the Making of the Atlantic World, 1400-1680. 2nd ed. Cambridge: Cambridge University Press, 1999.
22. Royde-Smith, John Graham, and Dennis E. Showalter. "World War I." Encyclopædia Britannica, Inc., March 27, 2020. *https://www.britannica.com/event/World-War-I.*
23. Hopkins, A. G. An Economic History of West Africa. Abingdon: Routledge, an imprint of the Taylor & Francis Group, 2020.
24. Choi, Jueun. "'Never Think That War ... Is Not a Crime,' and More Defining WWI Quotes." USA Today, April 4, 2017. *https://www.usatoday.com/story/news/world/2017/04/04/world-war-i-quotes/100031552/.*
25. The Guardian. "First World War: 15 Legacies Still with Us Today." The Guardian, January 15, 2014. *https://www.theguardian.com/world/2014/jan/15/firstworldwar.*
26. Cameron, Fraser. "The Impact of the First World War and Its Implications for Europe Today." Heinrich-Böll-Stiftung, June 2, 2014. *https://eu.boell.org/en/2014/06/02/impact-first-world-war-and-its-implications-europe-today.*
27. Talton, Benjamin. "The Challenge of Decolonization in Africa." Africana Age. Accessed April 30, 2020. *http://exhibitions.nypl.org/africanaage/essay-challenge-of-decolonization-africa.html.*

28. "African Leaders of Independence." African Studies Centre Leiden. Accessed May 18, 2020. *https://www.ascleiden.nl/content/webdossiers/african-leaders-independence.*
29. Snethen, John. D. "The Evolution of Sovereignty and Citizenship in Western Europe: Implications for Migration and Globalization." Indiana Journal of Global Legal Studies 8, no. 1 (2000).
30. Evans, Gareth. "The Limits of Sovereignty: The Case of Mass Atrocity Crimes." PRISM 5, no. 3 (2015): 2-11. Accessed June 21, 2020. *www.jstor.org/stable/26470407.*
31. Mazzone, Jason. "The Rise and Fall of Human Rights: A Sceptical Account of Multilevel Governance." Cambridge Journal of International & Comparative Law 3 (2014).
32. Mowat, R. B. The States of Europe, 1815-1871: A Study of Their Domestic Development. Edward Arnold & Co., 1932.
33. Doctor, Adi H. "Understanding Equality In the 20th Century." The Indian Journal of Political Science 37, no. 4 (1976): 127-34. Accessed March 18, 2020. *www.jstor.org/stable/41854763.*
34. de Warren, Nicolas. "The First World War, Philosophy, and Europe." Tijdschrift voor Filosofie, n.d., 715–37.
35. Schapiro, J. Salwyn, and James Thomson Shotwell. Modern and Contemporary European History (1815-1936). Houghton Mifflin Company, 1934.
36. Abbott, Lyman. The Rights of Man: A Study in Twentieth Century Problems. Houghton Mifflin and Company, 1901.
37. Darkwah, Kofi. "Nationalism and Independence." Transactions of the Historical Society of Ghana, New Series, no. 15 (2013): 71-89. Accessed July 11, 2020. *www.jstor.org/stable/43855012.*
38. Hitchcock, William I. "The Rise and Fall of Human Rights?: Searching for a Narrative from the Cold War to the 9/11 Era." Human Rights Quarterly 37, no. 1 (2015): 80-106.
39. Sellars, Kirsten. "The Rise and Rise of Human Rights: Drafting the Universal Declaration." Sutton Press, 2002.
40. Keith, K. J. "Sovereignty at the Beginning of the 21st Century: Fundamental or Outmoded?" The Cambridge Law Journal 63, no. 3 (2004): 581-604. Accessed April 1, 2020. *www.jstor.org/stable/4509140.*
41. Acemoglu, D., Johnson, S., and Robinson, J.A. (2001). The Colonial Origins of Comparative Development: An Empirical Investigation. American Economic Review, 91(5):1369–1401.
42. Acemoglu, D., and Robinson. J.A. (2010). Why is Africa Poor? Economic History of the Developing Regions, 25(1): 21–50.
43. Monga, Célestin, Justin Yifu Lin, and Gareth Austin. "The Economics of Colonialism in Africa." In The Oxford Handbook of Africa and Economics: Volume 1: Context and Concepts. : Oxford University Press, 2015-07-01. *https://www.oxfordhandbooks.com/view/10.1093/oxfordhb/9780199687114.001.0001/oxfordhb-9780199687114-e-4.*
44. Hayes, Carlton J.H. A Political and Social History of Modern Europe. Macmillan, 1925.
45. SEN, S.R. "From 20th To 21st Century — A Forecast." World Affairs: The Journal of International Issues 2, no. 1 (1993): 40-43. Accessed February 7, 2020. *www.jstor.org/stable/45064165.*
46. Mowat, R. B. The Concert of Europe. Macmillan, 1930.
47. Presbey, Gail M. Philosophia Africana 6, no. 1 (2003): 67-75. Accessed May 10, 2020. *www.jstor.org/stable/10.5325/philafri.6.1.0067.*
48. Jerven, Morten. Africa: Why Economists Get It Wrong (African Arguments). London: Zed Books , 2015.
49. Talton, Benjamin. "The Challenge of Decolonization in Africa." Africana Age. Accessed February 3, 2020. *http://exhibitions.nypl.org/africanaage/essay-challenge-of-decolonization-africa.html.*

50. Butsch, Joseph. "Catholics and the Negro." The Journal of Negro History 2, no. 4 (1917): 393–410.
51. Kivel, Paul. Uprooting Racism: How White People Can Work for Racial Justice. New Society Publishers, 1996.

Section Five
1. "Millennium Development Goals (MDGs)." World Health Organization, February 19, 2018. *https://www.who.int/news-room/fact-sheets/detail/millennium-development-goals-(mdgs).*
2. "Government Gross Debt (as % of GDP) vs Real GDP Growth (%)." United Nations Economic Commission for Africa. Accessed May 4, 2020. *https://ecastats.uneca.org/data/Debt.aspx?id=39.*
3. "About the Sustainable Development Goals." United Nations. Accessed April 30, 2020. *https://www.un.org/sustainabledevelopment/sustainable-development-goals/.*
4. "Figures at a Glance." United Nations High Commissioner for Refugees. Accessed March 5, 2020. *https://www.unhcr.org/en-us/figures-at-a-glance.html.*
5. "United Nations Statistical Commission Overview." United Nations Statistical Commission. Accessed May 17, 2020. *https://unstats.un.org/unsd/statcom.*
6. Our World in Data. Accessed February 15, 2020. *https://ourworldindata.org/.*
7. "Real Time World Statistics." Worldometer. Accessed April 27, 2020. *https://www.worldometers.info/.*
8. "International Statistics." World Statistics. Accessed April 29, 2020. *https://world-statistics.org/.*
9. "World Health Statistics." World Health Organization. Accessed March 25, 2020. *https://www.who.int/data/gho/publications/world-health-statistics.*
10. "World Health Statistics." World Health Organization. Accessed April 16, 2020. *https://www.who.int/gho/world-health-statistics.*
11. "People." The World Bank. Accessed February 5, 2020. *https://datatopics.worldbank.org/world-development-indicators/themes/people.html.*
12. "World Development Indicators." The World Bank. Accessed June 11, 2020. *https://databank.worldbank.org/indicator/NY.GDP.MKTP.KD.ZG/1ff4a498/Popular-Indicators.*
13. "Community: By Project." World Community Grid. Accessed February 23, 2020. *https://www.worldcommunitygrid.org/stat/viewProjects.do.*
14. Iea. "Data and Statistics." IEA. Accessed March 24, 2020. *https://www.iea.org/data-and-statistics?country=WORLD.*
15. "Statistics and Databases." International Labour Organization. Accessed June 20, 2020. *https://www.ilo.org/global/statistics-and-databases/lang--en/index.htm.*
16. "Free and Open Access to Labour Statistics." ILOSTAT. Accessed May 9, 2020. *https://ilostat.ilo.org/data/.*
17. Gapminder. Accessed May 15, 2020. https://www.gapminder.org/.
18. "Global Industry Market Sizing." NationMaster. Accessed May 20, 2020. *https://www.nationmaster.com/.*
19. "Trade and Tariff Data." World Trade Organization. Accessed April 12, 2020. *https://www.wto.org/english/res_e/statis_e/statis_e.htm.*
20. "WTO Data." World Trade Organization Data. Accessed April 5, 2020. *https://timeseries.wto.org/.*
21. "IMF Data." International Monetary Fund. Accessed April 28, 2020. *https://www.imf.org/en/Data.*
22. "World Economic Outlook Database April 2020." International Monetary Fund. Accessed March 26, 2020. *https://www.imf.org/external/pubs/ft/weo/2020/01/weodata/index.aspx.*
23. "Datasets Archives." UNICEF Data. Accessed February 21, 2020. *https://data.unicef.org/resources/resource-type/datasets/.*

24. "Global Homelessness Statistics." Homeless World Cup. Accessed May 26, 2020. *https://homelessworldcup.org/homelessness-statistics/.*
25. "Tracking the State of Open Government Data." Global Open Data Index. Accessed June 1, 2020. *https://index.okfn.org/.*
26. "A Short History of Human Rights." Human Rights Here and Now. Accessed May 7, 2020. *http://hrlibrary.umn.edu/edumat/hreduseries/hereandnow/Part-1/short-history.htm.*
27. Viljoen, Frans. "International Human Rights Law: A Short History." United Nations. Accessed June 28, 2020. *https://www.un.org/en/chronicle/article/international-human-rights-law-short-history.*
28. "Human Rights." United Nations. Accessed March 18, 2020. *https://www.un.org/en/sections/issues-depth/human-rights/.*
29. Graf, Timo Alexander. "Measuring State Failure: Development of a New State Index," July 4, 2012. *https://ecpr.eu/filestore/paperproposal/a7545b9d-ce86-4c1c-a673-fa530bfd8ea3.pdf.*
30. Brittain, Victoria. "The 20th Century: Africa." The Guardian, January 2, 1999. *https://www.theguardian.com/world/1999/jan/02/uganda.westafrica.*
31. Kaul, Inge. "Special Report: Collective Self-Interest – Global Public Goods and Responsible Sovereignty." The Broker, July 1, 2010. *https://www.thebrokeronline.eu/special-report-collective-self-interest/.*
32. Ersoy, Bernur Açıkgöz. "Globalization and Global Public Goods." IntechOpen, August 1, 2011. *https://www.intechopen.com/books/new-knowledge-in-a-new-era-of-globalization/globalization-and-global-public-goods.*
33. "Human Development Index (HDI)." Human Development Reports. Accessed February 11, 2020. *http://hdr.undp.org/en/content/human-development-index-hdi.*
34. "Africa." Human Development Reports. Accessed February 4, 2020. *http://hdr.undp.org/en/africa.*
35. HDRO. "Human Development Indices and Indicators: 2018 Statistical Update - World." ReliefWeb, September 14, 2018. https://reliefweb.int/report/world/human-development-indices-and-indicators-2018-statistical-update.
36. Rodríguez, Francisco. "What the New HDI Tells Us about Africa." Development Research Institute, *http://www.nyudri.org/what-the-new-hdi-tells-us-about-africa.*
37. Copley, Amy. "Figures of the Week: Human Development Progress in Africa and Globally." Brookings, March 24, 2017. *https://www.brookings.edu/blog/africa-in-focus/2017/03/24/figures-of-the-week-human-development-progress-in-africa-and-globally/.*
38. Ritchie, Hannah, Joe Hasell, Cameron Appel, and Max Roser. "Terrorism." Our World in Data, July 2013. *https://ourworldindata.org/terrorism.*
39. "Terrorism - Statistics & Facts." Statista Research Department, January 28, 2020. *https://www.statista.com/topics/2267/terrorism/.*
40. "Global Terrorism Index 2019: Measuring the Impact of Terrorism." Vision of Humanity, November 2019. *http://visionofhumanity.org/app/uploads/2019/11/GTI-2019web.pdf.*
41. OECD Better Life Index. Accessed May 1, 2020. *http://www.oecdbetterlifeindex.org/.*
42. "Countries With the Highest Quality of Life." U.S. News & World Report. Accessed April 25, 2020. *https://www.usnews.com/news/best-countries/quality-of-life-rankings.*
43. Standard Of Living By Country 2020. Accessed May 20, 2020. *https://worldpopulationreview.com/country-rankings/standard-of-living-by-country.*
44. "Quality of Life." WorldData.info. Accessed June 1, 2020. *https://www.worlddata.info/quality-of-life.php.*
45. Carment, David. "Assessing State Failure: Implications for Theory and Policy." Third World Quarterly 24, no. 3 (2003): 407-27. Accessed March 30, 2020. *www.jstor.org/stable/3993377.*

46. Alao, Charles Abiodun. "The Problem of the Failed State in Africa." Essay. In International Security Management and the United Nations, edited by Muthiah Alagappa and Takashi Inoguchi, 83–102. Tokyo: UNU Press, 1999.
47. Wolff, Stefan. "The Regional Dimensions of State Failure." Review of International Studies 37, no. 3 (2011): 951-72. Accessed April 24, 2020. *www.jstor.org/stable/23025406.*
48. Cogolatti, Samuel, Linda Hamid, and Nils Vanstappen. "Global Public Goods and Democracy: What Role for International Law?" Ku Leuven, 2015. *https://ghum.kuleuven.be/ggs/publications/working_papers/2015/159cogolatihamidvanstappen.*
49. Smith A.J. Fundamental Human Rights. Princeton University Press, 1972.
50. Richmond, Oliver P. Failed Statebuilding: Intervention, the State, and the Dynamics of Peace Formation. NEW HAVEN; LONDON: Yale University Press, 2014. Accessed April 2, 2020. www.jstor.org/stable/j.ctt13x1thc.
51. Lemay-Hébert, Nicolas. "The Bifurcation of the Two Worlds: Assessing the Gap between Internationals and Locals in State-building Processes." Third World Quarterly 32, no. 10 (2011): 1823-841. Accessed May 1, 2020. *www.jstor.org/stable/41341201.*
52. Keith, K. J. "Sovereignty at the Beginning of the 21st Century: Fundamental or Outmoded?" The Cambridge Law Journal 63, no. 3 (2004): 581-604. Accessed May 25, 2020. *www.jstor.org/stable/4509140.*
53. Cooper, Robert. The Breaking of Nations: Order and Chaos in the 21st Century. London: Atlantic Books, 2003.
54. Evans, Gareth. "The Limits of Sovereignty: The Case of Mass Atrocity Crimes." PRISM 5, no. 3 (2015): 2-11. Accessed July 11, 2020. *www.jstor.org/stable/26470407.*
55. Lowes, Sara, and Eduardo Montero. "The Legacy of Colonial Medicine in Central Africa." Scholars at Harvard, February 25, 2018. *https://scholar.harvard.edu/files/emontero/files/lowes_montero_colonialmedicine.pdf.*
56. Chazan, Naomi. Irredentism and International Politics. Boulder: Lynne Rienner Publishers, 1991.
57. Ramos, Jennifer M. Changing Norms through Actions: The Evolution of Sovereignty. Oxford University Press, 2013.
58. Smith, Richard D., and Landis MacKellar. "Global Public Goods and the Global Health Agenda: Problems, Priorities and Potential." Globalization and Health 3 (2007). *https://doi.org/doi.org/10.1186/1744-8603-3-9.*
59. Ersoy, Bernur A. "Globalization and Global Public Goods." IntechOpen, August 1, 2011. *https://doi.org/10.5772/21520.*
60. "The World Factbook." Central Intelligence Agency. Accessed May 28, 2020. *https://www.cia.gov/library/publications/the-world-factbook/.*
61. Ignatieff Michael: Blood and Belonging: Toronto, Viking Press 1993.
62. Tilly, Charles. Coercion, Capital, and European States, AD 990-1992. Cambridge, MA: B. Blackwell, 1992.

Section Six

1. Fanon, Frantz. The Wretched of the Earth. London: Mcgibbon and Kee, 1965.
2. Fanon, Frantz. Black Skin, White Masks. London: Grove Press, 1967.
3. Jinadu, L. Adele. Fanon: In Search of the African Revolution. Enugu: Fourth Dimension Publishers Ltd., 1980.
4. Obasanjo, Olusegun. Africa Embattled. Ibadan: Fountain Publishers Ltd., 1988.
5. Noonari, Majid Ali. "Chinese Involvement in Africa and Its Impact on United States." ResearchGate, December 2013. *https://www.researchgate.net/publication/337049773_Chinese_involvement_in_Africa_and_its_impact_on_United_States.*
6. Lenin, Vladimir Il'ich. The State and the Revolution, 1917.
7. Fraiman, A.L. Forpost Sotsialisticheskoi Revoliutsi. Leningrad, 1969.

8. Trotsky Archive, Houghton Library, Harvard University. "Trotsky's Diary ," bMS/ Russ 13, T-3731, p. 111. April 9, 2018.
9. Muravchik, Joshua. Heaven on Earth: The Rise and Fall of Socialism. San Francisco: Encounter Books, 2003.
10. Snow, Philip. The Star Raft: China's Encounter with Africa. London: Weidenfeld and Nicolson, 1988.
11. Andrew, Christopher M., and Vasili Mitrokhin. The World Was Going Our Way: The KGB and The Battle for the Third World. New York: Basic Books, 2005.
12. Figes, Orlando. A People's Tragedy: The Russian Revolution. New York: Penguin Putnam Inc., 1996.
13. "Full Text of President Jiang's Speech at China-Africa Forum." People's Daily, October 11, 2000.
14. People's Daily. May 16, 2006.
15. See China's Africa Policy (Beijing: Ministry of Foreign Affairs, 2006)
16. Troush, Sergei. "China's Changing Oil Strategy and Its Foreign Policy Implications." Brookings. Brookings, September 1, 1999. *https://www.brookings.edu/articles/chinas-changing-oil-strategy-and-its-foreign-policy-implications/.*
17. "U.S. Energy Information Administration - EIA - Independent Statistics and Analysis." U.S. Energy Information Administration (EIA). Accessed May 18, 2020. *http://www.eia.doe.gov/emeu/cabs/china.html.*
18. Jiang, Wenran. Fueling the Dragon: China's Quest for Energy Security and Canada's Opportunities. Vancouver: Asia Pacific Foundation of Canada, 2005.
19. Downs, Erica S. "The Chinese Energy Security Debate." The China Quarterly 177 (March 2004): 21–41. *https://doi.org/10.1017/s0305741004000037.*
20. China Daily. April 10, 1993.
21. "Human Rights Can Be Manifested Differently." China Daily. December 12, 2005.
22. New York Times, April 22, 2005.
23. Mallaby, Sebastian. "A Palace for Sudan: China's No Strings Aid Undermines the West." The Washington Post. February 5, 2007.
24. Oster, Shai, and Kate Linebaugh. "CNOOC Pays $2.27 Billion for Nigerian Oil and Gas Stake." The Wall Street Journal. January 10, 2006.
25. "Angola: Cautious Optimism for 2005." United Nations Office for the Coordination of Humanitarian Affairs, January 14, 2005.
26. "Zambia, China Sign Four Deals." Daily Mail. September 24, 2003.
27. "'Clear the Filth': Mass Evictions and Demolitions in Zimbabwe." Human Rights Watch, September 11, 2005. *http://hrw.org/backgrounder/africa/zimbabwe0905/zimbabwe0905.pdf.*
28. Dickie, Mure, and John Reed. "China Hails Mugabe's 'Brilliant Diplomacy'." Financial Times. July 27, 2005.
29. Wright, Logan. "Seizing an Opportunity: The Changing Character of Chinese Arms Sales to Africa." Armed Forces Journal. October 2001.
30. Goodman, Peter S. "Chinese Invests Heavily in Sudan's Oil Industry." The Washington Post, December 23, 2004.
31. Gary, Ian, and Terry Lynn Karl. Bottom of the Barrel: Africa's Oil Boom and the Poor. Baltimore: Catholic Relief Services, 2003.
32. "Global Trends 2015: A Dialogue About the Future with Nongovernment Experts." Office of the Director of National Intelligence, 2000. *https://www.dni.gov/files/documents/Global%20Trends_2015%20Report.pdf.*
33. Spence, Jonathan D. The Search for Modern China. New York: W.W. Norton & Company, 1990.
34. Engerman, Stanley L., and Joseph E. Inikori. The Atlantic Slave Trade: Effects on Economies, Societies and Peoples in Africa, the Americas, and Europeica, the Americas, and Europe. Duke Univ. Press, 1992.

35. Bernstein, Richard, and Ross H. Munro. The Coming Conflict With China. New York: Alfred A. Knopf, 1997.
36. Gourevitch, Philip. We Wish To Inform You That Tomorrow We Will Be Killed With Our Families: Stories From Rwanda. New York: Farrar, Straus, and Giroux, 1998.
37. Melvern, Linda. The Ultimate Crime: Who Betrayed the UN and Why? London: Allison & Busby, 1995.
38. UN Archives. UNAMIR Force Commander's Papers. UN Confidential. Interoffice Memo. File no. 1000. The Military Situation and Assessment of RGF and RPF Intentions. 23 February 1994.
39. Speke, John Hanning. Journal of the History of the Source of the Nile. London: J.M. Dent, 1969.
40. Semujanga, Josias. Origins of Rwandan Genocide. Amherst: Humanity Books, 2003.
41. Bagosora, Theoneste. The Assassination of President Habyarimana or the Ultimate Tutsi Operation to Take Power by Force in Rwanda, 1994.
42. Uvin, Peter. Aiding Violence: The Development Enterprise in Rwanda. Kumarian Press, 1998.
43. Salem, Torque. "Reps Begin Probe of N494bn Alleged School-Feeding Funds Fraud," June 17, 2020. *https://www.vanguardngr.com/2020/06/reps-begin-probe-of-n494bn-alleged-school-feeding-funds-fraud/.*
44. "L'Extermination Des Tutsi." Le Monde. February 4, 1964.
45. Bowen, Michael, Gary Freeman, and Kay Miller. Passing By: The United States and Genocide in Burundi. Geneva: Carnegie Endowment for International Peace, 1972.
46. Kuper, Leo. The Prevention of Genocide. New Haven: Yale University Press, 1985.
47. Melvern, Linda. Conspiracy to Murder: The Rwandan Genocide. London: Verso, 2004.
48. Melvern, Linda. A People Betrayed: The Role of The West in Rwanda's Genocide. New York: St. Martin's Press, 2000.
49. Ndiaye, B.W. "Report by Mr. B.W. Ndiaye, Special Rapporteur on His Mission to Rwanda, April 8-17, 1993." United Nations Digital Library, August 11, 1993.
50. Morgenthau, Hans J. Politics Among Nations. New York: The McGraw-Hill Companies, 1948.
51. Dougherty, James E., and Robert L. Pfaltzgraff. Contending Theories of International Relations: A Comprehensive Survey. New York: Longman, 2001.
52. Waltz, Kenneth Neal. Man, the State, and War: A Theoretical Analysis. New York: Columbia University Press, 1954.
53. Dallaire Roméo. Shake Hands With The Devil: The Failure of Humanity in Rwanda. New York: Carrol and Graf Publishers, 2003.
54. Ghosts of Rwanda, 2004.
55. Smerdon, Peter. "It's Genocide, Says UN as Rwandan Butchery Continues." The Guardian, April 29, 1994.
56. "The Orphan of Africa." The Guardian, May 4, 1994.
57. Luttwak, Edward. Coup D'Etat: A Practical Handbook. Cambridge, MA: Harvard University Press, 1968.
58. Martin, Lisa L. "Multilateral Organizations after the U.S.-Iraq War of 2003." Weatherhead Center for International Affairs, August 2003. *https://wcfia.harvard.edu/publications/multilateral-organizations-after-us-iraq-war-2003.*
59. Koh, Harold Hongju. "Forward: On American Exceptionalism," 2003.
60. Fukuyama, Francis. State-Building: Governance and World Order in the Twenty-First Century. Ithaca: Cornell University Press, 2004.
61. "Main Page." Wikipedia. Wikimedia Foundation, March 25, 2020. *https://www.wikipedia.org/. Sundry biographical information*
62. Ross, Dennis. Statecraft. New York: Farrar, Straus, and Giroux, 2007.
63. Tripp, Michael I, CPP. Background Data on Africa
64. Novak, Michael. The Spirit of Democratic Capitalism. Lanham, MD: Madison Books, 1991.

65. Muravchik, Joshua. Exporting Democracy: Fulfilling America's Destiny. Washington, D.C.: American Enterprise Institute, 1992.
66. Putnam, Robert D., Robert Leonardi, and Rafaella Y. Nanetti. Making Democracy Work: Civic Traditions in Modern Italy. Princeton, NJ: Princeton University Press, 1994.
67. De Tocqueville, Alexis. Democracy in America. Chicago: University of Chicago Press, 2002.
68. Boix, Carles, and Daniel N. Posner. Social Capital: Explaining Its Origins and Effects on Government Performance. British Journal of Political Science, 1998.
69. Fukuyama, Francis. Trust: The Social Virtues and the Creation of Prosperity. London: Hamish Hamilton, 1995.
70. Dewey, John. Democracy and Education. New York: Simon and Schuster Inc., 1997.
71. Bratton, Michael, and Peter Lewis. "The Durability of Political Goods. Evidence from Nigeria's New Democracy." Commonwealth and Comparative Politics 45, no. 1 (February 2007): 1–33.
72. Maslow, Abraham H. Towards a Psychology of Being. New York: John Wiley and Sons, 1999.
73. Inglehart, Ronald, and Christian Weizel. Modernization, Cultural Change, and Democracy: The Human Development Sequence. Cambridge University Press, 2005.
74. Tiruneh, Gizachew. "Towards Normal Democracy: Theory and Prediction with Special Reference to the Developing Countries." The Journal of Social, Political, and Economic Studies 29, no. 4 (2004).
75. Przeworski, Adam, Fernando Limongi, Michael E. Alvarez, and José Antonio Cheibub. Democracy and Development: Political Institutions and Well-Being in the World, 1950 - 1990. Cambridge University Press, 2000.
76. Dahl, Robert. Polyarchy: Participation and Opposition. New Haven: Yale University Press, 1971.
77. Plato. Republic. Translated by C. D. C. Reeve. Indianapolis: Hackett Publishing Company Inc., 2004.
78. Aristotle. Politics. Translated by Carnes Lord. University of Chicago Press, 1984.
79. Kreeft, Peter. A Shorter Summa: The Essential Philosophical Passages of St. Thomas Aquinas' Summa Theological Edited and Explained for Beginners. San Francisco: Ignatius Press, 1993.
80. Hobbes, Thomas. "Leviathan." SparkNotes. SparkNotes. Accessed April 11, 2020. *https://www.sparknotes.com/philosophy/leviathan/full-text/.*
81. Jefferson, Thomas, John Adams, Benjamin Franklin, Roger Sherman, and Robert R. Livingston. "Declaration of Independence of the United States of America," July 4, 1776.
82. Burke, Edmund. Reflections on the Revolution in France. London: Penguin Books, 2004.
83. Cobban, Alfred. The Debate on the French Revolution 1789-1900. London, 1960.
84. Burke: Select Works, by Payne, E.J., Three Volumes. (Oxford, 1874, 1875, 1878)
85. Copeland, Thomas Wellsted. Edmund Burke: Six Essays. London: Jonathan Cape, 1950.
86. Paine, Thomas. Common Sense. London: Penguin Books, 2004.
87. Kirk, Russell. The Roots of American Order. LaSalle, IL: Open Court, 1977.
88. McIlwain, Charles Howard. Constitutionalism Ancient and Modern. Ithaca, NY: Cornell University Press, 1983.
89. Pilon, Juliana Geran. Why America Is Such a Hard Sell: Beyond Pride and Prejudice. Lanham: Rowman & Littlefield, 2007.
90. Scott, R.B.Y. The Relevance of the Prophets. New York: Macmillan, 1968.
91. Barth, Hans. The Idea of Order: Contributions to a Philosophy of Politics. Translated by Ernest W. Hankamer and William M. Newell. Springer, 2013.
92. Berthoff, Rowland. An Unsettled People: Social Order and Disorder in American History. New York: Harper & Row, 1971.
93. Bryce, James. The American Commonwealth. 1. Vol. 1. New York, NY: Macmillan, 1919.
94. Weil, Simone, and Arthur Wills. Need for Roots: Prelude to a Declaration of Duties Towards Mankind. Boston, MA: Beacon Press, 1952.

95. Eisenstadt, Abraham Seldin. Reconsidering Tocqueville's Democracy in America. New Brunswick, NJ: Rutgers University Press, 1988.
96. Lieske, Joel. "Tocqueville and Democracy in America: Introduction." PS: Political Science & Politics 32, no.(1999): 194–96. doi:10.1017/S1049096500049271.
97. Siedentop, Larry. Tocqueville. Oxford: Oxford University Press, 1994.
98. Masugi, Ken. Interpreting Tocqueville's Democracy in America. Savage, MD: Rowman & Littlefield Publishers, 1991.
99. The Federalist Papers of the United States, No. 47
100. Mill, John Stuart. On Liberty. Edited by Elizabeth Rapaport. Indianapolis: Hackett, 2011.
101. Martin, Meredith. The Fate of Africa: A History of Fifty Years of Independence. New York, NY: Public Affairs, 2005.
102. Clark, J. Desmond, Fage, J. D., Crowder, Michael, Flint, John E., Gray, Richard, Oliver, Roland, Roberts, A. D., and G. N. Sanderson, eds. The Cambridge History of Africa. Vol. 1-8. Cambridge: Cambridge University Press, 1975-1982. doi:10.1017/CHOL9780521222150.
103. Shillington, Kevin. History of Africa. London: Macmillan, 1989.
104. Arnold, Guy. Africa: A Modern History. London: Atlantic, 2005.
105. Reader, John. Africa: A Biography of the Continent. New York: Vintage Books, 1999.
106. Crowder, Michael. "Africa under British and Belgian Domination 1935-45." Essay. In General History of Africa: Africa Since 1935VIII, edited by Ali Al'Amin Mazrui and Christophe Wondji, Vol. VIII. UNESCO, 1999.
107. Dumett, Raymond. "Africa's Strategic Minerals during the Second World War." The Journal of African History 26, no. 4 (1985): 381–408. *https://doi.org/10.1017/s0021853700028802.*
108. Curtis, Mark. Web of Deceit. New York: Vintage Books, 2003.
109. Diamond, Larry, and Marc F. Plattner. Civil-Military Relations and Democracy. Baltimore : Johns Hopkins University Press, 1996.
110. "Annual Statistical Bulletin 2005." OPEC. Accessed April 9, 2020. *https://www.opec.org/opec_web/static_files_project/media/downloads/publications/ASB2005.pdf.*
111. Powell, G. Bingham, Kaare Strøm, Gabriel A. Almond, and Russell J. Dalton. Comparative Politics Today: A World View . 8th ed. NY, NY: Pearson Longman, 2003.
112. Diamond, Larry, Juan J. Linz, Seymour Martin Lipset, and Jonathan Hartlyn. Democracy in Developing Countries: Latin America Edition: 2. Boulder: Lynne Rienner, 1992.
113. Gourevitch, Peter. Politics in Hard Times. Ithaca: Cornell University Press, 1986.
114. Diamond, Larry. Class, Ethnicity, and Democracy in Nigeria: The Failure of the First Republic. Syracuse University Press, 1988.
115. "USA Africa Dialogue Series." Google Groups, May 24, 2007. http://groups.google.com/group/USAAfricaDialogue.
116. Idonor, Daniel. "Nigeria: Obj-No Basis to Annual Poll-Seek Redress in Court-UN." Daily Champion 25 April, 2007 *http://allafrica.com/stories/200704250087.html.*
117. Olson, Mancur. "Dictatorship, Democracy and Development." American Political Science Review 87, no. 3 (September 1993).
118. Mazrui, Ali. "The Blood of Experience: The Failed State and Political Collapse In Africa," May 7, 1994.
119. Ojo, Bamidele. Problems and Prospects of Sustaining Democracy in Nigeria. Huntington: Nova Science Publishers, 2001.
120. Franck, Thomas. Why Federations Fail: An Inquiry into the Requisites for Successful Federalism. New York University Press, 1968.
121. Okafor, Victor Oguejiofor. Nigeria's Stumbling Democracy and Its Implications for Africa's Democratic Movement. Westport: Praeger Security International, 2008.
122. Agulana, Christopher. "Democracy and the Crisis of Leadership in Africa." Journal of Social, Political, and Economic Studies 31 (2006).

123. Ake, Claude. Is Africa Democratizing? Lagos: Malthouse Press, 1996.
124. Obi, Cyril I. The Changing Face of Identity Politics in Nigeria Under Economic Adjustment. Nordiska Afrikainstitutet, 2002.
125. Ikpuk, John Smith. Militarization of Politics and Neo-Colonialism: The Nigerian Experience 1966-90. London: Janus Publishing Company, 1995.
126. Bienen, Henry. Political Conflict and Economic Change In Nigeria. Frank Cass Publishers, 1985.
127. Dudley, Billy. An Introduction to Nigerian Government and Politics. Bloomington: Indiana University Press, 1982.
128. Ikenberry, John. "Why Export Democracy?" The Wilson Quarterly23, no. 3, 1999.
129. Alonge, Felix. Principles and Practice of Governing of Men: Nigeria and the World in Perspective. Ibadan: University Press PLC, 2005.
130. Burke, Edmund. Reflections on the Revolution in France. SMK Books, 2018.
131. Olurounbi, Ruth, and Emele Onu. "EU Observers Say Nigeria 2019 Elections Weren't Transparent." Bloomberg, June 15, 2019. *https://www.bloomberg.com/news/articles/2019-06-15/eu-observers-say-nigeria-s-2019-elections-weren-t-transparent.*
132. Smith A.J. Fundamental Human Rights. Princeton University Press, 1972.
133. "Handbook for EU Election Observation - 3rd Edition 2016." European External Action Service. *https://eeas.europa.eu/election-observation-missions/eom-nigeria- 2019_en.*
134. "Nigeria: Widespread Violence Ushers in President's New Term." Human Rights Watch, June 10, 2019. *https://www.hrw.org/news/2019/06/10/nigeria-widespread-violence-ushers-presidents-new-term.*
135. "Statement of the National Democratic Institute's International Observer Mission to Nigeria's March 28 Presidential and Legislative Elections." National Democratic Institute, March 30, 2015. *https://www.ndi.org/nigeria-election-observation-statement-march-2015.*
136. "2019 Country Reports on Human Rights Practices: Nigeria." U.S. Department of State. *https://www.state.gov/reports/2019-country-reports-on-human-rights-practices/nigeria/.*
137. "List of Massacres in Nigeria." Wikipedia. Accessed April 1, 2020. *https://en.wikipedia.org/wiki/List_of_massacres_in_Nigeria.*
138. "IRI/NDI Release Nigeria International Election Observation Mission." IRI, June 18, 2019. *https://www.iri.org/resource/irindi-release-nigeria-international-election-observation-mission-final-report.*
139. Afigbo, A. E. Nigerian History, Politics and Affairs: The Collected Essays of Adiele Afigbo. Edited by Toyin Falola. Trenton, NJ: Africa World Press, 2005.
140. Lakemfa, Owei. "A Fate Worse than Slavery," July 31, 2020. *https://www.vanguardngr.com/2020/07/a-fate-worse-than-slavery/.*
141. Sevastopulo, Demetri. "Huawei and ZTE Classified as Security Threat to US," July 1, 2020. https://www.ft.com/content/943f8c85-58f7-467b-b774-9963dfaa91b5.
142. Zengerle, Doina Chiacu and Patricia. "US Intelligence Officials All Say They Wouldn't Use a Chinese-Made Huawei or ZTE Phone for Fear of Spying." Business Insider. Business Insider, February 14, 2018. *https://www.businessinsider.com/us-intelligence-officials-say-chinese-made-huawei-zte-maybe-not-secure-2018-2.*
143. Doffman, Zak. "Huawei Employees Linked To China's Military And Intelligence, Reports Claim." Forbes. Forbes Magazine, July 8, 2019. *https://www.forbes.com/sites/zakdoffman/2019/07/06/huawei-employees-linked-to-chinas-state-intelligence-agencies-report-claims/.*
144. Ford, Christopher Ashley. "Huawci and Its Siblings, the Chinese Tech Giants: National Security and Foreign Policy Implications." U.S. Department of State, May 15, 2020. *https://www.state.gov/huawei-and-its-siblings-the-chinese-tech-giants-national-security-and-foreign-policy-implications/.*

References for Images

1. Total Deaths and Cases of Coronavirus, *Johns Hopkins*
2. Corporation of City of Kelowna Public Notice, *Kelowna Capital News: https://www.kelownacapnews.com/news/historical-photo-highlights-city-of-kelownas-response-to-1918-spanish-flu-pandemic/*
3. Policemen stand in a street in Seattle, Washington, wearing protective masks made by the Seattle Chapter of the Red Cross, during the influenza epidemic in 1918. *National Archives at College Park Maryland: https://www.theatlantic.com/photo/2018/04/photos-the-1918-flu-pandemic/557663/*
4. Emergency hospital during influenza epidemic, Camp Funston, Kansas, circa 1918. *National Museum of Health and Medicine: https://www.politico.com/news/magazine/2020/03/17/spanish-flu-lessons-coronavirus-133888*
5. Members of the American Red Cross carry a body during the 1918-20 "Spanish flu" pandemic which resulted in dramatic mortality rates worldwide: *https://en.wikipedia.org/wiki/Pandemic*
6. Nurses leaving Blackfriars Depot, Chippendale NSW, Australia, during the flu epidemic, in April of 1919. *NSW State Archives / Tara Majoor: https://www.theatlantic.com/photo/2020/07/photos-influenza-masks-1918/614272/*
7. OA telephone operator with protective gauze in 1918. Bettmann Archive / Getty : *https://www.theatlantic.com/photo/2020/07/photos-influenza-masks-1918/614272/*
8. Typist wearing mask, New York City, October 16, 1918*: National Archives at College Park Maryland*
9. Beatitudes for A Global Pandemic. *Cartoon Church*; *Illustrator: Dave Walker*
10. The Structure of our Ancestral Society: *Human Nature and Evolution of Society, by Alexandria Maryanski and Jonathan H. Turner, Stanford University Press*
11. Global terrorism split by number of casualties, 2018: *Statista*
12. Terrorist Attacks in 2015, Global Terrorism Index (2016): *Institute for Economics and Peace*
13. The Spread of Islam in Africa: *Ancient History Encyclopedia; Mark Cartwright*
14. Number of Far-right Attacks with more than 10 Fatalities (1970-2018): *StartGTD, IEP Calculations*
15. Comparing International & Domestic Terrorism Threats to the US: *C. Watts (Foreign Policy Research Institute)*
16. Terrorist Attack Spectrum: *C. Watts (Foreign Policy Research Institute)*
17. Mandela : *www.news.cn*
18. Tulsa, Oklahoma Arson: *Oklahoma Historical Society/ Getty images*
19. Racist Open Season Missouri Licence: *@MariaChapelleN. (August 2nd 2015)*
20. Civilization vanquishing barbarism, engraving: *Gustave Dore, Paris (1855)*
21. Priest with negro children: *scholarblogs.emory.edu*
22. Slavery ordained of God: *racialequitytools.org*
23. Slaves, obey your earthly masters: *Abraham Lincoln Presidential Library and Museum.*
24. Berlin conference. *https://en.wikipedia.org/wiki/Berlin_Conference#/media/File:Kongokonferenz.jpg*
25. Routes of European Explorers (1853): *Wikimedia Commons*
26. Wolff's Analytical Framework on State Failure: *Source: Wolff, Stefan & Dursun-Ozkanca, Oya. (2012). Regional and International Conflict Regulation: Diplomatic, Economic and Military Interventions.*
27. Smith's schematic on service and goods: Smith, 2004
28. UNDP HDI model: *UNDP HDI Reports*
29. Multidimensionally poor & out of school school-age children in South Asia: *Alkie, Ul Haq & Alim 2019*
30. IHDI loss from HDI from highest to lowest values (overall loss %): *A1HDR Team from UNDP, 2015*
31. Top terrorist countries as at 2018: *Statista*
32. Most active perpetrator groups worldwide in 2017, based on number of attacks: *Statista*
33. Top Ten Countries for economic cost of terrorism as a percentage of GDP (2018): *START GTD, IEP Calculations*
34. Economic Impact of Terrorism by Region: *IEP*
35. New asylum applications (Not inclusive of visa overstays*): UNHCR*
36. Figure 1. Covid:19 Spread Profile as at April, 2020: *Johns Hopkins Health*
37. Figure 2. Coronavirus Hotspots: *New York Times, April 9, 2020*
38. Figure 3. Tracking the spread of the novel coronavirus: *Reuters, April 10, 2020*
39. Figure 4. Religion waiting on Science*: @akinalabi. March 23, 2020*
40. Figure 5. Bye-bye Nigeria: *@saratu_ibrahim . April 12 2020*
41. Figure 6. Nigerian President Muhammadu Buhari meets Guinea Bissau's Prime Minister Umaro Embalo: *www.vanguardngr.com*

42. Figure 7. A strong correlation exists between Muslim population density in Africa and Islamic terrorism: *Pew Forum on Religion & Public Life, April 2010*
43. Figure 8. The folly and ignorance of racism: *Klressa*
44. Figure 9. Mayor Hal Marx : *Metro.co.uk*
45. Figure 10. The Rebel Flag: *Politico*
46. Figure 11. Trump and the rebel flag: *Politico*
47. Figure 12 Map of Africa, as conveniently drawn up at the Berlin conference: *scholarblogs.emory.edu*
48. Figure 13. Colonial map of Africa: *ThoughtCo*
49. Figure 14. Correlation between Failed States and Illicit Drug Activity: *US Department of State: Brookings, UNODC, IMO*
50. Figure 15. Failed States labeled as 'critical.': *www.foreign policy.com*
51. Figure 16. Failed States Index: *www.foreignpolicy.com*
52. Figure 17. Fragile States Index 2015: *www.fundforpeace.org*
53. Figure 18. Structure of the Global Multidimensional Poverty Index: *Oxford Poverty and Human Development Initiative 2018*
54. Figure 19. Multidimensional Poverty in love-income, lower-middle-income, and upper-middle-income countries: *Akine, Kanagaratnam & Suppa (2019) based on Human Development Report Office and Oxford Poverty and Human Development initiative calculations.*
55. Figure 20. Distribution of Indicators to overall multidimensional poverty: *Akine, Kanagaratnam & Suppa (2019) based on Human Development Report Office and Oxford Poverty and Human Development initiative calculations.*
56. Figure 21. Women's Empowerment Infographic: *Selim Jahan. Human Development Report Office 2016 (HDRO).*
57. Figure 22. Performance on Human Development Indices: *UNDP African Report, 2016*
58. Figure 23. African life expectancy data (gender split): *AfHDR Team from data in ILO 2015d.*
59. Figure 24. Income per capita for eight selected poor countries: *World Bank*
60. Figure 25. Most terrorism-related deaths take place in failed and failing States: *Global Terrorism Database (2018)*
61. Figure 26. Geographical density of terrorism-related deaths: *Global Terrorism Database (2018)*
62. Figure 27. *World Values Survey(2019)*
63. Figure 28. Global Terrorism Intensity Map (1): *Global Terrorism Index (GTI)*
64. Figure 29. Global Terrorism Intensity Map (2): *Global Terrorism Index (GTI)*
65. Figure 30. African Quality of Life Index: *World Population Review*
66. Figure 31 Concentration of Public Debt: *worldstatistics.org citing World Bank data*
67. Figure 32. Air freight as an indicator of commercial activity: *World Bank*
68. Figure 33. Ease of dealing with the Customs (darker colors represent better experiences with the Customs); Africa has a very unimpressive record, owing to inefficiency and corruption: *World Bank*
69. Figure 34. Rail infrastructure per kilometer; Africa performs very poorly, despite the billions of dollars that their governments claim to have spent on this vital sector: *World Bank*
70. Figure 35. Corruption Perception Index (deep red connotes a high score in Transparency and Integrity, while the lighter colors align with a high Corruption Perception); Africa still has a problem as a very corrupt Continent: *Transparency International*
71. Figure 36. A satellite image taken at night above Europe and Africa, for contrast. Private generating sets contribute to the flickers of electricity seen in Africa: *Geology.com*
72. Figure 37. The state of Nigeria: *Unknown*
73. Figure 38. Oil spillage caused by major oil corporations in the Niger Delta region of Nigeria. *Starconnect Media*
74. Figure 39. Utter despoliation in the Niger Delta, Nigeria: *africanarguments.org*
75. Figure 40. Oil spills in the Niger Delta, Nigeria: *Michael Uwemedimo/cmapping.net*
76. Figure 41. Ruined fish farm in Bodo, Nigeria: *Amnesty International*
77. Figure 42. Interconnected map of global risk trends. How would failing and failed States fare?: *World Economic Forum(2019)*
78. Figure 43. Global Risks Landscape(2020). Contemporary and Future Challenges of Statehood: *zurich.com*
79. Figure 44 Coronavirus: Cumulative Confirmed Cases (August 16, 2020): *Johns Hopkins coronavirus.jhu.edu/map.html*
80. Figure 45 Coronavirus: Active Cases (August 16, 2020): *Johns Hopkins https://coronavirus.jhu.edu/map.html*
81. Cycle of Dependency: Nadia Namko
82. Perennial Sovereign Nurslings: Nadia Namko
83. National Currency (Naira) Erosion vs the $: Nadia Namko
84. KRPC Annual Report (2018): NNPC KRPC Ltd. 2018 Financial Statements
85. The "Three Arms of Government" in Nigeria: @echwalu; June 7, 2017